P9-EJU-776

Better Homes and Gardens®

THE DIETER'S COOK BOOK

First Edition. Third Printing, 1983.
Library of Congress Catalog Card Number 81-67157
ISBN: 0-696-00745-2

BETTER HOMES AND GARDENS® BOOKS

Editor: Gerald M. Knox
Art Director: Ernest Shelton
Managing Editor: David A. Kirchner

Food and Nutrition Editor: Doris Eby
Department Head—Cook Books: Sharyl Heiken
Senior Food Editor: Elizabeth Woolever
Senior Associate Food Editors: Sandra Granseth, Rosemary C. Hutchinson
Associate Food Editors: Jill Burmeister, Julia Martinusen, Diana McMillen, Marcia Stanley, Diane Yanney
Recipe Development Editor: Marion Viall
Test Kitchen Director: Sharon Stilwell
Test Kitchen Home Economists: Jean Brekke, Kay Cargill, Marilyn Cornelius, Maryellyn Krantz, Marge Steenson

Associate Art Director (Managing): Randall Yontz
Associate Art Directors (Creative): Linda Ford, Neoma Alt West
Copy and Production Editors: Nancy Nowiszewski, Lamont Olson, Mary Helen Schiltz, David A. Walsh

Assistant Art Directors: Faith Berven, Harijs Priekulis
Graphic Designers: Mike Burns, Alisann Dixon, Mike Eagleton, Lynda Haupert, Deb Miner, Lyne Neymeyer, Trish Podlasek, Bill Shaw, D. Greg Thompson

Editor in Chief: Neil Kuehnl
Group Editorial Services Director: Duane Gregg
Executive Art Director: William J. Yates

General Manager: Fred Stines
Director of Publishing: Robert B. Nelson
Director of Retail Marketing: Jamie Martin
Director of Direct Marketing: Arthur Heydendael

THE DIETER'S COOK BOOK
Editor: Joyce Trollope
Copy and Production Editor: David A. Walsh
Graphic Designer: Lyne Neymeyer
Consultant: Michael P. Scott
Exercise Consultant: Dr. Arno L. Jensen

ON THE COVERS
Stir-Fried Vegetables (see recipe, page 181)
Fruit 'n' Yogurt Dazzler (see recipe, page 264)
Pared-Down Pizza (see recipe, page 127)
Elegant Chicken Crepes (see recipe, page 142)
Gingerbread with Lemon Sauce (see recipe, page 202)

Our seal assures you that every recipe in the *The Dieter's Cook Book* is endorsed by the Better Homes and Gardens Test Kitchen. Each recipe is tested for family appeal, practicality, and deliciousness.

FOREWORD

Whether you are overweight and need to trim a few pounds, or are now at your ideal weight and want to maintain it, this book will help you begin a lifelong pattern of eating nutritious foods and getting beneficial exercise. You'll soon discover it is just as easy to eat and exercise properly as it is not to. All it takes is careful thought about what foods you eat and the willpower to stick to the first few weeks of dieting and exercising. In *The Dieter's Cook Book* we have compiled for you some of the nutritious and calorie-reduced recipes we've published over the years. Besides delicious recipes, this book contains nutrition information and exercise ideas to help make positive changes in your health habits.

CONTENTS

GUIDE TO SENSIBLE EATING

Most of us have forgotten what little we learned in school about good nutrition, and it shows. The average American's diet is probably producing an overweight body. Combining a poor diet (one that contains too many calories, too much fat, too much sugar, too much salt, and too little fiber) with a sedentary and stress-filled life-style has contributed to national health problems.

The basics of good, nutritionally sound eating are not mysterious. To help you apply them, here is a recap that includes the Basic Five Food Groups, an explanation of calories, a chart listing calories in foods, and dietary pitfalls to avoid and advice to follow.

BUILD ON THE BASICS OF NUTRITION

Planning a well-balanced diet isn't all that difficult if you start by understanding the basics of good nutrition. That's the key to a successful, sensible diet. Basically, food is composed of proteins, fats, carbohydrates, vitamins, minerals, and water—about 50 essential nutrients in all. Most foods contain several of the basic nutrients, but no food has them all; so a balanced diet must have many kinds of foods. And the variety of foods necessary to achieve a well-balanced diet ensures that eating sensibly is anything but dull.

Protein: The Body Builder

Protein is often touted as a nutritional wonder, but it is only one of the essential parts of a healthy, well-rounded diet that also includes carbohydrates, fats, vitamins, and minerals.

Protein is necessary to build, maintain, and repair the body. It also helps produce antibodies that ward off disease, and produce enzymes and hormones that regulate many of our body processes.

With so many purposes, protein is quickly used in the body; so you need to replenish it frequently—preferably in small amounts at intervals during the day. Protein can be eaten in the form of three regular meals or four to six mini-meals. Adults, teenagers, and children require about 65 grams of protein daily. A pregnant or nursing woman requires additional protein to meet her special nutritional requirements.

Protein is made up of 22 different components called amino acids. Fourteen of the amino acids can be manufactured by the body if they aren't found in the food that is consumed. However, the remaining eight amino acids, known as essential amino acids, must be supplied by the food that is eaten. All eight of the essential amino acids must be eaten at the same meal for the protein to be properly used by the body.

Animal products make it easy to consume all of the essential amino acids simultaneously because they usually contain all eight of them. These top-quality protein sources include meat, fish, poultry, eggs, cheese, and milk.

Plant forms of protein such as dried beans and peas, whole grains and cereals, seeds and nuts are of lesser quality, failing to provide all needed amino acids, but can combine with high-quality protein sources to make them nutritionally valuable. Or, you can combine one plant protein with another to supply any missing essentials. For example, macaroni and cheese combines animal and plant proteins—milk, cheese, and enriched pasta. A bean-filled taco contributes protein from two good plant sources—beans and enriched grain.

Any of the following plant food combinations includes all eight essential amino acids: grains and legumes (dry beans, dry

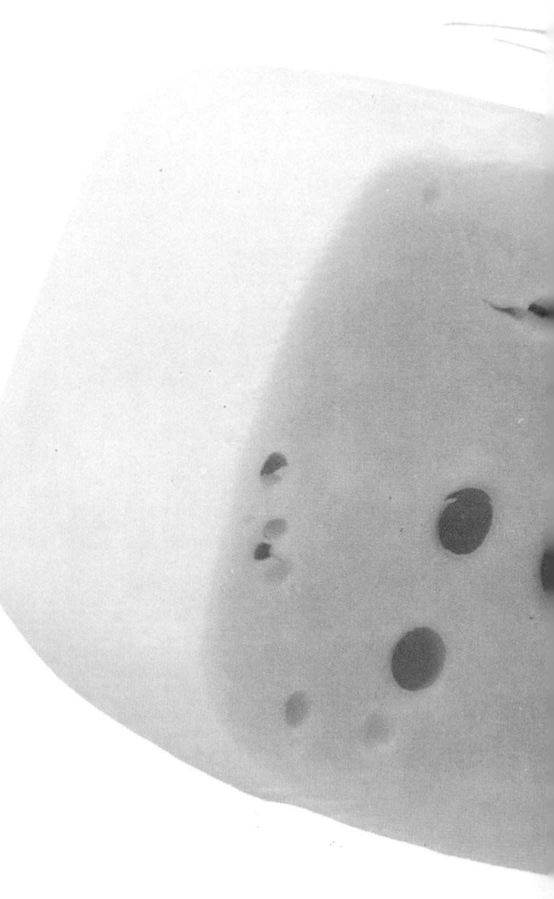

peas, or lentils); legumes and seeds or nuts; and combinations of seeds, nuts, grains, or legumes with milk products. Note that plant protein combinations must be eaten at the same time to perform effectively.

Fats: Concentrated Energy

Despite all of the negative attitudes about fats, they are in fact essential for your good health and are a necessary part of a well-balanced diet, even if you are on a diet and trying to lose weight.

Fats make it possible for your body to use carbohydrates and proteins to their best advantage. Fats are highly concentrated forms of energy, providing nine calories per gram compared with four calories each for proteins and carbohydrates.

Additionally, fats enable your body to use the fat-soluble vitamins—A, D, E, and K. Fat in small quantities makes food taste good, and because fats are digested slowly, they keep you from feeling hungry longer than do proteins or carbohydrates. Fat, a natural insulator, helps your body maintain its optimum temperature. And, fat provides some indispensable fatty acids that are necessary to life.

The most common sources of fat in your diet probably are oils, butter, margarine, shortenings, and meat. But "hidden" fats you don't generally see are in other foods such as baked products, fried foods, salad dressings, nuts, eggs, some milk products, and even lean meat.

Most fats that are solid at room temperature (particularly animal fats and some vegetable fats such as coconut oil) are called saturated fats. Unsaturated fats are usually liquid fats. Polyunsaturated fats (such as safflower, corn, peanut, and soybean oils) are a chemical variation of unsaturated fats and contain essential elements that the body can't manufacture. Some medical authorities think that saturated fats tend to increase blood cholesterol levels. And some researchers say that high cholesterol plays an important role in heart disease. Others think its role has been overstated. That is why nutrition experts have issued conflicting advice about the types of fats and amount of cholesterol we should include in our diets.

Fat should make up one-fourth to one-third of your total calories unless your doctor makes other recommendations.

Carbohydrates: Energy for the Body

Carbohydrates are another source of energy, but generally are lower in calories than are fats. They free protein for other uses and are important carriers of vitamins and minerals.

Carbohydrates are available in two basic forms: sugars and starches. They exist as natural sugars in fresh fruits, vegetables, and some dairy products. Pure or refined sugars—such as honey, corn syrup, brown sugar, molasses, and table sugar—provide carbohydrates. Foods such as potatoes, breads, cereals, and pasta are starch forms of carbohydrate.

The only nutritional contribution sugar itself (both natural and refined) can make to your diet is calories for energy. So the calorie content of foods high in refined sugars far outweighs the nutrient value. But, take note: Foods that contain natural sugars (such as fruits) will supply you with not only energy, but also nutrients that are essential. That's an important point to remember when you're concerned about limiting your calorie intake.

Starches have as much to offer nutritionally as foods that contain natural sugars, but watch what you eat. Americans often combine fats with starchy foods (for example, butter with potatoes and rich sauces with pasta). If you pay attention to the amount of fat in your diet, the starches aren't likely to cause undue problems.

Another caution related to carbohydrates: Some diets call for severe restrictions in carbohydrate intake. When that happens, your body compensates by manufacturing energy from protein, creating a nutritional deficit. The trade off—using valuable protein instead of carbohydrates for energy—isn't worth it.

Overall, the rule for carbohydrates is the same as that for proteins and fats in your diet—moderation is the key. It's your ticket to a well-balanced diet.

Vitamins

If you're concerned that cutting calories will shortchange you on vitamins, you should be. Each of the vitamins known to be required by our bodies for good health performs a specific function that no other nutrient can. A deficiency of just one of these special substances can have harmful effects on long-term fitness. On the other hand, excessive doses of some vitamins also can cause adverse reactions within the body.

Vitamins are essential for chemical reactions throughout the body. Our bodies cannot manufacture most vitamins, so they need to be in the foods we eat.

Here is a capsule list of some of the more important vitamins, along with their function in the body and some of their food sources:

• Vitamin A is needed for bone growth, healthy tooth structure, and development of normal skin. It aids in night vision, also. Large amounts of this vitamin can be stored in the liver, but excess doses may be toxic. Leafy green or yellow vegetables, liver, apricots, cantaloupe, tomatoes, and dairy products are good food sources.

• Vitamin C, also called ascorbic acid, is necessary for the framework of bones and teeth and for healthy gums and blood vessels. Vitamin C is an unstable vitamin and is easily destroyed, so it needs to be consumed every day. You'll find vitamin C in citrus fruits, green leafy vegetables, strawberries, tomatoes, and potatoes.

• Vitamin D aids in the proper use of calcium and phosphorus in bones. Vitamin D can be synthesized by the action of the sun's rays on the skin. Excess doses may have toxic effects. Food sources of vitamin D include fish liver oils and fortified milk.

• Thiamine (vitamin B_1) regulates appetite and digestion, maintains healthy nerves, and helps release energy from food. Thiamine is not stored in the body so it needs to be replenished in the diet every day. Thiamine is found in enriched cereals, whole grains, pork, nuts, and green peas.

• Riboflavin, another B vitamin, aids in the process of food metabolism, promotes a healthy mouth and skin, helps cells use oxygen, and aids vision in bright light. Riboflavin is not stored in the body and needs to be replenished at frequent intervals, although deficiency is rare. Milk, meats (variety meats in particular), eggs, dark green leafy vegetables, and cheese are rich in riboflavin.

• Niacin, another B vitamin, is involved in the conversion of sugars to energy and fat synthesis. It keeps the skin, digestive tract, and nervous system healthy. Niacin needs to be in a food source daily. Liver, poultry, fish, nuts, enriched cereals, and peanut butter are good sources of niacin.

• Vitamin E prevents the oxidation and breakdown of cells and substances such as vitamins A and D. Deficiencies of this vitamin are rare. Food sources include vegetable oils (such as cottonseed oil), margarine, and whole-grain cereals.

• Vitamin K is needed for normal blood clotting. Deficiency is rare. Good food sources include cauliflower, cabbage, spinach, and kale.

Minerals

Minerals occur in very small amounts, but they have an important effect on physical fitness. Minerals aid blood coagulation, and without them vitamins would not be stimulated to action. Here are some of the important minerals:

• Calcium gives strength and structure to bones, and rigidity and permanence to teeth. About 99 percent of the body's calcium is contained in bones and teeth. The remaining 1 percent is important for blood clotting, muscle contraction, and nerve impulses. Calcium is found in dairy products, sardines and salmon (with bones), and enriched cereals.

• Phosphorus produces firm and supple skin, and is present in food sources such as eggs, tuna, and bananas.

• Zinc helps maintain skin elasticity and aids in tissue respiration. Liver and shellfish are rich in it.

• Iron is an important constituent of every red blood cell in the body. It carries oxygen throughout the body. Blood loss or lack of sufficient iron in the diet can cause iron-deficiency anemia. Toxic levels of iron are extremely rare. Meats, bran cereals, dried beans, prunes, and spinach provide iron.

• Sodium (salt) helps regulate the passage of water and nutrients out of cells and helps maintain the proper acid-base balance in body fluids. The average diet fur-

nishes about three times as much sodium as is needed. The estimated safe and adequate daily intake of sodium is 1,100 to 3,300 milligrams for adults.

• Potassium helps regulate acid-base balance in body fluids. It also regulates muscular excitability and contraction, and aids in protein synthesis. A diet adequate in protein, calcium, and iron also contains adequate potassium. The estimated safe and adequate daily intake of potassium is 1,875 to 5,625 milligrams for adults.

Water

Although water isn't usually thought of as food, it is essential to all tissues. In fact, our body weight is two-thirds water. You should drink seven glasses of water each day in addition to the water that is naturally found in the foods that you eat.

DIETARY RECOMMENDATIONS

Now that you know more about the basic nutrients found in the foods that you eat, you may want to consider the following recommendations for changing your diet.

A surgeon general of the United States has said Americans could be healthier if they would consume: only enough calories to meet their body's needs and to maintain an appropriate weight (or consume fewer calories if overweight); less saturated fat and cholesterol; less salt; less sugar; more complex carbohydrates, such as whole grains, cereals, fruits, and vegetables; more fish, poultry, and legumes; and less red meat.

Add to those recommendations advice about consuming alcohol in moderate amounts, if at all, and you have the basics of a nutritious, lifelong eating plan.

Excessive Calories

Regardless of the foods we eat, most of us tend to eat too many calories. (A calorie is simply a measure of the energy that can be derived from the body's processing of foods. For more about calories, see page 20.) One goal of a balanced diet is to match the number of calories you eat with the amount of energy you expend in your daily routine and through exercise.

If you're overweight, you're asking for trouble. Obesity is linked with high blood pressure, diabetes, heart attack, stroke, and increased fat and cholesterol levels in the blood.

Too Much Fat in the Diet

Excessive fats (especially saturated fats) in the diet result in more than just being overweight: Some medical authorities say saturated fats are a prime contributor to high blood cholesterol in some people. Although fats provide energy and make foods taste better, some of us go overboard on them.

If you want to avoid excessive fats in your diet, here are some suggestions:

- Choose lean meat, fish, poultry, dried beans, and dried peas as your sources of protein.
- Eat eggs and organ meats (such as liver) in moderate amounts.
- Limit the amount of butter, cream, shortenings, and foods made with those products.
- Trim excess fat from meats.
- Broil, bake, or steam food instead of frying it whenever possible.

Too Much Salt

Salt (or sodium), a tasty addition to foods, contributes to the retention of body fluids. But, as is the case with many other dietary excesses, it is linked to high blood pressure and other diseases. Salt is present in almost any food you eat, but especially in processed foods. For example, two slices of bread contain enough salt to meet your body's daily requirement for salt.

Try to keep the salt shaker off the table, but if you must add salt at the table, use it sparingly.

Too Much Sugar

It's estimated that the average American eats more than 130 pounds of sugar and other sweeteners each year. The havoc that plays with your teeth is obvious.

Sugar also can contribute to obesity because it adds little more than calories to the diet. Only about 25 percent of the sugar consumed is added at home; a sizable portion of sugar that is consumed is found in purchased foods. These foods include soft drinks, bakery and cereal products, candy, jams, jellies, canned and frozen fruits. To cut back on sugar, here are some suggestions:

- Check labels on food products for other words that indicate the presence of sweeteners (sucrose, glucose, dextrose, fructose, corn syrups, or natural sweeteners, for example).
- Eat fewer of the foods that contain lots of sugar, such as pies, cakes, cookies, sweet rolls, ice cream, soft drinks, and candy.
- Substitute unsweetened fruit juices or water for soft drinks.
- Use unsweetened cereals.

Adequate Fiber

The evidence about the value of fiber in the diet is not yet conclusive. However, a normal healthy diet should include a certain amount of fiber—or roughage as it's sometimes called. Fiber has good water-binding capacity, or bulking properties; the result is it's discarded quickly by the body, carrying other substances with it.

Dietary fiber is a catchall term for a number of non-nutritive plant substances that can't be digested well by the body. Most fiber comes from the structural parts of plants—the leaves, flowers, seeds, fruits, stems, and roots. The most common fiber is cellulose, which is found in the cell walls of vegetables.

You can increase the amount of fiber in your diet by eating more foods made with whole grains (such as breads and cereals), bran, dried peas and dried beans, nuts, and fruits. Fruits and vegetables that have edible seeds or that can be eaten unpeeled are among the best sources of fiber.

Alcohol in Moderation

Alcoholic beverages are high in calories, and contribute very little else to the diet. Consumption of excessive amounts of alcohol often results in diminished appetite for essential foods, and contributes to liver and neurological disorders and birth defects among other problems.

The best advice about drinking alcohol remains: If you drink, do so in moderation.

Nutritional Labeling

When you're grocery shopping and are confronted with literally thousands of food choices, how can you possibly know which foods contain the essential vitamins and minerals? Which foods are too high in salt, sugar, or fat? Ounce for ounce, which foods are highest in calories? One handy source of dietary information is found on food labels themselves.

Since 1975, any food product with nutrients added and any for which nutritional claims are made must provide nutritional information on the label according to a standard format. Even if not required by law to do so, many food companies label their food products voluntarily. The Food and Drug Administration hopes that eventually all foods in the grocery store will be labeled so you can compare the nutritional value of the products just as you can now compare prices.

Information on nutrition labels is similar and contains the following:

- The number of calories and the gram weights of protein, fat, and carbohydrates must be listed for single serving amounts.
- The labels may show the amounts of cholesterol and salt (listed as sodium) in 100 grams of food or per serving.
- The percentage of U. S. Recommended Daily Allowances (U.S. RDA) for protein and for seven vitamins and minerals (A, C, thiamine, riboflavin, niacin, calcium, and iron) must follow.

Any of 12 other nutrients must be listed on the label when they are added by the food manufacturer.

- The label may include the amounts of polyunsaturated and saturated fats.

The U.S. RDAs reflect the highest amounts of various nutrients needed to meet the dietary needs of most healthy Americans.

NUTRITION ANALYSIS

Many recipes in this book have a nutrition analysis that gives values for the amount of calories, proteins, carbohydrates, fats, sodium, and potassium in an individual serving. The analysis also gives the percentages of the United States Recommended Daily Allowances (U.S. RDA) for protein and certain vitamins and minerals per serving. Use the analyses to compare nutritional values of recipes. Plan your daily menus by finding recipes that will meet your calorie and nutritional needs. For ease of comparison of recipes we have put the nutrition analyses at the beginning of the chapters.

The information for the nutrition analyses comes from a computerized method using Agriculture Handbook No. 456 by the United States Department of Agriculture as the primary source. The values found for the recipes in this cook book are as correct as possible.

To obtain the nutrition analyses, we made some assumptions:

- *Garnishes and ingredients listed as optional were omitted.*
- *If a food was marinated and then brushed with the marinade during cooking, the analysis includes the entire marinade amount.*
- *Dippers were not included with dip recipes.*
- *For main-dish meat recipes, the nutrition analyses were calculated using measurements for cooked lean meat, trimmed of fat.*
- *When two ingredient options appear in a recipe, the nutrition analysis was calculated using the first choice of ingredients.*
- *When a recipe ingredient has a variable weight (such as a 2½- to 3-pound broiler-fryer chicken), the nutrition analysis was calculated using the lesser weight.*

BASIC FIVE FOOD GROUPS

When planning menus, choose a variety of foods so that your nutritional requirements are met. To help in your selections use the Basic Five Food Groups system. This system takes into account Recommended Dietary Allowances (RDAs).

The RDAs tell the amounts of certain nutrients recommended to meet over time the nutritional needs of almost all healthy people in the United States. They were set up by the Food and Nutrition Board of the National Academy of Sciences—National Research Council.

By selecting the proper number of servings from the food groups every day, you obtain the nutrients essential to good health. Remember that a balanced variety of foods is the key.

Be sure to consider any medical problems in your family that require special menus. Your doctor is the best source of information for a special diet.

VEGETABLE-FRUIT GROUP

This group provides vitamins A and C, other nutrients, and fiber. Dark green and deep yellow vegetables are good sources of vitamin A. Vitamin C comes from dark green vegetables (if they're not overcooked), citrus fruits, melons, berries, and tomatoes. Unpeeled fruits and vegetables and foods with edible seeds (berries, for example) provide fiber in the diet.

Most vegetables and fruits are low in fat (two exceptions are olives and avocados), and none contain the cholesterol found in meats.

Recommended servings: Plan four servings from this group daily, including one good vitamin C source (citrus fruit or juice), and at least every other day include one good vitamin A source.

Serving size: One-half cup of fruit or vegetable counts as a serving. A serving might also be one medium orange, half a medium grapefruit, a wedge of lettuce, or a medium potato.

BREAD-CEREAL GROUP

The foods in this group are important sources of iron, thiamine, niacin, and riboflavin. Included in the bread-cereal group are products made with whole grains or enriched flour or meal. Bread, biscuits, muffins, waffles, cooked or ready-to-eat cereals, cornmeal, macaroni, spaghetti, noodles, rice, rolled oats, and barley are some of the items that are included in this food group.

Fortified breakfast cereals usually contain nutrients not normally found in cereals, such as vitamins B_{12}, C, and D.

Recommended servings: Plan four servings from this group each day.

Serving size: One slice of whole grain or enriched bread; ½ to ¾ cup cooked cereal, macaroni, noodles, or rice, or 1 ounce ready-to-eat cereal counts as a typical serving for this group.

MILK-CHEESE GROUP

These foods (including low-fat or skim milk products) are major sources of calcium. They also add riboflavin, protein, and vitamins A, B_6, and B_{12}. Additionally, they usually are fortified with vitamin D. Milk and cheese aren't the only beneficial foods in this group. Also choose yogurt, ice milk, cottage cheese, buttermilk, and any other form of milk. And, don't forget about the milk used in food preparation for such products as puddings.

Recommended servings: Each day—

children 9 to 12 . . . . 3 servings
teens . . . . 4 servings
adults . . . . 2 servings
pregnant women . . . . 3 servings
nursing mothers . . . . 4 servings

Serving size: Counting as one serving each are: one cup (8 ounces) of milk (whole, low-fat, or skim); 1 cup plain yogurt; 1⅓ ounces hard cheese; 2 ounces process cheese food; 1½ cups ice milk; ¼ cup Parmesan cheese; 2 cups cottage cheese.

MEAT, POULTRY, FISH, NUTS, AND BEANS GROUP

The foods in this group supply protein, iron, thiamine, niacin, riboflavin, and phosphorus. Foods in the group include beef, veal, pork, lamb, poultry, fish, shellfish, variety meats, eggs, dried beans or peas, soybeans, lentils, seeds, nuts, peanuts, and peanut butter.

Recommended servings: Plan two servings daily, varying the sources.

Serving size: Count as a serving—two to three ounces of lean, cooked meat, poultry, or fish, all without bone; two eggs; 1 cup cooked dried beans, peas, soybeans, or lentils. Or use 2 tablespoons peanut butter or ¼ to ½ cup nuts, sesame seed, or sunflower seed to count as one-half serving of meat, poultry, or fish.

FATS, SWEETS, AND ALCOHOL GROUP

Be judicious about selecting foods from this group because they are extremely high in calories and contribute little more than calories to the diet. Unenriched, refined bakery goods are in this group because they provide low levels of vitamins, minerals, and protein per calorie consumed.

Other foods in the group are butter, margarine, mayonnaise, salad dressings, candy, sugar, jams, syrups, soft drinks, wine, beer, and other alcoholic beverages.

When planning your diet, concentrate on foods in the four other food groups because of the nutrients and fiber they contain, and go easy on the foods in this fifth food group.

No serving sizes are suggested. The amount of these foods in your diet depends on how many calories you need.

SHOULD YOU REDUCE?

Whether you are thinking about losing weight or are already slim and trying to stay that way, for good health the diet rule is simple: Eat tasty, nutritious meals in the right amounts and enjoy every bite.

If you are more than 15 pounds overweight, ask your doctor whether you should reduce (that is, if you have not already been told to do so). Reduce, if your doctor says to; no "ifs" or "buts." Listen to medical advice.

Although correcting a weight problem seems simple enough to do on your own, never plunge into a diet without first consulting your doctor.

Doctor's Orders

The best reason for consulting a doctor is that a physical checkup will determine what ails you, if anything, besides your weight. The risks of hypertension, diabetes, gallbladder disease, joint disease aggravation, and cardiovascular disease increase as your degree of excess weight increases. Your doctor can check these things before you start out on a program to lose weight.

Your doctor probably will advise you to avoid any fad diet that extols one or two foods, supposedly bursting with slimming "miracles." Some reducing diets push kelp or other sources of iodine that can produce signs of iodine toxicity in the body. Some diets stress one class of foods at the expense of others. This can result in omission of foods that provide essential nutrients. Diets excessively high in one nutrient—fats, proteins, carbohydrates—can just as easily be looked on as low in another nutrient. For example, restrict your carbohydrate intake excessively and you'll likely be on a high-fat diet without knowing it.

Do not attempt a starvation diet or a protein-supplemented fast without close medical supervision. This book avoids that sort of thing as well as any "miracle" diets. Instead, this book recommends that you eat a variety of nutritious foods that are good for you in an appropriate amount.

Weight control is not a matter of crash reducing for brief periods of time. It is a lifetime proposition, and the foods you eat while reducing should be the kinds of foods that you would like to eat forever.

Telltale Bulges

To reduce safely you must have excess fat to lose. Believe it or not, a few people who are already beanpole slim want to reduce. (A doctor may be able to prevent such dangerous folly by giving sound medical guidance.) Generally, excess fat is all too visible. Stand naked in front of a full-length mirror. Look for telltale bulges, such as fleshy pads or "spare tires." Fat tends to cluster in slightly different areas of the body in men than in women.

On women, check for extra fat under the chin, at back of neck, the breasts, abdomen, upper arms, buttocks, hips, and thighs.

On men, check under the chin, at the back of the neck, the abdomen, and trunk.

Stand erect, sink your chin into your chest, and look down. If you can't see your toes without craning your neck, you have something to lose.

Tense your abdominal muscles as if someone were aiming a blow at you. While doing this, press your fingertips over your midriff. If the fat pad over the muscles feels soft and cushiony, you could spare some of it. A physically fit person should be able to feel the hardness of tensed muscles and even see a muscular ripple or two.

The "pinch test" gives another clue to excess body fat. Stand straight and have someone pinch just below your shoulder blades or at the back of your upper arm. Is there fat to spare?

Do last year's clothes have shrinking fits? Have your waistline and neckline measurements increased in the last five years or so? If you're more than 25 years old, could you get into the same clothes you wore then? Has the width of your shoe size increased? Do buttons and zippers have that strained look when they are closed?

Such signs may persuade you that you have fat to lose. Another way is to check your standing against a weight chart. Weight charts have the advantage of being completely impersonal and objective. Standards of average weight are given on page 31. Weigh yourself without shoes and clothing, check the chart, and find out how you measure up to the averages on the weight chart.

Normal weights in healthy persons will vary over a wide range because of individual differences in body structure. Persons with larger than average builds (wide shoulders and hips, large wrists and ankles) should generally weigh between the medium and large frame figures given in the table on page 31. Persons with small builds (narrow shoulders and hips, small wrists and ankles) probably should weigh somewhere between the average or medium frame and the low figures given for their height. Most people, however, have medium or average frames. Frequently, an overweight person will use a weight table to justify the extra weight by claiming a frame bigger than it really is. If your weight exceeds your desirable weight by 10 pounds or more, your doctor probably will tell you it's time to reduce.

Occasionally, excess weight is not caused by excess fat. Large amounts of water (which weighs more than fat) may accumulate in body tissue and tip the scales. Abnormal water retention is usually associated with some physical disorder. That's just another reason why you should consult your doctor before you start a reducing program of any kind so that your overall health status can be evaluated.

Why Reduce Your Weight?

Better personal appearance is a wonderful reason for keeping your weight normal, but there are other reasons, too. Obesity is frequently associated with high blood pressure and the onset of diabetes in susceptible persons. Excess fat makes breathing less efficient and puts a cruel and heavy load on joints that have to support it. Besides, overweight people usually will have shorter life-spans. And an impediment to vitality is lifted when useless dead weight is removed from the vital organs.

If you've just discovered that you need to shed a few extra pounds, you're not alone. One estimation has it that at least half the adults in the United States are either overweight or obese. With all the talk about fitness and diets, one would think that Americans are a slim bunch. Not so. As a group, Americans today are fatter than their counterparts a generation ago.

Many people manage to shed a few unwanted pounds. However, few people keep these pounds off. Instead, the unwanted, excess pounds come back when old eating habits are resumed. There's no easy solution for keeping off those excess pounds other than developing new eating and exercise habits that will become a way of life for you. Once you have set out to calorie-trim your cooking, or to master a system of weight control such as the Food Exchange System explained in chapter 12, you can lose those extra pounds and maintain your new weight.

HOW EXCESS WEIGHT COMES AND GOES

How does excess body fat pile up where it's not wanted? It comes from eating more food than we burn up through physical activity and the bodily processes that require energy.

To further explain, foods furnish energy that is measured in heat units called calories. You need a certain number of calories daily just to sustain life. And you obtain calories through foods, with each food varying in the amount of calories it supplies.

Protein, carbohydrate, and fat are the nutrient sources of calories. Proteins and carbohydrates provide four calories per gram; fats have nine calories per gram. Alcohol, another source of calories, provides seven calories per gram, but has little nutritional value.

It is important to evaluate foods for their nutrient makeup as well as their calorie count. Foods may have approximately the same amount of calories but vary greatly in their nutritional contribution to the diet. For example, an apple has 80 calories and adds vitamins to the diet; one cup of a carbonated cola beverage has 96 calories, yet it contributes next to nothing nutritionally.

Body weight is maintained when calorie intake equals calories used for energy. If we take in more calories from food and drink than we burn up through activity and basic body functions, the surplus calories are stashed away in the form of body fat and you gain weight. Each pound of excess body fat represents 3,500 calories of unused energy. The body acts as a sort of fat bank. If excessive intake of calories continues, the fat bank bulges and bulges from the heavy deposits.

Reducing is a matter of making withdrawals from the fat bank. There are only two safe ways to do this: Eat less and reduce calorie intake; or increase physical activity and burn up more calories. Or, you can combine the two and consume fewer calories and increase your physical activity.

In short, reducing requires a low-calorie diet combined when possible with more activity to help you lose weight faster and feel better.

Calorie Counters

Your body never fails to count a calorie, even if you fail to. You can look up the number of calories of general types of foods in the calorie tables on the following four pages. And you can check the nutrition analysis charts at the beginning of many of the chapters for calorie counts of specific recipes. Or, you can let Food Exchanges count calories for you.

As explained in chapter 12, Food Exchanges are units of the foods—such as meats, vegetables, fats, and fruits—that are foundations of good nutrition. The Food Exchanges, long used by professional dietitians, furnish definite amounts of calories. So, in planning meals, Food Exchanges not only help balance the diet and allow personal choices of foods you like, but also count your calories automatically so you don't have to struggle with the tallying.

One thing about dieting: You're sure to shed excess fat if your calorie deficit is sufficient to make withdrawals from your fat bank. It's also well to remember that everything that makes fat enters via the mouth. That's where fat control begins. And all too often that's where it ends.

When Extra Weight Comes

At various times in your life you must guard carefully against the perilous probability of weight gain. You, like many others, may allow a few too many extra pounds to accumulate after achieving adulthood—probably because of reduced physical activity with no change in food intake. Don't let those added pounds accumulate and go unnoticed.

As you grow older, your body requires fewer calories to fuel basic processes. Unless food intake is gradually reduced or physical activity increased, extra pounds surely will sneak up.

Women tend to gain weight at menopause and after the birth of children, especially if the first child comes when the woman is in her thirties.

Excess weight carried over from childhood can be a lifelong problem requiring constant vigilance. Sometimes emotional or psychological problems related to being overweight need medical attention.

Fallacies About Reducing

Misconceptions about reducing explain the appeal of many get-slim-quick schemes that seem to promise a loss of those excess pounds with no effort at all.

Novel diets of supposedly superior slimming power keep springing up and fading away. Sometimes a diet implies that the calories of certain foods or beverages are ignored by the body and that these foods can be eaten in any quantity. But *calories always count,* whatever their source. The only calories that don't count are those you don't swallow.

Sometimes, incredible virtues are attributed to exotic foods, or to one or two foods at the expense of others, although common wholesome foods in variety are the best and safest foundation for reducing diets. Only the magic of a balanced reducing diet, which provides a variety of nutritious foods, can result in years of eating and staying slim and healthy. The Food Exchange system is one way to provide good eating habits that help keep off those unwanted pounds.

Passive exercise (the kind in which all the effort is provided by another person or by a motor-driven machine) is useless for shedding fat or increasing muscle strength. This exercise system, however, may make you feel good. Massage, by hand or with vibrators, has valuable uses, but not for reducing. Fat won't melt away or rub off through massage. Local fat deposits can't be reduced by rollers or by shaking, shimmying gadgets. If so-called "spot-reducing" techniques seem to get results, it's because the subject has been made to eat less, get more exercise, or both.

Sweating from strenuous exercise, a hot bath, or baking in a steam cabinet can get rid of a pound or two of water (which is a part of your total body weight) in a hurry. But what you lose is merely water that is promptly replaced when you drink. Body fat can't be steamed off effectively.

"Reducing pills" prescribed by doctors are potent drugs, available only by prescription. Most common pills act on centers of the brain to depress appetite. This may make a low-calorie diet more satisfying during the first few weeks when the reducer is adjusting to the different diet and learning better eating habits.

Another drug prescribed by physicians is thyroid substance, which makes body fires burn more brightly. A few people who produce too little thyroid hormone may be sluggish and overweight and are prescribed a thyroid substance. However, if a person's thyroid production is normal (tests by your doctor are necessary to determine this), additional thyroid supplements can be hazardous to your health.

The place of drugs in weight reduction is simple. If your doctor prescribes them, take them. If he doesn't prescribe them for you, then leave them alone and avoid potential problems.

Some good dieting advice: Always avoid the quick weight-loss schemes.

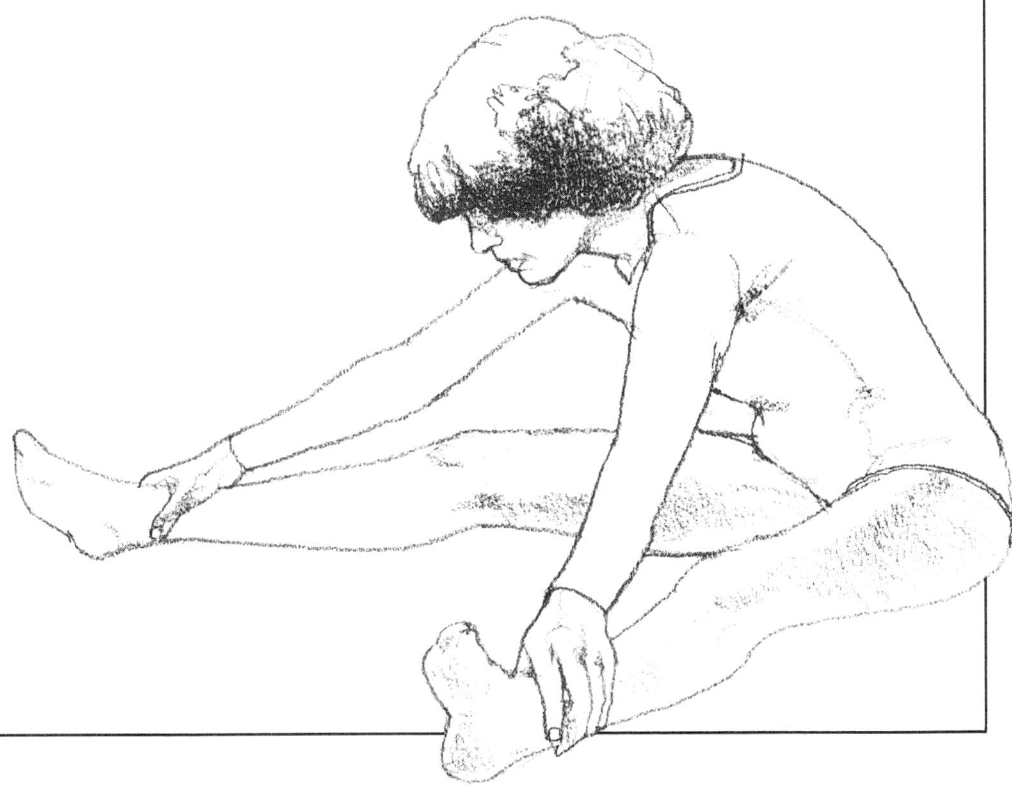

CALORIE COUNTS

A/B

ANCHOVY, canned; 5 fillets ... 35
APPLE
- fresh; 1 medium ... 80
- juice, canned; 1 cup ... 117

APPLESAUCE, canned
- sweetened; ½ cup ... 116
- unsweetened; ½ cup ... 50

APRICOT
- canned, in syrup; ½ cup ... 111
- dried, cooked, unsweetened, in juice; ½ cup ... 106
- fresh; 3 medium ... 55
- nectar; 1 cup ... 143

ASPARAGUS
- cooked, drained; 4 spears ... 12
- fresh cut spears; 1 cup ... 35

AVOCADO, peeled, all varieties
- ½ avocado ... 188

BACON
- 2 crisp strips, medium thickness ... 86
- Canadian-style, cooked; 1 slice ... 58

BANANA; 1 medium ... 101
BARBECUE SAUCE, bottled; ½ cup ... 114
BEANS
- baked, with tomato sauce and pork, canned; ½ cup ... 155
- green snap, canned; ½ cup ... 21
- green snap, fresh; ½ cup ... 17
- green snap, frozen; ½ cup ... 17
- lima, cooked; ½ cup ... 95
- red kidney, canned; ½ cup ... 115
- white, dry, cooked; ½ cup ... 112
- yellow or wax, cooked; ½ cup ... 14

BEAN SPROUTS, fresh; ½ cup ... 18
BEEF, dried, chipped; 2 ounces ... 116
BEEF CUTS
- corned, canned; 3 ounces ... 184
- ground beef, cooked
  - 10 percent fat; 3 ounces ... 186
  - 21 percent fat; 3 ounces ... 233
- pot roast, cooked
  - lean and fat; 3 ounces ... 246
  - lean only; 3 ounces ... 164
- rib roast, cooked
  - lean and fat; 3 ounces ... 375
  - lean only; 3 ounces ... 205
- round steak, cooked; 3 ounces ... 161
- sirloin steak, broiled; 3 ounces ... 329

BEEF LIVER, fried; 2 ounces ... 130
BEETS, cooked, diced; ½ cup ... 27
BEVERAGES, alcoholic
- beer; 1 cup ... 101
- dessert wine; 1 ounce ... 41
- gin, rum, vodka – 80 proof; 1 jigger ... 97
- table wine; 1 ounce ... 25

BISCUIT, enriched baking powder;
- 1 (2-inch diameter) ... 103

BLACKBERRIES
- canned in syrup; ½ cup ... 116
- fresh; ½ cup ... 42

BLUEBERRIES
- fresh; ½ cup ... 45
- frozen, sweetened; ½ cup ... 121

BOUILLON
- instant granules; 1 teaspoon ... 2

BOYSENBERRIES, frozen,
- unsweetened; ½ cup ... 30

BREAD
- Boston brown; 1 slice (3¼x½ inch) ... 95
- breadstick, plain; 1 (7¾ inches long) ... 19
- corn; 1 piece (2½ inches square) ... 161
- crumbs, dry; ¼ cup ... 98
- crumbs, soft; ¾ cup ... 30
- cubes; 1 cup ... 81
- French; 1 slice (½ inch thick) ... 44
- Italian; 1 slice (½ inch thick) ... 28
- pumpernickel; 1 slice ... 79
- raisin; 1 slice ... 66
- rye; 1 slice ... 61
- Vienna; 1 slice (½ inch thick) ... 73
- white; 1 slice ... 68
- whole wheat; 1 slice ... 56

BROCCOLI
- cooked; 1 medium stalk ... 47
- frozen chopped, cooked; ½ cup ... 24

BRUSSELS SPROUTS, cooked; ½ cup ... 28
BUTTER
- regular; 1 tablespoon ... 102
- whipped; 1 tablespoon ... 67

C

CABBAGE
- Chinese, raw; ½ cup ... 6
- common varieties, raw, shredded; 1 cup ... 17
- red, raw, shredded; 1 cup ... 22

CAKE, baked from home recipes
- angel, no icing; 1/12 cake ... 161
- chocolate, 2 layers, chocolate icing; 2-inch wedge ... 365
- fruitcake; 1 slice (¼x2x1½ inches) ... 57
- pound; 1 slice (3½x3x½ inches) ... 142
- sponge, no icing; 1/12 cake ... 131
- white, no icing; 1/12 cake ... 256
- yellow, chocolate icing; 1/12 cake ... 365

CANDY
- caramel; 1 ounce (3 medium) ... 113
- chocolate bar, milk; 1 ounce ... 147
- chocolate fudge; 1 piece (1 cubic inch) ... 84
- gumdrops; 1 ounce (2½ large or 20 small) ... 98
- hard; 1 ounce ... 109
- jelly beans; 1 ounce (10 pieces) ... 104
- peanut brittle; 1 ounce ... 119

CANTALOUPE (muskmelon)
- ¼ (5-inch diameter) ... 41

CARROT
- cooked, diced; ½ cup ... 22
- raw; 1 large or 2 small ... 30

CATSUP; 1 tablespoon ... 16
CAULIFLOWER
- cooked; ½ cup ... 14
- raw, whole flowerets; 1 cup ... 27

CELERY, raw, chopped; ½ cup ... 10
CEREAL, cooked
- oatmeal; ½ cup ... 66
- wheat, rolled; ½ cup ... 90

CEREAL, ready-to-eat
- bran flakes; ½ cup ... 53
- cornflakes; ½ cup ... 47
- oats, puffed; ½ cup ... 50
- rice, crisp cereal with sugar; ½ cup ... 70
- rice, puffed; ½ cup ... 30
- wheat flakes; ½ cup ... 53
- wheat, puffed; ½ cup ... 27

CHEESE
- American, process; 1 ounce ... 105
- blue; 1 ounce ... 104
- brick; 1 ounce ... 105
- Camembert; 1 ounce ... 85
- cheddar; 1 ounce ... 113
- cottage, dry; 1 cup ... 125
- cottage, from skim milk, cream-style; 1 cup ... 223
- cream cheese; 1 ounce ... 106
- Edam; 1 ounce ... 105
- Gruyère; 1 ounce ... 110
- Limburger; 1 ounce ... 98
- Neufchâtel; 1 ounce ... 70
- Parmesan, grated; 1 tablespoon ... 23
- spread, American; 1 ounce ... 82
- Swiss (natural); 1 ounce ... 105

CHERRIES
- canned (heavy syrup), tart or sweet, pitted; ½ cup ... 104
- canned (water pack), tart or sweet, pitted; ½ cup ... 52
- fresh, sweet, whole; ½ cup ... 41

CHEWING GUM, candy coated; 1 piece ... 5

CHICKEN
- dark meat, skinned, fried; 4 ounces ... 249
- dark meat, skinned, roasted; 4 ounces ... 209
- dark meat, with skin, fried; 4 ounces ... 263
- light meat, skinned, fried; 4 ounces ... 223
- light meat, skinned, roasted; 4 ounces ... 206
- light meat, with skin, fried; 4 ounces ... 234
- potpie; 1 individual (4½-inch diameter) ... 545

CHICK-PEAS, raw; ½ cup ... 360

CHILI SAUCE; 1 tablespoon ... 16

CHIVES, chopped; 1 tablespoon ... 1

CHOCOLATE
- bitter; 1 ounce ... 143
- semisweet; 1 ounce ... 144
- sweet plain; 1 ounce ... 150
- syrup, fudge-type; 1 tablespoon ... 62
- syrup, thin-type; 1 tablespoon ... 46

CLAMS, canned in liquor; ½ cup ... 57

COCOA, whole milk; 1 cup ... 243

COCOA POWDER, unsweetened; 1 tablespoon ... 14

COCONUT, shredded; ½ cup ... 138

COFFEE ... 2

COLA, carbonated beverage; 1 cup ... 96

COOKIES
- butter thin; 1 (2¼-inch diameter) ... 23
- chocolate chip; 1 ... 49
- cream sandwich, chocolate; 1 ... 49
- fig bars; 1 ... 50
- gingersnap; 1 ... 29
- sugar; 1 (2¼-inch diameter) ... 35
- vanilla wafer; 3 ... 42

CORN
- cream style; ½ cup ... 105
- sweet, cooked; 1 ear (5x1¾ inches) ... 70
- whole kernel; ½ cup ... 87

CORNSTARCH; 1 tablespoon ... 29

CORN SYRUP; 1 tablespoon ... 59

CRAB MEAT, canned; ½ cup ... 68

CRACKERS
- butter, rectangular; 1 ... 17
- cheese, round; 1 ... 15
- graham; 4 small pieces ... 55
- oyster; 10 ... 33
- rusk; 1 ... 38

CRACKERS (continued)
- rye wafer, crisp; 2 (1⅞x3½ inches) ... 45
- saltine; 2 (2-inch square) ... 24
- soda; 2 (2-inch square) ... 25

CRANBERRY JUICE COCKTAIL
- bottled; 1 cup ... 164

CRANBERRY-ORANGE RELISH; 1 cup ... 490

CRANBERRY SAUCE, sweetened, canned; 1 cup ... 404

CREAM
- half-and-half; 1 tablespoon ... 20
- heavy or whipping; 1 tablespoon ... 53
- light; 1 tablespoon ... 32
- light, whipped, unsweetened; 1 tablespoon ... 22

CUCUMBER; 6 large slices (1 ounce) ... 4

D/G

DATES, fresh or dried, pitted; 10 ... 219

DOUGHNUT
- cake type, plain; 1 (1½ ounces) ... 164
- yeast type; 1 (1½ ounces) ... 176

ECLAIR, with custard filling and chocolate icing; 1 (5x2x1¾ inches) ... 239

EGG
- fried; 1 large ... 99
- scrambled, plain; made with 1 large egg ... 111
- poached, hard- or soft-cooked; 1 medium ... 72
- white only; 1 medium ... 15
- whole; 1 large ... 82
- whole; 1 medium ... 72
- yolk only; 1 medium ... 52

EGGPLANT, cooked, diced; ½ cup ... 19

ENDIVE, raw; 1 cup ... 10

FIGS
- canned, in syrup; ½ cup ... 109
- dried; 1 large ... 52
- raw; 3 small ... 96

FISH
- bass, baked; 3 ounces ... 219
- flounder, baked; 3 ounces ... 171
- haddock, fried; 3 ounces ... 141
- halibut, broiled; 3 ounces ... 144

FISH (continued)
- herring, canned; 3 ounces ... 176
- herring, pickled; 3 ounces ... 189
- ocean perch, fried; 3 ounces ... 192
- salmon, broiled or baked; 3 ounces ... 156
- salmon, canned, pink; ½ cup ... 155
- sardines, canned, in oil, drained; 3 ounces ... 174
- swordfish, broiled; 3 ounces ... 138
- tuna, canned, in oil, drained; ½ cup ... 158
- tuna, canned, in water, drained; ½ cup ... 126

FISH STICK, breaded; 1 ... 50

FLOUR
- cake, sifted; 1 cup ... 349
- wheat, all-purpose enriched; 1 tablespoon ... 28
- wheat, all-purpose enriched, unsifted; 1 cup ... 455

FRANKFURTER, cooked; 1 ... 139

FROSTING
- caramel; 1 cup ... 1,224
- chocolate, home recipe; 1 cup ... 1,034
- white, boiled; 1 cup ... 297

FRUIT COCKTAIL
- canned, in syrup; ½ cup ... 97
- canned, water-pack; ½ cup ... 45

GARLIC, peeled; 1 clove ... 4

GELATIN
- dry, unflavored; 1 envelope ... 23
- dessert, plain, ready-to-serve; ½ cup ... 71

GINGER ALE; 1 cup ... 72

GOOSE, cooked; 3 ounces ... 198

GOOSEBERRIES, raw; 1 cup ... 59

GRAPE DRINK; 1 cup ... 135

GRAPEFRUIT
- canned sections, in syrup; ½ cup ... 89
- fresh; ½ medium ... 45

GRAPEFRUIT JUICE
- canned, sweetened; 1 cup ... 133
- canned, unsweetened; 1 cup ... 101
- fresh; 1 cup ... 96
- frozen, sweetened, reconstituted; 1 cup ... 117
- frozen, unsweetened, reconstituted; 1 cup ... 101

GRAPES
- concord, fresh; ½ cup ... 35
- green, fresh; ½ cup ... 52
- juice, canned; 1 cup ... 167

GRIDDLE CAKE
- buckwheat; 1 (4-inch diameter) ... 54
- plain; 1 (4-inch diameter) ... 61

H/O

HAM, fully cooked, lean; 3 ounces 159
HONEY; 1 tablespoon 64
HONEYDEW MELON; ¼ medium
(6½-inch diameter) 124
HORSERADISH, prepared; 1 tablespoon 6
ICE CREAM, vanilla,
10 percent fat; 1 cup 257
ice milk; 1 cup 199
soft serve; 1 cup 266
JAM; 1 tablespoon 54
JELLY; 1 tablespoon 49
KALE, cooked; ½ cup 22
KOHLRABI, cooked; ½ cup 20
LAMB, cooked
loin chop, lean; 3 ounces 159
rib chop, lean; 3 ounces 180
roast leg, lean; 3 ounces 158
LARD; 1 tablespoon 117
LEMON; 1 medium 20
LEMONADE, frozen, sweetened,
reconstituted; 1 cup 107
LEMON JUICE; 1 tablespoon 4
LENTILS, cooked; ½ cup 106
LETTUCE
Boston; ¼ medium head 6
iceberg; ¼ medium compact head 18
leaves; 2 large or 4 small 10
LIME; 1 medium 19
LIME JUICE; 1 tablespoon 4
LIVERWURST; 2 ounces
(3¼-inch diameter, ¼ inch thick) 175
LOBSTER, canned; ½ cup 69
LUNCHEON MEAT
bologna; 1 ounce 79
ham, boiled; 1 ounce 66
salami, cooked; 1 ounce 88
MACARONI, cooked; ½ cup 78
MACARONI AND CHEESE, baked;
½ cup 215
MALTED MILK; 1 cup 244
MAPLE SYRUP; 1 tablespoon 50
MARGARINE; 1 tablespoon 102
MARMALADE, orange; 1 tablespoon 51
MARSHMALLOWS; 1 ounce 90
MELBA TOAST; 1 slice 15
MILK
buttermilk; 1 cup 88
chocolate drink; 1 cup 190
condensed, sweetened, undiluted;
1 cup 982
dried nonfat, instant, reconstituted;
1 cup 81
evaporated, undiluted; 1 cup 345
skim; 1 cup 88
skim, 2-percent fat; 1 cup 145
whole; 1 cup 159
MOLASSES, light; 1 tablespoon 50
MUFFIN
blueberry; 1 (2⅜-inch diameter) 112
bran; 1 (2⅝-inch diameter) 104
corn; 1 (2¼-inch diameter) 126
plain; 1 (2¾-inch diameter) 118
MUSHROOMS, raw; 1 cup 20
MUSTARD, prepared; 1 tablespoon 12
MUSTARD GREENS, cooked; ½ cup 16
NECTARINE, raw; 1 (2½-inch diameter) 88
NOODLES
cooked; ½ cup 100
dry; 1 ounce 110
NUTS
almonds, shelled, chopped;
1 tablespoon 48
Brazil nuts; 3 89
cashews, roasted; 4 or 5 75
peanuts, roasted, shelled, chopped;
1 tablespoon 52
pecans, chopped; 1 tablespoon 52
pistachio; 1 ounce 168
walnuts, chopped; 1 tablespoon 52
OILS
corn; 1 tablespoon 120
olive; 1 tablespoon 119
peanut; 1 tablespoon 119
safflower; 1 tablespoon 120
sesame; 1 tablespoon 120
soybean; 1 tablespoon 120
OKRA
fresh, cooked; 10 pods (3x⅝ inch) 31
frozen, cooked; ½ cup 35
OLIVES, green; 4 medium 15
ripe; 3 small 15
ONION
cooked; ½ cup 30
green, without tops; 6 small 14
mature, raw; 1 medium 32
mature, raw, chopped; 1 tablespoon 4
ORANGE; 1 medium 64
ORANGE JUICE
canned, unsweetened; 1 cup 120
fresh; 1 cup 112
frozen concentrate, reconstituted;
1 cup 122
OYSTERS
fried; 1 ounce 68
raw; ½ cup (6 to 10 medium) 79

P/S

PANCAKE; 1 (4-inch diameter) 61
PARSLEY, raw; 1 tablespoon 2
PARSNIPS, cooked; ½ cup 51
PEACHES
canned; 1 half and 2 tablespoons
syrup 96
canned (water-pack); ½ cup 35
fresh; 1 medium 38
frozen, sweetened; ½ cup 110
PEANUT BUTTER; 1 tablespoon 94
PEARS
canned; 2 halves and
2 tablespoons syrup 91
fresh; 1 medium 100
PEAS, green, cooked; ½ cup 57
PEPPER, GREEN, sweet, chopped; ½ cup .. 16
PICKLE RELISH, sweet; 1 tablespoon 21
PICKLES
dill; 1 large (4 x 1¾ inches) 15
sweet; 1 medium (2¾x¾ inch) 30
PIE (⅙ of a 9-inch pie)
apple 404
blueberry 382
cherry 412
custard 331
lemon meringue 357
mince 428
pumpkin 321
PIE SHELL, baked; one 9-inch 900
PIMIENTO; 2 tablespoons 7
PINEAPPLE
canned, in syrup; ½ cup 86
canned, water-pack; ½ cup 48
fresh, diced; ½ cup 40
PIZZA, cheese; ⅛ of 14-inch pie 153
PLUMS
canned, syrup pack; ½ cup 107
canned, water-pack; ½ cup 57
fresh; 1 (2-inch diameter) 6
POMEGRANATE, raw; 1 medium 97

POPCORN
oil and salt; 1 cup 41
plain; 1 cup 23
POPOVER, home recipe; 1 90
PORK, cooked
chop, loin center cut, lean only; 3 ounces 198
picknic shoulder, fresh, lean; 3 ounces . 180
sausage, links or patty; 3 ounces 291
POTATO CHIPS; 10 medium 114
POTATOES
baked; 1 medium (oblong) 145
boiled; 1 medium (round) 104
french fried, homemade; 10 medium .. 214
french fried, frozen, oven-heated; 10 medium 172
hash-brown; ½ cup 177
mashed with milk; ½ cup 68
scalloped and au gratin, with cheese; ½ cup 178
scalloped and au gratin, without cheese; ½ cup 128
sweet, baked; 1 medium 148
sweet, candied; 1 medium 295
sweet, canned, vacuum packed; ½ cup 108
POTATO STICKS; 1 cup 190
PRETZELS; 10 small sticks 23
PRUNE JUICE, canned; 1 cup 197
PRUNES, dried
cooked, unsweetened; ½ cup 127
uncooked, pitted; 1 cup 459
PUDDING, cornstarch
chocolate; ½ cup 192
vanilla; ½ cup 141
PUMPKIN, canned; 1 cup 81
RABBIT, domestic; 3 ounces 183
RADISHES, raw; 5 medium 5
RAISINS; 1 cup 419
RASPBERRIES
black, fresh; ½ cup 49
red, canned; ½ cup 43
red, fresh; ½ cup 35
red, frozen, sweetened; ½ cup 122
RHUBARB
cooked, sweetened; ½ cup 191
raw, diced; 1 cup 20
RICE
brown, cooked; ½ cup 116
quick-cooking, cooked; ½ cup 90
white, cooked; ½ cup 112
RICE PRODUCTS, ready-to-eat breakfast cereals
oven-popped, sweetened; 1 cup 117
puffed, unsweetened; 1 cup 60
shredded, sweetened; 1 cup 98

ROLL
bun (frankfurter or hamburger); 1 119
hard; 1 medium 156
plain; 1 medium 119
sweet; 1 medium 179
RUSK, 3¾-inch diameter, ½ inch thick; 1 38
RUTABAGAS, cooked; ½ cup 30
SALAD DRESSING
blue cheese; 1 tablespoon 76
French; 1 tablespoon 66
home-cooked; 1 tablespoon 26
Italian; 1 tablespoon 83
mayonnaise; 1 tablespoon 101
mayonnaise-type; 1 tablespoon 65
mayonnaise-type, low cal; 1 tablespoon 22
Russian; 1 tablespoon 74
Thousand Island; 1 tablespoon 80
SAUERKRAUT, canned; ½ cup 21
SCALLOPS, cooked; 3 ounces 99
SHERBET, orange; ½ cup 130
SHORTENING; 1 tablespoon 111
SHRIMP
canned; 3 ounces 100
french-fried; 3 ounces 192
fresh, boiled; 3 ounces 98
SOUP, condensed, canned, diluted with water unless specified otherwise
bean with pork; 1 cup 168
beef bouillon broth, consommé; 1 cup .. 31
beef noodle; 1 cup 67
chicken noodle; 1 cup 62
clam chowder, Manhattan-style; 1 cup .. 81
cream of asparagus, diluted with milk; 1 cup 147
cream of celery, diluted with milk; 1 cup 169
cream of mushroom, diluted with milk; 1 cup 216
split-pea; 1 cup 145
tomato; 1 cup 88
tomato, diluted with milk; 1 cup 173
vegetable with beef broth; 1 cup 78
SOY SAUCE; 1 tablespoon 12
SPINACH
canned; ½ cup 22
frozen, chopped, cooked; ½ cup 23
raw, torn; 1 cup 14
SQUASH
frozen, cooked; ½ cup 45
summer, cooked, diced; ½ cup 15
winter, baked, mashed; ½ cup 65

STRAWBERRIES
fresh, whole; ½ cup 28
frozen, sweetened, whole; ½ cup 117
SUCCOTASH, frozen; ½ cup 75
SUGAR
brown, packed; 1 tablespoon 51
granulated; 1 tablespoon 46
powdered; 1 tablespoon 31

T/Z

TANGERINE; 1 medium 39
TAPIOCA, granulated; 1 tablespoon 30
TARTAR SAUCE; 1 tablespoon 74
TEA 0
TOMATO
canned; ½ cup 25
fresh; 1 medium 27
juice, canned; 1 cup 46
paste, canned; 6 ounces 139
purée; 1 cup 88
sauce; 1 cup 70
TOMATO CATSUP; 1 tablespoon 16
TOMATO CHILI SAUCE; 1 tablespoon 16
TURKEY, roasted;
3 slices (4x2x¼ inch) 162
TURNIP GREENS, cooked; ½ cup 15
TURNIPS, cooked, diced; ½ cup 18
VEAL, cooked
cutlet; 3 ounces 184
loin chop; 3 ounces 198
rib roast; 3½ ounces 229
VEGETABLE JUICE COCKTAIL; 1 cup 41
VEGETABLES, mixed, frozen, cooked; ½ cup 58
VINEGAR; 1 tablespoon 2
WAFFLE; 1 (4½ x4½ x⅝ inch) 140
WATER CHESTNUTS; 4 55
WATERCRESS, raw, chopped; ½ cup 12
WATERMELON; 1 wedge (8x4 inches) 111
YEAST, active, dry; 1 envelope 20
YOGURT
low-fat, fruit-flavored; ½ cup 115
plain, made from skim milk; ½ cup 61
plain, made from whole milk; ½ cup 76
ZUCCHINI; 1 medium 26
ZWIEBACK; 1 piece 30

DO-IT-YOURSELF
REDUCING

Put in the simplest of terms, the secret of losing weight is no more complicated than consuming less energy (fewer calories) than you burn up. Maintaining your "ideal" weight is equally simple: Balance the amount of energy you expend with the number of calories you consume. But, as is often true with simple formulas, there's a catch: You'll have to make some changes in your eating and exercise habits. To get you started, here are a few pointers for estimating your caloric needs, some dieting tips, plus suggestions for planning your daily menus.

BEHAVIOR MODIFICATION

Successful dieters quickly realize they were eating more from habit, to relieve stress, or because of social customs than to meet their body's energy needs. Once a dieter realizes that all calories count in the day's tally, she will want to make calorie counting and nutrition awareness a daily habit. Don't give up watching the diet once a desired weight is attained, or those excess, unwanted pounds may slowly reappear.

Whatever the cause of your weight problem, you should be able to apply some, if not all, of these dieting tips and suggestions as you start to change when you eat and the reasons why you eat:

• **Keep a meal record.** Before you begin to change the way you eat, keep a record for a week or two of what, when, where, and how much you eat. (A small notebook is handy for such record keeping.) Then, use a calorie chart, such as the one on pages 22 to 25, to figure out your daily caloric intake.

Total energy needs vary from person to person, but the height and weight chart on page 31 will help you approximate your ideal weight.

• **Identify the trouble spots and work on them.** After studying your diet record, look for ways to make changes. Have you acquired the habit of skipping meals, then gorging later to compensate? Are you snacking on high-calorie foods? Do you eat only to be sociable? Do you eat automatically, even if you're not really hungry?

Can you spot extra calories you can eliminate easily? If so, you're ready to change the why, when, and where of your eating habits by modifying your behavior.

Many of us are overweight because we associate eating with certain "cues," such as specific times of the day (coffee breaks, for instance), a particular mood (depression or boredom), even certain television commercials.

Behavior modification—a commonsense approach to dieting—teaches you to recognize your own cues and replace them with other forms of behavior. For instance, instead of eating while watching television, try knitting. Try substituting a good, brisk walk for a snack if you're bored or depressed.

• **Limit the areas where you eat.** Eat all your meals and snacks in the kitchen or dining room; consider all other rooms out of bounds.

• **Concentrate on eating.** If you eat while reading or watching television you can unconsciously overeat.

• **Eat formally.** Whenever you eat, serve the food on a plate, even if you are having just a light snack. Sit yourself down at the kitchen or dining room table. A dislike for washing extra dishes from snacks may help curb your appetite.

• **Eat less, but more frequently.** If your record shows you're eating three big meals a day, you may want to change your eating pattern. Instead of a big breakfast, lunch, and dinner, reduce the size of each meal. Between meals, substitute low-calorie snacks. Or, try setting aside a part of your normal meal for your "between meals," so you have four or five mini-meals a day. Frequent meals may help reduce your eating "extra" foods. By eating less food more often, you avoid feeling hungry all the time.

• **Use smaller plates.** Like many people, you're probably conditioned to clean every bit of food from your plate. And like many of us, you're probably overfilling your plate. So by limiting the size of the plate, you also limit the amount of food you consume at one sitting. By using smaller plates, you are still able to eat everything on it, only now the plate contains less food.

• **Change your snacking habits.** Substitute low-calorie foods for cookies, cakes, candy, chips and other traditional, high-calorie snacks. Fresh fruit and vegetables will satisfy your craving to munch, yet contribute fewer calories.

• **Eat slowly.** Doing so allows your brain time to register the food you eat and stop the impulses that make you think you're hungry. By eating fast you override the brain-to-stomach circuitry that tells you when to quit. You become full—and over-full—before the brain can turn off the desire to eat. By eating slowly, you know when to quit and can easily employ one of the best dieting exercises: pushing yourself away from the table.

• **Use positive reminders.** Try using the mnemonic "Think." The first four letters spell "thin;" the middle letter is "I." This "I think thin" becomes an easy-to-remember, positive memory device to help you change your eating habits. And here's a gimmick to avoid because of the negative associations. Don't paste a picture of a fat person on the refrigerator door. Instead, find a photo of a person who looks like you'd *like* to look and post it in a variety of locations. Today, the photo might be on the refrigerator door, two days later move it to the mirror in your bathroom, then to the clothes closet, your car, and to the top of the TV set. This constant shuffling simply keeps a positive image of your eventual goal in front of you all the time.

• **Make calorie counting and exercise a way of life.** As people get older, they tend to become more sedentary, and the disparity between food intake and energy expended causes them to gain weight. The body's basic requirements for calories decreases with age, meaning a person will gain weight unless he consumes fewer calories. The healthiest people are those who reach their adult weight level and remain stable thereafter. In other words, an adult's weight should be the same at age 50 as it was at age 25. Unfortunately for most of us, that means gradually cutting down on what we eat as we get older. Hard, yes; but the rewards of maintaining the proper weight are worth the sacrifice.

How To Make It Work

Here's a step-by-step guide to assuring success with your individual weight reduction program:

• **Ask for help if you need it.** You can begin a weight reducing diet by yourself, but if you're low on willpower, ask for help from your family doctor, friends, or one of the many reputable dieting organizations.

• **Resolve to take it slow and easy.** The surest way to fail at losing weight is to set unrealistic goals. No doubt it took considerable time to put on those pounds, and it'll take time (but not as much) to get them off. Medical authorities recommend a weight loss goal of no more than two pounds a week.

• **Keep a written record of progress.** This will help you evaluate your success at periodic intervals.

• **Prepare for some setbacks.** Losing weight is sometimes hard work. Don't worry if you suddenly find you've put a few pounds back on. Take heart that you've progressed as far as you have. Even if there are temporary setbacks, it probably won't seem as difficult to re-lose those few extra pounds as it did when you began.

• **Schedule rewards for yourself along the way.** For instance, the first time you're able to wear a smaller size, buy a new outfit. Your friends will notice the change and their compliments will be further impetus to continue dieting.

Fad Diets—Do They Work?

Fad diets (including fasting or modified fasting; one-emphasis diets such as the so-called "grapefruit" diet; and low-carbohydrate, low-protein, or high-fiber diets) can be dangerous because they often restrict or eliminate many essential nutrients necessary for a nutritionally balanced diet. Often such fad diets are "rapid weight loss" schemes that seldom prove successful for more than a short time.

In fact, the up-and-down, roller-coaster effect of repeated weight loss and gain may have more serious repercussions than maintaining a consistent weight, even if it is excessive.

The best dieting advice is to stay away from all quick weight-loss schemes. Instead, stick to a diet that contains the following characteristics:

• It provides all the necessary nutrients but supplies fewer calories than you're now consuming.

• It includes foods from each of the Basic Five Food Groups, with only limited choices from the fifth group—the fats, sweets, and alcohol group. The diet should include a *variety* of foods.

• It conforms to your individual tastes, habits, and budget.

• It doesn't leave you continually hungry, tired, and irritable.

• It is easy to follow both at home and away from home without making you feel "different" from others.

• It helps you learn eating habits you can continue for the rest of your life.

ACTIVITY CHART

CALORIES BURNED PER HOUR BY A 150-POUND PERSON ENGAGED IN VARIOUS ACTIVITIES

Rest and Light Activity	**50-200**
Lying down or sleeping	80
Sitting	100
Driving an automobile	120
Standing	140
Domestic work	180
Moderate Activity	**200-350**
Bicycling (5½ mph)	210
Walking (2½ mph)	210
Gardening	220
Canoeing (2½ mph)	230
Golf	250
Lawn mowing (power mower)	250
Bowling	270
Lawn mowing (hand mower)	270
Fencing	300
Rowboating (2½ mph)	300
Swimming (¼ mph)	300
Walking (3¾ mph)	300
Badminton	350
Horseback riding (trotting)	350
Square dancing	350
Volleyball	350
Roller skating	350
Vigorous Activity	**over 350**
Table tennis	360
Ditch digging (hand shovel)	400
Ice skating (10 mph)	400
Wood chopping or sawing	400
Tennis	420
Water skiing	480
Hill climbing (100 ft. per hr.)	490
Skiing (10 mph)	600
Squash and handball	600
Cycling (13 mph)	660
Scull rowing (race)	840
Running (10 mph)	900

CALORIC NEEDS

To estimate the number of calories needed to keep your weight at its ideal level (see the height-and-weight chart on the opposite page), multiply your desired weight by 15 (multiply by 12 if you lead a less-than-active life). That gives you the approximate number of daily calories needed to maintain that weight. Thus, if you are a moderately active person and you wish to maintain your weight at 120 pounds, you can eat foods totaling no more than 1,800 calories. Remember that these calories are maintenance calories. To shed fat, you'll have to consume fewer calories than those needed to maintain your present weight. Therefore, if you're over (or under) your ideal weight, you're going to have to reduce (or increase) your caloric intake accordingly.

It takes 3,500 calories to make one pound of fat; so if you want to lose two pounds a week, you'll have to take in about 1,000 fewer calories per day than you burn up. Or you can decrease your caloric intake by 500 calories per day and exercise enough or increase your physical activity enough to burn the remaining 500 calories.

Diet and Exercise "Mystery" Solved

It's no secret that excess pounds and inches have a tendency to mysteriously creep up on us all. No doubt you've heard it said (or have even said it yourself): "I don't eat any more than I ever did, and I still put on weight."

The mystery evaporates when you study lifetime exercise and work habits. In that first job out of school, you may have been in a position that required manual labor or considerable activity. Then, as your experience and knowledge increased, your job may have changed from "doing" to managing. You probably aren't eating more than you did, but your activity level has decreased and you're burning up fewer calories than you once did.

The President's Council on Physical Fitness says that lack of physical activity is more often the cause of overweight than is overeating. The council cites lack of exercise as the most important cause of the "creeping" obesity in our mechanized society.

Put another way, with no increase in activity just one extra can of cola, an extra slice of buttered bread, or anything else that adds about 100 calories to your diet each day can add up to 10 extra pounds a year. But, if you skip those extra calories and walk an extra mile each day, you'll take off those excess pounds in a year.

Morever, exercise has benefits beyond weight loss. You'll look better, tone up flabby muscles, sleep better, and be better equipped to take life's frustrations in stride.

The chart at the left gives you a good idea of the number of calories expended per hour by a 150-pound person in various activities. The heavier you are, the more energy you expend for each activity because you also have to expend more energy just to move yourself around.

It's apparent that there's energy expenditure in everything you do, even sleeping. But your excess pounds will come off more quickly if you look for ways to increase the amount of energy you burn in activities that are pleasant to you, such as gardening, bicycling, walking, or even mowing the lawn.

HEIGHT-AND-WEIGHT CHART

Height without shoes, weight without clothes

This handy height-and-weight chart can tell you at a glance whether you may need to gain or lose weight. The figures in this chart are averages, so your ideal weight may vary by a few pounds from those listed.

MEN *Acceptable Weight Range (pounds)*

HEIGHT	SMALL FRAME	MEDIUM FRAME	LARGE FRAME
5′ 2″	112	123	141
5′ 3″	115	127	144
5′ 4″	118	130	148
5′ 5″	121	133	152
5′ 6″	124	136	156
5′ 7″	128	140	161
5′ 8″	132	145	166
5′ 9″	136	149	170
5′10″	140	153	174
5′11″	144	158	179
6′ 0″	148	162	184
6′ 1″	152	166	189
6′ 2″	156	171	194

WOMEN *Acceptable Weight Range (pounds)*

HEIGHT	SMALL FRAME	MEDIUM FRAME	LARGE FRAME
4′10″	92	102	119
4′11″	94	104	122
5′ 0″	96	107	125
5′ 1″	99	110	128
5′ 2″	102	113	131
5′ 3″	105	116	134
5′ 4″	108	120	138
5′ 5″	111	123	142
5′ 6″	114	128	146
5′ 7″	118	132	150
5′ 8″	122	136	154
5′ 9″	126	140	158
5′10″	130	144	163

DINNER MENU

Orange-Spiced Pork Chops*	**208**
Parslied Brown Rice	**116**
Peas and Pods*	**56**
Mixed salad greens with radish and celery	**14**
Diet Thousand Island Dressing (1 Tbsp.)*	**21**
Berry-Melon Fruit Cup*	**52**
Skim milk (1 cup)	**88**
Coffee	**2**
TOTAL CALORIES	**557**

Serve this hearty, nutritious dinner, pictured on the opposite page, to family or friends. Pork chops are the featured entrée. The calories are already counted for you and the recipes marked with an asterisk (*) are in this book. Check the index for the page numbers.

Do-It-Yourself Menu Planning

A personalized, well-balanced, and calorie-controlled eating plan is important in any reducing diet that produces lasting results. True, it does not offer the quick-and-easy solutions promised by many fad diets. There's no gimmick involved, no magic formula to follow, and no secret combination of foods. What it does provide is a commonsense approach to the problem of keeping your weight under control.

Getting to know your eating habits is the first step in putting together a custom-made eating plan aimed at reducing your weight. Your food likes, dislikes, and your particular way of life affect what, when, where, and how much you eat. Take a close look at your eating habits by keeping a record for one or two weeks of the types and amounts of foods you eat. Figure your daily calorie intake using a calorie chart.

After going through your completed inventory, check to see whether the number of calories you've been consuming is the amount you require for your daily activities. (See page 30 to determine your calorie requirements.) If you take in more calories than you need, the excess will be stored as fat. To lose, you'll need to lower your calorie intake or exercise more.

Devising a calorie-reduced eating plan that is well-balanced may sound complicated, but it doesn't require you to be a nutrition expert. If it's well-balanced you'll find the weight easier to keep off, because the variety of foods provided will help you stay with the diet.

To achieve a balanced diet, you must combine the right amounts from each of the basic food groups. The information on pages 16 and 17 outlines the types of foods that belong in each group, the nutrients they supply, and the suggested number of daily servings. This basic food group system takes into account the RDA (Recommended Dietary Allowance), which is a nutritional standard set by the Food and Nutrition Board. The RDA tells how much of the known nutrients are recommended to meet the needs of a healthy person. Each food group contains foods of similar nutrient content. By planning your meals to include the suggested number of servings from each essential group, you'll receive an adequate intake of nutrients. If you have any medical problems that may require a special diet, be sure to consult your doctor.

A Menu Plan for You

Plan your meal schedule taking into account the demands of your day. If a traditional three-meal plan doesn't fit in, try a meal pattern that works better for you. Decide the number of meals you want per day, and the types of food you want to eat at certain times of the day. Consider each day's menu as a whole, keeping in mind the foods' total calorie and nutrient content.

Begin your planning around a protein main dish from the meat group. Everyone requires 2 servings a day from the meat group. Pregnant women and nursing mothers need more. On a traditional three-meal plan you could serve a food from this group at two of the meals. If you're using a five-meal plan you could distribute the protein throughout the day by serving half portions at four of the meals.

Next choose four servings from the vegetable-fruit group and four from the bread-cereal group. Servings from the milk group vary. Children need three servings, teenagers require four servings, and adults two servings. Work the required number of servings into the number of daily meals that you have chosen.

3-MEAL PLAN

This plan uses the usual three-meal-a-day schedule along with snacks. To give you an idea how you can divide up the food groups in this plan, here is one suggestion:
For meal 1, plan 1 milk serving, 1 citrus fruit serving, and 1 bread/cereal serving.
For meal 2, plan 1 meat serving, 1 vegetable serving, and 1 bread/cereal serving.
For a snack, plan 1 milk serving for children and teenagers, and 1 bread/cereal serving for everyone.
For meal 3, plan 1 meat serving, 1 vegetable serving (deep green or yellow variety every other day), 1 bread/cereal serving, 1 fruit serving, and 1 milk serving.
For a snack, plan 1 milk serving for teenagers.

To use this plan, simply plug in foods of your choice, such as those listed in the sample at right. Keep in mind your total calorie intake. By choosing low-calorie foods from each of the four required food groups, you can establish a well-balanced eating plan that helps you lose weight.

BASIC FOOD GROUPS (number of servings)	SAMPLE 3-MEAL PLAN
MEAL 1	
MILK (1)	1 cup skim milk
FRUIT/VEGETABLE (1)	½ grapefruit
BREAD/CEREAL (1)	½ cup cooked oatmeal
MEAL 2	
MEAT (1), BREAD/CEREAL (1), AND FRUIT/VEGETABLE (½)	Beef and Sprout Sandwiches*
FRUIT/VEGETABLE (½)	3 carrot sticks (3 inch)
SNACK	
MILK (1)	1 ounce mozzarella cheese (*children and teenagers*)
BREAD/CEREAL (1)	1 English muffin, toasted
MEAL 3	
MEAT (1) AND FRUIT/VEGETABLE (1)	Sole Florentine*
BREAD/CEREAL (1)	1 slice whole wheat bread
FRUIT/VEGETABLE (1)	Fruit Medley Salad*
MILK (¼)	Orange Yogurt Pie*
MILK (¾)	¾ cup skim milk
FATS/SWEETS/ALCOHOL	1 teaspoon butter
SNACK	
MILK (1)	1 cup cocoa — made with skim milk (*teenagers*)
TOTALS	
MEAT	2 servings
FRUIT/VEGETABLE	4 servings
BREAD/CEREAL	4 servings
MILK	2 servings (3 for *children*, 4 for *teenagers*)
CALORIES	1344

**Recipe for this item is in this book. See the index for the page number.*

5-MEAL PLAN

To give you an idea how you can divide foods from the basic food groups into five meals, here is one suggestion: *For meal 1,* plan 1 milk serving and 1 bread/cereal serving. *For meal 2,* plan ½ meat serving, 1 citrus fruit serving, and 1 bread/cereal serving. *For meal 3,* plan ½ meat serving, 1 milk serving, and 1 vegetable serving (deep green or yellow variety every other day). *For meal 4,* plan 1 milk serving (for children and teenagers) 1 vegetable serving, and 1 bread/cereal serving. *For meal 5,* plan 1 meat serving, 1 milk serving (for teenagers), 1 bread/cereal serving, and 1 fruit serving.

To use this plan, substitute foods of your choice. To help you start planning, use the sample five-meal plan at right.

BASIC FOOD GROUPS (number of servings)	SAMPLE 5-MEAL PLAN
MEAL 1	
MILK (1)	1 cup fruit-flavored yogurt
BREAD/CEREAL (1)	1 English muffin, toasted
FATS/SWEETS/ALCOHOL	1 teaspoon butter
FATS/SWEETS/ALCOHOL	2 teaspoons jelly
MEAL 2	
MEAT (½), BREAD/CEREAL (1), AND FATS/SWEETS/ALCOHOL	Open-face sandwich: 1½ ounces cooked chicken breast (sliced), 1 slice whole wheat toast, and 1 tablespoon low-calorie mayonnaise
FRUIT/VEGETABLE (1)	1 orange
MEAL 3	
FRUIT/VEGETABLE (1), MEAT (½), AND MILK (½)	Cottage Tomato Cups*
MILK (½)	½ ounce cheddar cheese
MEAL 4	
FRUIT/VEGETABLE (1)	Garden Vegetable Dip* (½ cup vegetable dippers and ¼ cup dip)
BREAD/CEREAL (1)	3 rye wafers
MILK (1)	1 cup skim milk (*children and teenagers*)
MEAL 5	
MEAT (1) AND BREAD/CEREAL (1)	Veal Sauté with Mushrooms*
FRUIT/VEGETABLE (1)	Fruit with Creamy Banana Dressing*
MILK (½)	Mandarin Rice Pudding* (*teenagers*)
MILK (½)	½ cup skim milk (*teenagers*)

TOTALS	
MEAT	2 servings
FRUIT/VEGETABLE	4 servings
BREAD/CEREAL	4 servings
MILK	2 servings (3 for *children,* 4 for *teenagers*)
CALORIES	1596

**Recipe for this item is in this book. See the index for the page number.*

MEATBALL DINNER

Cherry Tomato Meatballs*	312
Broccoli spears (2 small stalks)	72
Hard roll (1 small)	78
Whipped butter or margarine (1 teaspoon)	23
Orange-apple slice salad (½ medium orange, ½ apple on lettuce)	73
Whipped Gelatin*	8
Glass of skim milk (¾ cup)	66
TOTAL CALORIES	**632**

Try this dinner as suggested with plain broccoli spears or add a little zest to the broccoli (and a few extra calories) with the Sesame Broccoli recipe. For low-calorie, edible plate garnishes, try parsley sprigs and carrot curls.

If you use regular butter instead of the whipped butter, add 11 calories to the menu.

*For further nutrition information, see the chart on page 46.

CHERRY TOMATO MEATBALLS/312*

You can make these ahead; simply shape meatballs, cover, and refrigerate—

1 beaten egg
¾ cup soft bread crumbs (1 slice bread)
½ cup skim milk
¼ cup finely chopped onion
¾ teaspoon salt
½ teaspoon dried oregano, crushed
Dash pepper
• • •
1 pound lean ground beef
12 cherry tomatoes

In mixing bowl combine beaten egg, bread crumbs, milk, chopped onion, salt, oregano, and pepper. Add the ground beef and mix well. Shape about ¼ *cup* of meat mixture evenly around each cherry tomato to form round meatballs. Place meatballs in a 13x9x2-inch baking pan. Bake in a 375° oven for 25 to 30 minutes. Makes 4 servings.

SESAME BROCCOLI/77*

Next time, try chilling Sesame Broccoli and add the spears to a tossed green salad—

1 pound fresh broccoli
• • •
1 tablespoon cooking oil
1 tablespoon vinegar
1 tablespoon soy sauce
4 teaspoons sugar
1 tablespoon sesame seed, toasted

Wash broccoli; remove outer leaves and tough part of stalks. Cut broccoli lengthwise into uniform spears, following the branching lines. Cook, covered, in 1-inch of boiling, lightly salted water 10 to 15 minutes or till spears are crisp-tender.

In a saucepan combine the cooking oil, vinegar, soy sauce, sugar, and toasted sesame seed; heat to boiling. Pour the sesame-soy mixture over broccoli spears. Turn spears to coat evenly. Serves 5.

WHIPPED GELATIN/8*

If you like, top each serving with a little prepared whipped topping—

1 4-serving envelope low-calorie raspberry- *or* **strawberry-flavored gelatin**
1 cup boiling water
• • •
1 cup cold water *or* **low-calorie lemon-lime carbonated beverage**

Dissolve the flavored gelatin in boiling water; cool to room temperature. Stir in the cold water or carbonated beverage. Chill till partially set or till mixture is the consistency of unbeaten egg whites. Turn mixture into a mixer bowl; beat till light and fluffy. Spoon whipped gelatin into serving dishes; chill till firm. Makes 4 servings.

Note: If desired, spoon fresh, cut-up fruit into bottoms of parfait glasses; top with the whipped gelatin. Chill.

SEAFOOD SUPPER FOR 2

Halibut Steaks for Two* 283
Fluffy Baked Potato* 90
Green beans (½ cup) .. 17
Lettuce wedge (⅙ head) 12
Low-cal French dressing (1 tablespoon) 15
Fruit-filled orange (½ small orange, ½ cup pear, 1 tablespoon diced dates) .. 114
Glass of white wine (3 ounces) 75

TOTAL CALORIES 606

This dinner for two is easy to prepare and includes some foods usually forbidden among dieting fare. Use a convenient bottled salad dressing for the lettuce topper or save a few calories and shake together the Zesty Tomato Dressing. Of course, skim milk can be substituted for the wine.

*For further nutrition information, see the chart on page 46.

HALIBUT STEAKS FOR TWO/283*

You can use chopped mushrooms or shredded zucchini instead of tomato and carrot –

1 12-ounce package frozen halibut steaks
2 tablespoons lemon juice
2 tablespoons dry white wine
½ teaspoon salt
⅓ cup peeled and chopped tomato (1 small tomato)
1 medium carrot, shredded
2 tablespoons sliced green onion
2 tablespoons snipped parsley
2 lemon wedges

Thaw halibut steaks. Place fish in a 10x6x2-inch baking dish; sprinkle with the lemon juice, white wine, and salt. Combine tomato, carrot, green onion, and parsley; sprinkle over fish. Cover and bake in a 350° oven for 25 to 30 minutes or till fish flakes easily when tested with a fork. With slotted spatula lift fish and vegetables to serving platter. Accompany individual servings with a lemon wedge. Makes 2 servings.

FLUFFY BAKED POTATO/90*

If you like, mash potato with 2 teaspoons diet margarine; add 17 calories per serving –

1 medium baking potato
2 tablespoons Neufchâtel cheese
Snipped chives *or* dried chives

Scrub potato thoroughly. Use fork tines to prick into the potato. Bake in a 350° oven 70 minutes or till done. Cut potato in half lengthwise. Scoop out the insides of the potato with a spoon; mash. Return mashed potato to potato shell. Beat the Neufchâtel cheese lightly; spoon cheese atop potato. Sprinkle tops of potatoes with snipped chives. Makes 2 servings.

ZESTY TOMATO DRESSING/6*

Enhance the flavor of salads with this spicy low-calorie dressing –

1 8-ounce can tomato sauce
4 teaspoons vinegar
2 teaspoons Worcestershire sauce
1 teaspoon sugar
1 teaspoon grated onion
¾ teaspoon prepared horseradish
¼ teaspoon salt
Dash pepper

In a screw-top jar combine the tomato sauce, vinegar, Worcestershire sauce, sugar, grated onion, prepared horseradish, salt, and pepper. Cover and shake the ingredients to mix well. Chill to store. Shake salad dressing again just before serving. Makes about 1 cup salad dressing, or 16 one-tablespoon servings.

BURGER FEAST

Tomato Bouillon*........ 32
Burgers Florentine*.....294
Orange Cucumber Salad*................ 57
Julienne carrots (½ cup)............... 24
Pear chunks with whipped dessert topping from mix (1 pear, ¼ cup topping)..............140

TOTAL CALORIES.........547

This sumptuous-looking meal isn't as calorie laden as you might expect. Here's proof positive that a dieter's dinner can be hearty, colorful, and nutritious, too. Your guests will think you outdid yourself, but only you will know that the meal cuts calories.

One trick to remember: To fill up the dinner plate, arrange the salad on the plate along with the meat and vegetables.

BURGERS FLORENTINE / 294*

1 10-ounce package frozen chopped spinach
½ cup small curd cream-style cottage cheese
1 tablespoon snipped parsley
Dash salt
• • •
1 beaten egg
⅓ cup fine dry bread crumbs
1 teaspoon salt
2 pounds lean ground beef
• • •
½ of an 8-ounce can (½ cup) tomato sauce
¼ cup dry red wine
2 tablespoons chopped green pepper
2 tablespoons chopped onion

Cook spinach according to package directions; drain well. Combine drained spinach, cottage cheese, parsley, and the dash salt; mix well and set aside. In a bowl combine egg, crumbs, and the remaining salt; add beef and mix well. On waxed paper form meat mixture in 16 thin patties, 3 inches in diameter. Place about *2 tablespoons* of the spinach filling on each of 8 patties; top with remaining patties and seal edges well. In skillet brown half the filled patties at a time. Set patties aside. Discard excess fat. In same skillet combine tomato sauce, red wine, green pepper, and onion. Return burgers to skillet; spoon some sauce over. Cover and simmer 15 to 20 minutes. Remove burgers to a serving platter; pour sauce over. (If desired, boil the sauce down to thicken.) Makes 8 servings.

TOMATO BOUILLON / 32*

1 14½-ounce can (1¾ cups) beef broth
1 12-ounce can (1½ cups) tomato juice
1 teaspoon Worcestershire sauce
Few drops bottled hot pepper sauce
Thin lemon slices (optional)

In saucepan combine beef broth, tomato juice, Worcestershire sauce, and hot pepper sauce. Bring to boiling. Serve tomato mixture in mugs; top each with a lemon slice, if desired. Makes 4 servings.

ORANGE CUCUMBER SALAD / 57*

Delicately flavored bibb lettuce is a good base for this refreshing salad —

½ large cucumber, thinly sliced (1 cup)
¼ teaspoon salt
Dash pepper
2 medium oranges, peeled and sectioned
½ cup chopped green pepper
2 tablespoons snipped parsley
• • •
½ cup plain yogurt
¼ teaspoon dried thyme, crushed
Salad greens (optional)

In small mixing bowl sprinkle cucumber with the salt and pepper; toss with orange sections, green pepper, and parsley. Combine yogurt and thyme; spoon onto salad mixture. Toss lightly to coat. Cover and chill. Serve on crisp greens, if desired. Serves 4.

**For further nutrition information, see the chart on page 46.*

BARGAIN BRUNCH

Ham Soufflé in Green Pepper Cups* 223
Tomato wedges on lettuce (½ tomato) ... 20
Bran muffin 104
Butter or margarine (1 teaspoon) 34
Pineapple chunks in juice (½ cup fruit) 70
Glass of skim milk (¾ cup) 66
Tea 0

TOTAL CALORIES 517

For an elegant way to start the day, try this interesting brunch combination. Pick up some muffins in the bakery section of the supermarket, or bake up a wholesome batch of Bran Buttermilk Muffins from scratch. Serve tomato wedges on Bibb lettuce for a no-fuss vegetable, or if you have the time, prepare Cucumber-Topped Tomatoes for a few additional calories. Decorate the plate with a green onion garnish. Trim pineapple chunks with fresh mint.

**For further nutrition information, see the chart on page 46.*

HAM SOUFFLÉ IN GREEN PEPPER CUPS/223*

4 large green peppers
1 cup cubed fully cooked ham (5 ounces)
¾ cup skim milk
1 tablespoon butter *or* margarine
3 tablespoons all-purpose flour
1 teaspoon prepared mustard
3 slightly beaten egg yolks
3 egg whites

Place pepper on side. Remove slice from side of pepper; scoop out seeds and pulp. Repeat with remaining peppers. (Save slices for chopped green pepper in other recipes.) Cook whole peppers, covered, in boiling, lightly salted water for 5 minutes. Drain and set aside.

Meanwhile, in blender container combine ham and milk. Cover and blend till ham is slightly chopped. (Or, combine ground ham and the milk; do not blend.) In 1-quart saucepan melt butter or margarine; stir in flour and mustard. Add milk-ham mixture all at once. Cook and stir till mixture thickens and bubbles. Remove from heat. Gradually beat mixture into egg yolks. Beat egg whites to stiff peaks (tips stand straight), about 1½ minutes; fold in yolk mixture. Spoon mixture into peppers; place in 10x6x2-inch baking dish. Bake in a 375° oven for 25 to 30 minutes or till knife inserted into the ham mixture just off-center comes out clean. Makes 4 servings.

CUCUMBER-TOPPED TOMATOES/32*

⅓ cup low-calorie Italian salad dressing
¼ cup water
½ teaspoon dried dillweed
1 medium cucumber, unpeeled
2 medium tomatoes, sliced
Bibb lettuce leaves

Combine salad dressing, water, dillweed, ½ teaspoon *salt,* and ⅛ teaspoon *pepper*. Using a vegetable parer, slice cucumber paper-thin into a shallow dish. Add salad dressing mixture; cover and chill 6 hours or overnight. To serve, arrange tomato slices atop lettuce leaves. Spoon cucumbers atop tomato slices; top with a little marinade. Makes 4 servings.

BRAN BUTTERMILK MUFFINS/112*

1½ cups buttermilk
1½ cups whole bran cereal
2 tablespoons sugar
2 tablespoons cooking oil
1 beaten egg
1¼ cups all-purpose flour
2 teaspoons baking powder
½ teaspoon baking soda
½ teaspoon salt

Add buttermilk to bran; let stand till liquid is absorbed. Beat together sugar, oil, and egg till light and fluffy. Stir together flour, baking powder, soda, and salt; blend into egg mixture alternately with bran mixture. Stir just till dry ingredients are moistened. Fill greased muffin cups ⅔ full. Bake in a 400° oven for 20 to 22 minutes. Serve muffins while warm. Makes 12 muffins.

CALORIE-CONSCIOUS ENTERTAINING

Just because you or your friends are dieting doesn't mean that you have to give up entertaining. In fact, invite friends over—they'll be delighted with your tasty party fare and may never guess that you're watching their waistlines (and your own). When entertaining, serve some of the appealing foods shown here, or select from other choices found on the following pages. To keep those away-from-home meals from ruining your diet, check out the special dining out dieting pointers at the end of this chapter.

Italian-Style Nibble Mix

Ruby Lemonade Punch

Creamy Clam Dip

Glazed Ham Kabobs

NUTRITION ANALYSIS

Per Serving

Percent U.S. RDA Per Serving

ENTERTAINING

	CALORIES	PROTEIN gms	CARBOHYDRATE gms	FAT gms	SODIUM mgs	POTASSIUM mgs	PROTEIN	VITAMIN A	VITAMIN C	THIAMINE	RIBOFLAVIN	NIACIN	CALCIUM	IRON
APPLECOT COOLER (p. 50)	60	0	15	0	1	154	1	9	15	1	1	1	1	3
BRAN-APPLE SQUARES (p. 58)	85	3	10	4	36	111	4	3	2	6	6	3	3	8
BUTTERMILK-BLUE CHEESE DRESSING (p. 59)	17	1	1	1	47	19	2	1	0	0	2	0	2	0
CHEESE-STUFFED EGGS (p. 48)	58	4	1	4	128	45	6	7	6	2	6	0	4	4
CRANANA DAIQUIRI (p. 51)	114	1	29	0	2	153	1	2	66	3	2	2	1	3
CRANBERRY WARMER (p. 50)	80	0	20	0	17	111	1	1	27	3	1	1	1	2
CREAM PUFFS MELBA (p. 52)	154	5	20	6	133	110	7	7	1	6	9	3	4	4
CREAMY CLAM DIP (p. 47)	30	2	1	2	90	25	3	3	0	0	2	1	1	2
CURRY-BASTED PORK KABOBS (p. 56)	331	16	12	25	192	486	24	82	31	38	14	19	5	15
DATE FLUFF (p. 60)	107	6	15	3	68	190	9	4	1	3	10	3	9	4
DIET RUSSIAN DRESSING (p. 59)	5	0	1	0	47	30	0	2	3	0	0	0	0	1
FRISKY SOURS (p. 50)	66	0	17	0	1	138	1	3	59	4	1	1	1	1
FRUIT WITH TOPPING (p. 60)	185	3	38	4	59	357	4	5	61	4	7	3	3	5
GLAZED HAM KABOBS (p. 56)	209	15	25	5	500	438	24	115	41	27	11	15	4	15
HEARTY HOT POT (p. 60)	285	39	15	8	2328	973	59	170	240	27	78	65	11	41
HERBED LAMB KABOBS (p. 57)	265	17	6	20	314	332	26	23	129	9	13	18	2	9
INDONESIAN BEEF SKEWERS (p. 56)	208	20	14	8	422	456	31	2	9	6	11	25	2	16
ITALIAN-STYLE NIBBLE MIX (p. 47)	57	2	9	2	59	29	3	4	2	4	3	3	2	3
MINT-FILLED CHOCOLATE ANGEL LOAF (p. 52)	150	5	28	2	79	106	7	3	0	1	8	1	4	3
PEACHY YOGURT SIP (p. 50)	74	1	15	0	9	101	1	8	38	1	3	2	2	2
PEANUT BUTTER DIP (p. 48)	23	1	2	2	21	41	2	0	4	1	1	2	1	0
RASPBERRY FIZZ (p. 50)	49	0	12	0	1	84	1	1	16	2	1	1	1	2
RUBY LEMONADE PUNCH (p. 50)	76	0	20	0	8	19	0	0	80	0	0	0	0	0
SEAFOOD PÂTÉ (p. 48)	27	2	0	2	31	33	4	4	0	1	1	1	1	1
SHRIMP AND VEGETABLES (p. 54)	250	26	20	8	1658	942	39	88	67	18	18	30	14	25
SHRIMP-CUCUMBER DIP (p. 48)	13	2	1	0	21	27	3	1	2	0	1	0	1	1
STIR-FRIED BEEF (p. 54)	252	24	20	9	1236	954	37	70	241	25	26	29	8	30
STRAWBERRY SPRITZER PITCHER (p. 51)	77	0	20	0	2	109	0	0	30	2	2	1	1	2
STUFFED TOMATOES (p. 47)	12	1	2	0	27	88	2	6	12	1	1	4	1	1
TOMATO-ZUCCHINI NIBBLES (p. 47)	12	1	2	0	39	88	2	6	13	1	1	1	1	1
TUNA NIBBLES (p. 48)	16	2	0	1	34	27	3	2	2	0	1	4	0	1
RECIPES FOR DO-IT-YOURSELF REDUCING MENUS														
BRAN BUTTERMILK MUFFINS (p. 42)	112	4	19	3	296	120	6	8	9	18	19	12	6	7
BURGERS FLORENTINE (p. 40)	294	24	7	18	515	391	37	62	25	9	18	25	7	21
CHERRY TOMATO MEATBALLS (p. 36)	312	24	11	18	526	532	38	20	38	12	19	27	8	20
CUCUMBER-TOPPED TOMATOES (p. 42)	32	1	5	1	428	260	2	16	33	4	3	3	3	6
FLUFFY BAKED POTATO (p. 38)	90	3	16	2	31	392	4	3	32	6	3	7	1	3
HALIBUT STEAKS FOR TWO (p. 38)	283	36	9	10	738	1044	55	115	58	9	9	60	6	11
HAM SOUFFLÉ IN GREEN PEPPER CUPS (p. 42)	223	18	15	10	456	570	28	25	351	28	26	14	10	17
ORANGE CUCUMBER SALAD (p. 40)	57	2	12	1	154	285	3	9	107	7	7	2	8	5
SESAME BROCCOLI (p. 36)	77	4	9	4	278	374	6	45	171	6	13	5	10	7
TOMATO BOUILLON (p. 40)	32	3	5	0	541	264	5	15	24	3	2	6	1	6
WHIPPED GELATIN (p. 36)	8	2	0	0	10	0	1	0	0	0	0	0	0	0
ZESTY TOMATO DRESSING (p. 38)	6	0	1	0	137	2	0	3	1	1	0	1	0	0

SELECTIONS FOR AN APPETIZER BUFFET

For unhassled hosting, nothing beats a buffet. Let guests help themselves to calorie-trimmed party beverages (see some suggestions on page 50) and low-calorie carbonated beverages for those watching their calories. Have plenty of ice and fresh fruit pieces available for garnishing the beverages.

To set a buffet table that will deliciously delight dieter and non-dieter alike, serve tasty snacks, such as those on this page and the next. Add plenty of fresh cut-up vegetables for low-calorie snacking, then lean back and enjoy the party.

ITALIAN-STYLE NIBBLE MIX/57

Pictured on pages 44 and 45—

¼ cup unpopped popcorn
2 cups bite-size shredded wheat squares
2 cups round toasted oat cereal
2 tablespoons butter *or* margarine, melted
¼ cup grated Parmesan cheese
1 tablespoon dry Italian salad dressing mix

Pop corn in heavy skillet or saucepan over medium-high heat, using no oil. Cover skillet and shake pan constantly till all corn is popped. In 13x9x2-inch baking pan combine corn, wheat squares, and oat cereal. Heat in 300° oven about 5 minutes. Remove. Drizzle with butter. Combine cheese and salad dressing mix; sprinkle over corn and stir. Makes about 9 cups, or 18 one-half-cup servings.

STUFFED TOMATOES/12

24 cherry tomatoes
1 3¾-ounce can tuna (water pack)
2 tablespoons plain yogurt
1 teaspoon snipped chives
½ teaspoon prepared mustard

Cut small slice off bottoms of cherry tomatoes so they will sit flat. Cut thin slice from tops. Carefully scoop out centers of tomatoes; discard. Sprinkle insides of tomatoes lightly with salt and pepper. Invert and chill. Drain tuna thoroughly. Combine tuna, yogurt, chives, mustard, and ¼ teaspoon *salt.* Chill. Fill tomatoes with tuna mixture, using 1 to 1½ teaspoons for each. Makes 24.

TOMATO-ZUCCHINI NIBBLES/12

24 cherry tomatoes
¾ cup finely chopped zucchini
½ cup low-fat cottage cheese
1 teaspoon snipped chives
¼ teaspoon garlic salt

Cut small slice off bottoms of cherry tomatoes so they will sit flat. Cut thin slice from tops of tomatoes. With small melon baller or spoon, carefully scoop out centers of tomatoes; discard or save for another use. Sprinkle insides of tomatoes lightly with *salt.* In medium bowl combine zucchini, cottage cheese, chives, and garlic salt. Fill tomatoes with cottage cheese mixture, using 1 rounded teaspoonful for each. Garnish each stuffed tomato with additional chives, if desired. Makes 24 servings.

CREAMY CLAM DIP/30

Pictured on pages 44 and 45

1 7½-ounce can minced clams
1 8-ounce package Neufchâtel cheese, cut into cubes and softened
1 green onion with top, sliced
Assorted vegetables for dipping (see tip, page 228)

Drain clams, reserving 1 to 2 tablespoons liquid. Set aside. In blender container place Neufchâtel cheese and green onion; cover and blend till mixture is smooth, adding enough reserved clam liquid to make dipping consistency. Stir in the drained clams. Turn mixture into serving dish. Garnish top with additional snipped green onion tops, if desired. Serve with vegetables. Makes 1½ cups dip, or 24 one-tablespoon servings.

SHRIMP-CUCUMBER DIP/13

- 1 medium cucumber, unpeeled
- 1 cup cream-style cottage cheese
- 2 tablespoons finely chopped onion
- 2 teaspoons vinegar
- ½ teaspoon prepared horseradish
- 1 4½-ounce can shrimp, drained and coarsely chopped
- Assorted vegetables for dipping (see tip, page 228)

Halve cucumber lengthwise; remove seeds, and discard. Shred enough cucumber to make 1 cup; drain. Combine the shredded cucumber, cottage cheese, onion, vinegar, and horseradish. Beat till smooth with electric mixer. Stir in shrimp. Serve with vegetable dippers. Makes about 2 cups dip, or 32 one-tablespoon servings.

PEANUT BUTTER DIP/23

- ¼ cup peanut butter
- 2 tablespoons frozen orange juice concentrate, thawed
- 1 cup plain yogurt
- Assorted fruits for dipping

In small mixer bowl combine peanut butter and orange juice; beat till fluffy. Stir in yogurt till smooth. Cover and chill. Serve with fruit. Makes 1½ cups dip, or 24 one-tablespoon servings.

SEAFOOD PÂTÉ/27

- 1 teaspoon unflavored gelatin
- ¼ cup cold water
- 1 4½-ounce can shrimp, drained and rinsed
- 8 ounces fresh *or* frozen whitefish, cooked, drained, and flaked, *or* one 6½-ounce can tuna (water pack), drained and flaked, *or* one 7¾-ounce can salmon, drained, skin and bones removed, and flaked
- 1 8-ounce package Neufchâtel cheese, softened
- ⅓ cup plain yogurt
- ½ cup finely chopped celery
- ½ teaspoon dried fines herbes, crushed
- 2 tablespoons dry sherry
- Non-stick vegetable spray coating
- Lettuce leaves
- Watercress *or* parsley sprigs
- Toasted pita bread *or* flour tortilla triangles
- Assorted fresh vegetables

In small saucepan soften gelatin in the cold water; stir over low heat till gelatin is dissolved. Reserve a few of the shrimp for garnish; chop remaining shrimp.

In a mixer bowl combine chopped shrimp, flaked fish, softened cheese, yogurt, chopped celery, fines herbes, sherry, and gelatin mixture. Beat till all ingredients are well mixed. Turn mixture into a 3-cup mold or bowl sprayed with non-stick vegetable spray coating. Cover; refrigerate several hours or overnight.

Unmold pâté onto a lèttuce-lined plate. Trim with watercress or parsley sprigs and the reserved shrimp. Serve with pita bread or tortilla triangles and vegetables. Makes 2⅔ cups, or 43 one-tablespoon servings.

CHEESE-STUFFED EGGS/58

- 6 hard-cooked eggs
- ¼ cup process cheese spread
- 2 tablespoons chopped canned green chili peppers
- Dash salt
- Paprika

Halve eggs lengthwise. Remove yolks; mash. Blend egg yolks with cheese spread, chili peppers, and salt. Refill whites with yolk mixture. Sprinkle each with paprika. Chill. Makes 12 servings.

TUNA NIBBLES/16

- 1 6½-ounce tuna (water pack), drained and flaked
- 3 ounces Neufchâtel cheese, softened
- 2 tablespoons finely chopped celery
- 2 teaspoons lemon juice
- ½ teaspoon Worcestershire sauce
- ¼ teaspoon salt
- ⅓ cup finely snipped parsley

In bowl blend the tuna and Neufchâtel cheese. Add celery, lemon juice, Worcestershire sauce, and salt; mix well. Shape mixture into small balls, using about 2 teaspoons for each. Roll in the snipped parsley. Chill well. Serve the tuna-cheese balls with wooden picks. Makes 30 appetizers.

Seafood Pâté

PARTY BEVERAGES

RUBY LEMONADE PUNCH/76

Pictured on pages 44 and 45—

1 6-ounce can frozen lemonade concentrate, thawed
4 cups low-calorie cranberry juice cocktail
1 16-ounce bottle low-calorie lemon-lime carbonated beverage
Ice cubes
8 thin lemon slices (optional)

Stir lemonade concentrate into cranberry juice cocktail. Slowly add carbonated beverage; stir gently with an up-and-down motion. Serve over ice. Garnish with lemon slices, if desired. Makes 8 servings.

FRISKY SOURS/66

2½ cups cold water
1 6-ounce can frozen orange juice concentrate
1 6-ounce can frozen lemonade concentrate
2 16-ounce bottles low-calorie citrus carbonated beverage, chilled
Crushed ice

In a blender container combine cold water and frozen juice concentrates. Cover; blend just till mixed. Pour in low-calorie beverage; stir gently to mix. Serve over crushed ice. Makes 12 servings.

PEACHY YOGURT SIP/74

1 cup plain yogurt
¼ cup peach brandy
1 10-ounce package frozen peaches, partially thawed
Ground nutmeg

In a blender container combine the plain yogurt and peach brandy. Add peaches; cover and blend just till smooth. Pour into serving glasses; sprinkle with ground nutmeg. Makes 5 servings.

RASPBERRY FIZZ/49

1½ cups unsweetened pineapple juice, chilled
1 10-ounce package frozen red raspberries, partially thawed
½ cup water
2 16-ounce bottles low-calorie lemon-lime carbonated beverage, chilled
Ice cubes
Mint sprigs

In blender container combine pineapple juice, berries, and water. Blend on medium speed till berries are pureed; strain. Pour mixture into pitcher. Slowly pour carbonated beverage down side of pitcher, stirring with an up-and-down motion. Serve over ice. Garnish each serving with a fresh mint sprig. Makes 10 servings.

APPLECOT COOLER/60

Pictured on page 227—

2 cups apple juice
1 12-ounce can apricot nectar
¼ cup lemon juice
¼ teaspoon aromatic bitters
2 cups carbonated water, chilled
Ice cubes
8 thin lemon slices

In pitcher combine apple juice, apricot nectar, lemon juice, and bitters; chill. Just before serving, carefully pour carbonated water down side of pitcher. Stir gently with an up-and-down motion. Serve in ice-filled glasses. Garnish each serving with a thin lemon slice. Makes 8 servings.

CRANBERRY WARMER/80

4 cups low-calorie cranberry juice cocktail
1 18-ounce can (2¼ cups) unsweetened pineapple juice
1 teaspoon whole allspice
1 teaspoon whole cloves
Dash salt
Dash ground nutmeg
3 inches stick cinnamon

In large saucepan combine all ingredients; slowly bring mixture to boiling. Reduce heat; cover and simmer 20 minutes. Remove from heat; strain to remove spices. Serve in mugs. Makes 8 servings.

CRANANA DAIQUIRI/114

1 6-ounce can frozen cranberry juice cocktail concentrate
¾ cup orange juice
1 medium banana, cut up
2 tablespoons lime juice
2½ cups ice cubes

In blender container combine cranberry concentrate, orange juice, banana, and lime juice; cover and blend till smooth. Add the ice cubes; cover and blend till slushy. Pour into stemmed cocktail glasses. Garnish with additional banana slices, if desired. Makes 6 servings.

STRAWBERRY SPRITZER PITCHER/77

3 10-ounce packages frozen strawberries, thawed
2 24-ounce bottles white grape juice, chilled
1 28-ounce bottle carbonated water, chilled

Place 2 packages of the strawberries in a blender container. Cover; blend till smooth. In large pitcher or punch bowl combine blended berries, grape juice, and remaining package of berries. To serve, add the chilled carbonated water; stir gently to mix. Makes 25 servings.

Cranana Daiquiri; Frisky Sours; Strawberry Spritzer Pitcher; Peachy Yogurt Sip

COME FOR DESSERT AND COFFEE

The idea of offering only dessert and coffee when entertaining, especially when there are some dieters in the group, isn't necessarily taboo when you select the dessert with care. Try to plan a calorie-trimmed dessert that helps fulfill nutritive requirements for the day.

When entertaining, most people want to serve a dessert that has eye appeal and lavish taste—something that's extra special. Select either of the desserts on this page, or check the calorie-trimmed desserts starting on page 201 for a selection of other recipes to choose from.

MINT-FILLED CHOCOLATE ANGEL LOAF/150

⅓ cup sifted cake flour
3 tablespoons unsweetened cocoa powder
¼ cup sugar
6 egg whites
½ teaspoon cream of tartar
1 teaspoon vanilla
Dash salt
½ cup sugar
Mint Filling
Powdered sugar

Sift cake flour and cocoa powder with the ¼ cup sugar twice; set aside. In large mixer bowl beat egg whites, cream of tartar, vanilla, and salt till soft peaks form (tips curl over). Add remaining ½ cup sugar, 2 tablespoons at a time, and continue beating till stiff peaks form (tips stand straight). Sift *one-third* of the flour-cocoa mixture over the whites; fold in. Repeat sifting and folding twice more.

Spoon batter into an *ungreased* 9x5x3-inch loaf pan. Bake in a 375° oven 25 minutes or till cake tests done. Invert cake in pan on wire rack; cool in pan completely. Remove cake from pan; cut in thirds horizontally. Place bottom third of cake, cut side up, on serving platter; spread with *half* of the Mint Filling. Add the middle cake slice; spread with remaining filling. Top with remaining cake layer, cut side down. Sift powdered sugar over top. If desired, garnish with a mint sprig. Makes 10 servings.

Mint Filling: In a 1½-quart saucepan combine ¼ cup *sugar,* 5 teaspoons *cornstarch,* and dash *salt.* Add 1 cup *milk* and 2 well-beaten *eggs* all at once. Cook and stir till mixture is thickened and bubbly. Cook and stir 2 minutes more. Remove from heat. Stir in 2 tablespoons *white crème de menthe.* Cover with clear plastic wrap; chill. Makes 1⅓ cups filling.

CREAM PUFFS MELBA/154

1 8½-ounce can pear halves
1 tablespoon cornstarch
½ cup raspberry yogurt
1 egg white
2 tablespoons sugar
Cream Puffs

Drain pears, reserving syrup. Chop pears; set aside. Add water to syrup to equal ½ cup liquid. In a small saucepan combine syrup mixture and cornstarch. Cook and stir till thickened and bubbly. Cook and stir 2 minutes more. Cool to room temperature. Stir in yogurt. Beat egg white to soft peaks (tips curl over). Gradually add sugar, beating to stiff peaks (tips stand straight). Fold into yogurt mixture along with pears. Cover and chill. Prepare Cream Puffs. Cool. To serve, spoon filling into Cream Puff bottoms; add tops. Makes 6 servings.

Cream Puffs: In small saucepan melt 2 tablespoons *butter or margarine* in ½ cup *boiling water.* Add ½ cup *all-purpose flour* and ⅛ teaspoon *salt* all at once. Stir vigorously. Cook and stir till mixture forms a ball that doesn't separate. Remove from heat; cool 5 minutes. Add 2 *eggs,* one at a time, beating dough till very smooth and shiny after each addition. Drop puffs 3 inches apart on a lightly greased baking sheet, forming 6 in all. Bake in a 450° oven 15 minutes. Reduce oven temperature to 325°. Bake 10 minutes more. Remove from oven; cut off tops. Remove soft centers. Turn oven off; return cream puff tops and bottoms to oven for 20 minutes. Cool on wire rack. Makes 6 puffs.

Cream Puffs Melba; Mint-Filled Chocolate Angel Loaf

ENTRÉES FOR SPUR-OF-THE-MOMENT PARTIES

Don't let drop-in company ruin your diet! Make a quick shopping trip for meat or shrimp and fresh vegetables, then set the chopping blocks and knives in motion. Get out the wok, stir-fry the entrée, and dinner is almost on the table. For a super-fun evening, try Stir-Fried Beef or Shrimp and Vegetables for the main dish.

Remember: When stir-frying use a long-handled utensil to frequently lift and turn the food with a folding motion.

STIR-FRIED BEEF/252

1 pound beef round steak, trimmed of fat
⅔ cup water
¼ cup chopped onion
3 tablespoons soy sauce
1 teaspoon instant beef bouillon granules
1 teaspoon Worcestershire sauce
1 clove garlic, minced
½ teaspoon salt
Dash pepper
• • •
2 medium carrots, bias sliced
1 small head cauliflower, broken into flowerets (2 cups)
2 tablespoons cooking oil
1 cup sliced fresh mushrooms
1 6-ounce package frozen pea pods, partially thawed
¼ cup cold water
1 tablespoon cornstarch

Slice beef thinly into bite-size strips. Combine the ⅔ cup water, the onion, soy sauce, bouillon granules, Worcestershire sauce, garlic, salt, and pepper. Add beef strips and stir to coat. Cover and let stand 1 hour. Stir once or twice. Drain the beef well, reserving marinade.

Cook carrots and cauliflower in boiling, lightly salted water 3 minutes; drain. Preheat wok or large skillet over high heat; add oil. Brown beef strips; remove. Add mushrooms; cook and stir 1 minute. Add pea pods, carrots, and cauliflower. Cook and stir 2 minutes or till crisp-tender. Add beef. Blend reserved marinade and the ¼ cup cold water into the cornstarch; add to wok. Cook and stir till bubbly. Makes 5 servings.

SHRIMP AND VEGETABLES/250

2 medium carrots
1 cup fresh mushrooms
1 pound fresh *or* frozen shrimp in shells
½ cup chicken broth
1 tablespoon cornstarch
¼ cup soy sauce
• • •
2 tablespoons cooking oil
1 clove garlic, minced
1 teaspoon grated gingerroot
1 cup thinly sliced cauliflower
2 cups chopped bok choy
1 cup fresh pea pods *or* one 6-ounce package frozen pea pods, thawed
1 cup fresh bean sprouts *or* ½ of a 16-ounce can bean sprouts, drained

Thinly slice carrots and mushrooms. Thaw shrimp, if frozen. Shell and devein shrimp; halve lengthwise. Blend chicken broth into cornstarch; stir in soy sauce and set aside. Preheat wok or large skillet over high heat; add oil. Stir-fry garlic and gingerroot in hot oil for 30 seconds. Add cauliflower and carrots; stir-fry 3 minutes. Add bok choy, pea pods, mushrooms, and bean sprouts; stir-fry 2 minutes more or till vegetables are crisp-tender. Remove vegetables to bowl. Add shrimp to wok; stir-fry 7 to 8 minutes or till done. Push shrimp away from center of wok. Stir chicken broth mixture and add to center of wok. Cook and stir till thickened. Stir in vegetables; cover and cook 1 minute. Makes 4 servings.

Stir-Fried Beef

DO-IT-YOURSELF KABOBS

When planning the main dish for a party, consider serving kabobs. Let each guest build his own kabob with some helpful suggestions from the hostess about cooking times and accompanying basting sauces. Whether you make one or several kabob recipes, you can set out the ingredients—meat, vegetables or fruit, and basting sauces—in serve-yourself containers.

To keep cleanup to a minimum, serve the food in disposable containers. Thread kabobs on bamboo skewers and serve grilled kabobs and accompaniments on colorful paper plates with plastic forks and cups. A party could be no simpler if cleaning up is as easy as filling a trash can.

CURRY-BASTED PORK KABOBS/331

1½ pounds boneless pork
4 large carrots
2 small zucchini
8 small whole onions, peeled
4 teaspoons curry powder
1 teaspoon paprika
1 teaspoon dried oregano, crushed
½ teaspoon salt
⅛ teaspoon pepper
1 clove garlic, minced
⅔ cup cooking oil

Cut pork, carrots, and zucchini into 1-inch pieces. In saucepan cook carrots, covered, in small amount of boiling, lightly salted water 15 minutes. Add onions; cover and cook 10 minutes more. For sauce, in small saucepan combine curry, paprika, oregano, salt, pepper, and garlic; stir in oil. Heat through. Thread pork and vegetables on 8 skewers. Grill over *hot* coals 10 to 12 minutes, turning once; baste often with sauce. Makes 8 servings.

INDONESIAN BEEF SKEWERS/208

Leave peel on bananas for grilling so they hold their shape. Peel them before eating—

2 pounds beef sirloin *or* boneless lamb, cut into 1-inch pieces
¼ cup peanut butter
2 tablespoons lime juice
1 tablespoon molasses
Few drops bottled hot pepper sauce
2 tablespoons soy sauce
3 bananas, cut into 1-inch slices

Thread meat on 8 skewers. For sauce, in saucepan combine peanut butter, lime juice, molasses, and pepper sauce. Stir in soy sauce and ¼ cup *water*. Bring just to boiling, stirring constantly. Keep warm. Baste meat with sauce. Grill over *hot* coals 10 to 15 minutes, turning once; baste often with sauce. Thread banana slices on skewers; add to grill 3 minutes before end of cooking time. Makes 8 servings.

GLAZED HAM KABOBS/209

Pictured on pages 44 and 45—

2 medium sweet potatoes (about 10 ounces)
¾ pound fully cooked boneless ham, trimmed of fat
1 small green pepper, cut into 8 strips
2 small onions, cut into wedges

• • •

¼ cup orange juice
1 tablespoon light molasses
1 tablespoon vinegar
1 teaspoon cornstarch

Cut off woody portion of sweet potatoes. In saucepan cook potatoes, covered, in enough boiling, lightly salted water to cover for 25 minutes or till tender. Drain; cool. Peel and cut into 1-inch pieces. Cut ham into 1-inch cubes. On four skewers, alternately thread ham pieces and pepper strips, sweet potato pieces, and onion wedges.

For glaze, in saucepan combine orange juice, molasses, vinegar, and cornstarch. Cook and stir till thickened and bubbly. Brush glaze over kabobs. Grill over *medium* coals about 15 minutes, brushing occasionally with glaze. Makes 4 servings.

HERBED LAMB KABOBS/265

Pre-cook the onion wedges in boiling water before threading on skewers—

½ cup cooking oil
½ cup chopped onion
¼ cup snipped parsley
¼ cup lemon juice
1 clove garlic, minced
1 teaspoon salt
1 teaspoon dried marjoram, crushed
1 teaspoon dried thyme, crushed
¼ teaspoon pepper
• • •
2 pounds boneless lamb, cut into 1-inch pieces
Onion wedges
Green pepper squares
Sweet red pepper squares

For the marinade, in a bowl combine the cooking oil, chopped onion, snipped parsley, lemon juice, minced garlic, salt, marjoram, thyme, and pepper. Stir in the lamb pieces. Cover the bowl and chill meat in marinade for 6 to 8 hours; stir occasionally.

Drain lamb pieces, reserving the marinade; set aside. In a saucepan cook the onion wedges in a small amount of boiling water for 5 minutes; drain the onion. Thread the lamb pieces, onion wedges, and green and red pepper squares onto 8 skewers. Grill over *hot* coals for 10 to 12 minutes, turning once. Baste often with the reserved marinade. Makes 8 servings.

Curry-Basted Pork Kabobs; Indonesian Beef Skewers; Herbed Lamb Kabobs

PARTICIPATION SALAD AND SANDWICH BARS

To cook up a great party, let all concoct their own dinners. Spread out the ingredients for Freewheeling Sandwiches on a long counter. Let guests add the ingredients they want to the patted-out dough, then seal the dough and mark it with initials for identification.

In another location, such as the table in the dining room, set out some salad greens, vegetables, and dressings for the salad bar. Two suggested dressings include Buttermilk-Blue Cheese Dressing and Diet Russian Dressing.

For dessert, arrange a plate of bar cookies or a tray of fresh fruit—or both! Offer a generous sampling of calorie-trimmed beverages, then get in there and enjoy the party.

FREEWHEELING SANDWICHES

Calorie counts and nutrition information will vary depending on ingredients selected. Check a calorie chart, such as the one starting on page 22, for calorie counts of ingredients—

Meat and cheese fillings—
diced cooked lamb
cooked ground beef
cooked Italian sausage
diced cooked ham
chopped sliced pepperoni
shredded cheeses
Vegetable fillings—
chopped onion
chopped boiled potatoes
chopped green pepper
chopped mushrooms
chopped cabbage
sliced olives
grated carrots
shredded zucchini
Herbs and spices
Assorted frozen bread dough, thawed, *or* prepared yeast dough

Choose the suggested fillings you like and need for the number of guests. Plan to use about ⅓ cup of a combination of ingredients for each sandwich. (A pound of cooked meat yields about 3 cups when chopped. You'll get about 2 cups cooked meat per pound of ground beef.)

If you're not much for bread making, offer a selection of thawed frozen bread dough. If you prepared yeast dough from scratch, chill dough in refrigerator 3 to 24 hours. When ready to use, remove bread dough from refrigerator; uncover and let stand 20 minutes before using.

To make filled sandwiches: Pinch off a piece of dough a little larger than a golf ball. On lightly floured surface, pat out dough to 5-inch circle. Place about ⅓ cup of the desired filling combination on half of the circle of dough; fold over other half and seal edge with fork. (Prick initial on top for easy identification.) Place on greased baking sheet; cover and let rest 20 minutes. Bake in a 375° oven for 18 to 20 minutes, or till done. Brush with a little butter or margarine, if desired.

BRAN-APPLE SQUARES/85

Non-stick vegetable spray coating
1 cup 40% bran flakes
½ cup wheat germ
½ cup nonfat dry milk powder
½ teaspoon baking powder
2 beaten eggs
½ cup packed brown sugar
½ cup peeled and finely shredded apple
2 tablespoons cooking oil
1 tablespoon light molasses
2 teaspoons vanilla
½ cup chopped walnuts

Spray a 9x9x2-inch baking pan with non-stick vegetable spray coating. In a large mixing bowl stir together bran flakes, wheat germ, dry milk powder, and baking powder. In a small bowl combine eggs, brown sugar, apple, oil, molasses, and vanilla. Add egg mixture to dry ingredients, mixing well. Stir in walnuts. Turn into prepared pan. Bake in a 350° oven about 25 minutes. Cool on wire rack. Cut into squares. Makes 20.

BUTTERMILK-BLUE CHEESE DRESSING/17

1 cup plain yogurt
½ cup buttermilk
3 ounces blue cheese, crumbled (¾ cup)
1 teaspoon celery seed
¼ teaspoon salt
¼ teaspoon dried tarragon, crushed
Dash pepper

In mixing bowl combine yogurt and buttermilk; stir in blue cheese, celery seed, salt, tarragon, and pepper. Transfer to storage container; cover and chill. Makes about 2 cups, or 32 one-tablespoon servings.

DIET RUSSIAN DRESSING/5

1 1¾-ounce package powdered fruit pectin
1 tablespoon sugar
½ teaspoon dried basil, crushed
¼ teaspoon dried tarragon, crushed
¼ teaspoon garlic salt
¾ cup spicy vegetable juice cocktail
¼ cup wine vinegar

Combine pectin, sugar, basil, tarragon, and garlic salt. Stir in remaining ingredients. Cover; refrigerate at least 1 hour. Serve dressing on vegetable salads. Makes 1¼ cups, or 20 one-tablespoon servings.

Freewheeling Sandwiches

COOK AROUND THE TABLE

For a good, fuss-free entrée, gather your friends together for Hearty Hot Pot. Simmer bite-size chicken, fish, and vegetable pieces in bubbling chicken broth. Use a small wire basket, chopsticks, or a fork to remove the food from the broth. After the meat and vegetable main course, ladle the broth into mugs for a terrific chaser.

For dessert, a refreshing fruit mixture would be in order. Date Fluff should be made ahead and chilled; Fruit with Topping is quickly made in the food processor.

HEARTY HOT POT/285

4 to 6 cups chicken broth
12 ounces fresh *or* frozen fish fillets, thawed, and cut into 1-inch squares
1 chicken breast, boned, skinned, and thinly sliced
6 ounces chicken livers, halved
2 cups Chinese cabbage, sliced
2 cups fresh spinach, torn
1 cup fresh mushrooms
1 medium zucchini, sliced
1 pound asparagus, bias sliced
1 sweet red pepper, cut up
1 green pepper, cut up
Soy Lime Sauce

Heat broth to boiling; transfer to wok, firepot, or fondue pot. Spear meats and vegetables with fondue forks and cook in hot broth about 4 minutes, or till done. Serve with Soy Lime Sauce and hot cooked rice, if desired. Makes 6 servings.

Soy Lime Sauce: Combine ½ cup *soy sauce,* ¼ cup fresh *lime juice,* and ⅛ teaspoon ground *ginger;* blend together. Use for dipping sauce. Makes ¾ cup sauce.

DATE FLUFF/107

½ envelope unflavored gelatin
1½ cups skim milk
2 egg yolks
2 tablespoons sugar
1 tablespoon creamy peanut butter
⅓ cup pitted dates, snipped
½ teaspoon vanilla
2 egg whites
Pitted dates, snipped (optional)

In saucepan sprinkle gelatin over milk; stir over medium heat till gelatin is dissolved. Slowly stir *half* of hot mixture into beaten yolks; return all to saucepan. Cook and stir over medium heat for 1 to 2 minutes or till slightly thickened. Remove from heat. Blend in sugar and peanut butter. Stir in the ⅓ cup dates and vanilla. Chill till partially set.

Beat egg whites to stiff peaks; fold into gelatin mixture. Spoon mixture into 6 individual dessert glasses. Chill till firm. Garnish each serving with snipped dates, if desired. Makes 6 servings.

FRUIT WITH TOPPING/185

2 medium bananas, peeled and halved lengthwise
3 ripe medium pears, quartered and cored
3 tablespoons lemon juice
Cheese Topping

Place slicing disk in food processor work bowl. Slice bananas and pears; remove to bowl. Add lemon juice and 2 cups *water.* Meanwhile, prepare Cheese Topping. Drain fruit thoroughly; divide fruit into sherbet dishes. Spoon Cheese Topping over each serving. Makes 6 servings.

Cheese Topping: With steel blade in food processor work bowl, start processor. Add 3 ounces *Neufchâtel cheese,* quartered, through feed tube; process till smooth. Add one 10-ounce package frozen *strawberries,* thawed, and ⅛ teaspoon ground *ginger* through feed tube. Process till the mixture is smooth.

Hearty Hot Pot

DINING-OUT POINTERS

You don't have to stay home to stay on your diet. A night out and an occasional rest from the cooking routine does everyone good. However, dining out should be relaxing and an occasion to talk about anything but your diet. Learn to enjoy your dining companions more than the food on your plate. Follow these simple, commonsense suggestions and you'll have a pleasant evening to remember with no diet regrets.

Pick the Spot

Look for a quiet restaurant where you can relax and where you won't be pushed into making irrational food choices. Make dinner reservations ahead and be on time. That way you won't be stuck waiting in the cocktail lounge, consuming calories to kill time until your table is ready.

Choose a restaurant with a widely varied menu. Many contemporary restaurants offer light entrées, such as crepes, quiches, kabobs, and main-dish salads, besides their regular fare. The variety gives dieters and non-dieters alike a chance to select what they want.

Oriental restaurants offer an alternative to the heavy American steak and potato routine. And the nouvelle cuisine is taking the place of the calorie-laden cuisine in many French restaurants.

Buffet or cafeteria-style restaurants are ideal for the willful dieter. You can survey the food before selecting and make sound choices a la carte: You're free to assemble a low-calorie meal by calculating calories as you go through the cafeteria line.

Occasionally, choose a restaurant well known for its salad bar. You'll find making a meal out of salads is a dining adventure your waistline can afford.

Of course, no matter how hard you try, you'll undoubtedly sometimes find yourself at a traditional restaurant with an unimaginative menu. Be realistic. Don't make a fuss by asking for impossible items not on the menu. Be flexible and take it as it comes. Remember: You need not clean your plate.

Apéritifs

These high-calorie, few-nutrient drinks by themselves can send your diet astray faster than any other food, and they'll stimulate your appetite besides. Check the chart at the right for some calorie counts.

You have several options to the "What do you want to drink?" question. First of all, stand firm and don't be pressured into something you don't need or want. You can order a nonalcoholic refresher. Consider a glass of tonic with a wedge of lime, one of the many low-calorie soft drinks with a slice of lemon, or a glass of soda on the rocks (no calories at all). Try a popular bottled mineral water with a slice of your favorite citrus fruit as a garnish. For a nutritive beverage, select orange juice or tomato juice to drink straight. Or, become a slow sipper or an ice muncher. Make one glass of wine or light beer last through the cocktail period and even into dinner.

If, despite good intentions, you wind up with a wait in the cocktail lounge, choose your seat carefully. Settle as far away from the appetizer offerings as possible. It doesn't take long to spoil dinner and your diet with a "few" nuts.

Menu Choices

First courses: Select bouillon, fresh melon in season, a fresh-fruit cup, or a juice as predinner food. Avoid the heavy soups such as a cream or cheese soup unless you want to combine it with a trip to the salad bar for the entire meal. Consider skipping the first course entirely to cut calories.

Main courses: If the restaurant has a limited, high-calorie menu, go ahead and order. Don't be too obvious, but leave many of the calories on the plate. Eat around the breading, fat, rich sauces, gravies, and poultry or pork stuffings. If you end up at a steak place, trim off all the visible fat, then cut off the portion you intend to eat. Save the rest to take home. The next day you can thinly slice the meat and toss it in a main-dish salad or make it into an open-face sandwich to enjoy at lunch.

Vegetables: If your order includes a baked potato, skip the sour cream and ask for the butter separately, so you can control the amount put on the potato. Keep it around a teaspoon (34 calories). Consider a double portion of carrots, peas, or whatever vegetable the restaurant has to offer, in place of calorie-laden hash browns or French fries.

Salads: When it comes to the leafy green salads, you have several choices of lower calorie dressings. You can go without entirely, or ask for vinegar and oil (a very light touch on the oil, please, one tablespoon equals 120 calories). For an unusual yet tasty dressing, try a touch of tomato juice or freshly squeezed lemon juice with a generous sprinkling of pepper.

The inevitable extras: You really don't need them. Pass up the crackers that go with the soup and skip the bread or rolls and butter that accompany your dinner.

Desserts: If fresh fruit is listed on the menu, you're in luck. If not, order a cup of coffee or tea with lemon for an after-dinner chaser.

ALCOHOLIC BEVERAGES

Want to know how many calories are in certain alcoholic beverages? We've counted calories for the cocktails at right using basic recipes. Because you have the option of adding your favorite soft drink, low-calorie carbonated beverage, or special mix, the calorie counts for the mixed drinks at right are approximate.

Remember to add alcohol calories to your calorie allowance, yet don't use them as a substitute for food.

Beverage	Calories
BEER 1 12-ounce can	151
BEER, LIGHT 1 12-ounce can	96
BLOODY MARY 1 5-ounce cocktail	121
CHAMPAGNE 1 4-ounce glass	84
CRÈME DE MENTHE 1 cordial glass	67
DAIQUIRI 1 cocktail glass	122
GIN AND TONIC 1 8-ounce cocktail	157
GRASSHOPPER 1 3½-ounce cocktail	176
HIGHBALL 1 8-ounce cocktail	166
MANHATTAN 1 3½-ounce cocktail	164
MARTINI 1 3½-ounce cocktail	140
OLD-FASHIONED 1 4-ounce cocktail	179
TOM COLLINS 1 10-ounce cocktail	180
WHISKEY SOUR COCKTAIL 1 3½-ounce cocktail	211
WINE, DESSERT (18% alcohol by volume) 3½ ounces	141
WINE, TABLE (12% alcohol by volume) 3½ ounces	87

FOODS WITH A FOREIGN FLAIR

Take a culinary trip around the world with the light but luscious recipes on the next few pages. Travel to several foreign areas and countries—the Orient, France, Greece, Mexico, Italy, and Spain. You'll find that the foods are as diverse as the countries themselves, but the calorie counts of most are affordably low. Start with the assortment shown here.

Spicy Beef and Asparagus

Greek Salad

Spanish Gazpacho

Mushroom and Ham Lasagna

NUTRITION ANALYSIS

Add variety to your menus by selecting recipes with a foreign flair. Main dishes with foreign origins are good ones to select when entertaining since the entrée generally establishes the menu theme. Select calorie-trimmed side dishes that go along with the theme. A few simple table decorations in keeping with the theme also add a festive note.

	Per Serving						Percent U.S. RDA Per Serving							
FOREIGN FLAIR	CALORIES	PROTEIN gms	CARBOHYDRATE gms	FAT gms	SODIUM mgs	POTASSIUM mgs	PROTEIN	VITAMIN A	VITAMIN C	THIAMINE	RIBOFLAVIN	NIACIN	CALCIUM	IRON
ARROZ CON TOMATE (p. 82)	162	3	27	5	360	119	4	5	36	11	2	7	2	6
ARTICHOKE-SHALLOT SOUFFLÉ (p. 74)	294	16	22	19	415	555	24	26	18	13	24	6	26	14
BEEF WITH PEA PODS (p. 70)	254	24	14	11	980	467	38	7	27	17	15	28	4	22
BOEUF EN DAUBE (p. 72)	251	20	11	10	420	405	30	96	12	5	11	16	5	18
BOUILLABAISSE (p. 74)	232	30	10	8	1057	796	46	13	36	11	8	18	15	27
BRAISED CHINESE VEGETABLES (p. 67)	103	4	12	5	534	349	6	7	29	11	7	8	4	8
CEVICHE (p. 78)	82	7	3	5	157	191	11	4	25	2	2	7	2	2
CHICKEN WITH WALNUTS (p. 69)	224	21	7	12	845	211	33	9	121	8	13	37	4	13
CHILIES RELLENOS BAKE (p. 78)	269	16	12	17	504	108	25	22	43	8	21	5	36	9
COQUILLES SAINT JACQUES (p. 74)	309	30	14	13	726	711	46	15	5	13	15	12	20	24
EGG DROP SOUP (p. 67)	47	5	4	1	617	131	7	4	2	1	3	5	2	7
FRIED RICE WITH SHRIMP (p. 67)	241	12	31	7	1603	205	18	7	10	14	8	11	7	18
FRUIT-AND-CHEESE FRENCH OMELETS (p. 72)	385	19	22	25	659	486	30	40	147	17	34	5	13	18
GREEK SALAD (p. 76)	133	3	5	12	295	270	4	14	22	5	4	2	8	6
LEMON ICE (p. 80)	104	0	27	0	1	44	0	0	24	1	0	0	0	0
MARINATED GARBANZO BEANS (p. 80)	175	7	22	7	116	285	11	0	0	7	3	4	5	14
MARINATED TIDBIT TRAY (p. 80)	253	7	11	22	264	436	11	4	122	9	6	8	6	10
MOUSSAKA FOR MANY (p. 76)	285	20	13	16	962	434	31	15	12	13	22	18	14	13
MUSHROOM AND HAM LASAGNA (p. 80)	306	20	28	12	566	440	30	21	18	29	30	22	27	13
PAELLA CASSEROLE (p. 82)	395	31	30	16	741	351	47	21	54	28	25	41	7	29
PASTITSIO (p. 76)	217	18	23	5	722	280	28	12	7	9	22	9	14	11
PESCADO A LA NARANJA (p. 78)	305	33	4	18	449	765	51	18	25	9	8	63	4	8
PORK STIR-FRY (p. 69)	206	17	12	11	803	734	26	94	70	39	25	22	9	26
RATATOUILLE (p. 72)	70	2	9	4	380	352	3	14	73	6	6	6	3	5
SIMMERED PORK WITH SPINACH (p. 70)	221	17	11	7	875	672	26	94	67	40	22	22	8	25
SPANISH GAZPACHO (p. 82)	49	1	4	3	404	215	1	13	42	3	2	3	1	4
SPICY BEEF AND ASPARAGUS (p. 69)	164	17	8	7	496	423	25	22	93	11	15	19	3	15
STIR-FRIED PEA PODS (p. 67)	85	3	11	4	314	205	5	6	17	12	7	7	2	7
SUKIYAKI (p. 70)	422	22	20	30	1504	877	33	105	83	16	24	20	18	35
TOSTADA COMPUESTA (p. 78)	453	24	30	27	959	580	36	21	23	15	20	23	21	24

ORIENTAL-STYLE SPECIALTIES

FRIED RICE WITH SHRIMP / 241

2 beaten eggs
1/3 cup soy sauce
2 tablespoons dry sherry
1/8 teaspoon pepper
2 tablespoons cooking oil
1 clove garlic, minced
1 teaspoon grated gingerroot
1/4 cup chopped onion
3 cups cooked rice
1 cup shelled cooked shrimp, halved lengthwise
1 cup cooked *or* canned peas

In small bowl combine beaten eggs, soy sauce, dry sherry, and pepper; set aside.

Preheat wok or large skillet over high heat; add the cooking oil. Stir-fry the garlic and the gingerroot in hot oil for 30 seconds. Add chopped onion; stir-fry about 1 minute or till onion is crisp-tender.

Stir in the cooked rice, shrimp, and peas. Cook, stirring frequently, for 6 to 8 minutes. While stirring constantly, drizzle the egg mixture over the rice mixture. Cook, stirring constantly, till eggs are set. Serve at once. Makes 6 servings.

EGG DROP SOUP / 47

2 13¾-ounce cans chicken broth
1 tablespoon cornstarch
1 well-beaten egg
2 tablespoons sliced green onion

In medium saucepan slowly stir the chicken broth into the cornstarch. Cook, stirring constantly, till slightly thickened. Slowly pour in the well-beaten egg; stir once gently. Remove the soup from the heat. Garnish soup with green onion. Makes 4 servings.

BRAISED CHINESE VEGETABLES / 103

Purchase the dried mushrooms and lily buds at an Oriental food store—

6 dried mushrooms
1/4 cup dried lily buds
Warm water

• • •

2 tablespoons cooking oil
2 cups chopped bok choy
1½ cups fresh pea pods *or* one 6-ounce package frozen pea pods, thawed
1 cup fresh bean sprouts
1/2 cup sliced water chestnuts
1/2 cup water
2 tablespoons soy sauce
1/2 teaspoon instant chicken bouillon granules
1/2 teaspoon sugar

• • •

2 tablespoons dry sherry
2 teaspoons cornstarch

Soak dried mushrooms and lily buds in enough warm water to cover for 30 minutes; squeeze to drain well. Chop mushrooms, discarding stems. Cut lily buds into thirds. Preheat wok or large skillet over high heat; add oil. Stir-fry bok choy, pea pods, bean sprouts, and water chestnuts in hot oil for 2 minutes. Add mushrooms, lily buds, 1/2 cup water, soy sauce, bouillon granules, and sugar. Cover and cook for 5 minutes. Blend dry sherry into cornstarch. Stir into vegetable mixture. Cook and stir till thickened and bubbly. Serve at once. Serves 6.

STIR-FRIED PEA PODS / 85

You can use fresh pea pods in this recipe when they're in season—

1½ teaspoons instant chicken bouillon granules
1/3 cup boiling water
1 tablespoon soy sauce
2 tablespoons cold water
2 teaspoons cornstarch

• • •

1 8-ounce can bamboo shoots
1 8-ounce can water chestnuts
1 6-ounce can whole mushrooms
2 tablespoons cooking oil
1 clove garlic, minced
2 6-ounce packages frozen pea pods, thawed
Sliced green onion (optional)

Dissolve chicken bouillon granules in the boiling water; stir in soy sauce. Blend the cold water into the cornstarch; stir into bouillon mixture. Set aside.

Drain the bamboo shoots, water chestnuts, and mushrooms; thinly slice the drained water chestnuts.

Preheat a wok or large skillet over high heat; add cooking oil. Stir-fry the garlic in hot oil for 30 seconds. Add bamboo shoots, water chestnuts, mushrooms, and pea pods; stir-fry 2 minutes. Stir chicken broth mixture; stir into vegetables. Cook and stir till the mixture is thickened and bubbly. Cover and cook 1 minute more. Serve at once. Garnish with sliced green onions, if desired. Makes 8 servings.

PORK STIR-FRY / 206

The fresh ingredients are shown in the photo at left—

1 pound lean boneless pork
½ teaspoon instant chicken bouillon granules
⅓ cup boiling water
3 tablespoons soy sauce
2 teaspoons cornstarch
2 tablespoons cooking oil
1 teaspoon grated gingerroot
6 cups small fresh spinach leaves
1 cup bias-sliced celery
10 green onions, bias sliced
2 cups thinly sliced fresh mushrooms
2 cups fresh bean sprouts *or* one 16-ounce can bean sprouts, drained
1 8-ounce can water chestnuts, drained and thinly sliced

Partially freeze pork; thinly slice the meat into bite-size pieces. Dissolve bouillon granules in the boiling water. Blend soy sauce into cornstarch; stir in bouillon. Preheat wok or large skillet over high heat; add oil. Stir-fry gingerroot in hot oil 30 seconds. Add spinach, celery, and green onions; stir-fry 2 minutes. Remove. (Add more oil, if needed.) Add mushrooms, bean sprouts, and water chestnuts. Stir-fry 1 minute. Remove. Add pork; stir-fry 2 minutes. Stir soy mixture; add to pork. Cook and stir till bubbly. Add all vegetables. Cover; cook 1 minute. Makes 6 servings.

Pork Stir-Fry

SPICY BEEF AND ASPARAGUS / 164

Pictured on pages 64 and 65—

1 pound beef top round steak, trimmed of fat
1 tablespoon cornstarch
1 tablespoon water
1 teaspoon dry sherry
½ teaspoon salt
¼ teaspoon pepper
Several dashes bottled hot pepper sauce
¼ cup beef broth
1 tablespoon soy sauce
1 tablespoon catsup
1 teaspoon red wine vinegar
½ teaspoon sugar
2 tablespoons cooking oil
1 clove garlic, minced
¾ pound fresh asparagus, cut into 1-inch lengths, *or* one 10-ounce package frozen cut asparagus, thawed
1 cup sliced cauliflower flowerets
1 small sweet red *or* green pepper, cut into narrow strips
1 small onion, cut into thin wedges

Partially freeze beef; thinly slice the meat across grain into strips. Combine cornstarch, water, sherry, salt, pepper, and hot pepper sauce. Add meat, mixing well. Combine beef broth, soy sauce, catsup, vinegar, and sugar; set aside.

Preheat wok or large skillet over high heat. Add *1 tablespoon* of the oil. Stir-fry garlic in hot oil for 30 seconds. Add *half* the meat. Stir-fry 2 to 3 minutes or till just browned. Remove from skillet. Stir-fry remaining meat 2 to 3 minutes. Remove meat from skillet. Add remaining oil if necessary. Add asparagus and cauliflower; stir-fry for 4 minutes. (If using frozen asparagus that you've thawed, add it 2 minutes after the cauliflower is added.) Add the red or green pepper and onion; stir-fry about 2 minutes more or till asparagus is crisp-tender. Return meat to skillet. Stir in soy sauce mixture. Cook and stir till bubbly. Cover and cook 1 minute more. Makes 6 servings.

CHICKEN WITH WALNUTS / 224

1½ pounds whole chicken breasts, skinned, split, and boned
3 tablespoons soy sauce
2 teaspoons cornstarch
2 tablespoons dry sherry
1 teaspoon sugar
1 teaspoon grated gingerroot
½ teaspoon salt
½ teaspoon crushed red pepper
2 tablespoons cooking oil
2 medium green peppers, cut into ¾-inch pieces
4 green onions, bias-sliced into 1-inch lengths
½ cup walnut halves

Cut chicken into 1-inch pieces. Set aside. In small bowl blend soy sauce into cornstarch; stir in sherry, sugar, gingerroot, salt, and red pepper.

Preheat a wok or large skillet over high heat; add cooking oil. Stir-fry green peppers and green onions in hot oil 2 minutes. Remove. Add walnuts to wok; stir-fry 1 to 2 minutes or till just golden. Remove. (Add more oil, if necessary.) Add *half* of the chicken to wok; stir-fry 2 minutes. Remove. Stir-fry remaining chicken 2 minutes. Return chicken to wok. Stir soy mixture; add to chicken. Cook and stir till bubbly. Stir in vegetables and walnuts; cover and cook 1 minute. Makes 6 servings.

BEEF WITH PEA PODS/254

1 pound beef top round steak, trimmed of fat
2 teaspoons cornstarch
1 teaspoon sugar
½ teaspoon salt
⅛ teaspoon pepper
¼ cup water
2 tablespoons soy sauce
• • •
2 tablespoons cooking oil
1 clove garlic, minced
½ teaspoon grated gingerroot
1½ cups fresh pea pods *or* one 6-ounce package frozen pea pods, thawed
½ of an 8-ounce can (½ cup) water chestnuts, drained and thinly sliced

Partially freeze beef; slice thinly across the grain into bite-size strips. In small bowl mix cornstarch, sugar, salt, and pepper. Blend in water and soy sauce. Set aside.

Preheat a wok or large skillet over high heat; add cooking oil. Stir-fry the garlic and gingerroot in hot oil for 30 seconds. Add pea pods and water chestnuts to wok. Stir-fry about 1 minute. Remove pea pods and water chestnuts from wok. (Add more oil if necessary.) Add *half* the beef to hot wok or skillet; stir-fry 2 to 3 minutes or till browned. Remove the beef. Stir-fry the remaining beef for 2 to 3 minutes. Return all the beef to the wok or skillet. Stir the soy mixture and stir into beef. Cook and stir till mixture is thickened and bubbly. Stir in pea pods and water chestnuts; cover and cook 1 minute. Makes 4 servings.

SUKIYAKI/422

½ pound beef tenderloin
6 ounces fresh tofu (bean curd)
2 ounces fresh water chestnuts, peeled, *or* ½ of an 8-ounce can water chestnuts, drained
1 tablespoon cooking oil
1 tablespoon sugar
½ teaspoon instant beef bouillon granules
¼ cup boiling water
3 tablespoons soy sauce
1 cup bias-sliced green onions with tops
½ cup bias-sliced celery
3 cups torn bok choy *or* spinach
1 cup fresh bean sprouts *or* ½ of a 16-ounce can bean sprouts, drained
½ cup thinly sliced fresh mushrooms
⅓ cup canned bamboo shoots, drained

Partially freeze beef; slice very thinly across grain. Cube tofu. Thinly slice fresh or canned water chestnuts.

Preheat a large skillet or wok; add oil. Add beef slices; cook quickly, turning meat over and over, just till browned, 1 to 2 minutes. Sprinkle with sugar. Dissolve bouillon granules in the boiling water; add soy sauce. Pour over meat. Remove meat from skillet with a slotted spoon. Let soy mixture bubble. Add onion and celery. Continue cooking and toss-stirring over high heat about 1 minute. Add tofu, water chestnuts, bok choy or spinach, bean sprouts, mushrooms, and bamboo shoots. Return meat to pan. Cook and stir just till heated through. Serve with hot cooked rice and pass additional soy sauce, if desired. Serves 3.

SIMMERED PORK WITH SPINACH/221

¾ pound lean boneless pork
1 cup grated Chinese white radish *or* radishes
¾ cup sake
2 tablespoons soy sauce
2 tablespoons water
1 tablespoon grated gingerroot
¼ teaspoon salt
1 cup sliced fresh mushrooms
• • •
4 cups small fresh spinach leaves
6 green onions, bias-sliced into 1-inch lengths
1 tablespoon cold water
1 tablespoon cornstarch

Partially freeze pork; thinly slice. Place grated radish in a double layer of paper toweling; press tightly to extract as much moisture as possible. Set aside.

In large skillet combine sake, soy sauce, 2 tablespoons water, gingerroot, and salt. Add pork and mushrooms. Simmer, covered, 10 minutes or till pork is tender; turn pork slices occasionally. Stir in spinach leaves and green onions. Cook, covered, for 2 to 3 minutes.

Remove pork and vegetables and arrange on heated serving platter. For sauce, measure 1 cup cooking liquid. Slowly blend 1 tablespoon cold water into the cornstarch; stir into cooking liquid. Cook and stir till thickened and bubbly. Pass sauce. Garnish pork and vegetables with the grated radish. Makes 4 servings.

Sukiyaki

FRENCH ENTRÉES

FRUIT-AND-CHEESE FRENCH OMELETS/385

Fruit-and-Cheese Filling
4 eggs
2 tablespoons water
¼ teaspoon salt
⅛ teaspoon pepper
2 tablespoons diet margarine

Prepare Fruit-and-Cheese Filling and keep sauce warm. Beat together eggs, water, salt, and pepper. In a 6- or 8-inch skillet with flared sides, heat *1 tablespoon* of the diet margarine over medium heat till it sizzles and browns slightly. Tilt the pan to coat the sides. Pour in *half* the egg mixture (about ½ cup); cook over medium heat. As eggs set, run a spatula around edge of skillet, lifting eggs to allow uncooked portion to flow underneath. When eggs are set but still shiny, remove from heat. Spoon *half* of the filling across the center. Using a spatula, carefully lift one-third of the cooked omelet over filling. Repeat with remaining one-third to overlap. Gently slide omelet to edge of skillet. Tilt skillet, then invert to roll the omelet out onto a warm serving plate. Repeat with remaining egg mixture to make second omelet. Makes 2 servings.

Fruit-and-Cheese Filling: In saucepan blend ½ cup *orange juice* and 2 teaspoons *lemon juice* into 2 teaspoons *cornstarch* and ⅛ teaspoon ground *nutmeg.* Cook and stir till bubbly. Keep warm. Combine ½ cup sliced fresh *strawberries* and 1 medium *orange,* peeled, sectioned, and halved. Fill omelets with fruit mixture. Spoon some sauce over the fruit. Fold omelet. Spoon remaining sauce atop filled omelet; sprinkle ½ cup shredded *Gouda or Edam cheese* over all.

RATATOUILLE/70

1 large onion, sliced into thin wedges
2 cloves garlic, minced
2 tablespoons olive oil *or* cooking oil
1 16-ounce can tomatoes, cut up
1½ teaspoons dried thyme, crushed
1 bay leaf
1 teaspoon salt
¼ teaspoon pepper
• • •
1 medium unpeeled eggplant
2 medium zucchini, cut into strips
2 green peppers, seeded and cut into strips

In Dutch oven cook onion and garlic in oil till tender. Add the *undrained* tomatoes, thyme, bay leaf, salt, and pepper. Cover and simmer for 10 minutes. Discard the bay leaf. Remove and set aside *2 cups* of the tomato mixture.

Slice eggplant in half lengthwise, then crosswise into ½-inch slices. Arrange *half* of the eggplant, zucchini, and peppers over tomato mixture in the pan. Sprinkle with *salt* and *pepper.* Cover with *1 cup* of the reserved tomato mixture. Arrange remaining vegetables atop; sprinkle with salt and pepper. Add remaining reserved tomato mixture. Cover and simmer 20 minutes. Uncover and simmer the vegetable mixture for 15 minutes. Makes 8 servings.

BOEUF EN DAUBE/251

2 cups dry red wine
1 medium onion, chopped (½ cup)
2 cloves garlic, minced
1 tablespoon vinegar
1 teaspoon salt
½ teaspoon dried rosemary, crushed
½ teaspoon dried thyme, crushed
½ teaspoon finely shredded orange peel
¼ teaspoon pepper
2 to 2½ pounds lean beef stew meat, cut into 1-inch cubes
2 ounces salt pork
½ cup beef broth
6 carrots, bias-cut into 1-inch pieces
3 onions, quartered
1 cup pitted ripe olives
2 tablespoons cornstarch
2 tablespoons cold water

Combine wine, the ½ cup onion, garlic, vinegar, salt, rosemary, thyme, orange peel, and pepper. Add beef; stir to coat. Cover and marinate at room temperature for 2 hours. Drain meat, reserving marinade; pat meat dry with paper toweling. In 4-quart Dutch oven cook salt pork till 2 to 3 tablespoons fat accumulate; discard pork. Brown meat in the hot fat. Add marinade and broth; bring to boiling. Cover; simmer 1 hour. Add vegetables and olives; simmer, covered, 30 to 40 minutes. Blend cornstarch and cold water; add to pot. Cook and stir till bubbly. Turn into bowl; top with some snipped parsley, if desired. Makes 10 servings.

Boeuf en Daube

COQUILLES SAINT JACQUES/309

1½ pounds fresh *or* frozen scallops
1 cup dry white wine
1 tablespoon lemon juice
2 sprigs parsley
1 bay leaf
½ teaspoon salt
• • •
1 cup chopped fresh mushrooms
2 tablespoons thinly sliced shallot *or* green onion
2 tablespoons butter *or* margarine
2 tablespoons all-purpose flour
¼ teaspoon salt
⅛ teaspoon ground nutmeg
Dash pepper
1 cup milk
2 egg yolks
1 cup soft bread crumbs
2 tablespoons butter *or* margarine, melted

Thaw scallops, if frozen. Halve any large scallops. In saucepan combine scallops, wine, lemon juice, parsley, bay leaf, and the ½ teaspoon salt. Bring to boiling; reduce heat. Cover and simmer for 2 to 4 minutes or till scallops are opaque in appearance. Remove scallops with a slotted spoon. Strain wine mixture through cheesecloth; reserve 1 cup liquid.

In skillet cook mushrooms and shallot or green onion in 2 tablespoons butter or margarine about 5 minutes or till tender. Stir in flour, ¼ teaspoon salt, nutmeg, and pepper. Add reserved 1 cup liquid and ½ cup of the milk. Cook and stir till thickened and bubbly. Remove from heat. Combine egg yolks and remaining ½ cup milk; beat well with a wire whisk. Gradually stir about *half* of the hot mixture into egg yolk mixture; return to remaining hot mixture in skillet. Add scallops. Heat and stir just till bubbly. Reduce heat; cook and stir over low heat for 2 minutes.

Place 6 buttered coquilles (baking shells), shallow individual casseroles, or 6-ounce custard cups in shallow baking pans. Spoon scallop mixture into shells.

Toss together bread crumbs and 2 tablespoons melted butter or margarine; sprinkle over scallop mixture. Bake in a 400° oven about 10 minutes or till browned. Makes 6 servings.

ARTICHOKE-SHALLOT SOUFFLÉ/294

⅓ cup finely chopped shallots *or* onion
6 tablespoons butter *or* margarine
⅓ cup all-purpose flour
¼ teaspoon salt
1½ cups skim milk
½ cup grated Parmesan cheese
6 egg yolks
1 14-ounce can artichoke hearts, drained and chopped
6 egg whites

In saucepan cook shallots in hot butter or margarine till tender but not brown. Stir in flour and salt. Add milk all at once. Cook and stir till thickened and bubbly. Remove from heat. Stir in cheese. Beat egg yolks about 6 minutes or till very thick and light colored. Slowly stir cheese mixture into yolks. Stir in artichokes. Cool slightly. Thoroughly wash beaters. Beat egg whites till stiff peaks form (tips stand straight); fold yolk mixture into whites. Turn into an *ungreased* 2-quart soufflé dish. Bake in a 350° oven for 55 to 60 minutes. Makes 6 servings.

BOUILLABAISSE/232

1 pound frozen small lobster tails
1 pound fresh *or* frozen sole fillets *or* cod fillets
12 ounces fresh *or* frozen scallops
12 clams in shells
• • •
2 large onions, chopped (2 cups)
¼ cup olive oil *or* cooking oil
4 cups coarsely chopped tomatoes
6 cups water
1 tablespoon salt
1 clove garlic, minced
2 sprigs parsley
1 bay leaf
1 teaspoon dried thyme, crushed
¼ teaspoon thread saffron, crushed
Dash pepper

Thaw frozen shellfish and fish. When lobster is partially thawed, halve lengthwise; halve crosswise to make 8 portions. Cut fish fillets into 2-inch pieces. Cut large scallops in half. Wash clams well.

In Dutch oven cook onions in hot olive or cooking oil till tender but not brown. Add tomatoes, water, salt, garlic, parsley, bay leaf, thyme, saffron, and pepper. Bring to boiling. Reduce heat; cover and simmer 30 minutes. Strain liquid into a kettle. Bring stock to boiling; add lobster and fish. Cook the mixture 5 minutes. Add scallops and clams; boil 5 minutes more or till clams open. Discard any clams that don't open. Makes 8 servings.

Bouillabaisse

GREEK CLASSICS

MOUSSAKA FOR MANY/285

This eggplant casserole can be made with ground beef or ground lamb—

2 large eggplants, peeled and cut into ½-inch slices
2 tablespoons cooking oil
Salt
2 pounds lean ground lamb *or* ground beef
1 cup chopped onion
1 clove garlic, minced
1 8-ounce can tomato sauce
¾ cup dry red wine
2 tablespoons snipped parsley
1 teaspoon salt
¼ teaspoon dried oregano, crushed
¼ teaspoon ground cinnamon
1 beaten egg
• • •
¼ cup butter *or* margarine
¼ cup all-purpose flour
1 teaspoon salt
Dash pepper
2 cups skim milk
3 beaten eggs
½ cup grated Parmesan cheese
Ground cinnamon

Brush both sides of eggplant slices with the oil; sprinkle lightly with salt. In large skillet brown eggplant slices, about 1½ minutes on each side. Drain and set aside.

In same skillet cook ground lamb or beef, onion, and garlic till the meat is brown and the onion is tender; drain off excess fat. Stir in tomato sauce, wine, parsley, the 1 teaspoon salt, oregano, and ¼ teaspoon cinnamon. Simmer, uncovered, for 10 minutes. Gradually stir the ground meat mixture into the 1 beaten egg.

Meanwhile, in saucepan melt butter or margarine; stir in flour, 1 teaspoon salt, and pepper. Add milk all at once; cook and stir till thickened and bubbly. Gradually stir hot sauce into the 3 beaten eggs.

In a 13x9x2-inch baking dish arrange *half* the eggplant. Pour all the meat mixture over; top with the remaining eggplant. Pour milk mixture over all. Top with Parmesan and additional cinnamon. Bake in a 325° oven for 40 to 45 minutes. Garnish with additional snipped parsley, if desired. Serves 10.

GREEK SALAD/133

This salad is pictured on pages 64 and 65—

1 medium head iceberg lettuce, torn
1 head curly endive, torn
¼ cup sliced red onion, separated into rings
2 medium tomatoes, cut into wedges
¾ cup crumbled feta cheese (3 ounces)
¼ cup sliced pitted ripe olives
1 2-ounce can anchovy fillets, drained (optional)
• • •
⅓ cup olive oil *or* salad oil
⅓ cup white wine vinegar
½ teaspoon salt
¼ teaspoon dried oregano, crushed
⅛ teaspoon pepper

In mixing bowl toss together the torn lettuce, curly endive, and onion rings; mound onto 8 individual salad plates. Atop the greens arrange tomatoes, feta cheese, olives, and the anchovies, if desired.

To make the dressing, in screw-top jar combine the olive oil or salad oil, wine vinegar, salt, oregano, and pepper. Cover and shake well to mix. Pour the dressing over the salads. Makes 8 servings.

PASTITSIO/217

1 cup elbow macaroni
¾ pound lean ground lamb
½ cup chopped onion
1 8-ounce can tomato sauce
¼ cup grated Parmesan cheese
½ teaspoon salt
½ teaspoon dried thyme, crushed
¼ teaspoon ground cinnamon
1½ cups skim milk
3 tablespoons all-purpose flour
½ teaspoon salt
2 slightly beaten eggs
Ground cinnamon

Cook macaroni according to package directions; drain and set aside. In medium saucepan cook lamb and onion till meat is browned; drain well. Stir in macaroni, tomato sauce, *2 tablespoons* of the Parmesan cheese, ½ teaspoon salt, the thyme, and the ¼ teaspoon cinnamon. Spread meat mixture in a 10x6x2-inch baking dish.

For sauce, in screw-top jar combine *½ cup* of the milk, the flour, and ½ teaspoon salt; cover and shake well. In saucepan combine remaining milk and the milk-flour mixture. Cook and stir till thickened and bubbly. Cook and stir 1 to 2 minutes more. Gradually stir about ½ cup of the sauce into beaten eggs; return to remaining sauce in saucepan, stirring rapidly. Stir in the remaining Parmesan cheese. Pour atop meat mixture in baking dish. Sprinkle with additional ground cinnamon. Bake, uncovered, in a 375° oven 30 to 35 minutes or till a knife inserted just off-center comes out clean. Let stand 10 minutes before serving. Serves 6.

Moussaka for Many

MEXICAN SELECTIONS

TOSTADA COMPUESTA/453

A main dish and salad all in one—

1 pound lean ground beef
½ cup chopped onion
1 clove garlic, minced
½ teaspoon chili powder
1 8-ounce can cut green beans
1 8-ounce can red kidney beans
Cooking oil
6 10-inch flour tortillas
1 large tomato, chopped
1 small head lettuce, shredded
1 cup shredded American cheese
Zesty Salad Dressing

In skillet cook beef, onion, and garlic till meat is brown and onion is tender. Drain off fat. Add chili powder and ½ teaspoon *salt.* Set meat mixture aside and keep warm. In saucepan combine *undrained* green beans and kidney beans; heat and drain. In heavy skillet heat ¼ inch cooking oil. Fry tortillas, one at a time, in hot oil for 20 to 40 seconds on each side or till crisp and golden. Drain well on paper toweling. Keep warm in foil in 250° oven. Place tortillas in center of dinner plates. Dividing ingredients equally among tortillas, layer them in the following order: meat mixture, beans, tomato, lettuce, and cheese. Spoon dressing over each serving. Serves 6.

Zesty Salad Dressing: In small saucepan combine 1 tablespoon *cornstarch,* 1 teaspoon *sugar,* and 1 teaspoon *dry mustard.* Stir in 1 cup *cold water.* Cook and stir till thick and bubbly. Remove from heat; cover surface with waxed paper. Cool 10 to 15 minutes. Remove the waxed paper and stir in ¼ cup *vinegar,* ¼ cup *catsup,* 1 teaspoon prepared *horseradish,* 1 teaspoon *Worcestershire sauce,* ½ teaspoon *salt,* ½ teaspoon *paprika,* and dash bottled *hot pepper sauce.* Beat till smooth. Add 1 clove *garlic,* halved. Transfer to storage container; cover and chill. Remove garlic from dressing before serving.

PESCADO A LA NARANJA/305

2 pounds fresh *or* frozen halibut steaks *or* other fish steaks
½ cup finely chopped onion
2 cloves garlic, minced
2 tablespoons cooking oil
2 tablespoons snipped cilantro *or* parsley
1 teaspoon salt
⅛ teaspoon pepper
½ cup orange juice
1 tablespoon lemon juice
1 hard-cooked egg, cut into wedges

Thaw fish, if frozen. Arrange fish in a 12x7½x2-inch baking dish. In small skillet cook onion and garlic in oil till onion is tender but not brown. Stir in cilantro or parsley, salt, and pepper. Spread mixture over fish. Combine orange juice and lemon juice; pour evenly over all. Bake, covered, in a 400° oven for 20 to 25 minutes or till fish flakes easily when tested with a fork. Arrange egg wedges atop fish. Sprinkle with paprika and garnish with orange slices, if desired. Serves 6.

CHILIES RELLENOS BAKE/269

2 4-ounce cans green chili peppers
6 ounces Monterey Jack cheese
4 beaten eggs
⅓ cup skim milk
½ cup all-purpose flour
½ teaspoon baking powder
¾ cup shredded cheddar cheese (3 ounces)

Drain peppers; halve lengthwise and remove seeds. Cut Monterey Jack cheese into strips to fit inside peppers. Wrap each pepper around a strip of cheese; place in greased 10x6x2-inch baking dish. Combine eggs and milk; beat in flour, baking powder, and ½ teaspoon *salt* till smooth. Pour over peppers. Sprinkle cheddar cheese atop. Bake in a 350° oven for 30 minutes. Makes 6 servings.

CEVICHE/82

1 pound fresh *or* frozen haddock *or* other fish fillets
1 cup fresh lime *or* lemon juice
1 small onion, thinly sliced and separated into rings
2 to 3 pickled serrano peppers, rinsed, seeded, and cut into strips
¼ cup olive oil *or* cooking oil
¾ teaspoon salt
¼ teaspoon dried oregano, crushed
⅛ teaspoon pepper
2 medium tomatoes, peeled, seeded, and chopped

Thaw fish, if frozen. Cut into ½-inch cubes. In nonmetal bowl cover fish with lime juice. Cover and chill 4 hours or overnight or till fish is opaque, turning occasionally. Add onion, peppers, oil, salt, oregano, and pepper to fish. Toss gently to combine; chill. Toss tomato with chilled fish mixture. Sprinkle with snipped parsley, if desired. Makes 12 appetizer-size servings.

Tostada Compuesta

ITALIAN FARE

MARINATED TIDBIT TRAY/253

3 medium artichokes *or* one 9-ounce package frozen artichoke hearts
Lemon juice
1 medium head cauliflower *or* one 10-ounce package frozen cauliflower
1 cup shelled cooked shrimp
• • •
1 cup cooking oil
½ cup wine vinegar
¼ cup sliced green onion
2 tablespoons snipped parsley
1 tablespoon sugar
1 tablespoon lemon juice
2 cloves garlic, minced
1 teaspoon salt
1 teaspoon dried thyme, crushed
⅛ teaspoon ground red pepper

Trim stems and remove loose outer leaves from fresh artichokes. Cut 1 inch off tops; snip off sharp leaf tips. Cut each artichoke lengthwise into 6 wedges; discard the fuzzy "choke." Brush cut edges with lemon juice. Cook, covered, in boiling salted water for 20 to 30 minutes or just till tender. Drain. Remove leaves and woody stem from fresh cauliflower. Break the head into flowerets. Cook, covered, in small amount of boiling salted water for 10 to 15 minutes or just till tender. (Or, cook frozen vegetables as directed on the packages.) Drain.

Place vegetables and shrimp in plastic bag; set in shallow pan. In screw-top jar combine remaining ingredients. Cover; shake well. Pour over vegetables and shrimp; close bag. Refrigerate several hours or overnight, turning occasionally. To serve, drain vegetables and shrimp and arrange on lettuce-lined platter, if desired. Add some rolled, sliced salami to the arrangement (add 88 calories for each one-ounce slice), if desired. Makes 10 servings.

LEMON ICE/104

½ cup sugar
½ cup boiling water
1 cup cold water
¼ teaspoon finely shredded lemon peel
½ cup lemon juice

Dissolve sugar in the ½ cup boiling water. Add cold water, lemon peel, and lemon juice. Pour into a shallow pan. Freeze about 2 hours or till nearly firm. Break up into a chilled small mixer bowl. Beat at low speed of electric mixer till fluffy. Freeze till nearly firm, stirring once or twice. Scrape lemon ice into small goblets. Makes 4 servings.

MARINATED GARBANZO BEANS/175

Garbanzo beans are also known as chick-peas and in Italy are called cece beans—

2 15-ounce cans garbanzo beans
1 cup water
1 clove garlic, minced
½ teaspoon dried rosemary, crushed
¼ cup olive oil *or* cooking oil
2 tablespoons wine vinegar
½ teaspoon salt
⅛ teaspoon pepper

In saucepan combine *undrained* beans, water, garlic, and rosemary. Bring to boiling. Reduce heat; cover and simmer 15 minutes. Drain. In screw-top jar combine remaining ingredients. Cover and shake well. Pour over beans; toss. Cover and chill several hours or overnight; stir occasionally. To serve, drain beans. Serves 10.

MUSHROOM AND HAM LASAGNA/306

Pictured on pages 64 and 65—

6 ounces lasagna noodles
1½ cups ricotta cheese
3 tablespoons skim milk
½ teaspoon salt
⅛ teaspoon pepper
3 cups sliced fresh mushrooms
¼ cup sliced green onion
2 tablespoons diet margarine
1 7½-ounce can tomatoes, cut up
4 ounces fully cooked ham, cut into thin strips
2 tablespoons snipped parsley
2 tablespoons dry white wine
½ teaspoon dried basil, crushed
½ cup grated Parmesan cheese

Cook pasta in boiling salted water just till tender; drain. Rinse and drain again. Combine ricotta, milk, salt, and pepper.

Cook mushrooms and onion in margarine just till tender. Stir in *undrained* tomatoes, ham, parsley, wine, and basil. Bring to boiling; reduce heat. Boil gently, uncovered, for 5 to 8 minutes or till liquid is almost evaporated.

Arrange a single layer of cooked pasta in bottom of a greased 10x6x2-inch baking dish. Spread with ⅓ of the ricotta mixture, ⅓ of the mushroom mixture, and ⅓ of the Parmesan cheese. Repeat the layers of pasta, ricotta, mushroom mixture, and Parmesan two more times. Cover with foil and bake in a 350° oven for 35 to 40 minutes or till heated through. Let stand 10 minutes before serving. Makes 6 servings.

Marinated Tidbit Tray; Marinated Garbanzo Beans

SPANISH FAVORITES

PAELLA CASSEROLE/395

½ pound chorizos *or* Italian sausage links, sliced
1 2½- to 3-pound broiler-fryer chicken, cut up
Salt and pepper
1 medium onion, chopped (½ cup)
1 medium sweet red pepper, chopped
1 medium green pepper, chopped
2 cloves garlic, minced
• • •
1½ cups long grain rice
2 medium tomatoes, peeled and chopped (1½ cups)
2 teaspoons salt
¼ teaspoon thread saffron, crushed
4 cups boiling water
• • •
1 pound fresh *or* frozen shelled shrimp
10 small clams in shells
1 10-ounce package frozen peas

In large skillet cook sausage over medium heat till done. Drain, reserving drippings in skillet; set aside.

Season chicken pieces with a little salt and pepper. Brown chicken in reserved drippings; remove chicken, reserve drippings in skillet.

Add chopped onion, red pepper, green pepper, and garlic to the reserved drippings; cook till onion is tender but not brown. Stir in *uncooked* rice, chopped tomatoes, the 2 teaspoons salt, and saffron. Stir in the boiling water; bring mixture to boiling. Stir in cooked sausage.

Turn rice mixture into a paella pan or a 4-quart casserole or Dutch oven; arrange chicken pieces atop mixture. Bake, covered, in a 375° oven for 30 minutes.

Meanwhile, thaw shrimp, if frozen. Thoroughly scrub clams. Place clams in a saucepan with ½ inch of *boiling water;* cover and cook 3 to 5 minutes or till shells open. Drain; discard any unopened clams.

Place frozen peas in a colander or strainer; rinse with hot water to thaw. Arrange peas, clams, and shrimp atop rice mixture. Bake, covered, 15 to 20 minutes longer or till chicken, shrimp, and rice are done. Makes 10 servings.

ARROZ CON TOMATE/162

"Arroz con Tomate" translates to Spanish rice, a favorite among Americans—

½ cup chopped green pepper
¼ cup chopped onion
1 clove garlic, minced
½ teaspoon dried basil, crushed
½ teaspoon dried rosemary, crushed
2 tablespoons olive oil *or* cooking oil
• • •
2 cups water
1 cup long grain rice
1 cup chopped, peeled tomato
1 teaspoon salt
⅛ teaspoon pepper
Tomato slices (optional)
Green pepper rings (optional)

In skillet cook chopped green pepper, chopped onion, garlic, basil, and rosemary in hot olive oil or cooking oil till vegetables are tender.

Stir in water, uncooked rice, chopped tomato, salt, and pepper. Cover and cook over low heat about 20 minutes or till the rice is done. Garnish with tomato slices and green pepper rings, if desired. Serves 6.

SPANISH GAZPACHO/49

This chilled appetizer soup is pictured on pages 64 and 65—

2 cups tomato juice
½ cup finely chopped cucumber
½ cup finely chopped celery
½ cup finely chopped green pepper
⅓ cup finely chopped green onion
2 to 3 tablespoons wine vinegar
2 tablespoons olive oil *or* cooking oil
2 teaspoons snipped parsley
1 teaspoon salt
½ teaspoon Worcestershire sauce
¼ teaspoon freshly ground pepper
1 small clove garlic, minced
• • •
Cucumber slices (optional)

In a bowl combine the tomato juice, finely chopped cucumber, finely chopped celery, finely chopped green pepper, finely chopped green onion, wine vinegar, olive oil, snipped parsley, salt, Worcestershire sauce, freshly ground pepper, and minced garlic. Cover the bowl and chill the mixture thoroughly, at least 4 hours. Serve in chilled bowls. If desired, serve over crushed ice in glass icers. Garnish each serving of the chilled soup with a cucumber slice, if desired. Makes 8 servings.

Paella Casserole

QUICK-AND-EASY

HEALTHFUL MEALS

If a busy schedule leaves you little time to plan healthful, balanced meals, take a few minutes to look through the next few pages. You'll find nine preplanned menus of nutritious, calorie-counted foods to help you with mealtime preparations. Look for a variety of menu plans, from a soup-and-sandwich lunch for everyday enjoyment to a special-day brunch and a company-best fish dinner.

Tuna Salad Sandwiches

Confetti Consommé

Apricots Melba

NUTRITION ANALYSIS

Cooking nutritious meals quickly and without fuss is easy if you take a few minutes to get organized. Plan your meals for several days or a week at a time. Then, select the recipes for each meal and compile one large grocery list. You'll eliminate any last-minute panic about what to serve and you'll cut down on the number of trips to the grocery store.

	Per Serving						Percent U.S. RDA Per Serving							
QUICK-AND-EASY MEALS	CALORIES	PROTEIN gms	CARBOHYDRATE gms	FAT gms	SODIUM mgs	POTASSIUM mgs	PROTEIN	VITAMIN A	VITAMIN C	THIAMINE	RIBOFLAVIN	NIACIN	CALCIUM	IRON
AD-LIB ANTIPASTO (p. 102)	84	11	10	2	160	399	17	8	19	6	5	24	6	9
APRICOTS MELBA (p. 87)	94	1	22	1	5	235	2	39	20	2	3	3	2	3
BERRIES WITH LEMON (p. 90)	75	1	18	1	1	193	1	1	115	2	5	3	2	6
CHEESY STRATA (p. 100)	208	13	15	11	801	235	20	13	1	9	25	3	28	8
COCONUT BISCUITS (p. 100)	158	3	20	8	183	63	5	0	1	10	7	6	4	4
CONFETTI CONSOMMÉ (p. 87)	30	3	3	2	499	41	5	17	13	1	2	8	0	1
FISH AND ASPARAGUS BUNDLES (p. 98)	172	20	10	5	285	817	31	27	76	16	17	18	5	12
GARDEN FRITTATA (p. 101)	187	16	7	11	367	382	24	73	50	9	23	5	10	13
GREEN BEAN-FISH AMANDINE (p. 88)	334	34	12	16	947	673	53	15	17	17	20	50	37	12
GREEN SALAD (p. 98)	97	1	2	10	138	104	1	4	6	2	2	1	1	2
HAM AND SALAD ROLLS (p. 87)	266	15	24	12	1122	224	22	1	3	28	11	14	5	15
HAWAIIAN SAUSAGE STIR-FRY (p. 96)	335	14	30	18	1420	525	22	77	43	28	14	19	5	21
HONEY FRUIT COMPOTE (p. 100)	208	2	54	1	5	396	3	11	120	12	5	4	7	7
INSTANT PEACH-ALMOND SHERBET (p. 96)	139	1	35	0	3	237	1	20	116	3	4	5	1	4
ITALIAN ROUND STEAK WITH NOODLES (p. 90)	435	29	46	13	536	381	45	21	19	39	24	40	4	26
MARINATED THREE-BEAN SALAD (p. 92)	165	6	25	5	97	307	9	3	25	6	4	4	5	13
MEXICAN-STYLE QUICHES (p. 92)	372	25	27	18	680	459	39	24	8	27	40	8	43	19
PERCOLATOR MINT ICED TEA (p. 93)	0	0	0	0	0	0	0	0	0	0	0	0	0	0
PINEAPPLE-LEMON DESSERT-IN-A-GLASS (p. 94)	146	5	31	1	66	267	8	1	9	6	13	1	17	1
POACHED PEARS WITH ORANGE SAUCE (p. 102)	79	1	11	4	46	156	2	5	34	3	3	1	1	1
PROSCIUTTO AND PASTA (p. 102)	268	17	32	7	344	327	26	11	23	40	21	21	12	15
QUICK APPLE MOLD (p. 90)	90	2	16	3	54	93	3	1	4	1	1	0	1	1
RAW VEGETABLE PLATTER WITH DIP (p. 88)	67	4	12	1	96	475	6	86	31	6	10	3	12	8
SPARKLING FRUIT (p. 93)	43	0	11	0	5	156	1	3	4	1	1	2	1	2
SPECIAL SPICED APRICOTS (p. 98)	77	1	19	0	10	326	2	42	9	2	3	2	4	3
SPINACH-BLUE CHEESE SALAD (p. 96)	49	6	4	2	146	301	9	90	48	4	11	2	9	10
STRAWBERRY-BANANA FREEZE (p. 88)	97	3	17	3	38	333	5	4	45	3	10	3	9	4
SUPER STRATA SALAD (p. 94)	207	17	9	11	1025	301	27	13	9	25	16	17	16	13
TUNA SALAD SANDWICHES (p. 87)	166	19	17	3	391	363	29	11	18	10	11	36	6	9
WHOLE WHEAT CROUTONS (p. 94)	62	2	9	3	120	46	3	2	0	4	1	2	2	3

TUNA SALAD SANDWICHES/166

1/3 cup cream-style cottage cheese
1/3 cup bias-sliced celery
1 tablespoon chopped onion
1 tablespoon low-calorie mayonnaise
1/4 teaspoon salt
4 slices rye bread
4 teaspoons low-calorie mayonnaise
Lettuce leaves
1 tomato, cut into 4 slices
1 6½-ounce can tuna (water pack), chilled, drained, and broken into chunks

In bowl mix together the cottage cheese, celery, onion, the 1 tablespoon low-calorie mayonnaise, and the 1/4 teaspoon salt. Spread bread slices (toasted if desired) with the 4 teaspoons low-calorie mayonnaise. Top each slice of bread with lettuce leaves and a tomato slice; sprinkle lightly with salt. Divide tuna atop the 4 tomato slices. Divide the cottage cheese mixture atop tuna. If desired, trim platter with parsley and a tomato peel rose. Serves 4.

HAM AND SALAD ROLLS/266

4 frankfurter buns, split
4 teaspoons prepared mustard
1 cup shredded lettuce
1/4 cup chopped cucumber
2 tablespoons low-calorie French salad dressing
8 slices boiled ham (about 8 ounces)
4 dill pickle strips

Spread cut sides of buns with mustard. Mix lettuce, cucumber, and salad dressing. Stack together 2 slices ham for each sandwich. Place *one-fourth* of the lettuce mixture on one end of a stack of 2 ham slices; top with 1 pickle strip. Roll up jelly-roll fashion. Place in a frankfurter bun. Repeat for remaining sandwiches. Makes 4 servings.

CONFETTI CONSOMMÉ/30

1 10¾-ounce can condensed chicken broth
3/4 cup water
1/4 cup shredded carrot
2 tablespoons finely chopped green pepper
2 tablespoons thinly sliced green onion

In saucepan combine chicken broth, water, carrot, green pepper, and onion. Heat to boiling. Serve hot. Makes 4 servings.

APRICOTS MELBA/94

8 fresh medium apricots, halved and pitted
3/4 cup raspberry sherbet
1/2 cup fresh red raspberries
Few drops almond extract

Place 4 apricot halves in each serving dish. Stir raspberry sherbet to soften; mix in fresh raspberries and almond extract. Spoon over apricots. (*Or,* return raspberry mixture to freezer and freeze till firm enough to scoop. Serve small scoops over apricot halves in dish.) If desired, trim with a few additional raspberries and fresh mint sprigs. Serves 4.

SOUP-AND-SANDWICH LUNCH

Menu is pictured on pages 84 and 85—

Confetti Consommé	**30**
Tuna Salad Sandwiches	**166**
Apricots Melba	**94**
Skim milk (1 cup)	**88**
TOTAL CALORIES	**378**

This easy-to-put-together lunch follows the familiar soup-and-sandwich pattern. Another time you can substitute Ham and Salad Rolls for the tuna sandwiches, but be sure to add the extra calories.

Note that you can make the Apricots Melba recipe two ways. Either spoon the softened sherbet mixture over the apricots, or refreeze the mixture till it's firm enough to scoop into small balls. Replacing the apricot dessert with a piece of fresh fruit would simplify the lunch even more.

DINNER IN A HURRY

Green Bean-Fish Amandine 334
Raw Vegetable Platter with Dip 67
Roll (1 medium) 119
Whipped butter (1 teaspoon) 23
Strawberry-Banana Freeze 97
Tea 0

TOTAL CALORIES 640

You can have several of the ingredients for this dinner stored in the freezer, ready for unexpected company. Just take the fish steaks, green beans, and strawberries right from the freezer, then quickly cook or use the ingredients without thawing them. Be sure to wrap and freeze the bananas for the dessert and give them enough time to freeze till firm.

Start dinner by preparing the relishes and dip; chill. Then, poach the frozen fish and cook the beans and cheese sauce. Finally, combine the sauce with the green beans and spoon over the fish. Fix the dessert just before serving.

RAW VEGETABLE PLATTER WITH DIP/67

Lettuce
2 carrots, crinkle-cut into strips
2 stalks celery, cut into ½-inch pieces
1 large cucumber, sliced
10 radishes
Herbed Yogurt Dip

On lettuce-lined plate arrange vegetables and Herbed Yogurt Dip. Makes 4 servings.

Herbed Yogurt Dip: Stir together one 8-ounce carton *plain yogurt;* 2 tablespoons chopped *onion;* 1 teaspoon *Worcestershire sauce;* 1 clove *garlic,* minced; and ¼ teaspoon dried *mixed salad herbs.* Cover and chill the dip.

STRAWBERRY-BANANA FREEZE/97

1 cup frozen whole unsweetened strawberries
2 small ripe bananas
½ cup evaporated skimmed milk
½ teaspoon vanilla

(If desired, for garnish, reserve 1 frozen strawberry, sliced, and 4 thin banana slices, brushed with lemon juice.)

Peel bananas; wrap in plastic wrap and freeze till firm. Cut bananas into chunks. In blender container or food processor bowl combine the bananas, evaporated skimmed milk, and vanilla. Cover and blend till smooth. With blender or food processor slowly running, add the frozen berries, a few at a time, through opening; blend till smooth. Serve at once. Garnish with reserved fruit, if desired. Makes 4 servings.

GREEN BEAN-FISH AMANDINE/334

4 frozen salmon *or* other fish steaks, cut ¾ inch thick
2 cups water
2 tablespoons lemon juice
1 teaspoon salt
1 9-ounce package frozen French-style green beans

• • •

1 cup skim milk
½ cup process Swiss cheese cut into cubes (2 ounces)
2 tablespoons all-purpose flour
1 tablespoon butter *or* margarine
¼ teaspoon salt
1 tablespoon dry sherry
2 tablespoons slivered almonds

Place frozen fish steaks in large skillet. Add water, lemon juice, and the 1 teaspoon salt. Bring to boiling; reduce heat. Cover and simmer about 10 minutes or till fish flakes easily when tested with a fork. Cook green beans according to package directions; drain the cooked green beans.

In blender container combine milk, cheese, flour, butter or margarine, and ¼ teaspoon salt. Cover and blend till ingredients are well-combined. Pour the mixture into a medium saucepan. Cook and stir till mixture is thickened and bubbly; cook and stir 2 minutes more. Stir in sherry and beans. Drain fish; transfer to a warm platter. Spoon bean sauce over; sprinkle with almonds. If desired, garnish with parsley and lemon wedges. Makes 4 servings.

Green Bean-Fish Amandine; Raw Vegetable Platter with Dip

BEEF AND PASTA DINNER

Italian Round Steak with Noodles	**435**
Cooked carrots (½ cup)	**22**
Quick Apple Mold	**90**
Berries with Lemon	**75**
Iced tea	**0**
TOTAL CALORIES	**622**

You can do much of this meal's preparation ahead of time: The meat can be marinated, the salad made, and the dessert stirred together. Or, if you prefer, marinate the meat and prepare the dessert 2 hours before mealtime. Yet another option is to quick-chill the salad in the freezer.

At serving time, broil the meat, cook the noodles and carrots, and unmold the salads. Keep the berry mixture in the refrigerator until dessert time. Serve meal with iced tea or your favorite beverage. If you indulge in a small glass of light beer, don't forget to add the extra calories.

ITALIAN ROUND STEAK WITH NOODLES/435

If you prefer, marinate the steak at room temperature for 2 hours—

1½ pound boneless beef round steak, trimmed of fat
½ cup dry white wine
1 tablespoon cooking oil
½ teaspoon salt
⅛ teaspoon pepper
• • •
12 ounces uncooked medium green noodles
1 8-ounce can tomato sauce
¼ cup chopped onion
1 clove garlic, minced
2 tablespoons butter *or* margarine
½ cup snipped parsley

With a sharp knife, score steak on both sides in a diamond pattern. Place steak in a shallow dish. Combine the wine, oil, salt, and pepper; pour over the meat. Cover; marinate in refrigerator for 8 hours or overnight, turning steak occasionally.

At serving time, cook the noodles according to package directions. Drain meat well, reserving the marinade. Place meat on unheated rack of broiler pan; broil 3 inches from heat for 4 to 5 minutes. Turn and broil about 4 minutes more for meat to be medium-rare doneness.

Meanwhile, in saucepan combine reserved marinade, tomato sauce, onion, and garlic. Bring to boiling; reduce heat and simmer, uncovered, for 5 minutes.

Drain noodles and toss with the butter or margarine and snipped parsley. Thinly slice the meat across the grain. Arrange meat slices on a warm platter alongside the cooked noodles; spoon some of the marinade mixture over meat. Pass remaining marinade mixture. Garnish platter with parsley sprigs, if desired. Makes 6 servings.

QUICK APPLE MOLD/90

1 3-ounce package lime-flavored gelatin
2 cups ice cubes
1 tablespoon lemon *or* lime juice
1 small apple, chopped
⅓ cup chopped celery
3 tablespoons chopped walnuts

Dissolve gelatin in 1 cup *boiling water.* Stir in ice and lemon juice. Stir about 3 minutes or till gelatin starts to thicken; remove any remaining ice cubes. Fold in apple, celery, and walnuts. Spoon mixture into 6 individual molds. Chill in refrigerator till firm. (*Or,* to set the gelatin quickly, place filled molds in the freezer for 20 minutes or till the gelatin is firm.) Unmold onto lettuce-lined plates, if desired. Makes 6 servings.

BERRIES WITH LEMON/75

If you use sherry, add 14 calories per serving—

1 quart strawberries *or* raspberries
¼ cup sugar
¼ cup lemon juice
¼ cup cream sherry (optional)

Crush *1 cup* of the berries. Place remaining berries in a bowl; halve large strawberries. Combine crushed berries, sugar, and lemon juice, stirring to dissolve sugar. Stir in sherry, if desired. Pour over berries; stir gently to mix. Cover and refrigerate for several hours or overnight; stir occasionally. Spoon into dessert dishes. Serves 6.

Italian Round Steak with Noodles

PLAN A QUICHE FOR A LUNCHEON

Mexican-Style Quiches	**372**
Marinated Three-Bean Salad	**165**
Sparkling Fruit	**43**
Percolator Mint Iced Tea	**0**
TOTAL CALORIES	**580**

The menu items for this luncheon are short-cutted to save you time. The crust for the quiches are tortillas—no hint of the messy mixing and rolling associated with the conventional pastry crusts. You use canned beans for the salad—stow the salad in the refrigerator while you prepare and bake the quiches. And for dessert, thaw frozen mixed fruit in warm water, then mix with bottled ginger ale and lemon juice. Make the iced tea ahead and allow it to cool while you prepare the rest of the luncheon.

MEXICAN-STYLE QUICHES/372

The cheese, together with the milk and eggs, adds a protein punch to this meatless entrée—

4 6-inch flour tortillas
4 ounces Monterey Jack cheese with peppers, sliced
1 medium onion, sliced and separated into rings
1 beaten egg
½ cup wheat germ
• • •
2 cups skim milk
4 beaten eggs
½ teaspoon salt
½ teaspoon chili powder
¼ teaspoon dry mustard

Gently press one flour tortilla in each of four individual au gratin casseroles; top with cheese slices.

Dip the onion rings into the 1 beaten egg then coat liberally with wheat germ. Top the cheese slices with about two-thirds of the onion rings; reserve remainder.

In saucepan heat milk till almost boiling. Gradually add the milk to the remaining 4 beaten eggs, blending well; stir in salt, chili powder, and mustard. Place casseroles in shallow baking pan; place on oven rack. Divide egg mixture evenly among the casseroles. Top with reserved onion rings. Bake in a 350° oven about 30 minutes or till knife inserted off-center comes out clean. Let quiches stand at room temperature for 5 minutes before serving. Garnish quiches with parsley sprigs and pickled peppers, if desired. Makes 4 servings.

MARINATED THREE-BEAN SALAD/165

Serve the leftover bean salad in lettuce cups for another meal—

1 8-ounce can cut green beans, drained
1 8-ounce can red kidney beans, drained
½ of a 15-ounce can (1 cup) garbanzo beans, drained
⅓ cup chopped sweet red *or* green pepper
¼ cup chopped onion
• • •
2 tablespoons vinegar
2 tablespoons lemon juice
2 tablespoons salad oil
2 tablespoons honey
½ teaspoon celery seed

In large bowl combine the drained green beans, kidney beans, garbanzo beans, the red or green pepper, and the onion.

In a screw-top jar combine vinegar, lemon juice, salad oil, honey, and celery seed; cover and shake well to mix. Pour vinegar mixture over the vegetables and stir lightly to mix.

Cover and refrigerate the bean mixture while preparing remainder of meal. (Or, prepare the bean mixture ahead and refrigerate several hours or overnight, stirring occasionally to distribute marinade.) Garnish with sweet red pepper or green pepper rings, if desired. Serve using a slotted spoon. Makes 6 servings.

PERCOLATOR MINT ICED TEA/0

Add the sugar if you like sweetening in your tea, but count the extra calories—

2 quarts cold water
1 cup loosely packed fresh mint leaves, slightly crushed
4 family-sized tea bags
¼ cup sugar (optional)
Ice cubes

Pour cold water into an 8-cup percolator. Place the mint, tea bags, and sugar, if desired, in the percolator basket. Perk for 5 minutes. Remove the basket and let the tea cool. Serve the tea over ice cubes. Garnish with fresh mint and lemon wedges, if desired. Makes 8 cups, or 8 one-cup servings.

SPARKLING FRUIT/43

1 10-ounce package frozen mixed fruit
½ cup ginger ale, chilled
1 teaspoon lemon juice

Place unopened pouch of fruit in large bowl of warm water and let stand for 10 minutes, turning occasionally. Empty fruit into serving bowl. Combine ginger ale and lemon juice; pour over fruit. Makes 4 servings.

Mexican-Style Quiches; Marinated Three-Bean Salad

SPEEDY SALAD SUPPER

Super Strata Salad ... 207
Roll (1 medium) 119
Butter (1 pat) 36
Pineapple-Lemon Dessert-in-a-Glass ... 146

TOTAL CALORIES 508

Raid your cupboards and refrigerator and dazzle your family with this no-cook (unless you make homemade croutons) supper salad and blender-made drink that can pass as a dessert, too. If you make the Whole Wheat Croutons, start your meal preparations by popping the croutons into the oven. Then, whirl the dessert drink in the blender, pour into your prettiest glasses, and chill till serving time. To complete dinner preparations, shake together the dressing and chill while layering the salad ingredients in a bowl. Garnish the beverage with mint leaves, if desired.

SUPER STRATA SALAD/207

If time is extra short, use any desired flavor of purchased croutons—

1 8-ounce can tomato sauce
2 tablespoons tarragon vinegar
½ teaspoon dry mustard
½ teaspoon dried basil, crushed
½ teaspoon Worcestershire sauce
½ teaspoon onion juice
¼ teaspoon salt

• • •

6 cups torn lettuce
2 6¾-ounce cans chunk-style ham, drained and broken up
1 cup shredded mozzarella cheese (4 ounces)
1 4½-ounce jar sliced mushrooms, drained
½ cup Whole Wheat Croutons *or* any flavor packaged croutons

For dressing, in screw-top jar combine tomato sauce, vinegar, mustard, basil, Worcestershire sauce, onion juice, and salt. Cover and shake; chill the dressing.

In a large bowl layer *half* of the torn lettuce, *half* of the ham, *half* of the mozzarella cheese, *half* of the sliced mushrooms, and *half* of the croutons. Repeat layers with remaining lettuce, ham, mozzarella cheese, mushrooms, and croutons. Drizzle some of the dressing atop and toss. Pass remaining dressing. Makes 6 servings.

WHOLE WHEAT CROUTONS/62

Cover and refrigerate the leftover croutons. Use them to sprinkle over soups or salads—

5 slices whole wheat bread
3 tablespoons diet margarine

Spread both sides of bread slices with diet margarine; cut bread into ½-inch cubes. Spread bread cubes in a 15x10x1-inch baking pan. Bake in a 400° oven for 15 to 20 minutes or till bread cubes are dry and crisp. Cool. Store in covered container in refrigerator. Makes 2 cups, or 8 servings.

PINEAPPLE-LEMON DESSERT-IN-A-GLASS/146

This drink doubles as a dessert—

1 15¼-ounce can crushed pineapple (juice pack)
2 8-ounce cartons lemon yogurt
1 cup skim milk
4 to 6 ice cubes (about 1 cup)
1 tablespoon sugar
Fresh mint (optional)

Place the *undrained* crushed pineapple, the yogurt, and milk in a blender container. Cover and blend till smooth. Add ice cubes, one at a time, blending after each addition till chopped. Blend in sugar. Pour into glasses and chill while preparing remainder of meal. To serve, garnish with fresh mint, if desired. Makes 6 servings.

Super Strata Salad; Pineapple-Lemon Dessert-in-a-Glass

NO-CHOP WOK DINNER

Hawaiian Sausage Stir-Fry **335**
Chow mein noodles (½ cup) **110**
Spinach-Blue Cheese Salad **49**
Instant Peach-Almond Sherbet **139**
Skim milk (¾ cup) **66**

TOTAL CALORIES **699**

By adding a little ingenuity to an already fast way of cooking food, you can get dinner on the table very quickly. The stir-fry main dish calls for convenience foods that eliminate the need for time-consuming chopping.

Begin the menu preparations by blending the sherbet; freeze till serving time. Next, tear the spinach for the salad and prepare the dressing. Chill spinach and dressing separately in the refrigerator till just before serving. Finally cook the sausage stir-fry, and serve over the chow mein noodles.

SPINACH-BLUE CHEESE SALAD / 49

Serve extra dressing another time over fruit or a lettuce wedge—

1 small clove garlic, halved
4 cups torn fresh spinach
½ cup Blue Cheese Dressing (see recipe, page 324)

Rub wooden salad bowl with cut garlic clove; discard garlic. In the bowl place the torn spinach. Cover and chill. Just before serving, pour the ½ cup Blue Cheese Dressing over the torn spinach and toss gently to coat. Makes 4 servings.

INSTANT PEACH-ALMOND SHERBET / 139

You'll want to try this quick dessert idea with frozen strawberries, too—

½ cup water
2 tablespoons orange-flavored instant breakfast drink powder
2 10-ounce packages frozen peaches
¼ teaspoon almond extract
Shredded coconut (optional)

Place water and breakfast drink powder in blender container. Break up frozen peaches with a fork; add to blender container along with extract. Cover and blend on high speed till smooth and sherbetlike in texture. If necessary, stop blender and push ingredients toward blades with rubber spatula. Spoon mixture into sherbet dishes; store in freezer till serving time. Garnish with shredded coconut, if desired. Makes 4 servings.

HAWAIIAN SAUSAGE STIR-FRY / 335

If served over chow mein noodles, add 110 calories per half cup of noodles—

⅔ cup cold water
1 tablespoon cornstarch
½ of a 6-ounce can frozen pineapple juice concentrate, thawed
2 tablespoons soy sauce
1 teaspoon instant chicken bouillon granules

• • •

1 6-ounce package frozen pea pods
8 ounces smoked sausage links, cut crosswise into fourths
1 10-ounce package frozen Hawaiian-style vegetables
Chow mein noodles (optional)

In small bowl blend the cold water into the cornstarch; stir in the pineapple juice concentrate, the soy sauce, and the chicken bouillon granules; set aside.

Pour hot tap water over pea pods to thaw. Drain and set aside. In a wok or large skillet stir-fry sausage pieces about 5 minutes or till browned. Stir the pineapple juice mixture; stir into the wok or skillet along with the frozen Hawaiian-style vegetables. Cook and stir till mixture thickens and bubbles, breaking vegetables apart as they begin to thaw. Cover and cook 2 minutes longer; stir in the thawed pea pods. Cover and cook about 1 minute longer or till the mixture is heated through. Serve at once over chow mein noodles, if desired. Serves 4.

Hawaiian Sausage Stir-Fry; Instant Peach-Almond Sherbet; Spinach-Blue Cheese Salad

FAST-AND-FANCY FISH DINNER

Fish and Asparagus Bundles	**172**
Green Salad	**97**
Hard roll (1 roll)	**156**
Whipped butter (1 teaspoon)	**23**
Special Spiced Apricots	**77**
Coffee	**2**
TOTAL CALORIES	**527**

Feast on these fancy fish bundles. To begin the menu preparations, start with last things first—the dessert. Simmer the apricot syrup a mere 5 minutes before adding the apricots. Then chill till serving time. The fish bundles are slightly more complicated but well worth the effort. Precook the asparagus and cut up the ingredients for the tomato-based sauce. Assemble the fish rolls and simmer in a skillet along with the sauce. Meanwhile, the salad is a breeze to make. If you decide to serve wine with dinner, one 3½-ounce glass of table wine adds 87 calories.

FISH AND ASPARAGUS BUNDLES/172

4 fresh *or* frozen sole, flounder, *or* other fish fillets, ¼ inch thick
¾ pound fresh asparagus *or* one 8-ounce package frozen asparagus spears
2 medium tomatoes, peeled and cut up (1 cup)
½ cup sliced fresh mushrooms
¼ cup thinly sliced celery
¼ cup chopped onion
¼ cup dry white wine
1 clove garlic, minced
2 teaspoons snipped fresh mint *or* ½ teaspoon dried mint, crushed
½ teaspoon dried basil, crushed
¼ teaspoon salt

Thaw fish, if frozen. Cut fresh asparagus into about 6-inch lengths. In a covered saucepan cook cut fresh asparagus in a small amount of boiling, lightly salted water for 8 to 10 minutes or till almost tender. (Or, cook frozen asparagus according to package directions.) Drain asparagus well.

Sprinkle fish with a little salt. Place cooked asparagus across fish fillets; roll fish around asparagus and fasten securely with wooden picks. Place fish rolls, seam sides down, in 10-inch skillet. Add tomatoes, mushrooms, celery, onion, wine, garlic, mint, basil, and salt. Cover skillet tightly; simmer over low heat for 7 to 8 minutes or till the fish flakes easily when tested with a fork. Remove fish rolls to a warm platter; discard wooden picks. Cover the fish rolls and keep warm.

In the skillet boil tomato mixture gently, uncovered, about 3 minutes or till slightly thickened. Spoon the tomato mixture over the fish rolls. Garnish with fresh mint, if desired. Makes 4 servings.

GREEN SALAD/97

4 cups torn mixed salad greens such as iceberg, leaf, and Bibb lettuce, curly endive, escarole, and romaine
¼ teaspoon salt
3 tablespoons olive oil *or* salad oil
2 tablespoons wine vinegar

Place desired salad greens in a large salad bowl. Sprinkle with salt. Drizzle with olive oil or salad oil; toss to coat greens. Drizzle with vinegar. If desired, sprinkle with 1 tablespoon snipped parsley. Toss salad mixture till greens are well coated. If desired, sprinkle with crumbled blue cheese. Serves 4.

SPECIAL SPICED APRICOTS/77

1 16-ounce can apricot halves (water pack)
2 tablespoons brown sugar
1 teaspoon lemon juice
6 inches stick cinnamon
¼ cup plain yogurt

Drain apricot halves, reserving juice; set apricots aside. In small saucepan combine reserved apricot juice, brown sugar, lemon juice, and stick cinnamon. Simmer apricot juice mixture, uncovered, for 5 minutes. Add apricot halves; heat through. Chill thoroughly. Remove stick cinnamon before serving. Top each serving with a tablespoon of yogurt. Makes 4 servings.

Fish and Asparagus Bundles; Green Salad

FRITTATA FOR BRUNCH

Garden Frittata 187
Coconut Biscuits (1 biscuit) 158
Honey Fruit Compote . 208
Mexican-Style Hot Chocolate (½ cup) . 51

TOTAL CALORIES 604

You need not get up early to prepare this healthful brunch. Start by preparing the fruit mixture, then store it in the refrigerator till serving time. Next, stir up the biscuits. You don't have to bother with rolling—just drop the dough onto a baking sheet. While the biscuits bake, fix the frittata, a delicious open-faced omelet that you can serve from the skillet. At the last minute, whip up the hot chocolate. (Make six half-cup servings from the hot chocolate recipe.) If desired, top each serving of chocolate with a marshmallow, but don't forget to add 23 calories per large marshmallow.

Another time, change the menu by preparing Cheesy Strata instead of the frittata. Both the strata and fruit mixture can be made ahead and chilled. When serving the strata, omit biscuits from menu.

COCONUT BISCUITS/158

2 cups all-purpose flour
¾ cup coconut, toasted
2 tablespoons sugar
1 tablespoon baking powder
½ teaspoon salt
⅓ cup shortening
1 cup skim milk
½ teaspoon vanilla

In mixing bowl stir together the flour, coconut, sugar, baking powder, and salt. Cut in shortening till mixture resembles coarse crumbs. Combine milk and vanilla. Make a well in the center of the dry ingredients; add milk mixture all at once. Stir just till dough clings together. Use a knife or narrow spatula to push dough from a tablespoon onto a greased baking sheet. Bake in a 450° oven for 10 to 12 minutes or till biscuits are golden. Serve the biscuits immediately. Makes 12 biscuits.

HONEY FRUIT COMPOTE/208

Here's a sunny combination of fruits, lightly sweetened with honey—

1 20-ounce can pineapple chunks (juice pack)
2 11-ounce cans mandarin orange sections, drained
1½ cups seedless green *or* red grapes, seeded and halved
3 kiwis, peeled, halved lengthwise, and sliced
½ cup orange juice
¼ cup honey
1 tablespoon lemon juice

Drain pineapple, reserving juice. In a large bowl combine drained pineapple chunks, mandarin orange sections, grapes, and kiwi slices. Set the fruit aside.

Add water, if necessary, to the reserved pineapple juice to make 1 cup liquid. Combine pineapple juice mixture, orange juice, honey, and lemon juice; pour over fruit mixture. Cover and chill till serving time. Serve in dessert cups or stemmed glasses. Makes 6 servings.

CHEESY STRATA/208

3 cups dry bread cubes (about 4 slices bread)
1½ cups shredded process cheese spread *or* American cheese (6 ounces)
4 beaten eggs
1¾ cups skim milk
1 tablespoon finely chopped onion
½ teaspoon salt
¼ teaspoon dry mustard

Place *2 cups* of the bread cubes in an 8x8x2-inch baking pan. Top with shredded cheese, then with remaining bread cubes. Thoroughly stir together eggs, milk, onion, salt, and dry mustard. Pour evenly over mixture in pan. Cover; chill several hours or overnight. Bake, uncovered, in a 325° oven about 40 minutes or till knife inserted near center comes out clean. Let stand 5 minutes before serving. Makes 6 servings.

GARDEN FRITTATA/187

You can use vegetables fresh from the garden in this egg-based main dish—

1½ cups fresh broccoli cut into bite-size pieces *or* one 10-ounce package frozen cut broccoli
1 cup thinly sliced carrots
• • •
8 eggs
1 cup low-fat cottage cheese
¼ teaspoon salt
⅛ teaspoon pepper
1 cup sliced fresh mushrooms
2 tablespoons diet margarine
6 thin tomato slices
1 tablespoon grated Parmesan cheese

Place broccoli and carrots in steamer basket. Place basket over boiling water. Cover; steam for 8 to 10 minutes or just till vegetables are tender. In medium bowl beat the eggs with the cottage cheese, salt, and pepper. Stir in the steamed vegetables and mushrooms. In a 10-inch oven-proof skillet or omelet pan melt the diet margarine. Pour in egg mixture and cook over medium heat, lifting edges occasionally to allow uncooked portion to flow underneath until top is almost set and bottom is lightly browned. Place skillet under broiler, 5 inches from heat, for 1 to 2 minutes. Top with the thin tomato slices. Sprinkle with grated Parmesan cheese; broil about 1 minute more or till tomatoes are heated through. Makes 6 servings.

Garden Frittata; Coconut Biscuits; Honey Fruit Compote; Mexican-Style Hot Chocolate (see recipe, page 302)

ITALIAN-STYLE DINNER

Ad-Lib Antipasto	**84**
Prosciutto and Pasta ..	**268**
Breadsticks (2)	**38**
Poached Pears with Orange Sauce	**79**
Skim Milk (¾ cup)	**66**
TOTAL CALORIES	**535**

Use the top of the range to prepare this Italian feast. Once you've assembled the ingredients, start the water boiling for the pasta. Then prepare the dessert, but wait till serving time to add the cream cheese topper. Arrange the antipasto platter and place in the refrigerator till serving time. Finally, toss together the pasta main dish and place on a platter. The breadsticks are optional—by omitting them from the menu, you can save 38 calories.

POACHED PEARS WITH ORANGE SAUCE/79

1 16-ounce can pear halves (juice pack)
¼ cup frozen orange juice concentrate
1 inch stick cinnamon
Dash salt
½ of a 4-ounce container whipped cream cheese
Ground cinnamon

Drain pears, reserving liquid. In a medium saucepan stir the orange juice concentrate into the pear liquid, stirring till concentrate is dissolved; add stick cinnamon and salt. Bring to boiling. Add the pear halves. Cook, uncovered, 1 to 2 minutes or till pears are heated through. Let pears stand in the liquid till serving time; remove cinnamon.

To serve, spoon the cooked pear halves and the spiced liquid into 6 dessert dishes. Top each serving with a dollop of the whipped cream cheese. Sprinkle lightly with ground cinnamon. Makes 6 servings.

AD-LIB ANTIPASTO/84

Serve this tuna and vegetable assortment on a lettuce-lined platter as an appetizer—

1 9-ounce jar marinated artichoke hearts, drained
1 6½-ounce can tuna (water pack), drained and broken into large chunks
½ cup cherry tomatoes
½ cup pitted ripe olives
½ cup pickled sliced beets
Leaf lettuce
Lemon wedges (optional)

Arrange artichoke hearts, tuna, cherry tomatoes, ripe olives, and pickled beets on a large lettuce-lined serving platter. If desired, garnish platter with lemon wedges. Cover and chill till serving time. Serves 6.

PROSCIUTTO AND PASTA/268

8 ounces linguini, fettucini, spaghetti, *or* other pasta
1 10-ounce package frozen asparagus spears
½ cup grated Parmesan cheese
½ cup plain yogurt
⅓ cup dry white wine
2 tablespoons diet margarine, melted
6 ounces thinly sliced prosciutto *or* very thinly sliced smoked ham, cut into 1-inch-wide strips
Grated Parmesan cheese (optional)

Cook pasta in large amount of boiling, lightly salted water about 10 to 12 minutes or till tender. Meanwhile, cook asparagus according to package directions just till tender; drain well. In small bowl combine the ½ cup Parmesan cheese, yogurt, wine, and melted diet margarine; stir in cooked asparagus and prosciutto or ham. Drain pasta well (do not rinse). Transfer to warm serving platter; toss with cheese mixture. Sprinkle with additional Parmesan cheese, if desired. Serve immediately. Makes 6 servings.

Prosciutto and Pasta; Ad-Lib Antipasto; Poached Pears with Orange Sauce

CALORIE-TRIMMED CLASSICS

This is the section to check when looking for calorie-trimmed versions of old favorites. You'll find main-dish classics as well as side-dish salads, appetizers, soups, and desserts. The four classics shown here are just some of the favorites.

Canneloni Crepes

Sweet and Sour Pork Skillet

Orange Chiffon Cheesecake

Shrimp-Cucumber Mousse

NUTRITION ANALYSIS

Don't—even if you are a serious dieter—think you must forever forsake enjoying classic delights such as a rich stroganoff or a slice of cheese-cake. With some artful cooking skills, you can reduce calories in classic dishes. Here are some of our techniques for trimming calories. In meat dishes we use leaner cuts of meats and less oil (or none at all!) for browning. In some recipes we substitute yogurt or skim milk for sour cream and light cream—just as tasty but with fewer calories. The serving sizes are a bit smaller, too; not much, but enough to make a difference when trying to trim some calories from the day's tally.

	Per Serving						Percent U.S. RDA Per Serving							
CLASSICS	CALORIES	PROTEIN gms	CARBOHYDRATE gms	FAT gms	SODIUM mgs	POTASSIUM mgs	PROTEIN	VITAMIN A	VITAMIN C	THIAMINE	RIBOFLAVIN	NIACIN	CALCIUM	IRON
MAIN DISHES														
CALORIE COUNTER'S CREPES (p. 108)	37	2	6	0	44	40	3	1	0	4	4	2	3	1
CALORIE-REDUCED BEEF STROGANOFF (p. 110)	308	20	33	8	916	460	31	2	5	15	24	28	9	18
CALORIE-REDUCED MOUSSAKA (p. 107)	388	28	15	21	859	577	43	14	15	14	26	28	15	24
CANNELONI CREPES (p. 108)	337	24	25	15	745	560	36	84	29	18	30	19	30	20
CHICKEN PAPRIKA (p. 110)	301	32	19	11	311	192	49	15	15	12	19	58	6	14
DILLED SCALLOP SALAD (p. 109)	294	28	13	15	1409	876	43	19	45	12	7	11	17	23
OVEN BEEF STEW (p. 110)	184	18	20	3	705	584	28	98	33	12	14	23	6	17
PINEAPPLE-STUFFED CORNISH HENS (p. 107)	291	40	11	9	335	130	61	11	11	11	22	75	4	16
SWEET AND SOUR PORK SKILLET (p. 107)	347	17	47	10	916	380	26	81	44	43	12	22	4	19
VEAL PARMESAN (p. 110)	229	22	5	13	363	263	34	11	26	5	15	19	15	13
SIDE DISHES														
ASPARAGUS IN CREAM SAUCE (p. 112)	96	6	7	5	215	253	10	22	40	12	18	9	11	6
LOW-CALORIE ORANGE ALASKAS (p. 113)	108	2	21	2	13	274	4	5	110	9	4	3	5	3
MOCHA SPONGE CAKE (p. 113)	133	4	23	3	116	67	6	5	0	5	7	3	3	4
MOCK HOLLANDAISE SAUCE (p. 112)	17	0	1	1	9	20	1	1	1	0	1	0	2	0
MUSHROOM APPETIZER SUPREME (p. 111)	115	6	12	5	331	258	10	6	6	6	17	11	14	5
ORANGE CHIFFON CHEESECAKE (p. 113)	158	5	14	9	175	78	7	7	7	4	7	2	5	2
SHERRIED TOMATO SOUP (p. 112)	97	2	14	3	793	494	3	55	57	7	4	8	3	11
SHRIMP-CUCUMBER MOUSSE (p. 111)	47	6	4	1	44	133	9	4	9	2	5	2	6	4
STUFFED MUSHROOMS (p. 111)	18	1	1	1	63	65	1	2	1	1	4	3	0	1
VICHYSSOISE (p. 112)	168	7	20	7	525	517	10	6	27	7	16	6	19	3
WATERCRESS-ENDIVE ORANGE SALAD (p. 111)	78	2	7	5	40	275	3	52	54	6	7	3	8	8

MAIN-DISH CLASSICS

CALORIE-REDUCED MOUSSAKA / 388

- **1 small eggplant (about 14 ounces), peeled and cut into ¼-inch slices**
- **¾ pound ground lamb**
- **½ cup chopped onion**
- **1 clove garlic, minced**
- **½ cup tomato sauce**
- **⅓ cup dry red wine**
- **1 tablespoon snipped parsley**
- **Dash ground cinnamon**
- **1 beaten egg**
- **4 teaspoons all-purpose flour**
- **⅛ teaspoon ground cinnamon**
- **Dash ground nutmeg**
- **¾ cup skim milk**
- **1 beaten egg**
- **3 tablespoons grated Parmesan cheese**
- **Ground cinnamon**

In saucepan place eggplant slices in steamer basket over boiling water; cover and steam about 8 minutes. Drain on paper toweling. In skillet cook meat, onion, and garlic till meat is browned; drain. Stir in tomato sauce, wine, parsley, dash cinnamon, and ½ teaspoon *salt*. Simmer, uncovered, 8 minutes. Remove from heat. Gradually stir *half* of the hot mixture into 1 beaten egg; return all to skillet.

Meanwhile, prepare sauce. In saucepan combine flour, ⅛ teaspoon cinnamon, the nutmeg, ½ teaspoon *salt,* and dash *pepper;* gradually stir in milk till smooth. Cook and stir till bubbly. Remove from heat. Gradually stir *half* of the hot sauce into 1 beaten egg; return all to saucepan. In 8x8x2-inch baking pan place *half* the eggplant. Pour meat mixture over eggplant; top with remaining eggplant. Pour sauce over all. Sprinkle with Parmesan and additional cinnamon. Bake in a 325° oven about 30 minutes. Makes 4 servings.

SWEET AND SOUR PORK SKILLET / 347

This Oriental-style main dish is pictured on pages 104 and 105—

- **¾ pound boneless pork**
- **1 tablespoon cooking oil**
- **1 large green pepper, cut into ¾-inch pieces**
- **2 medium carrots, thinly bias sliced**
- **1 clove garlic, minced**
- **1¼ cups water**
- **¼ cup sugar**
- **¼ cup red wine vinegar**
- **1 tablespoon soy sauce**
- **1¼ teaspoons instant chicken bouillon granules**
- **¼ cup cold water**
- **2 tablespoons cornstarch**
- **2 cups hot cooked rice**

Partially freeze pork; slice thinly across the grain into bite-size strips. In skillet over high heat, quickly cook pork strips in oil about 4 minutes or till browned. Remove pork from skillet; drain pork well on paper toweling.

Add green pepper, sliced carrots, and garlic to drippings in skillet; cook about 4 minutes or till vegetables are crisp-tender but not brown. Drain off fat. Stir in the 1¼ cups water, the sugar, vinegar, soy sauce, bouillon granules, and pork strips. Bring to boiling; boil rapidly for 1 minute. Blend the ¼ cup cold water into the cornstarch. Stir into vegetables and meat mixture. Cook and stir till mixture is thickened and bubbly. Serve the thickened mixture over hot cooked rice. Makes 4 servings.

PINEAPPLE-STUFFED CORNISH HENS / 291

- **3 1- to 1¼-pound Cornish game hens**
- **½ cup quick-cooking rice**
- **⅓ cup chopped onion**
- **⅓ cup chopped celery**
- **1 tablespoon butter *or* margarine**
- **1 cup chopped fresh mushrooms**
- **½ cup crushed pineapple (juice pack), drained**
- **3 tablespoons snipped parsley**
- **¾ teaspoon salt**
- **¼ teaspoon dried marjoram, crushed**
- **¼ teaspoon dried thyme, crushed**
- **1 beaten egg**
- **1 tablespoon butter *or* margarine, melted**

Have butcher halve Cornish game hens lengthwise. Rinse poultry and pat dry. Rub cavities using salt, if desired. For stuffing, cook rice according to package directions. Cook onion and celery in 1 tablespoon butter or margarine till tender but not brown. In mixing bowl stir together cooked rice, the onion-celery mixture, chopped mushrooms, drained pineapple, snipped parsley, salt, marjoram, and thyme. Stir in the beaten egg.

In a 15x10x1-inch baking pan, place 6 equal mounds of the stuffing mixture. Place each poultry half, cut side down, over one of the mounds of stuffing. Cover poultry loosely with foil. Bake in a 375° oven for 30 minutes. Using a poultry baster, remove excess fat from pan. Uncover poultry; bake 30 minutes more or till done, basting occasionally with the 1 tablespoon melted butter or margarine and pan drippings. Makes 6 servings.

SLICK TRIMMING TRICKS

Cooking oils and shortening, at about 120 calories per tablespoon, can slyly hamper your calorie-watching efforts if you don't keep a careful eye on them. To cut some of their calories, panfry and brown foods in small amounts of fat—or in none at all. For no additional calories in your cooking, use pots and pans with non-stick coatings, or apply a non-stick vegetable spray coating to your utensils.

CANNELONI CREPES/337

This entrée is pictured on pages 104 and 105—

8 Calorie Counter's Crepes (see recipe, right)
½ of a 10-ounce package frozen chopped spinach
½ pound lean ground beef *or* ground pork
¼ cup chopped onion
¼ cup chopped celery
¼ cup shredded carrot
1 small clove garlic, minced
2 tablespoons grated Parmesan cheese
2 tablespoons dry white wine
2 tablespoons tomato paste
1 beaten egg
½ teaspoon salt
½ teaspoon dried basil, crushed
¼ teaspoon dried oregano, crushed

• • •

½ cup cold skim milk
2 tablespoons all-purpose flour
½ cup water
½ teaspoon instant chicken bouillon granules
¼ teaspoon salt
Dash white pepper
½ cup shredded mozzarella cheese (2 ounces)

Prepare Calorie Counter's Crepes; set aside. Cook frozen spinach according to package directions. Drain well, squeezing out excess liquid. Set aside. For filling, in skillet cook meat, onion, celery, carrot, and garlic till meat is browned and vegetables are tender; drain. Stir in spinach, Parmesan cheese, wine, tomato paste, beaten egg, the ½ teaspoon salt, the basil, and oregano.

For sauce, in saucepan gradually stir cold milk into flour till smooth. Add water, bouillon granules, the ¼ teaspoon salt, and the white pepper. Cook and stir till mixture is thickened and bubbly. Remove the saucepan from heat.

To assemble crepes, spoon about ¼ cup meat filling down center of unbrowned side of each crepe; roll up. Place filled crepes, seam side down, in a 12x7½x2-inch baking dish. Pour sauce over all. Cover; bake in a 375° oven about 20 minutes. Sprinkle with the shredded mozzarella cheese; bake, uncovered, 3 minutes longer. Makes 4 servings.

CALORIE COUNTER'S CREPES/37

1 cup all-purpose flour
1½ cups skim milk
1 egg
¼ teaspoon salt

In bowl combine flour, milk, egg, and salt; beat with a rotary beater till blended. Heat a lightly greased 6-inch skillet. Remove from heat; spoon in about 2 tablespoons batter. Lift and tilt skillet to spread batter. Return to heat; brown on one side only. Invert pan over paper toweling; remove crepe. Repeat to make about 18 crepes, greasing skillet occasionally.

To freeze crepes for future use, stack crepes between layers of waxed paper. Overwrap the stack in a moisture-vapor-proof bag, then place in a plastic container. Freeze up to 4 months. Thaw the crepes before using.

DILLED SCALLOP SALAD/294

- ½ pound fresh *or* frozen scallops
- 1 cup water
- ½ teaspoon salt
- 1 medium tomato, seeded and chopped
- ½ cup chopped celery
- 2 tablespoons sliced green onion
- 1 tablespoon snipped fresh dillweed *or* 1 teaspoon dried dillweed

• • •

- 2 tablespoons dry white wine
- 2 tablespoons lemon *or* lime juice
- 2 tablespoons cooking oil
- 1 teaspoon sugar
- ½ teaspoon salt
- Dash pepper
- Lettuce

Thaw scallops, if frozen. Cut large scallops in half. Heat the 1 cup water and the ½ teaspoon salt to boiling; add scallops. Reduce heat; simmer for 1 minute or till scallops are opaque. Drain; cool. In bowl combine cooled scallops, tomato, celery, onion, and dillweed.

For dressing, in screw-top jar combine wine, fruit juice, oil, sugar, the ½ teaspoon salt, and dash pepper. Cover and shake well. Pour over scallop mixture; toss to coat. Chill. To serve, drain the scallop-vegetable mixture and spoon onto a lettuce-lined plate. Makes 2 servings.

Dilled Scallop Salad; Watercress-Endive-Orange Salad (see recipe, page 111)

OVEN BEEF STEW / 184

¾ pound lean boneless beef, cut into ¾-inch cubes
2 medium carrots, cut into ¾-inch pieces
1 potato, peeled and quartered
1 stalk celery, sliced
1 8-ounce can tomato sauce
1 tablespoon *regular* dry onion soup mix
1 tablespoon quick-cooking tapioca
1 teaspoon instant beef bouillon granules
½ teaspoon dried thyme, crushed
1 9-ounce package frozen cut green beans, thawed

In 2-quart casserole combine beef cubes, carrots, potato, and celery. In a mixing bowl combine tomato sauce, dry soup mix, tapioca, bouillon granules, thyme, and ¼ cup *water;* stir into meat mixture.

Cover and bake in a 325° oven for 1 hour. Stir in beans; cover and bake about 45 minutes more or till meat and vegetables are tender. Makes 4 servings.

CHICKEN PAPRIKA / 301

2 whole medium chicken breasts (about 1½ pounds), split and skinned
2 tablespoons butter *or* margarine
1 small onion, thinly sliced
¾ cup tomato juice
1 tablespoon paprika
1 tablespoon cornstarch
½ cup plain yogurt
1⅓ cups hot cooked noodles

In skillet over medium heat, brown chicken in butter about 15 minutes total. Remove chicken; drain on paper toweling. Add onion to skillet; cook till tender. Drain. Stir tomato juice, paprika, ¼ teaspoon *salt,* and dash *pepper* into skillet. Add chicken. Cover; simmer 35 to 40 minutes or till tender. Remove chicken to platter. Skim fat from juices. Stir cornstarch into yogurt. Stir ½ cup pan juices into yogurt; return all to skillet. Cook and stir till thickened; *do not boil.* Serve with noodles. Serves 4.

VEAL PARMESAN / 229

1 pound veal leg round steak
½ cup chopped onion
1 clove garlic, minced
1 tablespoon butter *or* margarine
2 tablespoons grated Parmesan cheese
¼ cup chopped green pepper
½ cup tomato sauce
¼ teaspoon sugar
¼ teaspoon dried basil, crushed
½ cup shredded mozzarella cheese (2 ounces)

Cut veal into 4 pieces; pound to ¼-inch thickness. In skillet cook onion and garlic in butter till almost tender. Push to one side of skillet; add meat to skillet and brown on both sides. Sprinkle with Parmesan; add green pepper. Combine tomato sauce, sugar, and basil. Pour over meat, stirring in the onion mixture. Cover; cook over low heat for 20 to 25 minutes or till meat is tender. Sprinkle mozzarella over meat. Cover; cook 1 to 2 minutes more to melt cheese. Skim fat from remaining juices; pass juices with meat. Makes 4 servings.

CALORIE-REDUCED BEEF STROGANOFF / 308

¾ pound beef round steak, cut ½ inch thick and trimmed of fat
1 tablespoon cooking oil
2 cups sliced fresh mushrooms
½ cup dry sherry
½ cup water
½ teaspoon instant beef bouillon granules
1 8-ounce carton plain yogurt
1 tablespoon all-purpose flour
1 teaspoon sugar
¾ teaspoon salt
Dash pepper
2 cups hot cooked rice

Partially freeze steak. Thinly slice across grain into bite-size strips. In skillet brown meat, *half* at a time, in hot oil for 2 to 4 minutes. Remove meat from skillet. Add sliced mushrooms to skillet; cook for 2 to 3 minutes or till tender. Remove mushrooms. Add sherry, water, and bouillon granules to skillet; bring to boiling. Cook, uncovered, over high heat about 3 minutes or till liquid is reduced to ⅓ cup. Combine yogurt, flour, sugar, salt, and pepper; mix well. Stir yogurt mixture into liquid in skillet; stir in meat and mushrooms. Cook and stir over low heat till thickened and heated through; *do not boil.* Serve over hot cooked rice. Sprinkle the stroganoff mixture with snipped parsley, if desired. Makes 4 servings.

SIDE-DISH CLASSICS

SHRIMP-CUCUMBER MOUSSE/47

Pictured on pages 104 and 105—

¼ cup evaporated skimmed milk
1 envelope unflavored gelatin
1 cup cold water
½ cup plain yogurt
1 tablespoon lemon juice
2 teaspoons prepared horseradish
1 teaspoon sugar
¼ teaspoon onion juice
⅛ teaspoon paprika
Dash salt
½ cup chopped seeded cucumber
1 tablespoon chopped pimiento
1 4½-ounce can shrimp, drained
Lettuce

Pour evaporated skimmed milk into a small bowl; freeze till ice crystals form around edges of the milk in the bowl.

Meanwhile, in a saucepan soften gelatin in the cold water; heat, stirring constantly, till gelatin dissolves. Remove from heat. Cool slightly. Beat in plain yogurt, lemon juice, horseradish, sugar, onion juice, paprika, and salt. Chill mixture till partially set. (Gelatin is partially set when it has the consistency of unbeaten egg whites.) Fold chopped cucumber and pimiento into the gelatin mixture.

On high speed of electric mixer beat icy milk till soft peaks form (the tips of the peaks will bend over in soft curls when beaters are removed). Fold the beaten milk into gelatin mixture. Reserve 8 of the shrimp; fold remainder into gelatin. Turn mixture into 8 individual molds. Chill till firm. At serving time, unmold salads and serve on lettuce. Garnish salads with the reserved shrimp. Makes 8 servings.

WATERCRESS-ENDIVE-ORANGE SALAD/78

Pictured on page 109—

2 tablespoons salad oil
4 teaspoons cider vinegar
1 tablespoon olive oil
1 tablespoon Dijon-style mustard
½ teaspoon honey
1 large bunch watercress *or* Bibb lettuce, torn (about 3 cups leaves)
3 heads Belgian endive, cut diagonally into thin strips
2 medium oranges, peeled and thinly sliced

For dressing, in screw-top jar combine salad oil, vinegar, olive oil, mustard, and honey. Cover; shake well. On individual plates arrange watercress or Bibb lettuce, endive, and orange slices. Drizzle dressing over salad. Garnish with snipped parsley, if desired. Makes 6 servings.

STUFFED MUSHROOMS/18

16 large fresh mushrooms
2 tablespoons sliced green onion
2 teaspoons butter *or* margarine
2 ounces Neufchâtel cheese
1½ teaspoons prepared mustard
½ teaspoon Worcestershire sauce
¼ teaspoon salt

Remove stems from mushrooms; chop stems. Set mushroom caps aside. Cook chopped stems and onion in butter or margarine till vegetables are tender and liquid is absorbed. Remove from heat. Combine cheese, mustard, Worcestershire, and salt. Add cooked mushroom mixture; mix well. Fill mushroom caps with mixture. Place on a baking sheet; bake in a 375° oven for 8 to 10 minutes or till tender. Drain on paper toweling. Makes 16 appetizers.

MUSHROOM APPETIZER SUPREME/115

½ pound fresh mushrooms, sliced
1 tablespoon butter *or* margarine
2 tablespoons all-purpose flour
¼ teaspoon salt
¼ teaspoon instant chicken bouillon granules
Dash pepper
¾ cup skim milk
¼ cup water
½ cup shredded *process* Swiss cheese (2 ounces)
2 tablespoons snipped parsley
1 tablespoon dry white wine
3 slices whole wheat bread, toasted and cut diagonally into quarters

In saucepan cook mushrooms in butter or margarine about 5 minutes or till tender. Stir in flour, salt, bouillon granules, and pepper. Add milk and water all at once; cook and stir till thickened and bubbly. Add cheese, stirring to melt. Stir in parsley and wine.

To serve, place 2 toast quarters on each plate. Top with the mushroom mixture. Makes 6 appetizer servings.

ASPARAGUS IN CREAM SAUCE / 96

¾ pound fresh asparagus *or* one 8-ounce package frozen cut asparagus
1½ teaspoons butter
1 tablespoon all-purpose flour
Dash ground nutmeg
½ cup skim milk
¼ cup shredded Swiss *or* cheddar cheese (1 ounce)
1 2½-ounce jar sliced mushrooms, drained
1 hard-cooked egg, chopped
2 tablespoons crushed saltine crackers (about 3 crackers)
1 teaspoon butter, melted

For fresh asparagus, wash and scrape off scales. Break off woody bases at point where spears snap easily. Cut spears into 1-inch pieces. In covered saucepan cook cut-up fresh asparagus in small amount of boiling salted water for 8 to 10 minutes or till crisp-tender. (*Or,* cook frozen asparagus according to package directions.) Drain asparagus; set aside.

For sauce, in small saucepan melt the 1½ teaspoons butter. Blend in flour, nutmeg, and ¼ teaspoon *salt.* Add milk. Cook and stir till bubbly. Reduce heat; add cheese, stirring till melted.

In 1-quart casserole combine asparagus, mushrooms, and chopped egg. Gently fold in cheese sauce. Combine cracker crumbs and the 1 teaspoon melted butter; sprinkle over mixture in casserole. Bake in a 350° oven for 20 minutes or till heated through. Makes 5 servings.

Microwave directions: For fresh asparagus, break off ends; cut into 1-inch pieces. Combine asparagus and ¼ cup *water* in a 1-quart non-metal casserole. Cover and cook in counter-top microwave oven on high power for 3 to 4 minutes, rearranging once. (*Or,* place the unwrapped frozen asparagus in a 1-quart non-metal casserole. Micro-cook 6 minutes, turning after 3 minutes.) Drain asparagus.

In a 2-cup glass measure micro-melt the 1½ teaspoons butter for 30 seconds. Blend in flour, nutmeg, and ¼ teaspoon *salt;* add milk all at once, stirring well. Micro-cook, uncovered, 1 minute. Stir. Micro-cook 2 minutes or till thickened and bubbly, stirring every 30 seconds. Add cheese; stir to melt. In the casserole combine asparagus, mushrooms, and chopped egg. Gently fold in cheese sauce. Combine cracker crumbs and the 1 teaspoon melted butter or margarine; sprinkle atop. Micro-cook, covered, about 1½ minutes or till heated through.

SHERRIED TOMATO SOUP / 97

⅓ cup chopped onion
⅓ cup shredded carrot
1 tablespoon butter *or* margarine
4 teaspoons cornstarch
1 teaspoon instant beef bouillon granules
Dash ground nutmeg
3 cups tomato juice
¼ cup dry sherry
2 tablespoons snipped parsley
1 teaspoon sugar

In saucepan cook onion and carrot in butter or margarine till tender but not brown. Blend in cornstarch, bouillon granules, nutmeg, and ½ teaspoon *salt.* Add tomato juice and 1 cup *water* all at once. Cook and stir till thickened and bubbly. Stir in sherry, snipped parsley, and sugar; simmer, uncovered, for 5 minutes. Makes 4 servings.

VICHYSSOISE / 168

2 leeks
1 small onion, sliced
1 tablespoon butter *or* margarine
2½ cups peeled and sliced potatoes
2⅔ cups water
1 tablespoon instant chicken bouillon granules
½ teaspoon salt
1 13-ounce can evaporated skimmed milk

Remove tops from leeks; slice leeks (should yield about ⅔ cup). In 2-quart saucepan cook leeks and onion in butter till tender but not brown. Stir in potatoes, water, bouillon granules, and salt. Bring to boiling. Reduce heat; cover and simmer for 30 to 40 minutes or till potatoes are very tender.

In blender container or food processor bowl process potato mixture, *half* at a time, till smooth. Pour into a 2-quart bowl. Stir in evaporated skimmed milk. Season to taste with *salt* and *pepper.* Cool. Cover; chill thoroughly before serving. Garnish the chilled soup with snipped chives, if desired. Makes 6 servings.

MOCK HOLLANDAISE SAUCE / 17

¼ cup dairy sour cream
¼ cup plain yogurt
1 teaspoon lemon juice
½ teaspoon prepared mustard

In small saucepan combine all ingredients. Cook and stir over very low heat till heated through; *do not boil.* Serve over poultry, fish, and cooked vegetables. Makes ½ cup, or 8 one-tablespoon servings.

ORANGE CHIFFON CHEESECAKE / 158

Pictured on pages 104 and 105—

1 cup finely crushed zwieback
2 tablespoons sugar
¼ cup butter *or* margarine, melted
1 envelope unflavored gelatin
¼ cup water
2 beaten egg yolks
½ cup skim milk
⅓ cup ricotta cheese
⅓ cup orange juice
2 tablespoons sugar
2 tablespoons orange liqueur
1 1½-ounce envelope dessert topping mix
½ cup skim milk
4 egg whites
Orange slices (optional)
Mint sprigs (optional)

Combine crushed zwieback and 2 tablespoons sugar. Add melted butter; mix till blended. Reserve 2 tablespoons of the mixture. Press remaining mixture onto bottom of a buttered 7-inch springform pan. Chill. Soften gelatin in the water.

In saucepan combine the egg yolks, ½ cup milk, the cheese, orange juice, 2 tablespoons sugar, the liqueur, and the softened gelatin. Cook and stir over medium heat about 20 minutes or till gelatin is dissolved and mixture coats a metal spoon; *do not boil.* Remove from heat; chill till partially set, stirring occasionally.

Prepare topping mix according to package directions using the ½ cup skim milk; fold in gelatin mixture. In large bowl beat egg whites till stiff peaks form. Fold in gelatin-topping mixture. Turn into crumb-coated springform pan; cover and chill till firm. To serve, remove sides of pan and sprinkle the reserved crumb mixture atop cheesecake. Place cheesecake on platter. Garnish platter with orange slices and mint, if desired. Makes 10 servings.

LOW-CALORIE ORANGE ALASKAS / 108

Cut the hollowed-out orange tops into julienne strips. Twist and use as a garnish—

4 medium oranges
⅓ of a 4-ounce container frozen whipped dessert topping, thawed
1 egg white
¼ teaspoon vanilla
⅛ teaspoon cream of tartar
1 tablespoon sugar

Cut a very thin slice off bottom of each orange to make a flat base. Cut off tops of oranges a fourth of the way down; remove tops. Carefully scoop out pulp from tops and bottoms, reserving pulp, juice, and bottom shells. Set aside top shells of the oranges to use for the garnish.

Place orange pulp and juice in blender container or food processor bowl. Cover; process till smooth. Fold in thawed whipped dessert topping. Pour mixture into a shallow pan; cover and freeze several hours or till the orange mixture is firm.

Before serving, break up frozen orange mixture; spoon into orange shell bottoms. Place shells in freezer. In small mixer bowl beat on high speed of electric mixer the egg white with vanilla and cream of tartar till soft peaks form; gradually add sugar, beating to stiff peaks. Remove oranges from freezer. Cover tops of oranges with meringue, sealing to edges of oranges all around. Place in an 8x8x2-inch baking pan. Bake in a 500° oven for 1½ to 2 minutes or till lightly browned. Serve immediately. Makes 4 servings.

MOCHA SPONGE CAKE / 133

1 tablespoon instant coffee crystals
6 egg yolks
1 teaspoon vanilla
1 cup sugar
6 egg whites
¾ teaspoon cream of tartar
1¼ cups all-purpose flour
3 tablespoons unsweetened cocoa powder
1 teaspoon baking powder
1 1½-ounce envelope dessert topping mix
½ cup skim milk
1 teaspoon instant coffee crystals

Dissolve 1 tablespoon coffee crystals in 3 tablespoons *hot water;* set aside. Beat egg yolks at high speed of electric mixer till thick and lemon-colored. Add dissolved coffee and vanilla, beating at low speed till blended. Beat at medium speed till slightly thickened. Gradually add ½ *cup* of the sugar, beating till dissolved. Set aside. Wash beaters.

In large bowl beat egg whites and cream of tartar with electric mixer to soft peaks. Gradually add the remaining ½ cup sugar, beating to stiff peaks. Carefully fold in yolk mixture. Thoroughly stir together flour, cocoa powder, baking powder, and ½ teaspoon *salt.* Carefully fold dry ingredients, one-fourth at a time, into egg mixture. Turn into an ungreased 10-inch tube pan. Bake in a 325° oven for 45 to 50 minutes or till done. Invert cake in pan; cool completely. Using a spatula, loosen cake from pan; invert onto serving plate. Using an electric mixer beat together the dessert topping mix, milk, and 1 teaspoon coffee crystals till soft peaks form. Frost top and sides of cake with mixture. Refrigerate to store. Makes 16 servings.

CALORIE-TRIMMED
MAIN DISHES

Because main dishes provide most of your daily protein requirements and contribute the majority of the calories in a meal, you need to plan them carefully. Use recipes in this section to prepare calorie-trimmed meat, poultry, fish, egg, and cheese dishes.

Poached Halibut with Spinach

Stir-Fried Beef and Vegetables

Shrimp Stack-Ups

Pork Turnovers

Vegetable-Filled Omelet

NUTRITION ANALYSIS

Per Serving

MAIN DISHES

MEAT	CALORIES	PROTEIN gms	CARBOHYDRATE gms	FAT gms	SODIUM mgs	POTASSIUM mgs	Percent U.S. RDA Per Serving: PROTEIN	VITAMIN A	VITAMIN C	THIAMINE	RIBOFLAVIN	NIACIN	CALCIUM	IRON
APPLE HAM SLICE (p. 133)	252	21	17	11	792	371	32	6	6	33	12	19	2	18
BAKED ORANGE-SAUCED CHOPS (p. 131)	180	13	9	10	166	239	20	2	35	34	9	15	1	10
BARBECUED BEEF AND BEANS (p. 122)	250	26	17	9	545	458	40	17	6	8	15	21	15	22
BEEF AND SPROUT SANDWICHES (p. 122)	208	21	18	6	203	461	32	15	30	11	15	21	6	19
BEEF-BROCCOLI STIR-FRY (p. 120)	221	20	12	10	860	604	30	118	127	10	20	20	11	19
BEEFY TOSSED SALAD (p. 122)	173	19	8	8	147	601	30	32	98	11	17	17	17	19
BELGIAN LAMB STEW (p. 139)	242	19	19	10	605	685	30	22	65	12	17	24	7	14
CASSOULET SOUP (p. 137)	299	20	36	8	316	859	31	41	8	31	13	15	10	29
CHINESE VEAL STEAK (p. 128)	223	23	4	12	454	319	35	1	5	5	15	23	2	17
CREAMY LAMB CREPES (p. 138)	275	16	18	14	424	237	24	10	3	12	19	12	16	7
CURRIED YOGURT KABOBS (p. 137)	215	23	18	5	262	796	36	8	35	16	29	35	8	13
DELUXE BEEF PATTIES (p. 126)	306	23	7	20	500	441	35	19	42	10	15	26	3	20
DILLED CABBAGE ROLLS (p. 133)	244	14	17	13	628	277	21	6	17	20	15	14	8	12
FESTIVE PORK ROAST (p. 129)	177	18	4	9	135	227	28	1	1	45	12	20	1	14
GRILLED BEEF KABOBS (p. 124)	240	24	14	8	738	321	37	3	55	7	12	19	3	20
HAM AND CHEESE CASSEROLE (p. 136)	293	22	16	16	815	491	34	142	37	30	25	19	29	16
HAM AND COTTAGE CHEESE MOLD (p. 135)	128	16	5	5	252	271	24	7	20	14	15	9	10	7
HAM AND VEGETABLE ROLL-UPS (p. 135)	203	17	4	14	863	256	25	12	14	15	12	8	23	11
HAM PATTIES WITH APPLE RINGS (p. 136)	275	25	20	10	716	406	38	5	4	36	20	20	8	20
HAM STEW (p. 135)	159	15	17	4	282	543	22	112	47	26	12	19	4	18
HAM WITH PINEAPPLE SAUCE (p. 135)	165	18	5	7	664	268	28	2	18	31	10	17	2	14
HERBED LAMB STEW (p. 139)	249	19	22	10	269	782	29	85	82	15	16	25	6	13
HUNGARIAN ROUND STEAK (p. 125)	187	18	15	6	145	626	28	80	19	8	14	17	8	14
ITALIAN POT ROAST (p. 121)	221	29	7	8	619	240	44	15	8	7	14	26	1	21
LAMB ZUCCHINI CASSEROLE (p. 139)	176	18	6	9	390	449	28	117	46	9	19	12	29	13
LIVER KABOBS (p. 121)	307	33	16	12	868	865	50	1228	110	26	288	102	6	62
LUAU BURGERS (p. 126)	390	22	17	25	649	430	34	8	23	12	15	28	3	22
MARINATED CHUCK STEAK (p. 120)	198	21	4	11	303	190	32	0	0	3	11	17	1	16
MARINATED LAMB KABOBS (p. 137)	137	14	7	6	272	521	22	7	44	11	23	26	4	9
MEXICAN MEATBALL SOUP (p. 127)	281	17	14	17	1219	458	26	30	38	11	12	22	3	17
MINT-GLAZED LAMB CHOPS (p. 137)	109	14	4	4	171	155	21	0	1	5	8	15	1	7
MINUTE STEAK AU POIVRE (p. 121)	307	23	0	20	150	368	35	5	0	7	12	28	2	19
ONION BRAISED LAMB CHOPS (p. 138)	228	22	5	13	190	323	34	0	5	9	16	23	5	9
ORANGE BEEF STEW (p. 124)	262	24	12	13	503	445	37	120	15	6	13	20	6	21
ORANGE-GINGER HAM GRILL (p. 133)	332	17	14	23	875	373	27	1	23	51	12	21	2	15
ORANGE-SAUCED LAMB CHOPS (p. 138)	134	14	10	4	35	284	22	2	41	8	9	16	1	6
ORANGE-SPICED PORK CHOPS (p. 131)	208	18	14	9	132	383	28	4	80	48	13	21	3	14
ORIENTAL PORK CHOPS (p. 131)	193	18	5	11	424	308	28	1	5	43	14	21	2	14
PARED-DOWN PIZZA (p. 127)	252	16	24	10	355	372	24	19	82	17	17	18	16	13
PEPPER BEEF STEW (p. 124)	243	25	24	6	641	612	38	25	123	15	18	24	4	24
PORK AND VEGETABLE STIR-FRY (p. 129)	265	15	26	11	1235	527	24	99	74	39	14	20	6	20
PORK PAPRIKASH (p. 133)	263	20	25	9	155	320	30	7	14	45	18	22	7	16
PORK TURNOVERS (p. 132)	366	18	40	14	766	290	28	3	29	46	19	23	6	20

Per Serving — Percent U.S. RDA Per Serving

MAIN DISHES	CALORIES	PROTEIN gms	CARBOHYDRATE gms	FAT gms	SODIUM mgs	POTASSIUM mgs	PROTEIN	VITAMIN A	VITAMIN C	THIAMINE	RIBOFLAVIN	NIACIN	CALCIUM	IRON
POT ROAST (p. 126)	238	31	14	7	259	739	47	91	41	11	26	32	5	26
ROAST BEEF CARBONNADE (p. 119)	205	24	15	4	196	631	36	130	66	9	15	25	5	19
SAUCY PEPPER BURGERS (p. 127)	260	18	15	13	528	368	27	12	92	10	14	22	4	16
SAUERKRAUT AND PORK SKILLET (p. 131)	220	17	12	12	682	348	26	1	18	42	13	19	4	15
SPICED POT ROAST (p. 121)	186	24	5	7	202	318	37	40	6	4	13	18	4	17
SPICY PORK SKILLET (p. 130)	283	19	26	13	833	353	29	36	78	39	17	24	7	17
SPINACH-FILLED BEEF ROLLS (p. 119)	199	20	10	9	391	627	31	139	55	10	17	19	15	23
STEAK-TOMATO STEW (p. 120)	240	23	17	9	349	747	36	174	66	11	14	25	6	20
STIR-FRIED BEEF AND VEGETABLES (p. 119)	183	20	12	7	1200	913	31	195	83	12	25	23	12	31
SWEET-SOUR LAMB (p. 138)	295	16	35	10	640	369	25	13	55	17	11	21	3	13
TARRAGON BEEF AND NOODLES (p. 122)	310	22	30	10	252	268	34	4	4	23	19	26	2	19
VEAL CHOPS WITH LEMON SAUCE (p. 128)	219	20	5	13	477	315	30	3	5	5	18	21	6	13
VEAL SAUTÉ WITH MUSHROOMS (p. 129)	281	21	24	11	278	339	32	4	9	12	17	27	3	17
VEAL STEW (p. 128)	263	22	19	10	459	794	34	60	32	17	28	50	4	24
VEAL STEW OVER RICE (p. 128)	296	19	23	14	706	519	29	24	92	15	14	26	4	18
YOGURT BEEFWICHES (p. 126)	295	18	24	14	672	300	27	10	33	14	18	18	16	14
YOGURT-SAUCED PORK BALLS (p. 132)	264	21	12	15	673	288	32	5	3	28	17	19	6	15
POULTRY														
CHICKEN AND PEA PODS (p. 144)	247	34	14	6	2111	241	53	18	30	23	22	62	6	27
CHICKEN-CAULIFLOWER CASSEROLES (p. 141)	249	24	16	10	927	570	37	15	94	8	25	23	37	8
CHICKEN DIVAN (p. 141)	169	24	10	3	217	514	36	51	111	7	15	36	14	8
CHICKEN IN WINE SAUCE (p. 147)	267	29	7	12	631	76	44	20	15	7	14	56	3	11
CHICKEN LIVERS TARRAGON (p. 150)	248	32	11	8	455	377	50	285	48	16	185	69	7	55
CHICKEN MARENGO (p. 142)	202	25	9	6	198	473	38	9	30	6	15	48	3	13
CHICKEN 'N' SWISS STACKS (p. 140)	234	19	7	15	287	402	29	18	44	6	14	19	31	8
CHICKEN VERONIQUE (p. 145)	218	28	9	6	67	98	44	5	27	6	14	54	3	11
CLAYPOT CHICKEN (p. 144)	160	24	0	6	89	4	37	19	2	6	29	36	2	14
CREAMY CHICKEN SALAD (p. 142)	282	28	12	13	640	708	42	75	21	8	21	34	29	9
CURRY-SAUCED CHICKEN (p. 145)	171	29	5	3	220	78	44	4	4	5	17	56	2	10
ELEGANT CHICKEN CREPES (p. 142)	278	26	21	10	530	490	40	32	58	13	29	27	31	11
FRUITED BARBECUE CHICKEN (p. 144)	237	25	16	8	267	103	38	29	25	10	30	38	4	17
GARDEN CHICKEN SALAD (p. 142)	183	25	12	4	252	627	39	19	57	10	17	33	11	15
HERBED TOMATO CHICKEN (p. 146)	185	29	7	3	569	170	45	13	31	8	16	57	3	12
LEMON CHICKEN BREASTS (p. 147)	221	30	4	9	294	146	45	9	7	7	21	58	5	10
MANDARIN CHICKEN (p. 149)	282	27	17	12	1404	337	42	5	46	8	16	50	7	16
PLUM-SAUCED CHICKEN (p. 145)	236	24	17	6	451	88	38	20	18	7	30	36	3	16
QUICK CHICKEN VEGETABLE SOUP (p. 141)	155	19	15	2	573	754	30	142	86	9	9	37	5	11
SAUCED CHICKEN OVER RUSKS (p. 141)	236	25	24	4	406	572	38	6	13	7	21	38	14	8
SAVORY SAUCED CHICKEN (p. 146)	163	21	7	6	178	195	32	16	19	6	11	38	6	9
SPICY TURKEY DRUMSTICKS (p. 150)	259	35	6	10	191	638	54	19	42	6	17	26	3	17
STIR-FRIED CHICKEN WITH ALMONDS (p. 147)	357	36	19	15	707	533	55	21	48	26	35	73	8	25
THREE-CHEESE CHICKEN BAKE (p. 140)	318	23	22	15	656	288	35	19	36	17	23	21	24	10
TOMATO-BROCCOLI CHICKEN (p. 144)	244	31	9	9	486	416	48	60	121	12	20	59	8	15
TURKEY-BROCCOLI PILAF (p. 149)	267	27	23	7	346	528	42	39	85	12	16	36	7	13

MAIN DISHES

	Per Serving						Percent U.S. RDA Per Serving							
	CALORIES	PROTEIN gms	CARBOHYDRATE gms	FAT gms	SODIUM mgs	POTASSIUM mgs	PROTEIN	VITAMIN A	VITAMIN C	THIAMINE	RIBOFLAVIN	NIACIN	CALCIUM	IRON
TURKEY-FRUIT SALAD (p. 149)	238	24	28	5	216	1081	36	185	138	18	26	27	19	28
TURKEY LOAF (p. 149)	184	26	5	6	411	355	40	27	13	5	12	31	2	11
TURKEY-VEGETABLE BAKE (p. 150)	142	16	6	6	302	395	25	48	35	5	14	17	9	8
VEGETABLE-STUFFED CHICKEN BREASTS (p. 146)	260	30	6	12	349	307	47	16	18	9	27	64	5	12
FISH & SEAFOOD														
BAKED CURRIED FISH (p. 151)	184	19	9	8	483	443	29	3	11	4	6	15	7	7
BAKED RED SNAPPER (p. 153)	162	32	3	1	181	655	49	5	26	20	3	2	4	9
CREAMED CRAB WITH TOMATO (p. 160)	280	21	21	12	1222	451	33	29	22	11	28	12	43	8
FISH AND VEGETABLE BAKE (p. 154)	201	19	16	7	283	870	30	52	79	12	7	16	10	10
GRAPEFRUIT-SOLE SALAD (p. 153)	178	14	23	4	581	566	21	14	98	9	7	14	7	10
MAIN-DISH TUNA TOSS (p. 157)	167	19	10	6	574	498	30	19	37	10	16	34	10	13
MARINATED SOLE (p. 151)	173	18	11	6	329	390	28	3	17	4	5	15	5	7
MARINATED TUNA AND VEGETABLES (p. 157)	245	28	33	1	878	1092	43	189	240	38	22	61	11	30
NEWBURG-STYLE CRAB (p. 160)	278	15	25	12	807	320	24	28	19	20	20	11	18	12
ORIENTAL SCALLOPS (p. 160)	120	21	8	1	889	632	33	14	66	9	7	8	12	19
POACHED HALIBUT WITH SPINACH (p. 151)	268	36	6	11	398	994	56	131	53	9	15	54	18	15
RICE-VEGETABLE STUFFED FISH (p. 157)	305	23	13	17	678	516	36	92	15	16	13	22	5	7
SALMON-CAULIFLOWER CASSEROLE (p. 155)	222	18	11	12	1023	512	28	8	73	5	18	28	27	8
SALMON-STUFFED TOMATOES (p. 154)	273	21	18	15	493	1003	33	47	83	15	24	35	25	15
SESAME-SKEWERED SCALLOPS (p. 160)	177	19	12	6	385	625	29	15	81	11	6	9	11	16
SHRIMP AND PEPPER STIR-FRY (p. 159)	226	18	21	8	659	292	28	7	49	8	4	18	7	13
SHRIMP JAMBALAYA (p. 157)	284	22	21	12	356	434	34	17	37	18	7	24	6	17
SHRIMP KABOBS (p. 158)	169	23	12	3	435	488	36	12	40	8	4	22	9	13
SHRIMP STACK-UPS (p. 159)	176	15	20	4	280	327	23	15	21	11	12	13	10	13
SHRIMP THERMIDOR BAKE (p. 158)	257	26	13	10	743	218	39	14	8	4	9	9	23	17
SOLE FLORENTINE (p. 153)	163	21	12	4	394	792	32	115	57	11	18	13	24	15
SPICY SHRIMP SKILLET (p. 159)	209	24	12	8	437	461	36	5	20	5	6	20	11	15
TUNA TACOS (p. 155)	312	24	32	10	274	376	37	17	22	10	11	46	24	20
TUNA-ZUCCHINI BAKE (p. 155)	160	18	9	6	472	350	27	10	37	5	17	23	18	7
VEGETABLE-SAUCED FISH FILLETS (p. 153)	193	18	9	8	467	437	28	10	20	4	4	16	5	8
VEGETABLE-TOPPED HALIBUT STEAKS (p. 151)	272	36	9	10	745	1060	55	156	40	9	9	60	6	11
WILD RICE SHRIMP CREOLE (p. 158)	229	19	27	5	594	533	29	28	57	13	5	22	7	16
EGGS & CHEESE														
BROCCOLI-YOGURT OMELET (p. 164)	237	13	6	18	572	279	21	54	60	9	21	2	11	13
CHEESE-CAULIFLOWER CHOWDER (p. 161)	266	17	12	17	1017	371	27	18	83	5	25	5	47	7
CHEESE SOUFFLÉ (p. 161)	282	17	8	20	501	180	26	26	4	6	23	1	35	9
CRAB AND EGG CASSEROLE (p. 164)	233	19	5	15	819	287	29	29	3	8	22	4	15	10
EGG SALAD STUFFED TOMATOES (p. 164)	184	15	9	9	440	504	24	46	57	12	23	5	12	15
INDIVIDUAL CRUSTLESS QUICHES (p. 164)	225	22	7	12	1293	264	33	14	3	7	26	5	34	13
POACHED EGGS WITH CHEESE SAUCE (p. 162)	197	13	10	12	498	186	20	18	1	8	19	4	18	11
SPICY POACHED EGG STACKS (p. 162)	271	16	21	14	944	333	24	20	9	27	19	13	7	16
TACO SCRAMBLED EGGS (p. 162)	287	17	10	20	583	422	26	52	48	11	27	4	25	14
VEGETABLE-FILLED OMELET (p. 161)	246	15	8	18	802	400	22	44	52	12	24	6	8	17

MEAT MAIN DISHES

SPINACH-FILLED BEEF ROLLS/199

- **¾ pound boneless beef top round steak, cut ½ inch thick and trimmed of fat**
- **1 10-ounce package frozen chopped spinach, cooked and drained**
- **¼ cup shredded carrot**
- **¼ cup shredded sharp cheddar cheese (1 ounce)**
- **¼ teaspoon dried oregano, crushed**
- **¼ teaspoon pepper**
- **½ cup chopped onion**
- **1 clove garlic, minced**
- **1 tablespoon cooking oil**
- **1 cup tomato juice**
- **½ cup water**
- **1 teaspoon instant beef bouillon granules**
- **1 teaspoon Worcestershire sauce**
- **1 tablespoon cornstarch**

Cut meat into four rectangles; pound to ⅛-inch thickness. Sprinkle with salt and pepper, if desired. Combine spinach, carrot, cheese, oregano, and pepper. Spread spinach mixture over meat. Roll up jelly-roll style. Secure with wooden picks. In skillet cook onion and garlic in hot oil till tender but not brown; push aside. Add meat rolls to skillet; brown on all sides. Drain off excess fat. To skillet add tomato juice, the ½ cup water, bouillon granules, and Worcestershire sauce. Cover; simmer about 40 minutes or till meat is tender. Transfer rolls to serving platter; discard wooden picks and keep meat warm. Skim excess fat from pan drippings. Stir cornstarch into ⅓ cup *cold water;* stir into pan juices. Cook and stir till mixture is thickened and bubbly. Cook and stir 1 to 2 minutes more. Spoon mixture over meat rolls. Makes 4 servings.

STIR-FRIED BEEF AND VEGETABLES/183

This Oriental-inspired main dish is pictured on pages 114 and 115—

- **¾ pound beef top round steak, trimmed of fat**
- **½ teaspoon instant beef bouillon granules**
- **⅓ cup boiling water**
- **3 tablespoons soy sauce**

• • •

- **1 tablespoon cooking oil**
- **1 clove garlic, minced**
- **1 medium onion, sliced and separated into rings**
- **1 cup thinly sliced carrot**
- **1 cup bias-sliced celery**
- **1 cup sliced fresh mushrooms**
- **6 cups torn spinach leaves**

Partially freeze meat. Slice meat very thinly across the grain into bite size strips. Dissolve the instant beef bouillon granules in the boiling water. Add soy sauce; set aside.

Preheat a wok or large skillet over high heat; add oil. Stir-fry garlic in hot oil for 30 seconds. Add onion, carrot, celery, and mushrooms. Stir-fry 2 minutes. Remove vegetables. Add *half* the meat to hot wok or skillet; stir-fry 2 minutes. Remove meat. Stir-fry remaining meat 2 minutes. Return all meat to wok. Stir soy mixture; stir into meat. Cook and stir till bubbly. Stir in cooked vegetables and the spinach. Cover and cook 1 minute. Serve the beef-vegetable mixture immediately. Makes 4 servings.

ROAST BEEF CARBONNADE/205

- **2 pounds lean boneless beef top round, bottom round, *or* eye round steak, cut 1½ to 2 inches thick and trimmed of fat**
- **Non-stick vegetable spray coating**
- **1 12-ounce can beer**
- **2 tablespoons catsup**
- **1 clove garlic, minced**
- **½ teaspoon dried thyme, crushed**
- **1 10-ounce package frozen brussels sprouts**
- **6 medium carrots, bias sliced into ½-inch pieces (1 pound)**
- **2 medium onions, cut into wedges**
- **2 tablespoons cold water**
- **1 tablespoon cornstarch**
- **¼ teaspoon salt**
- **⅛ teaspoon pepper**

Sprinkle meat with a little salt and pepper. Spray bottom of 4-quart Dutch oven with non-stick vegetable spray coating. Place over medium heat. Add meat; brown on both sides. Combine beer, catsup, garlic, and thyme; pour over meat. Cover and bake in a 325° oven for 1¼ hours. Rinse brussels sprouts with warm water just to separate; add to Dutch oven along with carrots and onions. Cover and bake about 45 minutes more or till vegetables and meat are tender. Remove meat and vegetables to serving platter; keep warm. Skim fat from pan juices.

To make gravy, measure 1¼ cups pan juices, adding water if necessary. Combine the 2 tablespoons cold water and cornstarch; stir into pan juices. Cook and stir till thickened and bubbly. Cook and stir 1 to 2 minutes more. Season gravy with the salt and pepper; pass with meat and vegetables. Makes 8 servings.

BEEF-BROCCOLI STIR-FRY/221

Stir-frying requires a small amount of oil and constant stirring—

¾ pound beef top round steak, trimmed of fat
2 cups broccoli flowerets
2 medium carrots, bias sliced
• • •
1 teaspoon cornstarch
½ teaspoon sugar
¼ teaspoon salt
2 tablespoons soy sauce
2 tablespoons dry sherry
2 tablespoons cooking oil
1 medium onion, cut into thin wedges

Partially freeze the beef round steak. Slice the meat thinly across the grain into bite-size strips.

Cook the broccoli flowerets and carrot slices, covered, in boiling water 2 minutes; drain. Mix the cornstarch, sugar, and salt. Stir into the soy sauce and sherry. Set the soy sauce-cornstarch mixture aside.

Preheat a wok or large skillet over high heat; add *1 tablespoon* of the oil. Stir-fry broccoli, carrots, and onion in hot oil over high heat about 3 minutes or till crisp-tender. Remove vegetables. Add the remaining 1 tablespoon oil. Add the beef to wok or skillet; stir-fry 2 to 3 minutes or till browned. Stir soy mixture; stir into beef. Cook and stir till thickened and bubbly. Stir in broccoli, carrots, and onion; cover and cook 1 minute more. Serve immediately. Makes 4 servings.

STEAK-TOMATO STEW/240

¾ pound beef round steak, trimmed of fat and cubed
1 clove garlic, minced
1 tablespoon cooking oil
3 medium carrots, sliced ½ inch thick (1½ cups)
¾ cup water
1 teaspoon instant beef bouillon granules
¼ teaspoon dried basil, crushed
¼ teaspoon dried thyme, crushed
1 7½-ounce can tomatoes, cut up
9 pearl onions *or* one 8-ounce can peeled small whole onions, drained
¼ cup chopped green pepper
1 tablespoon cold water
2 teaspoons cornstarch

In medium saucepan brown *half* the meat and the garlic in hot oil. Remove from saucepan; brown remaining meat. Return all meat to saucepan. Stir in carrots, the ¾ cup water, bouillon granules, basil, and thyme. Simmer, covered, for 30 minutes. Stir in *undrained* tomatoes, onions, and green pepper. Simmer, covered, for 20 minutes more. Combine the 1 tablespoon cold water and cornstarch; add to stew. Cook and stir till the stew mixture is thickened and bubbly. Makes 3 servings.

MARINATED CHUCK STEAK/198

⅓ cup red wine vinegar
1 tablespoon cooking oil
1 clove garlic, minced
½ teaspoon salt
½ teaspoon dried basil, crushed
¼ teaspoon dried thyme, crushed
1½ pounds beef chuck blade steak, cut 1 inch thick and trimmed of fat
4 teaspoons cornstarch
2 tablespoons cold water
1 2½-ounce jar sliced mushrooms, drained
¼ teaspoon Kitchen Bouquet (optional)

For marinade, combine red wine vinegar, oil, garlic, salt, basil, and thyme. Pierce all surfaces of meat with long-tined fork. Place meat in plastic bag; set in shallow dish. Add marinade to bag; turn bag to coat all surfaces of meat. Close bag. Refrigerate for 8 hours or overnight, turning plastic bag several times to distribute marinade. Drain meat; reserve *3 tablespoons* marinade. Add water to reserved marinade to equal 1 cup liquid. Place meat on unheated rack of broiler pan. Broil meat 4 inches from heat till desired doneness (allow 12 to 14 minutes total for medium); turn meat once halfway through cooking time.

Meanwhile, in small saucepan stir cornstarch into cold water. Add reserved marinade mixture. Cook and stir till thickened and bubbly. Add mushrooms and Kitchen Bouquet, if desired; heat through. Season to taste with additional salt. Slice meat across the grain into thin slices. Serve with mushroom mixture. Makes 4 servings.

ITALIAN POT ROAST/221

1 3-pound beef chuck pot roast, trimmed of fat
8 cloves garlic
2 tablespoons cooking oil
3 8-ounce cans tomato sauce
2 tablespoons vinegar
6 to 8 whole cloves
1 teaspoon ground nutmeg
½ teaspoon ground cinnamon
½ teaspoon ground allspice

Make slits in top of roast using the tip of a knife; insert garlic cloves. Sprinkle roast with salt and pepper. In large skillet brown meat on both sides in hot oil. Combine tomato sauce, vinegar, and spices; pour over meat in skillet. Cover and simmer for 1½ hours or till meat is tender. Remove meat to cutting board; keep warm. Bring juices in skillet to boiling; boil, uncovered, about 5 minutes or till liquid is reduced to 3 cups. Strain sauce. Remove garlic cloves from meat, if desired. Slice meat. Spoon some of the sauce over meat; pass remaining sauce. Makes 8 servings.

LIVER KABOBS/307

1 cup tomato juice
2 tablespoons minced dried onion
1 teaspoon salt
1 teaspoon dried oregano, crushed
⅛ teaspoon garlic powder
⅛ teaspoon pepper
1 pound beef liver, cut into 1-inch-wide strips
3 medium zucchini, cut into ¾-inch chunks

In deep bowl combine tomato juice, onion, salt, oregano, garlic powder, and pepper. Add liver, stirring to coat. Let stand at room temperature 30 minutes, stirring occasionally. Meanwhile, cook zucchini in boiling unsalted water for 3 minutes or till nearly tender; drain. Lift liver from marinade, reserving marinade. On four skewers thread strips of liver loosely, accordion-style, alternating with the zucchini. Grill over *medium-hot* coals for 4 to 5 minutes, brushing occasionally with marinade. Turn. Grill and baste 4 to 5 minutes more. (*Or,* broil 4 to 5 inches from heat for 8 to 10 minutes, basting occasionally with the marinade; turn once.) Makes 4 servings.

MINUTE STEAK AU POIVRE/307

4 beef cubed steaks (about 1 pound)
1 to 1½ teaspoons freshly ground pepper
2 tablespoons butter *or* margarine
Salt
¼ cup brandy

Sprinkle cubed steaks on both sides with pepper, pressing in firmly with fingers. In skillet brown steaks in butter or margarine about 1 minute on each side. Sprinkle with a little salt. Add brandy to skillet; ignite. Remove steaks to warm serving platter; pour pan drippings over steaks on the serving platter. Makes 4 servings.

SPICED POT ROAST/186

Caraway seed, cloves, and buttermilk enhance the flavor of this dish—

1 2½-pound beef chuck arm pot roast, trimmed of fat
2 tablespoons cooking oil
2 medium carrots, finely chopped
2 stalks celery, thinly sliced
1 medium onion, thinly sliced
1½ cups water
2 teaspoons instant beef bouillon granules
½ teaspoon caraway seed
5 whole black peppercorns
2 whole cloves

• • •

½ cup buttermilk
1 tablespoon cornstarch
¼ teaspoon Kitchen Bouquet (optional)

Sprinkle meat with salt and pepper. In Dutch oven brown meat on all sides in hot oil. Remove meat; add carrot, celery, and onion to Dutch oven. Cook vegetables till tender. Drain off excess fat. Return meat to Dutch oven. Add water, bouillon granules, and caraway seed. In double layer of cheesecloth tie together peppercorns and cloves; add to Dutch oven. Cover and simmer about 1½ hours or till meat is tender. Remove meat to warm serving platter. Discard cheesecloth bag. Skim excess fat from pan juices.

In screw-top jar combine buttermilk and cornstarch; shake well. Add to drippings in Dutch oven. Cook and stir till thickened and bubbly. Add Kitchen Bouquet, if desired. Pour some gravy over meat; pass remainder. Makes 8 servings.

BARBECUED BEEF AND BEANS/250

½ pound cooked lean beef, trimmed of fat
½ cup tomato sauce
¼ cup water
2 tablespoons finely chopped onion
2 tablespoons red wine vinegar
2 teaspoons brown sugar
2 teaspoons Worcestershire sauce
2 teaspoons prepared mustard
1 teaspoon paprika
1 teaspoon chili powder
¼ teaspoon salt
1 8-ounce can red kidney beans, drained
2 cups shredded lettuce
½ cup shredded cheddar cheese (2 ounces)

Cut cooked beef into thin strips; set aside. In saucepan combine tomato sauce, water, onion, red wine vinegar, brown sugar, Worcestershire sauce, mustard, paprika, chili powder, and salt. Bring to boiling; reduce heat. Simmer, covered, for 10 minutes, stirring occasionally. Stir in beef strips and kidney beans. Heat through. Serve atop shredded lettuce. Sprinkle shredded cheese atop each serving. Makes 4 servings.

Microwave directions: Cut beef into thin strips. In non-metal mixing bowl combine tomato sauce, water, onion, vinegar, brown sugar, Worcestershire, mustard, paprika, chili powder, and salt. Cover; cook in counter-top microwave oven on high power for 6 minutes or till onion is tender. Add beef and kidney beans; micro-cook 2 minutes more or till heated through. Serve as above.

BEEFY TOSSED SALAD/173

Creamy Salad Dressing (see recipe, page 186)
6 ounces cooked lean beef, cut into thin bite-size strips
4 cups torn iceberg lettuce
3 cups torn romaine
2 cups cauliflower flowerets
1 cup cherry tomatoes, halved
½ cup shredded cheddar cheese
¼ cup sliced green onion

Prepare dressing. Chill. Season beef with salt. In large salad bowl combine beef with remaining ingredients. Spoon dressing over all. Toss. Serves 4.

BEEF AND SPROUT SANDWICHES/208

⅓ cup plain yogurt
2 tablespoons finely chopped cucumber
2 teaspoons snipped parsley
2 teaspoons chili sauce
4 slices rye bread, toasted
4 leaves leaf lettuce
8 ounces thinly sliced cooked beef
2 medium tomatoes, sliced (8 slices)
½ cup alfalfa sprouts

For yogurt sauce, in bowl combine yogurt, cucumber, parsley, and chili sauce.

Top each slice of toasted bread with leaf lettuce, 2 ounces sliced beef (season with salt and pepper, if desired), 2 tomato slices, 2 tablespoons alfalfa sprouts, and 2 tablespoons of the yogurt sauce. Makes 4 servings.

TARRAGON BEEF AND NOODLES/310

¾ pound beef stew meat, trimmed of fat and cut into ¾-inch cubes
1 clove garlic, minced
1 tablespoon cooking oil
1 cup water
¼ cup red wine vinegar
1 teaspoon sugar
1 teaspoon instant beef bouillon granules
½ teaspoon dried tarragon, crushed
¼ teaspoon salt

• • •

1 4-ounce can sliced mushrooms, drained
¼ cup sliced green onion
¼ cup cold water
1 tablespoon cornstarch
3 ounces medium noodles, cooked

In large saucepan cook meat and garlic in cooking oil till meat is browned. Drain off excess fat. Add the 1 cup water, the vinegar, sugar, beef bouillon granules, tarragon, and salt. Cover and simmer for 1 to 1¼ hours or till meat is tender. Add mushrooms and green onion; simmer 10 minutes more. Measure pan juices. If necessary, add water to pan juices to measure ¾ cup liquid; return to saucepan. Combine the ¼ cup cold water and the cornstarch; stir into meat mixture. Cook and stir till thickened and bubbly. Season to taste. Serve over noodles. Makes 4 servings.

Beefy Tossed Salad; Ham and Cottage Cheese Mold (see recipe, page 135)

PEPPER BEEF STEW/243

Look for pork-flavored Oriental noodles in the supermarket's soup section—

Non-stick vegetable spray coating
1 pound beef stew meat, trimmed of fat and cut into 1-inch cubes
1 16-ounce can tomatoes, cut up
½ cup chopped onion
1 clove garlic, minced
1 teaspoon instant beef bouillon granules
2 green peppers, cut into ¾-inch pieces
• • •
1 3-ounce package pork-flavored Oriental noodles
2 tablespoons cornstarch
1 tablespoon soy sauce
1 tablespoon cold water
1 cup bean sprouts

Spray medium saucepan with non-stick vegetable spray coating. In prepared saucepan brown the meat. Stir in *undrained* tomatoes, onion, garlic, and beef bouillon granules. Bring to boiling; reduce heat. Cover and simmer 1¼ to 1½ hours or till meat is nearly tender. Add green pepper pieces. Simmer the mixture, covered, for 10 to 15 minutes more.

Meanwhile, prepare pork-flavored noodles according to package directions; drain well. Combine cornstarch, soy sauce, and cold water; add to meat mixture. Cook and stir till thickened and bubbly; cook and stir 1 to 2 minutes more.

Toss together pork-flavored noodles and bean sprouts. Serve meat mixture over noodle mixture. Makes 4 servings.

GRILLED BEEF KABOBS/240

You can cook these kabobs over hot coals or under the broiler—

1 pound beef stew meat, trimmed of fat and cut into 1-inch cubes
½ cup bottled teriyaki sauce
⅓ cup dry red wine
1 tablespoon Worcestershire sauce
½ teaspoon garlic salt
Unseasoned instant meat tenderizer
½ small pineapple
1 large green pepper, cut into 1-inch squares

Place meat in bowl. Mix teriyaki sauce, wine, Worcestershire sauce, and garlic salt. Pour over meat. Cover and refrigerate overnight or let stand at room temperature 2 hours, stirring occasionally. Drain meat, reserving marinade. Sprinkle meat with the tenderizer according to package directions.

Remove crown from pineapple; cut off peel and remove eyes. Slice pineapple, then cut into wedges.

On four skewers thread meat alternately with green pepper and pineapple. Grill over *hot* coals 8 minutes; baste with marinade. Turn; grill 7 minutes more. (*Or,* broil 4 to 5 inches from heat for 8 minutes. Turn; brush with marinade. Broil 7 minutes more.) Brush meat, pineapple, and pepper again with marinade. Makes 4 servings.

ORANGE BEEF STEW/262

2 cups dry red wine
½ cup chopped onion
2 cloves garlic, minced
1 tablespoon vinegar
1 teaspoon salt
½ teaspoon dried rosemary, crushed
½ teaspoon dried thyme, crushed
½ teaspoon finely shredded orange peel
¼ teaspoon pepper
2 pounds beef stew meat, trimmed of fat and cut into 1-inch cubes
• • •
2 ounces salt pork
½ cup water
½ teaspoon instant beef bouillon granules
6 carrots, bias sliced into 1-inch pieces
3 medium onions, quartered
1 cup pitted ripe olives
2 tablespoons cornstarch
2 tablespoons cold water

Combine wine, the ½ cup onion, garlic, vinegar, salt, rosemary, thyme, orange peel, and pepper. Add beef; stir to coat. Cover and marinate at room temperature for 2 hours. Drain meat, reserving marinade; pat meat dry with paper toweling.

In 4-quart Dutch oven cook salt pork till 2 to 3 tablespoons fat accumulate; discard pork. Brown meat in the hot fat. Add marinade, ½ cup water, and bouillon granules; bring to boiling. Cover; simmer 1 hour. Add carrots, quartered onions, and olives; simmer, covered, 30 to 40 minutes more or till meat and vegetables are tender. Combine cornstarch and 2 tablespoons cold water; add to Dutch oven. Cook and stir till bubbly. Garnish with snipped parsley, if desired. Makes 8 servings.

HUNGARIAN ROUND STEAK/187

¾ pound boneless beef round steak, trimmed of fat
2 teaspoons cooking oil
½ cup water
½ teaspoon instant beef bouillon granules
2 medium parsnips, sliced
2 medium carrots, halved and quartered
¼ cup sliced celery

• • •

2 teaspoons cornstarch
¼ teaspoon paprika
½ cup plain yogurt

Cut the round steak into 4 serving-size pieces. In a 10-inch skillet brown the meat on both sides in cooking oil. Season meat with a little salt and pepper. Add water and instant beef bouillon granules to meat in skillet; cover and simmer the meat 30 minutes.

Halve any large parsnip slices. Add parsnips, carrots, and celery to meat; cover and simmer about 30 minutes more or till vegetables are tender. Remove meat and vegetables to a serving platter; keep warm while preparing sauce.

Measure pan juices; add water if necessary to make ½ cup liquid. To make sauce, in same skillet stir cornstarch and paprika into yogurt. Stir in the ½ cup pan juices. Cook and stir till thickened and bubbly. Cook and stir 1 to 2 minutes more. Serve the thickened sauce over steak pieces and vegetables. Makes 4 servings.

Hungarian Round Steak

POT ROAST/238

- **1 3-pound beef chuck arm pot roast, trimmed of fat**
- **1 tablespoon cooking oil**
- **½ cup dry red wine**
- **1 tablespoon instant beef bouillon granules**
- **½ teaspoon dried rosemary, crushed**
- **½ teaspoon dried basil, crushed**
- **16 large fresh mushrooms**
- **4 large carrots, cut into julienne strips**
- **8 small whole onions**
- **4 tomatoes, quartered**

In Dutch oven brown meat on all sides in hot oil. Add wine, bouillon granules, herbs, and ½ teaspoon *pepper.* Cover and cook in a 325° oven for 1 to 1¼ hours or till meat is nearly done. Add mushrooms, carrots, and onions; spoon juices over vegetables. Cover; continue cooking 40 minutes. Add tomatoes; cover and cook 5 to 10 minutes more or till vegetables and meat are tender. Remove meat and vegetables to platter. Skim fat from juices; pass with meat and vegetables. Serves 8.

YOGURT BEEFWICHES/295

- **½ pound lean ground beef**
- **¼ cup chopped green pepper**
- **2 tablespoons chopped onion**
- **1 small clove garlic, minced**
- **1 teaspoon all-purpose flour**
- **½ cup plain yogurt**
- **½ teaspoon Worcestershire sauce**
- **2 individual French rolls**
- **1 medium tomato, sliced**
- **½ cup shredded American cheese**

Cook beef, pepper, onion, and garlic till meat is browned. Drain off fat. Stir flour into yogurt; stir yogurt mixture, Worcestershire, ½ teaspoon *salt,* and dash *pepper* into meat mixture. Heat through; *do not boil.*

Slice rolls in half lengthwise. Place cut side up on baking sheet. Broil 4 to 5 inches from heat for 2 minutes or till toasted. Spread ¼ of the meat mixture atop each roll half. Place a tomato slice atop each. Place on baking sheet; broil 3 minutes. Sprinkle cheese atop; broil 2 minutes more. Makes 4 servings.

LUAU BURGERS/390

- **1 beaten egg**
- **1 8-ounce can tomato sauce**
- **½ cup finely crushed saltine crackers (14 crackers)**
- **½ cup chopped onion**
- **⅓ cup chopped green pepper**
- **2 tablespoons soy sauce**
- **½ teaspoon ground ginger**
- **2 pounds lean ground beef**
- **1 15½-ounce can pineapple slices, drained (8 slices)**
- **4 maraschino cherries, drained and halved**

In bowl combine egg, tomato sauce, crushed crackers, onion, green pepper, soy sauce, and ginger. Add ground beef; mix well. Shape meat mixture into eight 4-inch patties; grill over *medium* coals for 6 to 8 minutes; turn. Top each patty with a pineapple slice and cherry half. Continue to grill 6 to 8 minutes longer or till desired doneness. Serves 8.

DELUXE BEEF PATTIES/306

- **1 beaten egg**
- **¼ cup tomato juice**
- **2 tablespoons fine dry bread crumbs**
- **1 teaspoon Worcestershire sauce**
- **½ teaspoon salt**
- **½ teaspoon dried oregano, crushed**
- **¼ teaspoon pepper**
- **Dash bottled hot pepper sauce**
- **1 pound lean ground beef**

• • •

- **¼ cup chopped onion**
- **¼ cup chopped green pepper**
- **1 clove garlic, minced**
- **2 teaspoons butter *or* margarine**
- **1 7½-ounce can tomatoes, cut up**
- **¼ teaspoon dried oregano, crushed**
- **Dash bottled hot pepper sauce**

Combine egg, tomato juice, bread crumbs, Worcestershire sauce, salt, ½ teaspoon oregano, pepper, and dash hot pepper sauce. Add meat; mix well. Shape into 4 patties, each ¾ inch thick. Broil patties 3 inches from heat for 6 minutes; season with salt and pepper. Turn patties; broil 6 minutes more for medium doneness.

Meanwhile, prepare sauce. In small saucepan cook onion, green pepper, and garlic in butter or margarine till tender. Add *undrained* tomatoes, ¼ teaspoon oregano, and dash hot pepper sauce. Bring to boiling. Simmer, uncovered, 5 to 8 minutes or till sauce reaches desired consistency. Spoon over patties. Serves 4.

PARED-DOWN PIZZA/252

This recipe makes enough dough for two pizza crusts; use one now and freeze the other. A baked pizza is pictured on the cover—

½ pound lean ground beef
1 clove garlic, minced
1 16-ounce can tomatoes, finely cut up
½ cup coarsely chopped onion
1 teaspoon dried oregano, crushed
½ teaspoon fennel seed
¼ teaspoon salt

• • •

1¾ to 2 cups all-purpose flour
1 package active dry yeast
¼ teaspoon salt
⅔ cup warm water (115° to 120°)
1 tablespoon cooking oil
Non-stick vegetable spray coating
1 green pepper, cut into rings
1 cup shredded mozzarella cheese (4 ounces)

In medium saucepan cook ground beef and garlic till meat is browned; drain well. Stir in *undrained* tomatoes, onion, oregano, fennel seed, and ¼ teaspoon salt. Bring to boiling; reduce heat. Boil gently, uncovered, about 30 minutes or till of desired consistency.

Meanwhile, in small mixer bowl combine ¾ cup of the flour, the yeast, and remaining ¼ teaspoon salt. Add water and oil. Beat at low speed of electric mixer ½ minute, scraping bowl constantly. Beat 3 minutes at high speed. Stir in as much of the remaining flour as you can mix in with a spoon. Turn out onto lightly floured surface. Knead in enough of the remaining flour to make a moderately stiff dough that is smooth and elastic (6 to 8 minutes total). Divide dough in half. Cover dough and let rest 10 minutes.

On lightly floured surface roll each half into a 13-inch circle. Transfer circles to 12-inch pizza pans or baking sheets sprayed with non-stick vegetable spray coating. Build up edges slightly. Bake in a 425° oven about 12 minutes or till lightly browned. Freeze one crust for later use. Spread remaining crust with the meat-tomato mixture. Top with green pepper rings. Sprinkle with mozzarella cheese. Bake for 12 to 15 minutes more or till the topping is bubbly. Makes 6 servings.

SAUCY PEPPER BURGERS/260

¼ cup fine dry bread crumbs
2 tablespoons milk
½ teaspoon dried basil, crushed
½ teaspoon dried oregano, crushed
¼ teaspoon garlic powder
¼ teaspoon salt
Dash pepper
¾ pound lean ground beef
2 medium onions, thinly sliced
¾ cup tomato sauce
¼ cup dry red wine
2 medium green peppers, cut into strips

In a bowl combine bread crumbs, milk, basil, oregano, garlic powder, salt, and pepper. Add meat; mix well. Shape meat mixture into four ¾-inch-thick patties. In 10-inch skillet brown meat patties on both sides. Drain off fat. Add onions to skillet with meat patties. Combine tomato sauce and wine; pour over patties. Cover and simmer for 10 minutes; add green pepper strips. Cover and simmer 8 to 10 minutes more or till pepper is just tender. Serves 4

MEXICAN MEATBALL SOUP/281

1 beaten egg
½ cup chopped onion
¼ cup cornmeal
1 4-ounce can green chili peppers, rinsed, seeded, and chopped
1 clove garlic, minced
¾ teaspoon salt
¼ teaspoon dried oregano, crushed
⅛ teaspoon pepper
1 pound lean ground beef

• • •

3 cups water
1 16-ounce can tomatoes, cut up
1 8-ounce can tomato sauce
⅓ cup chopped onion
1 clove garlic, minced
1 tablespoon sugar
1½ teaspoons salt
1½ teaspoons chili powder
¼ teaspoon pepper
¼ teaspoon dried oregano, crushed

In bowl combine egg, ½ cup chopped onion, cornmeal, *half* the chopped chili peppers, 1 clove garlic, the ¾ teaspoon salt, ¼ teaspoon oregano, and the ⅛ teaspoon pepper; add ground beef. Mix well.

Using 1 rounded teaspoonful per meatball, shape mixture into 48 meatballs; set aside. In large saucepan or Dutch oven combine water, *undrained* tomatoes, tomato sauce, ⅓ cup onion, 1 clove garlic, sugar, 1½ teaspoons salt, chili powder, ¼ teaspoon pepper, ¼ teaspoon oregano, and the remaining chili peppers. Bring to boiling. Add meatballs. Return to boiling. Cover; reduce heat and simmer 30 minutes. Makes 6 servings.

VEAL STEW/263

1¼ pounds lean boneless veal, cut into 1-inch cubes
1 clove garlic, minced
1 tablespoon butter *or* margarine
1¾ cups water
¼ cup dry white wine
• • •
2 medium potatoes, peeled and cubed
2 medium carrots, bias sliced into 1-inch pieces
½ medium onion, cut into 1-inch pieces
1 cup frozen peas
18 fresh mushrooms, halved
2 tablespoons snipped parsley
2 teaspoons instant chicken bouillon granules
½ teaspoon dried marjoram, crushed
½ teaspoon salt
¼ teaspoon pepper
2 tablespoons cold water
1 tablespoon cornstarch

In 4-quart Dutch oven cook meat and garlic in butter or margarine till meat is brown. Stir in the 1¾ cups water and the wine. Bring to boiling. Reduce heat; cover and simmer for 30 minutes. Stir in potatoes, carrots, onion, peas, mushrooms, parsley, bouillon granules, marjoram, salt, and pepper. Cover and cook about 30 minutes more or till meat and vegetables are tender. Skim off fat. Combine the 2 tablespoons water and cornstarch; stir into meat mixture. Cook and stir till thickened and bubbly. Cook and stir 1 to 2 minutes more. Makes 6 servings.

VEAL CHOPS WITH LEMON SAUCE/219

2 veal loin chops, cut ½ inch thick (½ pound)
1 2-ounce can mushroom stems and pieces
2 teaspoons butter *or* margarine
⅓ cup skim milk
1½ teaspoons cornstarch
2 teaspoons lemon juice
Dash dried tarragon, crushed

Place chops on unheated rack of broiler pan. Broil chops 3 to 4 inches from heat for 5 minutes. Turn chops; sprinkle with salt and pepper. Broil about 5 minutes more or till done. Meanwhile, in saucepan combine *undrained* mushrooms and butter. Cook over low heat till butter is melted. In screw-top jar combine milk and cornstarch; shake well. Add to mushrooms. Cook and stir over medium heat till thickened and bubbly. Remove from heat; stir in lemon juice, tarragon, ¼ teaspoon *salt,* and dash *pepper.* Spoon sauce over chops. Makes 2 servings.

CHINESE VEAL STEAK/223

1 pound veal leg round steak
1 tablespoon cooking oil
½ cup chopped onion
¼ cup bias-sliced celery
1 2½-ounce jar sliced mushrooms, drained
1 tablespoon soy sauce
½ teaspoon instant chicken bouillon granules
2 teaspoons cornstarch

Cut veal into 4 pieces; pound with meat mallet to ¼-inch thickness. In large skillet brown veal in hot cooking oil. Drain off excess fat. Add onion, celery, mushrooms, soy sauce, bouillon granules, and ½ cup *water.* Cover and simmer for 30 minutes or till veal is tender. Remove veal to warm serving platter. Combine cornstarch and 2 tablespoons *cold water;* stir into mixture in skillet. Cook and stir till thickened and bubbly. Pour some mushroom mixture over veal; pass remainder. Makes 4 servings.

VEAL STEW OVER RICE/296

¾ pound lean boneless veal, cut into ¾-inch cubes
¾ cup chopped onion
1 clove garlic, minced
2 tablespoons cooking oil
4 medium tomatoes, peeled, seeded, and chopped
¼ cup water
1 tablespoon paprika
1 teaspoon instant chicken bouillon granules
Dash bottled hot pepper sauce
1 large green pepper, cut into thin strips
1⅓ cups hot cooked quick-cooking rice

In Dutch oven cook veal, onion, and garlic in hot oil till meat is browned and onion is tender. Drain off fat. Add tomatoes, water, paprika, bouillon granules, hot pepper sauce, and ¾ teaspoon *salt.* Cover and simmer for 30 minutes or till meat is tender, stirring occasionally. Add green pepper. Cover; simmer for 5 to 10 minutes more or till green pepper is tender. Serve over rice. Makes 4 servings.

VEAL SAUTÉ WITH MUSHROOMS/281

- **¾ pound boneless veal leg round steak, trimmed of fat**
- **1 tablespoon butter *or* margarine**
- **1 teaspoon Worcestershire sauce**
- **1 clove garlic, minced**
- **1 medium onion, sliced and separated into rings**
- **1 cup sliced fresh mushrooms**
- **⅓ cup water**
- **1 tablespoon lemon juice**
- **1½ teaspoons instant beef bouillon granules**
- **¼ cup cold water**
- **2 teaspoons cornstarch**
- **2 cups hot cooked noodles**
- **Lemon wedges**

Cut veal into 4 pieces; pound with meat mallet to ¼-inch thickness. In 10-inch skillet combine butter or margarine, Worcestershire sauce, and garlic. Cook over medium-high heat till garlic is lightly browned. Add veal and onion; cook meat on both sides till lightly browned. Arrange mushrooms over meat. Add water, lemon juice, and bouillon granules to meat and vegetables in skillet. Reduce heat; cover and simmer about 5 minutes or till meat is done. Remove meat; keep warm. Combine the ¼ cup cold water and the cornstarch; stir into meat mixture. Cook and stir till slightly thickened and bubbly. Cook and stir 1 to 2 minutes more. Serve meat and sauce over hot noodles. Garnish with lemon wedges. Makes 4 servings.

FESTIVE PORK ROAST/177

- **½ cup dry red wine**
- **¼ cup packed brown sugar**
- **3 tablespoons water**
- **3 tablespoons vinegar**
- **3 tablespoons catsup**
- **1 tablespoon cooking oil**
- **1 tablespoon soy sauce**
- **1 clove garlic, minced**
- **1 teaspoon curry powder**
- **¼ teaspoon ground ginger**
- **¼ teaspoon pepper**

• • •

- **1 5-pound boneless rolled pork loin roast**
- **¼ cup cold water**
- **2 teaspoons cornstarch**

For marinade, combine wine, sugar, 3 tablespoons water, vinegar, catsup, oil, soy sauce, garlic, curry powder, ginger, and pepper. Trim fat from meat (see note). Place meat in plastic bag; set in shallow dish. Pour marinade into bag; close bag. Marinate meat in refrigerator for 6 to 8 hours or overnight, turning bag several times to distribute marinade. Drain meat, reserving 1 cup marinade; set aside reserved marinade. Pat meat dry with paper toweling. Place meat on rack in shallow roasting pan. Roast in a 325° oven about 2 hours or till meat thermometer registers 160°.

Meanwhile, in small saucepan combine ¼ cup cold water and cornstarch; add reserved marinade. Cook and stir till mixture is thickened and bubbly. Cook and stir 1 to 2 minutes more. Brush roast with marinade mixture. Continue roasting about 1 hour or till meat thermometer registers 170°. Brush roast frequently with marinade mixture. Spoon remaining marinade mixture over meat before serving. Serves 20.

Note: Untie the rolled roast to trim fat. Reroll roast into a compact shape; tie with kitchen string.

PORK AND VEGETABLE STIR-FRY/265

If you don't have a wok, use a large skillet to prepare this colorful stir-fry—

- **1 pound lean boneless pork, trimmed of fat**

• • •

- **¼ cup soy sauce**
- **2 tablespoons dry sherry**
- **1 tablespoon cornstarch**
- **¼ teaspoon ground ginger**

• • •

- **2 tablespoons cooking oil**
- **1½ cups thinly bias-sliced carrots**
- **1½ cups bias-sliced celery**
- **1 large green pepper, cut into strips**
- **2 cups torn fresh spinach leaves**
- **2 cups hot cooked rice**

Partially freeze pork; slice thinly into bite-size strips. Stir together soy sauce, sherry, cornstarch, and ginger; set mixture aside.

Preheat a wok or large skillet over high heat; add oil. Stir-fry carrots, celery, and green pepper for 2 minutes. Remove vegetables. Add another tablespoon of oil if necessary. Add the pork to wok or skillet; stir-fry for 2 to 3 minutes. Stir soy mixture; stir into pork. Cook and stir till thickened and bubbly. Stir in cooked vegetables and spinach; cover and cook the mixture for 1 minute. Serve the pork and vegetables over hot cooked rice. Makes 6 servings.

SPICY PORK SKILLET/283

- ¾ pound boneless pork, cut into thin strips and trimmed of fat
- 1 medium onion, thinly sliced
- 1 tablespoon cooking oil
- 1 8-ounce can tomato sauce
- ⅓ cup water
- 1½ teaspoons chili powder
- 1 teaspoon Worcestershire sauce
- ¼ teaspoon salt
- ¼ teaspoon ground red pepper

• • •

- 1 12-ounce can whole kernel corn, drained
- 1 large green pepper, cut into strips (1 cup)
- 1 2-ounce jar sliced pimiento, drained
- ¼ cup shredded cheddar cheese (1 ounce)

In 10-inch skillet brown pork strips and sliced onion in hot cooking oil. Combine tomato sauce, water, chili powder, Worcestershire sauce, salt, and red pepper; add to meat in skillet. Cover and simmer for 15 minutes or till meat is tender. Stir in the drained corn, green pepper strips, and drained pimiento. Simmer, uncovered, for 10 minutes or till green pepper is tender and some of the liquid has evaporated. Sprinkle cheese atop before serving. Makes 4 servings.

Lamb Zucchini Casserole (see page 139); *Spicy Pork Skillet*

ORIENTAL PORK CHOPS/193

6 pork loin rib chops (2 pounds), cut ½ inch thick and trimmed of fat
1 tablespoon cooking oil
1 4-ounce can sliced mushrooms
½ cup sliced celery
¼ cup chopped onion
1 tablespoon soy sauce
1 teaspoon instant chicken bouillon granules
2 teaspoons cornstarch
8 water chestnuts, sliced

In large skillet brown chops in hot oil. Drain off fat. Add *undrained* mushrooms, celery, onion, soy sauce, bouillon granules, and ½ cup *water*. Cover and simmer for 40 minutes or till tender. Remove chops from skillet. Combine cornstarch and ¼ cup *cold water;* stir into mixture in skillet. Add water chestnuts. Cook and stir till mixture is thickened and bubbly. Cook and stir 1 to 2 minutes more. Pour some sauce over chops; pass remainder. Makes 6 servings.

BAKED ORANGE-SAUCED CHOPS/180

4 pork loin rib chops (1 to 1½ pounds), cut ½ inch thick and trimmed of fat
1 tablespoon cooking oil
1 tablespoon brown sugar
½ teaspoon finely shredded orange peel
¼ teaspoon salt
¼ teaspoon ground ginger
⅔ cup orange juice
2 teaspoons cornstarch

In skillet brown chops slowly in hot oil. Remove chops to 9x9x2-inch baking pan. Combine sugar, orange peel, salt, and ginger; stir in orange juice. Pour over chops. Cover; bake in 350° oven for 45 to 50 minutes or till tender. Transfer chops to platter; keep warm. Skim fat from cooking liquid. Measure cooking liquid. If necessary, add water to cooking liquid to measure ¾ cup. In saucepan combine cornstarch and 1 tablespoon *cold water;* add the ¾ cup liquid. Cook and stir till bubbly; cook and stir 2 minutes more. Spoon some sauce over chops; pass remainder. Makes 4 servings.

SAUERKRAUT AND PORK SKILLET/220

4 pork chops (about 1¼ pounds), cut ½ inch thick and trimmed of fat
1 tablespoon cooking oil
1 medium onion, sliced and separated into rings
1 clove garlic, minced
1 16-ounce can sauerkraut, drained and snipped
½ cup apple juice *or* cider
1 teaspoon caraway seed
¼ teaspoon dried thyme, crushed
1 small apple, cored and sliced

In skillet brown chops in hot oil; remove chops. Reserve drippings in skillet. Cook onion and garlic in drippings till tender. Add sauerkraut, apple juice, caraway, thyme, ½ teaspoon *salt*, and ¼ teaspoon *pepper*. Place chops atop; sprinkle with salt. Cover and simmer 20 minutes or till chops are tender. Add apple slices to skillet; cover and simmer 5 minutes or till apple is just tender. Serves 4.

ORANGE-SPICED PORK CHOPS/208

The menu on page 32 suggests other foods to complement this main dish—

Non-stick vegetable spray coating
6 pork top loin chops, cut ½ inch thick and trimmed of fat
¼ teaspoon salt
⅛ teaspoon pepper
¼ cup orange juice
2 oranges
1 cup water
1 tablespoon sugar
1 tablespoon cornstarch
1 cup orange juice
⅛ teaspoon ground allspice

Spray bottom of a 12-inch skillet with non-stick vegetable spray coating; brown pork chops on both sides. Season with the salt and pepper; add the ¼ cup orange juice. Cover and simmer 25 to 30 minutes or till the meat is tender.

Meanwhile, using a vegetable peeler, remove a very thin layer of the peel from one of the oranges. Slice the peel into julienne strips. Peel and section both oranges and cut sections into ½-inch pieces; set aside. Simmer orange peel strips in the water for 15 minutes; drain well and set aside the orange peel strips.

To make sauce, in small saucepan combine sugar and cornstarch. Stir in the 1 cup orange juice. Cook and stir till thickened and bubbly. Add the orange pieces, peel, and allspice. Cook and stir 1 to 2 minutes more. Serve warm sauce over pork chops. Makes 6 servings.

BROIL PORK CHOPS FOR LOW-CAL EATING

Broiling is an excellent calorie-cutting cooking technique because it adds no extra fat. Pork chops are excellent for broiling because of their lean meat; after being broiled the chops are tender and juicy.

To broil pork chops, choose pork rib or loin chops that are ¾ to 1 inch thick. Set the oven temperature to "broil" and preheat if desired (check range instruction booklet). Place chops on unheated rack of broiler pan (food will stick to a hot broiler rack). Place chops 3 to 4 inches from heat. (To position the rack, measure the distance from the top of the pork chops to the heat source.) Season chops with salt and pepper. Broil for 10 to 13 minutes, then turn using tongs. Continue broiling chops for 10 to 12 minutes more or till done.

Before serving, trim away excess fat. One 5-ounce raw pork loin chop (with bone) that has been broiled has 151 calories. If desired, serve broiled pork chops with a low-calorie sauce.

YOGURT-SAUCED PORK BALLS/264

1 beaten egg
⅓ cup fine dry bread crumbs
3 tablespoons plain yogurt
4 teaspoons finely chopped onion
½ teaspoon salt
¼ teaspoon pepper
1 pound ground pork
1 tablespoon cooking oil
• • •
1½ teaspoons instant beef bouillon granules
1 cup boiling water
2 tablespoons catsup
1 teaspoon Worcestershire sauce
½ teaspoon dried basil, crushed
3 tablespoons cold water
1 tablespoon cornstarch
⅓ cup plain yogurt

In bowl combine egg, the bread crumbs, 3 tablespoons yogurt, onion, salt, and pepper. Add ground pork; mix well. Shape into 32 meatballs. In skillet brown meatballs in hot oil. Drain off fat. Dissolve bouillon granules in boiling water; add catsup, Worcestershire sauce, and basil. Add to skillet. Bring to boiling. Reduce heat; cover and simmer 20 minutes.

Remove meatballs to serving dish. Skim fat from pan juices. Measure pan juices. Add water, if necessary, to measure ¾ cup liquid. Return to skillet. Stir cold water into cornstarch; add to liquid in skillet. Cook and stir till thickened and bubbly. Stir in ⅓ cup plain yogurt. Heat through but *do not boil.* Serve immediately. Makes 4 servings.

PORK TURNOVERS/366

This meal-in-a-sandwich, sprinkled with sesame seed, is pictured on pages 114 and 115—

½ cup chopped green pepper
¼ cup chopped onion
1 tablespoon butter *or* margarine
• • •
2 cups chopped cooked pork
1 8-ounce can applesauce
2 tablespoons Dijon-style mustard
½ to ¾ teaspoon ground ginger
¼ teaspoon salt
• • •
2 packages (6 biscuits each) refrigerated biscuits
Milk (optional)
Sesame seed (optional)

In a medium saucepan cook green pepper and onion in butter or margarine till tender. Remove from heat; stir in pork, applesauce, mustard, ginger, and salt. On floured surface roll each biscuit to a 5-inch circle. Place about ⅓ cup of the pork mixture on 6 of the dough rounds, spreading meat mixture to within ½ inch of edge. Top with remaining dough rounds. Moisten and press edges together; seal with tines of fork. Brush with milk and sprinkle with sesame seed, if desired. Place on an ungreased baking sheet. Bake in a 400° oven for 10 to 12 minutes or till golden brown. Serve warm. Makes 6 servings.

DILLED CABBAGE ROLLS/244

8 large cabbage leaves
½ pound ground pork
½ cup chopped fresh mushrooms
¼ cup chopped onion
1 cup cooked rice
½ cup plain yogurt
1 beaten egg
½ teaspoon dried dillweed
¼ teaspoon salt
• • •
2 teaspoons instant chicken bouillon granules
1 cup boiling water
¼ cup plain yogurt
Snipped parsley

Cut about 2 inches of heavy center vein out of each cabbage leaf. Immerse leaves in boiling salted water about 3 minutes or just till limp; drain.

In 10-inch skillet cook ground pork, mushrooms, and onion till meat is browned and onion is tender. Remove from heat. Stir in cooked rice, ½ cup yogurt, egg, dillweed, and salt. Place about ¼ cup of the meat mixture in center of each leaf; fold in sides. Fold ends of cabbage leaves so they overlap atop meat mixture.

Place cabbage rolls, seam side down, in a 10-inch skillet. Dissolve bouillon granules in boiling water; pour over cabbage rolls. Cover and simmer about 25 minutes. Using a slotted spoon, remove cabbage rolls to serving platter. Top each cabbage roll with a dollop of yogurt and snipped parsley. Serve the cabbage rolls immediately. Makes 4 servings.

PORK PAPRIKASH/263

1 pound pork tenderloin, trimmed of fat
Non-stick vegetable spray coating
1 cup chopped onion
2 teaspoons paprika
1 teaspoon instant chicken bouillon granules
1 tablespoon cornstarch
¾ cup plain yogurt
¼ cup snipped parsley
2½ cups hot cooked noodles

Partially freeze pork; slice diagonally into ¼-inch slices. Spray bottom of 10-inch skillet with vegetable spray coating; heat skillet. In prepared skillet cook meat, half at a time, over medium-high heat about 4 minutes or till browned, stirring occasionally. Return all meat to skillet. Add onion, paprika, bouillon granules, and ¾ cup *water*. Cover and simmer about 15 minutes or till pork is tender. Stir cornstarch into yogurt; blend some of the pan juices into yogurt mixture, stirring constantly. Return all to skillet. Cook and stir till bubbly; cook and stir 1 to 2 minutes more. Stir in parsley. Serve over noodles. Serves 5.

ORANGE-GINGER HAM GRILL/332

2 tablespoons dry white wine
2 tablespoons frozen orange juice concentrate, thawed
½ teaspoon dry mustard
⅛ teaspoon ground ginger
1 1½-pound fully cooked ham slice, cut 1 inch thick and trimmed of fat
6 canned pineapple slices

Combine wine, orange juice concentrate, dry mustard, and ginger. Slash edge of ham slice. Brush sauce over ham. Grill over *medium* coals for 10 to 15 minutes, brushing with sauce occasionally. Turn ham; grill 10 to 15 minutes more or till done, brushing with sauce. Grill pineapple slices alongside the ham during the last 5 to 10 minutes of grilling. Makes 6 servings.

APPLE HAM SLICE/252

2 tablespoons butter *or* margarine
1 2-pound fully cooked ham slice, cut 1 inch thick and trimmed of fat
¼ cup sliced green onion
¾ cup apple juice *or* apple cider
½ teaspoon ground cinnamon
1 tablespoon cornstarch
1 tablespoon cold water
2 medium apples
¼ cup raisins

In large skillet melt butter. Brown ham on both sides in butter; remove from skillet. Cook onion in butter till tender. Stir in apple juice and cinnamon; bring to boiling. Combine cornstarch and water; stir into apple juice mixture. Cook and stir till thickened and bubbly. Return ham to skillet. Cover; simmer for 10 minutes. Peel, core, and slice apples. Place apple slices atop ham and add raisins to skillet. Cook, covered, 5 to 7 minutes more or till apples are just tender. Transfer ham to warm platter; spoon some sauce and fruit atop. Pass remaining sauce. Makes 6 servings.

HAM AND COTTAGE CHEESE MOLD/128

This main-dish salad, prepared in individual molds, is pictured on page 123—

1 envelope unflavored gelatin
1 cup cold water
1 teaspoon instant chicken bouillon granules
1 cup plain yogurt
• • •
1 cup ground fully cooked ham
½ cup finely chopped celery
½ cup cream-style cottage cheese
2 tablespoons chopped pimiento
2 tablespoons chopped green pepper
1 tablespoon sliced green onion
Lettuce (optional)
Shredded carrot (optional)

Soften gelatin in cold water; add bouillon granules. Heat, stirring constantly, till gelatin and bouillon granules dissolve. Remove from heat. Add yogurt; beat with rotary beater till smooth. Chill mixture till partially set (consistency of unbeaten egg whites). Fold in ham, celery, cottage cheese, pimiento, green pepper, and green onion. Pour into 4 individual molds. Chill till firm. Unmold onto individual lettuce-lined plates, if desired. Garnish with shredded carrot, if desired. Makes 4 servings.

Chicken 'n' Swiss Stacks (see recipe, page 140); *Ham and Vegetable Roll-Ups*

HAM STEW/159

1 16-ounce can tomatoes, cut up
1 16-ounce can mixed vegetables
1 cup diced fully cooked ham
¼ cup water
1 tablespoon snipped parsley
½ teaspoon dried thyme, crushed
½ teaspoon instant chicken bouillon granules
Dash pepper
Dash bottled hot pepper sauce

Combine *undrained* tomatoes, *undrained* mixed vegetables, ham, water, parsley, thyme, chicken bouillon granules, pepper, and hot pepper sauce. Bring to boiling; reduce heat. Cover and simmer about 10 minutes, stirring occasionally. Serves 4.

HAM AND VEGETABLE ROLL-UPS/203

¼ cup coarsely chopped cucumber
¼ cup coarsely chopped tomato
¼ cup sliced fresh mushrooms
2 tablespoons sliced pitted ripe olives
2 tablespoons sliced green onion
⅓ cup low-calorie Italian salad dressing
1 6-ounce package sliced fully cooked ham (8 slices)
4 large outer leaves head lettuce
1 cup shredded mozzarella cheese (4 ounces)

In a small bowl combine cucumber, tomato, mushrooms, olives, and green onion; stir in salad dressing. Cover and chill for 6 hours or overnight; drain well. To assemble roll-ups, center two ham slices atop each lettuce leaf. Top each with ¼ cup *drained* vegetable mixture and ¼ cup shredded mozzarella cheese. Roll up lettuce and ham, turning edges of lettuce in toward center while rolling; secure each roll-up with a wooden pick. Makes 4 servings.

HAM WITH PINEAPPLE SAUCE/165

1 2-pound fully cooked boneless ham
1 8-ounce can crushed pineapple (juice pack)
1 teaspoon cornstarch
½ teaspoon finely shredded orange peel
¼ teaspoon ground cinnamon
Dash ground cloves
1 large orange
2 teaspoons butter *or* margarine

Place ham on rack in shallow baking pan. Insert meat thermometer. Bake in a 325° oven for 1 hour or till meat thermometer registers 140°.

Meanwhile, in saucepan combine *undrained* pineapple, cornstarch, orange peel, cinnamon, and cloves. Peel and section orange, reserving juice. Chop orange sections; add sections and reserved juice to pineapple mixture. Cook and stir till thickened and bubbly. Stir in butter till melted. To serve, slice ham; spoon sauce over. Makes 8 servings.

COOKING WITH YOGURT

Yogurt is used often in this book because it is low in calories yet adds a delightful flavor to foods. Try substituting yogurt for mayonnaise or sour cream to cut calories in your favorite recipes. A tablespoon of low-fat plain yogurt has only 8 calories compared with 101 for mayonnaise and 26 for sour cream. When using yogurt in a sauce, stir it in at the end of cooking; heat through but do not boil. Also when adding it to a hot or cold mixture, blend yogurt gently. Vigorous stirring causes it to become thin.

HAM PATTIES WITH APPLE RINGS/275

2 beaten eggs
½ cup applesauce
1½ cups soft bread crumbs (2 slices)
⅓ cup nonfat dry milk powder
¼ cup chopped onion
½ teaspoon dry mustard
¼ teaspoon salt
¾ pound ground fully cooked ham
½ pound ground pork

• • •

1 tablespoon brown sugar
2 teaspoons cornstarch
¼ teaspoon dry mustard
Dash ground cloves
¾ cup applesauce
1 tablespoon vinegar
1 medium apple, cored and sliced into 6 rings
Snipped parsley (optional)

In mixing bowl combine beaten eggs, the ½ cup applesauce, and the bread crumbs; stir in nonfat dry milk powder, chopped onion, ½ teaspoon dry mustard, and the salt. Add ground ham and ground pork; mix well. Shape meat mixture into 6 patties; place in a 13x9x2-inch baking pan. Bake in a 350° oven for 40 to 45 minutes or till the ham patties are done.

Meanwhile, prepare sauce. In saucepan combine brown sugar, cornstarch, ¼ teaspoon dry mustard, and the cloves. Stir in the ¾ cup applesauce and the vinegar. Cook and stir till thickened and bubbly. Add apple rings; cover and simmer about 15 minutes or till apple rings are just tender. To serve, arrange an apple ring atop each patty. Spoon sauce over. Garnish with parsley, if desired. Makes 6 servings.

HAM AND CHEESE CASSEROLE/293

1 cup sliced fresh mushrooms
½ cup chopped onion
¼ cup chopped green pepper
2 tablespoons butter *or* margarine
1⅓ cups *reconstituted* nonfat dry milk
4 teaspoons cornstarch
¼ teaspoon dry mustard
¼ teaspoon pepper
¾ cup shredded *process* Swiss cheese (3 ounces)
1¼ cups chopped fully cooked ham
1 10-ounce package frozen peas and carrots, thawed

In 2-quart saucepan cook mushrooms, chopped onion, and green pepper in butter or margarine till vegetables are tender but not brown. In screw-top jar combine reconstituted milk, cornstarch, dry mustard, and pepper; shake well to mix. Stir into mushroom mixture. Cook, stirring constantly, over medium heat till mixture is thickened and bubbly. Stir in ½ *cup* of the shredded Swiss cheese and stir to melt the cheese. Stir in the chopped ham and the peas and carrots. Transfer ham-vegetable mixture to a 1½-quart casserole. Cover and bake in a 350° oven for 30 minutes or till heated through. Sprinkle remaining shredded Swiss cheese atop ham-vegetable mixture. Bake 5 minutes more or till cheese is melted. Makes 4 servings.

CURRIED YOGURT KABOBS/215

1 8-ounce carton plain yogurt
¼ cup finely chopped green onion
3 tablespoons skim milk
1 teaspoon curry powder
½ teaspoon Worcestershire sauce
1½ pounds boneless leg of lamb, cut into 1-inch cubes
6 large fresh mushrooms
6 small boiled potatoes
6 cherry tomatoes

Combine first 5 ingredients and ½ teaspoon *salt;* set aside. Thread meat alternately with mushrooms and potatoes on 6 skewers. Brush yogurt mixture on kabobs. Broil kabobs about 4 inches from heat for 10 to 12 minutes, brushing with yogurt mixture and giving a quarter turn every 3 minutes. Add a cherry tomato to the end of each skewer before serving. Serves 6.

MARINATED LAMB KABOBS/137

Use a salad dressing with no more than 25 calories per tablespoon—

¾ pound lean boneless lamb, trimmed of fat
½ cup low-calorie Italian salad dressing
2 tablespoons lemon juice
8 fresh large mushrooms
¼ teaspoon Kitchen Bouquet (optional)
4 small zucchini, cut into 1-inch pieces

Cut meat into 1-inch pieces. Place meat in a plastic bag; add salad dressing and lemon juice. Close bag and place in a bowl. Refrigerate meat several hours or overnight, turning bag occasionally to distribute marinade. Drain meat, reserving the marinade. Add Kitchen Bouquet to marinade, if desired.

In bowl pour boiling water on mushrooms; drain immediately. Thread meat on skewers alternately with mushrooms and zucchini. Place on unheated rack of broiler pan. Broil 4 inches from heat for 10 to 12 minutes; turn and baste with marinade occasionally. Makes 4 servings.

MINT-GLAZED LAMB CHOPS/109

¼ cup cold water
1 teaspoon cornstarch
3 tablespoons finely snipped fresh mint leaves *or* 4 teaspoons dried mint flakes, crushed
1 tablespoon light corn syrup
½ teaspoon finely shredded lemon peel
¼ teaspoon salt
4 lamb leg sirloin chops (about 1¼ pounds), cut ¾ inch thick

For glaze, in saucepan combine water and cornstarch. Add mint, corn syrup, lemon peel, and salt. Cook and stir till thickened and bubbly.

Place lamb chops on unheated rack of broiler pan. Broil 3 to 4 inches from heat for 5 minutes. Brush some glaze over chops. Turn chops; broil 5 to 6 minutes more, brushing the lamb chops occasionally with glaze. Makes 4 servings.

CASSOULET SOUP/299

1 cup dry navy beans
4 cups cold water
3 cups hot water
½ cup chopped onion
½ cup chopped celery
½ cup chopped carrot
2 teaspoons instant chicken bouillon granules
¼ pound lean boneless lamb, cut into ½-inch cubes
½ cup diced fully cooked ham
1 bay leaf
3 tablespoons dry white wine
1 teaspoon Worcestershire sauce
½ teaspoon dried basil, crushed
½ teaspoon dried oregano, crushed

Rinse beans. In large saucepan combine beans and 4 cups cold water. Bring to boiling; reduce heat. Cover and simmer 2 minutes. Remove from heat. Cover and let stand 1 hour. (*Or,* soak beans in 4 cups cold water overnight in covered pan.) Drain beans and rinse. In same saucepan combine the rinsed beans, the 3 cups hot water, onion, celery, carrot, and bouillon granules. Cover and simmer 30 minutes. Add lamb, ham, and bay leaf. Simmer, covered, 30 minutes longer. Remove bay leaf. Stir in wine, Worcestershire sauce, basil, and oregano. Turn mixture into a 2-quart casserole. Cover and bake in a 350° oven for 45 minutes. Uncover and bake for 40 to 45 minutes more, stirring occasionally. Serve in bowls. Makes 4 servings.

ONION BRAISED LAMB CHOPS/228

4 lamb loin chops, cut 1 inch thick and trimmed of fat
1 tablespoon cooking oil
1 small onion, sliced
½ cup water
½ teaspoon instant chicken bouillon granules
⅛ teaspoon dried thyme, crushed
2 tablespoons skim milk
1 teaspoon cornstarch
2 tablespoons plain yogurt

In skillet brown chops on both sides in hot oil. Drain off excess fat. Add onion, water, bouillon granules, and thyme. Cover and simmer for 15 to 20 minutes or till meat is tender. Remove meat to platter; keep warm. Skim excess fat from skillet juices. Stir milk into cornstarch; add to skillet. Cook and stir over medium heat till mixture is thickened and bubbly. Stir in yogurt; heat through (*do not boil*). Spoon sauce over chops. Makes 2 servings.

ORANGE-SAUCED LAMB CHOPS/134

1 tablespoon cornstarch
¼ teaspoon finely shredded orange peel
⅛ teaspoon ground nutmeg
¾ cup orange juice
1 teaspoon lemon juice
4 lamb loin chops, cut ¾ inch thick
½ cup seedless green grapes, halved

In saucepan combine cornstarch, peel, and nutmeg; stir in orange juice. Cook and stir till bubbly. Stir in lemon juice. Brush chops with sauce. Broil chops 3 to 4 inches from heat for 4 minutes; turn and brush with sauce again. Broil chops 5 to 6 minutes longer. Stir grapes into remaining sauce; heat through. Spoon sauce atop chops. Makes 4 servings.

SWEET-SOUR LAMB/295

2 tablespoons cooking oil
1¼ pounds lean boneless lamb, cut into thin slices
1 medium sweet red *or* green pepper, cut into strips
½ of an 8-ounce can bamboo shoots, drained
6 green onions, bias sliced into 1-inch pieces
1 8-ounce can pineapple chunks (juice pack)
2 tablespoons wine vinegar
2 tablespoons catsup
1 teaspoon instant chicken bouillon granules
4 teaspoons cornstarch
3 cups hot cooked rice

Preheat a 12-inch skillet over high heat; add cooking oil. Cook lamb till browned. Stir in pepper strips, bamboo shoots, and green onions. Cook and stir about 3 minutes or till crisp-tender. Drain pineapple, reserving juice. Add enough water to pineapple juice to make ¾ cup liquid. Stir pineapple liquid, pineapple chunks, vinegar, catsup, bouillon granules, and ¼ teaspoon *salt* into lamb mixture; bring to boiling. Combine 3 tablespoons *cold water* and the cornstarch; stir into lamb mixture. Cook and stir till thickened and bubbly. Cook and stir 1 to 2 minutes more. Serve over hot rice. Makes 6 servings.

CREAMY LAMB CREPES/275

8 Calorie Counter's Crepes (see recipe, page 108)
½ pound lean boneless lamb, cut into thin strips and trimmed of fat
1 tablespoon all-purpose flour
½ teaspoon salt
Dash pepper
¼ cup chopped onion
1 tablespoon butter *or* margarine
¼ cup water
3 tablespoons dry sherry
⅛ teaspoon dried marjoram, crushed
Dash ground nutmeg
3 ounces Neufchâtel cheese, cubed
2 tablespoons skim milk
¼ cup shredded Swiss cheese (1 ounce)

Prepare Calorie Counter's Crepes. Coat meat strips in a mixture of the flour, salt, and pepper. In skillet brown meat strips and onion in butter or margarine. Stir in water, sherry, marjoram, and nutmeg. Simmer, covered, 15 to 20 minutes or till lamb is tender. Stir in Neufchâtel cheese and skim milk. Spoon meat filling along center of unbrowned side of each crepe; fold two opposite edges so they overlap atop filling. Place the crepes, seam side down, in a 12x7½x2-inch baking dish. Bake, covered, in a 350° oven 10 minutes. Sprinkle with Swiss cheese. Bake, uncovered, 5 minutes more or till cheese is melted. If desired, sprinkle with snipped parsley. Makes 4 servings.

LAMB ZUCCHINI CASSEROLE/176

Pictured on page 130—

1 pound lean boneless lamb, cut into thin bite-size strips and trimmed of fat
¾ cup chopped onion
1 clove garlic, minced
1 tablespoon cooking oil
2 10-ounce packages frozen chopped spinach, thawed and well drained (see note)
½ teaspoon dried basil, crushed
Dash ground nutmeg
1½ cups shredded mozzarella cheese (6 ounces)
½ teaspoon salt
⅔ cup cold water
1 teaspoon instant chicken bouillon granules
1 teaspoon cornstarch
2 small zucchini, thinly sliced
¼ cup grated Parmesan cheese
¼ teaspoon dried basil, crushed

In skillet brown the meat, onion, and garlic in hot oil. Drain off the fat. In large bowl combine spinach, ½ teaspoon basil, and nutmeg; stir in drained meat mixture, mozzarella cheese, and salt. Combine water, bouillon granules, and cornstarch; add to spinach mixture. Mix well; turn mixture into a 10x6x2-inch baking dish or other oblong baking dish. Arrange zucchini slices atop, overlapping as necessary. Sprinkle with Parmesan cheese and ¼ teaspoon basil. Bake, covered, in a 350° oven for 30 minutes or till zucchini is crisp-tender. Uncover and bake 5 to 10 minutes more or till golden. Makes 8 servings.

Note: Press out any excess liquid from the thawed and drained spinach.

HERBED LAMB STEW/249

1 pound lean boneless lamb, trimmed of fat
½ cup chopped onion
1 tablespoon cooking oil
1 cup water
¼ cup dry white wine
1½ teaspoons instant chicken bouillon granules
½ teaspoon dried basil, crushed
½ teaspoon dried thyme, crushed
¼ teaspoon dry mustard

• • •

2 carrots, cut into 1-inch pieces
2 potatoes, peeled and cubed
2 stalks celery, sliced into 1-inch pieces
1 cup fresh green beans
1 green pepper, cut into 1-inch pieces
1 tablespoon cornstarch
2 tablespoons cold water

In Dutch oven brown the meat and onion in hot oil. Drain off fat. Add water, wine, bouillon granules, basil, thyme, and dry mustard. Bring to boiling. Reduce heat; cover and simmer about 30 minutes or till meat is tender. Add carrots, potatoes, celery, beans, and green pepper. Cover and simmer for 20 to 25 minutes or till vegetables are tender. Combine cornstarch and cold water; stir into stew. Cook and stir till thickened and bubbly. Cook and stir 1 to 2 minutes more. Makes 4 servings.

BELGIAN LAMB STEW/242

Turnips, endive, herbs, and spices give this easy stew its unique flavor—

2 tablespoons cooking oil
2 pounds boneless lamb, cut into 1-inch cubes
2 cloves garlic, minced
1 large onion, chopped
1½ cups water
1 10½-ounce can condensed beef broth
1 teaspoon salt
1 bay leaf
½ teaspoon dried thyme, crushed
⅛ teaspoon ground cloves
⅛ teaspoon pepper
8 tiny new potatoes
4 small turnips, quartered
3 bunches Belgian endive
3 tablespoons cornstarch
3 tablespoons cold water
¼ cup snipped parsley

In 4½-quart Dutch oven heat cooking oil over medium heat. Add *half* of the lamb, turning to brown on all sides. Remove lamb; set aside. Cook remaining lamb and garlic till browned. Add first half of lamb and onion; cook till onion is tender. Add the 1½ cups water, the beef broth, salt, bay leaf, thyme, cloves, and pepper. Bring to boiling; simmer, covered, 40 minutes. Add unpeeled potatoes and turnips; simmer, covered, 30 minutes more.

Trim off base of each bunch of endive; slice into ½-inch lengths. Place endive atop stew; simmer 5 to 8 minutes. Stir cornstarch into the 3 tablespoons cold water. Add to stew. Bring to boiling over medium heat, stirring constantly; boil 1 minute. Stir in the snipped parsley. Serve in soup bowls. Makes 8 servings.

POULTRY MAIN DISHES

LOW-CALORIE COOKING TIPS FOR POULTRY

When preparing poultry remove its skin for fewer calories. This will decrease the calories in a serving by about 20 calories.

Also, try to prepare poultry recipes using light meat (breasts) rather than dark meat (thighs and legs). One cup of chopped cooked light meat (without skin) has 232 calories; a cup of chopped cooked dark meat (without skin) has 246 calories.

CHICKEN 'N' SWISS STACKS/234

Pictured on page 134—

½ cup plain yogurt
3 tablespoons mayonnaise *or* salad dressing
1 tablespoon snipped parsley
1 teaspoon prepared horseradish
1 teaspoon prepared mustard
⅛ teaspoon dried rosemary, crushed
⅛ teaspoon garlic powder
• • •
1 head lettuce
2 medium green peppers, thinly sliced into rings
6 ounces Swiss cheese, sliced
6 thin slices onion
6 ounces sliced cooked chicken *or* turkey
1 medium cucumber, sliced
2 medium tomatoes, thinly sliced

Combine yogurt, mayonnaise, parsley, horseradish, mustard, rosemary, and garlic powder. Mix well; cover and chill.

Slice off core end of lettuce head. Continue cutting crosswise slices to get 6 slices that are ½ inch thick. For each stack, top lettuce slice with 2 green pepper rings, 1 ounce cheese, 1 slice onion, 1 ounce of sliced chicken or turkey, 4 cucumber slices, and 2 tomato slices. Serve each stack topped with 2 tablespoons of the chilled yogurt mixture. Makes 6 servings.

THREE-CHEESE CHICKEN BAKE/318

This dish is similar to a baked lasagna—

8 ounces lasagna noodles
½ cup chopped onion
½ cup chopped green pepper
3 tablespoons butter *or* margarine
1 10¾-ounce can condensed cream of chicken soup
1 4-ounce can sliced mushrooms, drained
½ cup chopped pimiento
⅓ cup skim milk
½ teaspoon dried basil, crushed
1½ cups cream-style cottage cheese
2 cups chopped cooked chicken *or* turkey
1½ cups shredded American cheese (6 ounces)
½ cup grated Parmesan cheese

Cook lasagna noodles in boiling salted water according to package directions; drain well. Cook onion and green pepper in butter or margarine till tender. Stir in condensed soup, mushrooms, pimiento, skim milk, and basil.

Lay *half* the noodles in a 13x9x2-inch baking dish; top with *half* each of the soup mixture, cottage cheese, chicken, American cheese, and Parmesan cheese. Repeat layers of the noodles, sauce, cottage cheese, and chicken.

Bake in a 350° oven for 45 minutes. Top with remaining American and Parmesan cheese; bake 2 minutes more or till cheese is melted. Makes 10 servings.

CHICKEN-CAULIFLOWER CASSEROLES / 249

¼ cup chopped onion
¼ cup water
1 cup skim milk
1 tablespoon cornstarch
1 teaspoon instant chicken bouillon granules
¼ teaspoon salt
Dash pepper
¼ cup shredded American cheese (1 ounce)
• • •
½ of a 10-ounce package frozen cauliflower, cooked and drained
½ cup chopped cooked chicken
2 tablespoons chopped pimiento
¼ cup shredded American cheese (1 ounce)

Combine onion and the ¼ cup water. Bring to boiling. Cover and simmer for 5 minutes. Drain. Combine skim milk, cornstarch, bouillon granules, salt, and pepper. Add to onion. Cook and stir till thickened and bubbly. Add ¼ cup cheese; stir to melt. Remove from heat. Halve any large pieces of cauliflower. Stir cauliflower, chicken, and pimiento into the cheese sauce. Spoon mixture into 2 individual baking dishes. Bake in a 325° oven for 15 minutes. Sprinkle remaining shredded cheese atop mixture in both baking dishes. Bake 5 minutes more. Serve immediately. Makes 2 servings.

QUICK CHICKEN VEGETABLE SOUP / 155

1 cup water
1 7½-ounce can tomatoes, cut up
1 cup sliced carrot
½ cup chopped onion
¼ cup chopped green pepper
1½ teaspoons instant chicken bouillon granules
½ teaspoon dried thyme, crushed
¼ teaspoon ground sage
⅛ teaspoon pepper
¾ cup chopped cooked chicken

In saucepan combine water, *undrained* tomatoes, carrot, onion, green pepper, bouillon granules, thyme, sage, and pepper. Bring to boiling. Cover; simmer for 15 minutes or till vegetables are tender. Stir in chicken; heat through. Makes 2 servings.

CHICKEN DIVAN / 169

Use the white meat of the chicken to lower the calorie count even more—

2 10-ounce packages frozen chopped broccoli
1⅓ cups cold water
3 tablespoons cornstarch
⅔ cup skim milk
3 tablespoons dry sherry
1½ teaspoons instant chicken bouillon granules
Dash ground nutmeg
Dash pepper
12 ounces thinly sliced cooked chicken
¼ cup grated Parmesan cheese
Paprika

Cook broccoli according to package directions; drain well. Arrange in an 8x8x2-inch baking dish. To make sauce, in a saucepan combine cold water and cornstarch. Stir in milk, sherry, chicken bouillon granules, nutmeg, and pepper. Cook and stir till thickened and bubbly. Cook and stir 1 to 2 minutes more. Pour *half* of the sauce over broccoli. Arrange sliced chicken atop; cover with remaining sauce. Sprinkle Parmesan cheese over sauce; sprinkle with paprika. Bake, uncovered, in a 350° oven about 20 minutes or till heated through. Makes 6 servings.

SAUCED CHICKEN OVER RUSKS / 236

1 cup sliced fresh mushrooms
½ cup chopped onion
½ cup chopped celery
1½ cups skim milk
4 teaspoons cornstarch
1 teaspoon instant chicken bouillon granules
¼ teaspoon salt
⅛ teaspoon dried thyme, crushed
Dash pepper
½ pound cooked chicken, cut into strips
2 tablespoons snipped parsley
2 tablespoons dry white wine
8 rusks

In saucepan cook mushrooms, onion, and celery in a small amount of boiling water till onion is tender; drain. Combine milk, cornstarch, bouillon granules, salt, thyme, and pepper. Add to vegetables in saucepan. Cook and stir till mixture is thickened and bubbly. Stir in the chicken, parsley, and dry white wine. Heat chicken mixture through. To serve, spoon chicken mixture over rusks. Makes 4 servings.

CREAMY CHICKEN SALAD/282

1 teaspoon minced dried onion
2 tablespoons skim milk
½ cup plain yogurt
2 ounces Neufchâtel cheese, softened
¼ cup shredded Swiss cheese
½ teaspoon Worcestershire sauce
¾ cup chopped cooked chicken
¾ cup sliced celery
½ cup shredded carrot
Lettuce
Alfalfa sprouts

In bowl soak onion in milk 5 minutes. Stir in yogurt, cheeses, Worcestershire, and ¼ teaspoon *salt*. Stir in chicken, celery, and carrot. Chill. To serve, spoon chicken mixture onto lettuce-lined plates; top with sprouts. Serves 2.

GARDEN CHICKEN SALAD/183

Pictured on page 148—

½ cup lemon yogurt
3 tablespoons skim milk
1 tablespoon snipped parsley
1 tablespoon tarragon vinegar
2 teaspoons Dijon-style mustard
½ teaspoon celery seed
2 cups cubed cooked chicken *or* turkey
2 cups torn romaine
2 cups torn bibb lettuce
1 cup cauliflower flowerets
1 cup alfalfa sprouts
½ of a small red onion, sliced and separated into rings

For dressing, in small bowl combine lemon yogurt, skim milk, parsley, vinegar, mustard, celery seed, and ¼ teaspoon *salt*. Chill.

Season chicken or turkey lightly with salt and pepper. On 4 individual salad plates, arrange chicken or turkey, romaine, bibb lettuce, cauliflower, alfalfa sprouts, and onion. Spoon dressing over each serving. Makes 4 servings.

CHICKEN MARENGO/202

1 3-pound broiler-fryer chicken, cut up
1 tablespoon cooking oil
18 small boiling onions, peeled, *or* one 8-ounce can stewed onions, drained
1 7½-ounce can tomatoes, cut up
1 4-ounce can sliced mushrooms, drained
½ cup water
¼ cup dry sherry
1 clove garlic, minced
1 teaspoon instant beef bouillon granules
2 tablespoons cold water
1 tablespoon cornstarch

Remove skin from chicken pieces. In 10-inch skillet brown chicken pieces in hot oil. Drain off excess fat. Stir in onions, *undrained* tomatoes, mushrooms, ½ cup water, sherry, garlic, and bouillon granules. Cover and cook over low heat 30 to 35 minutes or till chicken is tender. Transfer chicken, mushrooms, and onions to platter. Combine the 2 tablespoons cold water and cornstarch; stir into tomato mixture in skillet. Cook and stir till thickened and bubbly. Cook and stir 1 to 2 minutes more. Serve sauce over chicken. Makes 6 servings.

ELEGANT CHICKEN CREPES/278

Also pictured on the back cover—

12 Calorie Counter's Crepes (see recipe, page 108)
¼ cup chopped onion
¼ cup water
1 cup skim milk
2 tablespoons cornstarch
¼ teaspoon salt
⅛ teaspoon pepper
1 cup shredded *process* Swiss cheese (4 ounces)
1 4-ounce can sliced mushrooms, drained
2 cups finely chopped cooked chicken
1 10-ounce package frozen chopped broccoli, cooked and drained

Prepare Calorie Counter's Crepes; set aside. In saucepan combine onion and water. Cook, covered, 5 minutes. *Do not drain.* Combine milk, cornstarch, salt, and pepper; add to onion. Cook and stir till thickened and bubbly. Cook and stir 1 minute more. Add cheese; stir to melt. Reserve ½ cup of the cheese mixture. Add mushrooms to remaining cheese mixture. Cover; set aside the cheese-mushroom mixture.

For filling, combine cooked chicken, cooked broccoli, and the ½ cup reserved cheese mixture. Spoon about ¼ cup filling on the unbrowned side of each crepe; roll up. Arrange crepes in a 13x9x2-inch baking dish. Cover and bake in a 350° oven for 20 minutes. Meanwhile, heat cheese-mushroom mixture in the saucepan; serve over crepes. Makes 6 servings.

Elegant Chicken Crepes

FRUITED BARBECUE CHICKEN/237

1 2½- to 3-pound broiler-fryer chicken, cut up
1 8-ounce can tomato sauce
2 tablespoons vinegar
2 tablespoons brown sugar
2 teaspoons cooking oil
1 teaspoon minced dried onion
1 teaspoon Worcestershire sauce
¾ teaspoon paprika
Dash garlic powder
Dash pepper
1 8-ounce can crushed pineapple (juice pack), drained
1 tablespoon cold water
2 teaspoons cornstarch
1 11-ounce can mandarin orange sections, drained

Remove skin from chicken pieces. In skillet combine tomato sauce, vinegar, brown sugar, cooking oil, minced dried onion, Worcestershire sauce, paprika, garlic powder, and pepper. Bring to boiling. Stir in drained pineapple. Add chicken pieces. Cover; simmer about 40 minutes or till chicken is tender, basting with sauce occasionally. Remove chicken to platter; keep warm. Skim fat from sauce in skillet. Combine cold water and cornstarch; add to sauce. Cook and stir till bubbly. Stir in mandarin orange sections; heat through. Spoon sauce over chicken. Serves 6.

CLAYPOT CHICKEN/160

1 2½- to 3-pound broiler-fryer chicken
1 tablespoon lemon juice
1 teaspoon dried marjoram, crushed
¼ teaspoon salt
Dash pepper
Paprika

Presoak a claypot lid and bottom in water for 10 minutes; drain. Remove skin from chicken. Sprinkle lemon juice over chicken. Combine marjoram, salt, and pepper; rub over outside of chicken. Tie chicken legs to tail; twist wing tips under back. Place chicken, breast side up, in pot. Sprinkle lightly with paprika. Cover tightly and place in unheated oven; set oven temperature at 400°. Bake for 1 hour or till chicken is tender. Season to taste. (*Or*, use a covered roaster instead of a claypot.) Makes 6 servings.

CHICKEN AND PEA PODS/247

1 whole medium chicken breast, skinned, boned, and halved lengthwise
3 tablespoons water
3 tablespoons soy sauce
½ teaspoon grated gingerroot
1 6-ounce package frozen pea pods
2 tablespoons sliced green onion
1 teaspoon butter *or* margarine

Place each chicken breast half between two pieces of clear plastic wrap. Pound with flat side of meat mallet to ¼-inch thickness. Remove plastic wrap; place chicken in shallow dish. Combine water, soy sauce, and gingerroot; pour over chicken. Cover and marinate in refrigerator for 1 hour. Drain chicken; reserve marinade.

Broil chicken 3 to 4 inches from heat for 2 to 3 minutes per side, brushing with reserved marinade occasionally. Cook pea pods and onion in boiling salted water according to directions on package. Toss cooked vegetables with the butter or margarine; turn onto a platter. Top with chicken pieces. Garnish with lemon slices, if desired. Makes 2 servings.

TOMATO-BROCCOLI CHICKEN/244

2 whole medium chicken breasts, skinned, boned, and halved lengthwise
¼ cup chopped onion
2 tablespoons butter *or* margarine
1 10-ounce package frozen cut broccoli, thawed
1 teaspoon lemon juice
¾ teaspoon salt
¼ teaspoon dried thyme, crushed
3 medium tomatoes, cut into wedges

Sprinkle chicken lightly with a little salt and pepper. Cut chicken into ½-inch-wide strips. In medium skillet cook chicken and onion in butter or margarine till chicken no longer is pink. Stir in broccoli, lemon juice, salt, thyme, and ⅛ teaspoon *pepper*. Cover; simmer 6 minutes. Add tomatoes. Simmer, covered, 3 to 4 minutes more. Makes 4 servings.

PLUM-SAUCED CHICKEN/236

- **1 2½- to 3-pound broiler-fryer chicken, cut up**
- **½ teaspoon salt**
- **¼ teaspoon pepper**
- **⅓ cup plum preserves**
- **¼ cup finely chopped onion**
- **2 tablespoons frozen orange juice concentrate, thawed**
- **1 tablespoon soy sauce**
- **1 teaspoon prepared mustard**
- **½ teaspoon ground ginger**
- **¼ cup dry white wine**
- **1 tablespoon cornstarch**
- **1 tablespoon cold water**
- **½ teaspoon instant chicken bouillon granules**
- **Few drops Kitchen Bouquet (optional)**

Remove skin from chicken pieces; season chicken with the salt and pepper. In large skillet combine preserves, onion, orange juice concentrate, soy sauce, mustard, and ginger. Simmer, uncovered, for 10 minutes. Stir in wine. Add chicken pieces; spoon plum mixture over chicken. Cover and simmer for 40 to 45 minutes or till chicken is tender; baste occasionally with plum mixture. Remove chicken to warm serving platter; keep warm.

Skim excess fat from pan juices. Measure 1 cup juices; return to skillet. Stir together cornstarch, cold water, and bouillon granules; add to pan juices. Cook and stir till thickened and bubbly. Stir in Kitchen Bouquet, if desired. Spoon some sauce atop chicken. Pass remaining sauce. Makes 6 servings.

CURRY-SAUCED CHICKEN/171

- **¾ cup water**
- **½ cup chopped apple**
- **2 tablespoons sliced green onion**
- **1 teaspoon instant chicken bouillon granules**
- **1 teaspoon curry powder**
- **1 small clove garlic, minced**
- **Dash pepper**
- **2 whole medium chicken breasts, skinned and halved lengthwise**
- **1 4-ounce can sliced mushrooms**
- **1 tablespoon cornstarch**

In 10-inch skillet combine water, apple, green onion, bouillon granules, curry powder, garlic, and pepper; bring to boiling. Add chicken; reduce heat. Cover and simmer for 25 to 30 minutes or till chicken is tender. Remove chicken to warm platter. Drain mushrooms, reserving ⅓ cup liquid. Combine ⅓ cup mushroom liquid and cornstarch; stir into pan juices. Cook and stir over medium heat till bubbly. Stir in the mushrooms. Spoon sauce over chicken. Makes 4 servings.

Microwave directions: In 2-quart nonmetal casserole combine water, apple, green onion, bouillon granules, curry powder, garlic, and pepper. Cook in countertop microwave oven on high power for 2 minutes. Add chicken pieces; micro-cook, covered, 12 to 15 minutes or till chicken is tender, rearranging chicken after 8 minutes. Remove chicken to platter. Drain mushrooms, reserving ⅓ cup liquid. Combine reserved mushroom liquid and cornstarch; stir into juices with mushrooms. Micro-cook for 3 minutes or till thickened and bubbly, stirring after each minute. Spoon sauce over chicken.

CHICKEN VERONIQUE/218

- **2 whole medium chicken breasts, skinned, boned, and halved lengthwise**
- **½ small lemon**
- **1 tablespoon butter *or* margarine**
- **⅓ cup dry white wine**
- **2 tablespoons water**
- **¼ teaspoon instant chicken bouillon granules**
- **Paprika**
- **1 tablespoon cold water**
- **2 teaspoons cornstarch**
- **¾ cup seedless green grapes, halved**
- **Lemon slices (optional)**

Rub chicken well with the lemon; sprinkle lightly with salt. In skillet brown chicken slowly in hot butter or margarine about 10 minutes, turning chicken pieces as necessary to brown evenly. Drain off fat. Add wine, 2 tablespoons water, and the chicken bouillon granules. Cover and simmer for 25 to 35 minutes or till chicken is tender, spooning wine mixture over chicken occasionally. Remove chicken to serving platter. Sprinkle with paprika; keep warm. Skim fat from pan juices. Measure juices, adding water if necessary to make ¾ cup. Return juices to pan. Stir 1 tablespoon cold water into cornstarch; stir into juices. Cook and stir over medium heat till mixture is thickened and bubbly. Add grapes and heat through. Spoon the grape sauce over chicken. Garnish with lemon slices, if desired. Makes 4 servings.

SAVORY SAUCED CHICKEN/163

1 small onion, sliced and separated into rings
1 tablespoon butter *or* **margarine**
• • •
1 cup vegetable juice cocktail
2 tablespoons snipped parsley
1 tablespoon cornstarch
¼ teaspoon dried marjoram, crushed
¼ teaspoon dried basil, crushed
• • •
2 whole small chicken breasts, skinned and halved lengthwise
2 tablespoons grated Parmesan cheese

In a saucepan cook onion in butter or margarine till onion is tender but not brown. Combine vegetable juice cocktail, snipped parsley, cornstarch, marjoram, and basil; stir into onion mixture. Cook and stir over medium heat till mixture is thickened and bubbly. Cook and stir 1 to 2 minutes more. Arrange chicken breasts in an 8x8x2-inch baking dish. Pour sauce mixture over chicken. Bake, covered with foil, in a 350° oven 50 to 55 minutes or till chicken is tender. Remove foil; sprinkle with Parmesan cheese. Bake 5 to 10 minutes more. Makes 4 servings.

VEGETABLE-STUFFED CHICKEN BREASTS/260

2 whole medium chicken breasts, skinned, boned, and halved lengthwise
2½ cups sliced fresh mushrooms
2 tablespoons sliced green onion
2 tablespoons finely chopped celery
¼ teaspoon dried thyme, crushed
1 tablespoon butter *or* **margarine**
1½ teaspoons lemon juice
¼ teaspoon salt
Dash pepper
1 medium tomato, peeled, seeded, and chopped
2 tablespoons butter *or* **margarine**
½ cup water
¾ teaspoon instant chicken bouillon granules
Skim milk
2 teaspoons cornstarch
Dash dried thyme, crushed
Dash salt
1 tablespoon dry white wine

Place each chicken breast half between two pieces of clear plastic wrap; working from center, pound with flat side of meat mallet to ⅛-inch thickness. Remove plastic wrap; season chicken with salt and pepper. Cook mushrooms, onion, celery, and ¼ teaspoon thyme in the 1 tablespoon butter or margarine till vegetables are tender and most of the liquid has evaporated. Remove from heat. Stir in lemon juice, the ¼ teaspoon salt, and pepper. Gently stir in tomato. Spoon some of the mixture onto each chicken piece. Fold in sides; roll up jelly-roll style. Secure with wooden picks.

In skillet slowly brown chicken on all sides in 2 tablespoons butter. Add water and bouillon granules. Cover; simmer for 20 minutes or till chicken is tender. Remove chicken; keep warm. Measure pan juices; add enough skim milk to measure ½ cup liquid. In screw-top jar combine milk mixture, cornstarch, dash thyme, and the dash salt. Cover and shake till combined. Pour into skillet. Cook and stir till bubbly. Stir in wine. To serve, spoon sauce over chicken. Makes 4 servings.

HERBED TOMATO CHICKEN/185

2 medium onions, sliced
2 cloves garlic, minced
3 whole medium chicken breasts, skinned and halved lengthwise
1 7½-ounce can tomatoes, cut up
½ cup tomato sauce
1 2½-ounce jar sliced mushrooms, drained
¼ cup chopped green pepper
1 teaspoon dried basil, crushed
1 teaspoon salt
1 bay leaf
¼ cup dry white wine

In skillet combine onions, garlic, and ½ cup *water.* Bring to boiling. Cover and simmer 10 minutes or till onion is tender. Drain. Add chicken to skillet. Combine *undrained* tomatoes, tomato sauce, mushrooms, green pepper, basil, salt, bay leaf, and dash *pepper.* Pour over chicken. Cover and simmer for 30 minutes. Stir in wine. Cook, uncovered, 15 minutes more. Remove bay leaf. Skim excess fat from juices. Transfer chicken and sauce to serving platter. Makes 6 servings.

CHICKEN IN WINE SAUCE / 267

½ cup chopped onion
2 tablespoons snipped parsley
1 clove garlic, minced
½ teaspoon dried marjoram, crushed
3 tablespoons butter *or* margarine
2 whole medium chicken breasts, skinned and halved lengthwise
• • •
⅔ cup tomato purée
⅓ cup dry red wine
⅓ cup water
½ teaspoon salt
⅛ teaspoon pepper
2 teaspoons cornstarch
1 tablespoon cold water
Snipped parsley

In heavy skillet cook onion, the 2 tablespoons parsley, garlic, and marjoram in *1 tablespoon* of the butter or margarine till onion is tender but not brown. Remove from skillet and set aside. Add the remaining 2 tablespoons butter or margarine to skillet; brown chicken on all sides.

Combine tomato purée, dry red wine, ⅓ cup water, salt, and pepper. Add to skillet along with the onion mixture. Cover and simmer for 45 minutes or till chicken is tender. Remove chicken to serving platter; keep warm. Spoon excess fat from sauce. Combine cornstarch and 1 tablespoon cold water; add to sauce in skillet. Cook and stir over medium heat till sauce is thickened and bubbly. Cook and stir 1 to 2 minutes more. To serve, pour sauce over chicken; sprinkle additional snipped parsley over all. Makes 4 servings.

LEMON CHICKEN BREASTS / 221

3 whole medium chicken breasts, skinned, boned, and halved lengthwise
2 cups chopped fresh mushrooms
¼ cup sliced green onion
1 tablespoon butter *or* margarine
½ cup skim milk
2 teaspoons cornstarch
¼ teaspoon salt
¼ teaspoon dried thyme, crushed
1 tablespoon snipped parsley
2 teaspoons lemon juice
2 tablespoons butter *or* margarine
½ cup water
1½ teaspoons instant chicken bouillon granules
1 teaspoon lemon juice
1½ teaspoons cornstarch
2 tablespoons cold water

Place each chicken breast half between two pieces of clear plastic wrap; working from center, pound with flat side of meat mallet to ⅛-inch thickness. Remove the plastic wrap.

In saucepan cook mushrooms and onion in 1 tablespoon butter or margarine till onion is tender and most of the liquid is evaporated. Combine milk, 2 teaspoons cornstarch, salt, thyme, and dash *pepper*. Add to mushroom mixture. Cook and stir till thickened and bubbly. Cook and stir 2 minutes more. Remove from heat; stir in parsley and 2 teaspoons lemon juice. Cool without stirring. Spoon some of the mixture on each chicken piece. Fold in sides and roll up jelly-roll style. Secure with wooden picks.

In skillet brown chicken rolls in 2 tablespoons butter. Add ½ cup water, bouillon granules, and 1 teaspoon lemon juice. Cover and simmer for 20 minutes or till chicken is tender. Remove chicken to serving platter; remove wooden picks. Keep chicken warm while preparing sauce.

Skim fat from skillet juices. Measure pan juices; if necessary, add water to equal ¾ cup liquid. Return to skillet.

Combine cornstarch and 2 tablespoons cold water. Add to juices; cook and stir till thickened and bubbly. Cook and stir 2 minutes more. Spoon sauce over chicken rolls. Makes 6 servings.

STIR-FRIED CHICKEN WITH ALMONDS / 357

1½ pounds chicken breasts, skinned and boned
⅓ cup chicken broth
2 tablespoons soy sauce
4 teaspoons cornstarch
2 tablespoons cooking oil
¼ cup sliced almonds
6 green onions, bias sliced into 1-inch pieces
1 6-ounce package frozen pea pods, thawed
2 cups sliced fresh mushrooms

Cut chicken into 1-inch pieces. Stir chicken broth and soy sauce into cornstarch; set the soy sauce-broth mixture aside.

In wok or skillet heat oil over high heat. Add almonds and stir-fry 1 minute or till just brown. Remove almonds. Add chicken and stir-fry 2 to 3 minutes or till done; remove chicken. Add green onion and pea pods and stir-fry 1 minute; remove vegetables. Add mushrooms and stir-fry 1 minute. Stir broth mixture; add to mushrooms. Cook and stir till bubbly. Stir in chicken and pea pod mixture. Cover; cook 1 minute. Stir in almonds. Makes 6 servings.

MANDARIN CHICKEN/282

1 whole large chicken breast, skinned and boned (1 pound)
2 tablespoons soy sauce
½ teaspoon grated gingerroot
1 tablespoon cooking oil
1 8-ounce can water chestnuts, drained and thinly sliced
¾ cup bias-sliced celery
1 tablespoon cooking oil
¼ cup water
1 tablespoon soy sauce
2 teaspoons cornstarch
¼ teaspoon instant chicken bouillon granules
1 orange, peeled and sectioned

Cut chicken into 1-inch pieces. Combine 2 tablespoons soy sauce and the gingerroot; add chicken. Let stand for 20 minutes. Heat the 1 tablespoon oil in wok or large skillet; add water chestnuts and celery. Stir-fry for 1 to 2 minutes or till celery is crisp-tender. Remove from wok or skillet. Heat remaining 1 tablespoon oil in wok; add chicken mixture and stir-fry for 2 to 3 minutes or till done. Return vegetables to wok. Combine water, 1 tablespoon soy sauce, cornstarch, and bouillon granules. Stir into wok. Cook and stir till bubbly. Add orange sections. Cover; cook for 1 minute more. Makes 3 servings.

Turkey-Fruit Salad; Garden Chicken Salad (see recipe, page 142)

TURKEY-FRUIT SALAD/238

8 cups torn spinach leaves
1 cup sliced celery
1 8-ounce can pineapple chunks (juice pack)
2 medium apples
1 orange, peeled and sectioned
½ pound cooked turkey, cut into strips
• • •
½ cup plain yogurt
2 tablespoons buttermilk
½ teaspoon celery seed
Dash bottled hot pepper sauce

In salad bowl combine spinach and celery. Drain pineapple, reserving juice. Core apples; cut into wedges. Dip apple wedges in reserved pineapple juice. Arrange pineapple chunks, apple wedges, orange sections, and turkey atop spinach. For dressing combine yogurt, buttermilk, celery seed, and hot pepper sauce. Pass dressing. Makes 4 servings.

TURKEY LOAF/184

1 beaten egg
1 2-ounce can mushroom stems and pieces, drained and chopped
½ cup shredded carrot
¼ cup orange juice
¼ cup fine dry bread crumbs
2 tablespoons snipped parsley
¾ teaspoon salt
¼ teaspoon poultry seasoning
Dash pepper
1 pound ground raw turkey

In bowl combine egg, mushrooms, carrot, orange juice, bread crumbs, parsley, salt, poultry seasoning, and pepper. Add ground raw turkey; mix well. Press evenly into a 9-inch pie plate. Bake in a 350° oven about 35 minutes or till done. Drain off any excess fat. Let stand 10 minutes; loosen edges and transfer to serving platter. Sprinkle with additional snipped parsley, if desired. Makes 6 servings.

TURKEY-BROCCOLI PILAF/267

2 cups water
2 teaspoons instant chicken bouillon granules
½ cup regular brown rice
¼ cup sliced green onion
1 small bay leaf
1 teaspoon dried thyme, crushed
⅛ teaspoon pepper
1 10-ounce package frozen cut broccoli
½ cup water
10 ounces cooked turkey, cut into strips (2 cups)
2 tablespoons slivered almonds, toasted

In saucepan bring 2 cups water to boiling; add chicken bouillon granules. Stir in *uncooked* brown rice, the green onion, bay leaf, thyme, and pepper. Reduce heat; cover and simmer 45 to 50 minutes or till rice is tender. Meanwhile, cook broccoli in the ½ cup water according to package directions *Do not drain.* Remove bay leaf. Stir turkey, almonds, and *undrained* broccoli into cooked rice mixture. Cover and simmer about 5 minutes more or till heated through. Makes 4 servings.

SPICY TURKEY DRUMSTICKS/259

If using frozen turkey legs, be sure to thaw them before you start cooking preparations—

2 fresh *or* frozen turkey legs (2 to 2½ pounds total)
1 7½-ounce can tomatoes, cut up
½ cup chopped onion
2 tablespoons chopped canned green chili peppers
2 tablespoons chopped pimiento
1 clove garlic, minced
¼ teaspoon Kitchen Bouquet
⅛ teaspoon ground red pepper
• • •
2 tablespoons cold water
2 teaspoons cornstarch

Remove skin from turkey legs. Place turkey legs in an 11x7x1½-inch baking pan. Season with salt and pepper. In small saucepan combine *undrained* tomatoes, onion, chili peppers, pimiento, garlic, Kitchen Bouquet, and red pepper. Bring to boiling; reduce heat and simmer 3 to 4 minutes or till onion is tender. Pour sauce over turkey legs in baking pan. Bake, covered, in a 375° oven for 1 to 1½ hours or till turkey is tender. Remove turkey legs to serving platter; keep warm. Skim fat from pan juices. Transfer juices to small saucepan. Combine cold water and cornstarch; stir into juices. Cook and stir till thickened and bubbly. Spoon some sauce over turkey legs; pass remainder. Makes 4 servings.

CHICKEN LIVERS TARRAGON/248

1 medium zucchini, thinly sliced
½ cup thinly sliced celery
½ cup chopped onion
1 tablespoon butter *or* margarine
1 pound chicken livers
¾ cup water
½ cup skim milk
1½ teaspoons instant beef bouillon granules
½ teaspoon dried tarragon, crushed
¼ teaspoon salt
Dash pepper
1 tablespoon cornstarch
1 tablespoon cold water

In 10-inch skillet cook zucchini, celery, and onion in butter or margarine till tender. Add chicken livers; cook about 5 minutes or till just browned. Stir in the ¾ cup water, the skim milk, bouillon granules, tarragon, salt, and pepper. Cover and simmer 5 minutes. Combine cornstarch and the 1 tablespoon cold water; stir into liver mixture. Cook and stir till mixture is thickened and bubbly. Cook and stir 1 to 2 minutes more. Makes 4 servings.

Microwave directions: In a 2-quart nonmetal casserole, cook zucchini, celery, and onion in butter or margarine in countertop microwave oven on high power about 2 minutes or till vegetables are tender. Add livers to onion mixture. Stir in cornstarch; mix in ¾ cup water, the skim milk, bouillon granules, tarragon, salt, and pepper. Omit the 1 tablespoon cold water. Micro-cook, covered, for 6 minutes or till livers are barely pink, stirring after 3 minutes.

TURKEY-VEGETABLE BAKE/142

1 cup chopped carrot
1 cup sliced celery
½ cup chopped onion
½ cup chopped green pepper
• • •
1½ cups chopped cooked turkey *or* chicken
1 4-ounce can sliced mushrooms, drained
½ teaspoon dried marjoram, crushed
¼ teaspoon ground sage
¼ teaspoon salt
Dash pepper
2 beaten eggs
½ cup skim milk
¼ cup shredded cheddar cheese (1 ounce)

In covered saucepan cook chopped carrot, sliced celery, chopped onion, and chopped green pepper in a small amount of boiling water for 10 minutes or till vegetables are tender. Drain.

In an 8x8x2-inch baking pan combine drained vegetable mixture, cooked turkey or chicken, drained mushrooms, marjoram, sage, salt, and pepper. In a bowl combine eggs and milk; pour over turkey mixture in baking pan. Sprinkle shredded cheddar cheese atop. Bake in a 325° oven 30 to 35 minutes or till set. Let stand 5 minutes before serving. Cut into squares. Makes 6 servings.

FISH & SEAFOOD MAIN DISHES

BAKED CURRIED FISH/184

See the tip on page 154 for types of fish to use in this recipe—

- 1½ **pounds fresh *or* frozen fish fillets**
- 2 **medium onions, thinly sliced**
- 1 **cup sliced celery**
- 1 **teaspoon curry powder**
- 1 **tablespoon butter *or* margarine**
- ¼ **cup skim milk**
- ¾ **teaspoon salt**

Thaw fish, if frozen. In small covered saucepan cook onion, celery, and curry powder in butter or margarine over medium heat 8 to 10 minutes or till onion is tender. Remove from heat. Stir in milk. Place fish in a lightly greased 12x7½x2-inch baking dish. Sprinkle with the salt. Spoon vegetables over fish. Bake, uncovered, in 350° oven for 25 minutes or till fish flakes easily when tested with a fork. Makes 6 servings.

POACHED HALIBUT WITH SPINACH/268

Pictured on pages 114 and 115—

- 1 **10-ounce package frozen chopped spinach**
- ¼ **teaspoon ground nutmeg**
- 4 **cups water**
- ⅓ **cup lemon juice**
- 1 **small onion, sliced**
- ¼ **cup chopped celery**
- ¼ **teaspoon salt**
- 4 **halibut steaks (about 1⅓ pounds total)**
- ¼ **cup grated Parmesan cheese**
- **Lemon wedges**

Cook spinach according to package directions. Drain well. Stir in nutmeg. In a 10-inch skillet combine water, lemon juice, onion, celery, salt, and ⅛ teaspoon *pepper.* Simmer 5 minutes. Add fish; simmer, covered, 5 to 10 minutes or till fish flakes easily when tested with a fork. Carefully remove fish to a 12x7½x2-inch baking dish or a broiler-proof platter. Spread spinach over each halibut steak. Sprinkle cheese atop each. Broil fish portions 4 to 5 inches from heat for 1 to 2 minutes. Garnish with lemon wedges. Makes 4 servings.

MARINATED SOLE/173

- 1 **pound fresh *or* frozen sole fillets**
- ½ **cup unsweetened pineapple juice**
- 2 **tablespoons snipped parsley**
- 1 **tablespoon lemon juice**
- 2 **teaspoons Worcestershire sauce**
- 1 **teaspoon minced dried onion**
- ½ **teaspoon dry mustard**
- ¼ **teaspoon salt**

Thaw fish, if frozen. Separate into fillets; place in plastic bag in bowl. Combine pineapple juice, parsley, lemon juice, Worcestershire sauce, minced dried onion, dry mustard, and salt. Pour over fish in bag. Marinate in refrigerator for 6 hours. Drain fish, reserving marinade. Place fillets on unheated rack of broiler pan. Turn under any thin edges. Broil 4 inches from heat for 4 to 5 minutes or till fish flakes easily when tested with a fork, brushing occasionally with the marinade. Makes 4 servings.

VEGETABLE-TOPPED HALIBUT STEAKS/272

- 1 **12-ounce package frozen halibut steaks**
- **Lemon juice**
- ½ **teaspoon salt**

• • •

- 2 **medium carrots, shredded (1 cup)**
- 2 **tablespoons sliced green onion**
- 2 **tablespoons snipped parsley**
- ½ **teaspoon dried marjoram, crushed**
- 1 **small tomato, cut into wedges and seeded**

Thaw fish. Place in a 10x6x2-inch baking dish; brush with a little lemon juice and sprinkle with the salt. Toss together carrot, onion, parsley, and marjoram; spoon atop fish. Top with tomato wedges. Bake, covered, in a 350° oven for 25 to 30 minutes or till fish flakes easily when tested with a fork. With a slotted spatula, carefully lift the halibut steaks and the vegetables to serving platter. Makes 2 servings.

Microwave directions: Arrange fish and vegetables as above in a nonmetal casserole. Cover with clear plastic wrap. Cook in a counter-top microwave oven on high power about 5 minutes or till fish flakes easily when tested with a fork; turn dish after 2½ minutes. With a slotted spatula, carefully lift the halibut steaks and the vegetables to a serving platter.

SOLE FLORENTINE/163

1 pound fresh *or* frozen sole fillets *or* other fish fillets
1 10-ounce package frozen leaf spinach
1 medium onion, sliced and separated into rings
¼ teaspoon salt
4 whole black peppercorns
½ cup chicken broth
2 tablespoons dry white wine
½ cup evaporated skimmed milk
1 tablespoon all-purpose flour
½ teaspoon dried dillweed
¼ teaspoon dried oregano, crushed

Thaw fish, if frozen. Cook spinach according to package directions; drain well. Set aside and keep warm.

Meanwhile, in 10-inch skillet layer fish fillets and onion. Sprinkle with salt; add peppercorns. Add chicken broth and wine; bring to boiling. Reduce heat. Cover skillet and simmer for 7 to 8 minutes or till fish flakes easily with a fork. Remove fish; keep warm.

Meanwhile, for sauce combine evaporated milk, flour, dillweed, and oregano; stir till smooth. Stir into mixture in skillet. Cook, stirring gently, over medium heat till thickened and bubbly. Cook and stir 1 to 2 minutes more. Remove peppercorns. Serve fish and sauce over cooked spinach. Garnish with lemon peel curls and fresh dillweed, if desired. Makes 4 servings.

Sole Florentine

BAKED RED SNAPPER/162

2 pounds fresh *or* frozen red snapper fillets *or* other fish fillets
2 tablespoons lemon juice
¾ cup vegetable juice cocktail
½ cup chopped celery
½ cup chopped onion
¼ cup chopped green pepper

Thaw fish, if frozen. Place fish in greased baking pan. Season with salt and pepper. Drizzle lemon juice over fish. Bake fish in a 350° oven for 10 minutes. Meanwhile, in saucepan combine remaining ingredients. Simmer, uncovered, 10 minutes. Remove fish from oven. Drain off all excess liquid. Pour simmered vegetable sauce over fish. Return fish to oven; bake 15 minutes more or till fish flakes easily when tested with a fork, basting with vegetable sauce occasionally. Makes 6 servings.

GRAPEFRUIT-SOLE SALAD/178

3 cups shredded lettuce
½ pound sole fillets, cooked, flaked, and chilled
2 grapefruits, peeled and sectioned
½ cup chopped celery
½ cup Tomato Salad Dressing (see recipe, page 184)

Arrange lettuce in bottom of a salad bowl. Place cooked fish, grapefruit sections, and celery atop. Drizzle the Tomato Salad Dressing over all. Serve the salad immediately. Makes 3 servings.

VEGETABLE-SAUCED FISH FILLETS/193

4 fresh *or* frozen fish fillets (1 pound)
1 medium tomato, peeled, seeded, and chopped
3 tablespoons finely chopped celery
2 tablespoons snipped parsley
2 tablespoons thinly sliced green onion
½ teaspoon salt
¼ teaspoon dried rosemary, crushed
2 teaspoons butter *or* margarine
¼ cup water
¼ cup dry white wine
¼ teaspoon Worcestershire sauce
1 tablespoon cold water
2 teaspoons cornstarch

Thaw fish, if frozen. Arrange fish fillets in a single layer in a 10-inch skillet. Combine chopped tomato, celery, parsley, green onion, salt, and rosemary. Top fillets with the tomato mixture. Dot each fillet with ½ teaspoon of the butter or margarine. Combine ¼ cup water, wine, and Worcestershire sauce; pour into skillet. Cover and simmer for 10 to 12 minutes or till fish flakes easily when tested with a fork. Remove fish to serving platter; keep warm.

Strain pan juices; measure ¾ cup juices. Combine 1 tablespoon cold water and the cornstarch; stir into skillet with the reserved ¾ cup pan juices. Cook and stir over medium heat till thickened and bubbly. Cook 1 minute more. Spoon sauce over fish. Serve immediately. Makes 4 servings.

COOKING FISH

Whether broiled, baked, steamed, or poached, fish is an excellent quick-cooking, low-caloried main dish. To determine which cooking method to use, check the fat content of the fish.

"Fat" fish have oil throughout the flesh; "lean" fish have a drier flesh. Fat fish can be broiled or baked because their fat helps keep them from drying out during cooking. Lean fish generally are steamed or poached to keep the flesh moist. However, lean fish can be baked or broiled if basted with a little melted butter or margarine.

Fat fish include lake trout, whitefish, eel, mackerel, salmon, and tuna. Lean fish include catfish, perch, cod, flounder, sole, haddock, and red snapper.

The size of the fish pieces also helps determine the cooking method. Thin fillets are best broiled, whereas thicker steaks and pan-dressed fish are better when they are poached or baked.

During cooking, doneness is indicated by a change in flesh color from a translucent pinkish white to an opaque white. To check for doneness, place fork tines into the fish at a 45-degree angle and twist the fork. If the fish resists flaking and still looks translucent, it is not done. At the just-right stage, the fish will flake apart easily when the fork is twisted. It also will have a milky white color. If cooked too long, fish becomes mealy, tough, and dry.

FISH AND VEGETABLE BAKE/201

2 medium potatoes, peeled and cubed
1 large carrot, sliced ¼ inch thick
1 small onion, sliced ¼ inch thick
2 tablespoons butter *or* margarine, melted
1 teaspoon dried dillweed
1 teaspoon dried basil, crushed
¼ teaspoon salt
¼ teaspoon pepper
1 16-ounce package frozen fish fillets, thawed and separated
1 small green pepper, cut into rings
2 teaspoons lemon juice
1 medium tomato, coarsely chopped

In an 8x8x2-inch baking dish place potatoes, carrot, and onion. Combine melted butter or margarine, dillweed, basil, salt, and pepper; spoon *half* of the butter mixture atop vegetables. Cover and bake in a 425° oven for 25 minutes. Place fish fillets, skin side down, atop vegetables; add green pepper rings. Combine lemon juice and remaining butter mixture; spoon over fish. Cover; bake about 15 minutes or till fish flakes easily with fork and vegetables are tender. Uncover; add chopped tomato. Return to oven; bake about 5 minutes more or till tomato is hot. Makes 4 servings.

SALMON-STUFFED TOMATOES/273

1 cup dairy sour cream
¼ cup chopped cucumber
¼ cup skim milk
1 tablespoon lemon juice
2 teaspoons snipped fresh dillweed *or* ½ teaspoon dried dillweed
¼ teaspoon salt
3 fresh artichokes *or* one 9-ounce package frozen artichoke hearts
1 tablespoon lemon juice
1 15½-ounce can salmon, drained and broken into chunks
1 cup sliced fresh mushrooms
3 hard-cooked eggs, chopped
¼ teaspoon salt
Dash pepper
6 large tomatoes, chilled

For dressing, combine sour cream, cucumber, milk, 1 tablespoon lemon juice, dillweed, and ¼ teaspoon salt. Chill.

Add fresh whole artichokes to large amount of boiling salted water; add 1 tablespoon lemon juice. Cover; reduce heat and simmer about 20 to 30 minutes or till stem is tender and leaf pulls easily from the base. Drain and cool. Pull off outer leaves; scoop out choke. Chop remaining heart into pieces. (*Or,* cook frozen artichoke hearts according to package directions; drain and chop. Omit the 1 tablespoon lemon juice.) In mixing bowl combine chopped artichoke hearts, salmon, mushrooms, egg, ¼ teaspoon salt, and pepper; chill the salmon mixture.

Starting at top, and cutting to, but not through base of tomato, cut each tomato into quarters. Place on serving plate and spread wedges open; fill with salmon mixture. Spoon dressing over. Garnish with fresh dill, if desired. Makes 6 servings.

SALMON-CAULIFLOWER CASSEROLE / 222

1 10-ounce package frozen cauliflower
¼ cup chopped onion
1 tablespoon butter *or* margarine
1 10¾-ounce can condensed cream of celery soup
1 4-ounce can chopped mushrooms, drained
½ cup grated Parmesan cheese
1 tablespoon lemon juice
½ teaspoon dried dillweed
Dash pepper
1 7¾-ounce can pink salmon, drained and broken into chunks
Lemon twist

In covered saucepan cook cauliflower in a small amount of boiling salted water for 3 minutes. Drain; cut cauliflower into small pieces. Set aside. In saucepan cook onion in butter till tender. Remove from heat. Stir in condensed soup, mushrooms, *half* of the Parmesan cheese, the lemon juice, dillweed, and pepper. Fold in salmon and cauliflower. Turn mixture into a 1-quart casserole. Sprinkle remaining cheese atop. Bake, uncovered, in a 350° oven for 25 to 30 minutes or till heated through. Garnish with lemon twist. Makes 4 servings.

Microwave directions: Place unwrapped package of cauliflower atop paper toweling in counter-top microwave oven. Micro-cook on high power for 3 to 4 minutes. Cut cauliflower into small pieces. In a 1-quart nonmetal casserole micro-cook onion in butter, uncovered, 2 minutes or till onion is tender. Stir in condensed soup, mushrooms, *half* of the cheese, the lemon juice, dillweed, and pepper. Stir in salmon and cauliflower. Micro-cook, uncovered, for 3 minutes; stir mixture. Micro-cook 2 to 3 minutes more or till heated through. Stir; sprinkle with remaining cheese and with *paprika.*

TUNA TACOS / 312

2 6½-ounce cans tuna (water pack), drained and flaked
½ cup chopped celery
2 tablespoons sliced green onion
⅛ teaspoon garlic powder
5 drops bottled hot pepper sauce
¼ cup low-calorie French salad dressing *or* reduced-calorie cucumber salad dressing
12 taco shells
1½ cups chopped tomato
1½ cups shredded lettuce
¾ cup shredded cheddar cheese (3 ounces)
Taco sauce

In medium bowl combine tuna, celery, green onion, garlic powder, and hot pepper sauce; mix well. Stir in desired low-calorie or reduced-calorie salad dressing.

Spoon tuna mixture into taco shells; top with tomato, lettuce, and cheese. Pass taco sauce. Makes 6 servings.

TUNA-ZUCCHINI BAKE / 160

A good recipe to remember when zucchini are abundant—

5 cups sliced zucchini
½ cup sliced fresh mushrooms
¼ cup chopped onion
¼ cup chopped green pepper
1 10¾-ounce can condensed cream of celery soup
1 tablespoon cornstarch
1½ cups dry cottage cheese
1 6½-ounce can tuna (water pack), drained and flaked
¾ teaspoon dried dillweed
¼ teaspoon garlic powder
¾ cup shredded mozzarella cheese (3 ounces)
2 tablespoons grated Parmesan cheese
Paprika

In large saucepan cook zucchini, mushrooms, onion, and green pepper in small amount of boiling water 4 to 5 minutes or just till crisp-tender. Drain well and set aside. In same saucepan combine soup and cornstarch; cook and tir till thickened and bubbly. Cook and stir 1 to 2 minutes more. Remove from heat. Gently stir in cottage cheese, tuna, dillweed, garlic powder, and the cooked vegetables. Turn into a 12x7½x2-inch baking dish. Sprinkle with mozzarella, Parmesan, and paprika. Bake, uncovered, in a 375° oven 20 to 25 minutes or till heated through. Let stand 10 minutes before serving. Makes 8 servings.

RICE-VEGETABLE STUFFED FISH / 305

1 1½-pound fresh *or* frozen pan-dressed white-fleshed fish (with head and tail)
½ cup quick-cooking rice
1 4-ounce can sliced mushrooms, drained
½ cup sliced celery
½ cup thinly sliced carrot
¼ cup sliced green onion
2 tablespoons butter *or* margarine
1 tablespoon snipped parsley
1 tablespoon lemon juice
¾ teaspoon salt
½ teaspoon dried marjoram, crushed
¼ teaspoon pepper
2 teaspoons butter *or* margarine, melted
1 teaspoon lemon juice

Thaw fish, if frozen. Prepare rice according to package directions, *except* omit the butter or margarine. In saucepan cook mushrooms, celery, carrot, and onion in the 2 tablespoons butter till vegetables are tender. Stir in parsley, 1 tablespoon lemon juice, ¾ teaspoon salt, marjoram, and pepper. Stir in the cooked rice.

Sprinkle fish cavity with salt. Spoon rice-vegetable mixture into fish. Skewer fish closed; place in a greased shallow baking pan. Combine the 2 teaspoons melted butter or margarine and 1 teaspoon lemon juice; brush over fish. Bake, uncovered, in a 350° oven about 25 minutes or till fish flakes easily when tested with a fork. Transfer fish and stuffing to platter. Serves 4.

Rice-Vegetable Stuffed Fish

MARINATED TUNA AND VEGETABLES / 245

2 large carrots, cut into 2-inch-long julienne strips
½ small head cauliflower, broken into flowerets (1½ cups)
1 10-ounce package frozen peas
½ cup thinly sliced celery
¼ cup sliced green onion
1 6½-ounce can tuna (water pack), well drained
¾ cup Tomato Salad Dressing (see recipe, page 184)

Cook carrots and cauliflower together in a small amount of boiling salted water for 10 minutes. Add peas. Cook 5 minutes more or till all vegetables are crisp-tender. Drain. In bowl combine cooked vegetables, celery, and green onion. Add tuna and Tomato Salad Dressing; toss. Cover and chill the mixture before serving. Serves 3.

MAIN-DISH TUNA TOSS / 167

½ cup plain yogurt
3 tablespoons chili sauce
Skim milk
8 cups torn salad greens
1 6½-ounce can tuna (water pack), drained
2 hard-cooked eggs, sliced
1 small red onion, sliced and separated into rings
½ cup sliced pimiento-stuffed olives
3 tablespoons chopped canned green chili peppers

For dressing, combine yogurt and chili sauce. Add a little skim milk if necessary to make desired consistency. Chill. In salad bowl combine torn salad greens, tuna, hard-cooked egg slices, onion, olives, and chili peppers. Pour dressing over all; toss to coat. Makes 4 servings.

SHRIMP JAMBALAYA / 284

½ cup chopped onion
¼ cup chopped green pepper
1 clove garlic, minced
2 tablespoons butter *or* margarine
2 tablespoons all-purpose flour
1 16-ounce can stewed tomatoes
1 cup cubed fully cooked ham
½ cup water
2 bay leaves
½ teaspoon dried thyme, crushed
¼ teaspoon salt
¼ teaspoon dried basil, crushed
¼ teaspoon ground red pepper
Dash pepper
1 cup quick-cooking rice
1 pound frozen shelled medium shrimp

In saucepan cook onion, green pepper, and garlic in butter or margarine till tender. Stir in flour, blending well. Stir in *undrained* tomatoes, ham, water, bay leaves, thyme, salt, basil, red pepper, and pepper. Stir in *uncooked* rice and shrimp. Bring to boiling; reduce heat. Cover and cook over medium heat, stirring frequently, for 10 to 15 minutes or till rice and shrimp are done. Remove bay leaves. Serve in bowls. Makes 6 servings.

CLEANING SHRIMP

To shell shrimp, open the shell lengthwise down the body. Hold the shrimp in one hand and carefully peel back the shell starting with the head end. Leave the last section of the shell and tail intact. You can either cut the body portion of the shell off, leaving the tail shell in place, or gently pull on the tail portion of the shell and remove the entire shell.

Remove the sandy black vein in shrimp by making a shallow slit with a sharp knife along the back of the shrimp. Look for the vein that appears as a dark line running down the center of the back. If it is present, use the tip of the knife to scrape it out and discard it. Some shrimp may be already deveined when purchased.

WILD RICE SHRIMP CREOLE/229

1 pound fresh *or* frozen shrimp in shells
½ cup chopped onion
⅓ cup chopped green pepper
2 tablespoons butter *or* margarine
1 28-ounce can tomatoes, cut up
1¾ cups water
¼ teaspoon garlic salt
¼ teaspoon dried rosemary, crushed
¼ teaspoon paprika
1 6-ounce package regular long grain and wild rice mix
Bottled hot pepper sauce

Thaw shrimp, if frozen. Shell and devein shrimp. In 3-quart saucepan cook onion and green pepper in butter about 5 minutes or till tender. Add *undrained* tomatoes, next 4 ingredients, ½ teaspoon *salt,* and ¼ teaspoon *pepper.* Stir in *both* packets from rice mix. Cover; simmer 20 minutes. Add shrimp. Cover; simmer 10 minutes. Pass pepper sauce. Serves 6.

SHRIMP KABOBS/169

1 pound fresh *or* frozen large shrimp in shells
1 8-ounce can pineapple slices (juice pack)
3 tablespoons lemon juice
2 teaspoons cooking oil
½ teaspoon dry mustard
¼ teaspoon pepper
Few dashes bottled hot pepper sauce
8 cherry tomatoes

Thaw shrimp, if frozen. Shell and devein shrimp. Drain pineapple, reserving juice. Halve pineapple slices. Combine reserved pineapple juice with next 5 ingredients and ½ teaspoon *salt;* pour over shrimp. Cover; refrigerate 2 hours, spooning marinade over shrimp occasionally. Drain shrimp; reserve marinade. On 4 skewers alternate shrimp and pineapple slices. Broil 4 inches from heat for 4 minutes; brush occasionally with marinade. Turn kabobs; put two tomatoes on end of each skewer. Broil about 4 minutes more, brushing with marinade. Makes 4 servings.

SHRIMP THERMIDOR BAKE/257

¼ cup chopped onion
¼ cup chopped celery
1 11-ounce can condensed cheddar cheese soup
½ cup skim milk
2 tablespoons dry sherry
¾ pound fresh *or* frozen shelled shrimp, cooked
2 tablespoons snipped parsley
Dash bottled hot pepper sauce
¾ cup soft bread crumbs
1 tablespoon butter *or* margarine, melted
Dash paprika

In a covered saucepan cook onion and celery in a small amount of water for 5 minutes; drain. Stir soup, milk, and sherry into saucepan with vegetables. Stir in shrimp, parsley, and hot pepper sauce. Spoon mixture into four individual baking shells. Toss together the bread crumbs, melted butter or margarine, and paprika. Sprinkle atop each shell. Bake in a 375° oven for 15 to 20 minutes. Makes 4 servings.

SHRIMP AND PEPPER STIR-FRY / 226

Use either a wok or a large skillet to prepare this Oriental-style main dish—

¾ pound fresh *or* frozen shelled shrimp
½ teaspoon instant chicken bouillon granules
⅓ cup hot water
• • •
1 teaspoon cornstarch
⅛ teaspoon pepper
1 tablespoon lemon juice
2 teaspoons soy sauce
• • •
2 tablespoons cooking oil
½ cup bias-sliced green onions
1 large green pepper, cut into 1-inch pieces
1⅓ cups hot cooked rice

Thaw shrimp, if frozen. (Halve large shrimp lengthwise.) Dissolve chicken bouillon granules in the hot water. Combine cornstarch and pepper; stir in lemon juice and soy sauce. Stir in bouillon. Set aside.

Heat wok or large skillet over high heat; add oil. Add green onion and green pepper; stir-fry 2 to 3 minutes. Remove from wok. Add shrimp; stir-fry 2 to 4 minutes or till done. Stir in lemon juice mixture; cook till thickened and bubbly. Add the green onion and green pepper. Cover and cook the mixture for 1 minute. Serve with the hot cooked rice. Makes 4 servings.

SHRIMP STACK-UPS / 176

Pictured on pages 114 and 115—

2 4½-ounce cans shrimp, drained and chopped
2 hard-cooked eggs
2 tablespoons chopped celery
2 tablespoons chopped sweet pickle
2 tablespoons thinly sliced green onion
• • •
½ cup plain yogurt
¼ cup cream-style cottage cheese
1 tablespoon lemon juice
Dash pepper
Lettuce leaves
12 tomato slices
6 slices bread, toasted and quartered

Rinse shrimp. Chop hard-cooked eggs, reserving one of the egg yolks. Cover and chill the reserved yolk. In a small bowl combine the chopped shrimp, chopped eggs, celery, sweet pickle, and green onion.

In a bowl stir together the yogurt, cottage cheese, lemon juice, and pepper. Add to shrimp mixture. Mix lightly and chill the mixture.

To serve, on 6 individual lettuce-lined plates place two tomato slices. Spoon about ½ cup of the shrimp mixture atop tomato slices on each plate. Sieve the reserved egg yolk; sprinkle some atop each mound of shrimp. Accompany with toast quarters. Makes 6 servings.

SPICY SHRIMP SKILLET / 209

This quick-cooking shrimp dish is one from southern India—

1 pound fresh *or* frozen shrimp in shells
2 tablespoons cooking oil
2 cups chopped onion
2 cloves garlic, minced
1 teaspoon grated gingerroot
⅛ teaspoon ground red pepper
1 bay leaf
1 tablespoon water
½ teaspoon ground coriander
• • •
½ of a 9-ounce package frozen cut green beans, cooked and drained
2 tablespoons vinegar
½ teaspoon salt

Thaw shrimp, if frozen. Shell and devein shrimp. Heat the cooking oil in a 10-inch skillet. Add chopped onion, minced garlic, gingerroot, red pepper, and bay leaf; cook and stir 3 to 5 minutes. Add the 1 tablespoon water and the coriander. Cook and stir 3 to 5 minutes more. (Add more water by teaspoons, if needed, to keep the spice mixture moist.)

Add the shelled and deveined shrimp, cooked and drained green beans, vinegar, and salt to the mixture in the skillet. Cook and stir the mixture for 5 minutes or till the shrimp is just tender. Remove and discard the bay leaf before serving the shrimp mixture. Makes 4 servings.

SESAME-SKEWERED SCALLOPS/177

- **1 pound fresh *or* frozen scallops**
- **¼ cup dry sherry**
- **2 tablespoons cooking oil**
- **1 tablespoon sesame seed, toasted and crushed**
- **1 teaspoon grated onion**
- **1 clove garlic, minced**
- **½ teaspoon salt**
- **⅛ teaspoon pepper**

• • •

- **1 8-ounce can pineapple chunks (juice pack), drained**
- **2 medium green peppers, cut into 1-inch pieces**
- **12 cherry tomatoes**

Thaw scallops, if frozen. Place in a plastic bag. For marinade, combine sherry, cooking oil, sesame seed, onion, garlic, salt, and pepper. Pour marinade over scallops. Close bag. Marinate in the refrigerator for several hours, turning bag occasionally. Drain, reserving marinade. Thread scallops on 6 skewers, alternating them with pineapple and green pepper. Place skewers in a 15x10x1-inch baking pan. Pour remaining marinade over skewers. Bake in a 425° oven for 10 to 12 minutes or till scallops are tender, turning skewers once or twice during the cooking time. Thread tomatoes on ends of skewers. Bake 5 minutes more. Makes 6 servings.

ORIENTAL SCALLOPS/120

- **¾ pound fresh *or* frozen scallops**
- **2 tablespoons soy sauce**
- **1 tablespoon lemon juice**
- **½ teaspoon ground ginger**
- **¼ teaspoon dry mustard**
- **8 cherry tomatoes**
- **1 medium green pepper, cut into 1-inch squares**

Thaw scallops, if frozen. Place in a shallow glass dish. Combine soy sauce, lemon juice, ginger, and dry mustard; pour over scallops. Cover; let stand at room temperature 1 hour. Drain, reserving marinade. On 4 skewers, alternate scallops, tomatoes, and green pepper. Place on unheated rack of broiler pan. Broil 5 inches from heat for 7 to 8 minutes per side, basting occasionally with marinade. Makes 4 servings.

NEWBURG-STYLE CRAB/278

- **1 tablespoon butter *or* margarine**
- **1 tablespoon cornstarch**
- **¼ teaspoon salt**
- **1¼ cups skim milk**
- **2 beaten egg yolks**
- **1 6-ounce package frozen crab meat, thawed**
- **½ of a 10-ounce package frozen peas, cooked and drained**
- **3 tablespoons dry white wine**
- **2 teaspoons lemon juice**
- **6 Whole Wheat Biscuit Crackers (see recipe, page 224)**

Melt butter or margarine; stir in cornstarch and salt. Add milk all at once. Cook and stir till bubbly. Cook and stir 2 minutes more. Stir *half* of the hot mixture into yolks. Return to hot mixture in saucepan. Cook and stir till bubbly. Add crab and peas; heat through. Stir in wine and lemon juice. Serve over Whole Wheat Biscuit Crackers. Makes 3 servings.

CREAMED CRAB WITH TOMATO/280

- **1 cup sliced fresh mushrooms**
- **½ cup sliced green onion**
- **¼ cup finely chopped celery**
- **1 tablespoon butter *or* margarine**
- **1¾ cups skim milk**
- **2 tablespoons cornstarch**
- **½ teaspoon salt**
- **½ teaspoon dried thyme, crushed**
- **¼ teaspoon pepper**

• • •

- **1 cup shredded process Swiss cheese (4 ounces)**
- **1 7-ounce can crab meat, drained, flaked, and cartilage removed**
- **1 medium tomato, peeled, seeded, and chopped**
- **2 slices bread, toasted and quartered**

In saucepan cook mushrooms, onion, and celery in butter or margarine till onion is tender. Stir together milk, cornstarch, salt, thyme, and pepper. Add to onion mixture all at once. Cook and stir till thickened and bubbly. Stir in Swiss cheese till melted. Carefully stir in crab and chopped tomato. Heat through. Serve over toast quarters. Makes 4 servings.

EGG & CHEESE MAIN DISHES

VEGETABLE-FILLED OMELET/246

Pictured on pages 114 and 115—

1 medium zucchini, thinly sliced
½ cup sliced fresh mushrooms
¼ cup sliced green onion
¼ cup chopped green pepper
1 7½-ounce can tomatoes, cut up
½ teaspoon dried basil, crushed
½ teaspoon salt
¼ teaspoon sugar
1 tablespoon cold water
2 teaspoons cornstarch
8 eggs
¼ cup water
½ teaspoon salt
⅛ teaspoon pepper
2 tablespoons butter *or* margarine

For filling, in saucepan cook zucchini, mushrooms, green onion, and green pepper in a small amount of boiling salted water about 5 minutes or till vegetables are crisp-tender. Drain well. Add *undrained* tomatoes, basil, ½ teaspoon salt, and sugar. Bring to boiling; reduce heat. Combine the 1 tablespoon cold water and cornstarch; add to tomato mixture. Cook and stir till thickened and bubbly. Keep filling warm while preparing omelets.

To make omelets, beat together eggs, water, ½ teaspoon salt, and the pepper till blended but not frothy. In a 6- or 8-inch skillet with flared sides heat ¼ of the butter or margarine till it sizzles and browns slightly. (Use less butter for pan with nonstick surface.) Lift and tilt the pan to coat the sides. Add ¼ of the egg mixture (about ½ cup); cook over medium heat. As eggs set, run spatula around edge, lifting eggs to allow uncooked portion to flow underneath. When eggs are set but still shiny, remove from heat. Spoon ¼ of the filling mixture (about ⅓ cup) across center. Fold ⅓ of omelet over center. Overlap remaining third atop filling. Slide omelet out onto hot serving plate. Keep warm. Repeat to make 3 more omelets. Makes 4 servings.

CHEESE-CAULIFLOWER CHOWDER/266

½ cup chopped onion
1¼ cups water
1 10-ounce package frozen cauliflower
1 4-ounce can sliced mushrooms
2 teaspoons instant chicken bouillon granules
½ teaspoon dry mustard
¾ cup skim milk
4 teaspoons cornstarch
2 cups shredded American cheese (8 ounces)
2 tablespoons chopped pimiento

In saucepan cook onion in water till tender. Add cauliflower, *undrained* mushrooms, bouillon granules, and dry mustard. Bring to boiling. Reduce heat; cover and simmer the vegetable mixture about 8 minutes or till cauliflower is just tender.

In screw-top jar combine milk and cornstarch; shake well. Stir into hot vegetable mixture. Cook and stir over medium heat till thickened and bubbly. Stir in shredded cheese and pimiento. Heat through, stirring to melt cheese. Makes 4 servings.

CHEESE SOUFFLÉ/282

4 eggs
¼ cup sliced green onion
1 clove garlic, minced
1 tablespoon butter *or* margarine
2 tablespoons cornstarch
½ teaspoon dried basil, crushed
¼ teaspoon salt
Dash ground red pepper
¾ cup skim milk
1¼ cups shredded sharp cheddar cheese (5 ounces)

Place a buttered foil collar on an ungreased 1½-quart soufflé dish, extending 2 inches above dish. Secure the foil strip using tape or a piece of string.

Separate the eggs; set aside. In a heavy saucepan cook onion and garlic in butter or margarine till onion is tender. Stir in cornstarch, basil, salt, and red pepper. Add the milk all at once; cook and stir over medium heat till thickened and bubbly. Add cheese; stir till melted. Remove from heat; set aside. In small mixer bowl beat the egg yolks till thick and lemon-colored (about 4 minutes). Slowly add the cheese mixture to egg yolks, stirring constantly. Wash beaters thoroughly before beating egg whites.

Using clean beaters and large mixer bowl, beat egg whites till stiff peaks form. Gradually pour the egg yolk mixture over beaten whites; fold to blend. Pour into prepared soufflé dish.

For a top hat that puffs in the oven, use a knife to trace a 1-inch-deep circle through the mixture about 1 inch from edge. Bake in a 300° oven about 1 hour or till knife inserted near center comes out clean. Serve immediately by breaking apart with two forks. Makes 4 servings.

POACHED EGGS WITH CHEESE SAUCE/197

- **½ cup skim milk**
- **½ teaspoon cornstarch**
- **¼ teaspoon salt**
- **¼ teaspoon dry mustard**
- **1 beaten egg yolk**
- **½ cup shredded American cheese (2 ounces)**
- **1 2-ounce can mushroom stems and pieces, drained and chopped**
- **4 eggs**
- **2 slices whole wheat bread, toasted and quartered**

In saucepan combine milk, cornstarch, salt, and dry mustard. Cook and stir over medium heat till thickened and bubbly. Cook and stir 2 minutes more. Stir *half* of the hot mixture into the beaten yolk; return all to saucepan. Add cheese and mushrooms. Stir over low heat 2 to 3 minutes or till thickened and cheese is melted. Keep sauce warm.

To poach eggs, lightly grease a 10-inch skillet. Heat about 1½-inches of water in skillet to boiling. Reduce heat to simmer. Break one egg into a sauce dish. Carefully slide egg into water, holding lip of dish as close to water as possible. Repeat with remaining eggs so each has about ¼ of the space. Simmer, uncovered, over low heat for 3 to 5 minutes or till eggs are cooked to desired doneness. During cooking, smooth the edges of eggs by using a spoon to gently pull away any trailing strings of egg white. Lift eggs out of water using a slotted spoon. Place 1 egg atop 2 toast quarters. Spoon some cheese sauce over each. Makes 4 servings.

SPICY POACHED EGG STACKS/271

- **1 teaspoon minced dried onion**
- **1 6-ounce can vegetable juice cocktail (⅔ cup)**
- **2 teaspoons cornstarch**
- **¼ teaspoon dried marjoram, crushed**
- **Dash salt**
- **Dash bottled hot pepper sauce**
- **4 slices Canadian-style bacon, cut ¼ inch thick**
- **4 eggs**
- **2 English muffins, split and toasted**

In saucepan soften onion in the vegetable juice cocktail for 5 minutes. Stir in cornstarch. Add marjoram, salt, and hot pepper sauce. Cook and stir till mixture is thickened and bubbly. Keep sauce warm.

In skillet heat Canadian-style bacon over medium heat about 5 minutes. Keep the Canadian-style bacon warm.

Lightly grease a 10-inch skillet. Heat about 1½ inches of water in skillet to boiling. Reduce heat to simmer. Break one egg into sauce dish. Carefully slide egg into water. Repeat with remaining eggs. Simmer, uncovered, over low heat for 3 to 5 minutes or till eggs are cooked to desired doneness. Do not let water boil. Smooth edges of eggs during cooking by using a spoon to gently pull away any trailing strings of egg white. When eggs are cooked to desired doneness, remove with slotted spoon.

Place a slice of Canadian-style bacon atop each English muffin half. Top each with a poached egg. Spoon on vegetable sauce. Serve immediately. Makes 4 servings.

TACO SCRAMBLED EGGS/287

- **6 beaten eggs**
- **½ cup *reconstituted* nonfat dry milk**
- **½ cup shredded cheddar cheese (2 ounces)**
- **½ teaspoon salt**
- **Few dashes bottled hot pepper sauce**
- **½ cup chopped onion**
- **¼ cup chopped canned green chili peppers**
- **2 tablespoons butter *or* margarine**
- **2 medium tomatoes, peeled, seeded, and chopped**
- **Shredded lettuce (optional)**
- **⅔ cup plain yogurt**
- **2 teaspoons chili powder**

In bowl combine eggs, milk, cheese, salt, and hot pepper sauce. In skillet cook onion and green chili peppers in butter or margarine till onion is tender but not brown. Add the egg mixture. Cook without stirring till egg mixture begins to set on bottom and around edges. Lift and fold the partially cooked eggs with a spatula so uncooked portion flows underneath. Continue cooking 5 to 8 minutes or till eggs are cooked throughout but still glossy and moist. Add the chopped tomato. Cover and cook 1 minute. Serve eggs on shredded lettuce, if desired. Combine yogurt and chili powder; pass to dollop atop eggs and lettuce. Serve eggs immediately. Makes 4 servings.

Spicy Poached Egg Stacks; Taco Scrambled Eggs

BROCCOLI-YOGURT OMELET/237

½ of a 10-ounce package frozen chopped broccoli *or* 1 cup chopped fresh broccoli
¼ cup sliced green onion
⅓ cup plain yogurt
1 teaspoon cornstarch
¼ teaspoon dried basil, crushed
Dash pepper
5 eggs
2 tablespoons water
½ teaspoon salt
⅛ teaspoon pepper
2 tablespoons butter *or* margarine

In saucepan combine broccoli and onion. Cook according to broccoli package directions. (*Or*, cook fresh broccoli and onion in a small amount of boiling salted water about 10 minutes or till tender.) Drain broccoli and onion thoroughly. In saucepan combine yogurt, cornstarch, basil, and dash pepper. Stir in cooked broccoli. Heat through stirring constantly just till bubbly; keep warm.

For omelets beat together eggs, 2 tablespoons water, salt, and ⅛ teaspoon pepper. In 6-inch skillet with flared sides, heat ⅓ of the butter till it sizzles and browns slightly. Lift and tilt the pan to coat the sides. Add ⅓ of the egg mixture; cook over medium heat. As eggs set, run a spatula around edge of skillet lifting eggs to allow uncooked portion to flow underneath. When eggs are set but still shiny, remove from heat. Spoon ⅓ of the broccoli mixture across center. Fold ⅓ of omelet over center. Overlap remaining third atop filling. Slide omelet out onto hot plate. Keep omelet warm. Repeat to make 2 more omelets. Makes 3 servings.

INDIVIDUAL CRUSTLESS QUICHES/225

1 3-ounce package sliced dried beef
½ of a medium onion, thinly sliced
3 beaten eggs
1½ cups skim milk
2 teaspoons all-purpose flour
¼ teaspoon salt
Dash ground nutmeg
¾ cup shredded Swiss cheese (3 ounces)

Finely chop the sliced dried beef; set aside. In skillet cook sliced onion in a small amount of boiling water till tender; drain. In bowl thoroughly stir together the eggs, milk, flour, salt, and nutmeg. Stir in the chopped dried beef, onion, and cheese; mix well. Place four 10-ounce custard cups in a 13x9x2-inch baking pan; pour egg mixture into the custard cups. Place pan on oven rack; pour hot water into pan around custard cups to depth of 1 inch. Bake in a 325° oven about 30 minutes or till knife inserted near center comes out clean. Let stand about 5 minutes before serving. Makes 4 servings.

CRAB AND EGG CASSEROLE/233

4 ounces Neufchâtel cheese
5 beaten eggs
1 cup skim milk
½ teaspoon salt
Dash pepper
1 6-ounce can crab meat, drained, flaked, and cartilage removed
½ cup finely chopped celery

In small mixer bowl beat cheese till softened and fluffy. Combine eggs, milk, salt, and pepper. Gradually add to cheese; beat till blended. Stir in crab and celery. Turn into a buttered 9-inch pie plate or quiche dish. Bake in a 325° oven for 15 minutes; stir. Continue baking for 10 to 15 minutes or till knife inserted near center comes out clean. Makes 4 servings.

EGG SALAD STUFFED TOMATOES/184

3 hard-cooked eggs, chopped
¼ cup plain yogurt
¼ cup dry cottage cheese
2 tablespoons finely chopped celery
2 tablespoons thinly sliced green onion
½ teaspoon dry mustard
¼ teaspoon salt
Dash ground red pepper
2 medium tomatoes
1 tablespoon snipped parsley
Lettuce (optional)

In bowl combine eggs, yogurt, cottage cheese, celery, green onion, dry mustard, salt, and red pepper. Cover and chill. For tomato shells, cut a slice off the top of each tomato. Scoop out seeds and flesh. Invert tomatoes on paper toweling to drain. Chill. To serve, sprinkle inside of tomatoes with salt and pepper. Spoon *half* of the egg mixture into each tomato shell. Sprinkle with snipped parsley. Arrange tomatoes on lettuce-lined plates, if desired. Makes 2 servings.

COOKING TO CUT CALORIES

STEAM

Steam cooking ensures the optimum in natural freshness and flavor because steamed foods retain their shape, texture, and nutrients. Although specialized appliances are available, an inexpensive metal steamer basket works just as well. Place the basket in a saucepan or skillet containing a shallow layer of boiling water. Steam cooks food placed in the basket suspended above boiling water in the covered saucepan or skillet.

POACH

Foods traditionally sautéed and served with a rich buttery sauce are just as delicious poached in a fat-free liquid that doubles as the base for a delicate sauce. Poaching pans are available for fish or eggs, but standard skillets and saucepans can also be used. To poach, place foods in a shallow simmering liquid (a broth, an inexpensive wine, or water with lemon, herbs, and spices). Cover the pan and simmer just till the food is done. Don't overcook. As the food cooks in the liquid, it picks up subtle seasonings and creates a flavorful stock. When done, fish flakes easily when tested with a fork, chicken loses its translucency, and eggs appear set.

STIR-FRY

Although not created as a low-calorie cuisine, most stir-fry dishes consist of a minimum of high-calorie foods combined with a generous selection of low-calorie fresh vegetables, all cooked in a small amount of cooking oil. Once you've mastered the basic stir-frying technique, experiment with your own combinations of meat and vegetables.

For stir-frying, cut foods into thin strips or small pieces. Then cook quickly in hot oil over high heat with constant stirring. The brief cooking time helps food retain its texture, color, and flavor. A bowl-shaped metal wok is designed for stir-frying, but a large skillet will deliver the same results. Use a long-handled spoon or spatula to frequently lift and turn the food, using a folding motion. The constant stirring of the foods helps ensure that all the ingredients are cooked as evenly as possible.

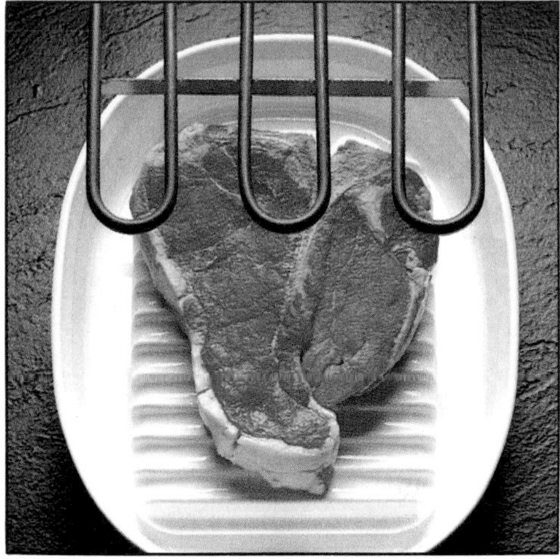

BROIL

Broiling is a fast, foolproof way to hold natural flavor and juices inside foods. It's a calorie-cutting technique, too, because no added butter or oil is necessary and fats naturally present in foods are left behind in the broiler pan. Foods lacking natural oils or juices need brushing with a liquid during broiling to keep them moist. (Soy sauce and fruit juices add flavor without adding excessive calories.) For proper cooking, place food on an unheated rack in a broiler pan. To position the rack, measure the distance from the top of the food surface to the heat element or heat source. (Check manufacturer's directions for your range to adjust broiler height or oven rack and to position the door.) Broil foods according to the time given in recipe instructions.

CALORIE-TRIMMED
SIDE DISHES

If you're in the rut of serving plain tossed salads and vegetables for side dishes, look through this section for an array of tempting ideas you can choose from. Vegetables (from artichokes to zucchini), salads (both fruit and vegetable), and salad dressings all receive special treatment in this chapter.

Pineapple Carrots

Marinated Tomato-Vegetable Salad

steamed cauliflower and broccoli

Stuffed Potatoes

Tomato Salad Dressing

NUTRITION ANALYSIS

Instead of thinking of vegetable and salad side dishes simply as plate-fillers, think of them as nutritional and flavorful complements to the protein main dishes. They also add color to the meal.

A generous amount of vegetables in your diet contributes to sound health and vitality. And there is such a wide variety to choose from.

Salads rate high with dieters because most of their ingredients are low-calorie and versatile. You can combine crisp greens, other vegetables, fruits, and meat or fish in an endless variety of tempting dishes. Whatever your salad choice, avoid rich dressings. Instead keep several tangy low-calorie dressings on hand to avoid unwanted calories. Or try just a splash of lemon juice, herb-flavored vinegar, or red wine vinegar on salad greens for a low-calorie change of taste.

	Per Serving						Percent U.S. RDA Per Serving							
SIDE DISHES	CALORIES	PROTEIN gms	CARBOHYDRATE gms	FAT gms	SODIUM mgs	POTASSIUM mgs	PROTEIN	VITAMIN A	VITAMIN C	THIAMINE	RIBOFLAVIN	NIACIN	CALCIUM	IRON
VEGETABLES														
ASPARAGUS PIQUANT (p. 171)	45	3	10	0	74	367	5	21	67	14	14	9	3	7
BAKED LIMA BEANS WITH TOMATOES (p. 173)	97	6	15	2	314	315	9	12	24	4	4	4	8	14
BROCCOLI-CAULIFLOWER SOUP (p. 182)	71	6	10	1	337	314	10	20	77	5	15	2	17	3
CARAWAY BRUSSELS SPROUTS (p. 173)	70	4	10	2	342	315	6	10	105	6	10	2	7	4
CAULIFLOWER CASSEROLE (p. 174)	58	3	6	3	444	230	5	4	69	3	7	4	7	4
CHEESE-BROCCOLI BAKE (p. 171)	65	4	7	3	117	231	6	21	78	4	10	2	10	3
CHILLED ASPARAGUS SOUP (p. 182)	52	5	9	0	223	348	8	16	47	11	18	6	12	5
CHILLED CUCUMBER SOUP (p. 183)	62	2	6	3	252	151	4	4	9	2	7	1	8	1
CHILLED SPINACH BISQUE (p. 182)	95	5	4	7	514	299	8	121	38	5	10	2	10	9
CHIVE CREAMED CORN (p. 176)	113	4	18	4	203	215	6	9	12	6	7	6	5	4
COMPANY CABBAGE (p. 173)	61	1	4	5	203	174	2	25	40	4	2	1	3	2
CORN PUDDING (p. 174)	131	7	16	5	478	203	11	11	9	5	13	3	10	5
CREAMY BROCCOLI CASSEROLE (p. 172)	63	5	7	2	200	242	7	39	85	4	10	2	10	3
CREAMY CORN AND ZUCCHINI (p. 178)	106	6	14	4	107	279	9	10	26	7	11	7	6	3
CRUSTLESS VEGETABLE QUICHE (p. 180)	75	6	4	4	97	301	9	82	47	5	12	2	9	11

SIDE DISHES	CALORIES	PROTEIN gms	CARBOHYDRATE gms	FAT gms	SODIUM mgs	POTASSIUM mgs	PROTEIN	VITAMIN A	VITAMIN C	THIAMINE	RIBOFLAVIN	NIACIN	CALCIUM	IRON
	Per Serving						Percent U.S. RDA Per Serving							
CURRIED POTATOES (p. 177)	145	3	21	6	209	494	4	5	44	8	3	9	2	4
DILLED ZUCCHINI (p. 180)	50	2	5	3	38	255	2	11	41	4	6	6	4	3
FRESH PEA SOUP (p. 183)	116	8	17	2	306	518	12	48	60	22	15	12	11	14
HERBED BRUSSELS SPROUTS (p. 173)	70	4	9	3	118	360	7	12	147	6	8	4	4	8
HERBED GREEN BEANS (p. 173)	42	2	5	2	76	174	2	16	26	4	6	3	3	5
HERBED VEGETABLE COMBO (p. 180)	39	2	6	2	94	237	2	11	46	5	5	4	4	3
ITALIAN ARTICHOKES (p. 171)	21	2	7	0	180	233	3	6	13	4	2	3	3	5
ITALIAN VEGETABLE SKILLET (p. 181)	91	2	10	6	111	220	3	9	54	5	4	2	3	5
KOHLRABI SOUP (p. 183)	52	4	10	0	354	396	6	3	87	5	9	2	11	3
LEMON-GLAZED CARROTS (p. 174)	65	1	9	3	78	320	2	202	18	4	3	3	4	4
LEMON-SESAME ASPARAGUS (p. 171)	56	2	5	4	171	251	4	18	49	10	10	7	2	5
MUSHROOM-BARLEY CASSEROLE (p. 176)	144	3	23	5	332	121	5	9	15	3	4	6	1	5
ORIENTAL PEA PODS AND SPINACH (p. 176)	55	3	7	3	247	276	4	64	57	7	7	4	4	10
PARMESAN STEAMED VEGETABLES (p. 181)	76	3	8	4	90	337	4	112	96	6	6	3	5	5
PEA AND CELERY MEDLEY (p. 176)	44	2	7	1	119	192	4	7	22	9	3	4	3	5
PEAS AND PODS (p. 177)	56	4	9	1	98	210	5	10	28	13	6	8	3	7
PINEAPPLE CARROTS (p. 174)	60	1	14	0	185	406	2	240	21	6	4	4	5	5
QUICK RATATOUILLE-STYLE VEGETABLES (p. 182)	46	2	6	2	101	266	2	16	70	5	4	5	2	4
SAUTÉED MUSHROOMS (p. 176)	51	2	4	3	108	254	3	7	9	4	15	11	1	3
SESAME GREEN BEANS (p. 172)	55	2	5	4	183	182	2	10	20	3	4	2	4	3
STEAMED SUMMER SQUASH (p. 178)	54	2	6	3	172	289	3	15	60	5	7	7	4	4
STEAMED VEGETABLE MEDLEY (p. 181)	60	2	5	4	240	235	3	43	51	4	6	4	2	4
STIR-FRIED TOMATOES AND PEPPERS (p. 174)	44	1	5	2	537	198	2	11	69	3	3	2	2	4
STIR-FRIED VEGETABLES (p. 181)	92	4	10	5	542	451	6	8	24	11	8	7	3	7
STUFFED POTATOES (p. 177)	70	3	13	1	563	308	5	2	24	5	5	5	6	3
TANGY GREEN BEANS (p. 172)	61	4	7	2	188	172	6	12	18	4	8	2	1	4
TANGY POTATO TOPPER (p. 177)	11	2	1	0	80	23	2	1	1	0	2	0	2	0
ZUCCHINI OREGANO (p. 178)	35	1	6	1	57	260	7	12	42	4	5	5	3	3
ZUCCHINI-STUFFED GREEN PEPPERS (p. 178)	62	2	9	2	182	378	4	12	181	8	11	12	3	6
SALADS AND SALAD DRESSINGS														
APPLE AND COTTAGE CHEESE SLAW (p. 188)	137	13	12	5	216	229	19	5	30	4	17	1	13	3
APPLE-BANANA FROST (p. 196)	66	1	15	1	15	173	2	3	23	3	4	1	4	2
ARTICHOKE AND ASPARAGUS SALAD (p. 189)	37	3	10	0	113	345	5	12	30	9	8	7	5	7
BANANA LOGS (p. 197)	118	3	19	5	60	317	4	7	17	4	5	3	2	4
BROCCOLI-SPROUT TOSSED SALAD (p. 186)	71	2	5	5	9	222	3	13	59	5	8	4	3	4
BULGUR SALAD (p. 192)	87	2	12	4	112	189	3	13	28	5	3	4	2	6
CABBAGE-CARROT MOLD (p. 193)	70	2	3	6	298	106	2	41	21	1	1	1	2	1
CALORIE-COUNTER'S COLESLAW (p. 188)	41	1	9	0	78	185	2	33	28	2	4	1	5	2
CAULIFLOWER SLAW (p. 187)	54	2	7	3	95	189	3	22	56	4	5	2	4	3
CITRUS SALAD TOSS (p. 197)	88	3	16	2	35	368	5	14	17	7	10	5	9	5
COTTAGE CHEESE AND FRUIT SALAD (p. 196)	117	4	26	0	57	339	7	9	51	9	7	3	6	5
COTTAGE TOMATO CUPS (p. 187)	116	10	9	5	224	423	16	27	67	7	8	7	7	10
CRANBERRY ORANGE MOLD (p. 195)	103	2	25	0	3	109	2	2	62	4	2	1	2	3
CREAMY GELATIN SALAD (p. 195)	70	3	14	1	15	245	5	5	87	7	5	2	5	1

SIDE DISHES

SIDE DISHES	Per Serving: CALORIES	PROTEIN gms	CARBOHYDRATE gms	FAT gms	SODIUM mgs	POTASSIUM mgs	Percent U.S. RDA Per Serving: PROTEIN	VITAMIN A	VITAMIN C	THIAMINE	RIBOFLAVIN	NIACIN	CALCIUM	IRON
CREAMY SALAD DRESSING (p. 186)	20	1	1	1	57	20	2	3	1	1	2	1	2	1
CREAMY STRAWBERRY MOLD (p. 193)	81	2	13	3	8	100	3	3	49	1	3	2	3	3
CRUNCHY APPLESAUCE MOLD (p. 193)	77	3	15	1	30	156	5	2	4	2	6	1	7	2
CUCUMBER-CHEESE MOLD (p. 187)	42	7	3	0	203	92	11	1	8	2	7	1	4	2
DIET BLUE CHEESE DRESSING (p. 184)	13	1	1	1	15	21	1	0	0	0	2	0	2	0
DIET SALAD DRESSING (p. 184)	22	1	2	1	98	29	2	2	0	1	3	0	2	1
DIET TARTAR SAUCE (p. 184)	24	1	3	1	126	36	2	3	2	1	3	0	2	1
DIET THOUSAND ISLAND DRESSING (p. 184)	21	1	3	1	98	35	1	3	5	1	2	0	2	1
DILLED CUCUMBER SALAD (p. 189)	34	3	4	1	108	142	5	4	13	2	5	1	5	4
DILLED VEGETABLE MEDLEY SALAD (p. 189)	33	1	4	2	17	195	2	9	19	2	4	1	5	5
FRUIT MEDLEY SALAD (p. 197)	79	2	19	1	15	358	2	5	60	4	5	4	3	6
FRUIT MOLD (p. 195)	90	3	20	1	32	258	5	2	13	4	6	2	7	2
FRUIT WITH CREAMY BANANA DRESSING (p. 196)	94	3	19	1	43	284	5	6	49	4	6	3	3	5
GARDEN VINAIGRETTE SALAD (p. 190)	95	3	7	7	10	376	4	12	119	8	7	6	3	6
GINGER FRUIT SLAW (p. 188)	135	3	34	0	30	503	4	98	98	9	6	6	6	10
GINGER-WINE VINAIGRETTE (p. 184)	48	0	1	5	0	8	0	0	0	0	0	0	0	0
HERBED CARROT POTATO SALAD (p. 192)	72	2	12	2	183	300	3	54	20	4	3	4	3	3
HERBED TOMATOES (p. 187)	138	2	7	12	361	350	3	29	58	6	4	5	3	5
ITALIAN SALAD BOWL (p. 190)	57	4	6	3	294	419	6	131	84	6	10	3	11	12
LOW-CAL CELERY SEED DRESSING (p. 186)	13	0	3	0	13	21	0	0	3	0	0	0	0	0
MARINATED POTATO SALAD (p. 190)	47	1	9	1	294	218	2	3	29	4	2	4	1	3
MARINATED TOMATO-VEGETABLE SALAD (p. 186)	55	1	7	2	93	232	2	14	33	4	4	3	3	4
MARINATED VEGETABLE SALAD (p. 189)	93	2	15	4	536	208	2	118	11	3	3	3	6	10
MINT-DRESSED SPINACH APPLE TOSS (p. 192)	55	2	13	0	63	308	2	60	48	5	6	2	5	9
MINTED FRUIT CUP (p. 196)	79	1	19	1	9	230	2	4	48	6	4	2	4	2
MOLDED STRAWBERRY SALAD (p. 193)	62	3	12	1	18	139	4	1	49	2	5	2	5	3
MUSHROOM-ZUCCHINI SALAD (p. 189)	61	2	4	5	184	272	2	7	20	4	12	10	2	3
ORANGE WALDORF SALAD (p. 195)	81	2	19	1	27	273	3	5	61	6	5	2	7	3
PEACH AND CHEESE MOLD (p. 194)	151	4	24	3	100	172	6	7	5	1	6	2	9	2
PEAR AND BLUE CHEESE SALAD (p. 197)	74	1	14	2	9	167	2	5	10	2	4	1	3	3
PINEAPPLE-PEAR MOLD (p. 193)	94	3	22	0	4	286	4	4	83	9	3	3	2	3
RAINBOW FRUIT SALAD (p. 196)	125	3	25	2	35	494	5	43	122	9	9	5	8	5
RED CABBAGE SLAW (p. 188)	74	2	18	0	149	267	3	1	58	4	3	1	3	5
SESAME APPLE TOSS (p. 193)	60	2	13	1	39	220	2	5	8	3	4	1	5	3
SPARKLING CHERRY-BERRY MOLD (p. 195)	35	2	7	0	2	64	3	1	24	1	1	1	1	1
SPICED FRUIT MOLD (p. 194)	62	2	14	0	2	178	2	3	47	4	2	1	2	3
SPICED FRUIT SALAD (p. 194)	73	1	17	0	2	247	1	8	22	3	3	3	1	3
SWEET-SOUR PLUM TOSS (p. 197)	129	2	12	9	117	221	2	5	17	4	4	3	2	5
TOMATO SALAD DRESSING (p. 184)	6	0	1	0	166	6	0	3	2	1	0	1	0	0
TOMATO VEGETABLE ASPIC (p. 187)	44	3	9	0	190	301	4	31	39	4	3	5	2	6
VINAIGRETTE DRESSING (p. 186)	62	0	1	7	0	10	0	0	0	0	0	0	0	0
WILTED SPINACH SALAD (p. 190)	43	3	5	2	80	328	4	80	50	6	10	4	5	11
ZUCCHINI SALAD (p. 190)	105	1	4	10	71	150	1	5	24	2	3	3	2	2
ZUCCHINI SALAD PIE (p. 192)	105	5	15	3	114	149	8	20	16	2	6	1	4	2

VEGETABLE SIDE DISHES

ITALIAN ARTICHOKES/21

- **2 pounds fresh tiny artichokes *or* medium artichokes, quartered**
- **Lemon juice**
- **1¾ cups water**
- **2 tablespoons tomato paste**
- **2 teaspoons instant chicken bouillon granules**
- **½ teaspoon dried tarragon, crushed**

Wash, trim stems, and remove loose outer leaves from artichokes. If using quartered medium artichokes, scoop out choke and discard. Cut off 1 inch of tops; snip off sharp leaf tips. Brush cut edges with lemon juice. In 10-inch skillet combine water, tomato paste, instant chicken bouillon granules, and tarragon. Bring to boiling. Reduce heat; add artichokes. Cover and simmer for 18 to 20 minutes or till a leaf pulls out of artichoke easily; stir occasionally. Remove artichokes with slotted spoon. Pour sauce into individual bowls for dipping the artichoke leaves. Makes 6 servings.

ASPARAGUS PIQUANT/45

- **1 pound fresh asparagus, bias sliced into 1-inch pieces**
- **1 small onion, thinly sliced**
- **2 tablespoons wine vinegar**
- **1 teaspoon sugar**
- **¼ teaspoon mustard seed**
- **⅛ teaspoon salt**

Place asparagus and onion in steamer basket. Place basket over boiling water. Cover and steam about 13 minutes or just till vegetables are tender. Meanwhile, in small bowl combine vinegar, sugar, mustard seed, and salt.

Transfer vegetables to a serving bowl. Pour vinegar mixture over vegetables; toss to coat. Serve immediately. Serves 4.

LEMON-SESAME ASPARAGUS/56

- **12 ounces fresh asparagus spears *or* one 8-ounce package frozen asparagus spears**
- **1 tablespoon butter *or* margarine**
- **2 teaspoons sesame seed**
- **2 teaspoons lemon juice**
- **¼ teaspoon salt**

Wash and trim fresh asparagus. Cook, covered, in boiling, lightly salted water 10 to 15 minutes or till crisp-tender. (*Or,* cook frozen asparagus spears according to the directions on the package.)

Meanwhile, in small saucepan heat and stir butter and sesame seed over low heat about 5 minutes or till seeds are golden brown. Add lemon juice and salt. Drain asparagus; remove to heated serving dish. Pour lemon mixture over hot asparagus. Serve immediately. Serves 4.

CHEESE-BROCCOLI BAKE/65

- **½ pound fresh broccoli *or* one 10-ounce package frozen cut broccoli**
- **1 cup frozen small whole onions**
- **1 tablespoon cornstarch**
- **⅛ teaspoon salt**
- **Dash pepper**
- **⅔ cup skim milk**
- **2 ounces Neufchâtel cheese**
- **2 tablespoons grated Parmesan cheese**

Remove the tough part of the fresh broccoli stalks. Cut the fresh broccoli stalks lengthwise into uniform spears, following the branching lines. Cut off buds and set aside. Cut the remaining part of the broccoli spears into 1-inch pieces.

In medium covered saucepan cook the 1-inch fresh broccoli pieces in boiling, lightly salted water for 10 to 12 minutes or just till tender, adding the reserved broccoli buds for the last 5 minutes of the cooking time. (*Or,* cook the frozen broccoli according to package directions.) Drain well. Cook the frozen onions according to package directions; drain well.

In small saucepan combine cornstarch, salt, and pepper; stir in skim milk. Cook and stir till thickened and bubbly. Cook and stir 1 to 2 minutes more. Reduce heat; stir in Neufchâtel cheese till smooth.

Combine broccoli, onions, and milk mixture; stir gently to mix. Turn into a 1-quart casserole. Sprinkle with Parmesan cheese. Bake, uncovered, in a 350° oven for 20 to 25 minutes or till the mixture is heated through. Makes 6 servings.

STEAMING FRESH VEGETABLES

It is easy to steam-cook fresh vegetables if you follow these simple steps and timings. Prepare the fresh vegetables by thoroughly rinsing them in cool water. Depending upon the type of vegetable, trim stems, remove outer leaves, or peel. Place vegetable in steamer basket (see note below); place over, but not touching, boiling water. Cover; reduce heat. Steam following timings below or till desired doneness. Drain; season to taste. If a combination of vegetables is desired, start with the longest cooking vegetable; add others at the appropriate time.

Asparagus, cut up . . . . . 13 minutes
Beans, cut into
½-inch pieces . . . . . . 23 minutes
Broccoli, spears . . . . 20 minutes
cut up . . . . 16 minutes
Brussels sprouts . . . . 20 minutes
Cabbage, wedges . . . . . 15 minutes
Carrots . . . . 23 minutes
Cauliflower,
flowerets . . . . 15 minutes
Onions, quartered . . . . 25 minutes
Squash, summer, cut into
¼-inch slices . . . . 13 minutes
Squash, winter, cut into
¼-inch slices . . . . 18 minutes

Note: *If you don't own a metal steamer basket, you can improvise with a metal can and rack. Simply remove the top and bottom of a metal can about 3 inches tall and 4 inches wide; place it in a large saucepan. Place a wire rack on top of the can. Add water to just below rack; bring to boiling. Position food in a heat-proof serving dish atop the wire rack. Cover; cook just till food is done.*

CREAMY BROCCOLI CASSEROLE/63

1 10-ounce package frozen cut broccoli
¼ cup chopped onion
½ cup *reconstituted* nonfat dry milk
1½ teaspoons cornstarch
¼ teaspoon salt
¼ teaspoon dried thyme, crushed
Dash pepper
1 ounce Neufchâtel cheese
1 tablespoon grated Parmesan cheese

Cook frozen broccoli according to package directions. Drain, reserving cooking liquid. Cook onion in reserved cooking liquid for 5 minutes or till tender. *Do not drain.* In screw-top jar combine milk, cornstarch, salt, thyme, and dash pepper. Stir into onion. Cook and stir till bubbly. Stir in Neufchâtel cheese. Add broccoli. Gently stir to mix. Turn into serving bowl. Sprinkle Parmesan atop. Makes 4 servings.

TANGY GREEN BEANS/61

1 9-ounce package frozen French-style green beans
¼ cup chopped onion
2 tablespoons snipped parsley
1½ teaspoons cornstarch
¼ teaspoon salt
Dash pepper
¼ cup water
½ cup plain yogurt
3 tablespoons shredded cheddar cheese

Cook frozen beans according to package directions along with the onion; drain.

Meanwhile, in medium saucepan combine parsley, cornstarch, salt, and pepper; stir in water. Cook and stir till thickened and bubbly. Cook and stir 1 to 2 minutes more. Stir in yogurt and drained bean mixture; heat through. Turn into serving dish; sprinkle with the shredded cheese. Serves 4.

SESAME GREEN BEANS/55

½ pound fresh green beans *or* **one 9-ounce package frozen French-style green beans**
1 tablespoon butter *or* **margarine**
2 teaspoons sesame seed
¼ cup thinly sliced celery
2 tablespoons chopped onion
¼ teaspoon salt

Slice fresh green beans diagonally end to end. In covered saucepan cook fresh beans in a small amount of boiling, lightly salted water for 10 to 12 minutes or just till tender. (*Or,* cook frozen beans according to package directions.) Drain; turn into serving bowl.

Meanwhile, in small saucepan heat butter or margarine and sesame seed over low heat about 5 minutes or till sesame seed is golden brown, stirring constantly. Add celery, onion, and salt; cook and stir till vegetables are tender. Pour over hot beans. Toss beans with celery mixture and serve immediately. Makes 4 servings.

HERBED GREEN BEANS/42

1 9-ounce package frozen cut *or* whole green beans
¼ cup sliced green onion
2 teaspoons butter *or* margarine
1 2-ounce can mushroom stems and pieces, drained
2 tablespoons chopped pimiento
¼ teaspoon dried marjoram, crushed
¼ teaspoon dried basil, crushed

In saucepan cook frozen beans according to package directions; drain well. In another saucepan cook onion in butter till tender. Stir in mushrooms, pimiento, marjoram, basil, dash *salt,* and dash *pepper.* Stir in drained beans. Toss to coat; heat. Serve at once. Serves 4.

BAKED LIMA BEANS WITH TOMATOES/97

1 16-ounce can lima beans, drained
1 8-ounce can stewed tomatoes, cut up
2 tablespoons finely chopped onion
1 small clove garlic, minced
¼ teaspoon dried basil, crushed
¼ teaspoon dried marjoram, crushed
¼ cup shredded Swiss cheese (1 ounce)

Combine lima beans, *undrained* tomatoes, onion, garlic, basil, marjoram, and dash *pepper.* Turn into a 1-quart casserole. Bake, uncovered, in a 350° oven for 30 minutes. Sprinkle with cheese. Serve in sauce dishes. Makes 5 servings.

CARAWAY BRUSSELS SPROUTS/70

1 10-ounce package frozen brussels sprouts
¼ cup chopped onion
2 teaspoons butter
½ cup skim milk
2 teaspoons cornstarch
1 teaspoon caraway seed
1 teaspoon Worcestershire sauce
¼ cup plain yogurt

Cook brussels sprouts according to package directions; drain. Cook onion in butter till tender. In screw-top jar combine milk, cornstarch, caraway, Worcestershire, ½ teaspoon *salt,* and dash *pepper;* shake well. Add to onion. Cook and stir till thickened and bubbly. Stir in yogurt. Stir sprouts into sauce; heat through. Serves 4.

HERBED BRUSSELS SPROUTS/70

¾ pound brussels sprouts
1 small onion, cut into thin wedges
1 clove garlic, minced
1 tablespoon butter *or* margarine
¼ teaspoon dried thyme, crushed
⅛ teaspoon dried oregano, crushed

Place brussels sprouts and onion in steamer basket. Place basket over boiling water. Cover and steam about 20 minutes or till vegetables are tender.

In 10-inch skillet cook garlic in butter or margarine till lightly browned. Stir in steamed brussels sprouts, onion, thyme, oregano, ⅛ teaspoon *salt,* and dash *pepper.* Cook for 3 to 5 minutes or till vegetables are heated through, stirring occasionally. Makes 4 servings.

COMPANY CABBAGE/61

2 teaspoons instant chicken bouillon granules
⅓ cup water
4 cups coarsely shredded cabbage
½ cup coarsely shredded carrot
¼ cup sliced green onion
½ teaspoon dillseed
⅛ teaspoon pepper
3 tablespoons chopped pecans
1 tablespoon butter *or* margarine, melted
½ teaspoon prepared mustard

In a large saucepan heat chicken bouillon granules in the water till dissolved. Add cabbage, carrot, green onion, dillseed, and pepper. Toss to mix. Cook, covered, over medium heat about 5 minutes or till tender, stirring once during cooking. Stir together pecans, butter or margarine, and mustard. Pour over vegetables; toss to mix. Makes 6 servings.

LEMON-GLAZED CARROTS/65

5 medium carrots
1 tablespoon butter *or* margarine
1 tablespoon lemon juice
⅛ teaspoon ground nutmeg
Dash salt
1 tablespoon snipped parsley

Quarter carrots. In medium covered saucepan cook carrots in a small amount of boiling, lightly salted water 12 to 15 minutes or just till tender; drain and set aside. In same saucepan melt butter or margarine. Stir in lemon juice, nutmeg, and salt. Boil gently, uncovered, for 1 minute. Add carrots; toss gently. Turn into serving bowl; sprinkle with parsley. Makes 4 servings.

PINEAPPLE CARROTS/60

Pictured on pages 166 and 167—

½ of an 8-ounce can crushed pineapple (juice pack)
½ cup water
¼ teaspoon salt
4 large carrots, cut into julienne strips (2 cups)
1 teaspoon cornstarch
1 tablespoon snipped parsley

Drain pineapple, reserving 2 tablespoons juice. In saucepan combine drained crushed pineapple, the water, and salt. Add carrots. Cover and simmer 12 to 15 minutes or till tender. Combine the reserved pineapple juice and the cornstarch. Add to carrots; cook and stir over low heat till bubbly. Stir in the snipped parsley. Season to taste with salt and pepper. Serves 4.

CAULIFLOWER CASSEROLE/58

2 10-ounce packages frozen cauliflower
1 10¾-ounce can condensed cream of celery soup
1 4-ounce can mushroom stems and pieces, drained
¼ cup sliced green onion
½ teaspoon dried basil, crushed
¼ teaspoon salt
¼ cup grated Parmesan cheese
½ teaspoon paprika

Cook cauliflower according to package directions; drain well. Halve any large pieces. In 2-quart casserole combine soup, mushrooms, onion, basil, salt, and dash *pepper*. Carefully stir in cauliflower. Sprinkle Parmesan cheese and paprika atop. Bake, uncovered, in a 375° oven for 25 minutes or till the cauliflower mixture is heated through. Makes 8 servings.

CORN PUDDING/131

⅓ cup chopped onion
2 teaspoons butter *or* margarine
1 cup skim milk
½ teaspoon salt
⅛ teaspoon pepper
2 beaten eggs
1 8-ounce can whole kernel corn, drained

Cook onion in butter or margarine till tender but not brown. Stir in milk, salt, and pepper; heat almost to boiling. Gradually stir milk mixture into beaten eggs; add corn. Turn into four 6-ounce custard cups. Place in an 8x8x2-inch baking pan; pour hot water into pan around custard cups to depth of 1 inch. Bake in a 350° oven for 20 to 25 minutes or till knife inserted near center comes out clean. Makes 4 servings.

STIR-FRIED TOMATOES AND PEPPERS/44

1 teaspoon instant beef bouillon granules
¼ cup boiling water
2 tablespoons soy sauce
2 teaspoons cornstarch
¼ teaspoon ground ginger
Several dashes bottled hot pepper sauce
1 tablespoon cooking oil
6 green onions, bias sliced into 1-inch pieces
½ cup bias-sliced celery *or* bok choy
2 medium green peppers, cut into strips
1 cup halved cherry tomatoes

Dissolve bouillon granules in boiling water. Stir together soy sauce, cornstarch, ginger, and hot pepper sauce; stir in bouillon. Set the soy-bouillon mixture aside.

Preheat a wok or large skillet over high heat; add cooking oil. Add green onions and celery; stir-fry 2 minutes. Remove vegetables. Add green pepper to wok or skillet; stir-fry 2 minutes. Stir soy mixture; stir into green pepper. Cook and stir till thickened and bubbly. Stir in green onions, celery, and tomatoes. Cover and cook for 1 minute. Serve immediately. Makes 6 servings.

Stir-Fried Tomatoes and Peppers

CHIVE CREAMED CORN/113

1 **10-ounce package frozen whole kernel corn**
¼ **cup chopped onion**
2 **teaspoons butter *or* margarine**
½ **cup skim milk**
1½ **teaspoons cornstarch**
¼ **teaspoon dried marjoram, crushed**
1 **ounce Neufchâtel cheese**
1 **tablespoon snipped chives**

Cook corn according to package directions; drain well. In medium saucepan cook onion in butter till tender. In screw-top jar combine skim milk, cornstarch, marjoram, ¼ teaspoon *salt,* and dash *pepper;* cover and shake well. Add to onion. Cook and stir till thickened and bubbly. Cook and stir 1 to 2 minutes more. Stir in cheese and chives till cheese is blended. Stir corn into cheese mixture; heat through. Serves 4.

SAUTÉED MUSHROOMS/51

3 **cups sliced fresh mushrooms (8 ounces)**
½ **cup sliced green onion**
2 **tablespoons dry white wine**
1 **tablespoon butter *or* margarine**
¼ **teaspoon pepper**
⅛ **teaspoon salt**

In skillet combine mushrooms, onion, wine, butter, pepper and salt. Cook over medium-high heat about 5 minutes or till mushrooms are lightly browned and some of the liquid has evaporated. Serve immediately. Makes 4 servings.

MUSHROOM-BARLEY CASSEROLE/144

⅔ **cup quick-cooking barley**
¼ **cup chopped onion**
2 **tablespoons butter *or* margarine**
1 **4-ounce can mushroom stems and pieces**
2 **tablespoons chopped pimiento**
2 **tablespoons snipped parsley**
2 **teaspoons instant chicken bouillon granules**
¼ **teaspoon dried rosemary, crushed**

In small skillet cook barley and onion in butter till barley is lightly browned and onion is tender. Drain mushrooms, reserving 3 tablespoons liquid. Add mushrooms and reserved liquid, pimiento, parsley, chicken bouillon granules, rosemary, and 1¾ cups *water* to skillet; stir to combine ingredients.

Turn into a 1-quart casserole. Cover and bake in a 350° oven for 1 hour or till barley is tender. Uncover and bake 10 minutes more or till liquid is absorbed. Serves 5.

ORIENTAL PEA PODS AND SPINACH/55

1 **tablespoon soy sauce**
2 **teaspoons lemon juice**
1 **teaspoon sugar**
1 **tablespoon cooking oil**
½ **teaspoon grated gingerroot**
½ **pound fresh small spinach leaves (6 cups)**
6 **ounces fresh pea pods *or* one 6-ounce package frozen pea pods**

Combine soy sauce, lemon juice, and sugar; set aside. Preheat a wok or large skillet over high heat; add cooking oil. Stir-fry gingerroot in hot oil for 30 seconds. Add spinach and fresh or frozen pea pods. (If using frozen pea pods, run under cold water to separate before adding to wok; drain.) Stir-fry vegetables about 1 minute or till crisp-tender. Stir soy mixture; stir into vegetables. Heat through, tossing gently to mix. Serve immediately. Makes 6 servings.

PEA AND CELERY MEDLEY/44

⅓ **cup water**
1½ **cups frozen peas**
1½ **cups sliced celery**
3 **green onions, sliced**
1 **teaspoon instant chicken bouillon granules**
½ **teaspoon dried basil, crushed**
Dash pepper
1 **teaspoon butter *or* margarine**

In saucepan bring water to boiling; stir in peas, celery, green onion, bouillon granules, basil, and pepper. Cover and simmer for 6 to 8 minutes or just till vegetables are tender. Drain; stir in butter or margarine. Makes 6 servings.

PEAS AND PODS/56

Pictured on page 33—

- **2 cups shelled fresh peas *or* one 10-ounce package frozen peas**
- **¼ cup sliced green onion**
- **1 6-ounce package frozen pea pods***
- **1 teaspoon butter *or* margarine**
- **¼ teaspoon salt**
- **⅛ teaspoon dried thyme, crushed**
- **Dash pepper**

Place fresh or frozen shelled peas and green onion in steamer basket. Place basket over boiling water. Cover and steam 5 minutes. Add frozen pea pods; cover and steam about 2 minutes more or till crisp-tender. Turn into serving bowl. Add butter or margarine, salt, thyme, and pepper; toss to coat. Makes 6 servings.

Note: If desired, use 6 ounces *fresh pea pods* instead of the frozen pea pods. Steam shelled peas and green onion for 3 minutes; add fresh pea pods and steam about 4 minutes more.

CURRIED POTATOES/145

Pictured on page 179—

- **1 pound new potatoes, halved**
- **1 small onion, sliced**
- **1 clove garlic, minced**
- **¼ teaspoon curry powder**
- **2 tablespoons butter *or* margarine**
- **1 tablespoon snipped parsley**
- **1 teaspoon lemon juice**
- **¼ teaspoon salt**
- **Dash ground red pepper**

In medium covered saucepan cook *unpeeled* potatoes and sliced onion in boiling, lightly salted water about 15 minutes or till potatoes are just tender; drain.

Meanwhile, in small saucepan cook garlic with curry powder in butter or margarine about 1 minute. Stir in parsley, lemon juice, salt, and red pepper. Add butter mixture to potatoes and onion; toss gently to mix. Makes 4 servings.

STUFFED POTATOES/70

Pictured on pages 166 and 167—

- **2 large potatoes**
- **¼ cup plain yogurt**
- **2 tablespoons snipped chives**
- **1 tablespoon skim milk**
- **1 teaspoon salt**
- **⅛ teaspoon garlic powder**
- **Dash pepper**
- **2 tablespoons grated Parmesan cheese**
- **Paprika**

Scrub potatoes; prick with a fork. Bake potatoes in a 375° oven for 70 minutes or till done. Slice potatoes in half lengthwise. Scoop out inside, leaving shells intact. Mash potatoes. Add yogurt, chives, milk, salt, garlic powder, and pepper. Beat till fluffy. Spoon or pipe the potato mixture into each potato shell. Sprinkle the top of each potato with cheese and paprika. Return to oven; bake 10 minutes or till heated through. If desired, place under broiler to lightly brown tops. Makes 4 servings.

TANGY POTATO TOPPER

Baked potatoes aren't fattening until you pile on the butter and sour cream. Then the calories really mount up! For a nutritious topping substitute, try this low-calorie creamy alternative.

In blender container combine ½ cup dry cottage cheese; 3 tablespoons skim milk; ¼ teaspoon salt; ¼ teaspoon dried basil, crushed; ¼ teaspoon onion powder; and dash pepper. Cover and blend till smooth. Stir in ¼ cup plain yogurt and 1 tablespoon snipped parsley. Serve over baked potatoes. Makes ⅔ cup. (11 calories per tablespoon)

ZUCCHINI OREGANO/35

4 small zucchini, sliced (1 pound)
4 green onions, bias sliced into ½-inch pieces
2 tablespoons dry white wine
1 teaspoon lemon juice
1 teaspoon butter *or* margarine
½ teaspoon dried oregano, crushed
⅛ teaspoon salt
Dash pepper
2 small tomatoes, cut into thin wedges
1 tablespoon snipped parsley

In 10-inch skillet combine zucchini, green onions, wine, lemon juice, butter or margarine, oregano, salt, and pepper. Cook, uncovered, over medium-high heat about 5 minutes or till zucchini is crisp-tender and some of the liquid has evaporated, stirring occasionally. Stir in tomato wedges and parsley. Cover and cook for 1 minute. Makes 6 servings.

CREAMY CORN AND ZUCCHINI/106

4 fresh ears of corn *or* one 10-ounce package frozen whole kernel corn
2 medium zucchini, sliced
½ cup cream-style cottage cheese
¼ cup dairy sour cream
2 tablespoons grated Parmesan cheese
⅛ teaspoon salt
⅛ teaspoon pepper

Cut fresh corn off cob. In covered saucepan cook fresh or frozen corn and zucchini in a small amount of boiling, lightly salted water for 3 to 5 minutes or just till tender. Drain. Combine cottage cheese, sour cream, Parmesan cheese, salt, and pepper. Pour over hot cooked vegetables and stir gently to combine; heat through. Makes 6 servings.

STEAMED SUMMER SQUASH/54

6 small zucchini (1¼ pounds)
4 small yellow crookneck squash (1 pound)
½ cup thinly sliced onion
2 tablespoons butter *or* margarine
1 tablespoon lemon juice
½ teaspoon salt
½ teaspoon dried basil, crushed
⅛ teaspoon pepper
1 2-ounce can sliced pimiento, drained and chopped

Cut zucchini and crookneck squash into ½-inch-thick slices. Place sliced zucchini and yellow squash and sliced onion in steamer basket. Place basket over boiling water. Cover and steam about 13 minutes or till vegetables are tender.

Meanwhile, in saucepan melt butter or margarine. Stir in lemon juice, salt, basil, and pepper. Turn steamed vegetables into serving bowl. Stir in butter mixture and the chopped pimiento. Serve the squash mixture immediately. Makes 8 servings.

ZUCCHINI-STUFFED GREEN PEPPERS/62

These stuffed peppers are a side-dish version of the familiar main-dish favorite—

4 medium green peppers
Salt

• • •

2 teaspoons butter *or* margarine
2 cups chopped zucchini
1 cup sliced fresh mushrooms
¼ cup chopped onion
1 clove garlic, minced
½ teaspoon dried basil, crushed
¼ teaspoon salt
Dash pepper
⅓ cup plain croutons

Cut tops off green peppers; remove seeds and membrane. Precook peppers in boiling, lightly salted water about 5 minutes; drain. (*Or*, for crisp green peppers omit precooking of the peppers.) Sprinkle inside of peppers with a little salt.

In a medium skillet melt butter or margarine; stir in zucchini, mushrooms, onion, garlic, basil, ¼ teaspoon salt, and the pepper. Cook, uncovered, over medium-high heat for 10 to 15 minutes or till liquid has evaporated, stirring constantly. Stir in croutons; spoon mixture into peppers. Place in a 1½-quart casserole. Bake, covered, in a 350° oven for 15 minutes; uncover and bake about 10 minutes more. Makes 4 servings.

Creamy Corn and Zucchini; Curried Potatoes (see recipe, page 177)

VEGETABLE DRESS-UPS

To add that special touch to your vegetable cookery, dress up plain vegetables with these simple and low-calorie additions. Add crunch to cooked vegetables with sliced celery or green pepper. For a touch of tartness, add a teaspoon of lemon juice or a little plain yogurt. For color contrast, add chopped pimiento, sliced hard-cooked eggs, shredded carrot, or snipped chives or parsley.

HERBED VEGETABLE COMBO/39

½ pound green beans, bias sliced into 1-inch pieces (about 1½ cups)
2 small zucchini, sliced (about 2 cups)
¼ cup chopped green pepper
2 tablespoons chopped onion
2 teaspoons cooking oil
1 medium tomato, chopped
¼ teaspoon salt
¼ teaspoon dried thyme, crushed
¼ teaspoon dried rosemary, crushed
Dash pepper

Place green beans in steamer basket. Place basket over boiling water. Cover and steam for 10 minutes. Add zucchini; cover and steam about 13 minutes more or just till vegetables are tender.

Meanwhile, in small saucepan cook green pepper and onion in hot cooking oil till tender but not brown. Stir in tomato, salt, thyme, rosemary, and pepper. Heat through. Pour over beans and zucchini in serving bowl; toss gently. Makes 6 servings.

DILLED ZUCCHINI/50

3 medium zucchini, sliced ⅜ inch thick (1 pound)
¼ cup chopped onion
1 tablespoon butter *or* margarine
1 tablespoon snipped parsley
1 teaspoon lemon juice
¼ teaspoon dried dillweed

In covered saucepan cook zucchini and onion in small amount of boiling, lightly salted water about 5 minutes or just till tender. Drain well. Add butter or margarine, parsley, lemon juice, and dillweed; sprinkle with a little salt and pepper. Toss to coat. Makes 4 servings.

CRUSTLESS VEGETABLE QUICHE/75

A creamy quiche without a crust—

¾ pound spinach
⅔ cup thinly sliced green onion
1 cup chopped lettuce
¼ cup snipped parsley
• • •
3 eggs
⅓ cup plain yogurt
2 ounces Neufchâtel cheese, softened
¼ cup skim milk
⅛ teaspoon pepper
Dash salt
Dash Worcestershire sauce
1 tablespoon grated Parmesan cheese

Rinse and chop spinach, removing stems. Cook spinach and onion, covered, with just the water that clings to spinach till steam forms. Reduce heat and cook 3 to 5 minutes, turning spinach frequently. Drain. Stir in lettuce and parsley. With electric mixer beat together eggs, yogurt, Neufchâtel cheese, skim milk, pepper, salt, and Worcestershire till smooth. Stir in spinach mixture. Turn into a greased 9-inch pie plate; sprinkle with Parmesan cheese. Bake, uncovered, in a 375° oven for 25 to 30 minutes or till knife inserted just off-center comes out clean. Let stand 10 minutes before serving. Makes 8 servings.

ITALIAN VEGETABLE SKILLET/91

¼ cup chopped onion
1 clove garlic, minced
2 tablespoons cooking oil
1 medium zucchini, sliced
1 cup frozen whole kernel corn, thawed
1 small green pepper, cut into strips
½ teaspoon dried basil, crushed
½ teaspoon dried oregano, crushed
¼ teaspoon salt
1 small tomato, cut into wedges

In 10-inch skillet cook onion and garlic in oil till onion is tender. Stir in zucchini, corn, green pepper, basil, oregano, salt, and ⅛ teaspoon *pepper*. Cook over medium heat, stirring frequently, about 5 minutes or till zucchini is crisp-tender. Stir in tomato. Cover; cook about 1 minute more or till tomato is heated through. Serve immediately. Makes 5 servings.

PARMESAN STEAMED VEGETABLES/76

1 cup bias-sliced carrots
2 cups cauliflower flowerets (⅓ medium head)
1 small green pepper, cut into rings
2 tablespoons butter *or* margarine
⅛ teaspoon ground nutmeg
2 tablespoons grated Parmesan cheese
1 tablespoon snipped parsley

Place carrots in steamer basket. Sprinkle with salt, if desired. Place basket over boiling water. Cover and steam for 8 minutes. Add cauliflower to carrots in basket; cover and steam 10 minutes more. Halve any large pepper rings. Add pepper rings to vegetables in basket; cover and steam for 3 to 5 minutes more or till all vegetables are tender.

Meanwhile, in small saucepan melt butter or margarine; stir in nutmeg. Transfer vegetables to serving bowl; drizzle with melted butter mixture. Sprinkle with the grated Parmesan cheese and snipped parsley. Makes 6 servings.

STEAMED VEGETABLE MEDLEY/60

2 cups cauliflower flowerets
1 cup bias-sliced carrots
1 medium red onion, sliced and separated into rings
1 cup whole fresh mushrooms
2 tablespoons butter *or* margarine
1 tablespoon lemon juice
½ teaspoon salt
¼ teaspoon dried dillweed
⅛ teaspoon pepper

Place cauliflower, carrots, and onion in steamer basket. Place basket over boiling water. Cover and steam for 15 minutes. Halve any large mushrooms. Add mushrooms; cover and steam for 5 minutes more or till all vegetables are tender.

Meanwhile, in saucepan melt butter or margarine. Add lemon juice, salt, dillweed, and pepper. To serve, transfer vegetables to serving bowl. Pour lemon mixture over vegetables; toss the vegetables to coat. Makes 6 servings.

STIR-FRIED VEGETABLES/92

This vegetable dish is pictured on the cover—

½ teaspoon instant beef bouillon granules
¼ cup boiling water
2 teaspoons cornstarch
Dash crushed red pepper *or* ground red pepper
2 tablespoons soy sauce
2 tablespoons cooking oil
1 medium onion, sliced and separated into rings
1 cup bias-sliced celery *or* bok choy
1 clove garlic, minced
1 cup sliced fresh mushrooms
1 8-ounce can bamboo shoots, drained
1 cup fresh pea pods *or* one 6-ounce package frozen pea pods, thawed
1 medium tomato, cut into wedges

Dissolve beef bouillon granules in the boiling water. Stir together cornstarch, red pepper, and soy sauce. Stir in beef bouillon mixture; set aside.

Preheat a wok or large skillet over high heat; add cooking oil. Stir-fry onion rings, sliced celery or bok choy, and minced garlic in hot oil for 1 to 2 minutes. Remove vegetables from wok or skillet. Add mushrooms and drained bamboo shoots to the wok or skillet. Stir-fry the mushrooms and bamboo shoots 2 minutes.

Stir bouillon-soy mixture; stir into mushroom mixture. Cook and stir till bubbly. Stir in onion-celery mixture, pea pods, and tomato wedges. Cover and cook 1 minute. Serve immediately. Makes 6 servings.

QUICK RATATOUILLE-STYLE VEGETABLES/46

1 small onion, sliced and separated into rings
1 small clove garlic, minced
2 teaspoons butter *or* margarine
1 small green pepper, cut into strips
1 medium zucchini, cut into ¼-inch slices
1 7½-ounce can tomatoes, cut up
⅛ teaspoon dried oregano, crushed
Dash salt
Dash pepper

In medium saucepan cook onion and garlic in butter or margarine till tender. Add green pepper, zucchini, *undrained* tomatoes, oregano, salt, and pepper. Bring to boiling; reduce heat. Simmer, uncovered, for 15 to 20 minutes or till all vegetables are tender. Serve immediately. Makes 4 servings.

CHILLED ASPARAGUS SOUP/52

1 pound fresh asparagus, cut up, *or* one 10-ounce package frozen cut asparagus
¼ cup chopped onion
2 cups skim milk
½ teaspoon salt
Dash white pepper

Cook fresh asparagus and onion, covered, in small amount of boiling, lightly salted water for 6 to 8 minutes or just till tender. (*Or,* cook frozen asparagus according to package directions along with the onion.) Drain well. In blender container combine the drained asparagus-onion mixture, ½ *cup* of the milk, the salt, and pepper. Cover and blend about 15 seconds or till smooth. Add remaining milk; cover and blend to mix. Cover and chill at least 3 hours or overnight (chill in blender container, if desired). Stir or blend before serving. Makes 6 servings.

CHILLED SPINACH BISQUE/95

1 10-ounce package frozen chopped spinach
2 cups water
¼ cup sliced green onion
1 tablespoon instant chicken bouillon granules
⅛ teaspoon ground nutmeg
4 ounces Neufchâtel cheese, cubed
Lemon twists

In saucepan combine spinach, water, green onion, instant chicken bouillon granules, and nutmeg. Cover and simmer about 5 minutes or till vegetables are tender. *Do not drain.* Add Neufchâtel cheese. Pour *half* the spinach mixture at a time into blender container or food processor bowl; cover and blend till smooth. Pour into a bowl; cover and chill. Garnish with lemon twists. Makes 4 servings.

BROCCOLI-CAULIFLOWER SOUP/71

Use your blender to puree the broccoli, cauliflower, and onion mixture until smooth—

1 10-ounce package frozen chopped broccoli
1 10-ounce package frozen cauliflower
⅓ cup chopped onion
2 teaspoons instant chicken bouillon granules
1½ cups water

• • •

¼ teaspoon ground mace
3 cups skim milk
1 tablespoon cornstarch
½ teaspoon salt
Dash pepper
¼ cup shredded *process* Swiss cheese (1 ounce)

In large saucepan cook the frozen chopped broccoli and the cauliflower with the chopped onion and chicken bouillon granules in the 1½ cups water for 5 to 8 minutes or till vegetables are tender. *Do not drain.* In blender container blend *half* of the vegetable mixture at a time and the ground mace till the mixture is smooth. Return all blended vegetables to saucepan.

Combine ½ *cup* of the milk and the cornstarch; add to vegetable mixture in saucepan. Stir in the remaining milk, salt, and pepper. Cook and stir till mixture is thickened and bubbly. Cook and stir 1 to 2 minutes more. Add shredded Swiss cheese; stir till cheese is melted. Makes 8 servings.

FRESH PEA SOUP / 116

This soup has a flavor and texture reminiscent of a rich soup, minus some calories—

2 cups shelled fresh peas *or* one 10-ounce package frozen peas
3 ounces spinach (about 7 leaves)
2 ounces lettuce (about 10 leaves)
½ cup chopped leeks
2 teaspoons instant chicken bouillon granules
½ teaspoon dried chervil, crushed
⅛ teaspoon pepper
1¼ cups water
¾ cup skim milk
2 teaspoons butter *or* margarine

In a large saucepan combine the peas, spinach, lettuce, leeks, bouillon granules, chervil, and pepper; add water. Bring to boiling; reduce heat. Cover and simmer for 20 minutes. Pour into blender container or food processor bowl; cover and process till smooth. Sieve mixture back into saucepan. Add milk and butter or margarine; heat through. Makes 4 servings.

KOHLRABI SOUP / 52

4 medium kohlrabi, peeled and sliced (2 cups)
1 cup water
½ cup chopped onion
1½ teaspoons instant chicken bouillon granules
1 cup skim milk
¼ teaspoon salt
Dash white pepper
Snipped chives *or* parsley

In saucepan combine kohlrabi, water, onion, and bouillon granules. Bring to boiling; reduce heat. Cover; simmer about 20 minutes or till kohlrabi is tender. Pour mixture into blender container; cover and blend till smooth. Return mixture to saucepan. Stir in milk, salt, and pepper; heat through. To serve, ladle into bowls; top with chives. Makes 4 servings.

CHILLED CUCUMBER SOUP / 62

1 medium cucumber, peeled, seeded, and chopped (1 cup)
2 tablespoons sliced green onion
1 tablespoon butter *or* margarine
2 teaspoons cornstarch
¾ cup water
½ cup *reconstituted* nonfat dry milk
1 teaspoon instant chicken bouillon granules
¼ teaspoon dried dillweed
⅛ teaspoon salt
½ cup plain yogurt
Sliced green onion tops

In saucepan cook cucumber and onion in butter or margarine about 5 minutes or till tender. Stir in cornstarch. Add water, milk, bouillon granules, dillweed, and salt. Cook and stir till slightly thickened and bubbly. Cook and stir 2 minutes more. Pour mixture into blender container; cover and blend till smooth. Stir cucumber mixture into yogurt. Cover and chill. Garnish with sliced green onion tops. Makes 4 servings.

VERSATILE CUCUMBERS

Take advantage of a cucumber's bountiful uses: Slice it for a refreshing, low-calorie, and nutritious snack. Add it to tossed salads, molded salads, and relish trays. Combine it with onion slices in a vinegar dressing.

To keep plain or scored cucumber slices crisp, cut them very thin and place immediately in ice water. Refrigerate.

To make scored cucumber slices, run the tines of a fork lengthwise down an unpeeled cucumber, pressing to break through peel. Repeat around entire cucumber. Then, make slices by cutting straight across or on the bias.

SALAD SIDE DISHES

DIET SALAD DRESSING/22

1 tablespoon all-purpose flour
1 tablespoon sugar
1 teaspoon dry mustard
½ teaspoon salt
Dash ground red pepper
¾ cup skim milk
2 slightly beaten egg yolks
3 tablespoons vinegar

In a saucepan combine the flour, sugar, dry mustard, salt, and red pepper; stir in the milk. Cook and stir till mixture is thickened and bubbly. Gradually stir some of the hot mixture into the slightly beaten egg yolks. Return all to saucepan. Cook, stirring constantly, 2 minutes more. Place a piece of waxed paper over the surface; cool 10 to 15 minutes. Remove waxed paper; stir in the vinegar. Transfer to jar; cover tightly and chill. Makes ¾ cup salad dressing, or 12 one-tablespoon servings.

DIET TARTAR SAUCE/24

½ cup Diet Salad Dressing
2 tablespoons finely chopped dill pickle
1 tablespoon snipped parsley
1 tablespoon chopped green onion

In bowl combine the Diet Salad Dressing, chopped pickle, snipped parsley, and green onion. Transfer to jar; cover and chill. Serve with fish. Makes ½ cup, or 8 one-tablespoon servings.

DIET THOUSAND ISLAND DRESSING/21

Pictured on salad on page 33—

½ cup Diet Salad Dressing
1 tablespoon sliced green onion
1 tablespoon chopped green pepper
1 tablespoon catsup *or* chili sauce
1 tablespoon chopped pimiento
1 teaspoon prepared horseradish

In small mixing bowl stir together the Diet Salad Dressing, green onion, green pepper, catsup or chili sauce, chopped pimiento, and horseradish till well combined. Transfer to jar; cover tightly and chill. Makes ⅔ cup salad dressing, or about 10 one-tablespoon servings.

TOMATO SALAD DRESSING/6

Pictured on pages 166 and 167—

1 8-ounce can tomato sauce
2 tablespoons tarragon vinegar
1 teaspoon Worcestershire sauce
½ teaspoon salt
½ teaspoon dried dillweed
½ teaspoon dried basil, crushed
½ teaspoon onion juice

In a screw-top jar combine tomato sauce, tarragon vinegar, Worcestershire sauce, salt, dried dillweed, basil, and onion juice. Cover and shake well; chill thoroughly. Shake again before serving. Makes about 1 cup, or 16 one-tablespoon servings.

DIET BLUE CHEESE DRESSING/13

1 cup plain yogurt
2 tablespoons crumbled blue cheese
2 teaspoons sugar
½ teaspoon celery seed
Dash bottled hot pepper sauce

In a small mixer bowl combine the plain yogurt, 1 *tablespoon* of the crumbled blue cheese, the sugar, celery seed, and the bottled hot pepper sauce. Thoroughly beat dressing with rotary beater till smooth. Stir in the remaining crumbled blue cheese. Transfer to jar; cover tightly and chill. Makes about 1 cup, or 16 one-tablespoon servings.

GINGER-WINE VINAIGRETTE/48

½ cup red wine vinegar
6 tablespoons salad oil
2 teaspoons sugar
1 teaspoon grated gingerroot *or* ½ teaspoon ground ginger
1 teaspoon celery seed

In screw-top jar combine vinegar, oil, sugar, gingerroot or ground ginger, and celery seed. Cover tightly; shake well. Chill. Makes 1 cup, or 16 one-tablespoon servings.

For a light, low-calorie salad like that at right, toss fresh vegetables with a calorie-trimmed dressing in this section.

VINAIGRETTE DRESSING/62

- 2/3 cup vinegar
- 1/2 cup salad oil
- 2 teaspoons dry mustard
- 1 teaspoon paprika
- 1 teaspoon dried basil, crushed
- 1 teaspoon dried oregano, crushed
- 1/2 teaspoon dried dillweed
- 1/8 teaspoon bottled hot pepper sauce

In screw-top jar combine all ingredients; cover and shake well to mix. Chill. Shake again just before serving. Chill to store. Makes about 1 cup salad dressing, or 16 one-tablespoon servings.

LOW-CAL CELERY SEED DRESSING/13

- 1 1¾-ounce package powdered fruit pectin
- 1 teaspoon celery seed
- 1/8 teaspoon salt
- 1 cup unsweetened pineapple juice
- 2 tablespoons lemon juice
- 2 tablespoons honey

Combine powdered pectin, celery seed, and salt. Stir in pineapple juice, lemon juice, and honey. Cover; refrigerate at least 1 hour. Serve dressing on fruit salads. Makes 1⅓ cups salad dressing, or about 21 one-tablespoon servings.

CREAMY SALAD DRESSING/20

- 2 hard-cooked egg yolks
- 1 raw egg yolk
- 1/2 cup plain yogurt
- 2 teaspoons finely chopped onion
- 1 teaspoon lemon juice
- 1 teaspoon Dijon-style mustard
- 1/4 teaspoon salt
- Dash pepper

Sieve hard-cooked egg yolks into small bowl. Blend in raw egg yolk. Stir in yogurt, onion, lemon juice, mustard, salt, and pepper. Mix well. Cover and chill. (Use within several days.) Makes ¾ cup salad dressing, or 12 one-tablespoon servings.

BROCCOLI-SPROUT TOSSED SALAD/71

- 5 cups torn salad greens
- 1 cup fresh broccoli buds
- 1 cup fresh bean sprouts
- 1 cup sliced fresh mushrooms
- 1 medium red onion, sliced and separated into rings
- 1/2 cup green pepper strips
- 1/2 cup Ginger-Wine Vinaigrette (see recipe, page 184)

In salad bowl combine torn salad greens, broccoli buds, bean sprouts, sliced mushrooms, onion rings, and green pepper strips. Pass Ginger-Wine Vinaigrette to drizzle over all. Makes 8 servings.

MARINATED TOMATO-VEGETABLE SALAD/55

Pictured on pages 166 and 167—

- 1/2 of a 9-ounce package frozen cut green beans *or* one 8-ounce can cut green beans
- 2 medium tomatoes, cut into wedges
- 1 small onion, thinly sliced and separated into rings
- 1 medium zucchini, sliced
- 3 tablespoons snipped parsley

• • •

- 1/3 cup vinegar
- 2 tablespoons rosé wine
- 1 tablespoon salad oil
- 2 teaspoons sugar
- 1/4 teaspoon salt
- 1/4 teaspoon dried basil, crushed
- Lettuce (optional)

Cook frozen green beans according to package directions; drain. (*Or,* drain canned beans.) In bowl combine green beans, tomatoes, onion rings, zucchini slices, and parsley.

For marinade, in screw-top jar combine vinegar, rosé wine, salad oil, sugar, salt, and basil. Cover and shake well. Pour marinade over vegetables in bowl. Cover and refrigerate several hours or overnight, stirring occasionally. Drain to serve. Serve vegetables on lettuce-lined salad plates, if desired. Makes 6 servings.

COTTAGE TOMATO CUPS/116

6 medium tomatoes
¾ cup dry cottage cheese
¼ cup low-calorie mayonnaise
¼ cup chopped cucumber
¼ cup thinly sliced radishes
¼ cup chopped green pepper
2 tablespoons sliced green onion
½ teaspoon dried basil, crushed
¼ teaspoon garlic salt
1 4½-ounce can shrimp, rinsed and drained
6 leaves bibb lettuce

Place tomatoes, stem end down, on cutting surface. With sharp knife cut tomato into 6 wedges, cutting to but not through the base of the tomato. Cover and chill. In bowl combine cottage cheese and mayonnaise; mix well. Stir in cucumber, radishes, green pepper, green onion, basil, and garlic salt. Gently fold in the drained shrimp. Place the tomatoes on individual lettuce-lined salad plates and spread the wedges apart. Place about ⅓ cup of the cottage cheese mixture in the center of each tomato. Makes 6 servings.

HERBED TOMATOES/138

6 medium tomatoes
⅔ cup salad oil
¼ cup snipped parsley
¼ cup sliced green onion
¼ cup wine vinegar
2 teaspoons snipped fresh marjoram *or* ½ teaspoon dried marjoram, crushed
1 teaspoon salt
Lettuce

Peel and quarter tomatoes; place in a deep bowl. In a screw-top jar combine oil, parsley, green onion, vinegar, marjoram, salt, and ¼ teaspoon *pepper;* shake well. Pour over tomatoes. Cover and refrigerate several hours or overnight, spooning herb mixture over tomatoes occasionally. At serving time, lift tomatoes from marinade with slotted spoon. Serve on lettuce-lined platter. Spoon some of the herb mixture over tomatoes again. Makes 6 servings.

CUCUMBER-CHEESE MOLD/42

1 envelope unflavored gelatin
1¼ cups cold water
1½ teaspoons instant chicken bouillon granules
2 teaspoons lemon juice
1 teaspoon prepared horseradish
1½ cups dry cottage cheese
1 large cucumber, peeled, seeded, and shredded
2 tablespoons chopped green onion
Lettuce (optional)

In small saucepan soften gelatin in cold water; add bouillon granules. Stir over low heat till gelatin is dissolved; cool. Stir in lemon juice and horseradish. Add cottage cheese, shredded cucumber, and chopped green onion. Turn into a 4-cup mold. Chill till firm. Unmold onto lettuce-lined plate and garnish with cucumber slices, if desired. Makes 8 servings.

TOMATO VEGETABLE ASPIC/44

1 envelope unflavored gelatin
1½ cups tomato juice
3 tablespoons vinegar
1 tablespoon sugar
½ cup shredded zucchini
½ cup finely chopped cabbage
¼ cup shredded carrot

In saucepan soften gelatin in ½ *cup* of the tomato juice. Cook and stir over low heat till gelatin is dissolved. Add remaining tomato juice, the vinegar, and sugar, stirring till sugar is dissolved. Stir in zucchini, cabbage, and carrot; mix well. Pour into a 3-cup mold or four 6-ounce custard cups. Chill several hours or till firm. Unmold to serve. Makes 4 servings.

CAULIFLOWER SLAW/54

2 cups chopped cauliflower
½ cup shredded carrot
¼ cup chopped onion
½ cup plain yogurt
2 tablespoons salad dressing
2 teaspoons sugar
2 teaspoons lemon juice
¼ teaspoon celery seed
⅛ teaspoon salt
Snipped parsley

In a large bowl combine cauliflower, carrot, and onion. In a small bowl combine yogurt, salad dressing, sugar, lemon juice, celery seed, and salt; mix well. Pour yogurt mixture over vegetables; toss to coat. Garnish with parsley. Makes 6 servings.

SHREDDING CABBAGE

Save time by shredding cabbage in the blender. Begin by removing and discarding any wilted outer leaves; rinse cabbage. Cut into wedges; remove center core. Then, fill blender container no more than half full with cabbage wedges; cover with cold water. Blend till chopped to desired coarseness. Remove from blender container; drain well. Repeat with remaining cabbage wedges. Cover and chill. Before serving, drain cabbage again. (Or, drain and use as directed in recipe for coleslaw or similar dishes.)

GINGER FRUIT SLAW/135

1 8-ounce can crushed pineapple (juice pack)
5 cups shredded red cabbage (about 6 ounces)
3 large oranges, peeled and sectioned
2 large carrots, shredded
¾ cup snipped dried apricots
¼ cup honey
1 tablespoon lemon juice
½ teaspoon ground ginger

Drain pineapple, reserving ¼ cup of the juice; set aside. In a large bowl combine cabbage, orange sections, shredded carrots, snipped apricots, and crushed pineapple; cover and chill. In a screw-top jar combine reserved pineapple juice, honey, lemon juice, and ginger. Cover and chill. Just before serving, shake dressing; pour over cabbage mixture. Toss to mix dressing with cabbage mixture. Makes 8 servings.

CALORIE-COUNTER'S COLESLAW/41

2 cups shredded cabbage
¾ cup shredded carrot
½ cup thinly sliced celery
2 tablespoons sliced green onion
½ cup plain yogurt
2 teaspoons sugar
1 teaspoon prepared horseradish
⅛ teaspoon salt
Dash pepper

In salad bowl toss together shredded cabbage, shredded carrot, sliced celery, and sliced green onion. For dressing, stir together plain yogurt, sugar, horseradish, salt, and pepper. Toss dressing with cabbage mixture till all ingredients are well-coated. Cover; chill the cabbage salad for several hours. Makes 6 servings.

RED CABBAGE SLAW/74

1 16-ounce can shoestring beets
6 cups coarsely shredded red cabbage
1 medium onion, thinly sliced
½ cup vinegar
⅓ cup sugar

Drain beets, reserving ½ cup liquid. In large bowl combine beets, cabbage, and onion. In saucepan combine vinegar, sugar, and reserved beet liquid. Bring to boiling. Pour over vegetables. Toss lightly. Cover and refrigerate 4 to 5 hours; stir occasionally. Makes 8 servings.

APPLE AND COTTAGE CHEESE SLAW/137

2 cups shredded cabbage
1 medium apple, cored and diced
½ cup Diet Blue Cheese Dressing (see recipe, page 184)
1½ cups cream-style cottage cheese (12 ounces)

In salad bowl combine shredded cabbage and diced apple. Pour Diet Blue Cheese Dressing over cabbage mixture; toss to coat. Spoon cottage cheese in ring atop cabbage mixture. Makes 4 servings.

MUSHROOM-ZUCCHINI SALAD/61

8 ounces fresh mushrooms, sliced (2½ cups)
1 medium zucchini *or* cucumber, thinly sliced
1 medium tomato, chopped
¼ cup sliced green onion
2 tablespoons salad oil
2 tablespoons vinegar
½ teaspoon salt
½ teaspoon ground pepper
½ teaspoon dried marjoram, crushed

In salad bowl combine mushrooms, zucchini, tomato, and green onion. In a screw-top jar combine remaining ingredients. Cover. Shake well; toss dressing with vegetables. Cover and chill 4 hours. Makes 6 servings.

DILLED VEGETABLE MEDLEY SALAD/33

1½ cups thinly sliced cucumber
½ cup sliced radishes
¼ cup sliced green onion
¼ cup plain yogurt
2 tablespoons dairy sour cream
2 tablespoons tarragon vinegar
2 teaspoons snipped fresh dill *or* ½ teaspoon dried dillweed
Dash salt
4 leaves leaf lettuce

Combine cucumber, radishes, and onion. In small bowl combine yogurt, sour cream, tarragon vinegar, fresh or dried dill, and the salt; add to vegetable mixture and toss to coat. Chill thoroughly. Serve on individual lettuce-lined plates. Makes 4 servings.

ARTICHOKE AND ASPARAGUS SALAD/37

½ pound fresh asparagus spears, cooked crisp-tender
1 6-ounce jar marinated artichoke hearts
½ cup sliced fresh mushrooms
¼ cup sliced green onion
1 tablespoon vinegar
1 teaspoon sugar
1 teaspoon toasted sesame seed
¼ teaspoon salt
Several dashes bottled hot pepper sauce
6 leaves leaf lettuce

In 10x6x2-inch dish arrange asparagus spears. Drain artichoke hearts, reserving marinade. Slice any large artichoke hearts in half; add along with mushrooms and onion to dish.

Combine reserved marinade, vinegar, sugar, sesame seed, salt, and hot pepper sauce. Pour over vegetables in dish. Cover; refrigerate several hours. Remove vegetables from marinade with slotted spoon; arrange vegetables on lettuce-lined plates. Makes 6 servings.

MARINATED VEGETABLE SALAD/93

1 16-ounce can cut green beans, drained
1 16-ounce can cut wax beans, drained
1 16-ounce can diced carrots, drained
½ cup chopped celery
⅓ cup vinegar
¼ cup sugar
2 tablespoons salad oil
½ teaspoon salt
⅛ teaspoon pepper

In mixing bowl combine green beans, wax beans, carrots, and celery. Combine vinegar, sugar, salad oil, salt, and pepper; pour over vegetables. Toss. Cover and chill several hours or overnight, stirring occasionally to distribute marinade. Drain the vegetables to serve. Makes 8 servings.

DILLED CUCUMBER SALAD/34

½ cup cream-style cottage cheese
½ cup plain yogurt
¼ teaspoon dried dillweed
¼ teaspoon salt
2 medium cucumbers, thinly sliced
1 medium onion, thinly sliced

In blender container combine cottage cheese, yogurt, dillweed, and salt. Cover and blend till smooth. In bowl combine cucumber and onion. Stir in yogurt mixture. Cover and chill. Makes 8 servings.

WILTED SPINACH SALAD/43

8 cups spinach leaves
1 cup sliced fresh mushrooms
1 slice bacon
2 tablespoons finely chopped onion
2 tablespoons vinegar
1 tablespoon catsup
1 tablespoon water
1 teaspoon sugar
¼ teaspoon dried marjoram, crushed
½ cup alfalfa sprouts

Tear spinach leaves into bite-size pieces and place in a bowl; add mushrooms. Cut up bacon. In a deep 10-inch skillet cook bacon pieces till crisp; *do not drain.* Add onion, vinegar, catsup, water, sugar, and marjoram. Stir till bubbly. Remove skillet from heat. Stir spinach mixture into skillet, tossing till all the greens are slightly wilted and well coated. Turn salad into serving bowl; sprinkle alfalfa sprouts atop and toss. Makes 8 servings.

GARDEN VINAIGRETTE SALAD/95

½ head cauliflower, broken into small flowerets (3 cups)
2 medium zucchini, sliced
1 medium green pepper, cut into strips
½ cup Vinaigrette Dressing (see recipe, page 186)
12 cherry tomatoes
Lettuce (optional)

In covered saucepan cook cauliflower flowerets in small amount of boiling, lightly salted water for 2 minutes. Add zucchini and cook 2 minutes more or till vegetables are crisp-tender. Drain. Combine cooked vegetables and green pepper. Pour Vinaigrette Dressing over vegetable mixture; toss to coat vegetables. Cover and refrigerate several hours or overnight, stirring occasionally. At serving time, halve tomatoes and add to vegetable mixture; toss gently to coat. To serve, lift vegetables from dressing with slotted spoon and place in lettuce-lined bowl, if desired. Makes 8 servings.

MARINATED POTATO SALAD/47

⅓ cup low-calorie Italian salad dressing
2 cups hot cooked cubed potatoes (1 pound)
½ cup bias-sliced celery
½ cup thinly sliced red onion, separated into rings
¼ cup sliced radishes
2 tablespoons chopped green pepper
½ teaspoon salt
¼ teaspoon dried dillweed
2 tablespoons snipped parsley

In a large bowl pour dressing over hot potatoes; mix gently to coat. Cover and marinate in refrigerator for at least 2 hours. Add celery, onion, radishes, green pepper, salt, and dillweed; toss gently to combine. Sprinkle with parsley. Makes 6 servings.

ITALIAN SALAD BOWL/57

6 cups torn spinach leaves
1 cup sliced radishes
1 small green pepper, cut into strips
1 cup shredded carrot
¼ cup grated Parmesan cheese
⅔ cup low-calorie Italian salad dressing

In salad bowl combine spinach, radishes, green pepper, carrot, and cheese. Toss to mix. Cover and chill, if desired. Pour dressing over salad. Toss to coat. Makes 6 servings.

ZUCCHINI SALAD/105

2 small zucchini, cut into julienne strips
⅓ cup vinegar
3 tablespoons salad oil
1 tablespoon finely chopped onion
1 tablespoon chopped pimiento
1 clove garlic, minced
¼ teaspoon dried tarragon, crushed

Place zucchini in a bowl. Combine vinegar, salad oil, onion, pimiento, garlic, tarragon, ⅛ teaspoon *salt,* and dash *pepper;* mix well and pour over zucchini. Cover; refrigerate several hours or overnight, stirring the zucchini mixture occasionally. To serve, lift zucchini mixture from liquid with slotted spoon. Makes 4 servings.

Spiced Fruit Mold (see recipe, page 194); *Zucchini Salad*

HERBED CARROT POTATO SALAD/72

2 medium potatoes
2 medium carrots, thinly sliced (1 cup)
1/4 cup thinly sliced celery
4 or 5 pitted ripe olives, sliced
• • •
1/4 cup low-calorie mayonnaise
1/4 cup plain yogurt
1 1/2 teaspoons snipped chives
1 teaspoon lemon juice
1 teaspoon Worcestershire sauce
1/4 teaspoon salt
1/8 teaspoon dried dillweed
1/8 teaspoon dry mustard
Dash pepper
Leaf lettuce (optional)

Cook potatoes, covered, in boiling, lightly salted water about 25 minutes or till tender. Drain; peel and slice. In small saucepan heat a small amount of water to boiling; add carrots and simmer, uncovered, for 4 minutes. Drain; rinse with cold water and drain again. In large bowl toss together potatoes, carrots, celery, and olives.

Combine salad dressing, yogurt, chives, lemon juice, Worcestershire, salt, dillweed, mustard, and pepper till blended. Add to vegetables and gently toss to coat well. Cover and chill several hours. Serve the potato salad in a lettuce-lined bowl, if desired. Makes 6 servings.

BULGUR SALAD/87

1/3 cup bulgur wheat
1 medium tomato, peeled and chopped
1/2 cup chopped cucumber
1/4 cup snipped parsley
2 tablespoons sliced green onion
2 tablespoons lemon juice
4 teaspoons salad oil
1/4 teaspoon salt
2 1/2 cups shredded lettuce

Pour 1 cup *boiling water* over bulgur wheat; let stand for 1 hour. Drain well, pressing out excess water. Combine bulgur, tomato, cucumber, parsley, onion, lemon juice, salad oil, salt, and dash *pepper;* mix well. Cover and chill several hours. For each serving, spoon about 1/2 cup bulgur mixture atop 1/2 cup shredded lettuce in individual salad bowls. Makes 5 servings.

ZUCCHINI SALAD PIE/105

1 3-ounce package lime-flavored gelatin
1 cup boiling water
1 8-ounce can (1 cup) unsweetened applesauce
2 tablespoons lemon juice
1 cup shredded zucchini
1/2 cup shredded carrot
2 tablespoons chopped green pepper
2 tablespoons chopped green onion
1 cup dry cottage cheese
1/2 cup dairy sour cream
1 teaspoon finely shredded lemon peel

Dissolve gelatin in the boiling water. Add applesauce and lemon juice. Chill till partially set (consistency of unbeaten egg whites). Fold in the zucchini, carrot, green pepper, and green onion. Turn into a lightly oiled 9-inch pie plate. Chill till firm.

Combine the cottage cheese, sour cream, lemon peel, and dash *salt.* Spread atop the firm mixture in pie plate. Garnish with parsley sprigs and halved cherry tomatoes, if desired. Makes 8 servings.

MINT-DRESSED SPINACH APPLE TOSS/55

1 1 3/4-ounce package powdered fruit pectin
1/8 teaspoon salt
1 cup unsweetened pineapple juice
2 tablespoons lemon juice
2 teaspoons sugar
1 tablespoon sliced green onion
1 tablespoon chopped fresh mint *or* 1/2 teaspoon dried mint, crushed
10 ounces fresh spinach, torn
2 medium apples, cored and cubed
1 small cucumber, thinly sliced
1/3 cup sliced radishes

In small bowl combine powdered pectin and salt. Stir in pineapple juice, lemon juice, and sugar; add onion and mint. Cover; refrigerate at least 1 hour. In large bowl combine torn spinach, cubed apple, sliced cucumber, and sliced radishes. Pour 1/3 cup of the dressing over salad and toss to coat. (Refrigerate remaining dressing.) Makes 8 servings.

SESAME APPLE TOSS/60

1 cup halved seedless green grapes
1 cup sliced celery
1 cup chopped apple
½ cup orange yogurt
6 bibb lettuce cups
2 teaspoons sesame seed, toasted

Combine grapes, celery, and apple; toss to mix. Fold in orange yogurt. Serve in lettuce cups. Sprinkle with toasted sesame seed. Makes 6 servings.

CABBAGE-CARROT MOLD/70

1 envelope unflavored gelatin
½ cup cold water
1 cup boiling water
1 teaspoon instant chicken bouillon granules
¼ cup creamy Italian salad dressing
¼ teaspoon dried dillweed
1 cup finely shredded cabbage
1 cup finely shredded carrot
2 tablespoons finely chopped green pepper
Lettuce (optional)

Soften gelatin in ½ cup cold water. Add 1 cup boiling water and chicken bouillon granules; heat and stir till gelatin is dissolved. Remove from heat. Stir in salad dressing and dillweed. Chill till partially set. Fold in cabbage, carrot, and green pepper. Turn mixture into a 3-cup mold. Cover and chill several hours or overnight till firm. Unmold onto lettuce-lined plate, if desired. Makes 6 servings.

CREAMY STRAWBERRY MOLD/81

2 cups fresh strawberries
1 4-serving envelope low-calorie strawberry-flavored gelatin
1 cup boiling water
⅓ cup dairy sour cream
¼ cup cold water
½ teaspoon vanilla

In blender container or food processor bowl, puree *1 cup* of the strawberries. Slice the remaining berries; set aside. Dissolve gelatin in boiling water. Stir in pureed berries, sour cream, cold water, and vanilla. Chill till partially set (consistency of unbeaten egg whites). Beat at high speed of electric mixer till light and fluffy. Fold in remaining sliced berries. Turn into a 4-cup mold. Chill several hours or till firm. Unmold to serve. Makes 6 servings.

CRUNCHY APPLESAUCE MOLD/77

1 envelope unflavored gelatin
¾ cup cold water
1 cup lemon yogurt
½ cup unsweetened applesauce
⅛ teaspoon ground cinnamon
1 cup finely chopped apple
Lettuce

In saucepan soften gelatin in cold water; stir over low heat till dissolved. In bowl combine lemon yogurt, applesauce, and cinnamon; stir in gelatin. Chill till partially set. Fold in chopped apple. Turn into a 3-cup mold. Chill till firm. To serve, unmold onto lettuce-lined plate. Makes 5 servings.

MOLDED STRAWBERRY SALAD/62

2 cups frozen whole unsweetened strawberries
1 envelope unflavored gelatin
1 cup water
¾ cup lemon yogurt
1 tablespoon honey

Thaw strawberries. Press *1 cup* of the berries through a fine-meshed sieve with the back of a wooden spoon. Slice remaining berries. In saucepan soften gelatin in water; heat to dissolve gelatin. Stir in the mashed berries, lemon yogurt, and honey. Chill till partially set. Fold in the sliced strawberries. Turn mixture into a 3-cup mold. Chill till gelatin mixture is firm. Unmold salad onto serving platter. Makes 6 servings.

PINEAPPLE-PEAR MOLD/94

2 envelopes unflavored gelatin
2½ cups orange juice
1 20-ounce can crushed pineapple (juice pack)
2 medium pears, peeled, cored, and chopped
3 tablespoons finely chopped green pepper (optional)

In saucepan soften gelatin in *½ cup* of the orange juice. Stir over low heat till gelatin is dissolved. Stir in the *undrained* crushed pineapple and the remaining 2 cups orange juice. Chill till partially set. Fold in the chopped pears and green pepper, if desired. Turn mixture into a 6-cup mold. Chill till firm. Unmold onto a plate. Makes 8 servings.

UNMOLDING A GELATIN SALAD

Tower or ring gelatin salads aren't that tricky to unmold—they just seem it.

To begin, dip the mold just to the rim in warm water for a few seconds. Remove mold from water. Tilt mold slightly to ease gelatin away from one side and let air in. With the tip of a small metal spatula, loosen the gelatin from mold by carefully running the spatula around the edges. Place hand over the gelatin and tilt or rotate the mold to let air loosen the gelatin all the way around the salad. Invert mold onto lettuce-lined plate; shake the mold gently. Lift off the mold, being careful not to tear the gelatin. Garnish as desired.

SPICED FRUIT SALAD/73

1 8-ounce can peach slices
¼ cup orange juice
2 tablespoons dry white wine
¼ teaspoon ground cinnamon
Dash ground nutmeg
• • •
1 medium apple, cored and sliced
1 small banana, sliced

In mixing bowl combine *undrained* peach slices, orange juice, white wine, ground cinnamon, and ground nutmeg. Stir in apple and banana slices. Cover and chill for 1 hour. Serve the fruit salad in individual bowls. Makes 4 servings.

SPICED FRUIT MOLD/62

Pictured on page 191—

1 cup apple juice *or* apple cider
4 inches stick cinnamon
4 whole cloves
1 envelope unflavored gelatin
¾ cup orange juice
1 cup chopped apple (1 medium)
⅔ cup orange sections, chopped (2 medium)

In saucepan combine ¾ *cup* of the apple juice or cider, the cinnamon, and cloves. Simmer, covered, for 15 minutes; remove spices. Meanwhile, soften gelatin in the remaining ¼ cup apple juice or cider. Add to apple juice in saucepan; cook and stir over low heat till dissolved. Stir in orange juice. Chill till partially set (consistency of unbeaten egg whites). Fold apple and orange sections into gelatin mixture. Turn into a 3½-cup mold. Chill several hours or till firm. Unmold to serve. Makes 6 servings.

PEACH AND CHEESE MOLD/151

2 4-serving envelopes low-calorie lemon-flavored gelatin
2 cups boiling water
1 cup dry white wine
1 tablespoon lemon juice
1 8-ounce carton plain yogurt
1 16-ounce can peach slices, drained and cut into pieces
½ cup shredded cheddar, Swiss, or Monterey Jack cheese (2 ounces)

In bowl dissolve gelatin in boiling water; stir in wine and lemon juice. With rotary beater, gradually blend gelatin mixture into yogurt. Chill till partially set (consistency of unbeaten egg whites). Fold in peaches and cheese. Turn into a 5½- or 6 cup mold. Chill till firm. Unmold. Serves 8.

CRANBERRY ORANGE MOLD/103

1 cup fresh *or* frozen cranberries
2 tablespoons sugar
1 envelope unflavored gelatin
2 cups low-calorie cranberry juice cocktail
2 medium oranges, peeled, sectioned, and chopped

Using food processor or coarse blade of food grinder, grind cranberries. In bowl stir together cranberries and sugar; set aside. In saucepan soften gelatin in *1 cup* of the cranberry juice cocktail. Cook and stir over low heat till gelatin is dissolved. Cool. Stir in remaining 1 cup cranberry juice cocktail; chill till partially set (consistency of unbeaten egg whites). Fold cranberry mixture and chopped oranges into partially set gelatin mixture; pour into a 4½-cup mold. Chill several hours or till firm. Unmold to serve. Makes 6 servings.

ORANGE WALDORF SALAD/81

3 medium oranges, peeled and sectioned
1½ cups chopped apple
½ cup chopped celery
½ cup lemon yogurt
2 teaspoons honey
6 lettuce leaves

Cut up orange sections over bowl, reserving juice. Toss oranges and juice with apple and celery. Chill. Combine yogurt, honey, and dash *salt;* fold into fruit. Spoon about ½ cup of the salad onto each of 6 lettuce-lined plates. Makes 6 servings.

CREAMY GELATIN SALAD/70

2 envelopes unflavored gelatin
1 cup cold orange juice
2¼ cups orange juice
1 medium orange, peeled, sectioned, and chopped
1 cup plain yogurt
1 tablespoon sugar

Soften gelatin in the 1 cup cold orange juice. In medium saucepan heat 1¾ *cups* of the orange juice just to boiling. Add the softened gelatin; stir to dissolve. Set aside *1 cup* of the gelatin mixture and keep at room temperature.

Stir remaining ½ cup orange juice into remaining gelatin mixture. Chill till partially set. Add the cut-up orange sections. Pour into an 8x8x2-inch pan; chill till almost firm. Combine yogurt and sugar; beat in reserved gelatin. Spoon over fruit layer. Chill till firm. Makes 9 servings.

FRUIT MOLD/90

1 envelope unflavored gelatin
½ cup cold water
1 teaspoon sugar
1 tablespoon lemon juice
1 cup lemon yogurt
1 8-ounce can crushed pineapple (juice pack)
2 small bananas, thinly sliced (1 cup)
⅓ cup chopped celery
Lettuce (optional)

In saucepan soften gelatin in cold water; stir in sugar. Stir over low heat till gelatin and sugar are dissolved. Cool. Add lemon juice. Beat lemon yogurt into cooled mixture till smooth. Stir in *undrained* pineapple, bananas, and celery. Pour into a 3-cup mold; chill till firm. Unmold onto lettuce-lined plate, if desired. Makes 6 servings.

SPARKLING CHERRY-BERRY MOLD/35

1 envelope unflavored gelatin
¼ cup water
2 tablespoons lemon juice
1 tablespoon sugar
1 12-ounce can low-calorie strawberry carbonated beverage
½ cup pitted, halved, fresh *or* frozen dark sweet cherries
½ cup sliced fresh *or* frozen strawberries

In a small saucepan soften gelatin in water. Cook and stir over low heat till gelatin is dissolved. Add lemon juice and sugar; stir till sugar is dissolved. Stir in carbonated beverage; chill till partially set (consistency of unbeaten egg whites). Fold in cherries and strawberries. Pour into a 3-cup mold. Chill several hours or till firm. Unmold to serve. Makes 4 servings.

COTTAGE CHEESE AND FRUIT SALAD/117

- **1 11-ounce can mandarin orange sections, chilled**
- **1 8-ounce can pineapple chunks (juice pack), chilled**
- **½ cup dry cottage cheese**
- **1 medium banana**
- **1 medium apple**
- **Lemon juice**
- **4 lettuce leaves**

Drain orange sections and pineapple chunks; reserve ¼ cup of the fruit liquid. In blender container combine cottage cheese and reserved fruit liquid. Cover; blend till smooth. Slice banana. Core and chop apple. Dip banana slices and chopped apple into a little lemon juice. Combine all fruits; spoon onto lettuce-lined salad plates. Dollop cottage cheese mixture atop. Makes 4 servings.

MINTED FRUIT CUP/79

- **½ cup plain yogurt**
- **2 tablespoons lime juice**
- **2 or 3 teaspoons snipped fresh mint**
- **2 cups seedless green *or* red grapes, halved**
- **3 medium oranges, peeled and sectioned**
- **2 medium apples, cored and sliced**

Stir together yogurt, lime juice, and mint. Combine halved grapes, orange sections, and sliced apples. Pour yogurt mixture over fruit; toss to coat. Cover and chill. To serve, spoon fruit into 8 individual serving dishes. Makes 8 servings.

FRUIT WITH CREAMY BANANA DRESSING/94

- **½ cup small curd cream-style cottage cheese**
- **1 medium banana, cut up**
- **2 to 3 tablespoons orange juice**
- **1 tablespoon honey**
- **½ teaspoon sesame seed, toasted, *or* poppy seed**
- **1 medium orange, peeled, sectioned, and chopped**
- **1 medium apple, thinly sliced**
- **1 medium banana, sliced**
- **1 cup halved fresh strawberries**
- **6 lettuce leaves**

For dressing, in blender container combine cottage cheese, cut up banana, orange juice, and honey. Cover and blend till smooth. Stir in sesame seed or poppy seed.

In medium bowl combine orange, apple, sliced banana, and strawberries; toss to mix. Spoon fruit onto individual lettuce-lined plates. Top each serving of fruit with 2 tablespoons dressing. Makes 6 servings.

APPLE-BANANA FROST/66

- **⅓ cup evaporated skimmed milk**
- **1 cup unsweetened applesauce**
- **1 medium banana, mashed**
- **1 medium orange, peeled, sectioned, and chopped**
- **2 tablespoons honey**
- **8 leaves leaf lettuce**

Pour milk into small mixer bowl. Place in freezer till ice crystals just begin to form around edges. Beat with electric mixer till fluffy. In another bowl combine applesauce, banana, orange, and honey. Fold whipped milk into fruit mixture. Turn into muffin pan lined with paper bake cups; freeze till firm. To serve, remove paper bake cups and invert frozen salads onto lettuce leaves. Let stand 5 minutes before serving. Makes 8 servings.

RAINBOW FRUIT SALAD/125

- **½ medium cantaloupe, peeled and cubed (2 cups)**
- **1 cup halved fresh strawberries**
- **1 cup halved seedless green grapes**
- **1 medium apple, chopped**
- **½ cup evaporated skimmed milk, chilled**
- **½ of a 6-ounce can frozen orange juice concentrate, partially thawed (⅓ cup)**
- **6 lettuce leaves**

Combine cantaloupe, strawberries, grapes, and apple; toss to mix. Combine evaporated skimmed milk and orange juice concentrate; pour over fruit and toss to coat. Serve on individual lettuce-lined plates. Makes 6 servings.

FRUIT MEDLEY SALAD/79

¼ cup plain yogurt
1 tablespoon honey
½ teaspoon finely shredded lemon peel
½ teaspoon lemon juice
Dash salt
1 cup cubed honeydew melon (¼ melon)
1 cup sliced fresh strawberries
1 medium banana, sliced
1 medium apple, sliced
6 leaves leaf lettuce

For honey dressing combine yogurt, honey, lemon peel, lemon juice, and salt. Chill.

Combine melon, strawberries, banana, and apple. For each serving, place about ⅔ cup fruit mixture on a lettuce-lined plate. Spoon about 1 tablespoon honey dressing atop each serving. Makes 6 servings.

BANANA LOGS/118

3 ounces Neufchâtel cheese, softened
2 tablespoons chopped raisins
2 teaspoons brown sugar
⅛ teaspoon ground cinnamon
3 medium bananas
6 leaves leaf lettuce
2 to 3 tablespoons orange juice
4 teaspoons chopped walnuts

Divide cheese in half. Combine half of the cheese, the raisins, brown sugar, and cinnamon. Halve bananas lengthwise, then crosswise. For each serving, spread a banana quarter with about 2 teaspoons cheese mixture and top with another banana quarter; place banana pieces on individual lettuce-lined plate. Combine the remaining Neufchâtel cheese and enough orange juice to make of drizzling consistency; spoon over bananas. Sprinkle with walnuts. Makes 6 servings.

SWEET-SOUR PLUM TOSS/129

¼ cup salad oil
3 tablespoons vinegar
1 tablespoon sugar
1½ teaspoons soy sauce
⅛ teaspoon ground ginger
4 cups torn salad greens
4 fresh medium plums, pitted and sliced
1 small onion, thinly sliced and separated into rings
1 cup fresh bean sprouts

For dressing, in screw-top jar combine salad oil, vinegar, sugar, soy sauce, and ginger; cover and shake to mix. In salad bowl combine greens, plums, onion, and sprouts. Pour dressing over salad; toss to coat. Makes 6 servings.

PEAR AND BLUE CHEESE SALAD/74

3 tablespoons sour cream with blue cheese
1 tablespoon plain yogurt
2 fresh medium pears
Lemon juice
4 leaves leaf lettuce
Paprika

Combine sour cream and yogurt; set aside. Cut each pear in half; remove core. Cut each half into 4 wedges; brush wedges with lemon juice. Arrange pear wedges on 4 lettuce-lined plates. Top each serving with 1 tablespoon yogurt mixture. Sprinkle with paprika. Makes 4 servings.

CITRUS SALAD TOSS/88

4 cups torn bibb lettuce
1 16-ounce jar refrigerated fruits for salad, drained and cut up
½ medium cucumber, thinly sliced
⅓ cup lemon yogurt
6 tablespoons shelled sunflower seed

In salad bowl combine lettuce, fruits for salad, and cucumber. In small bowl combine yogurt and sunflower seed; mix well. Pour yogurt mixture over salad; toss to coat. Makes 4 servings.

CALORIE-TRIMMED DESSERTS

For those with a sweet tooth, we have some delicious suggestions. You can enjoy these desserts and still watch your weight. With moderation and the calorie-trimmed recipes in this chapter, that small portion of dessert at the end of a meal may be just the boost you need for successful dieting.

Ambrosia Cream Puffs

Lime Freeze
and Lemon Freeze

Chocolate Angel Cake

Apricot Spanish Cream

NUTRITION ANALYSIS

Per Serving

DESSERTS

							Percent U.S. RDA Per Serving							
	CALORIES	PROTEIN gms	CARBOHYDRATE gms	FAT gms	SODIUM mgs	POTASSIUM mgs	PROTEIN	VITAMIN A	VITAMIN C	THIAMINE	RIBOFLAVIN	NIACIN	CALCIUM	IRON
AMBROSIA CREAM PUFFS (p. 201)	131	4	18	5	103	157	6	7	16	6	8	3	5	4
APPLE SOUFFLÉ (p. 208)	138	4	14	6	83	119	7	10	24	5	8	2	4	3
APRICOT SPANISH CREAM (p. 215)	105	5	18	2	42	267	8	32	6	3	8	2	7	3
BERRY-MELON FRUIT CUP (p. 208)	52	1	11	1	6	219	1	28	86	3	3	3	2	4
BERRY NECTARINE FLAMBÉ (p. 207)	120	1	27	0	4	343	2	16	96	5	5	5	2	6
BERRY-RICE PUDDING (p. 214)	108	4	17	3	114	149	6	3	31	4	9	2	7	3
CHEESY BAKED APPLES (p. 206)	100	3	17	3	154	106	4	3	7	2	4	1	7	2
CHOCOLATE ANGEL CAKE (p. 204)	96	3	21	0	64	53	5	0	0	4	5	2	1	2
CHOCOLATE BAVARIAN (p. 214)	93	4	12	3	63	110	6	4	1	2	7	0	7	2
CHOCOLATE MOUSSE MERINGUES (p. 212)	126	3	21	4	37	106	5	4	8	1	7	1	6	3
CHOCO-MINT ROLL (p. 203)	125	4	21	3	111	96	7	6	0	2	7	1	5	4
CITRUS-CHEESE SAUCE (p. 215)	16	1	2	1	18	18	1	1	1	0	1	0	1	0
COFFEE MERINGUES (p. 212)	107	2	18	3	25	33	3	4	0	1	4	0	2	2
CREAM PUFFS (p. 201)	74	2	6	4	82	24	4	5	0	4	4	2	1	3
FRUIT CUSTARD PIZZA (p. 207)	180	5	31	5	145	202	7	6	15	9	10	5	7	4
FRUIT 'N' GINGER PEARS (p. 207)	174	2	43	1	7	397	3	3	26	4	6	3	3	6
GINGERBREAD WITH LEMON SAUCE (p. 202)	127	2	30	0	4	129	3	0	5	7	4	4	2	6
HONEYDEW ICE (p. 209)	61	1	15	0	14	293	2	1	46	3	2	4	2	3
HONEY FRUIT COMBO (p. 206)	115	1	29	0	3	239	2	3	51	5	4	2	3	3
INDIVIDUAL MERINGUE SHELLS (p. 212)	42	1	10	0	23	9	1	0	0	0	1	0	0	0
LEMON FREEZE (p. 211)	75	3	11	3	49	76	4	4	7	1	6	0	5	1
LEMON PUDDING CAKE (p. 204)	109	4	14	4	72	94	6	6	6	3	8	1	6	2
LEMON SOUFFLÉ (p. 208)	102	5	11	4	48	95	8	5	8	2	8	0	6	2
LIME FREEZE (p. 211)	74	3	11	3	33	72	4	4	5	1	6	0	5	1
MANDARIN RICE PUDDING (p. 214)	133	6	25	1	69	206	9	5	23	7	13	2	12	3
MAPLE DESSERT CUPS (p. 215)	90	4	11	4	48	127	6	2	1	1	7	0	9	1
ORANGE CAKE ROLL (p. 204)	135	4	22	3	113	73	5	6	17	5	6	2	2	3
ORANGE CHIFFON DESSERT (p. 201)	88	4	12	3	23	117	6	8	38	4	4	1	2	3
ORANGE SPONGE CAKE (p. 202)	87	3	15	2	52	58	4	4	14	2	3	1	1	2
ORANGE YOGURT PIE (p. 211)	149	4	20	7	55	221	6	2	10	6	7	1	10	3
PEACH DESSERT SAUCE (p. 215)	47	1	10	0	18	86	2	4	2	1	4	1	5	0
PEACH TORTE (p. 203)	131	3	22	3	30	106	5	8	2	2	5	2	3	3
PINEAPPLE FLUFF (p. 212)	97	4	14	3	46	148	7	6	8	5	9	1	6	4
POLYNESIAN PARFAITS (p. 208)	100	2	24	1	17	294	3	7	47	8	6	2	7	3
RUM CUSTARD SOUFFLÉ (p. 209)	88	5	11	3	118	105	8	6	1	2	9	0	7	3
STEAMED CRANBERRY PUDDING (p. 201)	137	2	30	1	142	174	3	0	3	8	4	4	3	7
STIRRED CUSTARD (p. 215)	112	7	12	4	88	181	11	7	2	4	16	0	13	4
STRAWBERRY CHIFFON PIE (p. 211)	186	4	23	9	148	103	6	1	46	8	7	6	1	5
STRAWBERRY SPONGE CAKE (p. 202)	120	3	21	3	26	101	5	4	37	2	6	1	3	4
TANGERINE FREEZE (p. 209)	63	2	13	0	38	155	4	3	18	3	7	0	8	1
WAIST-WATCHERS ZABAGLIONE (p. 207)	132	2	22	4	5	149	3	6	8	3	4	1	2	4
WALLBANGER SOUFFLÉ (p. 209)	184	5	15	11	131	87	8	14	7	4	9	1	4	4
WINE FRUIT MEDLEY (p. 206)	72	1	16	0	2	229	1	7	45	3	3	3	1	3
YOGURT-SAUCED PEACHES (p. 206)	87	3	18	1	44	316	5	36	16	3	8	7	5	4

DESSERT RECIPES

ORANGE CHIFFON DESSERT/88

This light dessert is a good suggestion for a company meal since it can be made ahead—

3 tablespoons sugar
1 envelope unflavored gelatin
Dash salt
1 cup orange juice
¼ cup water
3 beaten egg yolks
• • •
1 11-ounce can mandarin orange sections
3 egg whites
½ of a 4-ounce container frozen whipped dessert topping, thawed

In saucepan combine sugar, unflavored gelatin, and salt; stir in orange juice and water. Stir in beaten egg yolks. Cook and stir over medium heat 10 to 12 minutes or till slightly thickened and bubbly. Remove from heat. Chill, stirring occasionally, just till mixture mounds slightly when spooned.

Drain mandarin orange sections; reserve 8 mandarin orange sections for garnish. Chop remaining orange sections; fold into gelatin mixture.

Beat egg whites till stiff peaks form; fold into gelatin mixture. Turn orange mixture into eight 6-ounce custard cups. Cover and chill till firm. If desired, invert onto plate. Top each with about 1 tablespoon whipped dessert topping and a reserved mandarin orange section. Makes 8 servings.

AMBROSIA CREAM PUFFS/131

Pictured on pages 198 and 199—

½ cup orange juice
3 tablespoons sugar
1 tablespoon cornstarch
1 teaspoon finely shredded orange peel
1 cup plain yogurt
1 medium banana, finely chopped
1 egg white
Cream Puffs

In saucepan combine orange juice, *1 tablespoon* of the sugar, the cornstarch, and orange peel. Cook and stir till bubbly. Remove from heat; cool slightly. Fold in yogurt and banana. Chill 2 hours. Beat egg white on high speed of electric mixer to soft peaks; gradually add remaining sugar, beating to stiff peaks. Fold into yogurt mixture. Chill. Prepare Cream Puffs. Cool. To serve, split and fill Cream Puffs with the yogurt filling. Makes 8 servings.

Cream Puffs: In saucepan melt 2 tablespoons *butter or margarine* in ½ cup *boiling water.* Add ½ cup *all-purpose flour* and ⅛ teaspoon *salt* all at once. Stir vigorously. Cook and stir till mixture forms a ball that doesn't separate. Remove from heat; cool 10 minutes. Add 2 *eggs,* one at a time, beating about 30 seconds after each addition. Drop by heaping tablespoonfuls, 3 inches apart, on lightly greased baking sheet. Bake in a 400° oven about 30 minutes or till golden brown and puffy. Remove from oven; cut off tops. Remove soft center from each puff. Cool on rack. Makes 8 cream puffs. (74 calories per puff)

STEAMED CRANBERRY PUDDING/137

This pudding, served warm, is topped with a dollop of whipped topping—

1 cup all-purpose flour
1 teaspoon baking soda
¼ teaspoon ground cinnamon
¼ teaspoon ground nutmeg
Dash ground cloves
• • •
⅓ cup hot water
⅓ cup light molasses
¼ cup packed brown sugar
1 cup halved fresh *or* frozen cranberries
• • •
8 tablespoons thawed frozen whipped dessert topping

In a medium mixing bowl stir together the all-purpose flour, baking soda, ground cinnamon, ground nutmeg, and ground cloves. In a small mixing bowl combine the hot water, light molasses, and brown sugar; stir into flour mixture along with the halved cranberries. Pour batter into a greased 1-quart mold. Cover the mold with greased foil and tie securely with a string.

Place mold on rack in deep kettle; add boiling water to a depth of 1 inch to kettle. Cover; steam for 2½ hours, adding more boiling water to kettle, if necessary. Cool steamed pudding 10 minutes; unmold. Serve the pudding while warm with whipped topping. Makes 8 servings.

STRAWBERRY SPONGE CAKE/120

- **1 cup sifted cake flour**
- **1¼ cups sifted powdered sugar**
- **5 egg yolks**
- **½ teaspoon salt**
- **5 egg whites**
- **1 teaspoon vanilla**
- **½ teaspoon cream of tartar**
- **½ teaspoon almond extract**
- **1 1½-ounce envelope dessert topping mix**
- **½ cup skim milk**
- **¼ cup currant jelly**
- **4 cups fresh whole strawberries, sliced**

Combine flour and ½ *cup* of the powdered sugar; set aside. Beat egg yolks on high speed of electric mixer till thick and lemon-colored. Gradually add ½ cup of the remaining powdered sugar and ½ teaspoon salt, beating constantly. Wash beaters thoroughly. Beat egg whites with vanilla, cream of tartar, and extract till soft peaks form. Gradually add remaining ¼ cup powdered sugar, beating till stiff peaks form. Gently fold yolk mixture into whites. Sift flour mixture over batter, ⅓ at a time; gently fold in just till blended. Turn into an *ungreased* 10-inch tube pan. Bake in a 325° oven for 30 minutes or till cake tests done. Invert cake in pan; cool completely. Remove cake from pan.

At serving time, slice cake in half horizontally. Combine dessert topping mix and the skim milk; beat with electric mixer till soft peaks form. In a small saucepan heat jelly till melted. To assemble cake, place one half of cake on a serving plate; spoon *half* of the whipped dessert topping over top of cake. Arrange *half* the berries atop; drizzle with *half* the jelly. Top with remaining cake layer. Spoon remaining whipped topping over cake. Top with remaining berries and melted jelly. Serves 16.

ORANGE SPONGE CAKE/87

- **1 cup sifted cake flour**
- **1¼ cups sifted powdered sugar**
- **5 egg yolks**
- **¼ teaspoon salt**
- **1 tablespoon finely shredded orange peel**
- **5 egg whites**
- **1 teaspoon vanilla**
- **½ teaspoon cream of tartar**
- **1 cup orange juice**
- **1 tablespoon honey**
- **¾ teaspoon almond extract**

Combine cake flour and ½ *cup* of the sifted powdered sugar; set aside. In small mixer bowl beat egg yolks on high speed of electric mixer about 6 minutes or till thick and lemon-colored. Gradually add the remaining ¾ cup sifted powdered sugar and the salt, beating constantly about 4 minutes. Stir in the shredded orange peel.

Wash beaters thoroughly. In large mixer bowl beat egg whites, vanilla, and cream of tartar till soft peaks form. Gently fold yolk mixture into whites. Sift flour mixture over egg mixture, ⅓ at a time, and fold in gently. Turn into an *ungreased* 9-inch tube pan. Bake in a 325° oven about 55 minutes or till cake springs back and leaves no imprint when lightly touched. Invert cake in pan; cool thoroughly. Remove from pan.

With a long-tined fork, poke holes in top of cake at 1-inch intervals. For syrup, in a saucepan combine orange juice and honey. Simmer for 5 minutes. Remove from heat; stir in almond extract. Spoon syrup liquid evenly over cake, a small amount at a time, allowing cake to absorb the syrup. Chill, if desired. Makes 16 servings.

GINGERBREAD WITH LEMON SAUCE/127

As shown on the back cover—

- **1 cup all-purpose flour**
- **1 teaspoon baking soda**
- **¼ teaspoon ground ginger**
- **¼ teaspoon ground cinnamon**
- **¼ teaspoon ground nutmeg**
- **¼ cup packed brown sugar**
- **¼ cup water**
- **¼ cup light molasses**
- **½ teaspoon finely shredded lemon peel (set aside)**
- **2 tablespoons lemon juice**
- **Non-stick vegetable spray coating**

• • •

- **¼ cup sugar**
- **1 tablespoon cornstarch**
- **⅛ teaspoon salt**
- **⅛ teaspoon ground nutmeg**
- **¾ cup water**
- **2 tablespoons lemon juice**

In medium mixing bowl stir together the flour, baking soda, ginger, cinnamon, and ¼ teaspoon nutmeg. Mix well. In small bowl combine brown sugar, the ¼ cup water, molasses, and 2 tablespoons lemon juice; stir into flour mixture just till blended. Quickly pour batter into 3 soup cans (2½-inch diameter) sprayed with non-stick vegetable spray coating. Cover with foil. Bake in a 350° oven for 20 to 25 minutes or till wooden pick inserted in center comes out clean. Cool 10 minutes; remove from cans.

Meanwhile, for lemon sauce, in small saucepan combine sugar, cornstarch, salt, the ⅛ teaspoon nutmeg, and lemon peel. Stir in the ¾ cup water. Cook and stir till thickened and bubbly. Stir in 2 tablespoons lemon juice and a few drops yellow food coloring, if desired. Slice gingerbread and serve topped with lemon sauce. Makes 9 servings.

CHOCO-MINT ROLL/125

- **4 egg yolks**
- **Few drops red food coloring**
- **¼ cup sugar**
- **4 egg whites**
- **¼ cup sugar**
- **½ cup sifted cake flour**
- **¼ cup unsweetened cocoa powder**
- **1 teaspoon baking powder**
- **¼ teaspoon salt**
- **1 tablespoon powdered sugar**

• • •

- **⅓ cup sugar**
- **⅓ cup nonfat dry milk powder**
- **2 tablespoons cornstarch**
- **Dash salt**
- **1 cup water**
- **2 well-beaten eggs**
- **Few drops peppermint extract**

In small mixer bowl beat 4 egg yolks about 5 minutes or till thick and lemon-colored. Add food coloring. Gradually add ¼ cup sugar, beating till sugar dissolves. Wash beaters thoroughly.

In large mixer bowl beat 4 egg whites to soft peaks; gradually add ¼ cup sugar, beating to stiff peaks. Fold yolks into whites. Sift together flour, cocoa, baking powder, and ¼ teaspoon salt; fold into egg mixture. Spread evenly in a greased and waxed paper-lined 15x10x1-inch jelly-roll pan. Bake in a 375° oven for 10 to 12 minutes. Loosen sides of cake; turn out onto a towel sprinkled with the powdered sugar. Carefully peel off paper. Starting at narrow end, roll the warm cake and towel together; cool the rolled cake thoroughly on a wire rack.

To prepare filling, in a saucepan combine ⅓ cup sugar, the milk powder, cornstarch, and dash salt. Add the 1 cup water. Cook and stir over medium heat till mixture is bubbly; cook and stir 2 minutes more. Remove from heat. Stir about *half* of the hot mixture into the 2 beaten eggs; return all to saucepan. Cook and stir just till bubbly; cook and stir 2 minutes more. Remove from heat; add extract. Cover with clear plastic wrap; cool. Unroll cake; spread with filling. Roll up. Cover; chill. Slice to serve. Makes 12 servings.

PEACH TORTE/131

- **Non-stick vegetable spray coating**
- **⅔ cup sifted cake flour**
- **¼ cup sifted powdered sugar**
- **3 egg yolks**
- **¼ cup sifted powdered sugar**
- **¼ teaspoon salt**
- **3 egg whites**
- **½ teaspoon vanilla**
- **¼ teaspoon cream of tartar**
- **¼ teaspoon almond extract**
- **¼ cup sifted powdered sugar**

• • •

- **1 16-ounce can peach slices (juice pack)**
- **2 tablespoons sugar**
- **1 tablespoon cornstarch**
- **⅛ teaspoon almond extract**
- **1 1½-ounce envelope dessert topping mix**
- **½ cup skim milk**

Spray two 8x1½-inch round baking pans with non-stick vegetable spray coating; line with waxed paper. Set aside.

In a bowl combine flour and ¼ cup powdered sugar; set aside. Beat egg yolks on high speed of electric mixer about 6 minutes or till thick and lemon-colored. Gradually add ¼ cup powdered sugar and the salt, beating constantly. Wash beaters thoroughly.

Beat egg whites, vanilla, cream of tartar, and ¼ teaspoon almond extract till soft peaks form. Gradually add the remaining ¼ cup powdered sugar beating till stiff peaks form. Gently fold yolk mixture into whites. Sift flour mixture over egg mixture, ⅓ at a time, folding in gently just till blended. Turn into the prepared pans. Bake in a 325° oven about 20 minutes or till cakes spring back and leave no imprint when lightly touched. (Cakes will be light in color.) Invert cakes in pans; cool completely. Remove cakes from pans; remove waxed paper.

Meanwhile, drain peaches, reserving ½ cup juice. Coarsely chop peach slices; set aside. In saucepan combine sugar and cornstarch. Stir in the reserved peach juice. Cook and stir till thickened and bubbly; cook and stir 1 to 2 minutes more. Remove from heat. Stir in peaches and ⅛ teaspoon almond extract. Cover and cool.

Combine dessert topping mix and milk; beat with electric mixer till soft peaks form. To assemble torte, place one cake layer on serving plate; spoon *half* of the peach mixture over cake. Top with *half* of the dessert topping. Add second cake layer. Pipe or spread remaining dessert topping in a spiral atop cake. Fill spiral with remaining peach mixture. Chill. Makes 10 servings.

ORANGE CAKE ROLL/135

4 egg yolks
1 tablespoon frozen orange juice concentrate, thawed
½ teaspoon finely shredded orange peel
¼ cup sugar
4 egg whites
⅓ cup sugar
½ cup all-purpose flour
1 teaspoon baking powder
¼ teaspoon salt
Sifted powdered sugar
• • •
1 1½-ounce envelope dessert topping mix
1 medium orange, peeled, sectioned, and cut up
Orange slices (optional)
Finely shredded orange peel (optional)

In a small mixer bowl beat 4 egg yolks at high speed of electric mixer till thick and lemon-colored. Add orange juice concentrate and ½ teaspoon orange peel; beat at low speed till blended. Beat at medium speed till thick. Gradually add the ¼ cup sugar, beating till sugar is dissolved. Wash beaters thoroughly.

In a large mixer bowl beat 4 egg whites at medium speed of electric mixer till soft peaks form. Gradually add the ⅓ cup sugar; continue beating till stiff peaks form. Fold yolks into whites. Thoroughly stir together flour, baking powder, and salt; sprinkle over egg mixture. Gently fold in flour mixture just till blended. Spread batter evenly in a greased and floured 15x10x1-inch jelly roll pan. Bake in a 375° oven for 12 to 15 minutes or till done.

Immediately loosen edges of cake from pan and turn out onto towel sprinkled with sifted powdered sugar. Starting with the narrow end, roll the warm cake and towel together; cool on wire rack. Prepare topping mix according to package directions, using skim milk. Fold in cut-up orange. Unroll cake; spread topping mixture over cake, leaving a 1-inch rim. Roll up cake. If desired, garnish with orange slices and orange peel. Serves 10.

LEMON PUDDING CAKE/109

3 egg whites
Dash salt
¼ cup sugar
3 egg yolks
1 teaspoon finely shredded lemon peel
¼ cup lemon juice
2 tablespoons butter *or* margarine, melted
¼ cup sifted all-purpose flour
2 tablespoons sugar
1½ cups *reconstituted* nonfat dry milk

In a large bowl beat egg whites with salt on high speed of electric mixer till soft peaks form (tips curl over). Gradually add the ¼ cup sugar, beating to stiff peaks (tips stand straight). In another bowl beat egg yolks with lemon peel, lemon juice, and melted butter or margarine. Combine flour and 2 tablespoons sugar; stir along with milk into egg yolk mixture. Fold in egg whites. Pour batter into an ungreased 8x8x2-inch baking pan. Place in larger pan on oven rack. Pour hot water to a depth of 1 inch into larger pan. Bake in a 350° oven for 35 to 40 minutes. Serve warm or chilled. Makes 9 servings.

CHOCOLATE ANGEL CAKE/96

Pictured on pages 198 and 199—

1 cup sifted cake flour
¾ cup sifted powdered sugar
3 tablespoons unsweetened cocoa powder
10 egg whites
1½ teaspoons cream of tartar
1½ teaspoons vanilla
¼ teaspoon salt
1 cup sifted powdered sugar
Rum Royale Glaze

Sift together flour, ¾ cup powdered sugar, and cocoa powder into bowl; repeat sifting. Set aside.

In a large mixer bowl beat egg whites with cream of tartar, vanilla, and salt at medium speed of electric mixer till soft peaks form (tips curl over). Gradually add the 1 cup powdered sugar, 2 tablespoons at a time, beating at high speed till stiff peaks form (tips stand straight).

Sift about ¼ cup of the flour mixture over whites; fold in. Repeat, folding in remaining flour by fourths. Turn the batter into an *ungreased* 9-inch tube pan. Bake cake on the lower oven rack in a 375° oven for 30 to 35 minutes or till cake tests done.

Invert cake in pan; cool. Using a spatula, loosen cake from pan; remove. Drizzle Rum Royale Glaze over cake. Slice into thin wedges to serve. Makes 16 servings.

Rum Royale Glaze: In small bowl stir together ½ cup sifted *powdered sugar,* ¼ teaspoon *rum extract,* and enough *milk* (about 2 teaspoons) to make of drizzling consistency.

Orange Cake Roll; Berry-Rice Pudding (see recipe, page 214)

DESSERT TOPPING TIPS

The kind of whipped topping you use on your diet dessert makes a big difference in your dessert's total calorie count. For example, regular whipping cream, whipped and sweetened, has 28 calories per tablespoon; frozen whipped dessert topping has 14 calories per tablespoon; the same amount of topping from a mix (made with whole milk) totals just 10 calories.

FRESH FRUIT SUBSTITUTES

If your favorite fruits are not in season, you can purchase them canned or frozen for little difference in calories. For canned fruits, choose juice pack, water pack, or calorie-reduced pack (slightly sweetened). If you use regular syrup-pack fruits, rinse the fruit with water before using. In frozen fruit, look for the unsweetened loose-pack variety.

YOGURT-SAUCED PEACHES/87

You can substitute your favorite in-season fruits for the peaches—

- **½ cup cream-style cottage cheese**
- **⅓ cup skim milk**
- **2 tablespoons sugar**
- **1 teaspoon lemon juice**
- **⅛ teaspoon ground cardamom**
- **Few drops almond extract**
- **½ cup plain yogurt**
- **8 fresh medium peaches** ***or*** **two 16-ounce cans peach slices (juice pack)**

In blender container or food processor bowl combine cottage cheese, skim milk, sugar, lemon juice, cardamom, and almond extract. Cover; process till smooth. Fold in yogurt. Chill. At serving time, peel, pit, and slice fresh peaches (*or*, drain canned peaches). Divide peach slices among 8 sherbet dishes. Spoon sauce over peaches. Makes 8 servings.

HONEY FRUIT COMBO/115

- **3 medium oranges**
- **3 medium pears, cored and cut up**
- **1 cup pitted dark sweet cherries**
- **¼ cup honey**
- **1 tablespoon lemon juice**

Shred 1 teaspoon peel from oranges; set peel aside. Peel and cut up oranges; combine in bowl with pears and cherries. Combine honey, lemon juice, and reserved orange peel. Drizzle the honey mixture over fruit. Chill. Makes 8 servings.

CHEESY BAKED APPLES/100

- **4 medium baking apples, peeled, cored, and cut into eighths**
- **¼ cup water**
- **2 teaspoons lemon juice**
- **2 tablespoons sugar**
- **1 tablespoon all-purpose flour**
- **¼ teaspoon ground cinnamon**
- **½ cup shredded American cheese (2 ounces)**

Arrange apple slices in a shallow baking dish; sprinkle with the water and the lemon juice. Combine sugar, flour, ground cinnamon, and ⅛ teaspoon *salt;* sprinkle over apples. Bake, covered, in a 350° oven about 45 minutes or till apples are tender. Uncover; top with the shredded American cheese. Bake 5 minutes more or till cheese melts. Makes 6 servings.

WINE FRUIT MEDLEY/72

- **⅓ cup orange juice**
- **¼ cup port wine**
- **1 tablespoon sugar**
- **1 tablespoon lemon juice**
- **1 cup fresh whole strawberries, sliced**
- **1 medium peach, peeled, pitted, and sliced**
- **1 medium pear, peeled, cored, and diced**
- **1 medium banana, sliced**

Combine orange juice, port wine, sugar, and lemon juice. Place cut-up fruits in a bowl. Pour juice mixture over; toss lightly to mix. Cover the fruit mixture and chill thoroughly. Makes 6 servings.

BERRY NECTARINE FLAMBÉ/120

- **3 cups fresh strawberries**
- **2 tablespoons sugar**
- **2 teaspoons cornstarch**
- **½ of a 6-ounce can frozen pineapple-orange juice concentrate, thawed (⅓ cup)**
- **½ cup cold water**
- **2 or 3 drops red food coloring (optional)**
- **2 fresh medium nectarines, peeled and sliced**
- **½ teaspoon finely shredded orange peel**
- **2 tablespoons rum**

Mash ½ *cup* of the berries; halve remaining berries. In blazer pan of chafing dish combine sugar and cornstarch; gradually stir in mashed berries, juice concentrate, water, and food coloring, if desired. Cook and stir over medium heat till thickened and bubbly. Add halved berries, nectarines, and orange peel. Return to boiling. Warm rum in ladle. Ignite carefully and pour over fruit. When flame dies, spoon fruit into serving dishes. Makes 6 servings.

FRUIT 'N' GINGER PEARS/174

- **6 medium pears**
- **1 8¾-ounce can fruit cocktail**
- **⅓ cup orange juice**
- **2 teaspoons chopped candied ginger**
- **1 tablespoon cornstarch**
- **1 tablespoon water**
- **3 tablespoons dry sherry**

Core pears; peel, if desired. Drain fruit cocktail, reserving syrup. Add water to make ⅔ cup liquid. In medium skillet combine reserved syrup, orange juice, and candied ginger. Place whole pears in liquid and bring to boiling. Reduce heat; cover and set aside. Combine cornstarch and water; stir into hot liquid in skillet. Cook and stir till thickened and bubbly. Remove from heat; stir in sherry and fruit cocktail. Place pears in 6 large wineglasses or sherbets. Spoon fruit cocktail sauce into core cavity and over pears, crowning with cherry half. Serve the sauced pears warm or cool. Makes 6 servings.

WAIST-WATCHERS ZABAGLIONE/132

- **3 medium pears, sliced**
- **3 medium apples, sliced**
- **1 tablespoon lemon juice**
- **3 egg yolks**
- **¼ cup cream sherry**
- **2 tablespoons sugar**
- **Dash salt**
- **½ of a 4-ounce container frozen whipped dessert topping, thawed**

Sprinkle pears and apples with lemon juice; toss to coat. Set aside. In top of double boiler beat egg yolks and sherry till combined; stir in sugar and salt. Place over boiling water (water should not touch upper pan). Beat at high speed of electric mixer for 6 to 8 minutes or till mixture thickens and mounds. When thick, place pan over ice water (if using a glass pan, transfer contents to metal bowl). Continue beating 2 to 3 minutes or till cool. Fold in whipped dessert topping. Serve over fruit immediately. Makes 8 servings.

FRUIT CUSTARD PIZZA/180

- **½ cup small-curd cream-style cottage cheese**
- **¼ cup butter *or* margarine, softened**
- **1 cup all-purpose flour**
- **½ cup quick-cooking rolled oats**
- **1 teaspoon finely shredded lemon peel**
- **¼ teaspoon salt**
- **½ of a 2⅛-ounce package (1 envelope) low-calorie vanilla pudding mix**
- **2 cups skim milk**
- **½ cup low-calorie apricot jam**
- **1 banana, sliced**
- **1 small orange, peeled and sectioned**
- **1 8¼-ounce can pineapple slices, drained**
- **1 8¾-ounce can peach slices, drained**

In small mixer bowl combine cottage cheese and butter; beat till smooth and well blended. In large bowl stir together flour, rolled oats, lemon peel, and salt. Add cottage cheese mixture to dry ingredients; mix well. Form into ball. With hands, press evenly into greased 12-inch pizza pan, forming rim about ½ inch above edge. Crimp edge. Bake in a 400° oven for 15 to 20 minutes; cool.

In saucepan prepare pudding mix according to package directions, using the 2 cups skim milk. Cover surface with clear plastic wrap; chill. Spread in prepared crust. Heat jam till melted. Arrange fruit atop pudding; brush with melted jam. Chill. Makes 12 servings.

POLYNESIAN PARFAITS/100

½ cup plain yogurt
2 teaspoons sugar
1 medium banana, sliced
Lemon juice
1 11-ounce can mandarin orange sections, drained
1 8-ounce can pineapple chunks (juice pack), drained
Ground nutmeg

Combine yogurt and sugar. Dip banana slices into lemon juice to prevent darkening. Layer yogurt mixture with banana slices, orange sections, and pineapple chunks in 4 sherbet dishes. Sprinkle each serving with nutmeg. Cover and chill at least 1 hour. Makes 4 servings.

BERRY-MELON FRUIT CUP/52

Pictured in menu on page 33—

2 cups sliced fresh strawberries
2 cups cantaloupe balls (1 medium)
2 tablespoons shredded coconut, toasted
⅓ cup orange juice
1 tablespoon honey
1 tablespoon orange liqueur
¼ teaspoon ground ginger

In large bowl combine strawberries, cantaloupe, and coconut; toss to mix. In small bowl combine orange juice, honey, orange liqueur, and ginger; add to fruit mixture, stirring to coat. Cover and chill about 1 hour. Makes 8 servings.

APPLE SOUFFLÉ/138

It's important to serve the soufflé as soon as it comes out of the oven—

Non-stick vegetable spray coating
2 egg yolks

• • •

4 teaspoons butter *or* margarine
2 tablespoons all-purpose flour
¼ cup skim milk
2 tablespoons frozen apple juice concentrate, thawed
1 tablespoon apple brandy *or* brandy

• • •

2 egg whites
2 tablespoons sugar

Spray the bottom and sides of a 1-quart soufflé dish and a foil collar with the non-stick vegetable spray coating. Secure the foil collar around the top of the soufflé dish using tape or a piece of string.

In a small mixer bowl beat the egg yolks on high speed of electric mixer about 6 minutes or till thick and lemon-colored; set aside. In saucepan melt butter or margarine; stir in flour. Add the milk all at once. Cook and stir till mixture is very thick and bubbly. Remove from heat. Stir in apple juice concentrate and brandy. Slowly add egg yolks, stirring constantly. Wash beaters.

In large mixer bowl beat egg whites till soft peaks form. Gradually add sugar, beating till stiff peaks form; gently fold into yolk mixture. Turn into soufflé dish. Bake in a 300° oven about 60 minutes. Serve immediately. Makes 4 servings.

LEMON SOUFFLÉ/102

1 envelope unflavored gelatin
¼ cup lemon juice
¼ cup water
2 egg yolks
2 tablespoons sugar
1 cup skim milk
2 egg whites
1 1½-ounce envelope dessert topping mix
Shredded lemon peel (optional)
Lemon slices (optional)

In small saucepan soften unflavored gelatin in lemon juice and water; heat just till gelatin is dissolved. Remove from heat.

In small mixer bowl beat egg yolks on high speed of electric mixer; gradually add sugar, beating about 5 minutes or till thick and lemon-colored. Gradually beat in hot gelatin mixture; beat in milk. Cool till mixture is partially set (consistency of unbeaten egg whites). Wash beaters thoroughly. Beat egg whites just till stiff peaks form (tips stand straight); *do not overbeat.* Fold in gelatin mixture.

Prepare dessert topping mix according to package directions, *except* use skim milk. Fold ¼ cup of the prepared topping into gelatin mixture (refrigerate remaining topping for another use). Pour gelatin mixture into a 3-cup soufflé dish with foil collar. (*Or,* use a 4-cup soufflé dish without collar or use six ½-cup individual soufflé dishes.) Refrigerate at least 3 hours or till set. To serve, remove foil collar. Garnish with shredded lemon peel and lemon slices, if desired. Makes 6 servings.

Note: If desired, use the remaining whipped dessert topping to garnish each serving. Be sure to count the extra calories the garnish adds to the serving total.

WALLBANGER SOUFFLÉ/184

Butter *or* margarine
Sugar
5 egg yolks
¼ cup butter *or* margarine
¼ cup all-purpose flour
½ cup milk
¼ cup orange juice
3 tablespoons Galliano
5 egg whites
⅓ cup sugar

Lightly butter and dust a 2-quart soufflé dish with sugar about halfway up the sides. Attach a foil collar around the top. (To make a foil collar, cut a 30-inch-long piece of 12-inch-wide foil. Fold in fourths to form a 30x3-inch piece. Wrap foil around top of soufflé dish and secure it tightly with tape.)

In small mixer bowl beat egg yolks on high speed of electric mixer 5 to 6 minutes or till thick and lemon colored; set aside. In saucepan melt the ¼ cup butter or margarine. Blend in flour. Add milk all at once. Cook and stir till mixture thickens and bubbles. Stir in orange juice. Stir about ½ cup of the hot mixture into the beaten egg yolks; mix well. Return all to hot mixture in saucepan. Cook and stir 2 minutes more. Remove from heat; stir in Galliano.

In large mixer bowl beat egg whites till soft peaks form. Gradually add the ⅓ cup sugar, beating to stiff peaks. Fold the egg whites into the hot mixture. Turn into the soufflé dish. Bake in a 300° oven for 55 to 60 minutes. Serve at once. Makes 8 servings.

RUM CUSTARD SOUFFLÉ/88

½ cup nonfat dry milk powder
⅓ cup sugar
1 envelope unflavored gelatin
¼ teaspoon salt
1½ cups cold water
4 beaten egg yolks
½ teaspoon rum flavoring
4 egg whites
Ground nutmeg

In saucepan combine milk powder, sugar, gelatin, and salt; stir in cold water. Stir in egg yolks. Cook and stir over medium heat till mixture just coats a metal spoon. Remove from heat; stir in rum flavoring. Chill till partially set (consistency of unbeaten egg whites); stir occasionally. In a large mixer bowl beat egg whites on high speed of electric mixer to stiff peaks (tips stand straight); fold into gelatin mixture. Turn into a 4-cup soufflé dish with foil collar; sprinkle with nutmeg. Chill several hours or overnight or till firm. Makes 8 servings.

TANGERINE FREEZE/63

5 cups skim milk
½ of a 2⅛-ounce package (1 envelope) low-calorie vanilla pudding mix
1 6-ounce can frozen tangerine juice concentrate, thawed
½ cup sugar
1 teaspoon vanilla
3 drops red food coloring
2 drops yellow food coloring
Toasted coconut (optional)

In saucepan gradually stir *2 cups* milk into pudding mix. Cook and stir over medium heat till thickened and bubbly. Blend in remaining milk, tangerine juice concentrate, sugar, vanilla, and food coloring. Freeze in 4-quart ice cream freezer according to ice cream freezer manufacturer's directions. Let ripen by packing additional ice and salt into the outer freezer container, covering freezer, and letting it stand several hours till mixture hardens slightly. Garnish with toasted coconut, if desired. Serves 20.

HONEYDEW ICE/61

Pictured on page 213—

1 teaspoon unflavored gelatin
2 tablespoons water
4 cups cubed honeydew melon (1 medium)
2 tablespoons lime juice
2 tablespoons honey

In 1-cup glass measure or a custard cup soften gelatin in water; place in pan of water. Heat and stir till gelatin is dissolved. In blender container combine *1 cup* of the melon cubes, the lime juice, honey, and the gelatin mixture. Cover and blend at high speed for 30 seconds or till smooth. Add remaining melon; cover and blend at high speed 30 to 45 seconds or till smooth. Pour into an 8x8x2-inch pan. Freeze till almost firm.

In chilled large mixer bowl beat mixture at high speed of electric mixer till smooth. Return to pan; freeze several hours or till firm. To serve, let stand 15 to 20 minutes at room temperature. Scrape surface and spoon into serving dishes. If desired, garnish with lime twists. Makes 6 servings.

LIME FREEZE/74

Both lime and lemon variations are pictured on pages 198 and 199—

½ cup evaporated skimmed milk
2 egg yolks
⅓ cup sugar
½ teaspoon grated lime peel
2 tablespoons lime juice
Dash salt
3 or 4 drops green food coloring (optional)
• • •
2 egg whites
2 tablespoons lime juice
Lime *or* lemon twists

Pour milk into shallow container; freeze till icy cold. In a mixing bowl combine egg yolks, sugar, lime peel, 2 tablespoons lime juice, salt, and food coloring; set aside. In another bowl beat the icy milk and egg whites with electric mixer till fluffy. Add 2 tablespoons lime juice; beat till stiff peaks form (tips stand straight). Beat in egg yolk mixture. Pour into an 8x4x2-inch loaf pan; freeze firm. With a fork, break mixture into chunks. In chilled mixer bowl beat with electric mixer for 5 to 6 minutes or till smooth. Return to loaf pan; freeze firm. Scoop to serve; garnish with lime or lemon twists. Makes 8 servings.

Lemon Freeze: Prepare Lime Freeze as above *except* substitute *lemon peel* and *lemon juice* for the lime peel and juice. Add *yellow food coloring,* if desired.

Strawberry Chiffon Pie

STRAWBERRY CHIFFON PIE/186

Pastry Shell
2½ cups fresh strawberries
1 envelope unflavored gelatin
¾ cup water
2 egg whites
¼ cup sugar
1 1¼-ounce envelope low-calorie dessert topping mix

Prepare and bake Pastry Shell; cool. Reserve a few strawberries for garnish. In large mixing bowl crush enough of the remaining berries to measure 1¼ cups crushed berries. Set aside. In small saucepan combine gelatin and water; heat and stir till gelatin dissolves. Cool 20 minutes; stir into the crushed strawberries. Chill to the consistency of corn syrup, stirring occasionally. Remove from refrigerator (gelatin mixture will continue to set). Beat egg whites till soft peaks form. Gradually add sugar, beating till stiff peaks form. When gelatin is consistency of unbeaten egg whites, fold in stiff-beaten egg whites.

Prepare topping mix according to package directions. Fold into strawberry mixture. Chill till mixture mounds when spooned. Pile mixture into pastry shell; chill 8 hours or till firm. Garnish with reserved strawberries. Serve with additional whipped topping, if desired. Serves 8.

Pastry Shell: Stir together 1 cup *all-purpose flour* and ½ teaspoon *salt.* Cut in ⅓ cup *shortening* till pieces are the size of small peas. Sprinkle 1 tablespoon *cold water* over part of the mixture; gently toss with fork. Push to side of bowl; repeat with 2 to 3 tablespoons additional *cold water* until all flour mixture is moistened. Form into a ball.

On lightly floured surface, flatten dough with hands. Roll from center to edge forming a circle about 12 inches in diameter. Wrap pastry around rolling pin. Unroll onto 9-inch pie plate. Ease pastry into pie plate, being careful to avoid stretching pastry. Trim edge ½ to 1 inch beyond edge of pie plate; fold excess under. Flute edge. Prick bottom and sides. Bake in a 450° oven for 10 to 12 minutes. Cool.

ORANGE YOGURT PIE/149

1⅓ cups flaked coconut (1 3½-ounce can)
1 tablespoon butter *or* margarine, melted
1 20-ounce can crushed pineapple (juice pack)
1 envelope unflavored gelatin
2 8-ounce cartons orange yogurt

Place 1¼ *cups* of the coconut in a bowl; toss with melted butter or margarine. Press on the bottom and up sides of a 9-inch pie plate. Bake in a 325° oven about 15 minutes or till golden. Cool on wire rack. Place remaining coconut in a shallow pan and toast in a 325° oven about 1 minute. Set aside.

Drain pineapple, reserving juice. Set fruit aside. Add water, if necessary, to reserved juice to make ¾ cup liquid. In small saucepan soften gelatin in the pineapple liquid. Cook and stir over low heat till gelatin is dissolved. Chill till partially set (consistency of unbeaten egg whites). Beat partially set gelatin mixture till fluffy. Fold in yogurt and drained pineapple. Pile into cooled crust. Garnish with reserved toasted coconut. Chill till firm. Makes 8 servings.

CHOCOLATE MOUSSE MERINGUES/126

Individual Meringue Shells
¼ cup sugar
3 tablespoons unsweetened cocoa powder
1 teaspoon unflavored gelatin
½ cup evaporated skimmed milk
2 slightly beaten egg yolks
Dash salt
½ teaspoon vanilla
1 1½-ounce envelope dessert topping mix
½ cup skim milk
5 fresh strawberries, halved

Prepare Individual Meringue Shells. Cool the meringues thoroughly.

In a heavy saucepan combine sugar, cocoa powder, and gelatin. Stir in evaporated skimmed milk, egg yolks, and salt, mixing till well blended. Cook and stir over low heat about 3 minutes or till slightly thickened; stir in vanilla. Cool for 5 to 10 minutes. (If mixture appears curdled, stir well with wire whisk.)

In small mixer bowl combine dessert topping mix and skim milk; beat with electric mixer till soft peaks form. Fold *half* of the dessert topping into the chocolate mixture; cover and chill. Cover and chill remaining topping till serving time. At serving time, spoon *1 tablespoon* of the whipped dessert topping, then *3 tablespoons* of the chocolate mixture into each meringue shell. Top each with a strawberry half. Makes 10 servings.

Individual Meringue Shells: Let 2 *egg whites* come to room temperature. For meringue, in small mixer bowl combine the egg whites, ½ teaspoon *vanilla,* ¼ teaspoon *cream of tartar,* and dash *salt.* Beat on high speed of electric mixer till soft peaks form (tips curl over). Gradually add ½ cup *sugar,* beating till stiff peaks form (tips stand straight) and sugar is dissolved. Line a baking sheet with plain brown paper. Draw ten 2½-inch circles on paper; place a mound of meringue on each. Using back of spoon, shape meringue into shells. Bake in a 300° oven for 35 minutes. (For crisper meringues, turn off oven. Dry meringue shells in oven with door closed about 1 hour more.) Makes 10.

COFFEE MERINGUES/107

10 Individual Meringue Shells
3 beaten egg yolks
¼ cup sugar
¼ cup *reconstituted* nonfat dry milk
2 teaspoons instant coffee crystals
Dash salt
1 1½-ounce envelope dessert topping mix
1 stiff-beaten egg white

Prepare Individual Meringue Shells. Cool the meringues thoroughly.

In small saucepan combine egg yolks, sugar, ¼ cup milk, coffee crystals, and salt. Cook over low heat, stirring constantly, till mixture coats a metal spoon. Remove from heat. Cool quickly by placing pan in a bowl of ice water; stir till mixture is cooled.

Prepare topping mix according to package directions *except* use skim milk or reconstituted nonfat dry milk. Fold topping and egg white into cooled cooked mixture. Chill. To serve, spoon into meringue shells. Makes 10 servings.

PINEAPPLE FLUFF/97

Be sure to serve this light dessert right after the egg whites are folded in—

1 8-ounce can crushed pineapple (juice pack)
3 tablespoons nonfat dry milk powder
• • •
2 beaten egg yolks
1 tablespoon sugar
½ teaspoon vanilla
• • •
2 egg whites
1 tablespoon sugar

Drain pineapple well, reserving juice. Chill pineapple. Add water to reserved juice, if necessary, to make ½ cup. Dissolve dry milk powder in pineapple juice.

In a small heavy saucepan combine the milk mixture, egg yolks, and 1 tablespoon sugar; cook over low heat, stirring constantly till mixture thickens and coats a metal spoon. Remove from heat; place saucepan in a pan of ice water to cool. Stir in vanilla. When cooled, cover and chill the egg-milk mixture for 2 to 4 hours.

At serving time, fold pineapple into cooked mixture. In a small mixer bowl beat egg whites on high speed of electric mixer till soft peaks form (tips curl over); gradually add 1 tablespoon sugar, beating till stiff peaks form (tips stand straight). Gently fold egg whites into the pineapple mixture. Spoon into chilled serving dishes. Serve immediately. Makes 4 servings.

Chocolate Mousse Meringues; Honeydew Ice (see recipe, page 209)

CHOCOLATE BAVARIAN/93

⅔ cup nonfat dry milk powder
⅓ cup sugar
2 tablespoons cornstarch
2 tablespoons unsweetened cocoa powder
1 envelope unflavored gelatin
⅛ teaspoon salt
1½ cups cold water
3 beaten egg yolks

• • •

2 egg whites
1 teaspoon vanilla
¼ teaspoon cream of tartar
½ of a 4-ounce container frozen whipped dessert topping, thawed

In saucepan combine the dry milk powder, sugar, cornstarch, cocoa powder, gelatin, and salt. Stir in cold water. Cook and stir over medium heat till thickened and bubbly. Stir about *half* of the hot mixture into egg yolks; return all to saucepan. Bring to a gentle boil. Cook and stir 1 minute more. Set the mixture aside to cool.

In a medium mixer bowl beat egg whites, vanilla, and cream of tartar on high speed of electric mixer till stiff peaks form (tips stand straight). Fold into cooled chocolate mixture. Fold in whipped dessert topping. Turn into a 4- or 5-cup mold. Chill several hours or overnight or till firm. Garnish with additional whipped topping, if desired. Makes 10 servings.

BERRY-RICE PUDDING/108

This updated old favorite, but with fewer calories, is pictured on page 205—

1⅓ cups water
⅔ cup evaporated skimmed milk
⅓ cup long grain rice
1 beaten egg yolk
2 tablespoons sugar
2 tablespoons lemon juice
¼ teaspoon salt
1 teaspoon vanilla
¼ teaspoon grated lemon peel
3 egg whites
¼ teaspoon cream of tartar
2 tablespoons sugar
1 cup sliced fresh strawberries
Finely shredded lemon peel
8 whole fresh strawberries

In medium saucepan combine water, evaporated skimmed milk, and rice. Bring to boiling. Reduce heat; cook, covered, over low heat for 20 minutes, stirring often. Uncover; cook 5 minutes more. In a small bowl combine egg yolk, 2 tablespoons sugar, lemon juice, and salt. Stir about *1 cup* of the hot mixture into yolk mixture; return all to saucepan. Bring to a gentle boil. Cook and stir over low heat for 3 to 4 minutes or till slightly thickened. Remove from heat; stir in vanilla and ¼ teaspoon lemon peel. Cool mixture thoroughly.

In a medium bowl beat egg whites and cream of tartar on high speed of electric mixer till soft peaks form (tips curl over). Gradually add 2 tablespoons sugar, beating till stiff peaks form (tips stand straight). Fold egg whites into cooled pudding. Fold in sliced berries; spoon mixture into 8 sherbet dishes. Cover and chill several hours. To serve, garnish with finely shredded lemon peel and whole strawberries. Makes 8 servings.

MANDARIN RICE PUDDING/133

2 cups skim milk
⅓ cup long grain rice
1 beaten egg yolk
¼ teaspoon finely shredded orange peel (set aside)
2 tablespoons orange juice
2 tablespoons sugar
¼ teaspoon salt
1 teaspoon vanilla
3 egg whites
¼ teaspoon cream of tartar
2 tablespoons sugar
1 11-ounce can mandarin orange sections, chilled and drained
Mint sprigs

In medium saucepan combine milk and rice. Bring to boiling. Reduce heat; cook, covered, over low heat for 20 minutes, stirring occasionally. Uncover; cook the rice mixture 5 minutes more.

In a small bowl combine egg yolk and orange juice; stir in 2 tablespoons sugar and the salt. Gradually stir about *1 cup* of the hot rice mixture into yolk mixture; return all to saucepan. Bring mixture to a gentle boil. Cook and stir over low heat about 2 minutes or till slightly thickened. Remove from heat; stir in vanilla and orange peel. Cool thoroughly.

In a small mixer bowl beat egg whites and cream of tartar on high speed of electric mixer till soft peaks form. Gradually add 2 tablespoons sugar, beating till stiff peaks form. Fold egg whites into cooled rice mixture. Set aside 6 orange sections for garnish. Fold remaining orange sections into rice mixture. Cover and chill for several hours. To serve, garnish the rice pudding with reserved orange sections and mint sprigs. Makes 6 servings.

CITRUS-CHEESE SAUCE/16

4 ounces Neufchâtel cheese, softened
3 tablespoons sugar
1 teaspoon finely shredded orange peel
½ teaspoon finely shredded lemon peel
1 tablespoon orange juice
1 tablespoon lemon juice
⅓ cup nonfat dry milk powder

In small bowl beat together cheese, sugar, orange and lemon peel, and orange and lemon juice on low speed of electric mixer till smooth. Cover; chill. To serve, in mixing bowl combine milk powder and ⅓ cup *ice water;* beat till stiff peaks form (tips stand straight). Fold into cheese mixture (do not overmix). Serve over slices of cake or cut up fruit. Makes about 2 cups, or 32 one-tablespoon servings.

STIRRED CUSTARD/112

3 beaten eggs
3 tablespoons sugar
2 cups *reconstituted* nonfat dry milk
½ teaspoon vanilla
Ground nutmeg

In top of double boiler combine eggs, sugar, milk, and dash *salt.* Cook and stir over hot (not boiling) water till mixture coats a metal spoon. Remove from heat and cool slightly. Stir in vanilla. Cool completely. Turn into dessert dishes. Cover and chill. To serve the custard, sprinkle with ground nutmeg. Makes 5 servings.

Note: If desired, serve Stirred Custard over cut-up fresh fruit.

APRICOT SPANISH CREAM/105

This rich-tasting delight is pictured on pages 198 and 199—

1 16-ounce can unpeeled apricot halves
1 envelope unflavored gelatin
¼ cup sugar
Dash salt
1 cup *reconstituted* nonfat dry milk
2 beaten egg yolks
2 egg whites
Mint sprigs

Drain apricot halves, reserving ¾ cup liquid; halve apricot halves and set aside. In saucepan combine gelatin, sugar, and salt; stir in reserved apricot liquid, milk, and beaten egg yolks. Cook and stir over low heat till gelatin and sugar dissolve. Remove from heat; chill till partially set (consistency of unbeaten egg whites). Beat egg whites on high speed of electric mixer till stiff peaks form (tips stand straight). Fold into gelatin mixture. Turn into six individual molds. Chill till firm. Unmold. Garnish with reserved apricots and mint. Serves 6.

MAPLE DESSERT CUPS/90

1 envelope unflavored gelatin
2 tablespoons brown sugar
⅔ cup evaporated skimmed milk
½ teaspoon maple flavoring
1 egg white
1 tablespoon brown sugar
6 tablespoons thawed frozen whipped dessert topping

In saucepan combine gelatin and 2 tablespoons brown sugar; stir in ½ cup *cold water.* Cook and stir over medium heat till gelatin and sugar dissolve. Remove from heat; stir in evaporated skimmed milk and maple flavoring. Pour mixture into large bowl; chill till almost set.

Beat egg white and 1 tablespoon brown sugar till stiff peaks form (tips stand straight). Beat chilled gelatin mixture using electric mixer till light and fluffy. Fold in beaten egg white. Spoon into 6 sherbet dishes. Chill till firm. To serve, top each serving with a spoonful of the thawed whipped dessert topping. Makes 6 servings.

PEACH DESSERT SAUCE/47

Another time, try this dessert sauce over fresh raspberries instead of the frozen yogurt—

1½ cups chopped fresh *or* frozen unsweetened peaches
¼ cup sugar
2 teaspoons cornstarch
½ teaspoon finely shredded lemon peel
¼ teaspoon ground cinnamon
¼ teaspoon ground nutmeg
Dash salt
⅓ cup water
8 scoops (⅓ cup each) lemon *or* vanilla frozen yogurt

Mash ¾ *cup* of the chopped peaches; set aside. In saucepan stir together sugar, cornstarch, lemon peel, cinnamon, nutmeg, and salt. Add water; mix well. Stir in mashed peaches and chopped peaches. Cook and stir till thickened and bubbly. Reduce heat; simmer for 5 to 7 minutes or till desired consistency, stirring occasionally. Remove from heat; serve warm over scoops of lemon or vanilla frozen yogurt. Makes 8 servings.

CALORIE-TRIMMED
BEVERAGES & SNACKS

If you plan to snack between meals, make sure what you eat is as nutritious and as calorie-trimmed as possible. Try some of the appetizer, snack, and beverage suggestions in this chapter to help stave off those between-meal cravings.

Strawberry-Yogurt Drink

Cottage Cheese-Tomato Appetizers; Potted Pepper Dip

Raspberry Sparkle Punch

NUTRITION ANALYSIS

Snacks probably are the biggest offenders when it comes to upsetting the nutrition in a good diet. Too often they consist only of "empty" calories – calories accompanied by little, if any, nutritional value. Snacks also can sap your mealtime appetite, causing you to bypass more-nutritious foods throughout the day. Good snacks should be just enough to tide you to your next meal and be as nutritious and as appetizing as possible. The best snacks are small amounts of any meat, grain, fruit, vegetable, or milk-based food group. Limit them to two or three pieces. Keep protein snacks one-fourth to one-third the size of a main dish portion. To carry you over from one meal to another, try a hard-cooked egg, some fruit, a cold soup, or vegetable nibblers. And, don't forget about beverages for fast and easy perk-ups.

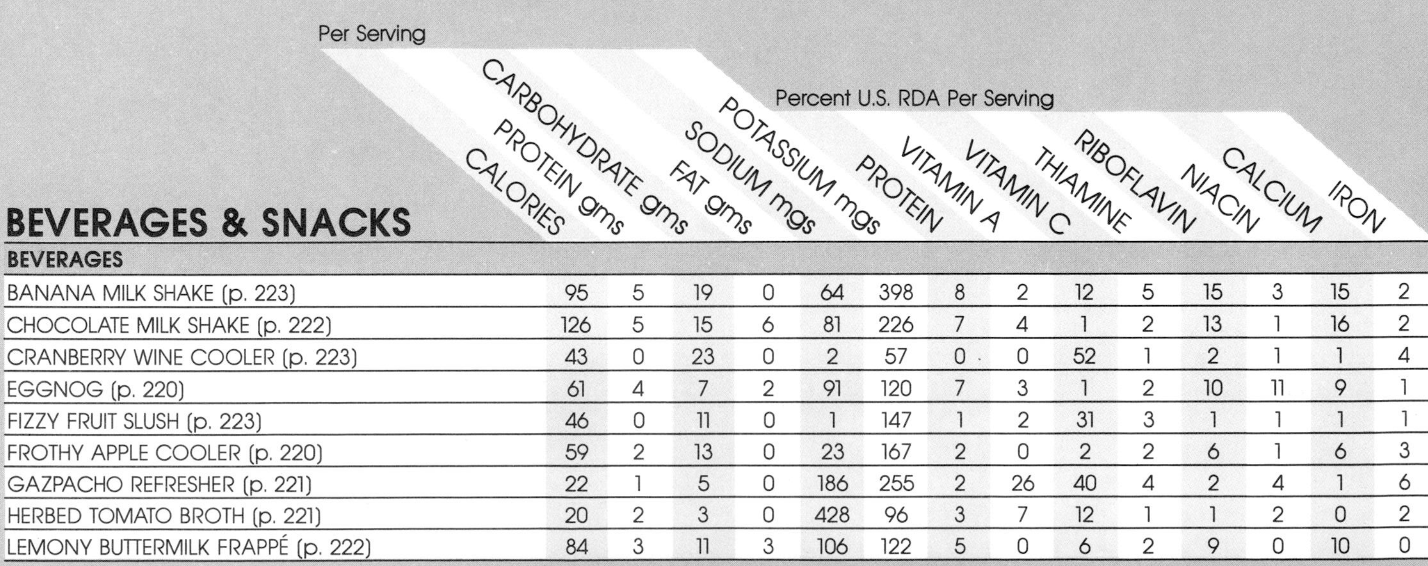

BEVERAGES & SNACKS	Per Serving						Percent U.S. RDA Per Serving							
	CALORIES	PROTEIN gms	CARBOHYDRATE gms	FAT gms	SODIUM mgs	POTASSIUM mgs	PROTEIN	VITAMIN A	VITAMIN C	THIAMINE	RIBOFLAVIN	NIACIN	CALCIUM	IRON
BEVERAGES														
BANANA MILK SHAKE (p. 223)	95	5	19	0	64	398	8	2	12	5	15	3	15	2
CHOCOLATE MILK SHAKE (p. 222)	126	5	15	6	81	226	7	4	1	2	13	1	16	2
CRANBERRY WINE COOLER (p. 223)	43	0	23	0	2	57	0	0	52	1	2	1	1	4
EGGNOG (p. 220)	61	4	7	2	91	120	7	3	1	2	10	11	9	1
FIZZY FRUIT SLUSH (p. 223)	46	0	11	0	1	147	1	2	31	3	1	1	1	1
FROTHY APPLE COOLER (p. 220)	59	2	13	0	23	167	2	0	2	2	6	1	6	3
GAZPACHO REFRESHER (p. 221)	22	1	5	0	186	255	2	26	40	4	2	4	1	6
HERBED TOMATO BROTH (p. 221)	20	2	3	0	428	96	3	7	12	1	1	2	0	2
LEMONY BUTTERMILK FRAPPÉ (p. 222)	84	3	11	3	106	122	5	0	6	2	9	0	10	0

BEVERAGES & SNACKS

	Per Serving						Percent U.S. RDA Per Serving							
	CALORIES	PROTEIN gms	CARBOHYDRATE gms	FAT gms	SODIUM mgs	POTASSIUM mgs	PROTEIN	VITAMIN A	VITAMIN C	THIAMINE	RIBOFLAVIN	NIACIN	CALCIUM	IRON
MOCHA MILK SHAKE (p. 222)	127	5	15	6	81	235	7	4	1	2	13	1	16	2
ORANGE BERRY WAKE-UP (p. 222)	157	5	31	2	61	366	8	6	115	8	15	3	13	5
ORANGE-PEACH REFRESHER (p. 220)	69	2	15	0	24	332	4	20	60	6	8	5	7	3
PINEAPPLE PUNCH (p. 223)	41	0	10	0	1	128	1	1	26	3	1	1	1	1
RASPBERRY SPARKLE PUNCH (p. 220)	46	0	12	0	0	34	0	0	16	1	1	1	0	1
RHUBARB-APPLE CRUSH (p. 223)	70	1	17	0	2	313	2	5	82	7	3	3	6	3
SPICED HOT COCOA (p. 221)	92	7	16	1	99	379	11	0	2	5	21	1	25	3
SPICED ICED COFFEE (p. 223)	38	2	7	0	32	116	3	0	1	1	7	2	8	0
STRAWBERRY COOLER (p. 222)	134	1	33	0	2	337	2	5	140	8	4	4	3	4
STRAWBERRY MILK SHAKE (p. 222)	120	5	13	6	75	232	7	4	25	2	14	1	16	2
STRAWBERRY SHAKE (p. 222)	67	3	14	0	39	205	5	1	60	3	10	2	10	3
STRAWBERRY SLUSH (p. 222)	134	1	33	0	2	337	2	5	140	8	4	4	3	4
STRAWBERRY-YOGURT DRINK (p. 220)	93	5	17	1	109	353	7	3	44	5	15	3	15	3
VEGETABLE BEEF BROTH (p. 221)	24	2	4	0	468	134	3	10	16	2	1	2	1	3
VEGETABLE REFRESHER (p. 220)	31	2	6	0	216	267	4	11	16	4	6	4	6	3
ZIPPY TOMATO COOLER (p. 221)	37	3	7	0	247	288	4	16	34	4	6	4	6	6
SNACKS														
BANANA ORANGE YOGURT POPS (p. 229)	115	5	23	1	61	236	7	1	4	3	10	1	12	1
BLUE CHEESE DIP (p. 229)	13	2	1	0	42	15	3	1	1	0	2	0	2	0
CARROT BALLS (p. 226)	40	2	3	3	68	52	3	22	4	3	4	2	4	1
COTTAGE CHEESE-TOMATO APPETIZERS (p. 224)	9	1	2	0	28	85	1	6	13	1	1	1	1	1
CRANBERRY FRUIT DIP (p. 224)	24	1	5	0	7	27	1	0	2	0	1	0	2	0
CREAMY CHEESE SNACKS (p. 224)	28	1	2	2	55	10	1	1	0	1	1	1	1	0
CURRIED-STUFFED EGGS (p. 226)	25	2	0	2	43	21	3	4	1	1	2	0	1	2
GARDEN VEGETABLE DIP (p. 229)	7	0	1	0	16	23	1	1	1	0	1	0	1	0
HOT CHEESE SNACKS (p. 231)	24	1	2	1	87	12	1	1	1	1	2	1	2	1
OATMEAL COOKIES (p. 231)	30	1	4	1	40	14	1	1	0	1	1	0	0	1
PICKLED CARROTS AND ZUCCHINI (p. 229)	43	0	11	0	9	97	1	40	6	1	1	1	1	1
PICKLED SHRIMP (p. 226)	60	11	3	0	214	162	17	1	3	1	1	9	4	6
PINEAPPLE YOGURT NUT LOAF (p. 230)	95	3	16	3	60	144	4	1	1	6	4	3	4	5
POTTED PEPPER DIP (p. 228)	15	1	1	1	73	30	1	1	18	1	1	1	1	0
QUICK WHOLE WHEAT BREAD (p. 231)	151	3	23	5	209	133	5	4	1	8	6	4	5	5
SMOKED OYSTER SNACKS (p. 225)	67	3	10	2	38	57	5	2	4	2	2	3	5	5
SPAGHETTI DIP (p. 228)	10	1	1	0	37	42	1	1	22	1	2	0	2	0
SPINACH DIP (p. 229)	39	1	1	4	69	47	1	10	9	1	2	0	2	1
TACO POPCORN SNACK (p. 226)	76	1	11	3	131	24	2	14	6	9	9	6	1	15
TOASTY OAT CRACKERS (p. 231)	19	1	2	1	23	12	1	1	0	2	1	1	0	1
VEGETABLE CHEESE DIP (p. 228)	22	1	1	2	37	36	1	10	9	0	1	0	1	0
WHOLE WHEAT BISCUIT CRACKERS (p. 224)	40	1	5	2	87	17	1	2	0	2	1	1	1	1
ZUCCHINI DIP (p. 226)	24	1	1	2	60	38	1	3	4	1	2	1	1	0

BEVERAGES

STRAWBERRY-YOGURT DRINK/93

Pictured on pages 216 and 217—

1 cup fresh *or* frozen unsweetened whole strawberries
1 cup buttermilk
1 8-ounce carton plain yogurt
1 ripe large banana, cut up
8 ice cubes

Thaw strawberries, if frozen. In blender container combine buttermilk, yogurt, banana, ice cubes, and strawberries. Cover and blend till mixture is smooth. Pour into 4 glasses. Makes 4 servings.

ORANGE-PEACH REFRESHER/69

2 medium peaches *or* 4 medium apricots
1 cup orange juice
¼ cup nonfat dry milk powder
8 ice cubes

Peel and pit peaches or apricots. In blender container combine orange juice, milk powder, ice cubes, and fruit. Cover and blend till the mixture is smooth. Pour into 2 glasses. Garnish with additional peach or apricot slices and mint sprigs, if desired. Makes 2 servings.

FROTHY APPLE COOLER/59

1½ cups apple juice, chilled
¼ cup nonfat dry milk powder
¼ teaspoon ground cinnamon
3 ice cubes

In blender container combine apple juice, milk powder, cinnamon, and ice cubes. Cover and blend till smooth. Serve immediately. Makes 4 servings.

RASPBERRY SPARKLE PUNCH/46

Pictured on pages 216 and 217—

1 10-ounce package frozen red raspberries, thawed
2 cups water
1 6-ounce can (¾ cup) frozen lemonade concentrate, thawed
Fruited Ice Ring
2 16-ounce bottles low-calorie lemon-lime carbonated beverage, chilled

Sieve raspberries; discard seeds. Combine water, sieved berries, and lemonade concentrate. Chill. At serving time pour the raspberry mixture into punch bowl. Add Fruited Ice Ring; carefully pour in the carbonated beverage. Stir gently to mix. Makes 16 four-ounce servings.

Fruited Ice Ring: Arrange orange slices, lemon slices, and mint sprigs in bottom of ring mold. Fill with cold water. Freeze till firm. Unmold before placing in punch bowl.

EGGNOG/61

4 egg yolks
¼ cup sugar
¼ teaspoon salt
4 cups *reconstituted* nonfat dry milk
1 teaspoon vanilla
¼ teaspoon brandy flavoring
4 egg whites
Ground nutmeg

Beat egg yolks, sugar, and salt; stir in *2 cups* of the milk. Cook and stir over medium heat till mixture coats a metal spoon. Remove from heat; add remaining milk. Stir in vanilla and brandy flavoring. Cover and chill.

To serve, beat egg whites till soft peaks form. Carefully fold yolk mixture into beaten egg whites. Serve eggnog in cups; sprinkle with nutmeg. Makes 14 four-ounce servings.

VEGETABLE REFRESHER/31

½ medium cucumber
2 cups vegetable juice cocktail, chilled
1 cup buttermilk

Peel cucumber; halve lengthwise and remove seeds. Cut cucumber into pieces. In blender container combine chilled vegetable juice cocktail, buttermilk, and cucumber. Cover and blend till cucumber is pureed. Serve cold. Serves 6.

SPICED HOT COCOA/92

Use a dollop of whipped nonfat dry milk for the cocoa topping—

¼ cup unsweetened cocoa powder
2 tablespoons sugar
Dash salt
1 cup water
6 inches stick cinnamon
6 whole cloves
• • •
1⅓ cups nonfat dry milk powder
3 cups water
¼ teaspoon vanilla
• • •
⅓ cup nonfat dry milk powder
⅓ cup ice water

In saucepan combine unsweetened cocoa powder, sugar, and salt; add the 1 cup water, stick cinnamon, and cloves. Bring to boiling, stirring constantly. Reduce heat; simmer for 5 minutes.

Reconstitute the 1⅓ cups nonfat dry milk powder in the 3 cups water. Add to chocolate mixture in saucepan. Bring just to boiling; stir in vanilla. Remove cinnamon sticks and the whole cloves.

In mixer bowl combine ⅓ cup nonfat dry milk powder and ⅓ cup ice water; beat at high speed of electric mixer till stiff peaks form.

Pour hot cocoa into 6 heatproof mugs; top with a dollop of the whipped milk. Serve with more stick cinnamon stirrers, if desired. Makes 6 servings.

VEGETABLE BEEF BROTH/24

This is good served warm or chilled—

1 12-ounce can vegetable juice cocktail
1 10½-ounce can condensed beef broth
½ cup water

In saucepan combine vegetable juice cocktail, beef broth, and water; heat through. Serve in mugs. Makes 6 servings.

ZIPPY TOMATO COOLER/37

½ medium cucumber
1 canned green chili pepper
• • •
1 18-ounce can tomato juice, chilled
1 cup buttermilk
1 teaspoon Worcestershire sauce
1 teaspoon lemon juice
Ice cubes

Peel cucumber; halve lengthwise and remove seeds. Cut into chunks. Drain and seed chili pepper. In blender container combine tomato juice, buttermilk, Worcestershire, lemon juice, cucumber, and chili pepper. Cover and blend till cucumber is pureed. Serve the mixture over ice cubes. If desired, serve with cucumber stick stirrers. Makes 6 servings.

HERBED TOMATO BROTH/20

1 10½-ounce can condensed beef broth
1 cup tomato juice
¼ teaspoon dried marjoram, crushed
¼ teaspoon dried thyme, crushed
1 tablespoon snipped parsley

Combine beef broth, tomato juice, marjoram, thyme, and ¾ cup *water.* Heat to boiling. Reduce heat and simmer 2 minutes. Ladle into mugs. Garnish with parsley. Serve immediately. Makes 6 servings.

GAZPACHO REFRESHER/22

Pictured on page 230—

1½ cups tomato juice, chilled
3 ice cubes
¼ medium green pepper
¼ medium carrot
¼ medium cucumber
2 sprigs parsley
2 teaspoons lemon juice
Dash garlic salt
Few drops bottled hot pepper sauce
½ medium cucumber, cut into spears

Place tomato juice in blender container. While blending at high speed, add ice cubes, one at a time, blending till smooth. Add green pepper, carrot, the ¼ medium cucumber, parsley, lemon juice, garlic salt, and hot pepper sauce. Cover and blend at high speed about 30 seconds. Serve with cucumber spears as stirrers. Serves 4.

LEMONY BUTTERMILK FRAPPÉ/84

2 cups buttermilk
1½ teaspoons finely shredded lemon peel
2 tablespoons lemon juice
2 tablespoons sugar
6 drops yellow food coloring (optional)
1 cup whipped low-calorie dessert topping

In blender container combine buttermilk, lemon peel, lemon juice, sugar, and food coloring, if desired. Cover and blend till mixture is frothy. Fold in the whipped dessert topping; pour the mixture into 6 chilled glasses. Makes 6 servings.

ORANGE BERRY WAKE-UP/157

1 cup orange juice
1 egg
1 10-ounce package frozen strawberries, partially thawed
½ cup nonfat dry milk powder
½ cup cold water

In blender container combine orange juice, egg, strawberries, milk powder, and cold water. Cover and blend till mixture is smooth. Serve in glasses. Garnish with orange twists and strawberries, if desired. Makes 4 servings.

STRAWBERRY SHAKE/67

2 cups fresh *or* frozen whole unsweetened strawberries
1½ cups skim milk
2 tablespoons sugar
Dash ground cinnamon

If using fresh strawberries, halve larger berries; freeze. In blender container combine milk, sugar, and cinnamon; gradually add frozen berries. Blend on medium speed till smooth. Serve in glasses. Makes 5 servings.

STRAWBERRY COOLER/134

2 cups orange juice
1 10-ounce package frozen strawberries, thawed
1 cup unsweetened pineapple juice
1½ cups carbonated water
Ice cubes

In blender container place orange juice, strawberries, and pineapple juice; cover and blend till frothy. Gently stir in carbonated water; pour over ice in tall glasses. Makes 5 eight-ounce servings.

Strawberry Slush: Prepare Strawberry Cooler as above *except* do not add the carbonated water. Pour mixture into a 9x9x2-inch pan; freeze solid. Remove from freezer and let stand at room temperature for 10 to 15 minutes. To make a slush, scrape spoon across surface of frozen mixture; spoon into bowl. Slowly add carbonated water; stir gently to mix. Spoon into glasses. (134 calories per serving)

CHOCOLATE MILK SHAKE/126

A rich, creamy drink that is surprisingly low in calories—

¾ cup evaporated skimmed milk
¼ cup cold water
2 tablespoons frozen whipped dessert topping, thawed
2 tablespoons chocolate-flavored syrup
1 teaspoon vanilla
• • •
6 1¼-inch ice cubes

In blender container combine the evaporated skimmed milk, water, thawed whipped dessert topping, chocolate-flavored syrup, and vanilla. Cover container. With blender running, add ice cubes one at a time through hole in lid, blending at lowest speed till mixture is thickened. Makes 3 eight-ounce servings.

Mocha Milk Shake: Prepare Chocolate Milk Shake as above *except* stir 1 teaspoon *instant coffee crystals* into the cold water before adding to the blender container. (127 calories per serving)

Strawberry Milk Shake: Prepare Chocolate Milk Shake as above *except* omit chocolate-flavored syrup and add ½ cup fresh *or* frozen whole unsweetened *strawberries* and 1 tablespoon *sugar* with evaporated skimmed milk to blender container. (120 calories per serving)

BANANA MILK SHAKE/95

1 medium-large banana
1 cup skim milk
½ teaspoon vanilla

Peel banana; cut into 1-inch pieces. Wrap in foil and freeze. In blender container combine milk, vanilla, and banana; cover and blend. Makes 2 servings.

FIZZY FRUIT SLUSH/46

Pictured on page 230—

1½ cups unsweetened pineapple juice
1½ cups water
½ of a 6-ounce can (⅓ cup) frozen orange juice concentrate, thawed
1 medium banana, pureed
1 tablespoon honey
2 12-ounce cans low-calorie lemon-lime carbonated beverage, chilled

In a 2-quart pitcher combine pineapple juice, water, orange juice concentrate, banana, and honey; mix well. Pour into a 9x5x3-inch loaf pan. Cover and freeze several hours or till firm. To serve, thaw juice mixture at room temperature about 30 minutes or till able to scrape surface of mixture to form a slush. For each serving place ⅓ *cup* of the slush in a glass and add ¼ *cup* of the lemon-lime carbonated beverage. Makes 12 servings.

RHUBARB-APPLE CRUSH/70

1 pound fresh rhubarb, cut into ½-inch pieces (3 cups)
3 cups water
2 tablespoons honey
1 6-ounce can frozen apple juice concentrate
1 teaspoon grenadine syrup
Crushed ice
1 16-ounce bottle low-calorie lemon-lime carbonated beverage, chilled

In saucepan combine rhubarb, water, and honey. Bring to boiling; reduce heat. Cover and simmer about 10 minutes or till rhubarb is very tender. Strain to remove pulp; chill the syrup and discard pulp. Combine rhubarb syrup, apple juice concentrate, and grenadine syrup; pour ½ *cup* mixture over crushed ice in each glass. Carefully pour ¼ *cup* carbonated beverage into each glass; stir. Serves 8.

SPICED ICED COFFEE/38

1½ cups skim milk
2 tablespoons sugar
2 tablespoons instant coffee powder
¼ teaspoon ground cinnamon
1 16-ounce bottle low-calorie cola beverage, chilled
Ice cubes

In blender container combine first 4 ingredients. Cover; blend till combined. Just before serving, carefully add chilled cola beverage. Stir gently. Serve immediately over ice. Makes 6 servings.

CRANBERRY WINE COOLER/43

1 32-ounce bottle low-calorie cranberry juice cocktail, chilled
1 12-ounce can low-calorie lemon-lime carbonated beverage, chilled
½ cup dry red wine, chilled
Ice cubes
8 whole fresh strawberries

In a 2-quart pitcher stir together chilled cranberry juice cocktail, carbonated beverage, and wine. Pour into ice-filled glasses. Garnish each serving with a strawberry. Makes 8 servings.

PINEAPPLE PUNCH/41

1½ cups water
6 inches stick cinnamon
12 whole cloves
Noncaloric sweetener equal to ¼ cup sugar
1 46-ounce can unsweetened pineapple juice
1½ cups orange juice
½ cup lemon juice
2 16-ounce bottles low-calorie lemon-lime carbonated beverage, chilled

In saucepan combine water, cinnamon, and cloves. Cover and simmer 15 minutes; strain into a large pitcher. Cool. Add sweetener and fruit juices; chill. Just before serving, pour into large punch bowl; slowly pour in lemon-lime carbonated beverage. Serve over ice cubes in punch cups. Makes 24 four-ounce servings.

SNACKS

SENSIBLE SNACKING

When watching your weight, remember to count calories from snacks. Here are some helpful calorie-cutting snack ideas

- *Reserve a part of a meal, such as the salad or dessert, for an afternoon or late-evening snack.*
- *Snack on foods that provide part of your nutritional needs, not "empty" calories. For example, a milk-based beverage supplies calcium, protein, and vitamins A and D, and a meat sandwich provides protein.*
- *Eat fresh fruits and vegetables that are low in calories for excellent snacks.*
- *Make sandwiches with thin-sliced bread. Or, serve open-face sandwiches.*
- *Cut calories by flavoring yogurt yourself. Just add crushed fruit and a little sugar to plain yogurt.*

CREAMY CHEESE SNACKS/28

½ of an 8-ounce package Neufchâtel cheese, softened
1 tablespoon sliced green onion
¼ teaspoon celery seed
Dash garlic powder
24 melba toast rounds
Paprika

In small mixer bowl combine cheese, green onion, celery seed, and garlic powder. Beat with electric mixer till smooth. Spread about *1 teaspoon* of the cheese mixture on each toast round; place on ungreased baking sheet. Sprinkle with paprika. Broil 5 inches from heat about 1 minute or just till cheese is hot. Serve immediately. Makes 24.

CRANBERRY FRUIT DIP/24

1 8-ounce carton vanilla yogurt
½ cup cranberry-orange relish
¼ teaspoon ground nutmeg
¼ teaspoon ground ginger
Assorted fruits for dipping (strawberries, apple slices, mandarin orange sections, and pineapple slices)

In a small bowl combine yogurt, cranberry-orange relish, nutmeg, and ginger; mix till well blended. Cover and chill. Serve with assorted fruits for dipping. If desired, garnish with a strawberry and mint sprigs. Makes about 1¼ cups, or 20 one-tablespoon servings.

WHOLE WHEAT BISCUIT CRACKERS/40

½ cup whole wheat flour
½ cup all-purpose flour
2 tablespoons sugar
1 teaspoon baking powder
½ teaspoon baking soda
¼ teaspoon cream of tartar
¼ teaspoon salt
¼ cup butter *or* margarine
⅓ cup buttermilk

In bowl combine dry ingredients; cut in butter till mixture resembles coarse crumbs. Add buttermilk. Stir with fork just till dough follows fork around bowl. On floured surface roll out to ¼-inch thickness. Using floured 2½-inch biscuit cutter, cut dough into 12 circles. Place on ungreased baking sheet. Bake in a 350° oven for 12 to 15 minutes or till lightly browned.

Reduce oven temperature to 300°. Split hot biscuits with sharp knife; place cut sides up on baking sheet. Dry in a 300° oven for 12 to 15 minutes. Makes 24.

COTTAGE CHEESE-TOMATO APPETIZERS/9

Pictured on pages 216 and 217—

24 cherry tomatoes
¼ cup dry cottage cheese
½ medium cucumber, shredded and drained
¼ teaspoon salt
Dash dried dillweed
Dash pepper

Cut small slice off bottoms of cherry tomatoes so they will sit flat. Cut thin slice from tops of tomatoes. With small melon baller or spoon carefully scoop out centers of tomatoes; discard. Sprinkle insides with a little salt and pepper. Invert and chill.

In bowl combine cottage cheese, shredded cucumber, salt, dillweed, and pepper. Cover and chill.

To serve, spoon a small amount of cottage cheese mixture into each cherry tomato. Makes 24.

SMOKED OYSTER SNACKS/67

A sophisticated tidbit for the appetizer tray—

24 shredded wheat wafers
1 3¾-ounce can smoked oysters, drained
2 tablespoons pimiento, drained and chopped
1 cup shredded Swiss, cheddar, brick, *or* Monterey Jack cheese (4 ounces)

Arrange the shredded wheat wafers on a baking sheet. Place one oyster on each wafer; top with some of the chopped pimiento and shredded cheese. Broil 3 to 4 inches from heat about 1 minute or till cheese begins to melt. Arrange on a plate and serve immediately. Makes 24.

Cranberry Fruit Dip

ZUCCHINI DIP/24

2 medium zucchini, chopped (2 cups)
½ cup tomato juice
1 tablespoon chopped onion
¼ teaspoon salt
⅛ teaspoon dried basil, crushed
1 8-ounce package Neufchâtel cheese, cut up
½ slice bacon, crisp cooked, drained, and crumbled (optional)
Assorted vegetables for dipping

In a saucepan combine the zucchini, tomato juice, onion, salt, and basil. Simmer, covered, for 10 minutes. Turn mixture into blender container. Add the cheese. Cover and blend till mixture is thoroughly combined. Remove from blender. Cover and chill. Just before serving, if desired, sprinkle top with crumbled bacon. Serve with desired vegetable dippers. Makes 1¾ cups dip, or 28 one-tablespoon servings.

TACO POPCORN SNACK/76

2 tablespoons unpopped popcorn
1 cup bite-size shredded wheat biscuits
¾ cup round toasted oat cereal
2 tablespoons butter *or* margarine, melted
½ teaspoon chili powder
⅛ teaspoon ground cumin
⅛ teaspoon onion salt

Pop the popcorn in a heavy skillet or saucepan over medium-high heat, using no oil. Be sure to cover pan and shake constantly until all the corn is popped. Combine popped corn (about 2½ cups) and cereals in a 13x9x2-inch baking pan. Heat in a 300° oven about 5 minutes or till cereal is warm. Remove from oven. Mix remaining ingredients; drizzle over cereal mixture, mixing well. Makes 4¼ cups, or 8 one-half-cup servings.

PICKLED SHRIMP/60

2 tablespoons mixed pickling spices
3 cups water
1 pound fresh *or* frozen medium shrimp, shelled and deveined
1 medium onion, sliced
½ cup white wine vinegar
½ cup water
1 tablespoon capers
1 teaspoon sugar
½ teaspoon celery seed
¼ teaspoon salt
¼ teaspoon dry mustard
1 clove garlic, minced
Few drops bottled hot pepper sauce
1 tablespoon snipped parsley

Tie the pickling spices in a cheesecloth bag. Heat the 3 cups water to boiling. Add shrimp, pickling spices, and onion. Return to boiling. Cover and simmer 1 to 3 minutes or till shrimp turn pink. Drain.

In plastic bag set in a deep bowl place the shrimp, onion, and spice bag. Combine the vinegar, ½ cup water, capers with liquid, sugar, celery seed, salt, dry mustard, garlic, and hot pepper sauce; mix well. Pour mixture over shrimp in bag. Close bag. Marinate shrimp in refrigerator at least 24 hours, turning bag occasionally. Stir in snipped parsley before serving. Makes 8 appetizer servings.

CURRIED-STUFFED EGGS/25

5 hard-cooked eggs
3 tablespoons dairy sour cream
1 tablespoon snipped parsley
2 teaspoons skim milk
½ teaspoon curry powder

Quarter hard-cooked eggs lengthwise. Remove yolks to bowl; mash. Combine yolks, next 4 ingredients, and ¼ teaspoon *salt.* If necessary, cut a thin slice off the bottom of each egg quarter so it will sit flat. Using pastry bag with star tip, pipe sour cream mixture into egg whites. Chill. Makes 20.

CARROT BALLS/40

3 ounces Neufchâtel cheese, softened
½ cup shredded cheddar cheese
1 teaspoon honey
1 cup finely shredded carrot
⅓ to ½ cup Grape Nuts cereal
2 tablespoons finely snipped parsley

In medium mixer bowl beat Neufchâtel cheese, cheddar cheese, and honey together till blended. Stir in shredded carrot. Cover and chill 30 minutes. Shape into fourteen 1-inch balls; cover and chill. Just before serving, roll balls in a mixture of cereal and parsley, pressing the cereal mixture into cheese to coat. Makes 14.

Applecot Cooler (see recipe, page 50); *Pickled Shrimp; Taco Popcorn Snack; Zucchini Dip*

VEGETABLE DIPPERS

Enjoy tasty dips and cut calories at the same time by serving raw vegetables for dipping. Crisp, cold carrots, celery, green pepper, green onion, cucumber, zucchini, broccoli, cherry tomatoes, cauliflower flowerets, mushrooms, and radishes are colorful and fresh tasting. Peel the vegetables if necessary, then serve whole or cut into slices, sticks, or strips, depending on the vegetable. For variety, use a scalloped cutter to make crinkle-cut carrot sticks or cucumber slices. Use a radish cutter to make radish roses.

POTTED PEPPER DIP/15

Pictured on pages 216 and 217—

4 large sweet red *or* green peppers
1 small onion, cut up
1 tablespoon lemon juice
2 teaspoons cooking oil
1 teaspoon salt
½ teaspoon prepared horseradish
Dash pepper

• • •

¾ cup plain yogurt
½ of an 8-ounce package Neufchâtel cheese, softened
Few dashes bottled hot pepper sauce
Assorted vegetables for dipping

Quarter peppers lengthwise; remove stem and seeds. Place peppers, peel side up, on baking sheet. Broil 2 to 3 inches from heat for 4 to 5 minutes or till peppers are charred. Cool, then peel peppers.

In blender container or food processor bowl place about ⅓ of the red or green peppers, the onion, lemon juice, cooking oil, salt, horseradish, and pepper. Cover and blend till smooth. Add another ⅓ of the peppers to mixture in blender container or food processor bowl; cover and blend till smooth. Repeat with remaining peppers. Transfer mixture to bowl. Cover and let stand at room temperature for 2 hours.

Sieve vegetable mixture, pressing gently to drain off excess liquid. In mixing bowl combine yogurt, Neufchâtel cheese, and hot pepper sauce. Stir in sieved vegetable mixture. Cover; chill. If desired, spoon into 2 hollow green pepper shells; keep 1 shell chilled while serving the other. Serve with vegetable dippers. Makes 2⅓ cups dip, or 37 one-tablespoon servings.

VEGETABLE CHEESE DIP/22

½ of an 8-ounce package Neufchâtel cheese
½ cup chopped carrot
¼ cup chopped green pepper
¼ cup chopped celery
2 tablespoons chopped pimiento
2 teaspoons lemon juice
1 teaspoon Worcestershire sauce
⅛ teaspoon pepper
Assorted vegetables for dipping

In blender container or food processor bowl combine Neufchâtel cheese, carrot, green pepper, celery, pimiento, lemon juice, Worcestershire sauce, and pepper; cover and blend till smooth. (Mixture may have curdled appearance.) Cover and chill. Serve with vegetable dippers. Makes about 1 cup, or 16 one-tablespoon servings.

SPAGHETTI DIP/10

1 large green pepper
1 8-ounce carton plain yogurt
2 tablespoons dry spaghetti sauce mix
Assorted vegetables for dipping

Remove top and seeds from green pepper. Remove stem from green pepper top and discard. Place green pepper top, yogurt, and spaghetti sauce mix in blender container; blend till green pepper is coarsely chopped. Chill well. Fill green pepper with dip. Serve with vegetable dippers. Makes 1 cup dip, or 16 one-tablespoon servings.

GARDEN VEGETABLE DIP / 7

- **1 8-ounce carton plain yogurt**
- **2 tablespoons finely chopped cucumber**
- **2 tablespoons finely chopped green onion**
- **1 tablespoon snipped parsley**
- **1 tablespoon chili sauce**
- **1/8 teaspoon garlic powder**
- **Dash bottled hot pepper sauce**
- **Assorted vegetables for dipping**

In a bowl combine yogurt, cucumber, green onion, parsley, chili sauce, garlic powder, and hot pepper sauce; stir gently to blend. Serve with vegetable dippers. Makes about 1¼ cups, or 20 one-tablespoon servings.

BLUE CHEESE DIP / 13

- **1 cup dry cottage cheese**
- **3 tablespoons buttermilk**
- **2 tablespoons crumbled blue cheese**
- **2 tablespoons chopped green onion**
- **1 tablespoon snipped parsley**
- **1 teaspoon Worcestershire sauce**
- **Dash bottled hot pepper sauce**
- **Assorted vegetables for dipping**

In blender container combine all ingredients except the vegetable dippers. Cover; blend till smooth. Cover and chill. Serve with vegetable dippers. Makes 1 cup dip, or 16 one-tablespoon servings.

SPINACH DIP / 39

- **1 cup finely torn and lightly packed fresh spinach leaves**
- **½ cup lightly packed parsley (stems removed)**
- **¼ cup water**
- **3 tablespoons chopped green onion**
- **¼ teaspoon dried tarragon, crushed**
- **⅔ cup plain yogurt**
- **⅓ cup mayonnaise *or* salad dressing**
- **¼ teaspoon salt**
- **Assorted vegetables for dipping**

In small saucepan combine torn spinach leaves, parsley, water, green onion, and tarragon. Bring to boiling. Reduce heat; cover and simmer for 1 minute. Drain vegetables, discarding liquid.

Puree vegetables; stir in yogurt, mayonnaise or salad dressing, and salt. Cover and chill. Serve the spinach mixture with desired vegetable dippers. Makes 1 cup dip, or 16 one-tablespoon servings.

BANANA ORANGE YOGURT POPS / 115

Next time, try another yogurt flavor—

- **2 egg whites**
- **2 tablespoons sugar**
- **1 ripe medium banana, mashed**
- **2 8-ounce cartons orange yogurt**
- **6 wooden sticks**

In a bowl beat egg whites till soft peaks form (tips curl over); gradually add the sugar, beating till stiff peaks form (tips stand straight). Fold the egg white mixture and banana into the orange yogurt. Divide mixture among six 5-ounce paper drink cups and insert a wooden stick into each. Freeze till mixture is firm. To serve, peel off the paper cups. Makes 6 servings.

PICKLED CARROTS AND ZUCCHINI / 43

Keep these pickled vegetables on hand in the refrigerator, ready for snacking—

- **½ cup sugar**
- **½ cup vinegar**
- **½ cup water**
- **1 tablespoon mustard seed**
- **2 inches stick cinnamon**
- **3 whole cloves**

• • •

- **3 medium carrots, cut into strips**
- **1 medium zucchini, cut into strips**

In saucepan combine sugar, vinegar, water, mustard seed, stick cinnamon, and cloves. Add carrots; cover and simmer till carrots are crisp-tender. Add zucchini; return to boiling. Transfer to bowl. Cover; chill at least 8 hours. Makes 3 cups, or 12 one-fourth cup servings.

PINEAPPLE YOGURT NUT LOAF/95

2½ cups whole wheat flour
½ cup 40% bran flakes
2 tablespoons wheat germ
1 teaspoon baking soda
1 teaspoon baking powder
1 beaten egg
2 8-ounce cartons pineapple yogurt
¼ cup milk
2 tablespoons cooking oil
2 tablespoons light molasses
2 tablespoons honey
1 teaspoon lemon juice
1 cup raisins
½ cup chopped walnuts
½ cup snipped, pitted whole dates
Non-stick vegetable spray coating

In a bowl stir together whole wheat flour, bran flakes, wheat germ, baking soda, baking powder, and dash *salt.* In a second bowl combine egg, yogurt, milk, cooking oil, molasses, honey, and lemon juice; stir into dry ingredients just till moistened. Stir in raisins, walnuts, and dates. Turn into two 7½x3½x2-inch loaf pans sprayed with non-stick vegetable spray coating. Bake in a 325° oven 50 to 60 minutes or till wooden pick inserted near center comes out clean. Cool 10 minutes on wire rack; remove from pans. Cool loaves completely on wire rack. Wrap and store overnight before slicing. Makes 2 loaves, or 32 servings.

Gazpacho Refresher (see recipe, page 221); *Pineapple Yogurt Nut Loaf; Fizzy Fruit Slush* (see recipe, page 223); *Toasty Oat Crackers*

QUICK WHOLE WHEAT BREAD / 151

1½ cups whole wheat flour
1 cup all-purpose flour
½ cup quick-cooking rolled oats
½ cup packed brown sugar
1 tablespoon finely shredded orange peel
2 teaspoons baking powder
½ teaspoon baking soda
½ teaspoon salt
1¾ cups buttermilk
1 slightly beaten egg
Wheat germ
Honey
Date Butter

In a large bowl combine whole wheat flour, all-purpose flour, rolled oats, brown sugar, orange peel, baking powder, baking soda, and salt till well blended. Add buttermilk and egg; stir just till ingredients are moistened.

Grease a 1½-quart casserole dish; sprinkle lightly with wheat germ. Pour batter into casserole. Bake in a 350° oven for 50 to 60 minutes or till bread tests done. If necessary, cover loaf with foil during the last 15 minutes of baking to prevent over-browning.

Cool in casserole for 10 minutes; turn out on wire rack. Brush top of loaf with honey. Serve warm or cool with Date Butter. Makes 1 loaf, or 20 servings.

Date Butter: In a small saucepan cook ½ cup snipped pitted *dates,* uncovered, with ¼ cup *water,* ½ teaspoon *lemon juice,* and a dash *salt* over medium heat till mixture is thick; cool. Whip ½ cup softened *butter or margarine* till light and fluffy; gradually beat in the thickened date mixture. Turn into bowl; cover and chill. To serve, garnish with orange slices, if desired. Makes about 1 cup.

HOT CHEESE SNACKS / 24

1 cup shredded low-calorie process cheese product (4 ounces)
2 tablespoons hot water
1 teaspoon minced dried onion
¼ teaspoon salt
Few drops bottled hot pepper sauce
2 tablespoons finely chopped canned green chili peppers
2 stiff-beaten egg whites
48 melba toast rounds

Have cheese product at room temperature. In small mixer bowl combine low-calorie cheese, water, onion, salt, and hot pepper sauce. Beat with electric mixer till smooth. Stir in chopped chili peppers. Stir about one-fourth of the stiff-beaten egg whites into cheese mixture; gently fold in remaining egg whites. Spoon about 1 teaspoon of the cheese mixture on each melba toast round and place on baking sheet. Broil 5 inches from heat for 1 to 1½ minutes or just till the cheese topping is lightly browned. Makes 48.

OATMEAL COOKIES / 30

½ cup all-purpose flour
¼ cup sugar
½ teaspoon baking soda
½ teaspoon baking powder
¼ cup packed brown sugar
¼ cup butter *or* margarine, softened
1 egg
2 tablespoons plain yogurt
¼ teaspoon vanilla
1 cup quick-cooking rolled oats

In bowl mix together flour, sugar, baking soda, baking powder, and ¼ teaspoon *salt.* Add brown sugar, butter, egg, yogurt, and vanilla; beat well. Stir in oats; chill. Drop from teaspoon onto greased cookie sheet. Bake in a 375° oven about 8 minutes. Makes 48 cookies.

TOASTY OAT CRACKERS / 19

1½ cups quick-cooking rolled oats *or* regular rolled oats
⅔ cup all-purpose flour
⅓ cup wheat germ
1 tablespoon sugar
1 tablespoon sesame seed
½ teaspoon salt, seasoned salt, *or* garlic salt
¼ cup butter *or* margarine
½ cup water

Place quick-cooking rolled oats or regular rolled oats in a blender container or food processor bowl. Cover and blend about 1 minute or till oats are evenly ground.

In a mixing bowl combine oats, flour, wheat germ, sugar, sesame seed, and salt. Cut in butter till mixture resembles coarse crumbs. Gradually add water, mixing till dry ingredients are moistened. Shape dough into a 9-inch-long roll. Wrap and chill for several hours. Cut into ⅛-inch slices; place on ungreased baking sheet. Flatten till very thin with tines of a fork. Bake in a 375° oven about 12 minutes or till edges are brown. Remove and cool on wire rack. Makes about 72.

GOOD EATING NATURALLY

Modern eating trends lend themselves to naturally good eating, which simply means incorporating nutritious foods into the diet. These include dairy foods, fruits and vegetables, and grain products, such as those shown here, plus others.

Buttermilk-Fruit Coolers (peach variation)

Sprout-Stuffed Tomatoes

Minestrone

Strawberries Romanoff

Triticale Banana Biscuits

NUTRITION ANALYSIS

Check out the nutrients in this assortment of naturally good recipes. You'll find main dishes, side dishes, beverages, and desserts in this section.

GOOD EATING NATURALLY	Per Serving						Percent U.S. RDA Per Serving							
	CALORIES	PROTEIN gms	CARBOHYDRATE gms	FAT gms	SODIUM mgs	POTASSIUM mgs	PROTEIN	VITAMIN A	VITAMIN C	THIAMINE	RIBOFLAVIN	NIACIN	CALCIUM	IRON
APRI-ORANGE-CARROT COOLER (p. 260)	80	1	19	0	12	334	2	67	75	6	2	3	2	2
BANANA NOG (p. 263)	130	6	15	5	67	211	9	8	4	3	13	1	12	2
BANANA PEACH FLAMBÉ (p. 268)	154	3	28	2	31	366	5	13	36	5	9	4	8	3
BEANY NOODLE BAKE (p. 241)	331	22	39	10	922	385	34	20	5	20	23	13	20	18
BELGIAN TOSSED SALAD (p. 252)	167	3	5	16	181	239	5	8	56	6	6	3	3	5
BERRY-BUTTERMILK SOUP (p. 267)	119	3	28	0	108	174	5	1	18	4	11	2	11	3
BERRY YOGURT (p. 244)	79	5	14	0	71	218	8	0	14	3	15	1	17	1
BREAKFAST DRINK (p. 242)	172	5	25	6	72	244	8	8	2	3	14	1	18	1
BROCCOLI-TOFU SOUP (p. 241)	282	18	19	16	883	493	28	48	90	9	26	5	49	13
BROWN NUT BREAD (p. 258)	125	3	21	4	150	163	5	1	1	8	5	4	5	6
BROWN RICE PUDDING WITH TOPPING (p. 258)	182	5	40	1	112	231	8	1	10	8	10	7	12	6
BULGUR WHEAT PILAF (p. 259)	132	6	18	4	627	143	9	3	1	4	3	9	1	6
BUTTERMILK-FRUIT COOLERS (p. 262)	76	5	15	0	160	232	7	8	5	4	14	2	15	1
CABBAGE SUPREME (p. 249)	73	4	9	3	151	311	6	5	89	5	8	2	13	3
CANTALOUPE FROST (p. 262)	108	5	18	2	64	347	7	48	39	4	12	3	15	2
CHEESE-TOPPED CANTALOUPE (p. 242)	89	2	13	4	68	278	4	64	62	4	5	4	3	4
CHEF'S CHOICE SALAD (p. 252)	329	18	21	20	269	426	28	10	57	8	10	27	14	8
CITRUS FRUIT SOUP (p. 268)	184	1	43	0	3	373	1	16	49	5	3	3	3	6
COLD SPICED PEACHES (p. 268)	87	1	22	0	90	246	1	20	24	4	3	5	2	3
COLESLAW SALAD BOWL (p. 252)	126	2	19	6	235	269	2	19	61	5	5	3	4	5
CURRIED FRUIT-AND-NUT SALAD (p. 252)	189	2	13	16	65	229	3	25	29	4	5	2	5	7
DILL-ONION BREAD IN THE ROUND (p. 254)	128	6	21	3	254	103	9	4	3	18	14	10	2	7
EGGPLANT SALAD (p. 249)	79	2	11	4	264	305	3	14	47	7	5	6	3	7
EGGS-IN-A-PUFF (p. 242)	399	16	17	30	525	230	25	48	49	16	25	6	14	16
EXOTIC FRUIT PLATTER (p. 267)	149	3	32	2	32	395	5	122	74	6	9	9	8	4
FLORENTINE SKILLET (p. 237)	260	17	22	12	525	859	27	81	77	14	26	9	16	17
FRESH FRUIT ALOHA (p. 264)	80	1	21	0	3	266	1	27	101	5	3	2	3	3
FROSTY SPICED TEA (p. 262)	23	0	6	0	0	0	0	0	0	0	0	0	0	0
FROZEN ORANGE MIST (p. 267)	85	3	14	2	51	214	5	3	28	4	10	1	12	1
FRUIT-AND-CHEESE MOLD (p. 267)	158	5	25	3	138	218	8	29	22	2	6	2	10	2
FRUIT 'N' YOGURT DAZZLER (p. 264)	146	3	29	3	32	374	5	28	55	6	10	4	8	6
FRUIT SHERBET (p. 266)	117	4	20	3	60	205	6	14	6	2	9	3	9	1
GARDEN-FRESH REFRESHER (p. 260)	49	4	8	1	302	382	6	27	63	6	5	11	3	5
GARDEN-STUFFED PEPPERS (p. 248)	98	4	15	3	247	362	6	16	191	10	7	6	2	8

GOOD EATING NATURALLY

GOOD EATING NATURALLY	Per Serving: CALORIES	PROTEIN gms	CARBOHYDRATE gms	FAT gms	SODIUM mgs	POTASSIUM mgs	Percent U.S. RDA Per Serving: PROTEIN	VITAMIN A	VITAMIN C	THIAMINE	RIBOFLAVIN	NIACIN	CALCIUM	IRON
GARDEN VEGETABLE STIR-FRY (p. 246)	92	3	11	5	459	345	4	59	61	6	7	4	5	7
GRANOLA FRUIT CRISP (p. 268)	188	2	33	6	224	162	3	6	13	12	9	7	3	5
HEALTH COOKIES (p. 255)	88	2	11	5	77	103	3	7	1	4	2	3	2	3
HEARTY BEAN STEW (p. 237)	336	19	43	10	452	874	30	57	32	14	14	12	29	27
HERBED LENTILS AND RICE (p. 238)	349	21	44	9	833	510	32	7	5	15	14	14	32	23
HOMEMADE YOGURT (p. 244)	6	1	1	0	9	25	1	0	0	0	2	0	2	0
HONEY BUTTERMILK ICE CREAM (p. 244)	127	4	20	4	157	151	7	4	4	3	10	1	10	1
MACARONI-CRUST PIZZA (p. 237)	318	19	28	14	516	168	29	14	13	19	23	9	29	11
MINESTRONE (p. 236)	278	17	49	3	928	1048	26	82	61	34	18	21	16	25
MINTED LIME SODA (p. 262)	166	3	29	3	45	152	5	3	7	2	9	1	10	0
NO-COOK APPLESAUCE (p. 269)	119	0	31	0	1	148	1	1	7	3	2	1	1	2
OATMEAL RAISIN ROLLS (p. 258)	150	4	30	3	70	120	6	2	0	12	6	7	1	7
ORANGE-ANA DRINK (p. 263)	94	1	23	0	2	339	2	5	78	7	3	3	2	3
PEA PODS WITH ALMONDS (p. 246)	132	5	11	8	412	294	8	12	26	15	12	13	3	9
PEASANT BREAD (p. 256)	70	2	14	1	127	59	3	1	1	8	6	5	1	4
PINEAPPLE-CARROT COCKTAIL (p. 262)	71	1	18	0	269	267	1	1	20	4	2	3	3	6
RAINBOW COMPOTE (p. 264)	99	1	25	0	5	230	2	3	80	5	4	3	3	5
RHUBARB SAUCE (p. 269)	111	1	28	0	2	230	1	2	14	2	4	1	9	4
RUSSIAN BLACK BREAD (p. 257)	126	3	25	2	256	122	5	5	4	15	12	11	2	8
RUTABAGA AND APPLE (p. 246)	119	1	21	4	54	194	1	12	34	4	3	3	6	4
RYE BREAD (p. 254)	93	3	18	1	145	105	4	1	0	8	6	5	2	5
SANGRIA (p. 262)	77	0	9	0	4	101	0	1	15	1	1	1	1	2
SEVEN-GRAIN BREAD (p. 258)	118	4	20	3	147	73	5	2	0	11	6	7	1	5
SNOWCAPPED BROCCOLI (p. 244)	123	5	5	10	211	250	8	52	110	5	10	3	8	4
SOYBEANS AU GRATIN (p. 238)	364	24	26	20	512	963	37	6	5	42	16	8	28	28
SPICY DATE SHAKE (p. 262)	140	7	30	0	85	429	10	0	3	6	19	4	21	5
SPICY PAELLA-STYLE VEGETABLES (p. 241)	465	21	55	18	947	888	32	67	276	34	32	24	26	29
SPINACH FRITTATA (p. 244)	380	23	8	29	762	711	35	222	98	15	36	4	36	35
SPINACH-PINEAPPLE DELIGHT (p. 260)	80	1	20	0	8	238	1	16	30	5	3	2	3	4
SPRINGTIME POTATOES (p. 249)	85	3	17	1	153	453	5	3	39	7	6	7	5	4
SPROUT-STUFFED TOMATOES (p. 249)	97	4	10	5	159	406	6	28	61	9	7	6	4	7
STRAWBERRIES ROMANOFF (p. 267)	118	3	18	4	29	217	4	4	81	3	9	3	8	5
TABOULEH (p. 257)	112	3	18	4	269	119	4	7	14	5	3	6	2	6
TANGY CHICKEN BOWL (p. 250)	327	16	16	23	240	458	25	12	19	6	8	23	10	10
TOASTED BARLEY BAKE (p. 259)	125	2	20	4	306	61	4	5	5	2	1	4	1	3
TOFU-BROCCOLI STRATA (p. 236)	285	18	16	17	860	263	27	36	48	11	22	5	40	12
TOFU MANICOTTI (p. 238)	322	18	26	17	317	241	28	13	4	20	23	10	33	12
TRITICALE BANANA BISCUITS (p. 259)	81	2	12	3	154	63	3	3	1	5	3	3	2	2
TRITICALE BERRY-RICE PILAF (p. 259)	122	5	23	2	425	164	8	0	5	8	6	14	2	5
TRITICALE WHEAT BREAD (p. 257)	139	5	22	4	215	121	8	3	1	13	10	7	4	6
VANILLA MALTED MILK (p. 260)	129	7	20	3	123	326	11	3	2	6	19	1	22	2
VEGETABLE SPINACH SALAD (p. 250)	199	5	8	17	235	339	8	102	46	7	10	4	6	12
WATERMELON FROST (p. 268)	69	0	15	0	1	98	1	9	15	2	2	1	1	2
WHOLE WHEAT BATTER ROLLS (p. 259)	103	3	19	2	152	66	4	1	0	10	6	7	1	5

MAIN DISHES WITHOUT MEAT

Add variety to your menus by occasionally planning meatless meals. Each main-dish serving should contribute about one-fourth of the day's protein requirements. Some meatless entrées may not be as low in calories as other main dishes. Sometimes the entrées are a meal-in-a-dish, requiring only a few items to round out the meal.

Not all protein-rich foods are alike. Animal products such as meat, poultry, fish, eggs, cheese, and milk usually contain all eight essential amino acids. But foods of plant origin, such as nuts, seeds, lentils, dry beans, and grains, may be short one or more of the essential amino acids. So, to plan nutritious meals using plant foods, you must use them in complementary combinations that are nutritionally equivalent to animal products. For your body to function properly, you must get all eight of the essential amino acids at the same meal.

Any of these combinations provide all eight essential amino acids: grains and legumes; legumes and seeds or nuts; and dairy products plus seeds or nuts, grains, or legumes.

MINESTRONE/278

Pictured on pages 232 and 233—

1 cup dry navy beans
1 28-ounce can tomatoes, cut up
2 medium carrots, cut into 2-inch sticks
2 stalks celery, bias sliced
1 10½-ounce can condensed beef broth
½ cup chopped onion
1 clove garlic, minced
2 teaspoons dried basil, crushed
2 large bay leaves
1 teaspoon sugar
1 teaspoon dried thyme, crushed
4 ounces spaghetti, broken into 2-inch lengths
2 medium zucchini, thinly sliced
⅓ cup grated Parmesan cheese

Rinse beans. In a Dutch oven or kettle combine beans and 9 cups *water.* Bring to boiling. Reduce heat and simmer 2 minutes. Remove from heat. Cover; let stand 1 hour. Drain beans and rinse. In same Dutch oven or kettle combine rinsed beans and 8 cups more *water.* Stir 1 teaspoon *salt* into beans and water. Bring to boiling; reduce heat. Cover and simmer for 45 minutes to 1 hour or till beans are tender. Drain; reserve 4 cups liquid.

To beans add *undrained* tomatoes, carrots, celery, beef broth, onion, garlic, basil, bay leaves, sugar, thyme, and reserved bean liquid. Bring to boiling. Stir in spaghetti. Reduce heat; cover and simmer about 20 minutes. Add zucchini; cover and simmer about 10 minutes or till vegetables are tender and spaghetti is tender yet firm. Remove bay leaves. Sprinkle *each* serving with about *1 tablespoon* of Parmesan cheese. Serves 6.

TOFU-BROCCOLI STRATA/285

1 10-ounce package frozen chopped broccoli
2 cups cubed day-old bread
4 ounces sliced Swiss cheese
8 ounces fresh tofu (bean curd), drained and cut into ½-inch cubes
2 tablespoons chopped pimiento, drained
4 ounces sliced Swiss cheese
2 cups cubed day-old bread
4 eggs
1¾ cups milk
1¼ teaspoons salt
Dash ground red pepper
1 cup cubed day-old bread
2 tablespoons butter *or* margarine, melted

In a medium saucepan cook chopped broccoli, covered, in a small amount of boiling, lightly salted water for 3 minutes; drain well. Place the 2 cups bread cubes on the bottom of an ungreased 8x8x2-inch baking dish. Top the bread cubes with 4 ounces sliced Swiss cheese. Top the Swiss cheese with all the cooked broccoli, cubed tofu, and chopped pimiento. Place 4 ounces sliced Swiss cheese and the 2 cups bread cubes atop.

In a bowl thoroughly beat the eggs; stir in the milk, salt, and ground red pepper. Pour the egg mixture over the ingredients in the baking dish. Cover and place strata in refrigerator to chill for 1 to 3 hours.

Toss the 1 cup bread cubes with the melted butter or margarine. Sprinkle atop the chilled mixture. Bake, uncovered, in a 325° oven for 55 to 60 minutes or till a knife inserted near center comes out clean. Let stand 10 minutes before serving. Serves 8.

FLORENTINE SKILLET/260

A good brunch main dish—

2 tablespoons cooking oil
3 cups shredded cooked potatoes
¼ cup chopped onion
¼ cup chopped green pepper
¼ cup chopped pimiento
• • •
½ of a 10-ounce package frozen chopped spinach, cooked
½ cup drained cottage cheese
• • •
1½ cups frozen egg substitute, thawed
½ teaspoon celery salt
Dash pepper
½ cup shredded low-calorie process cheese product
1 tomato, cut into wedges

Pour the cooking oil into a 10-inch skillet. Combine potatoes, onion, green pepper, and pimiento. Pat the mixture into the skillet. Sprinkle with salt and pepper. Cook, uncovered, over medium-low heat about 10 minutes. Drain spinach well.

Combine spinach and cottage cheese; set aside. Beat egg substitute, celery salt, and pepper. Spoon spinach mixture over potatoes; pour egg substitute mixture atop. Cover and cook over low heat 10 minutes or till set. Sprinkle with the shredded cheese. Cook, covered, 1 to 2 minutes more. To serve, cut into wedges. Trim with the tomato wedges. Makes 5 servings.

MACARONI-CRUST PIZZA/318

7 ounces elbow macaroni (2 cups)
2 beaten eggs
½ cup shredded Monterey Jack cheese (2 ounces)
¼ cup grated Parmesan cheese (1 ounce)
¼ cup milk
½ teaspoon dried basil, crushed
½ teaspoon dried oregano, crushed
⅛ teaspoon pepper
• • •
1 beaten egg
1 cup cream-style cottage cheese, drained
1 8-ounce can pizza sauce
¼ cup thinly sliced green onion
¼ cup finely chopped green pepper
¼ cup sliced pitted ripe olives
1 cup shredded Monterey Jack cheese (4 ounces)

To make crust, in a large saucepan cook macaroni according to package directions; drain well. In a mixing bowl combine the 2 beaten eggs, the ½ cup shredded Monterey Jack cheese, Parmesan cheese, milk, basil, oregano, and pepper. Add drained macaroni to egg and cheese mixture; mix well. Form macaroni mixture into a "crust" in a greased 10-inch pie plate or a greased 11-inch quiche dish. Bake in a 375° oven for 10 minutes.

For filling, in a bowl combine the 1 beaten egg and drained cottage cheese; pour on top of macaroni crust in pie plate or quiche dish. Pour pizza sauce over top of filling mixture; arrange green onion, chopped green pepper, and sliced ripe olives atop pizza sauce. Sprinkle with the 1 cup shredded Monterey Jack cheese. Return to 375° oven for 10 to 15 minutes more or till heated through. Let stand 10 minutes before serving. Makes 7 servings.

HEARTY BEAN STEW/336

2 15½-ounce cans red kidney beans
1 15-ounce can garbanzo beans
2½ cups water
2 medium potatoes, peeled, quartered lengthwise, and sliced
1 cup thinly sliced carrot
½ cup chopped onion
1 6-ounce can tomato paste
2 teaspoons chili powder
1 teaspoon salt
1 teaspoon dried basil, crushed
¼ teaspoon garlic powder
¼ teaspoon pepper
8 ounces Monterey Jack cheese, cut into ½-inch cubes (2 cups)

In a Dutch oven combine *undrained* kidney and garbanzo beans, water, potatoes, carrot, onion, tomato paste, chili powder, salt, basil, garlic powder, and pepper. Bring to boiling; reduce heat. Cover and simmer 30 minutes or till vegetables are tender. Top *each* serving with about ¼ *cup* of the cheese cubes. Makes 8 servings.

SOYBEANS AU GRATIN/364

1½ cups dry soybeans
4 cups water
4 cups water
1 cup chopped onion
• • •
2 tablespoons cooking oil
¼ cup whole wheat flour
1½ cups water
1 teaspoon salt
¼ teaspoon ground sage
¼ teaspoon dried savory, crushed
¼ teaspoon dried thyme, crushed
1 cup shredded cheddar cheese (4 ounces)
½ cup soft whole wheat bread crumbs

Rinse beans. In a Dutch oven or a kettle bring beans and 4 cups water to boiling. Reduce heat and simmer 2 minutes. Remove from heat. Cover and let stand 1 hour. (Or, soak beans in the water overnight in a covered pan.) Drain beans and rinse. In same Dutch oven or kettle combine rinsed beans and 4 cups more water. Bring to boiling; add onion. Reduce heat; simmer, covered, 2 hours or till tender. Drain.

In saucepan heat oil; blend in flour. Add the 1½ cups water, the salt, sage, savory, and thyme. Cook and stir till bubbly. Stir in drained beans. Pour into an ungreased 1½ quart casserole. Bake, uncovered, in a 350° oven for 15 minutes. Combine cheese and crumbs; sprinkle atop beans. Return to oven; bake, uncovered, 10 to 15 minutes more. Makes 6 servings.

TOFU MANICOTTI/322

8 manicotti shells (about 5 ounces)
½ cup chopped fresh mushrooms
¼ cup finely chopped onion
1 tablespoon cooking oil
1 tablespoon snipped parsley
½ teaspoon dried basil, crushed
¼ teaspoon salt
⅛ teaspoon paprika
Dash pepper
• • •
2 beaten eggs
10 ounces fresh tofu (bean curd), drained and mashed
¼ cup grated Parmesan cheese
2 tablespoons butter *or* margarine
2 tablespoons all-purpose flour
Dash pepper
1½ cups milk
1 cup shredded mozzarella cheese (4 ounces)
Ground nutmeg (optional)

Cook pasta shells in boiling salted water according to package directions. Rinse in cold water; drain. Cook mushrooms and onion in hot oil till tender. Add parsley, basil, salt, paprika, and dash pepper. Remove from heat; cool. Combine eggs, tofu, Parmesan cheese, and vegetable mixture. Stuff each manicotti shell with about ¼ cup tofu mixture; arrange in greased 12x7½x2-inch baking dish.

Melt butter; add flour and dash pepper. Add milk all at once. Cook and stir till thickened and bubbly. Remove from heat; stir in mozzarella cheese till melted. Pour cheese sauce over pasta; sprinkle with nutmeg, if desired. Cover with foil. Bake in a 350° oven 20 to 25 minutes or till heated through. Makes 6 servings.

HERBED LENTILS AND RICE/349

2⅔ cups chicken *or* vegetable broth
¾ cup dry lentils
¾ cup chopped onion
½ cup brown rice
¼ cup dry white wine
½ teaspoon dried basil, crushed
¼ teaspoon salt
¼ teaspoon dried oregano, crushed
¼ teaspoon dried thyme, crushed
⅛ teaspoon garlic powder
⅛ teaspoon pepper
½ cup shredded Swiss cheese (2 ounces)
• • •
8 thin strips Swiss cheese (2 ounces)

Combine the chicken or vegetable broth, lentils, onion, uncooked brown rice, wine, basil, salt, oregano, thyme, garlic powder, pepper, and shredded Swiss cheese. Turn mixture into an ungreased 1½-quart casserole with a tight-fitting lid. Bake, covered, in a 350° oven for 1½ to 2 hours or till lentils and rice are done, stirring twice.

Uncover casserole; top with the Swiss cheese strips. Bake 2 to 3 minutes more or till cheese melts. If desired, garnish the top of the casserole with watercress or sprigs of parsley. Makes 4 servings.

Herbed Lentils and Rice

BEANY NOODLE BAKE/331

2¼ cups (3 ounces) medium noodles
1 8-ounce can tomato sauce
½ teaspoon salt
½ teaspoon dried basil, crushed
½ teaspoon dried marjoram, crushed
½ teaspoon dried oregano, crushed
Dash garlic salt
• • •
1 slightly beaten egg
1 cup cream-style cottage cheese
1 15½-ounce can red kidney beans, drained and slightly mashed
½ cup shredded cheddar cheese (2 ounces)

Cook noodles according to package directions; drain. Meanwhile, in saucepan mix tomato sauce, salt, basil, marjoram, oregano, and garlic salt. Simmer, uncovered, for 10 minutes. Combine egg and cottage cheese. Place *half* the noodles in bottom of ungreased 9x5x3-inch loaf pan; top with beans, *half* the sauce, and *half* the cottage cheese mixture. Repeat layers of noodles, sauce, and cheese mixture. Bake, uncovered, in a 350° oven for 25 minutes. Sprinkle cheddar cheese atop. Bake for 5 minutes more. Let stand for 5 to 10 minutes before serving. Makes 4 servings.

Spicy Paella-Style Vegetables

SPICY PAELLA-STYLE VEGETABLES/465

This is a meal-in-a-dish. All you need add is a beverage and fruit for dessert—

¾ pound broccoli, sliced, *or* one 10-ounce package frozen chopped broccoli
2 small zucchini, sliced ¼ inch thick (2 cups)
2 medium green *or* red sweet peppers, chopped (1½ cups)
½ cup chopped onion
2 cloves garlic, minced
¼ cup olive oil *or* cooking oil
• • •
1 16-ounce can tomatoes, cut up
1 teaspoon salt
½ teaspoon ground red pepper
⅛ teaspoon pepper
2¾ cups chicken broth
1½ cups long grain rice
1 tablespoon lemon juice
• • •
1 cup shelled fresh *or* frozen peas, thawed
⅔ cup grated Parmesan cheese
6 eggs

Cook fresh broccoli in a small amount of boiling, lightly salted water for 5 minutes or till crisp-tender. (*Or,* if using frozen broccoli, cook according to package directions.) Drain. In a paella pan or a 12-inch oven-going skillet, cook zucchini, sweet pepper, onion, and garlic in olive oil till onion is tender. Stir in *undrained* tomatoes, salt, red pepper, and pepper. Stir in chicken broth, uncooked rice, and lemon juice; mix well. Bring to boiling.

Bake, covered, in a 350° oven for 10 minutes. Stir in broccoli, peas, and Parmesan cheese. Make 6 depressions in rice mixture with the back of a spoon. Carefully break the eggs into the depressions. Sprinkle eggs lightly with salt. Bake, covered, 15 to 18 minutes more or till eggs are set and rice is tender. Makes 6 servings.

BROCCOLI-TOFU SOUP/282

8 ounces fresh tofu (bean curd)
½ cup water
1 tablespoon minced dried onion
½ teaspoon instant chicken bouillon granules
¼ teaspoon dried basil, crushed
1 10-ounce package frozen chopped broccoli
1 10¾-ounce can condensed cream of potato soup
2 cups milk
¾ cup shredded Swiss cheese (3 ounces)

Place tofu in a double thickness of cheesecloth or paper toweling. Press gently to extract as much moisture as possible. Cut tofu into ½-inch cubes. In a saucepan combine the water, dried onion, bouillon granules, and basil. Bring to boiling. Stir in frozen broccoli; return to boiling. Reduce heat; cover and simmer 5 minutes or till tender. *Do not drain.* Stir in soup. Gradually add milk; bring to boiling. Reduce heat. Add tofu and cheese, stirring till cheese is melted. Makes 4 servings.

GREAT DISHES FROM THE DAIRY

Milk and other dairy products are excellent sources of protein and calcium. They are versatile as well and are ideal for supplementing plant proteins in main dishes. And they add their fair share of nutrition to other parts of the meal.

If you're limiting your fat intake, select from several low-fat milk and cheese products. Included among these are low-fat milk, skim milk, nonfat dry milk, evaporated skimmed milk, buttermilk, and yogurt made with skim or low-fat milk.

Certain process cheeses are made with low-fat or skim milk. Some natural cheeses are also made with part skim milk. Cottage cheese is available in three types: creamed, low-fat, and dry curd. Neufchâtel cheese is a good alternative to cream cheese because of its less fat and fewer calories.

Eggs are a good protein source. When eaten in moderation, the nutritional value of eggs is hardly questionable. And, eggs are an excellent low-cost source of protein for the amount they provide.

EGGS-IN-A-PUFF/399

½ cup butter *or* margarine
1 cup boiling water
1 cup all-purpose flour
¼ teaspoon salt
4 eggs
• • •
8 beaten eggs
⅓ cup milk
¼ teaspoon salt
Dash pepper
½ of a 10-ounce package frozen cut broccoli, cooked and drained, *or* ½ of a 6-ounce package frozen pea pods, thawed
½ small red *or* green sweet pepper, sliced or chopped
2 tablespoons butter *or* margarine
½ cup shredded cheddar cheese (2 ounces)

To make the puff, melt the ½ cup butter or margarine in boiling water. Add flour and ¼ teaspoon salt all at once; stir vigorously. Cook and stir till mixture forms a ball that doesn't separate. Remove from heat; cool slightly (about 5 minutes). Add the 4 eggs, one at a time, beating after each till smooth. Spread batter over the bottom and up the sides of a greased 9-inch glass pie plate. Bake in a 400° oven about 25 minutes or till golden brown and puffy.

Meanwhile, use a fork to beat together the 8 beaten eggs, milk, ¼ teaspoon salt, and pepper. Stir in broccoli or pea pods and sweet pepper. Heat the 2 tablespoons butter in a skillet till just hot enough to make a drop of water sizzle. Pour in the egg-vegetable mixture. Reduce heat to low. When egg mixture starts to set on the bottom and sides of the skillet, sprinkle with cheese. Lift and fold the egg mixture with a spatula till eggs are cooked and cheese is melted. Spoon into baked puff. Serves 7.

BREAKFAST DRINK/172

To cut a few extra calories, substitute ice milk and skim milk for the regular products—

1 pint vanilla ice cream
1½ cups peach yogurt
¾ cup peach nectar, chilled
½ cup milk
½ teaspoon vanilla

In blender container combine all ingredients. Cover and blend just till mixed. Pour into chilled glasses. Serves 6.

CHEESE-TOPPED CANTALOUPE/89

For a special brunch, top cantaloupe with berries and an orangy-cheese mixture—

3 ounces Neufchâtel cheese
½ teaspoon finely shredded orange peel
2 tablespoons orange juice
• • •
1 medium cantaloupe
1½ cups fresh *or* frozen unsweetened blueberries

Soften cheese; beat till fluffy. Stir in orange peel and juice. Seed and cut cantaloupe into wedges; top with blueberries. Pour some cream cheese mixture over top of each serving. Makes 6 servings.

Eggs-in-a-Puff; Cheese-Topped Cantaloupe; Breakfast Drink

SNOWCAPPED BROCCOLI/123

- **2 10-ounce packages frozen broccoli spears**
- **1 tablespoon butter *or* margarine, melted**
- **2 egg whites**
- **¼ teaspoon salt**
- **¼ cup mayonnaise *or* salad dressing**
- **Grated Parmesan cheese**

Cook broccoli according to package directions; drain well. Arrange broccoli in a 9-inch pie plate with stem ends toward the center; brush with melted butter. Beat egg whites and salt until stiff peaks form (tips stand straight); fold in mayonnaise. Spoon mixture into center of broccoli; sprinkle generously with Parmesan. Bake in a 350° oven 12 to 15 minutes or till egg white mixture is golden brown. Makes 6 servings.

HONEY BUTTERMILK ICE CREAM/127

- **1 8-ounce package Neufchâtel cheese, softened**
- **⅔ cup honey**
- **1 quart buttermilk (4 cups)**
- **1 cup unsweetened pineapple juice**
- **1 teaspoon vanilla**

In a bowl combine the cheese and honey; beat till smooth and creamy. Stir in the buttermilk, pineapple juice, and vanilla. Pour into an ice cream freezer container; freeze according to freezer manufacturer's directions. Serve with fresh fruit, if desired. Makes about 2 quarts, or 14 servings.

SPINACH FRITTATA/380

Serve this as a main dish—

- **½ pound fresh spinach, stems removed, *or* ½ of a 10-ounce package frozen chopped spinach, thawed**
- **2 tablespoons butter *or* margarine**
- **2 tablespoons chopped onion**
- **1 small clove garlic, minced**
- **⅓ cup shredded fontina cheese**
- **¼ teaspoon salt**
- **Dash pepper**
- **Dash ground nutmeg**
- **4 beaten eggs**

Finely chop fresh spinach. In saucepan melt *1 tablespoon* of the butter or margarine. Add onion, garlic, and spinach. Cook over medium heat, stirring frequently, about 15 minutes or till liquid is evaporated from spinach. Remove from heat; stir in cheese, salt, pepper, and nutmeg. Combine beaten eggs and spinach mixture.

In an 8-inch oven-going skillet, heat the remaining 1 tablespoon butter or margarine over medium-low heat. Pour egg mixture into skillet. As eggs set, run a spatula around edge of skillet, lifting egg mixture to allow uncooked portion to flow underneath. Continue cooking and lifting edges till almost set (surface will be moist). Place skillet under broiler 5 inches from heat; broil for 1 to 2 minutes or just till top is set. Sprinkle with additional shredded fontina, if desired. Makes 2 servings.

HOMEMADE YOGURT/6

The first batch, begun with commercial yogurt as the starter, may not set up as firmly as future batches begun with a homemade starter—

- **2 cups skim *or* whole milk**
- **¼ cup plain yogurt**

In saucepan heat the milk to just below boiling point (200°), stirring to prevent scorching. Cool to about 115°, checking temperature with candy thermometer. Place the yogurt in mixing bowl; blend in warm milk. Cover bowl with plastic wrap and a towel. Place in another bowl of warm water (115° to 120°) checking the temperature with a thermometer. Let stand 6 to 8 hours or till mixture is firm when shaken gently. Change the water every hour to maintain temperature. (To shorten standing time to 4 to 5 hours, place a bowl of warm water in a plastic foam cooler. Place the bowl of yogurt in the water. With this method you only change the water about every 2 hours.) Let stand 4 hours more to develop tangy flavor. After yogurt is firm, remove ¼ cup of the yogurt to use as a starter for the next batch of yogurt. Store yogurt and starter in refrigerator. (You can discard the free liquid that forms as yogurt sets up.) Makes 2 cups, or 32 one-tablespoon servings.

Berry Yogurt: Prepare the Homemade Yogurt as above. Combine 2 tablespoons *sugar or honey* with ⅓ cup crushed fresh *or* frozen *strawberries, raspberries, or blueberries.* Gently fold fruit into the chilled yogurt or spoon fruit atop the plain yogurt. Makes 4 servings. (79 calories per serving)

Snowcapped Broccoli

VEGETABLES WITH VARIETY

For too long people overcooked and overseasoned vegetables, never really tasting their true flavors. All that has changed. Fresh vegetables, full of vitamins and minerals, are in the limelight—the more unusual the vegetable the better, from rutabaga and eggplant to pea pods and zucchini.

Vegetables provide welcome variety to the diet with so many delicious flavors available at a minimum of calories. And because they're high in fiber, they're generally quite filling.

Vegetables, fresh from the store or garden, are delicious eaten raw—as a snack, with a vegetable dip, in a salad, or on a sandwich.

For cooked vegetables, steaming (see tip, page 172) and baking are two excellent cooking methods. When cooking vegetables in liquid, be sure to keep cooking time to a minimum. Stir-frying till vegetables are just crisp-tender in a minimum amount of fat is popular and helps retain nutrients.

PEA PODS WITH ALMONDS/132

1 tablespoon teriyaki sauce
1½ teaspoons cornstarch
1 teaspoon instant chicken bouillon granules
2 tablespoons butter
2 tablespoons slivered almonds
8 ounces pea pods
1 cup sliced fresh mushrooms

Combine teriyaki sauce, cornstarch, bouillon granules, and ½ cup *water;* set aside. Melt butter in skillet. Add almonds and stir-fry 2 minutes or till lightly browned. Add pea pods and mushrooms; stir-fry 2 minutes more. Stir cornstarch mixture. Add to pea pods. Cook and stir till thickened and bubbly. Makes 4 servings.

RUTABAGA AND APPLE/119

1 medium rutabaga (1 pound), peeled and cubed
1 medium apple, peeled, cored, and sliced
⅓ cup packed brown sugar
2 tablespoons butter *or* margarine

In covered pan cook rutabaga in small amount of boiling, lightly salted water 20 to 35 minutes or till just tender; drain well. Place *half* the rutabaga and *half* the apple in a 1-quart casserole. Sprinkle with *half* the brown sugar; dot with *half* the butter. Sprinkle with *salt.* Repeat layers of rutabaga, apple, sugar, butter, and *salt.* Bake, covered, in a 350° oven for 30 minutes. Serves 6.

GARDEN VEGETABLE STIR-FRY/92

2 medium carrots, cut into thirds
2 cups green beans bias sliced into 1-inch lengths
2 cups sliced cauliflower
2 tablespoons cold water
1½ teaspoons cornstarch
2 tablespoons soy sauce
1 tablespoon dry sherry
2 teaspoons sugar
Dash pepper
• • •
2 tablespoons cooking oil
1 medium onion, cut into thin wedges
1 cup sliced zucchini

Cut carrots into thin sticks. In covered saucepan cook carrots and green beans in boiling, lightly salted water for 3 minutes. Add cauliflower. Cover and cook 2 minutes more; drain well. In small bowl blend water into cornstarch; stir in soy sauce, dry sherry, sugar, and pepper. Set aside.

Preheat a wok or large skillet over high heat; add cooking oil. Stir-fry onion in hot oil for 1 minute. Add carrots, green beans, cauliflower, and zucchini; stir-fry 2 minutes or till vegetables are crisp-tender. Stir soy mixture; stir into vegetables. Cook and stir 3 to 4 minutes or till thickened and bubbly. Serve at once. Makes 6 servings.

Garden Vegetable Stir-Fry

GARDEN-STUFFED PEPPERS/98

Serve this stuffed pepper when the fresh vegetables are in season. It's a side dish—

4 large green peppers
3 or 4 fresh ears of corn
• • •
¼ cup chopped onion
2 tablespoons butter *or* margarine, melted
1 cup shelled baby lima beans, cooked and drained
1 large tomato, chopped
½ teaspoon dried rosemary, crushed
Salt
Pepper

Remove tops from green peppers. Cut peppers in half lengthwise and remove seeds. Cook peppers in boiling, lightly salted water for 3 to 5 minutes; invert to drain. Cut off tips of corn kernels. Carefully scrape cobs with dull edge of knife; measure 1½ cups corn. In covered pan cook fresh corn in a small amount of boiling, lightly salted water 12 to 15 minutes or till done; drain the corn.

Cook onion in butter or margarine till tender. Stir in cooked corn, lima beans, tomato, and rosemary.

Season green peppers with salt and pepper. Fill peppers with vegetable mixture. Place in a 13x9x2-inch baking dish. Bake the filled peppers in a 350° oven for 30 minutes. Makes 8 servings.

Garden-Stuffed Peppers

SPROUT-STUFFED TOMATOES/97

Pictured on pages 232 and 233—

4 medium tomatoes
1½ cups fresh mung bean sprouts
2 tablespoons chopped green onion
1 tablespoon butter *or* margarine
⅓ cup soft whole wheat bread crumbs
1 tablespoon grated Parmesan cheese
2 teaspoons butter *or* margarine, melted

Cut tops off tomatoes; remove centers, leaving shells. Drain tomatoes. Chop enough centers to make ⅓ cup. Cook sprouts and green onion in 1 tablespoon butter or margarine 3 to 5 minutes or till tender. Remove from heat; stir in chopped tomato and ⅛ teaspoon *salt.*

Sprinkle insides of tomatoes lightly with *salt.* Fill tomatoes with sprout mixture. Combine crumbs, cheese, and the 2 teaspoons melted butter or margarine. Sprinkle atop tomatoes. Place tomatoes in an 8x8x2-inch baking pan. Bake in a 375° oven for 20 to 25 minutes or till hot. Makes 4 servings.

SPRINGTIME POTATOES/85

1 pound tiny new potatoes
½ cup chopped seeded cucumber
¼ cup sliced green onion
¼ cup sliced radishes
¼ teaspoon salt
⅛ teaspoon celery seed
Dash pepper
½ cup plain yogurt

In covered saucepan cook *unpeeled* new potatoes in boiling, lightly salted water about 15 minutes or till the potatoes are just tender; drain. Halve any large potatoes. In small saucepan combine chopped cucumber, sliced green onion, sliced radishes, salt, celery seed, and pepper; stir in yogurt. Cook over low heat till heated through, stirring constantly. *(Do not boil.)* Pour yogurt mixture over hot potatoes. Serves 4.

CABBAGE SUPREME/73

1 medium head cabbage, cored and cut into 8 wedges
¼ cup chopped green pepper
¼ cup finely chopped onion
1 tablespoon butter *or* margarine
1 tablespoon cornstarch
1 cup skim milk
¼ teaspoon salt
Dash black *or* white pepper
⅓ cup plain yogurt
¼ cup shredded cheddar cheese (1 ounce)

In large skillet cook cabbage in a small amount of boiling, lightly salted water for 3 minutes; cover pan and cook 10 to 12 minutes more or just till tender. Drain well; place on serving platter and keep warm. Meanwhile, in saucepan cook green pepper and onion in butter or margarine till tender; add cornstarch and mix well. Stir in skim milk, salt, and black or white pepper. Cook and stir till thickened and bubbly. Cook and stir 1 to 2 minutes more. Stir in yogurt and cheese till cheese melts. Pour over cabbage to serve. Makes 8 servings.

EGGPLANT SALAD/79

Serve this vegetable warm or chilled—

2 medium eggplants
1 medium green pepper, finely chopped
2 medium onions, finely chopped
1 clove garlic, minced
2 tablespoons olive oil *or* cooking oil
1 large tomato, peeled and finely chopped (¾ cup)
¼ cup snipped parsley
½ teaspoon dried basil, crushed
¼ teaspoon salt
⅛ teaspoon pepper
1 8-ounce can tomato sauce

Cut eggplants lengthwise into quarters. If desired, sprinkle cut surfaces with *salt;* let stand ½ hour. Rinse and pat dry with paper toweling. Place eggplant, cut side up, in shallow baking pan. Bake, covered, in a 450° oven for 25 minutes. Meanwhile, cook green pepper, onion, and garlic in *1 tablespoon* of the olive oil till tender but not brown. Remove from heat. Add chopped tomato, parsley, basil, salt, and pepper. Cut a lengthwise slit down center of each eggplant quarter, cutting to but not through the other side. Spoon green pepper mixture into slits. Return to baking pan. Pour tomato sauce over wedges. Bake in a 450° oven for 30 minutes. Serve warm or chilled. Makes 8 servings.

SUPER SALADS

The ingredients you can put into salads for a super flavor are so boundless you can tailor salads to anyone's and everyone's liking.

Start with an assortment of salad greens. Besides iceberg lettuce are leaf lettuce, romaine lettuce, and Bibb lettuce. Bok choy, savoy cabbage, Chinese cabbage, red cabbage, kale, watercress, parsley, Swiss chard, spinach, and endive are equally interesting and flavorful ingredients.

Tomato, green pepper, celery, onion, mushrooms, cucumber, and radishes are frequently added to salads for texture and color, but you can add other ingredients to make the salad unique. Avocado slices, artichoke hearts, water chestnuts, orange sections, zucchini slices, cauliflower or broccoli flowerets, apple wedges, and cheese cubes or strips all add character and nutrition, as do toasted sesame and sunflower seeds, walnuts, and almonds. And, remember fresh bean and seed sprouts, such as alfalfa, mung beans, and lentils.

Salad dressings should complement a salad, not overpower it. So, apply salad dressings with discretion.

VEGETABLE SPINACH SALAD/199

1 small onion
½ cup salad oil
3 tablespoons catsup
1 tablespoon sugar
2 tablespoons vinegar
2 teaspoons Worcestershire sauce
¼ teaspoon salt
Dash pepper

• • •

4 slices bacon
7 cups torn fresh spinach *or* assorted greens
1 cup fresh bean sprouts *or* one 8-ounce can water chestnuts, drained and sliced
1 medium carrot, thinly bias sliced
2 hard-cooked eggs, cut into wedges

Halve onion crosswise; cut up half and slice remaining half. Separate slices into rings and set aside.

For dressing, in blender container combine cut up onion, oil, catsup, sugar, vinegar, Worcestershire, salt, and pepper. Cover and blend till dressing is smooth. Chill.

Cook bacon till crisp. Drain, crumble, and set bacon aside. Place spinach or assorted greens in salad bowl. Add sprouts or water chestnuts, carrot, onion rings, and bacon; toss. Drizzle desired amount of dressing over the salad; top with hard-cooked egg wedges. Refrigerate the remaining dressing. Makes 8 servings.

TANGY CHICKEN BOWL/327

You can use a blender to make the dressing for this main dish salad—

1 8-ounce can kidney beans, drained
1½ cups cooked chicken *or* turkey cut into strips (about 8 ounces)
2 ounces American *or* cheddar cheese, cut into strips
½ of a small cucumber, sliced
½ cup sliced celery

• • •

¼ cup vinegar
3 tablespoons sugar
1 teaspoon grated onion
¼ teaspoon salt
¼ teaspoon celery seed
¼ teaspoon dry mustard
⅛ teaspoon paprika
½ cup salad oil

• • •

4 cups torn salad greens
1 large tomato, cut into wedges

Combine beans, chicken strips, cheese strips, cucumber slices, and sliced celery; chill. In a mixer bowl combine the vinegar, sugar, onion, salt, celery seed, dry mustard, and paprika. Gradually add the salad oil, beating constantly. Chill the dressing. Toss greens with bean and chicken mixture. Shake dressing. Pour some over the salad; toss. Pass remaining dressing. Garnish with the tomato wedges. Makes 6 servings.

Tangy Chicken Bowl

BELGIAN TOSSED SALAD/167

1 pint fresh brussels sprouts
½ cup salad oil
⅓ cup vinegar
1 clove garlic, minced
1 teaspoon dried parsley flakes, crushed
¼ teaspoon dried basil, crushed
8 cups torn mixed salad greens
½ medium red onion, sliced and separated into rings
4 slices bacon, crisp-cooked, drained, and crumbled

Cook brussels sprouts in small amount of boiling, lightly salted water about 5 minutes or till barely tender; drain. In screw-top jar combine oil, vinegar, garlic, parsley, basil, ½ teaspoon *salt,* and ⅛ teaspoon *pepper.* Cover; shake well to mix. Cut brussels sprouts in half lengthwise; pour dressing over. Cover; chill well. Combine greens, onion rings, and bacon. Add brussels sprouts with dressing; toss well. Serves 8.

COLESLAW SALAD BOWL/126

⅓ cup red wine vinegar
¼ cup salad oil
1 tablespoon sugar
1 teaspoon salt
1 14-ounce jar spiced apple rings, drained
4 cups shredded red cabbage
3 cups shredded green cabbage
2 cups torn fresh spinach
1 cup fresh sliced mushrooms
Red cabbage leaves

In screw-top jar combine red wine vinegar, oil, sugar, salt, and ¼ teaspoon *pepper*. Cover and shake; chill. Quarter apple rings. In large bowl toss together red and green cabbage, spinach, mushrooms, and apple pieces. Shake dressing; pour over salad and toss to coat. Cover; chill in red-cabbage-lined bowl. Serves 10.

CHEF'S CHOICE SALAD/329

This is a main-dish salad—

⅓ cup honey
1 teaspoon paprika
1 teaspoon dry mustard
¼ teaspoon salt
¼ cup white wine vinegar
½ cup salad oil
2 teaspoons toasted sesame seed
3 cups desired fresh fruit
• • •
8 cups torn salad greens
12 ounces cooked chicken, turkey, beef, *or* ham, cut into strips
1 cup cubed American, Swiss, brick, *or* mozzarella cheese (4 ounces)

Combine honey, paprika, mustard, and salt. Stir in wine vinegar. Add salad oil in a slow, steady stream, beating constantly with electric mixer or rotary beater about 3 minutes or till thick. Beat in sesame seed. Fold in fresh fruit. Cover and refrigerate several hours. To serve, arrange greens, cooked meat, and cheese on individual serving plates. Spoon fruit mixture and dressing over. Makes 8 servings.

CURRIED FRUIT-AND-NUT SALAD/189

A sophisticated tossed salad full of fruits and toasted almonds—

1 head red leaf *or* romaine lettuce, torn
1 cup torn fresh spinach
1 cup grapes, halved and seeded
1 11-ounce can mandarin orange sections chilled and drained
• • •
½ cup salad oil
⅓ cup wine vinegar
1 clove garlic, minced
2 tablespoons brown sugar
2 tablespoons minced chives
1 tablespoon curry powder
1 teaspoon soy sauce
¼ cup toasted slivered almonds*
1 avocado, peeled, seeded, and sliced (optional)

Combine red leaf or romaine lettuce, torn spinach, seeded grapes, and mandarin oranges. In screw-top jar combine oil, vinegar, garlic, brown sugar, chives, curry powder, and soy sauce. Pour some dressing over salad, tossing lightly to coat. Pass remaining dressing. Trim top of salad with toasted slivered almonds and the avocado slices, if desired. Makes 8 servings.

Note: To toast the almonds, spread the slivered almonds in a shallow baking pan. Toast the nuts in a 300° oven for 20 minutes, stirring occasionally.

Curried Fruit-and-Nut Salad

WHOLE-GRAIN FOODS

People not only are realizing how nutritious whole grains are, but also are discovering their natural hearty flavors. And the choice of grain goes far beyond just wheat. Rye, oats, triticale (a hybrid of wheat and rye), buckwheat, barley, and rice all add wholesome goodness to many types of dishes.

Any whole grain can be ground into flour, but wheat is the most common. Wheat flour comes in whole wheat and all-purpose, and all-purpose comes in bleached or unbleached. Whole wheat flour still has the bran, germ, and endosperm.

Other variety flours are rye flour, triticale flour, barley flour, and soy flour. You also can get flour from oats, corn, rice, and buckwheat.

You don't have to totally give up refined grains and flour to get the advantages of whole grains. Just substitute whole-grain flour for part of the white flour in baking, or occasionally alternate whole or cracked grains with rice or breakfast cereal.

DILL-ONION BREAD IN THE ROUND/128

Spike is a seasoning mixture available at health food stores—

1 package active dry yeast
½ cup warm water (110° to 115°)
• • •
1 beaten egg
½ cup cream-style cottage cheese
⅓ cup finely chopped onion
1 tablespoon butter *or* margarine, melted
• • •
2 cups unbleached flour
⅓ cup whole bran cereal
½ cup wheat germ
1 tablespoon sugar
1 tablespoon dillseed
1 teaspoon salt
½ teaspoon Spike (optional)
¼ teaspoon baking soda

Soften yeast in warm water. Combine egg, cottage cheese, onion, and butter or margarine; mix well. In bowl stir together flour, bran cereal, wheat germ, sugar, dill, salt, Spike (if desired), and soda. Add cottage cheese and yeast mixtures, stirring well. Cover; let rise till double (1 hour). Stir dough down. Knead on floured surface 1 minute. With greased hands pat in a well-greased 9-inch round baking pan. Cover; let rise till double (1 hour). Score top in diamond pattern. Bake in a 350° oven 40 minutes. Remove from dish; cool on rack. Serve warm. Makes 1 loaf or 12 servings.

RYE BREAD/93

3 packages active dry yeast
1 cup warm water (110° to 115°)
½ cup dark molasses
½ cup boiling water
2 tablespoons butter *or* margarine
2 tablespoons caraway seed
2 teaspoons salt
½ cup wheat germ
2¾ cups rye flour
2½ to 2¾ cups unbleached flour

Dissolve yeast in warm water. In large bowl combine molasses, boiling water, butter or margarine, caraway seed, and salt, stirring till butter almost melts. Cool to lukewarm (110° to 115°). Stir in yeast and wheat germ. Stir in all of the rye flour and as much unbleached flour as you can mix in with a spoon. Turn out onto lightly floured surface. Knead in enough remaining flour to make a moderately stiff dough that is smooth and elastic (6 to 8 minutes). Shape dough into a ball. Place in greased bowl, turning once to grease surface. Cover; let rise till double (about 1½ hours). Punch dough down. Divide dough in half. Cover; let rest 10 minutes. Shape into loaves. Place in two greased 11x4x3-inch or two 9x5x3-inch loaf pans. Cover; let rise till almost double (about 1 hour). Brush loaves with water. With sharp knife, gently score tops of loaves diagonally at 3-inch intervals. Bake in a 350° oven for 45 minutes. Remove from pans; cool. Makes 2 loaves, or 32 servings.

HEALTH COOKIES/88

- ¾ cup whole wheat flour
- ¼ cup wheat germ
- ¼ cup nonfat dry milk powder
- ¾ teaspoon salt
- ¼ teaspoon baking powder
- ¼ teaspoon baking soda

• • •

- ½ cup butter *or* margarine
- ½ cup peanut butter
- ¾ cup honey
- 1 egg
- 1 teaspoon vanilla

• • •

- 1 cup raisins
- 1 cup dried apricots, snipped (5 ounces)
- ¾ cup quick-cooking rolled oats
- ½ cup chopped walnuts
- ⅓ cup unsalted sunflower seed
- ⅓ cup shredded coconut

Stir together flour, wheat germ, milk powder, salt, baking powder, and soda. In large mixer bowl beat together butter or margarine, peanut butter, and honey. Add egg and vanilla; beat well. Add flour mixture, mixing well. Stir together raisins, apricots, rolled oats, walnuts, sunflower seed, and shredded coconut; add to the creamed mixture. Mix well. Drop by rounded teaspoonfuls onto ungreased cookie sheet. Bake in a 350° oven 10 to 11 minutes. Let cool on cookie sheet 1 minute; remove to wire rack to cool. Makes 54.

Health Cookies; Rye Bread; Whole Wheat Batter Rolls (see recipe, page 259); *Brown Nut Bread* (see recipe, page 258); *Dill-Onion Bread in the Round*

PEASANT BREAD/70

- 3 to 3½ cups all-purpose flour
- 2 packages active dry yeast
- 1¾ cups water
- ¼ cup dark molasses
- 2 tablespoons cooking oil
- 2 teaspoons salt
- 1½ cups rye flour
- ½ cup whole bran cereal
- ⅓ cup yellow cornmeal
- 1 tablespoon caraway seed

In a large mixer bowl combine *2 cups* of the all-purpose flour and the yeast. In saucepan heat water, molasses, oil, and salt just till warm (115° to 120°); stir constantly. Add to flour mixture. Beat at low speed of electric mixer ½ minute, scraping bowl. Beat 3 minutes at high speed. Stir in rye flour, bran, cornmeal, caraway, and as much remaining all-purpose flour as you can mix in with a spoon. Turn out onto lightly floured surface. Knead in enough remaining all-purpose flour to make a moderately stiff dough that is smooth and elastic (6 to 8 minutes total). Shape into a ball. Place in a greased bowl; turn once to grease surface. Cover; let rise in a warm place till double (1 to 1¼ hours).

Punch down; turn out onto floured surface. Divide in half. Cover; let rest 10 minutes. Shape into 2 loaves; place in two greased 8x4x2-inch loaf pans. Cover; let rise till nearly double (30 to 45 minutes). Bake in a 375° oven 35 to 40 minutes or till the bread is done. Cool on wire rack. Makes 2 loaves, or 36 servings.

Russian Black Bread

RUSSIAN BLACK BREAD/126

3½ to 4 cups all-purpose flour
4 cups rye flour
2 cups whole bran cereal
2 packages active dry yeast
2 tablespoons instant coffee crystals
2 tablespoons caraway seed
1 tablespoon sugar
1 tablespoon salt
1 teaspoon fennel seed, crushed
2½ cups water
⅓ cup molasses
¼ cup butter *or* margarine
1 square (1 ounce) unsweetened chocolate
2 tablespoons vinegar
½ cup cold water
1 tablespoon cornstarch

In large mixer bowl combine *3 cups* of the all-purpose flour, *1 cup* of the rye flour, the whole bran cereal, the yeast, coffee crystals, caraway seed, sugar, salt, and fennel seed. In saucepan heat together the 2½ cups water, molasses, butter or margarine, chocolate, and vinegar just till warm (115° to 120°) and chocolate and butter are almost melted; stir constantly. Add molasses mixture to flour mixture in mixer bowl. Beat at low speed of electric mixer ½ minute, scraping bowl. Beat 3 minutes at high speed. Stir in remaining 3 cups rye flour and as much of the remaining all-purpose flour as you can mix in with a spoon.

Turn out onto lightly floured surface. Knead in enough of the remaining all-purpose flour to make a moderately stiff dough that is smooth and elastic (6 to 8 minutes total). (Dough may be slightly sticky because of the rye flour.) Shape into a ball. Place in greased bowl; turn once to grease surface. Cover; let rise in a warm place till nearly double (1¼ to 1½ hours).

Punch down; divide in half. Shape each half into a ball. Place on greased baking sheets. Flatten slightly with palm of hand to a 6- to 7-inch diameter. Cover; let rise till nearly double (30 to 45 minutes). Bake in a 375° oven for 50 to 60 minutes or till well browned and bread sounds hollow when tapped. Remove from baking sheets; cool on wire rack.

Meanwhile, in a small saucepan combine the ½ cup cold water and cornstarch. Cook and stir till mixture is thickened and bubbly; cook 1 minute more. Brush over *hot* bread. Makes 2 loaves, or 32 servings.

TABOULEH/112

1 cup bulgur wheat
2 cups hot water
3 tablespoons lemon juice
2 tablespoons olive oil *or* cooking oil
2 tablespoons sliced green onion tops
1 tablespoon snipped parsley
1 teaspoon salt
1 teaspoon crushed fresh mint
1 tomato, cubed and seeded
8 romaine leaves

Soak bulgur in water for 2 hours; drain. Stir in lemon juice, oil, onion, parsley, salt, and mint. Cover and chill. Just before serving, stir in tomatoes. To serve, spoon mixture onto a romaine leaf and fold or roll. Or, stuff mixture into pockets of pita bread rounds, if desired. Makes 4 cups, or 8 servings.

TRITICALE WHEAT BREAD/139

2½ cups all-purpose flour
1 cup whole wheat flour
2 packages active dry yeast
2½ cups milk
¼ cup honey
3 tablespoons butter *or* margarine
2 teaspoons salt
2 eggs
1 cup triticale flour *or* soy flour
¼ cup wheat germ
1 beaten egg white
¼ cup shelled sunflower seed

In large mixer bowl combine *1 cup* of the all-purpose flour, the 1 cup whole wheat flour, and the yeast. In saucepan heat together the milk, honey, butter, and salt just till warm (115° to 120°) stirring constantly till butter almost melts. Add liquid to flour mixture along with the eggs. Beat well. Stir in triticale, wheat germ, and the remaining all-purpose flour to make a soft dough. Cover dough; let rise in a warm place till double (about 1 hour). Stir down dough; spoon into two well-greased 1½-quart casseroles. Cover; let rise again in a warm place till double (30 to 45 minutes). Just before baking, brush surface of dough lightly with the beaten egg white; sprinkle with sunflower seed. Bake in a 375° oven for 20 minutes; cover with foil and bake 10 to 15 minutes more or till bread sounds hollow when lightly tapped. Remove from casseroles; cool on wire rack. Serve with butter and honey, if desired. Makes 2 loaves, or 24 servings.

BROWN NUT BREAD/125

Pictured on page 255—

- **2¼ cups whole wheat flour**
- **1¾ cups unbleached flour**
- **2 teaspoons baking soda**
- **1 teaspoon salt**
- **2 beaten eggs**
- **2 cups sour milk***
- **½ cup molasses**
- **⅓ cup honey**
- **2 teaspoons finely shredded orange *or* lemon peel**
- **1 cup chopped walnuts**
- **¾ cup raisins**

In large bowl stir together flours, soda, and salt; set aside. In separate bowl combine eggs, sour milk, molasses, honey, and citrus peel; add to dry ingredients, stirring till blended. Stir in nuts and raisins. Turn into two greased 8x4x2-inch loaf pans. Bake in a 350° oven for 55 minutes, covering with foil the last 15 to 20 minutes. Remove from pans and cool on wire rack. Makes 2 loaves, or 32 servings.

Note: To make sour milk, place 2 teaspoons *lemon juice or vinegar* in a glass measuring cup. Add fresh *milk* to make 1 cup liquid. Stir and let stand 5 minutes.

BROWN RICE PUDDING WITH TOPPING/182

- **2½ cups skim milk**
- **¼ cup packed brown sugar**
- **¼ teaspoon salt**
- **¼ teaspoon ground cinnamon**
- **1 cup quick-cooking brown rice**
- **Blueberry Topping**

In saucepan combine milk, brown sugar, salt, and cinnamon. Bring to boiling; stir in rice. Cover; simmer 30 minutes or till milk is nearly absorbed, stirring occasionally. Serve warm or cold with Blueberry Topping. Makes 8 servings.

Blueberry Topping: Mash 1 cup *blueberries;* add *water* to equal 1 cup. In saucepan combine 2 tablespoons *brown sugar* and 2 teaspoons *cornstarch;* stir in the crushed blueberry mixture. Cook and stir till mixture thickens and bubbles. Cook and stir the mixture 2 minutes more. Remove from heat; stir in 1 cup whole *blueberries* and 1 teaspoon *lemon juice.*

OATMEAL RAISIN ROLLS/150

- **2½ cups whole wheat flour**
- **1 cup rolled oats**
- **1 cup unprocessed wheat bran**
- **¾ cup raisins**
- **2 packages active dry yeast**
- **½ teaspoon salt**
- **2 cups water**
- **½ cup honey**
- **¼ cup butter *or* margarine**
- **2¼ cups unbleached flour**

Combine *1 cup* of the whole wheat flour, the oats, bran, raisins, yeast, and salt. In saucepan heat water, honey, and butter till lukewarm; add to flour mixture. Mix well. Stir in remaining whole wheat flour and enough unbleached flour to make a moderately stiff dough; knead 6 to 8 minutes. Shape into ball. Cover; let rise till double. Punch down; halve dough. Cover let rest 10 minutes. Shape each half into 12 rolls; place on greased baking sheets. Cover; let rise till nearly double.Bake in a 350° oven for 25 minutes. Makes 24 rolls.

SEVEN-GRAIN BREAD/118

- **2 cups boiling water**
- **1½ cups uncooked seven-grain cereal**
- **4 cups unbleached flour**
- **2 packages active dry yeast**
- **1 cup water**
- **6 tablespoons butter *or* margarine**
- **¼ cup packed brown sugar**
- **2 teaspoons salt**
- **2 eggs**
- **2 cups whole wheat flour**
- **1 tablespoon sesame seed *or* poppy seed**

Pour the 2 cups boiling water over cereal; cool to lukewarm. Combine *2 cups* of the unbleached flour and the yeast. In saucepan heat the 1 cup water, the butter, brown sugar, and salt just till warm (115° to 120°) and butter is almost melted; stir constantly. Add to flour mixture; add eggs and beat well. Stir in cereal and whole wheat flour; add as much remaining unbleached flour as you can mix in with a spoon. Turn out on lightly floured surface. Knead in enough remaining unbleached flour to make a moderately stiff dough that is smooth and elastic (8 to 10 minutes). Shape into a ball. Place in greased bowl; turn once. Cover; let rise in warm place till almost double (about 1¼ hours).

Punch down; divide dough in half. Cover; let rest 10 minutes. Shape each portion into a loaf; place in 2 greased 9x5x3-inch loaf pans. Cover; let rise in warm place till nearly double (about 45 minutes). Brush tops with a little water and sprinkle with sesame seed. Bake in a 375° oven for 30 to 35 minutes, covering with foil the last 10 minutes. Remove from pan and cool on wire rack. Makes 2 loaves, or 36 servings.

BULGUR WHEAT PILAF/132

2 tablespoons butter *or* margarine
¾ cup bulgur wheat
2 tablespoons chopped onion
2 cups beef broth *or* chicken broth
Salt and pepper

Melt butter. Add bulgur wheat and chopped onion; brown lightly, stirring often. Add broth. Bring to boiling. Cover; reduce heat and simmer about 20 minutes or until the bulgur wheat is done. Season with salt and pepper. Makes 6 servings.

TOASTED BARLEY BAKE/125

¾ cup quick-cooking barley
¼ cup finely chopped onion
2 tablespoons butter *or* margarine
2 cups water
1 teaspoon instant chicken bouillon granules
½ teaspoon salt
2 tablespoons snipped parsley

In large skillet cook barley and finely chopped onion in butter or margarine over low heat, stirring frequently, about 15 minutes or till onion is tender and barley is golden brown. Stir in water, chicken bouillon granules, and salt. Bring to boiling. Pour into a 1-quart casserole. Bake, covered, in a 325° oven for 45 minutes, stirring once or twice. Uncover and bake 15 minutes more. Stir in snipped parsley. Makes 6 servings.

TRITICALE BANANA BISCUITS/81

Pictured on pages 232 and 233—

1 cup unbleached flour
1 cup triticale flour
2 teaspoons sugar
1½ teaspoons baking powder
½ teaspoon baking soda
½ teaspoon salt
¼ cup butter *or* margarine
• • •
¾ cup milk
½ cup mashed banana
½ teaspoon vanilla

In a mixing bowl stir together the unbleached flour, the triticale flour, sugar, baking powder, baking soda, and salt. Cut in butter or margarine till mixture resembles coarse crumbs. In another bowl combine the milk, banana, and vanilla; add all at once to dry mixture, stirring with a fork just till moistened.

Drop dough into 18 mounds onto a greased baking sheet. Bake in a 375° oven for 18 to 20 minutes or till golden. Serve warm. Makes 18 biscuits.

WHOLE WHEAT BATTER ROLLS/103

Pictured on page 255—

1 package active dry yeast
1¼ cups warm water (110° to 115°)
2 cups unbleached flour
1 teaspoon salt
1 teaspoon Italian seasoning
2 tablespoons butter *or* margarine, softened
1 tablespoon honey
1 tablespoon dark molasses
1 cup whole wheat flour

In large mixing bowl dissolve yeast in warm water. Add unbleached flour, salt, Italian seasoning, butter, honey, and molasses; beat well. Stir in whole wheat flour, blending well. Cover; let rise 30 minutes. Punch dough down. Reserve about ½ cup batter. Spoon remaining batter into greased 2½-inch muffin cups, filling ⅔ full. Spoon an additional teaspoon of the reserved batter atop batter in each muffin cup to make top knot. Bake in a 375° oven for 10 to 15 minutes. Remove from pan. Cool on wire rack. Brush tops with melted butter or margarine, if desired. Makes 16 rolls.

TRITICALE BERRY-RICE PILAF/122

1½ cups water
1 10¾-ounce can condensed chicken broth
½ cup triticale berries
¼ teaspoon salt
½ cup regular brown rice
2 tablespoons minced dried onion
¼ teaspoon ground nutmeg
1 cup thinly sliced fresh mushrooms

In a 2-quart saucepan bring water and chicken broth to boiling; stir in triticale berries and salt. Reduce heat; cover and simmer 1 hour. Add rice, minced onion, and nutmeg. Return to boiling; reduce heat. Cook, covered, for 40 minutes. Add sliced mushrooms; cover and cook 5 to 10 minutes more or till tender. Drain off excess liquid, if necessary. Press mixture into a buttered 3-cup ring mold; unmold onto platter. Garnish with parsley, if desired. Makes 6 servings.

ENERGIZING BEVERAGES

Fruit, vegetable, milk, and yogurt drinks can provide significant amounts of vitamins, minerals, and protein to your diet. And they can give your day a burst of energy. If you have your own juicer at home, you can squeeze your own juices from fresh fruits and vegetables. The fresh flavors you get are a bonus.

For great-tasting drinks, mix some of your favorite fruit juices with yogurt or milk, or put them in a blender with a few ice cubes to make a slush. Add an egg and you have a nog—great for breakfast or between meal energy boosters.

You can make fruit swizzle sticks for your beverages, using almost any fruit. Just spear strawberries, pineapple, cantaloupe, honeydew, and peaches on bamboo skewers, and put them in glasses for stirring or nibbling. You can also drop pieces of fruit directly into glasses—try citrus fruits, strawberries, pineapple, peaches, or nectarines.

GARDEN-FRESH REFRESHER/49

2 ripe medium tomatoes, peeled, cored, and cut up
¾ cup chicken broth
½ small zucchini, cut into chunks (½ cup)
1 small green onion, cut up
3 sprigs parsley
⅛ teaspoon dried basil, crushed

In blender container combine tomato, chicken broth, zucchini, green onion, parsley, and basil. Cover and blend till mixture is chunky. Chill. To serve, pour into glasses. If desired, garnish with sprigs of watercress. Makes 2 servings.

APRI-ORANGE-CARROT COOLER/80

1 medium carrot, sliced (½ cup)
¼ cup water
1 5½-ounce can (¾ cup) apricot nectar, chilled
1 cup orange juice

In small saucepan cook carrot, covered, in the water for 10 minutes or till tender. Cover and chill. When ready to serve pour *undrained* carrots and ¼ *cup* of the apricot nectar into blender container. Cover and blend till smooth. Add the orange juice and the remaining apricot nectar. Cover and blend till mixed. Pour into serving glasses. Garnish with carrot sticks, if desired. Makes 3 servings.

VANILLA MALTED MILK/129

1 cup ice water
½ cup vanilla ice milk
⅓ cup nonfat dry milk powder
2 teaspoons malted milk powder
½ teaspoon vanilla
Ground cinnamon (optional)

In blender container combine ice water, ice milk, nonfat dry milk powder, malted milk powder, and vanilla. Cover and blend till mixture is smooth. If desired, lightly sprinkle ground cinnamon atop each serving. Makes 2 servings.

SPINACH-PINEAPPLE DELIGHT/80

1½ cups unsweetened pineapple juice, chilled
½ cup torn fresh spinach
1 tablespoon lemon juice
1 teaspoon honey

Freeze *1 cup* of the pineapple juice in freezer tray. In blender container combine remaining ½ cup pineapple juice, spinach, lemon juice, and honey. Cover and blend 10 to 15 seconds. Break up the frozen pineapple juice into chunks. Add to blender container. Cover and blend just till slushy. Serve immediately. Makes 3 servings.

Orange-Ana Drink (see recipe, page 263); *Garden-Fresh Refresher; Apri-Orange-Carrot Cooler; Vanilla Malted Milk; Spinach-Pineapple Delight*

FROSTY SPICED TEA/23

- ¾ cup water
- 3 tablespoons sugar
- 6 inches stick cinnamon, broken
- ½ teaspoon whole cloves
- ¼ teaspoon ground nutmeg
- 4 teaspoons loose tea *or* 4 tea bags
- 4 cups boiling water

In small saucepan combine the ¾ cup water with sugar, cinnamon, cloves, and nutmeg. Bring to boiling; reduce heat. Cover and simmer for 20 minutes. Strain to remove spices.

Place loose tea in tea ball; add tea ball or tea bags to teapot. Pour the 4 cups boiling water over loose tea or tea bags. Let tea steep. Combine sugar mixture with the brewed tea; pour over ice in glasses. Makes 6 (6-ounce) servings.

BUTTERMILK-FRUIT COOLERS/76

Pictured on pages 232 and 233—

- 3 cups buttermilk
- 2 tablespoons honey
- 1 teaspoon vanilla
- 1 cup frozen unsweetened sliced peaches, strawberries, *or* blueberries

In blender container combine buttermilk, honey, and vanilla. Add desired frozen fruit; cover and blend 30 seconds or till smooth. Pour into glasses; garnish with fresh mint, if desired. Makes 6 (5-ounce) servings.

CANTALOUPE FROST/108

- ¾ cup milk
- ½ medium ripe cantaloupe, seeded, peeled, and cut up (2 cups)
- 1 cup frozen orange yogurt

In blender container combine milk and melon. Cover; blend till smooth. Add yogurt; cover. Blend till smooth. Serves 4.

SPICY DATE SHAKE/140

- ½ cup pitted dates, cut up
- 2 cups skim milk
- ½ teaspoon vanilla
- ⅛ teaspoon ground cinnamon
- 6 to 8 ice cubes

In blender container combine dates and *half* the milk. Cover; blend till smooth. Add remaining milk, vanilla, and spice. Cover; blend well. Add ice cubes, one at a time, blending till finely crushed. Serve at once in chilled glasses. Serves 3.

PINEAPPLE-CARROT COCKTAIL/71

- 1 12-ounce can carrot juice, chilled
- 1 cup unsweetened pineapple juice, chilled
- 1 tablespoon lemon juice

In a pitcher combine carrot juice, pineapple juice, and lemon juice. Chill. Serve over ice cubes. Serves 3.

SANGRIA/77

- 1 orange, halved
- 1 lemon, halved
- 1 750-milliliter bottle rosé, burgundy, *or* other red wine
- 2 tablespoons honey
- 1 apple
- 2 cups carbonated water, chilled

Chill *half* of orange and *half* of lemon for garnish; squeeze juice from the other halves. Place juice, wine, and honey in a pitcher or bowl. Stir to dissolve honey; chill. Cut chilled orange half into wedges. Slice chilled lemon half into cartwheels. Cut apple into wedges; remove core. Thread fruit on wooden picks to stand in glasses. Slowly add carbonated water to mixture in pitcher. Pour into glasses and garnish with fruit. Makes about 12 (4-ounce) servings.

MINTED LIME SODA/166

- 3 tablespoons crème de menthe syrup
- ½ of a 6-ounce can frozen limeade concentrate
- 1 pint vanilla ice milk
- 1 12-ounce bottle carbonated water, chilled

Combine crème de menthe, limeade concentrate, *half* of the ice milk, and *half* of the carbonated water; stir till blended. Pour into 4 glasses. Place additional scoops of ice milk in glasses; fill with remaining carbonated water. Garnish with mint sprigs, if desired. Makes 4 (8-ounce) servings.

ORANGE-ANA DRINK/94

Pictured on page 261—

3 medium oranges
1 small ripe banana, cut up
½ cup white grape juice, chilled
1 tablespoon lemon juice

Squeeze juice from oranges to make 1 cup. In blender container combine orange juice and remaining ingredients. Cover; blend. Pour into glasses. If desired, trim with grapefruit or orange wedge. Serves 3.

BANANA NOG/130

3 egg yolks
2 tablespoons sugar
1 banana, mashed
¼ teaspoon vanilla
⅛ teaspoon ground nutmeg
3 cups cold milk
3 egg whites
3 tablespoons sugar

Beat egg yolks at high speed of electric mixer about 6 minutes or till they are thick and lemon colored. Gradually add the 2 tablespoons sugar, beating constantly; beat in banana, vanilla, and nutmeg. Stir in milk; chill well.

Beat egg whites till soft peaks form; gradually add the 3 tablespoons sugar and beat to stiff peaks. Fold into egg yolk mixture just till combined, leaving a few small fluffs of egg white. Serve at once. Sprinkle with additional nutmeg, if desired. Makes 8 (6-ounce) servings.

Sangria; Minted Lime Soda; Banana Nog; Frosty Spiced Tea

FRESH FRUIT DESSERTS

The naturally sweet flavors of fresh, ripe fruit in season are hard to beat. And with the assortment of fruit available in the marketplace today, you can have fresh fruit year-round.

Fresh fruits are good sources of vitamins A and C, minerals, natural sugars, and fiber. They also offer plenty of flavor and color, and some texture.

Of course you can serve plain fruit for dessert. Or, you can dress the fruit up as indicated in the following recipes. Some of these recipes are never out of season because you select the fruit you want to use.

RAINBOW COMPOTE/99

¼ cup honey
1 tablespoon lemon juice
½ teaspoon finely shredded orange peel
¼ teaspoon ground cinnamon
2 oranges, peeled and sliced crosswise
3 cups desired fresh fruits*

Combine honey, lemon juice, orange peel, and cinnamon. Drizzle over orange slices in bowl; cover and chill for several hours or overnight. Chill remaining fruits. Drain oranges; reserve liquid. Arrange oranges in bottom of glass bowl. Top with three layers of desired fruits (1 cup each). Pour reserved liquid over fruits. Makes 6 servings.

Fruit options: Choose three of the following: blueberries, strawberries (halve large berries); peeled and sliced or cut-up melon, bananas, kiwis, mangoes, papayas, peaches, or pineapples; sliced or cut-up apples, apricots, nectarines, pears, or plums; halved and pitted dark sweet cherries; or halved, seeded grapes.

FRESH FRUIT ALOHA/80

1 cup fresh pineapple chunks
1 papaya, peeled, seeded, and cubed
½ cup sliced fresh strawberries
1 teaspoon lime juice
2 tablespoons sugar

Combine pineapple, papaya, strawberries, lime juice, and sugar. Chill thoroughly. Makes 4 servings.

FRUIT 'N' YOGURT DAZZLER/146

Pictured on the cover—

3 egg yolks
⅓ cup honey
¼ cup water
1 teaspoon cornstarch
2 8-ounce cartons plain yogurt

• • •

2 cups sliced fresh strawberries
2 cups cantaloupe *or* honeydew melon pieces *or* combination of both
2 cups seedless grapes, halved
2 cups sliced banana
2 tablespoons toasted coconut
Fresh mint leaves (optional)

In a small saucepan combine egg yolks, honey, water, and cornstarch; mix well. Cook and stir over medium heat till mixture comes to a boil. Reduce heat; cook and stir 2 minutes longer. Spoon mixture into a small bowl or glass measure. Cover with plastic wrap; chill the egg-yolk mixture, without stirring, several hours.

At serving time, fold egg yolk mixture into yogurt, blending well. In a large glass bowl or individual parfait glasses, layer fruit and yogurt mixture, ending with yogurt on top. Sprinkle with toasted coconut and, if desired, garnish with whole fresh strawberries and fresh mint leaves. Store any leftover yogurt mixture in refrigerator. Makes about 10 servings.

Rainbow Compote

FRUIT SHERBET/117

Select the desired fruit flavor from the options listed at end of recipe—

1 envelope unflavored gelatin
½ cup sugar
Dash salt
½ cup water
• • •
2 cups desired fresh fruit puree*
1 13-ounce can (1⅔ cups) evaporated milk
2 egg whites
¼ cup sugar

In saucepan combine gelatin, the ½ cup sugar, and the salt. Stir in water; heat and stir till gelatin dissolves. Stir in desired fruit puree and evaporated milk. Turn into a 9x9x2-inch pan; cover and freeze till firm.

In small mixer bowl beat egg whites till soft peaks form (tips curl over); gradually add the ¼ cup sugar, beating till stiff peaks form (tips stand straight). Break frozen mixture into chunks; turn into a large chilled mixer bowl. Beat with electric mixer till fluffy. Carefully fold in egg whites. Return mixture to pan; cover and freeze firm. Let stand a few minutes before serving. Makes about 1½ quarts, or 12 servings.

***Fruit options:** Mash or blend 3 to 4 cups of one of the following fruit suggestions to obtain 2 cups puree: peeled and cut-up peaches, apricots, or melons; berries (if desired, sieve to remove seeds); or pitted dark sweet cherries.

Exotic Fruit Platter

EXOTIC FRUIT PLATTER/149

- ½ teaspoon finely shredded lemon peel
- ½ cup frozen whipped dessert topping, thawed
- 1 8-ounce carton lemon yogurt
- Ti leaves *or* lettuce
- 3 fresh medium mangoes, peeled, seeded, and sliced
- 2 kiwi fruits, peeled and sliced
- ⅓ cup pomegranate seeds (optional)

For sauce, fold the lemon peel and thawed dessert topping into the yogurt. Line a platter with ti leaves or lettuce. Arrange mango and kiwi fruit slices atop. If desired, sprinkle with pomegranate seeds. Serve fruit with sauce. If desired, garnish sauce with a lemon-peel twist. Makes 6 servings.

BERRY-BUTTERMILK SOUP/119

- 2 cups fresh blueberries *or* strawberries
- 1½ cups water
- ⅓ cup honey
- ½ teaspoon finely shredded orange peel
- 2 tablespoons orange juice
- 2 cups buttermilk

In 1½-quart saucepan combine berries, water, honey, orange peel, and orange juice. Bring to boiling. Reduce heat; cover and simmer 20 minutes. Cool 30 minutes.

Pour into blender container; cover and blend till smooth. Stir in buttermilk. Cover and chill thoroughly. Makes 6 servings.

FROZEN ORANGE MIST/85

- ¼ teaspoon finely shredded orange peel
- 1 cup orange juice
- ¼ cup sugar
- 1 tablespoon lemon juice
- 1 cup *reconstituted* nonfat dry milk
- ⅔ cup evaporated skimmed milk

Combine orange peel, orange juice, sugar, and lemon juice; stir till sugar dissolves. Gradually add to *reconstituted* nonfat dry milk, stirring constantly. Pour into a 10x6x2- or 8x8x2-inch dish; freeze till firm.

Meanwhile, pour evaporated skimmed milk into a small mixer bowl; freeze till ice crystals form around edges. Break frozen orange juice mixture into chunks; place in chilled large bowl. Beat the orange juice mixture with an electric mixer till smooth.

Beat the icy cold evaporated milk with electric mixer till stiff peaks form; fold into orange juice mixture. Turn into a 10x6x2- or 8x8x2-inch dish; freeze till firm. Scoop to serve. Makes 8 servings.

STRAWBERRIES ROMANOFF/118

Pictured on pages 232 and 233—

- 1 quart fresh strawberries
- 2 tablespoons sugar
- 1 pint strawberry ice cream
- ½ cup plain yogurt *or* dairy sour cream
- 2 tablespoons orange liqueur

Sprinkle berries with sugar. Cover and chill. Meanwhile, stir ice cream just to soften. Fold in yogurt or sour cream and liqueur. Cover and freeze for 1 hour. To serve, top each serving of berries with a dollop of ice cream mixture. Makes 8 servings.

FRUIT-AND-CHEESE MOLD/158

- 1 6-ounce package lemon-flavored gelatin
- 2 cups boiling water
- 1 cup dry white wine
- 1 cup plain yogurt
- 2 cups desired fresh fruits*
- ½ cup shredded cheddar, Swiss, *or* Monterey Jack cheese (2 ounces)

Dissolve gelatin in boiling water; stir in wine. Gradually beat gelatin mixture into yogurt. Chill till partially set (consistency of unbeaten egg whites). Fold in fruit and cheese. Turn mixture into a 5½- or 6-cup mold. Chill gelatin several hours or overnight till firm. Unmold. Makes 8 servings.

Fruit options: Choose one of the following: peeled and cut-up melons (except watermelon) or peaches; cut-up apples; or berries (halve large strawberries).

GRANOLA FRUIT CRISP/188

If fruit is very ripe or juicy, toss prepared fruit with 1 to 2 tablespoons flour—

½ cup whole wheat flour
½ cup granola cereal
¼ cup packed brown sugar
½ teaspoon salt
¼ cup butter *or* margarine
6 cups sliced apples, peaches, bananas, *or* plums
¼ cup orange juice
1 tablespoon lemon juice
¼ cup granulated sugar

In bowl combine whole wheat flour, granola, brown sugar, and salt; cut in butter or margarine till mixture resembles coarse crumbs. Set aside.

Arrange fruit in a 10x6x2-inch baking dish. Combine orange and lemon juices; pour over fruit. Sprinkle with the granulated sugar. Top with granola mixture. Bake in a 375° oven for 30 to 35 minutes. Serves 8.

COLD SPICED PEACHES/87

3 large fresh peaches
Lemon juice
2 teaspoons cornstarch
2 tablespoons honey
¼ teaspoon salt
½ of a 6-ounce can pineapple-orange juice concentrate, thawed (⅓ cup)
⅔ cup water
½ teaspoon finely shredded orange peel
4 inches stick cinnamon
5 whole cloves

Peel, halve, and pit peaches; sprinkle with lemon juice mixed with a little *water* to prevent darkening. In saucepan mix cornstarch, honey, and salt. Stir in juice concentrate, ¾ cup water, orange peel, cinnamon, and cloves. Cook and stir till thickened and bubbly; cook and stir 2 minutes more. Pour hot mixture over peaches; chill. Remove spices before serving. Makes 6 servings.

CITRUS FRUIT SOUP/184

1¾ cups apple cider *or* apple juice
1 12-ounce can (1½ cups) apricot nectar
2 tablespoons sugar
2 tablespoons cornstarch
4 inches stick cinnamon, broken
4 whole cloves
¾ cup orange sections
¾ cup grapefruit sections
½ cup grapes, halved and seeded
1 cup cubed peeled apples, peaches, pears, pineapple, *or* plums
½ cup dry white wine

In a saucepan stir together apple cider, apricot nectar, sugar, cornstarch, stick cinnamon, and cloves. Cook and stir till boiling; reduce heat. Cover and simmer 15 minutes, stirring occasionally. Remove from heat. Stir in fruit and wine. Cover and chill, stirring occasionally. Remove cinnamon sticks and whole cloves; stir the fruit mixture before serving. Makes 5 servings.

BANANA PEACH FLAMBÉ/154

2 ripe bananas, peeled and sliced
2 peaches, peeled and sliced
1 tablespoon lemon juice
1 tablespoon brown sugar
2 teaspoons cornstarch
⅔ cup orange juice
Ground cinnamon
3 tablespoons light rum
2 cups vanilla ice milk

Brush banana and peach slices with the lemon juice. In saucepan stir together the brown sugar and cornstarch. Stir in the orange juice. Cook and stir till mixture is thickened and bubbly. Gently stir in the banana and peach slices. Cook and stir gently 1 to 2 minutes more. Sprinkle lightly with cinnamon. Heat the rum in a small saucepan just till it *almost* simmers. Carefully ignite the rum and pour over the fruit. Serve the fruit mixture immediately over small scoops of ice milk. Makes 6 servings.

WATERMELON FROST/69

¼ cup orange liqueur
¼ cup sugar
3 tablespoons lemon juice
3 cups peeled, seeded, and cubed watermelon

In blender container place orange liqueur, sugar, lemon juice, and *half* the watermelon. Cover; blend till pureed. Add remaining melon. Cover; blend again till smooth. Pour into refrigerator trays. Cover; freeze at least 2 hours (mixture will not freeze hard). Serve in dessert glasses. Serves 6.

RHUBARB SAUCE/111

½ to ⅔ cup sugar
¼ cup water
1 orange peel strip (optional)
1 pound fresh rhubarb, cut into ½-inch pieces (3 cups)

In a medium saucepan combine the sugar, water, and the orange peel strip, if desired. Bring to boiling; add rhubarb pieces. Reduce heat. Cover and simmer 5 minutes or till rhubarb is tender. Remove the orange peel. Makes 4 servings.

NO-COOK APPLESAUCE/119

4 medium apples, peeled, quartered, and cored
¼ cup sugar
¼ cup water
1 tablespoon lemon juice
Ground cinnamon *or* nutmeg

Slice apples into container of blender or food processor. Add sugar, water, and lemon juice. Cover and blend till almost smooth. Spoon into dessert dishes and sprinkle each serving lightly with cinnamon or nutmeg. Or, transfer to saucepan and bring to boiling to keep apples from darkening. Makes 4 servings.

Banana Peach Flambé

COOKING WITH AND USING
FOOD EXCHANGES

Here's how to diet without counting calories; instead you add up Food Exchanges. With the Food Exchange plan to guide you, it's easy to guard against a growing girth. At the same time, the recipes in this chapter—all rated for Food Exchange values—demonstrate that dieting can mean tasty eating because this plan lets you savor a large variety of foods.

Polynesian Shrimp

Peach Fondue

Meat and Potato Loaf

Spinach Salad Toss

USING FOOD EXCHANGES

Do not let the term "Food Exchange" intimidate you. Although it sounds very technical, it's really a simple method used for many years by dietitians to balance diets carefully.

Each Food Exchange is merely a measurement of calories and nutrient values. Foods are divided into seven Exchange groups—Meat, Bread, Fruit, Vegetable, Milk, Fat, and a group of Free foods. The foods in each Exchange group contain similar amounts of proteins, fats, carbohydrates, and calories.

For example, a Bread Exchange is not necessarily bread. It can be a tortilla, cereal, or peas. Any differences in nutrients and calories are adjusted by the serving size. Because one slice of white bread furnishes the same amount of proteins, carbohydrates, and calories as one tortilla, one-half cup of peas, or one cup of puffed cereal, all count as one Bread Exchange. Thus, they are interchangeable on a menu. That is why we call the seven food groups Food "Exchanges." Using them in your daily eating pattern assures you'll have a varied diet.

Understanding Food Exchange Lists

Food Exchanges can simplify reducing for you by counting calories, assuring a well-balanced diet, permitting you to choose the foods you like best within a food group, and providing menus easily adapted for all members of the family. A reducing diet based on Food Exchanges will provide adequate nutrients for most people. A variety of foods will help ensure that your diet is nutritionally adequate.

Look at the Food Exchange Lists on pages 282 to 286. Notice that the foods in these lists are bulwarks of the everyday American diet. Each list has a color symbol for recognition at a glance. Check the tip box on the next page for a summary of the exchanges and color symbols.

The size of each serving is specified in each Exchange List, with the exception of the Free Exchanges. (Free foods specify no limit since they are insignificant in terms of calories.) Exchange units are usually expressed as ounces or as standard measuring cups and spoons. It is important for you to estimate and visualize these measures accurately. At first you may want to measure servings using standard measuring cups and spoons. But after a while, you'll be able to recognize quantities such as one-half cup of peas or one cup of puffed cereal. A small dietary scale may be useful for weighing meat.

Take a look at the Meat Exchange List on pages 282 and 283. You'll find it divided into three subcategories according to fat content. The three subcategories are Lean Meat, Medium-Fat Meat, and High-Fat Meat. These may be easier to think of as fat, fatter, and fattest. The Lean Meat Exchange provides seven grams of protein, three grams of fat, and 55 calories per serving. The Medium-Fat Meat Exchange provides seven grams of protein and five and one-half grams of fat. It contains 75 calories per serving because of its higher fat content. You must charge yourself an extra one-half Fat Exchange above and beyond the Lean Meat Exchange for each serving of Medium-Fat Meat. Each serving of High-Fat Meat provides seven grams of protein, eight grams of fat, and 100 calories. It costs one additional Fat Exchange.

But why all the calculations and talk about calories? You need not compute or worry about calories. When necessary, simply account for the appropriate number of Fat Exchanges per serving of Medium- or High-Fat Meat. You'll find that all the meal plans and recipes in this chapter are based on the Lean Meat Exchange plus a specified number of Fat Exchanges when Medium- or High-Fat Meats are used.

As you may expect, the Bread Exchange List on page 284 contains bread, cereals, and crackers. But it also lists dried beans and starchy vegetables such as corn, peas, and potatoes. At first glance, you may think the potatoes are out of place. Not so. One small potato delivers about the same cargo of proteins, carbohydrates, and calories as does one slice of bread. Also contained in the Bread Exchange List are various prepared foods for which one or two additional Fat Exchanges must be deducted when figuring Food Exchanges.

Most vegetables are in the Vegetable Exchange List on page 285. As mentioned, dried beans, peas, and lentils, and starchy vegetables, such as corn, peas, and potatoes, are in the Bread Exchange List. Some raw vegetables (chicory, Chinese cabbage, endive, escarole, lettuce, parsley, radishes, and watercress) can be eaten in any amount and merit a coveted Free Exchange rating.

No complicating factors are found in the Fruit Exchange List on page 285, because all fruits are fat free. One Fruit Exchange contains ten grams of carbohydrate and 40 calories. Cranberries are one fruit you can eat to your heart's content as long as you add no sugar to them.

The Milk Exchange List on page 285 is based on nonfat milk. Thus, if you choose an item from this list *not* made from nonfat or skim milk, you must account for the equivalent Fat Exchanges. (The number of accountable Fat Exchanges is listed after the lowfat and whole milk products in the Milk Exchange List.)

Fat Exchanges, found on page 286, include nuts, olives, and avocados, in addition to the more common fats and oils. The "note" with the Fat Exchange List tells you more about saturated and unsaturated fats.

In the Free Exchange List on page 286, you'll find flavor enrichers such as salt, pepper, herbs, and spices. A variety of other foods and beverages is offered to please your palate and fill you up without adding significant calories.

Not at all hard to understand, is it? Now you're ready to put the Food Exchanges to work in planning some meals.

Easy Meal Planning

The Daily Meal Plans on page 288 give you a choice of three "reducing speeds"—1,000, 1,200, or 1,500 calories a day. Choose a meal plan with a daily calorie deficit that lets you reduce no more than two pounds a week. From now on, think no more about counting calories.

Just select the foods you like from the respective Food Exchange Lists specified for each meal. For example, on the 1,000-calorie diet you can have one Fruit Exchange for breakfast. The Fruit Exchange List gives you many choices—one-half small banana, one fig if you feel exotic, or one-half cup unsweetened applesauce if you don't, one-half cup orange juice, or one-half of a grapefruit. Remember to read the Food Exchange Lists carefully. Serving sizes differ within a Food Exchange group and may be somewhat different from the serving sizes you are accustomed to eating.

Go over the other specified Food Exchanges for breakfast, lunch, and dinner on page 288, and make your selections from the Food Exchange Lists on pages 282 to 286. Choose any food you desire, as long as it fits into a Daily Meal Plan that helps you lose about two pounds in a week. One warning: If you exceed the Exchange allotments of your Daily Meal Plan, your reducing progress will be slow.

On the 1,000-calorie daily diet, you may have one Lean Meat Exchange at breakfast, two Lean Meat Exchanges at lunch, and two Lean Meat Exchanges at dinner. For an example of how to make appropriate meat selections for each of the three meals and how to incorporate them in the 1,000-calorie Daily Meal Plan, read the first column on page 274.

EXCHANGE SYMBOLS

You will find that the Exchange Lists on pages 282 to 286 are color-keyed. In addition, you will find corresponding color symbols on the Daily Meals Plans (page 288), suggested menus, and also following the recipes in this chapter. Below is a summary of these color symbols:

- ● Lean Meat Exchange
- ● Bread Exchange
- ● Vegetable Exchange
- Fruit Exchange
- ● Milk Exchange
- ● Fat Exchange
- Free Exchange

A typical Meat Exchange selection at breakfast might be a poached egg. But you won't find eggs on the Lean Meat Exchange. They're on the Medium-Fat Exchange. In this case, just deduct one-half Fat Exchange in addition to one Lean Meat Exchange from the breakfast meal plan.

At lunch, when two Lean Meat Exchanges are allotted, cottage cheese would be a logical choice. One Lean Meat Exchange is equivalent to one-fourth cup cottage cheese (2% milkfat), so two Exchanges would allow one half-cup cottage cheese (2% milkfat) at lunchtime.

At dinnertime, you could choose frankfurters as your Meat Exchanges, but only if you deduct one Fat Exchange in addition to one Lean Meat Exchange *per* frankfurter (because frankfurters are found on the High-Fat Meat Exchange List). So in order to fit two frankfurters into the dinner meal plan for the 1,000-calorie diet, you would have to subtract two Fat Exchanges in addition to two Lean Meat Exchanges. That takes care of the dinnertime allotment of both Meat and Fat Exchanges.

Breakfast and dinner meal plans on page 288 allow only one-half of a Milk Exchange at each meal. In this case, choose any item from the Milk Exchange List, but cut the quantity in half. For example, for one-half of a Milk Exchange, you may have one-half cup of skim milk instead of the one cup for a full Exchange.

Your selection of foods will add up automatically in round numbers to the number of calories in the Daily Meal Plan you choose. The number of Food Exchanges specified in your Daily Meal Plan takes care of the arithmetic for you. What a relief to make easy choices of your favorite foods instead of counting calories! Together, the Food Exchange List and the Daily Meal Plans will add variety to all your meals.

Helpful Meal Planning Hints

The Daily Meal Plans show the conventional three meals a day. But no law requires that you eat only three meals. You can divide your allotted Food Exchanges for the day into half a dozen small meals or three meals plus a coffee break or bedtime snack. In fact, spreading your supply of Food Exchanges over the entire day may help reduce hunger pangs between meals.

If you carry a lunch, you might want to borrow a breakfast or dinner bread allowance in order to enjoy a lunchbox sandwich. Or, you may be content with the Bread Exchanges the way they are, allowing you one exchange for each meal, except for the 1,500-calorie diet breakfast and lunch meal plans.

Remember, you can substitute one food for another in the *same* Food Exchange List, but you can't substitute foods of one Exchange List for foods of a different Exchange. You can't swap grapefruit juice for cottage cheese without risk of upsetting dietary balance or calorie contribution. Let the color code of the Food Exchange Lists be your guide. Substitute only those foods with the same color code. The Bread and Fruit Exchanges are the exceptions. Refer to pages 277 and 279 to find out how to substitute fruit for bread or vice versa.

"Mixed" foods, such as stews or casseroles, combine foods from different Exchange Lists. You can calculate their composition closely enough by looking at them carefully to determine the Meat, Bread, Vegetable, Fruit, Milk, Fat, or Free Exchanges that compose them. This was the procedure used to calculate the recipes starting on page 302. This calculation doesn't always give you enough calories or nutrients to equal one whole Food Exchange. As a result, one-half and sometimes even one-fourth Food Exchanges are used. Look for the following color symbols when whole or fractional Exchanges are used:

- 1 Milk Exchange
- ½ Milk Exchange
- ¼ Milk Exchange

Round out fractional Exchanges with *partial* servings of that particular Exchange.

The Menu Planning Steps and sample menus on pages 289 to 301 are a good place to begin your menu planning. We've devised several menus for the 1,000-, 1,200- and 1,500-calorie Daily Meal Plans that should help you plan your own menus.

Built-in Daily Variety

Endless variety is built into the Daily Meal Plans. Take full advantage of it when making your Food Exchange selections. Variety is a very important word in nutrition. Too much of one type of food or too little of another makes a diet lopsided. A *balance of a variety of foods* is the key to proper nutrition. The foods in each Exchange group make a specific nutritional contribution. No single Food Exchange group can supply all the nutrients needed for a well-balanced diet. It takes foods from all of the Exchange groups to supply your nutritional needs for good health.

The Daily Meal Plans furnish a fine balance of essential nutrients in the most convenient way. You can substitute foods that you happen to have on hand, foods that are in season and inexpensive when plentiful, or those that you just happen to like best. If there's no bread in the cupboard but there is a small leftover boiled potato in the refrigerator, it's nice to know you can substitute the potato for the bread. Making such choices provides variety in a mixed diet. The Food Exchange Lists are indeed good mixers.

Add to the Food Exchange Lists the recipes starting on page 302 and your mealtime choices grow. Tastefully seasoned, these imaginative recipes are based on Food Exchanges for easy incorporation into the Daily Meal Plans. These recipes are as easy and almost as sumptuous as any calorie-laden food you've ever tasted. You can indulge yourself with these dishes as long as you account for the appropriate number of Food Exchanges from your Daily Meal Plan. Non-dieting families and friends will also enjoy the reducing recipes.

The choices are yours. Select foods to fit your Daily Meal Plan from the variety of foods found on the Exchange Lists or from the recipes found in this chapter of the book. Then, enjoy a different menu each day.

Food Exchanges To Hold Your Weight Loss

The Daily Meal Plans are deficient only in calories (that's why they make excess fat disappear). After you have reduced to your ideal weight using the Daily Meal Plans, you will need more calories—but not a great number more—to maintain your weight without putting a load of fat back on your frame.

With your eating habits geared to weight reduction, it will be easy to increase your caloric intake to maintenance levels (page 341). You can use the Daily Meal Plans as the foundation of a balanced diet. For example, while keeping the same balance of good nutrition, you can increase the calories by adding a few extra servings from the Food Exchanges. You will recognize the values of the different Food Exchanges almost instinctively by the time you reach the happy stage when you need more calories to keep from wasting away to a shadow.

Food Exchanges can help ensure a lifetime of good balanced eating. Give them a try. Food is one of life's basic necessities, and eating is one of its greatest pleasures.

POINTS TO REMEMBER

One Food Exchange: *A measurement of calorie and nutrient values. Foods within the same Exchange are interchangeable; they contain similar amounts of nutrients and calories in each specified serving.*

Food Exchange Lists: *Seven lists of foods. Foods in each list have similar amounts of protein, fat, carbohydrate, and calories. Caloric values within an Exchange group are adjusted by serving size.*

Daily Meal Plans: *A daily guide of reducing menus that counts the calories for you (page 288).*

SEVEN FOOD-EXCHANGE GROUPS

MEAT EXCHANGE

The Meat Exchanges (pages 282 to 283) are the protein keystones of your meals. For good reason, the meat course is the *pièce de résistance.* Meat Exchanges aren't limited to poultry, meat, and fish, however. They also include other protein foods, such as cheese, eggs, dried peas and beans, and peanut butter.

All the foods found in the Meat Exchange List provide generous amounts of protein, the nutrient responsible for tissue building and repair. Many members of the Meat Exchange family are good sources of the B vitamins and minerals such as iron, zinc, and phosphorus. Foods in the Meat Exchange List contain similar amounts of all nutrients except fat. The Medium-Fat and High-Fat Meat Exchanges contain more fat than the Lean Meat Exchange.

Foods from the Medium-Fat Meat Exchange cost one-half additional Fat Exchange (except peanut butter, which costs two and one-half additional Fat Exchanges), and foods from the High-Fat Meat Exchange cost one additional Fat Exchange per serving.

Most foods in the Lean Meat Exchange are low in cholesterol and saturated fat. Peanut butter (a Medium-Fat Meat Exchange) contains no cholesterol and is also low in saturated fat.

Most of the Meat Exchanges are based on one-ounce servings of *cooked* meat. A three-ounce serving of cooked meat is about equal to four ounces of raw meat. Be sure to trim all fat from meat. If the meat is fried, count the fat used to fry it as a Fat Exchange. To brown meat, use diet margarine or a pan with a non-stick surface.

Don't forget about fish and seafood. One ounce of any fresh, frozen, or canned seafood is equivalent to one Lean Meat Exchange. Be sure to drain all canned seafood well and use the water-pack variety when possible. In practical measures, one-fourth cup of canned salmon, tuna, or mackerel is equivalent to one Lean Meat Exchange. That's also true for crab and lobster in any form. Five scallops, shrimp, oysters, or clams, or three *drained* sardines also equal one Lean Meat Exchange.

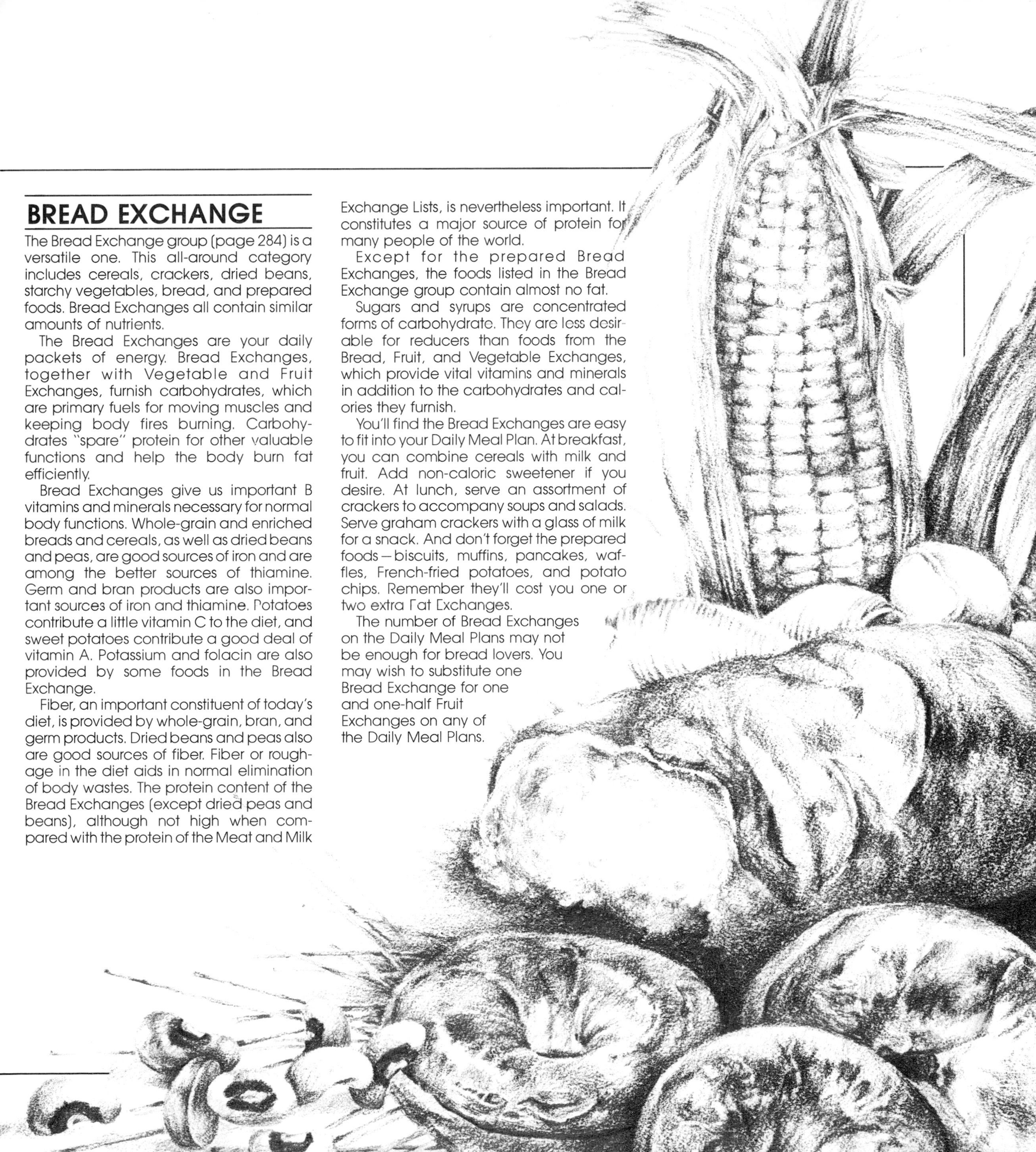

BREAD EXCHANGE

The Bread Exchange group (page 284) is a versatile one. This all-around category includes cereals, crackers, dried beans, starchy vegetables, bread, and prepared foods. Bread Exchanges all contain similar amounts of nutrients.

The Bread Exchanges are your daily packets of energy. Bread Exchanges, together with Vegetable and Fruit Exchanges, furnish carbohydrates, which are primary fuels for moving muscles and keeping body fires burning. Carbohydrates "spare" protein for other valuable functions and help the body burn fat efficiently.

Bread Exchanges give us important B vitamins and minerals necessary for normal body functions. Whole-grain and enriched breads and cereals, as well as dried beans and peas, are good sources of iron and are among the better sources of thiamine. Germ and bran products are also important sources of iron and thiamine. Potatoes contribute a little vitamin C to the diet, and sweet potatoes contribute a good deal of vitamin A. Potassium and folacin are also provided by some foods in the Bread Exchange.

Fiber, an important constituent of today's diet, is provided by whole-grain, bran, and germ products. Dried beans and peas also are good sources of fiber. Fiber or roughage in the diet aids in normal elimination of body wastes. The protein content of the Bread Exchanges (except dried peas and beans), although not high when compared with the protein of the Meat and Milk Exchange Lists, is nevertheless important. It constitutes a major source of protein for many people of the world.

Except for the prepared Bread Exchanges, the foods listed in the Bread Exchange group contain almost no fat.

Sugars and syrups are concentrated forms of carbohydrate. They are less desirable for reducers than foods from the Bread, Fruit, and Vegetable Exchanges, which provide vital vitamins and minerals in addition to the carbohydrates and calories they furnish.

You'll find the Bread Exchanges are easy to fit into your Daily Meal Plan. At breakfast, you can combine cereals with milk and fruit. Add non-caloric sweetener if you desire. At lunch, serve an assortment of crackers to accompany soups and salads. Serve graham crackers with a glass of milk for a snack. And don't forget the prepared foods—biscuits, muffins, pancakes, waffles, French-fried potatoes, and potato chips. Remember they'll cost you one or two extra Fat Exchanges.

The number of Bread Exchanges on the Daily Meal Plans may not be enough for bread lovers. You may wish to substitute one Bread Exchange for one and one-half Fruit Exchanges on any of the Daily Meal Plans.

VEGETABLE EXCHANGE

Not only are Vegetable Exchanges (page 285) great to taste, but they also supply valuable vitamins and minerals. Among the leading sources of vitamin A in the diet are the dark green and deep yellow members of the Vegetable Exchange. In addition, many of the vegetables of this group are notable sources of vitamin C, with asparagus, broccoli, brussels sprouts, beet greens, cabbage, cauliflower, collards, kale, dandelion, mustard and turnip greens, spinach, rutabagas, tomatoes, and turnips leading the way. Fiber, which helps promote regularity, is present in vegetables. Vegetables are loaded with other important vitamins and minerals, too.

Whether you serve them cooked or raw, wash all vegetables even if they look clean. And, if fat is added in preparation, deduct the equivalent number of Fat Exchanges.

Add zest to vegetables by cooking them with herbs and spices (Free Exchanges).

Vegetable salads serve the dieter in good stead, but be adventuresome! Start with a variety of greens (endive, escarole, Bibb, or Boston lettuce—they're all Free Exchanges), add a few of your favorite raw vegetables, and toss with a favorite low-calorie salad dressing.

Treat yourself to a glass of tomato juice or vegetable juice cocktail as an appetizer or snack. Dash in a squirt of lemon juice, Worcestershire sauce, or bottled hot pepper sauce. Sprinkle lightly with seasoned salt, onion salt, or celery salt for a change of pace.

Speaking of snack time, don't forget vegetable relishes. Devour radishes to your heart's content (they are a Free Exchange), but be sure to measure amounts of other vegetables such as celery, carrots, cucumbers, or cauliflower. One-half cup equals one Vegetable Exchange.

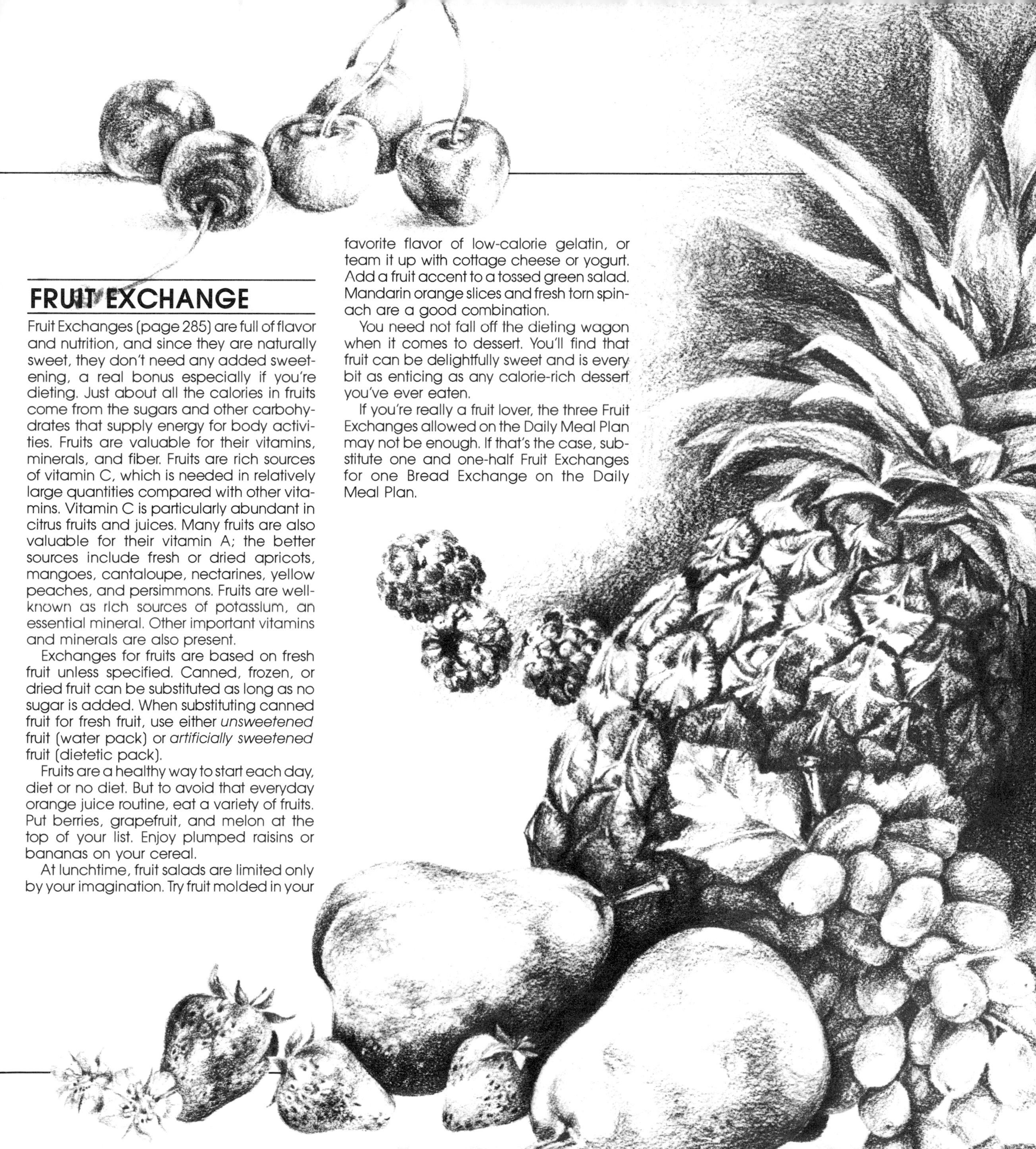

FRUIT EXCHANGE

Fruit Exchanges (page 285) are full of flavor and nutrition, and since they are naturally sweet, they don't need any added sweetening, a real bonus especially if you're dieting. Just about all the calories in fruits come from the sugars and other carbohydrates that supply energy for body activities. Fruits are valuable for their vitamins, minerals, and fiber. Fruits are rich sources of vitamin C, which is needed in relatively large quantities compared with other vitamins. Vitamin C is particularly abundant in citrus fruits and juices. Many fruits are also valuable for their vitamin A; the better sources include fresh or dried apricots, mangoes, cantaloupe, nectarines, yellow peaches, and persimmons. Fruits are well-known as rich sources of potassium, an essential mineral. Other important vitamins and minerals are also present.

Exchanges for fruits are based on fresh fruit unless specified. Canned, frozen, or dried fruit can be substituted as long as no sugar is added. When substituting canned fruit for fresh fruit, use either *unsweetened* fruit (water pack) or *artificially sweetened* fruit (dietetic pack).

Fruits are a healthy way to start each day, diet or no diet. But to avoid that everyday orange juice routine, eat a variety of fruits. Put berries, grapefruit, and melon at the top of your list. Enjoy plumped raisins or bananas on your cereal.

At lunchtime, fruit salads are limited only by your imagination. Try fruit molded in your favorite flavor of low-calorie gelatin, or team it up with cottage cheese or yogurt. Add a fruit accent to a tossed green salad. Mandarin orange slices and fresh torn spinach are a good combination.

You need not fall off the dieting wagon when it comes to dessert. You'll find that fruit can be delightfully sweet and is every bit as enticing as any calorie-rich dessert you've ever eaten.

If you're really a fruit lover, the three Fruit Exchanges allowed on the Daily Meal Plan may not be enough. If that's the case, substitute one and one-half Fruit Exchanges for one Bread Exchange on the Daily Meal Plan.

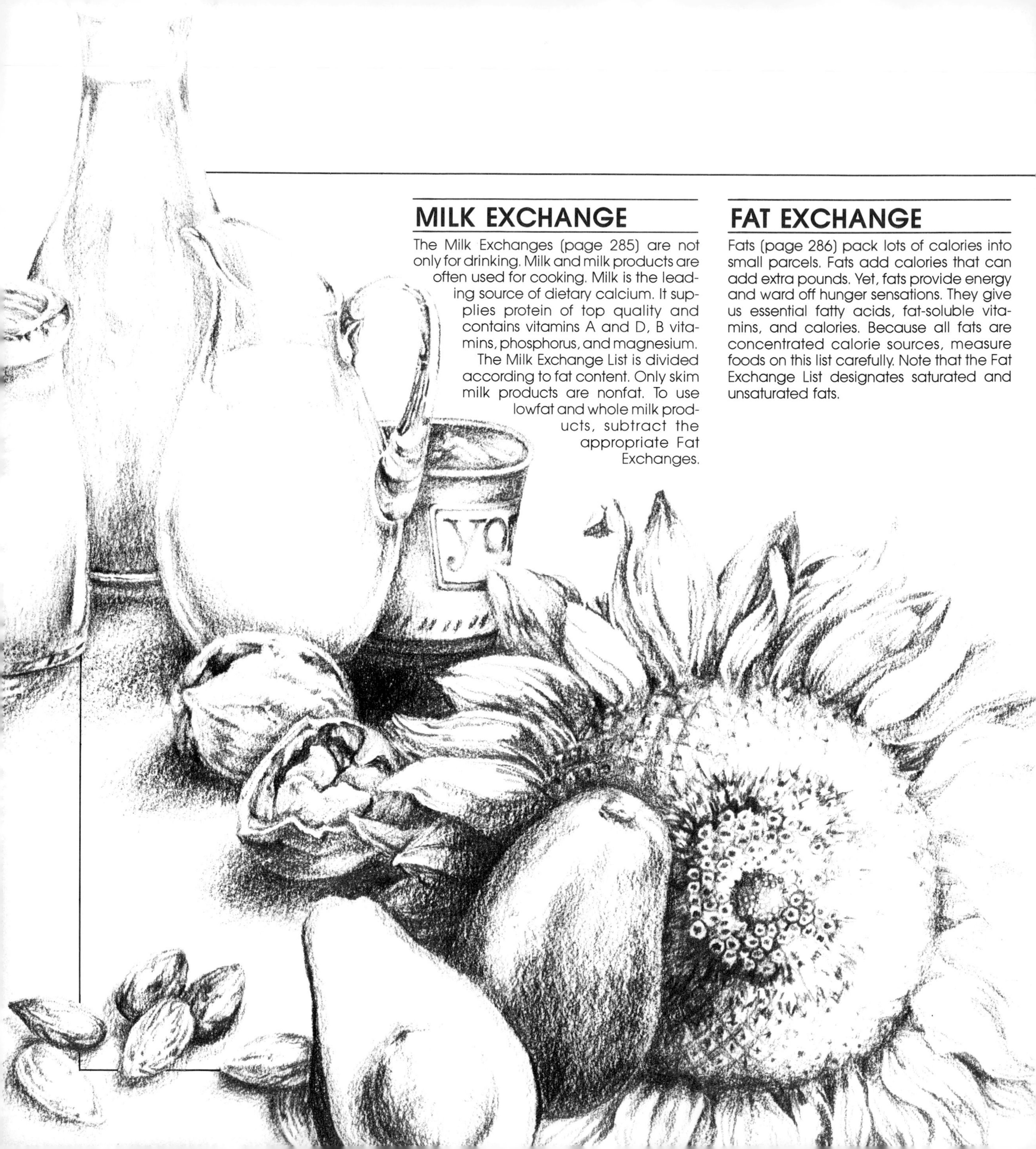

MILK EXCHANGE

The Milk Exchanges (page 285) are not only for drinking. Milk and milk products are often used for cooking. Milk is the leading source of dietary calcium. It supplies protein of top quality and contains vitamins A and D, B vitamins, phosphorus, and magnesium.

The Milk Exchange List is divided according to fat content. Only skim milk products are nonfat. To use lowfat and whole milk products, subtract the appropriate Fat Exchanges.

FAT EXCHANGE

Fats (page 286) pack lots of calories into small parcels. Fats add calories that can add extra pounds. Yet, fats provide energy and ward off hunger sensations. They give us essential fatty acids, fat-soluble vitamins, and calories. Because all fats are concentrated calorie sources, measure foods on this list carefully. Note that the Fat Exchange List designates saturated and unsaturated fats.

FREE EXCHANGE

The only limit on Free Exchanges (page 286) is your appetite. They are insignificant in terms of calories. Use the Free Exchanges to add the gourmet touches to your meals. Pep up your palate by using herbs and spices freely when you prepare your foods.

Use non-caloric sweetener only in moderate amounts, if at all, in place of sugar. It's available in liquid, tablet, and powdered form.

ALCOHOL CALORIES COUNT

Alcohol doesn't come without calories. In fact, alcohol contains more calories per ounce than do proteins or carbohydrates and nearly as many as fats do.

A balanced reducing diet furnishes essential nutrients. Therefore, never subtract foods from a reducing diet to make room for alcohol calories. Calories from an alcoholic beverage will have to be *added* to the calories of a reducing diet. This slows the speed of the reducing diet and indeed can impede progress.

To discover how quickly alcohol can add unwanted calories to a reducing diet, compare the figures for various alcoholic beverages on page 63.

Alcohol can be used *in moderation for cooking purposes.* Most of the calories from alcohol are burned off quickly when heated, leaving only its subtle flavor behind. If desired, for new aroma and flavor, add a dash of dry wine to some of your long-standing favorite recipes.

FOOD EXCHANGE LISTS

MEAT

LEAN MEAT EXCHANGE

Each serving in the list at right is based on cooked meat with fat trimmed. One Exchange provides seven grams protein, three grams fat, and 55 calories. Most Exchanges, except shellfish, are fairly low in saturated fat and cholesterol.

BEEF: 1 ounce	chuck dried beef flank steak plate short ribs plate skirt steak plate spareribs	round, bottom or top rump, all cuts sirloin tenderloin tripe
LAMB: 1 ounce	leg loin rib	shank shoulder sirloin
PORK: 1 ounce	fully cooked ham (center slices)	leg (whole rump, center shank)
VEAL: 1 ounce	cutlets leg loin	rib shank shoulder
FISH: fresh, canned, or frozen	bass, 1 oz. carp, 1 oz. catfish, 1 oz. clams, 1 oz. cod, 1 oz. crab, ¼ cup eel, 1 oz. flounder, 1 oz. haddock, 1 oz. hake, 1 oz. halibut, 1 oz. herring, 1 oz. lobster, ¼ cup mackerel, ¼ cup mullet, 1 oz. oysters, 1 oz.	perch, 1 oz. pike, 1 oz. pollock, 1 oz. pompano, 1 oz. red snapper, 1 oz. rockfish, 1 oz. salmon, 1 oz. canned, ¼ cup sardines, 3 scallops, 1 oz. shrimp, 1 oz. smelt, 1 oz. sole, 1 oz. swordfish, 1 oz. tuna, ¼ cup whitefish, 1 oz.
POULTRY: 1 ounce without skin	chicken Cornish game hen Guinea hen	pheasant turkey
CHEESES: 1 ounce	containing less than 5% milkfat	
COTTAGE CHEESE: ¼ cup	dry and 2% milkfat	
DRIED BEANS AND PEAS: ½ cup cooked	(omit 1 Bread Exchange)	

MEDIUM-FAT MEAT EXCHANGE

Each serving is based on cooked meat and counts as one Medium-Fat Meat Exchange. Because of their higher fat content, Medium-Fat Meat Exchanges count as one Lean Meat Exchange and one-half Fat Exchange. One Medium-Fat Meat Exchange supplies seven grams protein, five and one-half grams fat, and 75 calories. Only peanut butter is low in saturated fat and cholesterol.

BEEF: 1 ounce	corned beef (canned) ground beef (15% fat)	ground round (commercial) rib eye steak
PORK: 1 ounce	boiled ham Canadian-style bacon loin (all cuts tenderloin)	shoulder arm picnic shoulder blade Boston roast
VARIETY MEATS — beef, veal pork, or lamb: 1 ounce (high in cholesterol)	heart kidney	liver sweetbreads
CHEESE:	farmer cheese, 1 ounce mozzarella, 1 ounce Neufchâtel, 1 ounce	Parmesan, 3 Tbsp. ricotta, 1 ounce
COTTAGE CHEESE:	creamed, ¼ cup	
EGG: 1 (high in cholesterol)		
PEANUT BUTTER: 2 Tbsp.	(omit a total of 2½ Fat Exchanges)	

HIGH-FAT MEAT EXCHANGE

Each serving is based on cooked meat and counts as one High-Fat Meat Exchange. Because of their high fat content, foods in this Exchange List count as one Lean Meat Exchange and one Fat Exchange. One High-Fat Meat Exchange supplies seven grams of protein, eight grams of fat, and 100 calories.

BEEF: 1 ounce	brisket corned beef brisket ground beef (more than 20% fat) ground chuck (commercial)	hamburger (commercial) rib roast rib steak top loin steak
LAMB: 1 ounce	breast	
VEAL: 1 ounce	breast	
PORK: 1 ounce	cook-before-eating ham (country-style) deviled ham	ground pork loin back ribs spareribs
POULTRY: 1 ounce	capon duck (domestic)	goose
CHEESE: 1 ounce	cheddar types	
COLD CUTS:	4½ × ⅛-inch slice	
FRANKFURTER:	1 small	

BREAD

Each serving of the breads, cereals, crackers, dried beans, starchy vegetables, and prepared foods listed at right counts as one Bread Exchange. All items except those listed as prepared foods are lowfat. Be sure to charge yourself for the extra Fat Exchanges contained in the prepared foods. One Bread Exchange provides two grams of protein, 15 grams of carbohydrate, and 70 calories.

BREAD:	bagel, small, ½ dried bread crumbs, 3 Tbsp. English muffin, small, ½ frankfurter bun, ½ French, 1 slice hamburger bun, ½ Italian, 1 slice	plain dinner roll, 1 pumpernickel, 1 slice raisin, 1 slice rye, 1 slice tortilla, 6 inch, 1 white, 1 slice whole wheat, 1 slice
CEREAL:	bran flakes, ½ cup cooked barley, ½ cup cooked cereal, ½ cup cooked grits, ½ cup cooked pasta, macaroni, or noodles, ½ cup cooked rice, ½ cup cornmeal (dry), 2 Tbsp.	flour, 2½ Tbsp. other ready-to-eat unsweetened cereal, ¾ cup popcorn (popped, no fat added), 3 cups puffed cereal (unfrosted), 1 cup wheat germ, ¼ cup
CRACKERS:	arrowroot, 3 graham, 2½ inch, 2 matzo, 6×4 inch, ½ oyster, 20	pretzels, 3⅛×⅛ inch, 25 rye wafers, 3½×2 inch, 3 saltines, 6 soda, 2½-inch square, 4
BEANS, PEAS, AND LENTILS:	beans, peas, lentils (dried, cooked), ½ cup (omit 1 Lean Meat Exchange)	baked beans, no pork (canned), ¼ cup
STARCHY VEGETABLES:	corn, ⅓ cup corn on cob, 1 small lima beans, ½ cup parsnips, ⅔ cup peas (canned or frozen), ½ cup	potato (mashed), ½ cup potato (white), 1 small pumpkin, ¾ cup winter squash, ½ cup yam or sweet potato, ¼ cup
PREPARED FOODS:	biscuit, 2-inch diameter, 1 (omit 1 Fat Exchange) corn bread, 2×2×1 inch, 1 (omit 1 Fat Exchange) corn muffin, 2 inch, 1 (omit 1 Fat Exchange) crackers, round butter type, 5 (omit 1 Fat Exchange) muffin, plain small, 1 (omit 1 Fat Exchange)	pancake, 5x½ inch, 1 (omit 1 Fat Exchange) potatoes, French-fried, 8 (omit 1 Fat Exchange) potato or corn chips, 15 (omit 2 Fat Exchanges) waffle, 5×½ inch, 1 (omit 1 Fat Exchange)

VEGETABLE

Each half-cup serving counts as one Exchange and provides two grams protein, five grams carbohydrate, and 25 calories. Vegetables are nonfat. Free vegetables are listed separately and in the Free List, also. The free vegetables may be eaten in any amounts.

asparagus	celery	sauerkraut
beans, green or yellow	cucumbers	spinach and other greens
bean sprouts	eggplant	summer squash
beets	mushrooms	tomatoes
broccoli	okra	tomato juice
brussels sprouts	onions	turnips
cabbage	peppers	vegetable juice cocktail
carrots	rhubarb	zucchini
cauliflower	rutabaga	
FREE VEGETABLES:	chicory	lettuce
These raw vegetables	Chinese cabbage	parsley
may be eaten in any amounts	endive	radishes
	escarole	watercress

FRUIT

The amount of each fruit listed (with no sugar added) counts as one Fruit Exchange. Fruits are nonfat. One Exchange contains 10 grams of carbohydrate and 40 calories.

apple, 1 small	figs, fresh or dried, 1	orange juice, ½ cup
apple juice or cider, ⅓ cup	grapefruit, ½	papaya, ¾ cup
applesauce (unsweetened), ½ cup	grapefruit juice, ½ cup	peach, 1 medium
apricots, fresh, 2 medium	grape juice, ¼ cup	pear, 1 small
apricots, dried, 4 halves	grapes, 12	persimmon, native, 1 medium
banana, ½ small	mango, ½ small	pineapple, ½ cup
berries:	melon:	pineapple juice, ⅓ cup
strawberries, ¾ cup	cantaloupe, ¼ small	plums, 2 medium
other berries, ½ cup	honeydew, ⅛ medium	prune juice, ¼ cup
cherries, 10 large	watermelon, 1 cup	prunes, 2 medium
cranberries, as desired	nectarine, 1 small	raisins, 2 Tbsp.
dates, 2	orange, 1 small	tangerine, 1 medium

MILK

Milk Exchanges are shown in the list at right. Lowfat and whole milk products cost extra Fat Exchanges. One Milk Exchange equals eight grams of protein, 12 grams of carbohydrate, and 80 calories.

NONFAT FORTIFIED MILK:	buttermilk, made from skim milk, 1 cup	nonfat dry milk powder, ⅓ cup
	canned evaporated skim milk, ½ cup	skim or nonfat milk, 1 cup
		yogurt, made from skim milk (plain), 1 cup
LOWFAT FORTIFIED MILK:	1% fat milk, 1 cup (omit ½ Fat Exchange)	yogurt, made from 2% milk, (plain), ¾ cup (omit 1 Fat Exchange)
	2% fat milk, 1 cup (omit 1 Fat Exchange)	
WHOLE MILK:	buttermilk, made from whole milk, 1 cup (omit 2 Fat Exchanges)	whole milk, 1 cup (omit 2 Fat Exchanges)
	canned evaporated whole milk, ½ cup (omit 2 Fat Exchanges)	yogurt, made from whole milk (plain), 1 cup (omit 2 Fat Exchanges)

FAT

Each serving of the fats listed at right counts as one Fat Exchange. See the **Note** below for further explanation about fats and an explanation of the asterisk (*). One Fat Exchange provides five grams of fat and 45 calories.

avocado* (4-inch diameter), ⅛	cream, whipping, 1 Tbsp.	margarine, regular, 1 tsp.
bacon, crisp cooked, 1 slice	cream cheese, 1 Tbsp.	margarine,*** soft (tub or stick), 1 tsp.
bacon fat, 1 tsp.	French salad dressing,*** 1 Tbsp.	mayonnaise,*** 1 tsp.
butter, 1 tsp.	Italian salad dressing,*** 1 Tbsp.	olives,* 5 small
cream, light, 2 Tbsp.	lard, 1 tsp.	salad dressing,*** mayonnaise-type, 2 tsp.
cream, sour, 2 Tbsp.	margarine,** diet, 1 Tbsp.	salt pork, ¾-inch cube
NUTS	almonds,* 10 whole	pecans,* 2 large whole
	peanuts,* Spanish, 20 whole	walnuts,** 6 small
	peanuts,* Virginia, 10 whole	other,* 6 small
OIL: 1 tsp.	corn**	safflower**
	cottonseed**	soy**
	olive*	sunflower**
	peanut*	

FREE

Listed at right are flavor bonuses with Free Exchange ratings. Also included on this list are raw vegetables that can be eaten in any amount.

salt	tea	unsweetened pickles
pepper	coffee	chicory
herbs	nonfat bouillon	Chinese cabbage
spices	non-caloric sweetener	endive
lemon	low-calorie carbonated beverages	escarole
lime	low-calorie flavored gelatin	lettuce
horseradish	unflavored gelatin	parsley
vinegar		radishes
mustard		watercress

Note: Fats listed above are designated as saturated, monounsaturated, or polyunsaturated. Saturated fats are found primarily in animal food products and are thought to raise the level of cholesterol in the blood, a factor possibly associated with heart disease. Heart specialists recommend substituting unsaturated fats for the saturated fats in the diet whenever possible. Vegetable oils such as corn, cottonseed, safflower, soybean, and sunflower are low in saturated fats.

The fats listed above are saturated unless marked with an asterisk (*). One asterisk (*) indicates a fat content that is primarily monounsaturated. Two asterisks (**) indicate a fat content that is primarily polyunsaturated; three asterisks (***) indicate a polyunsaturated fat content only if the product is made with corn, cottonseed, safflower, soy, or sunflower oil.

Food exchange Lists on pages 282 to 286 are based on material in the booklet *Exchange Lists for Meal Planning* prepared by committees of the American Diabetes Association, Inc. and the American Dietetic Association.

MEAL PLANNING

Let Food Exchanges count calories for you as you choose foods from the seven Food Exchange Lists. Make your mealtime selections from the color-coded Exchanges—Meat, Bread, Vegetable, Fruit, Milk, Fat, and Free—based on the Daily Meal Plan of your choice (see page 288). Once you master the system, using it to plan meals will become second nature. Using this guide, you can shed unwanted pounds and keep them off.

Shown at left are some of the foods you can eat in one day and still lose weight. See page 297 for this 1,200-calorie Daily Meal Plan. The recipes pictured here are (clockwise from back): *Mexican-Style Hot Chocolate, Tapioca Pudding Parfait, Taco Compuesto,* and *Appetizer Tomato Soup* (see index for page numbers).

DAILY MEAL PLANS

Planning diet menus is almost easy—if you use the Food Exchanges to guide you. Select a meal plan giving a daily calorie deficit that lets you lose no more than two pounds a week (see page 30). Then, follow the food allotments in your Daily Meal Plan. Make menu selections from the Food Exchange Lists (see pages 282 to 286) and the recipe section beginning on page 302. Use the color symbols to aid you.

DAILY MEAL PLAN	NUMBER OF EXCHANGES		
BREAKFAST	1,000 CAL. PER DAY	1,200 CAL. PER DAY	1,500 CAL. PER DAY
Lean Meat Exchange	1	1	2
Bread Exchange	1	1	2
Fruit Exchange	1	1	1
Milk Exchange	½	½	½
Fat Exchange	1	2	2
Free Exchange	as desired	as desired	as desired
LUNCH			
Lean Meat Exchange	2	2	2
Bread Exchange	1	1	2
Vegetable Exchange	1	2	2
Fruit Exchange	1	1	1
Milk Exchange	1	1	1
Fat Exchange	1	1	2
Free Exchange	as desired	as desired	as desired
DINNER			
Lean Meat Exchange	2	4	4
Bread Exchange	1	1	1
Vegetable Exchange	1	2	2
Fruit Exchange	1	1	1
Milk Exchange	½	½	½
Fat Exchange	2	2	3
Free Exchange	as desired	as desired	as desired

MENU-PLANNING STEPS

Decide on the Daily Meal Plan that helps you lose no more than two pounds per week. Follow your Meal Plan and make menu selections from the Food Exchange Lists and recipes in this chapter.

Use the Menu-Planning Steps listed in the next column. These steps were used to plan the tasty dinner menu at the right from the 1,200-calorie meal plan for dinner.

1. Choose a main dish. It may be strictly meat or it may be a combination of Exchanges. Four ounces of broiled sirloin steak represent four Lean Meat Exchanges, the exact Meat Exchange allowance.

2. Select a Bread Exchange. One small potato that is baked equals one Bread Exchange.

3. Pick compatible vegetables. Two Exchanges are allowed. Tangy Vegetable Vinaigrette, found in the recipe section of this chapter, and one-half cup of cooked carrots account for the two Exchanges.

4. Decide on a Fruit Exchange as a meal accompaniment or dessert. Tapioca Pudding Parfait is the dessert in this menu. The recipe and Exchange values can be found in the recipe section of this chapter. One serving supplies one-half Milk Exchange in addition to one Fruit Exchange.

5. Add any Milk Exchanges not used in cooking. Because one-half Milk Exchange was used for the Tapioca Pudding Parfait, there's no need to add milk here.

6. Decide on any Fat Exchanges not used in cooking. Two tablespoons of dairy sour cream on the potato account for one Fat Exchange, and one tablespoon of diet margarine on the carrots equals the remaining Fat Exchange.

7. Add Free Exchanges to round out the meal. Have coffee or tea to accompany the meal or just with dessert.

MEAL PLAN

- 4 Lean Meat Exchanges
- 1 Bread Exchange
- 2 Vegetable Exchanges
- 1 Fruit Exchange
- ½ Milk Exchange
- 2 Fat Exchanges
- Free Exchanges

MENU

- 4 ounces broiled sirloin steak
- 1 small baked potato
- 2 Tbsp. dairy sour cream
- Tangy Vegetable Vinaigrette*
- ½ cup cooked sliced carrots
- 1 Tbsp. diet margarine
- Tapioca Pudding Parfait*
- coffee or tea

See index for page number of recipe.

1,000-CALORIE MENUS

Can the famished reducer's appetite really be appeased with only 1,000 calories a day? Yes! We have created three satisfying menus that provide only 1,000 calories to show that dieters, too, can enjoy hearty, flavorful foods. We used seven easy Menu-Planning Steps on page 289 to create the menus. Take a closer look and you'll discover some meals use extra Exchanges and others are missing an Exchange or two. Don't be mystified. The Exchanges simply have been moved from one meal to another meal.

Foods marked with an asterisk (*) are found in the recipe section of this chapter. Don't cut back to fewer than 1,000 calories daily. And, check to make sure you lose no more than two pounds a week.

On the pages immediately preceding each set of menus, you will find some menu planning tips, such as those at right.

Menu A

Wake up to a slice of crisp toast topped with a layer of bubbly-hot cheddar cheese. Fresh blackberries and skim milk round out breakfast with one-half Bread Exchange left over. Don't worry, you'll find a good use for that extra Exchange at dinner.

Lunch features healthful Vegetarian Sprout Sandwiches with fresh avocado and a side dish of cottage cheese served on a lettuce-lined plate. You may want to add a few radish slices to the cottage cheese for color—they're free.

The meal from the dinner menu is pictured on the opposite page. Fruited Lamb Chops team up with broccoli spears and almond-studded rice for a satisfying meal. The four teaspoons of sliced almonds (or 10 whole almonds) equal one Fat Exchange. We've borrowed that extra one-half Bread Exchange from breakfast so you can top off dinner with an icy Banana Freeze. Add a small glass of skim milk to fulfill the Milk Exchange allowance.

Menu B

Egg, raisin toast, diet margarine, apple juice, and skim milk combine to make breakfast in Menu B. Rye bread spread with cream cheese accents the Trimming Tuna Toss at lunch. Add carrot sticks, a peach, and a glass of skim milk and you ease those hunger pangs and still have one-half Lean Meat Exchange left for dinner. No-Crust Pizza adds an Italian flair to a dinner that's suitable for the whole family. And what a surprise: chocolate pudding with whipped topping (low-calorie, of course) for dessert.

Menu C

This menu features a hefty breakfast composed of a one-egg omelet and a bowl of puffed rice cereal topped with banana slices and skim milk. Good news for the dieter: It uses only those Exchanges allowed for breakfast on the 1,000-calorie Daily Meal Plan.

The roast beef sandwich for lunch makes a hearty entrée. Be sure to use roast beef from the Lean Meat Exchange only. Very thin bread and diet margarine help stretch the lunchtime Bread and Fat Exchanges. Choose vegetable relishes from the Vegetable Exchange List. Raw broccoli, carrots, cauliflower flowerets, celery, cucumbers, and mushrooms are among the possibilities. Round out the meal with an orange and a glass of skim milk.

For dinner, Turkey-Asparagus Pilaf is practically a meal in itself. It supplies all the Meat, Bread, Vegetable, and half the Fat Exchanges for the entire dinner. Mixed salad greens (chicory, Chinese cabbage, endive, escarole, lettuce, parsley, and watercress—take your choice) are free. So is the two-tablespoon serving of Italian salad dressing, as long as it provides no more than 8 calories per tablespoon. Read the label carefully; it states the calorie content of the salad dressing. Any meal goes better when you include a dessert like Plum Whip. This dessert supplies a Fruit Exchange and the other Fat Exchange. Add one-half cup of skim milk and your choice of coffee or tea, and you've satisfied your appetite and the Exchange requirements for the 1,000-calorie Daily Meal Plan.

1,000-CALORIE MENUS

These three menus each provide only 1,000 calories a day. The dinner meal for Menu A is pictured on page 291.

Note that in Menu A breakfast, one-half Bread Exchange was unused; however, it was used for the dinner meal for the same Menu plan. For Menu B, one-half Lean Meat Exchange was unused for lunch but was used for the dinner meal.

BREAKFAST

DAILY MEAL PLAN

- 1 Lean Meat Exchange
- 1 Bread Exchange
- 1 Fruit Exchange
- ½ Milk Exchange
- 1 Fat Exchange
- Free Exchanges

LUNCH

- 2 Lean Meat Exchanges
- 1 Bread Exchange
- 1 Vegetable Exchange
- 1 Fruit Exchange
- 1 Milk Exchange
- 1 Fat Exchange
- Free Exchanges

DINNER

- 2 Lean Meat Exchanges
- 1 Bread Exchange
- 1 Vegetable Exchange
- 1 Fruit Exchange
- ½ Milk Exchange
- 2 Fat Exchanges
- Free Exchanges

*See index for page number of recipe.

MENU A	MENU B	MENU C
1 slice broiled cheese toast made with: 1 oz. cheddar cheese 1 slice very thin bread ½ cup fresh blackberries ½ cup skim milk Exchanges not used: ½ Bread Exchange	1 soft-cooked egg 1 slice raisin toast 1½ tsp. diet margarine ⅓ cup apple juice ½ cup skim milk	1 egg omelet, made with 1½ tsp. diet margarine 1 cup puffed rice cereal ½ cup skim milk ½ small banana, sliced coffee or tea
Vegetarian Sprout Sandwiches* ⅛ avocado, sliced ¼ cup lowfat cottage cheese (no more than 2% milkfat) on lettuce-lined plate 1 small apple 1 cup skim milk coffee or tea	Trimming Tuna Toss* 1 slice rye bread 1 Tbsp. cream cheese ¼ cup carrot sticks 1 medium peach 1 cup skim milk Exchanges not used: ½ Lean Meat Exchange	1 roast beef sandwich made with: 2 oz. cooked lean roast beef 2 slices very thin white bread 1 Tbsp. diet margarine lettuce ½ cup vegetable relishes 1 small orange 1 cup skim milk coffee or tea
Fruited Lamb Chops* ½ cup cooked rice with 4 tsp. sliced almonds (10 whole) ½ cup cooked broccoli 1½ tsp. diet margarine Banana Freeze* ½ cup skim milk coffee or tea Extra Exchanges used: ½ Bread Exchange	No-Crust Pizza* 1 slice very thin bread Zippy Waldorf Salad* ½ cup low-calorie chocolate-flavored pudding 3 Tbsp. low-calorie whipped dessert topping Extra Exchanges used: ½ Lean Meat Exchange	Turkey-Asparagus Pilaf* mixed salad greens 2 Tbsp. low-calorie Italian salad dressing (no more than 8 calories per tablespoon) Plum Whip* ½ cup skim milk coffee or tea

1,200-CALORIE MENUS

If dieting has you down, our 1,200-calorie reducing menus will banish boredom from your diet with an array of imaginative ideas and robust recipes. To create these delicious diet menus, we applied the seven Menu-Planning Steps from page 289.

When you compare the menus to the 1,200-calorie Daily Meal Plan, you will discover that some meals appear to use an extra Exchange or two, and other meals are "short" Exchanges. To trace the moving Exchanges, we've used the headlines "Extra Exchanges used" and "Exchanges not used." An asterisk (*) denotes the foods found in the recipe section of this chapter.

Menu A

A well-balanced breakfast highlighted with fresh raspberries starts the dieter's day. Other breakfast items are a fried egg and a toasted bagel half spread with a specified amount of diet margarine.

The luncheon, pictured on the opposite page, features Confetti Cheese Quiche, pea pods, apple slices, and a mixed green salad accented with radish slices and tossed with Tangy Tomato Dressing. This light-tasting lunch saves you one Lean Meat Exchange for dinner, when you capitalize on Beef Burgundy with rice, cut green beans, and a peach, halved and topped with one-half cup cottage cheese. Don't let this shift of Food Exchanges from lunch to dinner confuse you. As long as the daily total of Food Exchanges remains the same as those allowed on the 1,200-calorie Daily Meal Plan, you can consume the Exchanges whenever you please—morning, afternoon, or night. Coffee, tea, and low-calorie carbonated beverages are all Free Exchanges and can be added anytime of the day.

Menu B

This menu features ham, a blueberry-topped pancake, and skim milk for breakfast. Be sure to use fully cooked center-cut ham slices and not boiled ham, because there's a difference of one-half Fat Exchange. Top the pancake with one-half cup of juicy blueberries and eliminate the need for butter or margarine. The Fat Exchange you save is used at lunch so you can enjoy the Corned Beef Slaw-Wiches. Vegetable relishes (your choice of any of the Vegetable Exchanges served raw), applesauce, and skim milk complete the lunch menu.

The Icy Tomato Tune-Up will prime your appetite for dinner. Or, if you can't wait, enjoy Icy Tomato Tune-Up as a midafternoon snack. Lemon Poached Salmon pairs up with a creamy Tartar Sauce at dinner. For the finale, serve refreshing Ruby Fruit Compote for dessert.

Menu C

The 1,200-calorie menu (some items are pictured on page 287) is a bit more complicated than some of the other menus. We've dropped a few Exchanges here and added other Exchanges there to bring you an imaginative menu. You can trace the Food Exchanges and tally the totals. Here are the menu mechanics:

By saying no to the breadbasket in the morning, you can indulge in two tacos at dinner. So you won't feel shortchanged at breakfast, we've borrowed one-half Milk Exchange from lunch to make room for a steaming mug of Mexican-Style Hot Chocolate. The main luncheon dish, Turkey-Asparagus Stacks, uses extra Lean Meat and Fat Exchanges from dinner. But you won't notice the missing Exchanges at dinner when you treat yourself to Taco Compuesto. If you think it's a case of "musical Exchanges," you're right; but it offers a lot of eating satisfaction for only 1,200 calories.

1,200-CALORIE MENUS

If you've selected the 1,200-calorie-per-day meal plan, here are three days' menus to start you off. The lunch for Menu A, featuring a quiche, is pictured on page 295.

Note that in Menu A one Lean Meat Exchange was not used for lunch but was used for the dinner menu. The extra Fat Exchange used for the lunch in Menu B comes from breakfast where one Fat Exchange wasn't used. You can trace where the extra Exchanges come from and are used in Menu C. What counts is the total exchange tally for the day.

BREAKFAST

DAILY MEAL PLAN

- 1 Lean Meat Exchange
- 1 Bread Exchange
- 1 Fruit Exchange
- ½ Milk Exchange
- 2 Fat Exchanges
- Free Exchanges

LUNCH

- 2 Lean Meat Exchanges
- 1 Bread Exchange
- 2 Vegetable Exchanges
- 1 Fruit Exchange
- 1 Milk Exchange
- 1 Fat Exchange
- Free Exchanges

DINNER

- 4 Lean Meat Exchanges
- 1 Bread Exchange
- 2 Vegetable Exchanges
- 1 Fruit Exchange
- ½ Milk Exchange
- 2 Fat Exchanges
- Free Exchanges

*See index for page number of recipe.

MENU A

1 egg, fried in 1 Tbsp. diet margarine
½ small bagel, toasted
1½ tsp. diet margarine
½ cup fresh raspberries
½ cup skim milk

Confetti Cheese Quiche*
1½ ounces cooked pea pods
mixed salad greens
Tangy Tomato Dressing*
1 small apple, sliced
1 cup skim milk
coffee or tea

Exchanges not used:
1 Lean Meat Exchange

Beef Burgundy*
½ cup cooked cut green beans
1 Tbsp. diet margarine
1 medium peach, halved
½ cup lowfat cottage cheese (no more than 2% milkfat)
½ cup skim milk
coffee or tea
Extra Exchanges used:
1 Lean Meat Exchange

MENU B

1 one-oz. fully cooked center-cut ham slice
1 five-inch pancake
½ cup blueberries
½ cup skim milk
coffee or tea

Exchanges not used:
1 Fat Exchange

Corned Beef Slaw-Wiches*
¾ cup vegetable relishes
½ cup unsweetened applesauce
1 cup skim milk

Extra Exchanges used:
1 Fat Exchange

Icy Tomato Tune-Up*
Lemon Poached Salmon*
Tartar Sauce*
½ cup cooked cut asparagus
1 refrigerated crescent roll
Ruby Fruit Compote*
1 Tbsp. dairy sour cream
½ cup skim milk

MENU C

1 hard-cooked egg
1½ slices cooked bacon
¼ small cantaloupe with lime
Mexican-Style Hot Chocolate*
Extra Exchanges used:
½ Milk Exchange
Exchanges not used:
1 Bread Exchange

Turkey-Asparagus Stacks*
Appetizer Tomato Soup*
Pineapple Pie*
iced tea

Extra Exchanges used:
½ Lean Meat Exchange
½ Fat Exchange
Exchanges not used:
½ Milk Exchange

Taco Compuesto*
Tapioca Pudding Parfait*

Extra Exchanges used:
1 Bread Exchange

Exchanges not used:
½ Lean Meat Exchange
½ Fat Exchange

1,500-CALORIE MENUS

The hearty 1,500-calorie menus offer more flavorful foods than you ever thought you'd be eating on a diet. These menus offer a lot of eating satisfaction, although reducing speed will be slower than that produced by 1,000- or 1,200-calorie menus. The seven Menu Planning Steps on page 289 were used to create the menu ideas. They're the same seven steps you will use to plan your own imaginative menus.

Remember it's possible to move Exchanges or "save" Exchanges to snack on later that day or night as long as the daily total of Exchanges remains the same. Foods marked with an asterisk (*) are found in the recipe section of this chapter.

Menu A

The eye-opening breakfast pictured on the opposite page features two crisp waffles topped with Peach-Berry Sauce. Two slices of Canadian-style bacon count as Medium-Fat Meat Exchanges. The extra Fat Exchange that makes this breakfast possible is borrowed from dinner Exchanges. A small glass of skim milk and hot tea with lemon are the beverages. Parsley makes an attractive, "free" garnish.

When lunch arrives, you will find Seafaring Salmon Salad and piping-hot tomato soup are a satisfying combination. Crackers or any other Bread Exchange can substitute for the toasted rye bread. If soup and salad are all you need at lunch, save the pear halves and cream cheese for a snack later in the day. Dinner consists of Barbecued Ham Slice, a small ear of corn with a little diet margarine, Coleslaw, and a generous portion of watermelon balls for dessert. A small glass of skim milk (½ cup) plus tea or coffee are the beverages.

Menu B

Wake up to a breakfast of pork breakfast strips, French toast, and blueberries on Menu B. Two slices of pork breakfast strips supply only one Fat Exchange and one Lean Meat Exchange. The French toast is prepared with the listed ingredients—egg, white bread, diet margarine, and a little milk. Serve the rest of the skim milk as a beverage or pour it over the fresh blueberries to finish off the meal.

Follow the list of Exchanges through the day and you will sample Fruity Ham Sandwiches, vegetable relishes, and Asparagus Bisque accompanied with saltine crackers for lunch. If you prefer, save the vegetable relishes (your choice of any of the crispy Vegetable Exchanges served raw) for a midafternoon snack.

Spicy Marinated Pork Chops, a slice of Italian bread, avocado salad topped with Tangy Tomato Dressing, and Orange Chiffon Soufflé are the foods planned for dinner. Marinate the chops 8 hours or overnight, then broil in short order before serving.

Menu C

This menu offers a hearty breakfast with a savings of two Lean Meat Exchanges and one Fat Exchange. Top the oatmeal with skim milk and add a couple of tablespoons naturally sweet raisins—you won't even miss the sugar. Feast on Onion Soup Gratiné and Chef's Salad Bowl at noon. Tender biscuits can be topped with one tablespoon diet margarine, but if you're yearning for butter, substitute one teaspoon for the Fat Exchange. Serve fresh strawberries for the lunchtime dessert.

Begin dinner with an appetizer of two Cheese and Carrot Balls. Bean-Stuffed Tomatoes complement savory French Herbed Chicken. A cluster of red grapes topped with a dab of dairy sour cream provides a delicious garnish. And for dessert, Mint Chocolate Cream Puffs plus coffee or tea are the grand finale.

1,500-CALORIE MENUS

Those able to "afford" a 1,500-calorie-per-day meal plan find a variety of foods in these three menus. Look on page 299 for a picture of the breakfast of Menu A.

You'll find that one Fat Exchange in Menu A was switched from the dinner to the breakfast meal. Also, in Menu C, the two Lean Meat Exchanges and one Fat Exchange not used at breakfast time are used for the lunch and dinner meals.

BREAKFAST

DAILY MEAL PLAN

- 2 Lean Meat Exchanges
- 2 Bread Exchanges
- 1 Fruit Exchange
- ½ Milk Exchange
- 2 Fat Exchanges
- Free Exchanges

LUNCH

- 2 Lean Meat Exchanges
- 2 Bread Exchanges
- 2 Vegetable Exchanges
- 1 Fruit Exchange
- 1 Milk Exchange
- 2 Fat Exchanges
- Free Exchanges

DINNER

- 4 Lean Meat Exchanges
- 1 Bread Exchange
- 2 Vegetable Exchanges
- 1 Fruit Exchange
- ½ Milk Exchange
- 3 Fat Exchanges
- Free Exchanges

*See index for page number of recipe.

MENU A	MENU B	MENU C
2 one-oz. slices cooked Canadian-style bacon 2 five-inch waffles Peach-Berry Sauce* ½ cup skim milk tea with lemon Extra Exchanges used: 1 Fat Exchange	2 pork breakfast strips 2 slices French toast: 1 egg 2 slices white bread 1½ tsp. diet margarine ½ cup fresh blueberries ½ cup skim milk	½ cup cooked oatmeal ½ cup skim milk 2 Tbsp. raisins 1 slice bread, toasted 1 Tbsp. diet margarine coffee or tea Exchanges not used: 2 Lean Meat Exchanges 1 Fat Exchange
Seafaring Salmon Salad* 1 slice rye bread, toasted 1½ tsp. diet margarine 10 oz. prepared condensed tomato soup 1 small pear, halved 1 Tbsp. cream cheese 1 cup skim milk coffee or tea	Fruity Ham Sandwiches* Asparagus Bisque* 3 saltine crackers ½ cup vegetable relishes 1 cup skim milk	Onion Soup Gratiné* Chef's Salad Bowl* 2 refrigerated buttermilk biscuits 1 Tbsp. diet margarine ¾ cup fresh strawberries 1 cup skim milk coffee or tea Extra Exchanges used: 2 Lean Meat Exchanges
Barbecued Ham Slice* 1 small ear of corn 1 Tbsp. diet margarine Coleslaw* 1 cup watermelon balls ½ cup skim milk coffee or tea Exchanges not used 1 Fat Exchange	Spicy Marinated Pork Chops* 1 slice Italian bread 1½ tsp. diet margarine ⅛ avocado, sliced and served on a lettuce-lined plate Tangy Tomato Dressing* Orange Chiffon Soufflé* ½ cup skim milk	Cheese and Carrot Balls* French Herbed Chicken* Bean-Stuffed Tomatoes* 12 red grapes 3 Tbsp. dairy sour cream Mint Chocolate Cream Puffs* coffee or tea Extra Exchanges used: 1 Fat Exchange

BEVERAGES, APPETIZERS, AND SOUPS

INCLUDE BEVERAGES IN EXCHANGE TALLY

You can include a number of beverages in your diet using the Food Exchange plan. Beverages that are Free Exchanges include low-calorie carbonated beverages, tea, coffee, and nonfat bouillon. Other beverages must be included in your daily Exchange tally. For example, 1/4 cup prune juice, 1/3 cup apple juice or cider, 1/3 cup pineapple juice, and 1/2 cup orange juice or grapefruit juice each counts as one Fruit Exchange. A one-half cup serving of tomato juice or vegetable juice cocktail each counts as one Vegetable Exchange.

MEXICAN-STYLE HOT CHOCOLATE

Pictured on page 287—

2/3 cup water
3 tablespoons unsweetened cocoa powder
Non-caloric liquid sweetener to equal 3 tablespoons sugar
3 1/2 inches stick cinnamon
3 cups skim milk
1/4 teaspoon vanilla

In saucepan combine water, unsweetened cocoa powder, non-caloric sweetener, and stick cinnamon. Bring to a boil, stirring constantly; boil 1 minute longer. Stir in the skim milk. Cook till heated through *(do not boil)*. Add the vanilla. Remove the stick cinnamon. Beat with a rotary beater. If desired, garnish each serving with an additional cinnamon stick. Makes 4 servings. One serving (6 ounces) equals:

1 Milk Exchange

CITRUS FROST

1 1/2 cups orange sherbet
1 cup cold water
1 6-ounce can frozen tangerine juice concentrate
4 ice cubes
3 12-ounce cans low-calorie grapefruit carbonated beverage, chilled

In blender container combine orange sherbet, cold water, tangerine juice concentrate, and ice cubes. Cover and blend till smooth. Pour into 6 tall glasses. Pour carbonated beverage down sides of glasses. Stir gently to mix. Makes 6 servings. One serving (10 ounces) equals:

1 Bread Exchange
1 Fruit Exchange

STRAWBERRY ROMANOFF SWIZZLE

2 cups orange juice
2 cups frozen whole unsweetened strawberries, partially thawed
2 12-ounce cans low-calorie strawberry carbonated beverage, chilled
1 12-ounce can low-calorie lemon-lime carbonated beverage, chilled

In blender container combine the orange juice and partially thawed berries. Cover; blend till pureed. Strain into large pitcher. Pour carbonated beverages down side of pitcher. Stir gently. Serve over ice in tall glasses. If desired, garnish with fresh strawberries. Makes 8 servings. One serving (7.5 ounces) equals:

1 Fruit Exchange

Citrus Frost; Strawberry Romanoff Swizzle; Asparagus Bisque (see recipe, page 305); *Dilled Garden Dip* (see recipe, page 304)

ICY TOMATO TUNE-UP

2½ cups tomato juice
2 tablespoons lemon juice
1 teaspoon Worcestershire sauce
⅛ teaspoon celery salt
5 drops bottled hot pepper sauce

Combine all ingredients. Chill well and serve *or* pour into an 8x8x2-inch baking dish and freeze about 1¼ hours or till slushy. Spoon into glasses. Makes 5 servings. One serving (4 ounces) equals:

● 1 Vegetable Exchange

OLIVE MEATBALLS

1 beaten egg
½ cup soft bread crumbs (⅔ slice bread)
⅓ cup pizza sauce
¼ cup finely chopped onion
½ teaspoon salt
1 pound ground beef (15% fat)
36 medium pimiento-stuffed olives, drained

In medium bowl combine egg, bread crumbs, pizza sauce, onion, salt, and dash *pepper*. Add ground beef; mix well. Shape about *1 tablespoon* of the meat mixture evenly around each olive to form round meatballs. Place in a 13x9x2-inch baking dish. Bake in a 375° oven about 20 minutes. Serve warm on wooden picks. Makes 18 servings. One serving (2 meatballs) equals:

● 1 Lean Meat Exchange
◖ ½ Fat Exchange

HERBED MUSHROOMS

⅔ cup dry red wine
1 small onion, sliced and separated into rings
½ teaspoon dried basil, crushed
¼ teaspoon salt
3 4-ounce cans whole mushrooms, drained
Lettuce leaves
2 tablespoons snipped parsley

In small saucepan combine wine, onion, basil, salt, and ⅛ teaspoon freshly ground *pepper*. Bring to boil; add mushrooms. Cook over medium heat for 15 minutes or till most of the liquid evaporates. Pour into a bowl; cover and chill. At serving time, drain and serve the mushrooms on a lettuce-lined plate. Sprinkle with parsley. Makes 8 servings. One serving (¼ cup) equals:

◖ ½ Vegetable Exchange

CHEESE AND CARROT BALLS

3 ounces Neufchâtel cheese, softened
½ cup shredded low-calorie process cheese product (2 ounces)
1 cup finely shredded carrot
⅓ cup Grape Nuts cereal
2 tablespoons finely snipped parsley

In bowl beat Neufchâtel cheese and process cheese. Pat shredded carrot dry with paper toweling. Stir shredded carrot into cheese mixture. Cover and chill at least 1 hour. Combine cereal and parsley; set aside. Shape cheese-carrot mixture into sixteen balls about 1 inch in diameter. Roll balls in cereal-parsley mixture, pressing into cheese-carrot balls to coat. Cover; chill up to 1 hour. Makes 8 servings. One serving (2 cheese and carrot balls) equals:

◖ ½ Lean Meat Exchange
◖ ½ Bread Exchange

DILLED GARDEN DIP

Pictured on page 303—

2 cups lowfat cottage cheese (no more than 2% milkfat)
2 tablespoons tarragon vinegar
1 tablespoon finely chopped green onion
1 tablespoon snipped parsley
1 teaspoon snipped fresh mint
½ teaspoon dried dillweed
Dash freshly ground pepper
4 cups fresh vegetable dippers (broccoli, carrots, cauliflower, celery, cucumber, mushrooms, cherry tomatoes, zucchini, green onion, and green pepper)
Radishes

In blender container combine cottage cheese and vinegar. Cover and blend till smooth. Stir in onion, parsley, mint, dried dillweed, and pepper. Cover and chill thoroughly. If desired, garnish with fresh dillweed. Serve dip with fresh vegetable dippers and radishes. Makes 8 servings. One serving (¼ cup dip and ½ cup vegetables except radishes, which can be eaten in any amount) equals:

● 1 Lean Meat Exchange
● 1 Vegetable Exchange

ASPARAGUS BISQUE

Pictured on page 303—

2 10-ounce packages frozen cut asparagus
3½ cups water
1 medium onion, quartered
2 tablespoons lemon juice
4 teaspoons instant chicken bouillon granules
1 to 2 teaspoons curry powder
Dash pepper

In a large saucepan combine asparagus, water, onion, lemon juice, bouillon granules, curry powder, and pepper. Bring to boil; simmer, covered, 8 to 12 minutes or till asparagus is just tender. Place *half* the asparagus mixture in a blender container. Cover and blend till smooth. Pour into a bowl. Repeat with remaining asparagus mixture. Serve hot in bowls or cover and chill at least 4 hours. If desired, garnish each serving of the soup with a lemon slice and an asparagus tip. Makes 6 servings. One serving (1 cup) equals:

● 1 Vegetable Exchange

CUCUMBER-BUTTERMILK SOUP

1 quart buttermilk, made from skim milk (no more than 0.5% milkfat)
2 cucumbers, peeled, seeded, and shredded (1 cup)
2 tablespoons snipped parsley
1 tablespoon sliced green onion
1 teaspoon salt
Dash pepper

In large bowl combine buttermilk, shredded cucumber, snipped parsley, sliced green onion, salt, and pepper. Cover and chill till serving time. Makes 5 servings. One serving (1 cup) equals:

● 1 Milk Exchange

APPETIZER TOMATO SOUP

Pictured on page 287—

2½ cups tomato juice
1 10½-ounce can condensed beef broth
1 tablespoon lemon juice
1 teaspoon Worcestershire sauce
¼ teaspoon dried basil, crushed
¼ teaspoon dried thyme, crushed
6 thin lemon slices *or* snipped parsley

In medium saucepan combine tomato juice, beef broth, lemon juice, Worcestershire sauce, basil, and thyme. Bring to boil; simmer, covered, 5 minutes. Ladle into bowls. Garnish each serving with a thin lemon slice or snipped parsley. Makes 6 servings. One serving (⅔ cup) equals:

● 1 Vegetable Exchange

ONION SOUP GRATINÉ

1 large onion, thinly sliced (1 cup)
1 tablespoon diet margarine
2 10½-ounce cans condensed beef broth
1½ cups water
1 to 2 tablespoons dry sherry
½ teaspoon Worcestershire sauce
Dash pepper
6 melba toast rounds
6 tablespoons grated Parmesan cheese

In a large saucepan cook the sliced onion in the diet margarine, covered, over low heat about 20 minutes or till onion is lightly browned, stirring occasionally. Add the condensed beef broth, water, dry sherry, and Worcestershire sauce. Bring to boil; season with the dash pepper. Pour soup into oven-proof cups or small bowls. Float melba toast rounds on top of the onion soup in each bowl; sprinkle each melba toast round with *1 tablespoon* of the grated Parmesan cheese. Broil 3 to 4 inches from heat about 2 minutes or till browned. Makes 6 servings. One serving (¾ cup) equals:

● 1 Lean Meat Exchange
◖ ½ Bread Exchange

MAIN DISHES

STIR-FRIED BEEF AND SPINACH

1¼ pounds boneless beef round steak, trimmed of fat
2 tablespoons soy sauce
¼ teaspoon Five Spice Powder (see recipe below)
¼ cup cold water
2 teaspoons cornstarch
¼ teaspoon instant beef bouillon granules
1 tablespoon cooking oil
1 teaspoon grated gingerroot
8 ounces small fresh spinach leaves (6 cups)
½ cup sliced water chestnuts

Partially freeze beef; slice thinly into bite-size strips. Combine beef, soy sauce, and Five Spice Powder; let stand at room temperature 15 minutes. In small bowl blend ¼ cup cold water into cornstarch; add bouillon granules and set aside. Preheat wok or large skillet over high heat; add oil. Stir-fry gingerroot in hot oil 30 seconds. Add *half* the beef to hot wok; stir-fry 2 to 3 minutes or till browned.

Remove beef. Stir-fry remaining beef 2 to 3 minutes. Return all beef to wok. Stir cornstarch mixture; stir into beef. Cook and stir till thickened and bubbly. Stir in spinach and water chestnuts; cook, covered, 1 to 2 minutes. Serve at once. Makes 6 servings.

Five Spice Powder: In small bowl combine 1 teaspoon ground *cinnamon;* 1 teaspoon crushed *aniseed or* 1 *star anise,* ground; ¼ teaspoon crushed *fennel seed;* ¼ teaspoon freshly ground *pepper or* ¼ teaspoon crushed *Szechwan pepper;* and ⅛ teaspoon ground *cloves.* Store in covered container. (Or, purchase five spice powder at Oriental food stores.)

One serving (⅔ cup) Stir-Fried Beef and Spinach equals:

●●●◖ 3½ Lean Meat Exchanges
● 1 Vegetable Exchange
◖ ½ Fat Exchange

NEW ENGLAND BOILED DINNER

1 3-pound corned beef round, trimmed of fat
2 cloves garlic, minced
2 bay leaves
8 tiny new potatoes
4 medium carrots, quartered
2 small onions, quartered
1 medium head cabbage, cut into 8 wedges

In Dutch oven cover corned beef with water. Add garlic and bay leaves. Bring to boil; simmer, covered, 2½ hours. Remove meat. Add potatoes, carrots, and onions. Cook, covered, 10 minutes; add cabbage. Cook, covered, 15 to 20 minutes. Add meat; heat through. Drain meat and vegetables; season the vegetables to taste. Makes 8 servings. One serving equals:

●●●◖ 3½ Lean Meat Exchanges
◖ ½ Bread Exchange
●● 2 Vegetable Exchanges

BEEF BURGUNDY

¾ pound boneless beef sirloin steak, trimmed of fat
4 teaspoons cooking oil
4 teaspoons cornstarch
1 medium onion, sliced and separated into rings
½ cup burgundy
½ cup water
1 teaspoon instant chicken bouillon granules
⅛ teaspoon dried oregano, crushed
⅛ teaspoon dried thyme, crushed
1 bay leaf
Dash pepper
1 cup sliced fresh mushrooms
2 cups hot cooked rice

Partially freeze beef; slice thinly into bite-size strips. In 2-quart saucepan cook *half* the beef in *half* the hot oil over medium-high heat till browned. Remove beef. Repeat with remaining beef and oil. Return all beef to pan. Stir in cornstarch. Add onion, burgundy, water, bouillon granules, oregano, thyme, bay leaf, and pepper. Cook, covered, over low heat 35 to 45 minutes or till tender, adding mushrooms 5 minutes before end of cooking time. Remove bay leaf. Serve beef mixture over hot cooked rice. Makes 4 servings. One serving (about ½ cup beef mixture and ½ cup cooked rice) equals:

●●● 3 Lean Meat Exchanges
● 1 Bread Exchange
● 1 Vegetable Exchange
● 1 Fat Exchange

New England Boiled Dinner; Stir-Fried Beef and Spinach; Skillet Spaghetti (see recipe, page 308)

FAT CONTENT OF GROUND BEEF

When labeled not less than 85% lean, ground beef contains not more than 15% fat and has a Medium-Fat Meat Exchange rating. Ground beef labeled not less than 80% lean usually rates a High-Fat Meat Exchange. You may find ground round or ground chuck in the meat case. They rate Medium-Fat and High-Fat Meat Exchanges respectively. Ground round can substitute for the 15% fat ground beef called for in Food Exchange recipes.

MEAT AND POTATO LOAF

Pictured on pages 270 and 271—

2 medium potatoes, peeled and cut up
1 tablespoon snipped parsley
1/8 teaspoon dried thyme, crushed
1/8 teaspoon dried marjoram, crushed
Salt
Pepper
• • •
2 beaten eggs
1/2 cup finely crushed saltine crackers (14 crackers)
1/3 cup tomato sauce
1/4 cup finely chopped onion
2 tablespoons finely chopped green pepper
3/4 teaspoon salt
1 1/2 pounds ground beef (15% fat)
• • •
1/4 cup catsup
1/4 teaspoon dry mustard

Cook potatoes, covered, in boiling salted water about 20 minutes or till tender; drain, reserving liquid. Mash potatoes, adding about *3 tablespoons* of the reserved liquid to make a stiff consistency. Stir in parsley, thyme, and marjoram. Season to taste with salt and pepper; set the potatoes aside.

In a large bowl stir together eggs, cracker crumbs, tomato sauce, onion, green pepper, and the 3/4 teaspoon salt. Add beef; mix well. On waxed paper pat beef mixture into a 10x8-inch rectangle; spoon potato mixture lengthwise down center of beef mixture. Fold sides over potato mixture; seal. Place loaf, seam side down, on 15 1/2x10 1/2x2-inch baking pan. Remove paper. Bake in a 350° oven 45 minutes or till done. Heat together catsup and dry mustard; spoon over meat loaf. If desired, garnish with endive. Makes 8 servings. One serving (1/8 meat loaf) equals:

3 Lean Meat Exchanges
1/2 Bread Exchange
1 Vegetable Exchange
1 1/2 Fat Exchanges

SKILLET SPAGHETTI

Pictured on page 307—

1 pound ground beef (15% fat)
3 cups water
1 18-ounce can tomato juice
1 6-ounce can tomato paste
2 tablespoons minced dried onion
1 1/2 teaspoons chili powder
1 teaspoon salt
1 teaspoon garlic salt
1 teaspoon dried oregano, crushed
1 7-ounce package spaghetti
7 tablespoons grated Parmesan cheese

In large skillet combine ground beef, the water, tomato juice, tomato paste, minced dried onion, chili powder, salt, garlic salt, and oregano. Bring to boil. Simmer, covered, 30 minutes; stir often. Add the uncooked spaghetti; simmer, covered, 30 minutes. Stir often. Serve with the grated Parmesan cheese. Makes 7 servings. One serving (1 cup) equals:

2 1/2 Lean Meat Exchanges
1 1/2 Bread Exchanges
1 1/2 Vegetable Exchanges
1 1/2 Fat Exchanges

NO-CRUST PIZZA

1 2-ounce can chopped mushrooms
1 slightly beaten egg
1 cup soft bread crumbs (1¼ slices bread)
½ teaspoon salt
½ teaspoon dried oregano, crushed
Dash pepper
1 pound ground beef (15% fat)
2 1-ounce slices mozzarella cheese
½ of an 8-ounce can (½ cup) pizza sauce
¼ cup chopped onion
2 tablespoons chopped green pepper

Drain mushrooms, reserving the liquid. Add *water* to equal ⅓ cup liquid. Combine the liquid, egg, bread crumbs, salt, oregano, and pepper; let stand 5 minutes. Add beef; mix well. Pat beef mixture into a 9-inch pie plate to form crust. Cut cheese into 8 triangles; layer *half* the cheese atop beef mixture. Top with pizza sauce, mushrooms, onion, and green pepper. Bake in a 350° oven 45 minutes. Top with remaining cheese; bake 5 minutes. Remove to serving platter, using two spatulas. Makes 8 servings. One serving (⅛ pizza) equals:

●●◖ 2½ Lean Meat Exchanges
● 1 Vegetable Exchange
● 1 Fat Exchange

TACO COMPUESTO

Pictured on page 287—

1 pound ground beef (15% fat)
½ cup chopped onion
2 tablespoons chopped canned green chili peppers
1 clove garlic, minced
1 teaspoon chili powder
½ teaspoon salt
• • •
1½ cups chopped tomato
3 tablespoons low-calorie Italian salad dressing (no more than 8 calories per tablespoon)
½ teaspoon seasoned salt
8 taco shells
1 cup shredded lettuce
½ cup shredded low-calorie process cheese product (2 ounces)
½ cup taco sauce

Cook beef, onion, chili peppers, and garlic till beef is browned; drain. Stir in chili powder and salt. Combine tomato, salad dressing, and seasoned salt. Spoon beef mixture into taco shells; top with tomato mixture, shredded lettuce, and shredded cheese. Pass taco sauce. Makes 4 servings. One serving (2 tacos and 2 tablespoons taco sauce) equals:

●●●◖ 3½ Lean Meat Exchanges
●● 2 Bread Exchanges
●● 2 Vegetable Exchanges
●◖ 1½ Fat Exchanges

OLD-FASHIONED BEEF STEW

1¼ pounds boneless beef round steak, cut into 1-inch cubes and trimmed of fat
1 tablespoon diet margarine
1½ cups hot water
1½ teaspoons salt
1 teaspoon Worcestershire sauce
2 bay leaves
1 clove garlic, minced
½ teaspoon paprika
¼ teaspoon pepper
Dash ground cloves
• • •
8 medium carrots, quartered
4 small potatoes, peeled and quartered
4 small onions, quartered
1 tablespoons cornstarch
¼ cup cold water

In Dutch oven brown beef in diet margarine. Add the 1½ cups hot water, the salt, Worcestershire sauce, bay leaves, garlic, paprika, pepper, and cloves. Cook, covered, 1¼ hours; stir often. Remove bay leaves; add vegetables. Cook, covered, 30 to 45 minutes. Drain; reserve liquid. Skim fat. Add water to liquid to equal 1¼ cups; return to Dutch oven. Combine cornstarch and the ¼ cup cold water; stir into hot liquid. Cook and stir till thickened and bubbly; stir in beef and vegetables. Heat through. Makes 8 servings. One serving (1 cup) equals:

●●◖ 2½ Lean Meat Exchanges
● 1 Bread Exchange
● 1 Vegetable Exchange

SPICY MARINATED PORK CHOPS

1 cup vegetable juice cocktail
3 tablespoons finely chopped onion
3 tablespoons finely chopped green pepper
3 tablespoons lemon juice
2 tablespoons low-calorie Italian salad dressing mix
2 tablespoons Worcestershire sauce
Few drops bottled hot pepper sauce
• • •
4 pork loin chops, cut ½ inch thick and trimmed of fat

For marinade, in plastic bag combine vegetable juice cocktail, onion, green pepper, lemon juice, salad dressing mix, Worcestershire sauce, and hot pepper sauce; add pork chops. Close bag securely; place in an 8x8x2-inch baking dish. Refrigerate 8 hours or overnight. Drain; reserve marinade. Place chops on unheated rack in broiler pan. Broil chops 3 to 4 inches from heat 6 minutes on each side or till done. Heat marinade and serve with chops. Makes 4 servings. One serving (1 chop and ¼ cup marinade) equals:

3 Lean Meat Exchanges
1½ Vegetable Exchanges
1½ Fat Exchanges

Veal and Peppers Italiano (see recipe, page 312); *Barbecued Ham Slice; Athenian Lamb Kabobs* (see recipe, page 312)

PINEAPPLE AND PORK STIR-FRY

12 ounces pork tenderloin *or* boneless pork, trimmed of fat
1 small fresh pineapple
½ cup orange juice
¼ cup soy sauce
½ teaspoon instant chicken bouillon granules
1 clove garlic, minced
⅛ teaspoon pepper
2 tablespoons cold water
4 teaspoons cornstarch
1 medium red *or* green pepper, cut into 1-inch squares
1 tablespoon cooking oil

Partially freeze pork; slice thinly into bite-size strips. Set aside. Remove pineapple crown. Cut off peel; remove all eyes from fruit by cutting diagonal wedge-shaped grooves in the pineapple. Cut pineapple lengthwise into 8 wedges, reserving any juice. Cut off center core from each wedge. In small bowl combine reserved pineapple juice, orange juice, soy sauce, bouillon granules, garlic, and pepper; set aside. In small bowl blend cold water into cornstarch; set aside.

In wok or large skillet stir-fry pork and red or green pepper in hot oil over high heat 3 to 4 minutes or till pork is just browned. Remove from wok. Pour juice mixture into wok; add pineapple wedges. Cook, covered, 2 minutes. Remove wedges with slotted spoon and arrange on platter; keep warm. Return pork and peppers to hot liquid in wok. Stir cornstarch mixture; add to wok. Cook and stir till thickened and bubbly. (If sauce is thick, add a few tablespoons water.) Spoon pork mixture atop pineapple wedges. Makes 4 servings. One serving (½ cup pork mixture and 2 wedges pineapple) equals:

3 Lean Meat Exchanges
2 Fruit Exchanges
½ Vegetable Exchange
2 Fat Exchanges

BARBECUED HAM SLICE

½ cup catsup
2 tablespoons finely chopped onion
1 tablespoon Worcestershire sauce
2 teaspoons lemon juice
2 teaspoons prepared mustard
¼ teaspoon chili powder
1 1½-pound fully cooked ham slice, cut 1 inch thick and trimmed of fat

For sauce, combine catsup, onion, Worcestershire sauce, lemon juice, mustard, and chili powder. Bring to boil. Slash edges of ham; brush with some sauce. Place ham on unheated rack in broiler pan. Broil 3 to 4 inches from heat 5 to 6 minutes on each side, brushing with sauce once. Makes 6 servings. One serving (4 ounces) equals:

4 Lean Meat Exchanges
1 Vegetable Exchange

VEAL SCALLOPINI

12 ounces boneless veal leg round steak, cut ¼ inch thick and trimmed of fat
2 tablespoons diet margarine
½ cup water
¼ cup dry sherry
¾ teaspoon instant chicken bouillon granules
⅛ teaspoon pepper
1 4-ounce can sliced mushrooms, drained
2 tablespoons snipped parsley

Cut veal into 4 pieces; pound to ⅛-inch thickness. Cook veal in hot margarine 1 to 1½ minutes on each side. Remove; keep warm. For sauce, in same pan add water, sherry, bouillon granules, and pepper to drippings. Boil sauce 3 to 4 minutes or till reduced to ⅓ cup. Stir in mushrooms and parsley. Heat through. Pour over veal. Makes 4 servings. One serving (1 piece veal and 3 tablespoons sauce) equals:

3 Lean Meat Exchanges
½ Fat Exchange

FRUITED LAMB CHOPS

Pictured on page 291—

1 16-ounce can peach slices (juice pack)
2 teaspoons cornstarch
½ teaspoon ground ginger
¼ teaspoon ground nutmeg
2 tablespoons diet margarine
1 tablespoon lemon juice
1 teaspoon soy sauce
8 lamb loin chops, cut ¾ inch thick

Drain peaches, reserving juice; halve peaches lengthwise. Set peaches aside. Combine cornstarch and spices; blend in juice. Cook and stir till thickened and bubbly; stir in margarine, lemon juice, and soy sauce. Trim fat from chops; brush chops with some sauce. Broil 3 to 4 inches from heat 9 to 10 minutes, turning and brushing with sauce once. Stir peaches into remaining sauce; heat through; serve with chops. Makes 8 servings. One serving (1 chop and ¼ cup sauce) equals:

2 Lean Meat Exchanges
½ Fruit Exchange
½ Fat Exchange

VEAL AND PEPPERS ITALIANO

Pictured on page 310—

1 pound lean boneless veal
1 tablespoon diet margarine
1 10½-ounce can tomato puree
1 cup chicken broth
1 clove garlic, minced
¾ teaspoon salt
½ teaspoon dried basil, crushed
½ teaspoon dried oregano, crushed
⅛ teaspoon pepper
2 medium green peppers, cut into strips
1 medium onion, sliced
2 cups hot cooked rice

Cut veal into 1-inch cubes; trim fat. Brown veal in diet margarine. Stir in tomato puree, chicken broth, garlic, salt, basil, oregano, and pepper. Simmer, covered, 25 minutes. Add green peppers and onion; cook, covered, 20 minutes. Serve with rice. Makes 4 servings. One serving (1 cup veal mixture and ½ cup rice) equals:

4 Lean Meat Exchanges
1 Bread Exchange
2 Vegetable Exchanges
½ Fat Exchange

ATHENIAN LAMB KABOBS

Pictured on page 310—

¾ cup low-calorie French salad dressing (no more than 25 calories per tablespoon)
3 tablespoons lime juice
½ teaspoon dried oregano, crushed
¼ teaspoon dried tarragon, crushed
1½ pounds lean boneless lamb, trimmed of fat
2 cups small fresh mushrooms
2 medium green peppers

For marinade, combine salad dressing, lime juice, and herbs. Cut lamb into 1-inch cubes; add to marinade. Cover; let stand 2 hours at room temperature, stirring occasionally. Drain; reserve marinade. Sprinkle lamb with *salt.* Pour boiling water over mushrooms; let stand 1 minute and drain. Cut green peppers into 1-inch squares. Alternate lamb and vegetables on 6 skewers. Broil 4 inches from heat 10 to 12 minutes, turning and basting with marinade occasionally. If desired, sprinkle with snipped parsley. Makes 6 servings. One serving (1 kabob) equals:

3 Lean Meat Exchanges
1 Vegetable Exchange
1 Fat Exchange

TERIYAKI CHICKEN KABOBS

Substitute the ground ginger if fresh gingerroot isn't available—

¼ cup soy sauce
¼ cup dry sherry
¼ cup water
1 clove garlic, minced
1 teaspoon grated gingerroot *or* ¼ teaspoon ground ginger
• • •
2 8-ounce whole chicken breasts, skinned, split, boned, and cut into 1-inch cubes
6 large green onions, bias sliced into 1-inch lengths
4 cherry tomatoes

Combine soy sauce, sherry, water, garlic, and gingerroot or ginger. Boil 1 minute; cool. Marinate chicken and green onion in soy mixture 30 minutes at room temperature, stirring once to coat all pieces. Drain; reserve marinade. Alternate chicken and onion pieces on 4 skewers. Broil kabobs 4 inches from heat 4 to 5 minutes. Place a cherry tomato on end of each skewer. Turn; broil kabobs 4 to 5 minutes longer, brushing occasionally with marinade. Makes 4 servings. One serving (1 kabob) equals:

●● 2 Lean Meat Exchanges
● 1 Vegetable Exchange

TURKEY-ASPARAGUS PILAF

1 6¾-ounce package quick-cooking long grain and wild rice mix
1 10-ounce package frozen cut asparagus
3 cups cooked turkey cut into strips
⅓ cup chicken broth
¼ cup sliced almonds
2 tablespoons dry sherry
2 tablespoons white wine vinegar

Prepare rice mix according to package directions *except* substitute *diet margarine* for the butter. Cook asparagus according to package directions; drain. Add asparagus, turkey, chicken broth, almonds, sherry, and vinegar to rice; heat through. Season to taste with salt and pepper. Makes 8 servings. One serving (1 cup) equals:

●● 2 Lean Meat Exchanges
● 1 Bread Exchange
● 1 Vegetable Exchange
● 1 Fat Exchange

SPICY BAKED CHICKEN

¼ cup all-purpose flour
2 tablespoons snipped parsley
1 tablespoon low-calorie Italian salad dressing mix
2 teaspoons diet margarine
½ teaspoon paprika
3 tablespoons water
1 3-pound broiler-fryer chicken, cut up

In small bowl stir together first 5 ingredients. Blend in water. Remove wing tips and skin from chicken. Spread flour mixture over skinned chicken pieces. Place chicken in ungreased 15x10x1-inch baking pan. Bake in a 375° oven for 50 to 60 minutes. *Do not turn.* Makes 4 servings. One serving (¼ recipe) equals:

●●●◖ 3½ Lean Meat Exchanges
◖ ½ Bread Exchange

CHEESE-STUFFED CHICKEN

2 8-ounce whole chicken breasts, skinned, split, and boned
4 3x1-inch slices Monterey Jack cheese
1 egg
2 teaspoons grated Parmesan cheese
1 teaspoon snipped parsley
½ teaspoon instant chicken bouillon granules
2 tablespoons all-purpose flour
2 tablespoons cooking oil

In thickest side of each chicken piece, cut a pocket just large enough for cheese slice. Place a cheese slice in each pocket. Beat together egg, Parmesan cheese, parsley, bouillon granules, and dash *pepper.* Coat chicken with flour and dip in egg mixture; brown in hot oil 2 to 3 minutes on each side. Transfer to a 10x6x2-inch baking dish. Bake in a 375° oven for 8 to 10 minutes. Makes 4 servings. One serving (1 piece) equals:

●●● 3 Lean Meat Exchanges
●● 2 Fat Exchanges

CHICKEN-BROCCOLI SKILLET

A colorful main dish that cooks quickly—

- **1 10-ounce package frozen cut broccoli**
- **2 8-ounce whole chicken breasts, skinned, split, boned, and cut into ½-inch-wide strips**
- **Salt**
- **Pepper**
- **¼ cup chopped onion**
- **2 tablespoons diet margarine**

• • •

- **1 teaspoon lemon juice**
- **¾ teaspoon salt**
- **¼ teaspoon dried thyme, crushed**
- **⅛ teaspoon pepper**
- **3 medium tomatoes, cut into wedges**

Thaw the frozen broccoli. Season chicken strips with salt and pepper. Cook chicken and chopped onion quickly in the hot diet margarine till chicken is just done. Stir in the thawed broccoli, lemon juice, ¾ teaspoon salt, thyme, and ⅛ teaspoon pepper. Cook, covered, 6 minutes. Add tomato wedges. Cook, covered, 3 to 4 minutes more. Makes 4 servings. One serving (1¼ cups) equals:

2½ Lean Meat Exchanges
2 Vegetable Exchanges
½ Fat Exchange

Chicken Cacciatore; Chicken-Broccoli Skillet; Lemon Poached Salmon and *Tartar Sauce* (see recipes, page 316)

CHICKEN CACCIATORE

- **½ of a 7½-ounce can (½ cup) tomatoes**
- **¾ cup sliced fresh mushrooms**
- **¼ cup chopped onion**
- **¼ cup chopped green pepper**
- **3 tablespoons dry red wine**
- **1 clove garlic, minced**
- **½ teaspoon salt**
- **½ teaspoon dried oregano, crushed**
- **Dash pepper**
- **2 8-ounce whole chicken breasts, skinned, split, and boned**
- **Paprika**
- **2 teaspoons cornstarch**
- **2 tablespoons cold water**

In medium skillet cut up *undrained* tomatoes. Add sliced mushrooms, chopped onion, chopped green pepper, red wine, garlic, salt, oregano, and pepper. Place chicken pieces atop mixture in skillet. Bring to boil; simmer, covered, 25 minutes. Remove chicken to serving dish; sprinkle with paprika. Keep warm.

Combine cornstarch and the 2 tablespoons cold water; stir into skillet mixture. Cook and stir till thickened and bubbly; cook 1 minute longer. Spoon sauce over chicken. If desired, garnish with a sprig of parsley. Makes 4 servings. One serving (½ breast and ⅓ cup sauce) equals:

2½ Lean Meat Exchanges
1 Vegetable Exchange

FRENCH HERBED CHICKEN

Buy a whole chicken and cut it up yourself or select one that's already cut up—

- **1 3-pound broiler-fryer chicken, cut up**
- **1 tablespoon cooking oil**
- **Salt and pepper**

• • •

- **1 cup sauterne**
- **1 8-ounce can (1 cup) stewed onions, drained**
- **1 cup sliced fresh mushrooms**
- **½ cup coarsely chopped carrot**
- **2 to 3 stalks celery, cut up**
- **2 tablespoons snipped parsley**
- **¼ teaspoon dried thyme, crushed**
- **1 clove garlic, minced**
- **1 bay leaf**

Remove wing tips and skin from chicken. Brown the chicken pieces in the hot cooking oil. Drain. Season chicken to taste with the salt and pepper. Add the sauterne, stewed onions, sliced mushrooms, chopped carrot, cut up celery, parsley, thyme, garlic, and bay leaf. Bring to boil; simmer, covered, 45 minutes. Remove celery and bay leaf; discard. Remove chicken and vegetables; keep warm while cooking sauce. Boil sauce 5 minutes or till reduced to ½ cup. Makes 6 servings. One serving (1/6 recipe) equals:

3½ Lean Meat Exchanges
½ Vegetable Exchange
½ Fat Exchange

POLYNESIAN SHRIMP

Pictured on pages 270 and 271—

12 ounces fresh *or* frozen shelled shrimp, halved lengthwise
1½ cups carrots bias sliced into ½-inch lengths
⅔ cup cold water
1 tablespoon cornstarch
½ of a 6-ounce can (6 tablespoons) frozen pineapple juice concentrate, thawed
2 tablespoons soy sauce
1 teaspoon instant chicken bouillon granules
• • •
1 tablespoon cooking oil
2 teaspoons grated gingerroot
1 clove garlic, minced
1 6-ounce package frozen pea pods, thawed
¼ cup green onion bias sliced into ½-inch lengths
2 cups hot cooked rice

Thaw shrimp, if frozen. In saucepan cook carrots in small amount of boiling, lightly salted water 5 to 7 minutes or till just tender; drain well. Blend the ⅔ cup cold water into the cornstarch; stir in pineapple juice concentrate, soy sauce, and chicken bouillon granules; set aside.

Preheat wok or large skillet over high heat; add oil. Stir-fry gingerroot and garlic in hot oil for 30 seconds. Add the carrots, pea pods, and green onion; stir-fry 1 minute or till heated through. Remove the vegetables and set aside.

Stir-fry the shrimp in hot oil 7 to 8 minutes or till shrimp are done. Push shrimp away from center of wok or skillet. Stir the soy mixture and add to center of wok or skillet. Cook and stir till thickened and bubbly. Stir in vegetables; cover and cook 1 minute. Serve shrimp mixture at once with hot cooked rice. If desired, sprinkle rice with snipped parsley. Makes 4 servings. One serving (1 cup shrimp mixture and ½ cup rice) equals:

●●● 3 Lean Meat Exchanges
● 1 Bread Exchange
●● 2 Vegetable Exchanges
●◐ 1½ Fruit Exchanges
● 1 Fat Exchange

LEMON POACHED SALMON

Pictured on page 314—

4 6-ounce fresh *or* frozen salmon steaks
4 cups water
⅓ cup lemon juice
1 small onion, sliced
¼ cup chopped celery
½ teaspoon salt
⅛ teaspoon freshly ground pepper
Lemon wedges
Tartar Sauce (see recipe at right) (optional)

Thaw salmon, if frozen. In large skillet combine water, lemon juice, onion, celery, salt, and pepper. Bring to boil; simmer 5 minutes. Add salmon; simmer, covered, 7 to 10 minutes or till fish flakes easily when tested with a fork. Remove salmon from liquid with spatula. Chill or serve hot. Serve salmon with lemon wedges. If desired, top salmon with Tartar Sauce and garnish with fresh dillweed. Makes 4 servings. One serving (1 salmon steak) equals:

●●●● 4 Lean Meat Exchanges

TARTAR SAUCE

Pictured on page 314—

½ cup whipped mayonnaise-type salad dressing substitute (no more than 20 calories per tablespoon)
¼ cup finely shredded carrot
1 tablespoon finely chopped dill pickle
1 teaspoon finely chopped onion
1 teaspoon snipped parsley
1 teaspoon finely chopped pimiento
1 teaspoon lemon juice

Combine salad dressing, carrot, dill pickle, onion, parsley, pimiento, and lemon juice. Cover and chill thoroughly. Serve with fish. Makes ¾ cup sauce. One serving (2 tablespoons) equals:

◐ ½ Fat Exchange

FISH CREOLE

16 ounces fresh *or* frozen fish fillets
1/3 cup chopped onion
1/3 cup chopped green pepper
1 clove garlic, minced
2 tablespoons water
• • •
1 16-ounce can tomatoes, cut up
1/2 cup water
2 tablespoons snipped parsley
1 tablespoon instant chicken bouillon granules
Dash bottled hot pepper sauce
1 tablespoon cornstarch
3 tablespoons cold water
3 cups hot cooked rice

Thaw fish, if frozen. Cut into 1-inch cubes. Combine onion, green pepper, garlic, and the 2 tablespoons water. Cook, covered, till tender. Add *undrained* tomatoes, 1/2 cup water, parsley, bouillon granules, and hot pepper sauce. Simmer, covered, 10 minutes. Blend cornstarch and the 3 tablespoons cold water; stir into tomato mixture. Cook and stir till thickened. Stir in fish. Simmer, covered, 5 to 7 minutes. Serve over rice. Makes 6 servings. One serving (2/3 cup fish mixture and 1/2 cup rice) equals:

2 1/2 Lean Meat Exchanges
1 Bread Exchange
1 Vegetable Exchange

TUNA-NOODLE NEWBURG

1 10 3/4-ounce can condensed cream of celery soup
2/3 cup evaporated skim milk
1/2 cup shredded low-calorie process cheese product
1/3 cup whipped mayonnaise-type salad dressing substitute (no more than 20 calories per tablespoon)
1/4 cup dry sherry
2 7-ounce cans tuna (water pack), drained
4 ounces medium noodles, cooked
1 cup thinly sliced celery
1/4 cup chopped pimiento

Combine soup and milk. Bring to boil; stir often. Remove from heat; stir in cheese, salad dressing, and 1/4 teaspoon *salt.* Stir till cheese melts. Blend in sherry. Add tuna, noodles, celery, and pimiento; mix well. Bake in a 1 1/2-quart casserole, covered, in a 350° oven 25 minutes. Makes 6 servings. One serving (1 cup) equals:

2 1/2 Lean Meat Exchanges
1 Bread Exchange
1 Vegetable Exchange
1/2 Milk Exchange

OVEN-FRIED FISH

1 pound fresh *or* frozen fish fillets
1 slightly beaten egg
1/2 of a 6-ounce can (6 tablespoons) frozen orange juice concentrate, thawed
2 tablespoons soy sauce
1/2 cup fine dry bread crumbs
2 tablespoons diet margarine
1/2 teaspoon lemon juice

Thaw fish, if frozen. Combine egg, orange juice concentrate, and soy sauce. Combine bread crumbs and 1 teaspoon *salt.* Dip fish in egg mixture, then in crumb mixture. Place skin side down in a 12x7 1/2x2-inch baking dish. Melt margarine; stir in lemon juice. Drizzle over fish. Bake in a 500° oven for 10 to 12 minutes. Makes 4 servings. One serving (4 ounces) equals:

4 Lean Meat Exchanges
1 Bread Exchange
1 Fruit Exchange
1 Fat Exchange

HEARTY SALMON PIE

1 tablespoon diet margarine
2 cups soft bread crumbs (2 1/2 slices bread)
2/3 cup skim milk
1 slightly beaten egg
2 tablespoons chopped onion
1 16-ounce can salmon, drained, boned, and finely flaked
3 hard-cooked eggs, chopped
2 cups plain mashed potatoes
3 tablespoons skim milk
1 egg

Melt margarine; stir in crumbs, the 2/3 cup milk, 1 egg, onion, and 1/2 teaspoon *salt.* Stir in salmon and hard-cooked eggs. Turn into a 9-inch pie plate. Combine potatoes and the 3 tablespoons milk. Beat in remaining egg and 1 teaspoon *salt.* Spoon around edge of pie. Bake in a 350° oven for 30 to 35 minutes. Makes 6 servings. One serving (1/6 pie) equals:

3 Lean Meat Exchanges
1 1/2 Bread Exchanges

ELEGANT EGGS FLORENTINE

- **½ cup sliced green onion**
- **2 tablespoons diet margarine**
- **6 tablespoons dry white wine**
- **2 tablespoons vinegar**

• • •

- **2 tablespoons diet margarine**
- **2 tablespoons cornstarch**
- **2 cups skim milk**
- **¼ teaspoon salt**
- **¼ teaspoon dried tarragon, crushed**
- **1 10-ounce package frozen chopped spinach, cooked and drained**
- **1 4-ounce can sliced mushrooms, drained**
- **3 small English muffins, split and toasted**
- **6 tomato slices**
- **6 eggs**

In small saucepan cook onion in the 2 tablespoons diet margarine till tender. Add dry white wine and vinegar. Simmer, reducing liquid by half. Meanwhile, in medium saucepan melt 2 tablespoons diet margarine. Blend in cornstarch. Add skim milk. Cook and stir till mixture is thickened and bubbly. Remove from heat; stir in salt and tarragon. Return to low heat; *gradually* stir in onion mixture. Add ¾ cup sauce mixture to cooked spinach; keep remaining sauce warm over low heat (*do not boil*). Stir mushrooms into spinach mixture. Spoon ⅓ *cup* of the spinach mixture onto each toasted English muffin half. Top with 1 tomato slice. Broil 3 inches from heat about 5 minutes or till heated through; keep warm.

Meanwhile, poach eggs in simmering water to desired doneness. Place poached eggs atop tomato slices. Top each egg with 3 tablespoons sauce. Makes 6 servings. One serving equals:

- 1 Lean Meat Exchange
- 1 Bread Exchange
- ½ Vegetable Exchange
- ½ Milk Exchange
- 1½ Fat Exchanges

CONFETTI CHEESE QUICHE

Pictured on page 295—

- **⅔ cup all-purpose flour**
- **¼ teaspoon salt**
- **3 tablespoons shortening**
- **⅓ cup lowfat cottage cheese (no more than 2% milkfat), sieved**

• • •

- **1 8½-ounce can mixed vegetables, drained**
- **¼ cup finely chopped green onion**
- **1 cup shredded low-calorie process cheese product (4 ounces)**
- **3 slightly beaten eggs**
- **1 cup evaporated skimmed milk**
- **½ teaspoon salt**
- **⅛ teaspoon pepper**

In small bowl combine flour and the ¼ teaspoon salt; cut in shortening till pieces are the size of small peas. Add cottage cheese. Toss mixture with fork till entire mixture is moistened. Form dough into a ball. Flatten on a very lightly floured surface by pressing with edge of hands 3 times across in both directions. Roll out to ⅛-inch thickness. Fit into a 9-inch pie plate or quiche pan; flute edges and set aside. In small bowl combine drained vegetables and onion. In cottage cheese pastry shell layer *half* the cheese and the entire vegetable mixture. In large bowl combine eggs, evaporated skimmed milk, ½ teaspoon salt, and pepper. Pour egg mixture over vegetables in pastry shell. Sprinkle with remaining cheese. Bake in a 325° oven for 45 to 50 minutes or till knife inserted off center comes out clean. Remove from oven and let stand 10 minutes before serving. (Texture may be soft.) Makes 8 servings. One serving (⅛ quiche) equals:

- 1 Lean Meat Exchange
- 1 Bread Exchange
- ½ Vegetable Exchange
- 1 Fat Exchange

CORNED BEEF SLAW-WICHES

- **½ cup whipped mayonnaise-type salad dressing substitute (no more than 20 calories per tablespoon)**
- **2 teaspoons prepared mustard**
- **4 cups finely shredded cabbage**
- **2 tablespoons sliced green onion**
- **12 slices very thin whole wheat bread, toasted**
- **1 12-ounce can corned beef, chilled**

Blend salad dressing and mustard. Combine cabbage and onion; toss with salad dressing mixture. Spoon ½ *cup* of the cabbage mixture onto 6 of the toasted bread slices. Cut corned beef into 12 slices; arrange 2 slices atop each sandwich. Top with remaining toasted bread. Makes 6 servings. One serving (1 sandwich) equals:

- 2 Lean Meat Exchanges
- 1 Bread Exchange
- ½ Vegetable Exchange
- 2 Fat Exchanges

FRUITY HAM SANDWICHES

½ cup whipped mayonnaise-type salad dressing substitute (no more than 20 calories per tablespoon)
2 tablespoons chili sauce
1 tablespoon finely chopped dill pickle
2 teaspoons skim milk

• • •

4 slices whole wheat bread, toasted
Lettuce
4 1-ounce slices Swiss cheese
4 1-ounce slices boiled ham
8 cantaloupe slices *or* one 16-ounce can peach slices (juice pack), drained

Combine first 4 ingredients. Layer each slice of toasted bread with lettuce, *1 tablespoon* dressing mixture, cheese, ham, and ¼ of cantaloupe or peach slices. Drizzle with remaining dressing mixture. Serves 4. One serving (1 sandwich) equals:

- 2 Lean Meat Exchanges
- 1½ Bread Exchanges
- 1 Fruit Exchange
- 2 Fat Exchanges

VEGETARIAN SPROUT SANDWICHES

1 cup thinly sliced cucumber
½ cup shredded carrot
2 tablespoons chopped green onion
⅓ cup low-calorie Italian salad dressing (no more than 8 calories per tablespoon)
4 ⅔-ounce slices low-calorie process cheese product
2 small English muffins, split and toasted
½ cup alfalfa sprouts
4 teaspoons shelled sunflower seed

Combine cucumber, carrot, onion, and salad dressing; set aside. Place 1 cheese slice atop each muffin half. Broil 5 inches from heat for 2 minutes. Spoon ⅓ *cup* of the vegetable mixture atop each half; add *2 tablespoons* of the alfalfa sprouts and *1 teaspoon* of the sunflower seed. Makes 4 servings. One serving (1 sandwich) equals:

- 1 Lean Meat Exchange
- 1 Bread Exchange
- 1 Vegetable Exchange

TURKEY-ASPARAGUS STACKS

A good use for leftover turkey—

¼ cup low-calorie French salad dressing (no more than 25 calories per tablespoon)
2 tablespoons finely chopped onion
⅛ teaspoon pepper
1 10-ounce package frozen asparagus spears, cooked and drained

• • •

2 bagels, halved and toasted
8 1-ounce slices cooked turkey
4 ⅔-ounce slices low-calorie process cheese product, halved diagonally

Combine salad dressing, onion, and pepper; pour over asparagus. Refrigerate several hours. Remove asparagus with slotted spoon. Spread some dressing mixture on the toasted bagel halves. Top with the sliced, cooked turkey; spread dressing mixture between turkey slices. Top with cooked asparagus spears. Broil 4 inches from heat 4 minutes. Place cheese atop asparagus. Broil 1 minute more. Makes 4 servings. One serving (1 sandwich) equals:

- 2½ Lean Meat Exchanges
- 1 Bread Exchange
- 1 Vegetable Exchange
- ½ Fat Exchange

SALADS AND VEGETABLES

CHEESE AND VEGETABLE MOLD

1 envelope unflavored gelatin
1½ cups chicken broth
1 tablespoon lemon juice
1½ teaspoons prepared horseradish
¼ cup thinly sliced cucumber
1½ cups dry cottage cheese (12 ounces)
⅓ cup seeded, shredded cucumber
⅓ cup shredded carrot
2 tablespoons chopped green onion

Soften gelatin in the chicken broth. Add lemon juice and horseradish; stir over low heat till dissolved. Cool. Arrange cucumber slices in a 4-cup mold. Pour ½ *cup* of the gelatin mixture into mold. Chill till almost firm. Combine remaining gelatin mixture with cottage cheese, shredded cucumber, shredded carrot, and green onion. Turn into the mold. Chill till firm. Makes 6 servings. One serving (about ⅔ cup) equals:

● 1 Lean Meat Exchange
◖ ½ Vegetable Exchange

SPARKLING CITRUS MOLD

1 8-ounce can grapefruit sections (juice pack)
Orange juice
1 envelope unflavored gelatin
1 cup low-calorie orange carbonated beverage, chilled
1 tablespoon lemon juice
½ cup orange sections

Drain grapefruit, reserving juice. Add enough orange juice to reserved juice to measure 1 cup liquid; soften gelatin in the juice mixture. Stir over low heat till dissolved. Add orange beverage and lemon juice. Chill till partially set (consistency of unbeaten egg whites). Cut up orange and grapefruit sections; fold into gelatin. Turn into a 3-cup mold. Chill till firm. Makes 4 servings. One serving (¾ cup) equals:

● 1 Fruit Exchange

MOLDED GAZPACHO SALAD

1 4-serving envelope low-calorie lemon-flavored gelatin
¾ cup boiling water
¾ cup vegetable juice cocktail
2 tablespoons low-calorie Italian salad dressing (no more than 8 calories per tablespoon)
4 teaspoons vinegar
½ cup sliced cauliflower flowerets
½ cup chopped, seeded tomato
½ cup chopped celery
¼ cup chopped green pepper

Dissolve gelatin in the boiling water. Stir in vegetable juice cocktail, salad dressing, and vinegar. Chill till partially set (consistency of unbeaten egg whites). Fold in cauliflower, tomato, celery, and green pepper. Turn into a 3-cup mold. Chill several hours or till firm. Makes 4 servings. One serving (about ⅔ cup) equals

● 1 Vegetable Exchange

TANGY VEGETABLE VINAIGRETTE

1 tablespoon cornstarch
1 teaspoon dry mustard
1 cup cold water
¼ cup vinegar
¼ cup catsup
1 teaspoon Worcestershire sauce
½ teaspoon salt
½ teaspoon prepared horseradish
¼ teaspoon paprika
⅛ teaspoon garlic powder

• • •

1 cup thinly sliced cauliflower flowerets
1 cup thinly sliced carrot
1 cup thinly sliced cucumber
1 cup thinly sliced celery
¼ cup thinly sliced green onion
Lettuce

In saucepan combine cornstarch and dry mustard; gradually stir in cold water. Cook and stir till thickened and bubbly. Remove from heat. Cover surface with waxed paper. Cool 10 to 15 minutes. Stir in vinegar, catsup, Worcestershire sauce, salt, horseradish, paprika, and garlic powder.

In large bowl combine cauliflower, carrot, cucumber, celery, and green onion. Add dressing; stir gently. Cover; refrigerate several hours or overnight, stirring occasionally. To serve, drain vegetables; mound in a lettuce-lined bowl. Makes 8 servings. One serving (½ cup) equals:

● 1 Vegetable Exchange

Cheese and Vegetable Mold; Carrot-Potato Boats (see recipe, page 325)

SHIMMERING ICEBERG RINGS

1 4-serving envelope low-calorie lime-flavored gelatin
¼ teaspoon salt
1 cup boiling water
⅔ cup cold water
1 tablespoon vinegar
1½ cups chopped iceberg lettuce
¼ cup finely chopped radishes

Dissolve gelatin and salt in the 1 cup boiling water. Stir in the ⅔ cup cold water and the vinegar. Chill till partially set (consistency of unbeaten egg whites). Fold in lettuce and radishes. Turn into 4 individual molds. Chill several hours or till firm. Makes 4 servings. One serving (½ cup) equals:

1 Free Exchange

COLESLAW

2 cups shredded cabbage
¾ cup shredded carrot
¼ cup thinly sliced bermuda onion
½ cup lowfat plain yogurt (no more than 2% milkfat)
2 teaspoons salad oil
1 teaspoon prepared horseradish
⅛ teaspoon salt
Dash pepper

Combine cabbage, carrot, and onion. Stir together yogurt, oil, horseradish, salt, and pepper. Toss yogurt mixture with cabbage mixture to coat. Chill several hours. Makes 4 servings. One serving (¾ cup) equals:

● 1 Vegetable Exchange
● 1 Fat Exchange

SPINACH SALAD TOSS

Pictured on pages 270 and 271—

2 tablespoons salad oil
1 teaspoon sesame seed, toasted
½ teaspoon finely shredded lime peel
4 teaspoons lime juice
¼ teaspoon dry mustard
⅛ teaspoon salt
• • •
3 cups torn fresh spinach
1 cup sliced fresh mushrooms
½ cup sliced radishes
2 hard-cooked eggs, sliced

For dressing, in small screw-top jar combine oil, sesame seed, lime peel, lime juice, dry mustard, and salt. Cover and shake well; chill. To serve, combine spinach, sliced mushrooms, sliced radishes, and egg slices. Shake dressing and toss with spinach mixture. Makes 4 servings. One serving (1½ cups) equals:

◖ ½ Lean Meat Exchange
◖ ½ Vegetable Exchange
●● 2 Fat Exchanges

TIJUANA TACO SALAD

Plan supper around this main-dish salad—

1 pound ground beef (15% fat)
¼ cup chopped onion
1 7½-ounce can tomatoes, cut up
2 teaspoons chili powder
¼ teaspoon garlic powder
¼ teaspoon salt
⅛ teaspoon ground cumin
⅛ teaspoon pepper
• • •
1 large head lettuce
3 medium tomatoes, cut into wedges
¾ cup shredded low-calorie process cheese product (3 ounces)

Cook ground beef and onion till beef is browned; drain. Stir in *undrained* tomatoes, chili powder, garlic powder, salt, cumin, and pepper. Bring to boil; simmer till most of the liquid evaporates, stirring occasionally. Line 6 individual salad bowls with large lettuce leaves; tear remainder of lettuce into bite-size pieces and divide among salad bowls. Spoon beef mixture onto lettuce. Arrange the tomato wedges atop; sprinkle with shredded cheese. Makes 6 servings. One serving (1 salad) equals:

●●◖ 2½ Lean Meat Exchanges
● 1 Vegetable Exchange
● 1 Fat Exchange

SEAFARING SALMON SALAD

1 7¾-ounce can salmon, drained, boned, and flaked
1 tablespoon lemon juice
2 hard-cooked eggs, coarsely chopped
¼ cup thinly sliced dill pickle
¼ cup whipped mayonnaise-type salad dressing substitute (no more than 20 calories per tablespoon)
2 tablespoons sliced green onion
¼ teaspoon salt
Dash pepper

Sprinkle salmon with lemon juice; stir in hard-cooked eggs, pickle, salad dressing, green onion, salt, and pepper. Mix gently and chill. If desired, serve on lettuce-lined plates. Makes 4 servings. One serving (⅓ cup) equals:

2 Lean Meat Exchanges
1 Vegetable Exchange
½ Fat Exchange

CHICKEN-STUFFED ORANGES

4 large oranges
1 cup thinly sliced celery
¼ cup orange yogurt
1 tablespoon thinly sliced green onion
½ teaspoon celery salt
1⅓ cups diced cooked chicken (8 ounces)

Cut tops off oranges; remove and chop fruit. Chill orange shells. Combine chopped orange, celery, yogurt, green onion, and celery salt. To serve, stir chicken into orange mixture; spoon mixture into the orange shells. Makes 4 servings. One serving (1 stuffed orange) equals:

2 Lean Meat Exchanges
1 Vegetable Exchange
1 Fruit Exchange

LAYERED VEGETABLE SALAD

1 small head lettuce, torn into pieces
2 small bermuda onions, thinly sliced and separated into rings
2 cups thinly sliced zucchini
2 cups cherry tomatoes, halved
½ of an 8-ounce package Neufchâtel cheese, softened
1 teaspoon Worcestershire sauce
½ teaspoon dry mustard
1 cup lowfat plain yogurt (no more than 2% milkfat)

In salad bowl layer lettuce, onions, zucchini, and cherry tomatoes. To prepare dressing, combine cheese, Worcestershire sauce, and mustard. Stir in yogurt. Spoon dressing over vegetables in bowl. If desired, sprinkle with paprika. Cover; refrigerate 4 to 6 hours or overnight. Toss just before serving. Makes 8 servings. One serving (1¼ cups) equals:

½ Lean Meat Exchange
1 Vegetable Exchange
½ Fat Exchange

CHEF'S SALAD BOWL

Feature this salad at a summer luncheon—

1½ cups thinly sliced cauliflower flowerets
1 cup sliced radishes
½ cup sliced green onion
½ cup low-calorie French salad dressing (no more than 25 calories per tablespoon)
• • •
4 cups torn mixed salad greens
4 ounces low-calorie process cheese product, cut into julienne strips
4 ounces fully cooked center-cut ham, cut into julienne strips
8 cherry tomatoes, halved
4 hard-cooked eggs, quartered

Combine cauliflower, radishes, and green onion. Add French salad dressing; toss. Refrigerate 4 hours, tossing occasionally. Place salad greens in 4 individual salad bowls. Arrange cheese, ham, cherry tomatoes, and eggs atop greens. To serve, drain vegetable mixture; reserve dressing. Spoon some of the vegetable mixture atop each salad. Drizzle the reserved dressing over the salads. Makes 4 servings. One serving (1 salad) equals:

3 Lean Meat Exchanges
2 Vegetable Exchanges
1 Fat Exchange

TRIMMING TUNA TOSS

¾ cup wine vinegar
1½ teaspoons dried basil, crushed
2 7-ounce cans tuna (water pack), drained
8 cups torn lettuce
1½ cups cherry tomatoes, halved
1 medium cucumber, sliced
½ medium onion, thinly sliced and separated into rings
½ cup sliced celery

Combine vinegar, basil, ¼ teaspoon *salt,* and dash *pepper;* chill. In large salad bowl break up tuna; add lettuce, cherry tomatoes, cucumber, onion, and celery. Add vinegar mixture and toss lightly. Makes 7 servings. One serving (1¾ cups) equals:

1½ Lean Meat Exchanges
½ Vegetable Exchange

ZIPPY WALDORF SALAD

3 medium apples, cored and chopped
½ cup chopped celery
½ cup apple yogurt
⅓ cup seeded, halved red grapes
¼ cup chopped walnuts

Combine all ingredients. Cover; chill 2 to 3 hours. If desired, turn into a romaine-lined bowl. Makes 8 servings. One serving (½ cup) equals:

1 Fruit Exchange
½ Fat Exchange

POTLUCK POTATO SALAD

Be sure to chill the salad thoroughly before serving—

5 medium potatoes
¼ cup low-calorie French salad dressing (no more than 25 calories per tablespoon)

• • •

1 cup chopped celery
⅓ cup chopped onion
4 hard-cooked eggs, sliced
1 teaspoon salt
1 teaspoon celery seed
½ cup whipped mayonnaise-type salad dressing substitute (no more than 20 calories per tablespoon)
2 teaspoons prepared mustard
½ to 1 teaspoon prepared horseradish

Cook unpeeled potatoes till tender in boiling water; peel and cube. Combine warm potatoes and French salad dressing; toss gently to coat. Chill 2 hours. Add celery, onion, eggs, salt, and celery seed. Combine salad dressing substitute, mustard, and horseradish; toss gently with potato mixture. Chill 4 hours. Makes 8 servings. One serving (¾ cup) equals:

½ Lean Meat Exchange
1 Bread Exchange
½ Vegetable Exchange
½ Fat Exchange

TANGY TOMATO DRESSING

Pictured on page 295—

2 teaspoons cornstarch
¼ teaspoon salt
1 cup vegetable juice cocktail
¼ cup chili sauce
1 tablespoon salad oil
1 tablespoon lime *or* lemon juice
2 teaspoons prepared horseradish

Combine cornstarch and salt. Add vegetable juice. Cook and stir till thickened; cook 1 minute more. Stir in chili sauce, salad oil, lime or lemon juice, and horseradish. Cover; chill. Makes 1⅓ cups. One serving (2 tablespoons) equals:

½ Vegetable Exchange

BLUE CHEESE DRESSING

1 cup lowfat cottage cheese (no more than 2% milkfat)
⅓ cup crumbled blue cheese
4 teaspoons lemon juice
½ cup skim milk

In blender container combine cottage cheese, *half* of the blue cheese, and the lemon juice. Cover; blend till creamy. Blend in skim milk a tablespoon at a time. Stir in remaining blue cheese. Cover; chill. Serve with vegetable or fruit salads. Makes 1⅔ cups. One serving (2 tablespoons) equals:

½ Lean Meat Exchange
¼ Fat Exchange

CARROT-POTATO BOATS

Pictured on page 321—

4 small baking potatoes
½ of an 8-ounce package Neufchâtel cheese, cut into chunks and softened
3 to 4 tablespoons skim milk
¼ teaspoon salt
Dash pepper
1 cup cooked chopped carrot, pureed
2 tablespoons chopped green onion

Bake potatoes in a 375° oven for 45 minutes or till done. Cool slightly; cut potatoes in half lengthwise. Scoop out potatoes into small mixer bowl, reserving shells. Add Neufchâtel cheese, milk, salt, and pepper. Beat till fluffy, adding more milk if necessary. Fold in carrot and green onion. Pipe or spoon potato mixture into potato shells. Bake on a baking sheet in a 375° oven for 12 to 15 minutes or till heated through. If desired, sprinkle with chives. Makes 8 servings. One serving (1 potato boat) equals:

◖ ½ Lean Meat Exchange
● 1 Bread Exchange

CREAMY SPINACH CUSTARD

8 ounces fresh spinach (6 cups)
2 eggs
1 cup skim milk
½ teaspoon salt
¼ teaspoon ground nutmeg
½ cup shredded Monterey Jack cheese (2 ounces)

Cook spinach in a small amount of boiling, lightly salted water 3 to 5 minutes or till tender; drain well. Coarsely chop the spinach and pat between paper toweling to remove excess liquid.

Beat eggs, skim milk, salt, and ground nutmeg till blended. Stir in the cheese and spinach. Turn mixture into four 6-ounce custard cups. Set cups in a shallow baking pan on oven rack. Pour hot water into pan to depth of 1 inch. Bake in a 350° oven 35 to 40 minutes. Remove from water; let stand 5 minutes before serving. Makes 4 servings. One serving (1 custard) equals:

● 1 Lean Meat Exchange
● 1 Vegetable Exchange
◖ ¼ Milk Exchange
◖ ½ Fat Exchange

BEAN-STUFFED TOMATOES

1 9-ounce package frozen Italian *or* cut green beans, cooked and drained
1 2½-ounce jar sliced mushrooms, drained
⅓ cup low-calorie Italian salad dressing (no more than 8 calories per tablespoon)
¼ cup sliced green onion
¼ teaspoon salt
Dash pepper
6 medium tomatoes

Combine beans, mushrooms, salad dressing, green onion, ¼ teaspoon salt, and the pepper; toss. Refrigerate 2 hours, tossing occasionally. Cut tops off tomatoes, scoop out pulp, leaving ¼-inch shells. (Reserve pulp for another use.) Invert shells on paper toweling; chill. To serve, season the tomato shells to taste with salt; fill tomatoes with bean mixture. Makes 6 servings. One serving (1 stuffed tomato) equals:

●◖ 1½ Vegetable Exchanges

VEGETABLE SKILLET

4 cups thinly sliced zucchini
1 cup coarsely shredded carrot
1 cup chopped onion
¾ cup bias-sliced celery
½ medium green pepper, cut into thin strips
½ teaspoon garlic salt
¼ teaspoon dried basil, crushed
Dash pepper
2 tablespoons cooking oil
¼ cup chili sauce
2 teaspoons prepared mustard
2 medium tomatoes, cut into wedges

In large skillet cook zucchini, carrot, onion, celery, green pepper, garlic salt, basil, and pepper, covered, in hot oil over medium-high heat 4 minutes, stirring occasionally. Combine chili sauce and mustard; stir into vegetable mixture. Add tomato wedges; cook 2 to 3 minutes or till heated through. Season to taste with salt. Serve from skillet or transfer to serving dish. Makes 8 servings. One serving (¾ cup) equals:

●◖ 1½ Vegetable Exchanges
● 1 Fat Exchange

DESSERTS

STRAWBERRY RIBBON PIE

Be sure to use the low-calorie products specified in the recipe—

¾ cup finely crushed graham crackers (11 crackers)
2 tablespoons diet margarine, melted
1 ⅝-ounce package (2 envelopes) low-calorie strawberry-flavored gelatin
2 cups boiling water
1 tablespoon lemon juice
½ cup cold water
• • •
½ cup cold water
2 cups fresh *or* frozen whole unsweetened strawberries, thawed
2 egg whites
¼ teaspoon cream of tartar
• • •
1 1¼-ounce envelope low-calorie dessert topping mix
1 teaspoon skim milk

Combine graham cracker crumbs and margarine. Press mixture firmly into a 9-inch pie plate. Chill. Dissolve gelatin in the 2 cups boiling water; add lemon juice. Measure ½ *cup* of the gelatin mixture; stir in the ½ cup cold water. Chill till partially set (consistency of unbeaten egg whites). Turn into chilled graham cracker crust; chill till almost firm.

To remaining gelatin mixture add the remaining ½ cup cold water and chill till partially set. Reserve a few strawberries for garnish. Sieve remaining strawberries; fold into partially set gelatin. In small mixer bowl beat egg whites with cream of tartar till stiff peaks form.

Prepare dessert topping mix according to package directions. Gently fold egg whites into partially set gelatin mixture. Fold in ¾ *cup* of the whipped topping. (Refrigerate remaining topping.) If necessary, chill strawberry mixture till it mounds. Pile strawberry mixture atop first layer in crust. Chill till firm. Stir skim milk into remaining topping till smooth and fluffy. Pipe or spoon whipped topping around edge of pie. Garnish with reserved strawberries. Makes 8 servings. One serving (⅛ pie) equals:

½ Bread Exchange
½ Fruit Exchange
1 Fat Exchange

MINT CHOCOLATE CREAM PUFFS

2 tablespoons butter *or* margarine
½ cup boiling water
½ cup all-purpose flour
⅛ teaspoon salt
2 eggs
• • •
1 4-serving-size envelope *regular* low-calorie chocolate pudding mix
¼ teaspoon peppermint extract
1 1¼-ounce envelope low-calorie dessert topping mix

In small saucepan melt butter or margarine in the boiling water. Add flour and salt all at once; stir vigorously. Cook and stir till mixture forms a ball that does not separate. Remove saucepan from heat; cool 5 minutes. Add the eggs one at a time, beating till dough is very smooth and shiny after each addition. Drop the dough by spoonfuls 3 inches apart on lightly greased baking sheet, making 8 mounds. Bake in a 450° oven for 15 minutes. Reduce heat to 325°. Bake 10 minutes more. Remove cream puffs from oven; cut off tops. Remove soft centers. Turn off oven; return the hollow cream puff tops and bottoms to oven for 20 minutes to dry. Cool cream puffs on a wire rack before filling.

Meanwhile, in a medium saucepan prepare the chocolate pudding mix according to package directions. Stir in the peppermint extract. Cover surface of the chocolate pudding with waxed paper; cool the chocolate pudding to room temperature. In small mixer bowl prepare the dessert topping mix according to package directions. Stir the chocolate pudding; fold the whipped topping into the chocolate pudding. Cover pudding mixture and chill in the refrigerator.

To serve, spoon about ½ *cup* of the chilled chocolate pudding mixture into each of the cream puff bottoms. Top with the cream puff tops. One serving (1 filled cream puff) equals:

½ Bread Exchange
½ Milk Exchange
2 Fat Exchanges

Ribbon Mocha Parfaits (see recipe, page 330); *Ruby Fruit Compote* (see recipe, page 331); *Strawberry Ribbon Pie*

PINEAPPLE PIE

This light-tasting pie has a coconut crust instead of a pastry shell—

¾ cup flaked coconut
1 tablespoon diet margarine, melted
1 4-serving-size envelope *regular* low-calorie vanilla pudding mix
1 20-ounce can crushed pineapple (juice pack)
1 envelope unflavored gelatin
2 tablespoons lemon juice
½ cup whipped low-calorie dessert topping

In small bowl combine flaked coconut and margarine; press on bottom and sides of a 9-inch pie plate. Bake coconut pie shell in a 325° oven about 15 minutes or till coconut is golden; cool.

Prepare pudding mix according to package directions. Cover surface of pudding with waxed paper; cool to room temperature. Meanwhile, drain pineapple, reserving juice in a 1-cup measure. Add water to juice to equal ¾ cup. Soften gelatin in pineapple juice mixture. Stir over low heat till gelatin is dissolved; stir in lemon juice. Chill gelatin mixture till partially set (consistency of unbeaten egg whites). Whip partially set gelatin till fluffy; fold in cooled pudding and *1¼ cups* of the crushed pineapple. (Reserve remainder of the pineapple for another use.) Pour pineapple mixture into the cooled pie shell. Garnish pie with dollops of whipped low-calorie dessert topping. Makes 8 servings. One serving (⅛ pie) equals:

1 Fruit Exchange
½ Milk Exchange
1 Fat Exchange

PEACH FONDUE

Pictured on pages 270 and 271—

1 16-ounce can peach halves (juice pack)
1 teaspoon cornstarch
¼ teaspoon ground cinnamon
⅛ teaspoon ground allspice
½ teaspoon vanilla
1 cup cut-up cantaloupe *or* honeydew melon
1 small apple, cored and cut into wedges
¾ cup fresh strawberries, hulled
½ small banana, cut into chunks

In blender container combine *undrained* peaches, cornstarch, cinnamon, and allspice. Cover; blend till nearly smooth. Pour into a saucepan; cook and stir till thickened. Stir in vanilla. Transfer to fondue pot; keep warm over fondue burner. Serve with melon, apple, berries, and banana as dippers. Makes 5 servings. One serving (¼ cup peach sauce and 1/5 fruit) equals:

2 Fruit Exchanges

PUMPKIN-SPICE CAKE

2¼ cups sifted cake flour
1 tablespoon baking powder
1½ teaspoons ground cinnamon
¾ teaspoon ground cloves
¾ teaspoon ground nutmeg
¼ teaspoon salt
7 egg yolks
½ of a 16-ounce can (1 cup) pumpkin
½ cup cooking oil
Non-caloric liquid sweetener equal to ½ cup sugar
½ teaspoon finely shredded orange peel
7 egg whites
½ teaspoon cream of tartar
1 1¼-ounce envelope low-calorie dessert topping mix, whipped

Sift together flour, baking powder, cinnamon, cloves, nutmeg, and salt. Combine egg yolks, pumpkin, oil, sweetener, and orange peel; beat till smooth. Wash beaters. Beat egg whites and cream of tartar till stiff peaks form. Fold pumpkin mixture into egg whites. Sprinkle ¼ of the dry ingredients atop. Fold in dry ingredients, adding ¼ at a time. Turn into an ungreased 9-inch tube pan. Bake in a 325° oven 45 minutes. Invert cake in pan; cool. Remove cake from pan. Serve slices of the cake with whipped topping. Makes 16 servings. One serving (1/16 cake and 2 tablespoons whipped topping) equals:

½ Lean Meat Exchange
1 Bread Exchange
2 Fat Exchanges

ORANGE CHIFFON SOUFFLÉ

⅓ cup nonfat dry milk powder
2 tablespoons cornstarch
⅛ teaspoon salt
¾ cup water
1 teaspoon finely shredded orange peel
½ cup orange juice
Non-caloric liquid sweetener equal to 2 tablespoons sugar
5 egg yolks
5 egg whites

• • •

4 teaspoons cornstarch
Dash salt
Non-caloric liquid sweetener equal to 1 tablespoon sugar
1 medium orange
8 drops almond extract
Red and yellow food coloring (optional)

In saucepan combine nonfat dry milk, 2 tablespoons cornstarch, and ⅛ teaspoon salt. Gradually stir in the water. Cook and stir till mixture is thickened and bubbly. Remove from heat; stir in orange peel, orange juice, and non-caloric sweetener equal to 2 tablespoons sugar.

Beat egg yolks till thick and lemon-colored. Slowly add thickened orange mixture to egg yolks, stirring constantly. Wash beaters thoroughly. Beat egg whites till stiff peaks form. Carefully fold egg yolk mixture into beaten egg whites. Gently pour mixture into an ungreased 2-quart soufflé dish with a foil collar. Bake in a 325° oven 65 to 70 minutes or till knife inserted off-center comes out clean.

Meanwhile, for sauce, in small saucepan combine 4 teaspoons cornstarch, dash salt, and the remaining sweetener. Peel and section orange over bowl to catch juice; cut up orange sections. Add enough water to reserved juice to equal 1 cup. Blend orange juice mixture into cornstarch mixture. Cook and stir till mixture is thickened and bubbly. Remove from heat; stir in orange sections and almond extract. If desired, tint orange sauce with food coloring. To serve, spoon sauce over individual servings of warm soufflé. Makes 8 servings. One serving (⅛ soufflé and about 2 tablespoons sauce) equals:

1 Lean Meat Exchange
1 Fruit Exchange

FRESH FRUIT MEDLEY

3 ounces Neufchâtel cheese, softened
⅔ cup strawberry yogurt
2¼ cups fresh *or* frozen whole unsweetened strawberries, thawed
2 small oranges, sectioned
2 small bananas, bias sliced

In small mixer bowl beat cheese till fluffy. Add *half* of the yogurt; beat till smooth. Stir in remaining yogurt. Cover; chill. Halve strawberries; combine with oranges and bananas. Chill. To serve, spoon *½ cup* of the fruit into each of 8 compotes; spoon yogurt mixture atop. Makes 8 servings. One serving (½ cup fruit and 2 tablespoons yogurt mixture) equals:

½ Lean Meat Exchange
1½ Fruit Exchanges

CRAN-CHERRY CREPES

1½ cups frozen pitted tart red cherries
1 egg
⅔ cup skim milk
½ cup all-purpose flour
2 teaspoons butter *or* margarine, melted
½ cup dairy sour cream
⅛ teaspoon ground cinnamon

• • •

2 teaspoons cornstarch
Non-caloric liquid sweetener equal to 2 tablespoons sugar
¾ teaspoon finely shredded orange peel
1 cup low-calorie cranberry juice cocktail

Thaw frozen cherries. Combine egg, skim milk, flour, and butter or margarine; beat till smooth. Lightly grease a 6-inch crepe pan; heat. Add 2 tablespoons batter; lift pan and tilt till batter covers bottom. Brown crepe on one side. Turn onto waxed paper. Repeat with remaining batter. Combine sour cream and ground cinnamon; spread unbrowned side of each crepe with *1 tablespoon* of mixture. Roll up; place in a 13x9x2-inch baking dish.

Combine cornstarch, sweetener, and orange peel. Stir in cranberry juice cocktail. Add cherries. Cook and stir till thickened and bubbly; pour over crepes. Bake in a 375° oven 15 minutes. Makes 8 servings. One serving (1 crepe and 3 tablespoons sauce) equals:

½ Bread Exchange
1 Fruit Exchange
1 Fat Exchange

RIBBON MOCHA PARFAITS

Pictured on page 327—

1 4-serving-size envelope *regular* low-calorie chocolate pudding mix
2 teaspoons instant coffee crystals
1¾ cups skim milk
2 stiff-beaten egg whites
1 1¼-ounce envelope low-calorie dessert topping mix

Combine pudding mix and coffee crystals; slowly stir in skim milk. Cook and stir till thickened and bubbly. Remove from heat. Cover surface of pudding with waxed paper and cool to room temperature. Fold in egg whites. Prepare topping mix according to package directions. Fold ½ *cup* of the topping into pudding. Alternately spoon pudding and remaining topping into 6 parfait glasses. Chill. If desired, top with mint leaves. Makes 6 servings. One serving (1 parfait) equals:

½ Milk Exchange
1 Fat Exchange

BANANA FREEZE

Pictured on page 291—

1 4-serving-size envelope *regular* low-calorie vanilla pudding mix
¼ teaspoon almond extract
2 small fully ripe bananas, mashed
2 stiff-beaten egg whites
5 maraschino cherries, halved

Prepare pudding mix according to package directions. Stir in extract. Cover surface of pudding with waxed paper; cool to room temperature. Fold in bananas and egg whites. Spoon into 10 paper bake cups in muffin pans. Freeze till firm. Let stand at room temperature 30 minutes before serving. To serve, trim with maraschino cherries. Serves 10. One serving (⅓ cup) equals:

½ Bread Exchange
½ Fruit Exchange

LAYERED PEACH DESSERT

1 4-serving envelope low-calorie lemon- *or* raspberry-flavored gelatin
¾ cup boiling water
¾ cup cold water
1 16-ounce can peach slices (juice pack), drained and cut up
¼ cup chilled evaporated skimmed milk
Few drops almond extract

Dissolve gelatin in boiling water. Stir in cold water. Add *1 cup* of the gelatin mixture to peaches; chill till partially set. Chill remaining gelatin till partially set (consistency of unbeaten egg whites). Add evaporated skimmed milk and almond extract to partially set gelatin *without* peaches. Beat till fluffy. In 6 parfait glasses layer the two gelatin mixtures, ending with whipped gelatin. Chill thoroughly before serving. Makes 6 servings. One serving (1 parfait) equals:

1 Fruit Exchange

TAPIOCA PUDDING PARFAIT

This dessert is pictured on page 287 and included in a menu on page 297—

2 cups skim milk
2 tablespoons quick-cooking tapioca
Non-caloric liquid sweetener equal to ¼ cup sugar
¼ teaspoon salt
2 slightly beaten egg yolks
½ teaspoon vanilla
• • •
2 egg whites
6 cups fresh *or* frozen whole unsweetened strawberries, thawed

In a saucepan combine skim milk, quick-cooking tapioca, sweetener, and salt. Let stand 5 minutes. Add egg yolks. Cook and stir till bubbly. Remove from heat (mixture will be thin); stir in vanilla. In small mixer bowl beat egg whites till soft peaks form. Gradually fold in the hot mixture.

Halve strawberries; reserve a few strawberries for garnish. Alternate layers of tapioca pudding with halved strawberries in 8 parfait glasses, ending with the tapioca mixture. Garnish tops of parfaits with reserved strawberries. Chill. Makes 8 servings. One serving (1 parfait) equals:

1 Fruit Exchange
½ Milk Exchange

PEACH-BERRY SAUCE

Pictured on page 299—

- **1 16-ounce can peach slices (juice pack)**
- **2 tablespoons water**
- **2 teaspoons cornstarch**
- **1 tablespoon peach brandy**
- **¾ cup fresh *or* frozen whole unsweetened strawberries, thawed and halved**
- **¼ teaspoon ground cinnamon**
- **⅛ teaspoon ground allspice**
- **Molded Crème de Cinnamon (see recipe, below), waffles, *or* pancakes (optional)**

Drain peaches; reserve juice. Blend water into cornstarch. Blend in reserved juice and peach brandy. Cook and stir till thickened and bubbly; stir in the peaches, strawberries, cinnamon, and allspice. Heat through. If desired, serve atop Molded Crème de Cinnamon, waffles, or pancakes. Makes 8 servings. One serving of sauce (about ⅓ cup) without molded Crème de Cinnamon, waffles or pancakes equals:

1 Fruit Exchange

MOLDED CRÈME DE CINNAMON

- **3 cups skim milk**
- **Non-caloric liquid sweetener equal to ¾ cup sugar**
- **9 inches stick cinnamon, broken**
- **2 envelopes unflavored gelatin**
- **1 cup dairy sour cream**
- **1 teaspoon vanilla**
- **Peach-Berry Sauce (see recipe, above) (optional)**

Combine skim milk, sweetener, and stick cinnamon. Cook over low heat 10 to 15 minutes, stirring occasionally. Remove cinnamon. Soften gelatin in ¼ cup *cold water.* Add to hot milk mixture; stir to dissolve. Chill till partially set (consistency of unbeaten egg whites). Combine sour cream and vanilla. Fold into gelatin mixture. Pour into a 4-cup mold or 8 individual molds. Chill till firm. If desired, serve with Peach-Berry Sauce. Makes 8 servings. One serving (½ cup) without sauce equals:

½ Milk Exchange
1 Fat Exchange

RUBY FRUIT COMPOTE

Pictured on page 327—

- **1 16-ounce package frozen pitted tart red cherries**
- **1 tablespoon cornstarch**
- **Non-caloric liquid sweetener equal to ½ cup sugar**
- **Dash salt**
- **1½ cups cold water**
- **1 tablespoon lemon juice**
- **4 drops red food coloring (optional)**
- **2 cups fresh *or* frozen whole unsweetened strawberries, thawed**

Thaw frozen cherries. Combine cornstarch, sweetener, and salt. Blend the cold water into cornstarch mixture. Cook and stir till thickened and bubbly. Add lemon juice and food coloring, if desired. Halve large strawberries. Stir strawberries and cherries into cornstarch mixture. Chill. To serve, spoon ½ *cup* of the fruit into each of 9 compotes. If desired, top with lemon peel twist. Makes 9 servings. One serving (½ cup fruit) equals:

1 Fruit Exchange

PLUM WHIP

- **1 envelope unflavored gelatin**
- **¼ cup cold water**
- **1 16-ounce can dietetic-pack red plums (artificially sweetened)**
- **1 tablespoon lemon juice**
- **6 to 8 drops red food coloring (optional)**
- **2 egg whites**
- **Dash salt**
- **1 1¼-ounce envelope low-calorie dessert topping mix**

Soften gelatin in cold water. Sieve *undrained* plums into saucepan; bring to boil. Stir in softened gelatin and lemon juice. Add food coloring, if desired. Stir till dissolved. Chill till partially set (consistency of unbeaten egg whites). In large mixer bowl beat egg whites with salt till soft peaks form; gradually add plum mixture and beat till fluffy. Prepare topping mix according to package directions; fold *half* into plum mixture. Chill till partially set. Mound into individual serving dishes; chill. Use remaining topping as garnish. Serves 6. One serving (about ½ cup) equals:

1 Fruit Exchange
1 Fat Exchange

FAMILY-STYLE REDUCING

No dieter likes being sentenced to nibble on carrots and celery while the rest of the family feasts on heartier fare. To solve this problem, we've concocted a series of recipes to satisfy the often-deprived dieter. Our family-style reducing plan works by a simple system of substitutions and omissions in the kitchen. The dieter will hardly notice the difference. The diet dinner and dessert look every bit as appetizing as the meal for the rest of the family. And because the diet portions taste so good, the satisfied dieter will find that it's much easier to stick to the reducing system.

To carry out this scheme, cooking habits need only minor changes. Remove the dieter's portion from the family's portion before adding calorie-laden ingredients. Serve butter, margarine, mayonnaise, and other high-calorie extras from separate containers at the table. Dieters can abstain, or if they prefer they can add their own low-calorie substitutes. Both the dieter and the rest of the family will find all these recipes equally satisfying.

ROUND-STEAK STROGANOFF

The dieter's version cuts down on calories by eliminating the sour cream.

1 pound boneless beef round steak, cut ¾ inch thick and trimmed of fat
1 tablespoon cornstarch
½ teaspoon salt
1¼ cups water
1 tablespoon tomato paste
1½ teaspoons instant beef bouillon granules

• • •

2 tablespoons diet margarine
1 2½-ounce can sliced mushrooms, drained
½ cup shredded carrot
½ cup chopped onion
1 clove garlic, minced
1 tablespoon cornstarch
2 tablespoons dry red wine
½ cup dairy sour cream
2¾ cups hot cooked noodles

Partially freeze the beef round steak; slice thinly into bite-size strips. Combine 1 tablespoon cornstarch and the salt. Coat the beef strips with the cornstarch mixture; set aside. In small bowl combine water, tomato paste, and instant beef bouillon granules; set aside.

In skillet brown meat in diet margarine. Push the meat to one side of skillet; add the drained mushrooms, shredded carrot, chopped onion, and minced garlic. Cook 2 to 3 minutes or till tender. Blend in the remaining 1 tablespoon cornstarch. Add the tomato paste mixture. Cook and stir till mixture is thickened and bubbly. Stir in the dry red wine.

Reserve ¾ *cup* of the beef-vegetable mixture for the dieter; keep warm. Stir sour cream into the remaining beef-vegetable mixture; heat through (*do not boil*). Reserve

½ *cup* of the hot, cooked noodles for dieter. Serve the remaining noodles with sour cream-beef mixture. Makes 3 regular servings and 1 diet serving. One diet serving (¾ cup beef-vegetable mixture and ½ cup noodles) equals:

3 Lean Meat Exchanges
1 Bread Exchange
1 Vegetable Exchange
½ Fat Exchange

CRANBERRY-ORANGE CHICKEN

The dieter's chicken, minus the skin, is served without browning—

- **1 3-pound broiler-fryer chicken, cut up**
- **1 10½-ounce can condensed beef broth**
- **¾ cup low-calorie cranberry juice cocktail**
- **2 tablespoons butter *or* margarine**
- **2 medium oranges, thinly sliced**
- **1 tablespoon cornstarch**
- **1 tablespoon cold water**

Combine chicken neck, giblets, and condensed beef broth. Simmer, covered, 1 hour; strain. Add cranberry juice cocktail to broth; boil till reduced to 1 cup. Skin and halve chicken breast lengthwise; place in small baking dish. Sprinkle with *salt;* cover. Brown remaining chicken in butter or margarine; place in a 12x7½x2-inch baking dish. Sprinkle with *salt.* Bake chicken, covered, in a 350° oven 40 minutes. Top breast with ¼ of the orange slices. Top remaining chicken with remaining orange slices. Bake, uncovered, 10 minutes more. Blend cornstarch into the 1 tablespoon cold water; stir into broth mixture. Cook and stir till thickened. Top breast with ¼ *cup* of the sauce. Pass remaining sauce. Makes 3 regular servings and 1 diet serving. One diet serving (1 breast and ¼ cup sauce) equals:

3½ Lean Meat Exchanges
1 Fruit Exchange

TROPICAL FRUIT CUP

The shredded coconut and brown sugar are omitted for the dieter—

- **1 20-ounce can pineapple chunks (juice pack)**
- **2 medium oranges, peeled and sliced**
- **1½ cups seedless green grapes**
- **½ cup shredded coconut**
- **6 ounces Neufchâtel cheese, softened**
- **2 tablespoons brown sugar**

Drain pineapple, reserving ⅓ cup of the juice. Halve orange slices. Combine fruits; reserve ½ *cup* for dieter. Add coconut to remainder. Chill fruit. Combine cheese and reserved pineapple juice. Spoon *1 tablespoon* of the cheese mixture atop dieter's portion. Stir brown sugar into the remaining cheese mixture; spoon atop regular servings of the fruit-coconut mixture. Makes 4 regular servings and 1 diet serving. One diet serving (1 fruit cup) equals:

½ Lean Meat Exchange
1½ Fruit Exchanges
¼ Fat Exchange

READ THE LABEL

Is your brand of process cheese or salad dressing really low-calorie? Don't stop at the words "diet" or "low-calorie" on the label—read on. A product that claims special nutritional qualities must prove it on the label. Among other things, it must specify exact amounts of protein, carbohydrate, fat, and calories provided by one serving.

Take time to read labels. When a recipe or a Food Exchange specifies a calorie or fat content for a food item, use only brands that measure up. Otherwise you'll be adding unnecessary and unwanted calories to your diet.

SPINACH-TOPPED HALIBUT

This recipe includes just enough rich cheese sauce to make the dieter's entrée special—

1½ pounds fresh *or* frozen halibut steaks
4 cups water
⅓ cup lemon juice
1 small onion, sliced and separated into rings
¼ cup chopped celery
¼ teaspoon salt
⅛ teaspoon freshly ground pepper
• • •
1 10-ounce package frozen chopped spinach
¼ teaspoon ground nutmeg
1 1¼-ounce envelope cheese sauce mix
1 cup skim milk
Lemon wedges

Thaw fish, if frozen. In a 12-inch skillet combine water, lemon juice, onion, celery, salt, and pepper. Bring to boil; simmer 5 minutes. Add halibut; simmer, covered, 5 to 10 minutes or till fish flakes easily when tested with a fork. Carefully remove fish to a 13x9x2-inch baking pan.

Meanwhile, cook spinach according to package directions, drain and stir in nutmeg. Reserve ¼ *cup* of the spinach mixture for dieter. Prepare cheese sauce mix according to package directions, *except* use the skim milk instead of whole milk. Spoon *1 tablespoon* of the cheese sauce into dieter's spinach mixture; spread atop *1* of the halibut steaks. Combine remaining cheese sauce and spinach; spread stop remaining steaks for regular servings.

Broil all halibut portions 4 to 5 inches from heat 2 to 3 minutes. Serve all halibut portions with lemon wedges. Makes 3 regular servings and 1 diet serving. One diet serving (1 halibut steak and ¼ cup spinach mixture) equals:

●●●● 4 Lean Meat Exchanges
● 1 Vegetable Exchange
◖ ½ Fat Exchange

Shrimp Mélange (family's portion, top right; dieter's portion, bottom left)

SHRIMP MÉLANGE

The dieter swaps wine sauce for the rich cheese sauce and sidesteps the crumb topping—

1 pound fresh *or* frozen shelled shrimp
1 9-ounce package frozen artichoke hearts
5 teaspoons cornstarch
½ teaspoon salt
½ teaspoon paprika
Dash pepper
1⅔ cups skim milk
¼ cup dry white wine
¾ cup shredded Swiss cheese (3 ounces)
• • •
2¼ cups cooked rice
⅛ teaspoon dried basil, crushed
⅛ teaspoon dried oregano, crushed
Paprika
1 tablespoon butter *or* margarine, melted
3 tablespoons fine dry bread crumbs

Thaw shrimp, if frozen. Prepare artichoke hearts according to package directions; set aside. In medium saucepan combine cornstarch, salt, the ½ teaspoon paprika, and the pepper. Gradually stir in skim milk. Cook and stir till mixture is thickened and bubbly. Stir in dry white wine; heat through. Reserve ½ *cup* of the sauce for dieter. Stir Swiss cheese into remaining sauce; cook and stir till cheese melts. Set aside. Combine rice, basil, and oregano. Place ¼ *cup* of the rice mixture in the bottom of a 10-ounce casserole for dieter. Place remaining rice in a 1-quart casserole.

Drop shrimp in 3 cups boiling, lightly salted *water;* reduce heat and simmer gently 1 to 3 minutes or till shrimp turn pink. Drain the shrimp. Combine shrimp and cooked artichokes. Top dieter's rice mixture with ¾ *cup* shrimp-artichoke mixture and the ½ cup reserved sauce. Top large casserole with remaining shrimp-artichoke mixture and cheese sauce. Sprinkle both dishes with additional paprika.

Combine butter or margarine with bread crumbs; sprinkle bread crumbs atop large casserole. Bake large casserole in a 350° oven 10 minutes, then place small casserole in oven. Bake both casseroles 20 to 25 minutes more. Makes 4 regular servings and 1 diet serving. One diet serving (1 individual casserole) equals:

●●● 3 Lean Meat Exchanges
◖ ½ Bread Exchange
● 1 Vegetable Exchange
◖ ½ Milk Exchange

SACK LUNCHES

Lunch sometimes must be portable, stowed in a brown bag, a lunch box, or even an attaché case. Don't let this limit your lunchtime creativity or stymie your slimming efforts. A brown-bag lunch can be appetizing and make a contribution to your weight-loss program.

Mainstay Sandwiches

A hearty sandwich is the traditional foundation of a brown-bag lunch. Weight watchers, too, can lunch on sandwiches.

Sandwich construction begins with bread. Choices include white, whole wheat, Italian, French, rye, pumpernickel, and raisin. English muffins, hamburger buns, and bagels are also suitable.

If you're following the 1,000- or 1,200-calorie Daily Meal Plans, you may wish to transfer one Bread Exchange from breakfast or dinner to lunch to allow two slices of bread for a sandwich. If not, try stretching the lunchtime allotment of one Bread Exchange in one of two ways. You can use very thin bread (white or whole wheat). Two slices count as one Bread Exchange. Or, you can pack sandwich ingredients separately and assemble an open-faced sandwich at lunchtime.

Spread your choice of bread with mustard, diet margarine, or low-calorie salad dressing substitute. Next, layer meat slices atop. Meats listed in the Lean Meat Exchanges are the best choices because they conserve fat for other uses. Cooked turkey, chicken, ham (center-cut, not boiled), and lean roast beef are possible selections that cost you no extra fat. Boiled ham and cooked pork are Medium-Fat Meat Exchanges; most common cold cuts are High-Fat Meat Exchanges.

Team your meat selection with a slice of cheese. One ounce of most cheddar types counts as one High-Fat Meat Exchange. Trim Fat Exchanges by selecting a low-calorie process cheese product. A one-ounce serving equals one Lean Meat Exchange. For a change of pace, try scrambled eggs or egg salad as sandwich fillers. Don't forget about canned foods such as tuna, chicken, salmon, ham, and shrimp for sandwich makings.

Lettuce adds crunch and freshness to a sandwich without adding extra Exchanges. Bean sprouts and slices of cucumber, green pepper, or onion are crisp sandwich ingredients, and they cost only one Vegetable Exchange per one-half cup.

Sandwiches normally need refrigeration if stored for long periods of time. If sandwiches must stand at room temperature, freeze them overnight. Remove from the freezer just before leaving for work, and they will thaw by lunchtime.

Sandwich Substitutes

Salads provide a tasty alternative to sandwiches. If refrigerator space is available, use it to store perishables. Otherwise use a wide-mouth vacuum bottle. Take along chicken, tuna, egg, or ham salad, and pack lettuce and tomato separately. Assemble the salad quickly at lunchtime. For variety, pack a chef's salad, cottage cheese, or your favorite yogurt. You'll appreciate the versatility a vacuum bottle (or refrigerator) allows.

You also can use a vacuum bottle to keep soup, chowder, chili, or stew piping hot. Pack a thick slice of crusty French bread, too.

Sandwich Supplements

Round out the sack lunch with suitable supplements. Fruit is a logical choice. Apples, oranges, bananas, plums, and pears all pack well. Or you can carry chilled canned fruit in a wide-mouth vacuum bottle. Freeze cans of fruit juice the night before and remove from the freezer in the morning. By lunchtime the juice will be thawed but still frosty. Vegetable relishes add a crisp accent. Dill pickles add tang and they're free.

DAILY MEAL PLANS

Planning diet menus is almost easy—if you use the Food Exchanges to guide you. Select a meal plan giving a daily calorie deficit that lets you lose no more than two pounds a week.

DAILY MEAL PLAN	NUMBER OF EXCHANGES		
BREAKFAST	1,000 CAL. PER DAY	1,200 CAL. PER DAY	1,500 CAL. PER DAY
Lean Meat Exchange	1	1	2
Bread Exchange	1	1	2
Fruit Exchange	1	1	1
Milk Exchange	½	½	½
Fat Exchange	1	2	2
Free Exchange	as desired	as desired	as desired
LUNCH			
Lean Meat Exchange	2	2	2
Bread Exchange	1	1	2
Vegetable Exchange	1	2	2
Fruit Exchange	1	1	1
Milk Exchange	1	1	1
Fat Exchange	1	1	2
Free Exchange	as desired	as desired	as desired
DINNER			
Lean Meat Exchange	2	4	4
Bread Exchange	1	1	1
Vegetable Exchange	1	2	2
Fruit Exchange	1	1	1
Milk Exchange	½	½	½
Fat Exchange	2	2	3
Free Exchange	as desired	as desired	as desired

CLIP-OUT

FOOD EXCHANGE LISTS

Remove this clip-out section and keep it handy as a quick reference of the seven Food Exchange Lists plus the Daily Meal Plans. Also check the sample restaurant menu and suggested selections.

FOOD EXCHANGE LISTS

MEAT

LEAN MEAT EXCHANGE

Each serving in the list below is based on cooked meat with fat trimmed. One Exchange provides seven grams protein, three grams fat, and 55 calories. Most Exchanges, except shellfish, are fairly low in saturated fat and cholesterol.

BEEF: 1 ounce	chuck dried beef flank steak plate short ribs plate skirt steak plate spareribs	round, bottom or top rump, all cuts sirloin tenderloin tripe
LAMB: 1 ounce	leg loin rib	shank shoulder sirloin
PORK: 1 ounce	fully cooked ham (center slices)	leg (whole rump, center shank)
VEAL: 1 ounce	cutlets leg loin	rib shank shoulder
FISH: fresh, canned, or frozen	bass, 1 oz. carp, 1 oz. catfish, 1 oz. clams, 1 oz. cod, 1 oz. crab, ¼ cup eel, 1 oz. flounder, 1 oz. haddock, 1 oz. hake, 1 oz. halibut, 1 oz. herring, 1 oz. lobster, ¼ cup mackerel, ¼ cup mullet, 1 oz. oysters, 1 oz.	perch, 1 oz. pike, 1 oz. pollock, 1 oz. pompano, 1 oz. red snapper, 1 oz. rockfish, 1 oz. salmon, 1 oz. canned, ¼ cup sardines, 3 scallops, 1 oz. shrimp, 1 oz. smelt, 1 oz. sole, 1 oz. swordfish, 1 oz. tuna, ¼ cup whitefish, 1 oz.
POULTRY: 1 ounce without skin	chicken Cornish game hen Guinea hen	pheasant turkey
CHEESES: 1 ounce	containing less than 5% milkfat	
COTTAGE CHEESE: ¼ cup	dry and 2% milkfat	
DRIED BEANS AND PEAS: ½ cup cooked	(omit 1 Bread Exchange)	

RESTAURANT MENUS

DINNER SELECTIONS

Using the Food Exchange formula will make eating dinner out fun. Just select foods within limits of your Daily Meal Plan. Look at the sample restaurant menu below. Using the Food Exchange framework, we've adjusted many of the menu offerings to meet your reducing requirements. Although you can't eat everything offered on the menu, you have plenty of choices. The possible menu selections are marked with an asterisk (*).

Here are some suggestions when selecting foods from this sample menu:

- For appetizers, order the fruit cup but leave the sherbet. Count the prosciutto as a High-Fat Meat. Order oysters or shrimp and use lemon instead of the cocktail sauce.
- In the "Chef's Specialties" section, remember that main-dish servings are typically larger than Exchange allotments. Take leftovers home. Order lobster without lemon butter; add fresh lemon instead. Order the "catch" if it's baked or broiled. Order lamb, but leave the jelly.
- For vegetables, request the asparagus or peas without butter or sauces—add your own. Ditto for the baked potato. Estimate serving sizes carefully.
- In the salad section, go easy on the dressing. Order spinach salad without bacon dressing; try lemon juice instead.
- For desserts, ask whether the peaches are prepared with sugar. Ask for strawberries and cream separately; add cream sparingly.
- For a beverage, coffee and tea are free. Milk is allowed, but avoid soft drinks unless low-cal brands are available.

DINNER

APPETIZERS	Fruit cup with sherbet* Prosciutto with melon* French-fried mushrooms	Gulf shrimp cocktail* Blue point oysters on the half shell*
CHEF'S SPECIALTIES	New York strip steak* Roast prime rib of beef* Beef en brochette* Rock Cornish hen with wild rice stuffing* Creamy chicken crepes	Broiled lobster tail with lemon butter* Batter-fried shrimp Crab-stuffed flounder Catch of the day* Lamb with mint jelly*
VEGETABLES	Steamed fresh asparagus* Fresh garden peas*	Baked Idaho potato* Hash brown potatoes Rice pilaf*
SALADS	Bouquet of fresh fruit* Green garden salad*	Fresh spinach salad with bacon dressing*
DESSERTS	French apple tart Spicy baked peaches* Cheesecake	Chocolate mousse Strawberries and cream*
BEVERAGES	Coffee* Tea*	Milk* Soft drinks

FAT

Each serving of the fats listed below counts as one Fat Exchange. See the **Note** below for further explanation about fats and an explanation of the asterisk (*). One Fat Exchange provides five grams of fat and 45 calories.

FREE

Listed below are flavor bonuses with Free Exchange ratings. Also included on this list are raw vegetables that can be eaten in any amount.

avocado* (4-inch diameter), ⅛	cream, whipping, 1 Tbsp.	margarine, regular, 1 tsp.
bacon, crisp cooked, 1 slice	cream cheese, 1 Tbsp.	margarine,*** soft (tub or stick), 1 tsp.
bacon fat, 1 tsp.	French salad dressing,*** 1 Tbsp.	mayonnaise,*** 1 tsp.
butter, 1 tsp.	Italian salad dressing,*** 1 Tbsp.	olives,* 5 small
cream, light, 2 Tbsp.	lard, 1 tsp.	salad dressing,*** mayonnaise-type, 2 tsp.
cream, sour, 2 Tbsp.	margarine,** diet, 1 Tbsp.	salt pork, ¾-inch cube
NUTS	almonds,* 10 whole	pecans,* 2 large whole
	peanuts,* Spanish, 20 whole	walnuts,** 6 small
	peanuts,* Virginia, 10 whole	other,* 6 small
OIL: 1 tsp.	corn**	safflower**
	cottonseed**	soy**
	olive*	sunflower**
	peanut*	
salt	tea	unsweetened pickles
pepper	coffee	chicory
herbs	nonfat bouillon	Chinese cabbage
spices	non-caloric sweetener	endive
lemon	low-calorie carbonated beverages	escarole
lime		lettuce
horseradish	low-calorie flavored gelatin	parsley
vinegar		radishes
mustard	unflavored gelatin	watercress

Note: Fats listed above are designated as saturated, monounsaturated, or polyunsaturated. Saturated fats are found primarily in animal food products and are thought to raise the level of cholesterol in the blood, a factor possibly associated with heart disease. Heart specialists recommend substituting unsaturated fats for the saturated fats in the diet whenever possible. Vegetable oils such as corn, cottonseed, safflower, soybean, and sunflower are low in saturated fats.

The fats listed above are saturated unless marked with an asterisk (*). One asterisk (*) indicates a fat content that is primarily monounsaturated. Two asterisks (**) indicate a fat content that is primarily polyunsaturated; three asterisks (***) indicate a polyunsaturated fat content only if the product is made with corn, cottonseed, safflower, soy, or sunflower oil.

Food exchange Lists on pages 282-286 in *The Dieter's Cook Book* are based on material in the booklet *Exchange Lists for Meal Planning* prepared by committees of the American Diabetes Association, Inc. and the American Dietetic Association.

MEDIUM-FAT MEAT EXCHANGE

Each serving is based on cooked meat and counts as one Medium-Fat Meat Exchange. Because of their higher fat content, Medium-Fat Meat Exchanges count as one Lean Meat Exchange and one-half Fat Exchange. One Medium-Fat Meat Exchange supplies seven grams protein, five and one-half grams fat, and 75 calories. Only peanut butter is low in saturated fat and cholesterol.

HIGH-FAT MEAT EXCHANGE

Each serving is based on cooked meat and counts as one High-Fat Meat Exchange. Because of their high fat content, foods in this Exchange List count as one Lean Meat Exchange and one Fat Exchange. One High-Fat Meat Exchange supplies seven grams of protein, eight grams of fat, and 100 calories.

BEEF: 1 ounce	corned beef (canned)	ground round (commercial)
	ground beef (15% fat)	rib eye steak
PORK: 1 ounce	boiled ham	shoulder arm picnic
	Canadian-style bacon	shoulder blade Boston roast
	loin (all cuts tenderloin)	
VARIETY MEATS – beef, veal pork, or lamb: 1 ounce (high in cholesterol)	heart	liver
	kidney	sweetbreads
CHEESE:	farmer cheese, 1 ounce	Parmesan, 3 Tbsp.
	mozzarella, 1 ounce	ricotta, 1 ounce
	Neufchâtel, 1 ounce	
COTTAGE CHEESE:	creamed, ¼ cup	
EGG: 1 (high in cholesterol)		
PEANUT BUTTER: 2 Tbsp.	(omit a total of 2½ Fat Exchanges)	
BEEF: 1 ounce	brisket	hamburger (commercial)
	corned beef brisket	rib roast
	ground beef (more than 20% fat)	rib steak
	ground chuck (commercial)	top loin steak
LAMB: 1 ounce	breast	
VEAL: 1 ounce	breast	
PORK: 1 ounce	cook-before-eating ham (country-style)	ground pork
	deviled ham	loin back ribs
		spareribs
POULTRY: 1 ounce	capon	goose
	duck (domestic)	
CHEESE: 1 ounce	cheddar types	
COLD CUTS:	4½ × ⅛-inch slice	
FRANKFURTER:	1 small	

BREAD

Each serving of the breads, cereals, crackers, dried beans, starchy vegetables, and prepared foods listed below counts as one Bread Exchange. All items except those listed as prepared foods are lowfat. Be sure to charge yourself for the extra Fat Exchanges contained in the prepared foods. One Bread Exchange provides two grams of protein, 15 grams of carbohydrate, and 70 calories.

BREAD:	bagel, small, ½ dried bread crumbs, 3 Tbsp. English muffin, small, ½ frankfurter bun, ½ French, 1 slice hamburger bun, ½ Italian, 1 slice	plain dinner roll, 1 pumpernickel, 1 slice raisin, 1 slice rye, 1 slice tortilla, 6 inch, 1 white, 1 slice whole wheat, 1 slice
CEREAL:	bran flakes, ½ cup cooked barley, ½ cup cooked cereal, ½ cup cooked grits, ½ cup cooked pasta, macaroni, or noodles, ½ cup cooked rice, ½ cup cornmeal (dry), 2 Tbsp.	flour, 2½ Tbsp. other ready-to-eat unsweetened cereal, ¾ cup popcorn (popped, no fat added), 3 cups puffed cereal (unfrosted), 1 cup wheat germ, ¼ cup
CRACKERS:	arrowroot, 3 graham, 2½ inch, 2 matzo, 6×4 inch, ½ oyster, 20	pretzels, 3⅛×⅛ inch, 25 rye wafers, 3½×2 inch, 3 saltines, 6 soda, 2½-inch square, 4
BEANS, PEAS, AND LENTILS:	beans, peas, lentils (dried, cooked), ½ cup (omit 1 Lean Meat Exchange)	baked beans, no pork (canned), ¼ cup
STARCHY VEGETABLES:	corn, ⅓ cup corn on cob, 1 small lima beans, ½ cup parsnips, ⅔ cup peas (canned or frozen), ½ cup	potato (mashed), ½ cup potato (white), 1 small pumpkin, ¾ cup winter squash, ½ cup yam or sweet potato, ¼ cup
PREPARED FOODS:	biscuit, 2-inch diameter, 1 (omit 1 Fat Exchange) corn bread, 2×2×1 inch, 1 (omit 1 Fat Exchange) corn muffin, 2 inch, 1 (omit 1 Fat Exchange) crackers, round butter type, 5 (omit 1 Fat Exchange) muffin, plain small, 1 (omit 1 Fat Exchange)	pancake, 5x½ inch, 1 (omit 1 Fat Exchange) potatoes, French-fried, 8 (omit 1 Fat Exchange) potato or corn chips, 15 (omit 2 Fat Exchanges) waffle, 5×½ inch, 1 (omit 1 Fat Exchange)

VEGETABLE

Each half-cup serving counts as one Exchange and provides two grams protein, five grams carbohydrate, and 25 calories. Vegetables are nonfat. Free vegetables are listed separately and in the Free List, also. The free vegetables may be eaten in any amounts.

FRUIT

The amount of each fruit listed (with no sugar added) counts as one Fruit Exchange. Fruits are nonfat. One Exchange contains 10 grams of carbohydrate and 40 calories.

MILK

Milk Exchanges are shown in the list below. Lowfat and whole milk products cost extra Fat Exchanges. One Milk Exchange equals eight grams of protein, 12 grams of carbohydrate, and 80 calories.

asparagus beans, green or yellow bean sprouts beets broccoli brussels sprouts cabbage carrots cauliflower	celery cucumbers eggplant mushrooms okra onions peppers rhubarb rutabaga	sauerkraut spinach and other greens summer squash tomatoes tomato juice turnips vegetable juice cocktail zucchini
FREE VEGETABLES: These raw vegetables may be eaten in any amounts	chicory Chinese cabbage endive escarole	lettuce parsley radishes watercress
apple, 1 small apple juice or cider, ⅓ cup applesauce (unsweetened), ½ cup apricots, fresh, 2 medium apricots, dried, 4 halves banana, ½ small berries: strawberries, ¾ cup other berries, ½ cup cherries, 10 large cranberries, as desired dates, 2	figs, fresh or dried, 1 grapefruit, ½ grapefruit juice, ½ cup grape juice, ¼ cup grapes, 12 mango, ½ small melon: cantaloupe, ¼ small honeydew, ⅛ medium watermelon, 1 cup nectarine, 1 small orange, 1 small	orange juice, ½ cup papaya, ¾ cup peach, 1 medium pear, 1 small persimmon, native, 1 medium pineapple, ½ cup pineapple juice, ⅓ cup plums, 2 medium prune juice, ¼ cup prunes, 2 medium raisins, 2 Tbsp. tangerine, 1 medium
NONFAT FORTIFIED MILK:	buttermilk, made from skim milk, 1 cup canned evaporated skim milk, ½ cup	nonfat dry milk powder, ⅓ cup skim or nonfat milk, 1 cup yogurt, made from skim milk (plain), 1 cup
LOWFAT FORTIFIED MILK:	1% fat milk, 1 cup (omit ½ Fat Exchange) 2% fat milk, 1 cup (omit 1 Fat Exchange)	yogurt, made from 2% milk, (plain), ¾ cup (omit 1 Fat Exchange)
WHOLE MILK:	buttermilk, made from whole milk, 1 cup (omit 2 Fat Exchanges) canned evaporated whole milk, ½ cup (omit 2 Fat Exchanges)	whole milk, 1 cup (omit 2 Fat Exchanges) yogurt, made from whole milk (plain), 1 cup (omit 2 Fat Exchanges)

HOW TO STAY SLIM

Once you've trimmed down to your ideal weight, you can maintain it. Food Exchanges make it easier, but staying slim requires a lifetime commitment. Remember that it's much easier to gain unwanted pounds than it is to lose them. Don't let extra pounds creep up on you. You've learned how to slim using the Food Exchange system to guide your eating habits. Now follow the four rules at left to help you stay that way.

Using Food Exchanges To Maintain Weight

As you approach your dietary goal and are shedding those last few unwanted pounds, think about your maintenance tactics. How are you going to stay slim?

Everything that you've learned about Food Exchanges, plus the good food habits you've acquired, apply to staying slim.

Food Exchanges provide a workable and reliable framework for maintaining your weight. Follow the 1,500-calorie Daily Meal Plan (page 288), then add your favorite Exchanges to raise your calorie consumption to maintenance levels. Calculate the number of calories necessary to maintain your desirable or ideal weight according to the directions found on page 30. Remember that there are individual differences of size and shape and variations in calorie needs, but for practical purposes, the figure of 15 calories per pound gives a yardstick of desirable calorie intake by men and women who aren't running marathons or playing basketball all day long.

For example, someone whose desirable weight is 100 pounds could follow the 1,500-calorie Daily Meal Plan exactly. The person whose desirable weight is 130 pounds must add enough Exchanges to the 1,500-calorie Daily Meal Plan to add 450 calories. You'll find the calorie values of the various Exchange groups listed on pages 282 to 286. When adding extra Food Exchanges to the Daily Meal Plan, you will keep the same balance of good nutrition by adding proportionate amounts of the seven Exchanges. It's often as simple as increasing the size of your serving. For example, you could eat a six-ounce sirloin steak instead of a four-ounce steak. This adds two extra ounces of lean meat or two Lean Meat Exchanges. That's 110 additional calories, about one-fourth the amount a 130-pound person needs to increase the 1,500-calorie diet to maintenance levels. You'll find that it's simple to add those maintenance calories. Capitalize on a variety of wholesome foods in your diet.

A reducing diet based on Food Exchanges will provide adequate nutrients for most people. A variety of foods will help ensure that your diet is nutritionally adequate.

Basic Rules To Help You Stay Slim

Follow these rules to stay slim:
1. Follow the 1,500-calorie Daily Meal Plan listed on page 288.
2. Add only those Exchanges needed to bring calories to a maintenance level.
3. Weigh once a week and cut back on calories if your weight creeps up a few pounds.
4. Exercise regularly.

GUIDE TO GOOD FITNESS

If you're not yet convinced that personal fitness is a major part of the "wellness" revolution, just throw open your doors and windows. Listen for the rhythmic slap-slap-slap of countless jogging shoes, and look at the sweaty (but happy) faces of your slim friends returning from the nearest community exercise class. But if the mere thought of exercising conjures up visions only of repetitive calisthenics, you're missing the benefits of tennis, swimming, bicycling, running, and cross-country skiing. Oh, sure, your long-unused muscles will ache at first, but after the first few days, those aches will be forgotten and replaced with a growing sense of pride and enthusiasm.

THE WHOLE-PERSON APPROACH TO WELLNESS

"Wellness" is the state of being in good health, according to the dictionary. That's the basic definition—but it doesn't suggest the many nuances of meaning the word wellness has acquired in recent years.

In fact, if you talk to health experts, or read what they have to say about wellness, you'll find almost as many different definitions as there are experts. What they all seem to agree on is this: Wellness is a way of living that maximizes those aspects of your life-style contributing to your physical, mental, and emotional well-being.

Wellness is more than just being healthy. Indeed, most people want more out of life than health—they want happiness. Life would be like walking on eggs if you tried to practice all the disease and accident prevention measures touted today.

You Are in Charge

The key ingredient in a wellness life-style is you. You—and you alone—have the ability to make most of the important changes that can elevate the quality of your life to a state of what one authority calls "high-level wellness."

The first, and often most difficult, step in achieving wellness is to make up your mind that you want to change the way you live for the better. After you've made that important personal commitment, you'll have lots of help achieving your goals: books, magazines, self-help groups, family, friends, and your own physician.

No one can afford to overlook the most fundamental measures: having immunizations, obtaining adequate rest, practicing good hygiene, developing sensitivity to the early signs of mental illness, avoiding excess alcohol consumption, practicing good safety habits, and not smoking.

Coping, Diet, and Exercise

Beyond these measures, you'll want to focus your efforts on three broader areas: coping with the many factors in your life that cause physical and mental stress; changing your diet to make sure you give your body the best possible chance to maintain a state of physical wellness; and exercising, which, besides being an essential ingredient in the physical wellness recipe, helps you cope with stresses in your life.

• *Learning to cope with stress* is a real challenge because stress is so pervasive in life, and it's hard to distinguish between normal and harmful stress. Yet a long list of disorders is thought to be directly or indirectly related to negative stress. Coping effectively with stress may help you avoid some of the more common pitfalls en route to wellness—smoking, overeating, drinking too much, and drug abuse.

• *How you eat and what you eat* are two of the most critical factors in achieving wellness. Nutrition experts have no "perfect" diet, but they do agree on some of the basics.

• *A regular exercise program,* besides improving your physical health, has psychological benefits. It can help you feel more fit and in control, minimize negative emotional stress, and alleviate depression.

Your Ultimate Goal

As you study our strategies for wellness, remember that the ultimate reward of a healthful life-style is more than just being free of disease, having a trim figure, or developing the ability to cope with the hassles of everyday living. The real reward is the knowledge that you're making the most of what you have, living your life to the best of your ability—and enjoying yourself in the process.

FACTS ABOUT STRESS AND COPING

The notion that all stress is bad is a major misconception. Stress is present when you gear up to present a really exciting proposal to your boss, play a winning game of tennis, laugh at a funny movie, or cry because you're happy.

Normally your body copes with stressful events by preparing for them, resolving them, and returning to equilibrium, or "normal" stress.

What's happening is this: Your body is preparing to fight or flee from a stressful situation in much the same way a prehistoric person fought or fled from attacking animals. Adrenalin and other hormones are pumped into the bloodstream, and the heart, muscles, brain, and lungs prepare to react to the stressful situation. If the challenge is resolved, your body resumes its state of equilibrium; if the challenge is unresolved, one stress builds on another.

What Causes Stress Today?

Scientists have attempted to rate the relative importance of various events in modern life in terms of negative stress. Among the major stress-producing events are death of a spouse, loss of a job, serious illness, trouble with your boss, and divorce.

Unfortunately, instead of being able to deal with just one or two isolated stressful events at a time, many of us lead lives filled with a never-ending series of unresolved conflicts. With each event, our bodies prepare—automatically and without conscious effort—to deal with the new stress.

But, because many of us have been taught to try to control or sublimate our emotions, we are often not able to resolve stressful situations physiologically or emotionally. No matter how much some people want to lash out at someone or something, they can't or won't because it's "nonproductive" to react openly. Thus, we're often denied opportunities to let the stress cycle complete its normal course.

Stress Indicators

Scientists have devised laboratory tests for measuring stress, including blood pressure readings, assessment of hormone levels in the bloodstream, and measurements of brain activity.

But you can recognize some stress symptoms, too. (Of course, these symptoms often are caused by conditions other than stress—it's always wise to check with your doctor.) Some of these symptoms are:

- An overall sense of depression or nervousness; the urge to cry or laugh without reason; the inability to sit still for any length of time; irrational behavior; anxiety without good cause; or being startled easily.
- A pounding or racing of your heart.
- Insomnia; grinding of teeth; profuse sweating; frequent urination; diarrhea; or an upset stomach.
- Headaches; back and neck pain.
- Loss of appetite or—depending on your own attitude about food—an increased appetite.

The Right Way To Cope

Most authorities agree that the first step in coping is to recognize that a certain degree of stress is a normal part of your life, and that you can't—and don't want to—eliminate it all.

Recognize your own stress limits. You're unique—what's stressful for you may or may not be stressful for others. Study the events and situations in your life that cause you excessive stress, change those you can, and find outlets for pent-up stress. You'll be better off accepting and coping effectively with stress than trying to eliminate it from your life.

Stress Relievers

To help cope with stress, try one or more of these techniques:

- *Exercise.* It really works. In fact, some psychiatrists today advise exercise therapy to treat cases of mild depression. Exercise rechannels the hormonal and emotional changes that occur because of mental stress into a "healthy" physical outlet.
- *Consciously relax.* Meditation, or even a hobby, may help divert your mind and provide a natural period of relaxation.
- *Practice biofeedback.* Such training may help you relax tense muscles and has been particularly successful in helping people manage migraine headaches.
- *Do something for someone else who needs your help.* You'll earn the gratitude of the beneficiary and, for a few minutes at least, be able to focus on something or someone other than yourself.
- *Talk about it.* The compassionate ear and strong shoulder of a good friend may help you "talk off" your stress. Specially trained psychological counselors, ministers, or close friends may all qualify as good listeners.
- *Seek medical help.* If negative stress seems to be beyond your control, a doctor may be able to help you clear up a physical condition that, in itself, is causing stress in your life and your body. Medications such as tranquilizers and antidepressants may be prescribed, too—but beware of drug dependency.

HOW TO KICK YOUR BAD HEALTH HABITS

Bad habits aren't something you are born with, they are learned. If you really want to take charge of your life and make it better, you have to swear off the bad habits and acquire some new, good ones.

Behavioral psychologists are researching many methods to help people make such changes and then stick to them. Here's one step-by-step approach to kicking your bad habits.

What's Going To Go?

First, decide which of your bad habits have to go. Do you smoke? Do you eat or drink too much? Are you spending too much time in an easy chair?

You have to make up your mind that things are going to change. It may be enough for you to just resolve to break a bad habit, or you may need to write a contract with yourself in which you promise that you will develop a plan to change. Perhaps enlisting a relative or friend will provide you with support during the transition period.

Decide on Your Tactics

One of the best things about the "wellness movement" is that making positive changes in your life-style no longer has to be a solitary and Spartan effort with no outside encouragement.

If you've already tried to quit smoking or to lose weight but failed, maybe it was because there was no one around to offer you support.

Today self-help groups abound. There are numerous clinics—free and at minimal cost—available to help you kick your bad habits. Check into one or more of the sensible private or community self-help groups around today that will help you shed your unneeded pounds. If giving up tobacco is your problem, stop-smoking clinics and other similar programs sponsored by hospitals, churches, the American Lung Association, and the American Cancer Society can help.

Exercise classes offered at the local Y, in fitness centers, or as part of an adult education curriculum may provide the necessary incentive for you to get moving again.

Start Slow

Resolve to make the changes slowly and methodically. If you're trying to cut down on eating, make your first steps small and manageable. Eat a little less each day, exercise a little more. Set realistic goals and, when you meet them, give yourself rewards for your good behavior.

It helps to remember that bad habits didn't occur overnight and eliminating them will take time, too.

Record Your Progress

Keep a written record of your progress to help manage the situations that make you backslide.

Carry note cards or a notebook with you every day. Keep your recorded observations in an appropriate place—by the scales or in the pocket where you ordinarily kept your cigarettes.

Evaluate Your Gains

Check at regular intervals to make sure the results are what you want—whether it's the number of pounds you're losing, or the number of cigarettes you're *not* smoking.

Anticipate Backsliding

Don't despair if you backslide a little bit—these are tough habits you're trying to break. Be prepared to renew your efforts any time you find yourself regressing.

Take heart in the fact that you've come this far: You won't have to put out as much effort to maintain change as you did at the beginning.

Reward Yourself

Do reward yourself for your efforts. If you made a contract with yourself to lose weight so you could wear a stylish new suit—buy it when you've reached your weight-loss goal. Little rewards along the way are important, too.

If one of the benefits of stopping smoking was to save money, compute how much you've saved at the end of a given cigarette-free period and spend it on something that gives you as much pleasure as the cigarettes used to.

FALLACIES ABOUT EXERCISE

There's (almost) no such thing as a good excuse for not exercising. Even if you have a physical condition that you think precludes an exercise program, chances are there's an exercise routine—or part of one—that would be good for you.

Nevertheless, excuses for not exercising abound, and often they're based on erroneous information. Here are some of the most common fallacies about exercise as well as the facts.

FALLACY: Exercise increases the appetite.

The truth, surprisingly, is that exercise just before mealtimes actually decreases the appetite—especially if you're overweight.

If you're among those who are overweight, exercise will use up calories stored in the body's excess fat, and your appetite isn't likely to be stimulated at all.

If you're not overweight, some increase in appetite may occur, but it will be offset by the number of calories burned up by exercise.

One study of overweight adults showed that obesity began with a decline, not an increase, in physical activity.

Once you've built up to a regular daily exercising schedule, you'll probably find that you can eat anything you want to, safe in the knowledge that your physical activity will compensate for any reasonable amount of extra calories consumed.

FALLACY: Exercise is time consuming.

Think of it this way: A week has 168 hours in it. Subtract the 40 hours you spend on the job, and 56 hours for sleeping and you have 72 hours left. Even if you exercised an hour a day, you would still have an average of more than nine hours a day to spend any way you choose.

Once into a routine, you'll be able to put a reverse twist on Parkinson's Law: Your time will expand to accommodate exercise. It's simply a matter of reordering priorities: watching the TV news while you're doing stretching exercises; taking a shorter lunch hour so you can have a brisk walk; jogging before you read the paper and eat dinner.

A good exercise program needn't be a daily affair. Many authorities think a three-times-a-week exercise routine is sufficient to keep you in shape.

FALLACY: To be beneficial, exercise must be exhausting.

Wrong again. It's true that you need to work up a good sweat and breathe hard if exercise is to do you any good. But you don't have to exercise until you're exhausted. A good exercise program is one that gives your heart and lungs a workout—sustained for 15 to 20 minutes—but doesn't tax them to capacity.

FALLACY: Exercising once in a while is better than not exercising at all.

The experts say if you don't exercise regularly, you're just as well off not exercising at all. Sporadic bursts of energy subject your body to undue strain, and any headway you might make will dissipate during the periods of inactivity.

Set an exercise schedule you can live with and adhere to—every other day, three times a week; or more often if you can do so comfortably.

FALLACY: Exercise automatically extends your life.

So many factors determine longevity (heredity is a very important one) that it's impossible to guarantee a longer life simply because you exercise.

But most experts do think that a regular exercise program can help extend life, especially if you're combining exercise for your heart and lungs with changes in your life-style that eliminate negative health influences—such as smoking, excessive stress, lack of sleep, and poor nutrition. Although many people who exercise think they'll live longer and be healthier, the real reason they continue to exercise is because the quality of their life is better.

FALLACY: Exercise is risky for persons older than 40 and isn't needed at all for the elderly.

Precluding accidents, exercise is seldom risky for a healthy person who is accustomed to it, regardless of age. But especially if you're approaching middle age, are obviously out of shape, or haven't exercised before, you should observe these precautions:

- Get a medical checkup before plunging into an exercise program.

• Take a few minutes to warm up and cool down before and after you perform vigorous exercise.

• Resist the temptation to keep up with younger people, or those who are in better condition than you. Pace yourself according to your age and condition.

• Pay attention to these warning signals: nausea, extreme shortness of breath, pounding in the head, or pain in the chest—all signals to stop your activity and check with your doctor.

Older adults need exercise as much as, perhaps more than, younger ones who are less apt to be troubled with stiffening joints and poor circulation. Of course, no one expects senior citizens to be running marathons or participating in all-day cross-country skiing expeditions (although some do). But an exercise program that gives joints and muscles regular workouts, and provides an opportunity to keep heart and lungs working at peak capacity should be a part of every person's routine, regardless of that person's age.

FALLACY: All exercises are alike.

Exercises are alike only in the sense that they contribute in some measure to your overall fitness.

You must choose the type of exercise that best suits your condition, and the goal you have in mind.

Exercises requiring muscular action and moderate amounts of additional oxygen (aerobic exercises) are generally more beneficial than isometric exercises because the aerobic exercises step up the action of the heart and circulatory systems to a beneficial level without demanding excessive expenditures of energy.

One axiom about exercise that applies to everyone, regardless of condition, is that it should be a part of your regular routine.

HOW TO EVALUATE AN EXERCISE PROGRAM

No exercise program is able to transform an overweight, out-of-shape, and lethargic person into a fit and trim Olympic athlete overnight.

Just as it took you months or years to get out of shape, it's going to take time to get back in shape.

Pause just a minute before that beginning step and examine what you want to accomplish, how you want to accomplish it, and which of many options will suit your purpose best.

The following questions will help ensure that your first step won't be a misstep:

Is It Compatible with Your Physical Condition?

If you're a great deal overweight, or have a history of health problems (such as hypertension, diabetes, or heart disease), check with your doctor before you start. You won't have to abandon your plans for an exercise program if you get less than a perfect bill of health, but you may have to wait until a health problem is cleared up or under treatment before beginning.

Does It Suit the Purpose That You Have in Mind?

Is your eventual goal to get back in shape and stay there? Are you just trying to lose a little weight? Do you simply want to tone up some flabby muscles? Do you want to combine exercise with recreation? The exercise options explained on pages 352 to 369 will help you decide which sort of activity is best for you.

Will It Enhance Your Overall Physical Condition?

No matter what your eventual goal, include aerobic exercises in your exercise plan. Your heart is the most important muscle in your body, so be sure to include exercises that contribute to a healthier life by strengthening the heart and improving respiratory efficiency.

Will It Fit Easily into Your Schedule?

If you decide on ambitious goals that take more time than you have to spare, it's a good bet that your exercise program will take a backseat to other demands on your time. Make sure the program fits comfortably into your schedule. You'll probably have to make some changes in your daily routine (forgoing half an hour of television-viewing for example, or maybe exercising while watching TV) to accommodate your exercise schedule. But remember: Even a comprehensive exercise program requires less than an hour of your time each day to accomplish.

And if your schedule is so hectic that you can't see how to get started, remember that a regular program of as little as 30 minutes of exercise done three times a week is far more beneficial than no exercise at all.

Will You Enjoy It?

To get the most out of exercise, you have to stay with it; to stay with it, you have to enjoy it. If exercise looms as a bore or a chore, you might as well forget it. Don't be discouraged by the first few days, they're always the least enjoyable. After a week or two, pride in your improving condition makes exercising easier.

If the thought of solitary jogging doesn't appeal to you, find a jogging partner or check out group exercise options. Conversely, if you dislike participating in a competitive sport, you're a perfect candidate for an exercise program that has built-in solitary activities.

The point is, preferences in exercise vary according to individual tastes, so don't forget to consider yours before you start.

EXERCISING OPTIONS: WHICH ROUTE TO FITNESS?

America's perception of how the classic physically fit person looks has changed drastically in the past generation. The burly football player's position as the quintessence of fitness has been superseded by a downright skinny marathon runner, or a lean gymnast.

Of course, you don't have to be a marathon runner to be "in shape." Today you have many equally good exercise paths to physical fitness—from aerobic dancing to cross-country skiing. Even such sports as volleyball or soccer can be part of an exercise prescription designed to get you on the road to good shape.

What is the principal purpose of exercise? Physical fitness, of course. That means your heart and lungs function efficiently, and that you have muscular strength, flexible joints, agility, coordination, and a reservoir of endurance and stamina. Here's how different types of activity can help you reach those goals.

Four Major Types of Exercise

Exercises are generally classified in one (or a combination) of the following four categories: isometric, isotonic, anaerobic, and aerobic.

- *Isometric exercises* increase the size and strength of muscles by tensing one set of muscles against another, or against an immovable object—for instance, pushing against opposite sides of a doorjamb.
- *Isotonic exercises* increase muscular strength, agility, coordination, and joint flexibility by repetitive contraction and relaxation of muscles—for instance, weightlifting or calisthenics.
- *Anaerobic exercises* build up stamina by demanding maximum energy output for brief periods of time—for instance, a 100-yard dash, or a bicycle sprint.
- *Aerobic exercises* tone up the body and build heart and lung endurance by subjecting the body to sustained vigorous activity—for instance, swimming, long-distance running, or aerobic dancing.

If you're seriously interested in exercise for your health, and not just exercise for fun, you should include at least one of the aerobic exercises described on pages 358 to 360 in your daily routine.

Team and Individual Sports

You have many sports exercise options to choose from: group activities such as team sports; solitary activities such as running or swimming; or even activities such as aerobic dancing that are not strictly considered sports but still fulfill the cardiorespiratory requirements outlined on page 358. Here's more on individual and team sports.

- *Vigorous individual sports* such as tennis, racquetball, and handball can be played for fun, as meaningful exercise, or both. The style of play you choose determines whether these sports or any sport will be beneficial. Each combines physical activity with companionship, is inexpensive, requires little in the way of athletic equipment, and can be just plain fun.

Individual sports are excellent for agility, reaction time, speed, and coordination. But, like anything else that's done halfheartedly, you won't do your body much good if you just "fool around" at these sports.

- *Vigorous team sports* (such as basketball, volleyball, baseball, touch football, softball, soccer, field hockey, and rugby) are characterized by alternating periods of intense and relaxed play.

Such sports can be considered a form of aerobic exercise. Remember that unless those periods of intense play let you work your heart and lungs sufficiently, and for a long enough time, the sport is probably enhancing nothing more than your coordination and your flexibility.

No matter how fast-moving or exciting they are, such sports are not intended to be the keystone of your physical fitness program. Instead, include them as one facet of your overall fitness strategy.

Tips for Your Exercise Program

As you start your exercise program, remember these hints:

- If you have a health problem, get your doctor's okay. This is a good idea even if you have no health problem. And if you're older than 35, ask about the need for a stress electrocardiogram.
- Select a regular time for exercise and stick with it.
- Don't try to do all the exercises on the first day of the program. Nothing discourages a beginning exerciser more than overly stiff muscles on the second day. Start with a few exercises done slowly, and gradually add others as your fitness improves.
- Keep track of your progress. Use the charts on pages 350 and 351 to record your improvement. Seeing your progress written on paper will help keep you motivated.

PERSONAL FITNESS CHARTS

FLEXIBILITY EXERCISES

EXERCISE	GOAL	WEEK 1	WEEK 2	WEEK 3	WEEK 4
Side-to-Side Bend (p. 352)	5				
Waist Twist (p. 352)	5-10				
Toe Touch (p. 353) Toe Touch (alternate) (p. 353)	10 4				
Broomstick Shoulder Flexibility (p. 354)	3-5				
Arm Circles (p. 354)	20				
Neck Roll (p. 354)	3				
Forward Bend (legs together) (p. 355)	6				
Forward Bend (legs split) (p. 355)	3				
Calf Stretch (p. 355) Calf Stretch (alternate) (p. 355)	6 3				
Groin Muscle Stretch (p. 356) Groin Muscle Stretch (alternate) (p. 356)	8 3-5				
Hurdler's Stretch (p. 356)	4				
Spine Rock (p. 357)	5-10				
The Plow (p. 357) The Plow (alternate 1) (p. 357) The Plow (alternate 2) (p. 357)	1-5 1-5 1-5				

HEART-LUNG EXERCISES

We've left blanks for you to fill in the names of the heart-lung exercises you choose. Your eventual goal is to keep your heart at 65 to 70 percent of its maximum rate for 15 to 20 minutes. The chart will help you keep track of your improvement in the distance (D) you cover (or the number of repetitions if you choose jumping rope, jogging in place, or stepping up and down on a stool), the time (T) it takes you to do it, and your heart rate (HR). Remember, you won't be able to jog or jump rope 15 to 20 minutes at first. Start slowly and exercise as long as you can at the 65 to 70 percent maximum heart rate. You probably won't see daily improvement, so you should fill in the chart at the beginning and end of each of the four weeks.

EXERCISE	MHR 70%	WEEK 1						WEEK 2						WEEK 3						WEEK 4					
		D	T	HR	D	T	HR	D	T	HR	D	T	HR	D	T	HR	D	T	HR	D	T	HR	D	T	HR

Heart-Lung Goals

The goal of all cardiorespiratory exercise is to keep your heart beating at 65 to 70 percent of its maximum rate for 15 to 20 minutes. The accompanying chart shows approximate ranges for maximum heart rates (MHR) and 70-percent levels. To be more precise about your MHR, subtract your age from 220. Then multiply that figure by .7 to obtain your 70-percent level.

Five minutes after you've finished your heart-lung exercise, check your pulse. If your rate is more than 120, you probably have overexerted. The next time out slow down your pace a bit so your maximum heart rate falls into the proper range.

AGE	MHR	70%
20-29	**200-191**	**140-134**
30-39	**190-181**	**133-127**
40-49	**180-171**	**126-120**
50-59	**170-161**	**119-113**
60-69	**160-151**	**112-106**

How To Take Your Pulse

You'll want to check your pulse often, especially when you're beginning the exercise program. The best way is to find the "pulse point" on the palm side of the wrist near the thumb. Place your second and third fingertips over the point for ten seconds and count the beats. Multiply that figure by six to get your pulse rate for one minute.

STRENGTH EXERCISES*

EXERCISE	GOAL	WEEK 1					WEEK 2					WEEK 3					WEEK 4				
Squats (p. 361)	15/10																				
Lunges (p. 361)	20																				
Inside Thigh Exercise (p. 362)	3																				
Outside Thigh Exercise (p. 362)	3																				
Back of Thigh Exercise (p. 362)	6																				
Calf Exercise (p. 363)	10-20																				
Push-Ups (p. 363) Push-Ups (alternate) (p. 363) Push-Ups (alternate) (p. 364)	10-15 10-15 10-15																				
Chin-Ups (p. 364)	5/10																				
Fly (p. 365)	10																				
Pull-Overs (p. 365)	10																				
Isometric Chest Exercise (p. 365)	10																				
Forward Lift (p. 366)	10																				
Side Lift (p. 366)	10																				
Bend and Lift (p. 366)	10																				
Sit-Ups (p. 367)	20-25																				
Negative Sit-Ups (p. 367)	10																				
Head-Knee Curl-Ups (p. 367)	20																				
Leg Raises (p. 367)	30																				
Sitting Leg Tucks (p. 368)	15-20																				
Back Lift (p. 368)	3-5																				
The Locust (p. 369)	5																				
Neck Exercises (p. 369)	4																				
Forearm and Hand Exercise (p. 369)	20																				

*These exercises should be done two or three times a week, on non-consecutive days. Always allow at least one day of rest (indicated by the gray columns in the chart) after you perform strength exercises before doing them again.

FLEXIBILITY EXERCISES

To prevent injury, you need to prepare your body before working out by stretching and warming up. Start by hopping up and down, or walking briskly for a few minutes. The key to effective stretching is to do the exercises slowly and smoothly. *Do not bounce.* Jerking or bouncing movements can cause more harm than good. *Stretch till you feel some discomfort, back off a bit (exercise shouldn't be painful), and then hold the position from five to ten seconds,* release and repeat. The exercises offered here will keep joints flexible but are not very time consuming.

Side-to-Side Bend: Start with your arms overhead, feet shoulder-width apart, and body erect. Bend laterally to the right at the waist. Hold five to ten seconds, then bend to the left and hold five to ten seconds. Repeat five times. Excellent for firming the waistline.

Side-To-Side Bend

Waist Twist

Waist Twist: Stand erect with hands on waist. Twist as far to the right as possible and hold that position for a few seconds. Then twist to the left and hold a few more seconds. Repeat this twisting and holding sequence five to ten times.

Toe Touch: (See ***Note** on page 369.) Stand erect with feet slightly wider apart than your shoulder width. Bend down, not twisting the body, and touch the left foot with the right hand. Stand erect again, then bend and touch the right foot with the left hand. Work up to repeating the sequence ten times. This exercise is excellent for firming the waistline and stretching the hamstring muscles in your thighs.

Toe Touch (alternate): (See ***Note** on page 369.) From a standing position with your feet shoulder-width apart, bend forward and reach for your left foot with *both* hands. Do not bounce. Try to keep your legs straight. Hold for five to eight seconds. Stand erect again, then reach for the right foot and hold the stretch. Repeat four times for each foot.

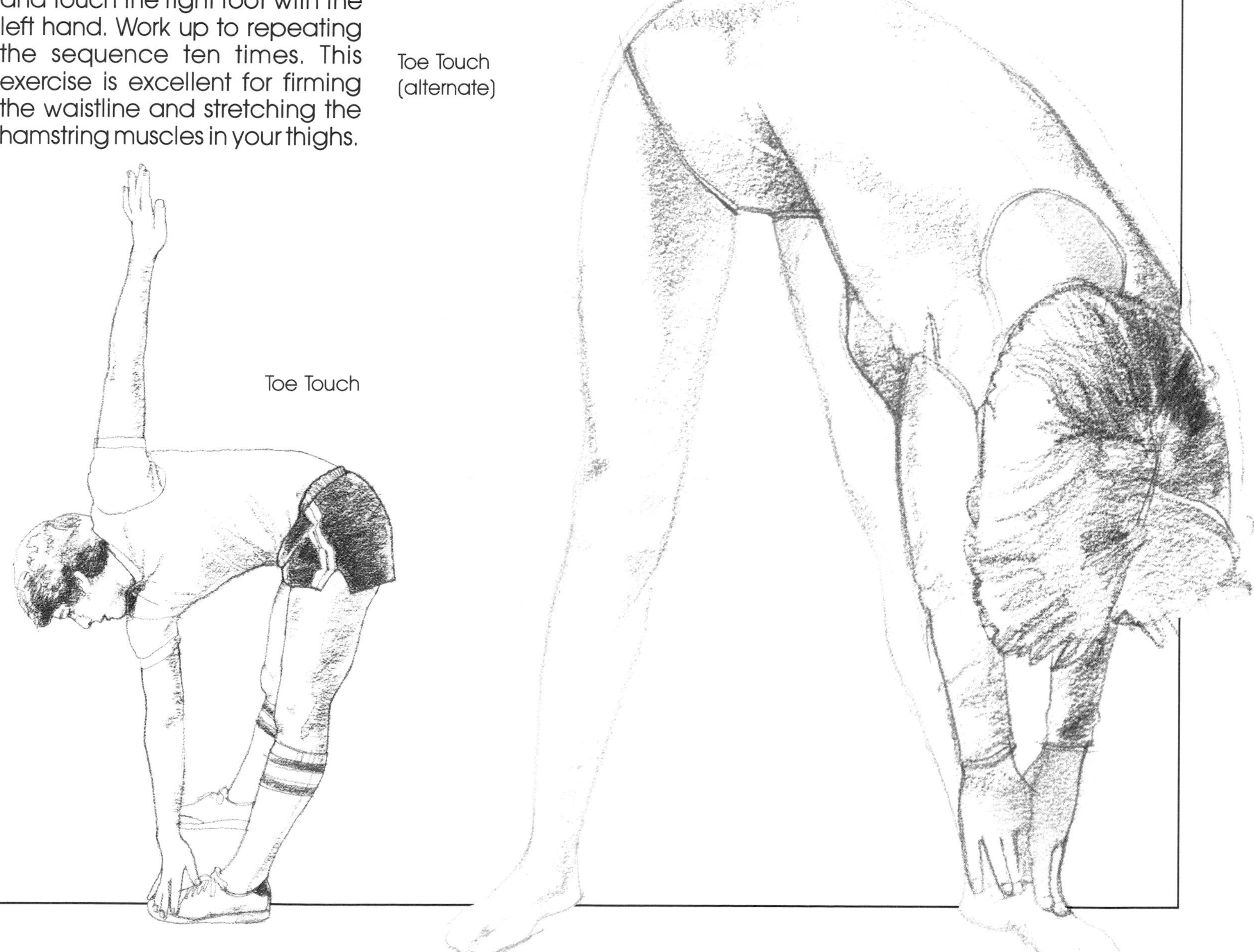

Toe Touch (alternate)

Toe Touch

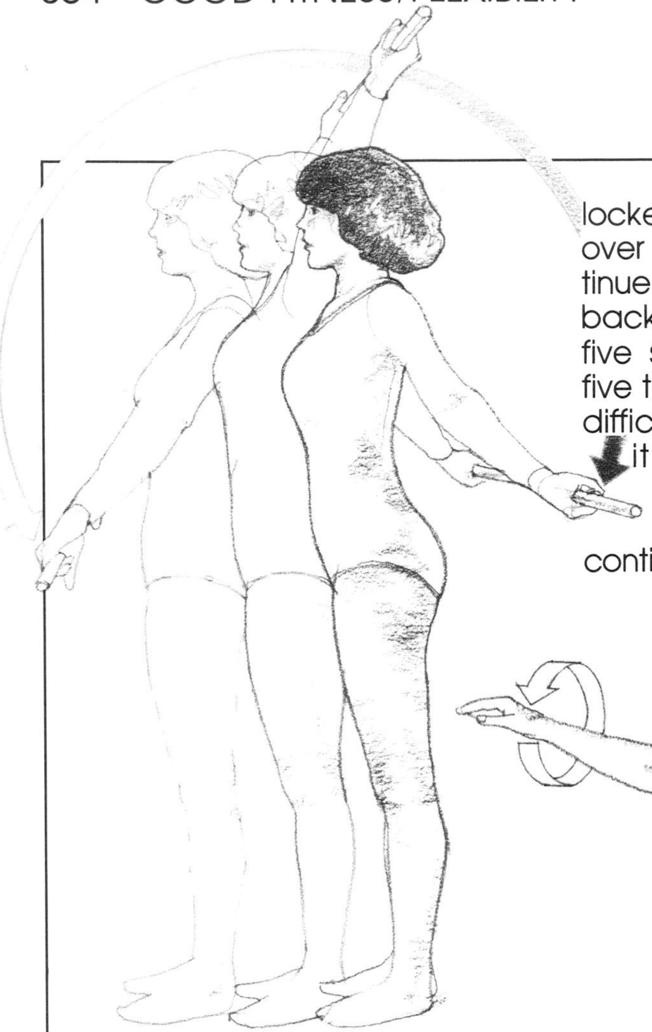

Broomstick Shoulder Flexibility

Broomstick Shoulder Flexibility: Begin by grasping a broomstick or longer pole (if you don't have a broomstick or pole, just use a bath towel stretched between your hands) in front of you with your palms down, your arms and hands spread to about two times your shoulders' width, and your elbows locked. Be sure to keep your elbows locked while bringing the pole over your head as shown. Continue bringing the pole straight back behind you as shown. Hold five seconds. Repeat three to five times. This exercise may be difficult to do the first time, but it's great for developing shoulder flexibility and will become easier as you continue to practice it.

Arm Circles: Stand and stretch your arms straight out in opposite directions, parallel to the floor. Rotate your arms from the shoulders in gradually enlarging circles. Return to the starting position and rotate your arms in the *opposite* direction. Repeat *ten times in each direction.*

Arm Circles

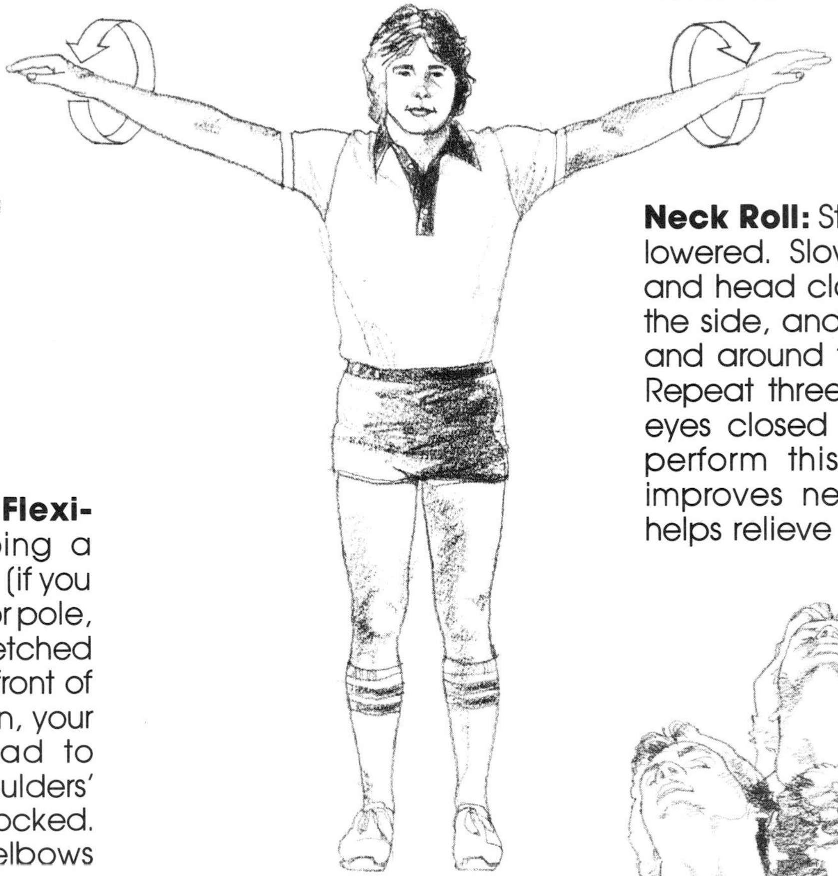

Neck Roll: Start with your head lowered. Slowly roll your neck and head clockwise around to the side, and all the way back and around to the front again. Repeat three times. Keep your eyes closed and relax as you perform this exercise, which improves neck flexibility and helps relieve tension.

Neck Roll

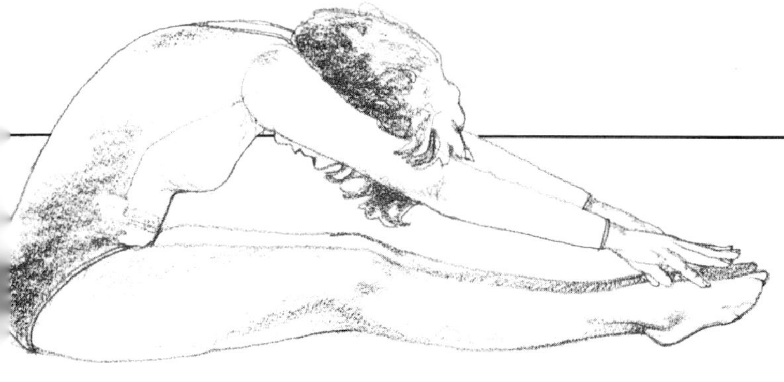

Forward Bend (legs together)

Forward Bend (legs together): Sit with arms at side and feet in front, toes straight up. Bend forward as far as you can. Your goal eventually is to bring chest to thighs with hands grasping toes. Hold five seconds; repeat three times. Repeat the exercise—this time with your toes pointed *forward.* Good for back of legs and your back.

Forward Bend (legs split): Sit erect with legs apart. Bend at the waist and slide your hands as far forward as possible along your legs. Eventually you'll be able to grasp your ankles with your hands. Hold five seconds and repeat three times. Excellent for back of legs and back.

Calf Stretch: From a standing position, place your right leg 3 or 4 feet in front of your left leg. Then, keeping your left heel on the floor and your left leg straight, lean forward on your right knee. As you lean forward on your right knee, you stretch your left calf. The toes of the left leg should be directly under the knee of the left leg. Hold this stretch for five to eight counts. Switch legs and repeat three times with each leg.

Calf Stretch (alternate): Stand an arm's length from a wall. Place your palms on the wall, lean forward on one or both legs, keeping your heels on the floor and your body straight. Hold the position for five to ten seconds and repeat three times.

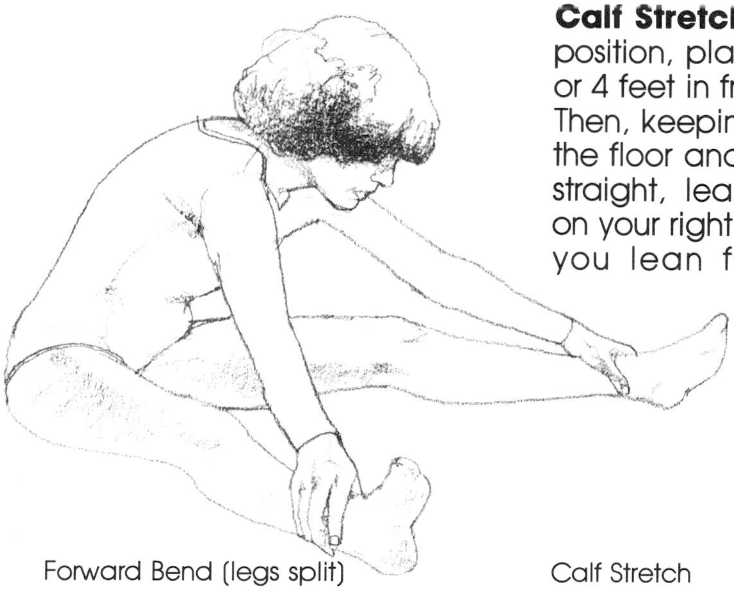

Calf Stretch (alternate)

Forward Bend (legs split)

Calf Stretch

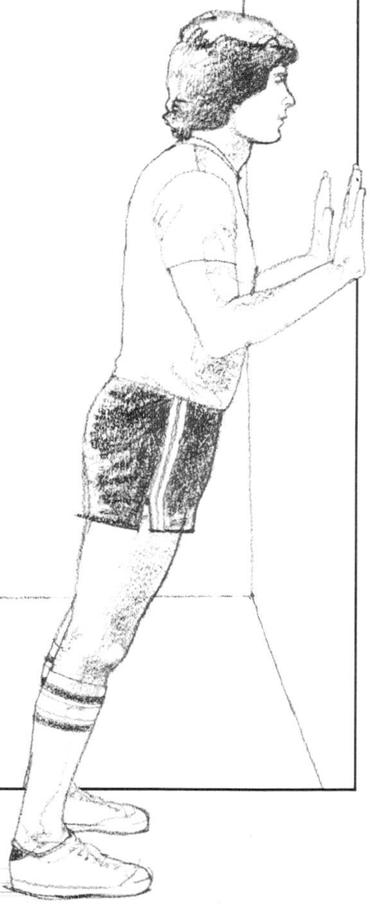

Groin Muscle Stretch: Stand with your feet 3 to 4 feet apart, and your hands on your knees. Slowly bend the right knee and, while still facing forward, lean out toward the right knee. Hold this leaning position for five to ten seconds. Return to the starting position and repeat, leaning toward the bent left knee. Repeat the exercise four times for each leg.

Groin Muscle Stretch (alternate)

Hurdler's Stretch: Assume the sitting position shown, with one foot tucked up next to your seat and the other extended out in front of you. First reach out toward the toes of your extended leg and hold for five to eight seconds. Then lean backward and rest on your elbow for five to eight counts. This allows the muscles on the front side of the thigh of your bent leg to be stretched. Repeat this procedure one more time on the same leg. Then switch leg positions and repeat the sequence. *Do not bounce.*

Groin Muscle Stretch

Groin Muscle Stretch (alternate): Sit on floor with the soles of your feet together as shown. Grasp your toes *or* ankles and pull yourself forward from the waist. Hold the position for 10 to 15 seconds; relax and repeat three to five times. Another way to do this exercise is to push down on your knees with your elbows, while grasping your toes or ankles to keep your feet tucked in toward your body.

Hurdler's Stretch

Spine Rock

Spine Rock: (See ***Note** on page 369.) Sit on the floor, clasp your hands together under your knees, and bring your knees up to your chest to touch your chin. Rock back and forth five to ten times. This will help to limber the spine. You'll have to do this exercise gradually if you have trouble getting your trunk all the way back with your feet touching the floor. And don't worry if you can't completely master this exercise immediately. Stop rocking and return to the sitting position any time your neck starts to hurt. Excellent for your spine and the back of your neck.

The Plow

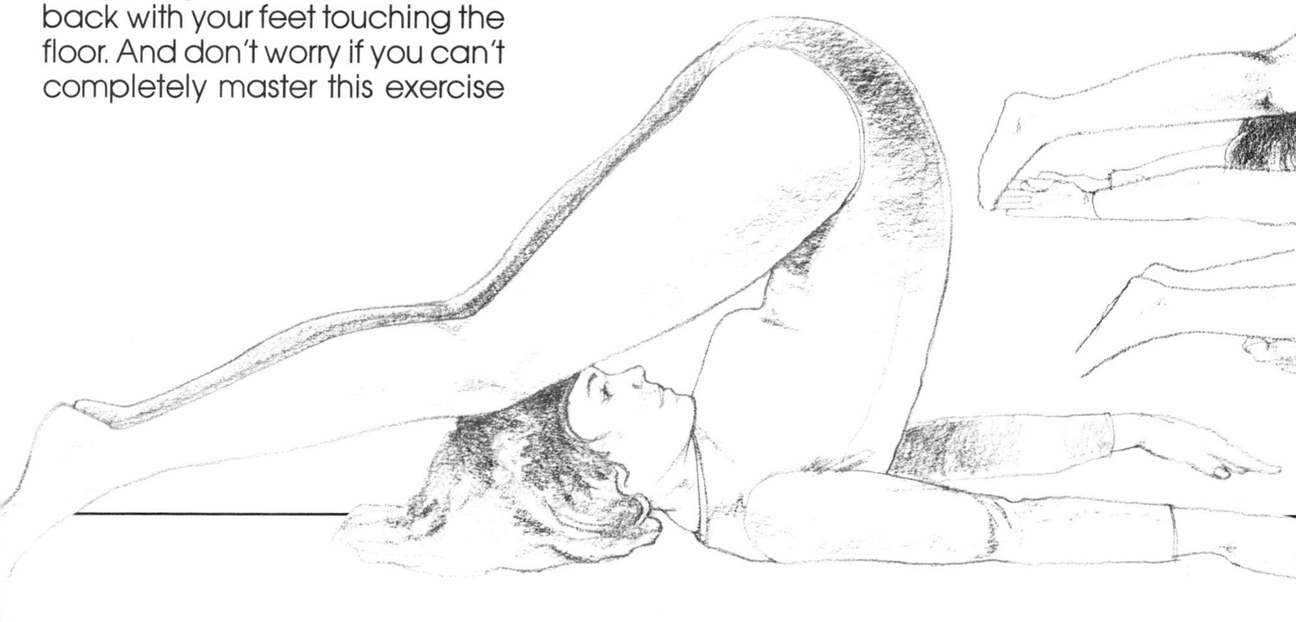

The Plow: (See ***Note** on page 369.) With arms at your sides and palms on floor, slowly raise your legs straight overhead and as far back as possible, or till your toes touch the floor. Hold five to ten seconds. Repeat one to five times.

First alternate: Your head should be between slightly spread legs. Grasp legs with arms and cover ears with palms. Rock backward; hold for five to ten seconds. **Second Alternate:** Put arms overhead and your legs together. Raise legs up and over till toes and fingers touch. Hold five to ten seconds. Repeat alternates one to five times.

The Plow (alternates)

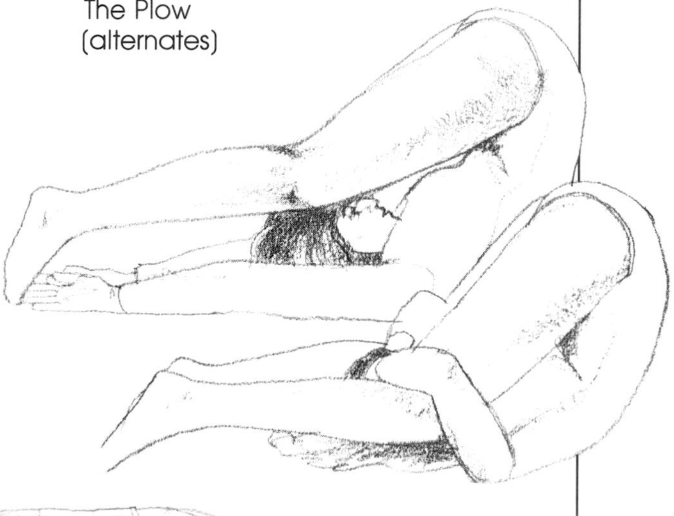

HEART-LUNG EXERCISES

The goal of all of the following heart-lung or aerobic exercises is to give the most important muscle in your body—your heart—and your lungs a vigorous workout.

You want to work up to keeping your heart beating at 65 to 70 percent of its maximum rate (see page 351 for an explanation of how to figure your maximum heart rate) for 15 to 20 minutes at a time. It may take several months to work up to maintaining that level, and once you've reached it, you may want to work up to exercising at 75 to 80 percent of your maximum heart rate. *BUT AT NO TIME SHOULD YOUR HEART RATE EXCEED 80 PERCENT OF YOUR MAXIMUM.*

Beginners who are badly out of shape often try to do too much at the start and become discouraged. Just remember that you'll have to start at less than your desired goal and work up to the optimum level of performance.

For your heart-lung exercises, pick one—or a combination—of the following exercises and keep at it for at least 15 to 20 consecutive minutes each time you exercise.

Walking, Walking and Jogging, Jogging

Walking, Walking and Jogging, or Jogging: Start slowly. Gradually increase the time you walk, walk and jog, or jog until you can continue for 15 to 20 minutes at the 65 to 70 percent of maximum level. If you're out of shape, start by walking. As your condition improves, substitute jogging steps for walking steps to bring yourself up to your goal. Eventually (it may take several months) you'll have to jog continuously to reach 65 to 70 percent of your maximum heart rate level.

Running in place, or stationary jogging, is an acceptable substitute for the real thing, but make sure you run in place on carpet or a jogging pad to prevent foot and leg injuries.

Swimming: Swimming is one of the best all-around exercises. Also, swimming puts into play muscles that aren't used in some other exercises, such as jogging. Keeping afloat and moving in the water for 15 to 20 minutes at 65 to 70 percent of your maximum heart rate is different from spending 15 minutes splashing around in the pool. You'll really have to swim laps to make this exercise worthwhile.

Jumping Rope: Boxers know the value of this cardiorespiratory exercise. All it takes is a piece of rope and a pair of well-cushioned shoes. Rope-jumping makes a perfect foul-weather substitute for outdoor cardiovascular exercises. A jump rope takes little space in a suitcase, so you can always exercise away from home when you travel. Take it easy when you begin so you won't end up with sore feet. If you find yourself without a rope, simply go through the motions—the aerobic benefits are identical.

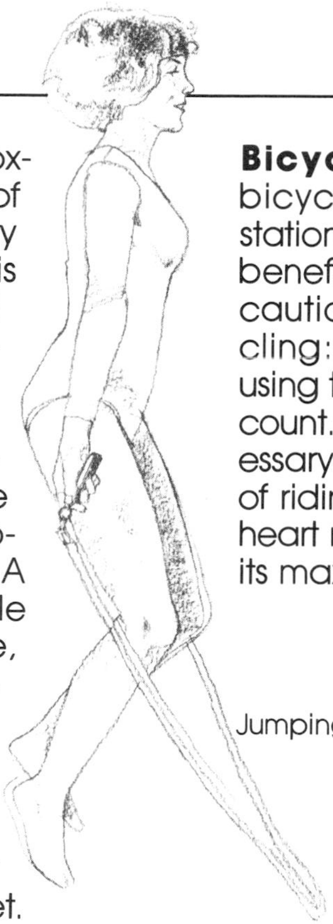

Stationary Bicycling: Pedal without stopping for 15 to 20 minutes. Start with little resistance on the tire. Gradually increase the resistance as your fitness improves till you reach your maximum heart-rate goal.

Bicycling: Whether you bicycle outdoors or on a stationary bicycle inside, the benefits are equal. One precautionary note about bicycling: Coasting downhill and using the "easier" gears doesn't count. Use the highest gear necessary to sustain 15 to 20 minutes of riding at a pace where your heart rate is 65 to 70 percent of its maximum.

Jumping Rope

Bicycling

Cross-Country Skiing

Cross-Country Skiing: This sport provides a good workout for your heart and lungs while you take in the scenery and crisp winter air. Start slowly and work toward mastering a rhythmic combination of swinging your arms from front to back while your legs maintain a skating motion. Plodding along doesn't count. It takes a little practice to develop a good gliding rhythm, so stay with it. Make sure you're dressed properly and have all the necessary equipment before you start.

Aerobic Dancing: So-called "aerobic" dancing appeals to many because it combines all the heart-lung exercise requirements with a pleasant time. The goal during aerobic dance is the same as for the other heart-lung exercises—to reach 65 to 70 percent of your maximum heart rate and keep it there for 15 to 20 minutes. Many community organizations offer aerobic dance classes. Or you can purchase instructional books and records that will teach you a few basic steps. This is a good exercise for when you're traveling.

Aerobic dancing is also a good all-around exercise because it contributes to flexibility and strength while exercising your heart and lungs.

Step-Ups: If you've ever run up a flight or two of stairs, you know you'll be breathing hard after 15 minutes of doing step-ups. A small step stool is all that's needed. If one is unavailable, simply use the nearest stairway. Start by putting your left foot on the stool (or step), then bring your right foot up. Next return the left foot to the floor and then the right foot. The object is to get a steady 1-2-3-4 rhythm established. Remember to start slowly and increase gradually. This is an excellent exercise, but it can quickly become boring. Use it on rainy days or when you're away from home.

Step-Ups

STRENGTH EXERCISES

A good time to do strength exercises is after you've completed the heart-lung and stretching routine, and before you cool down with a few more stretching exercises. *Do these exercises two or three times a week. If you let more than 96 hours pass between strength exercises, your muscles start to lose ground.* However, doing these exercises more often than every other day doesn't give muscle tissue a chance to recover and prepare for another exercise session.

Begin with only a few repetitions, then gradually work up to the recommended goal. Perform each exercise slowly and deliberately.

One last word of caution: Don't immediately follow these, or any, exercises with a hot shower or a session in the sauna. *The heat dilates superficial skin blood vessels and robs vital organs of blood needed during the post-exercise period.*

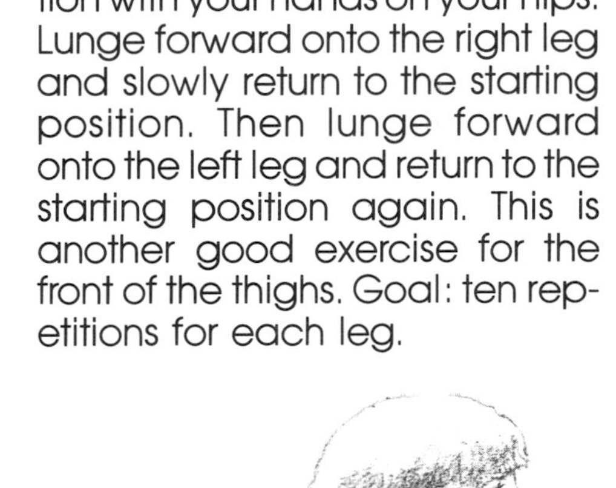

Lunges: Start in a standing position with your hands on your hips. Lunge forward onto the right leg and slowly return to the starting position. Then lunge forward onto the left leg and return to the starting position again. This is another good exercise for the front of the thighs. Goal: ten repetitions for each leg.

Squats

Lunges

Squats: This is a good exercise for the front of the thighs. Begin by standing with your arms extended in front of you or on your hips. Squat slowly until your thighs are parallel to the floor, or until your buttocks almost touch the seat of a chair. Slowly rise again until you are standing. Goal: 15 for men, ten for women.

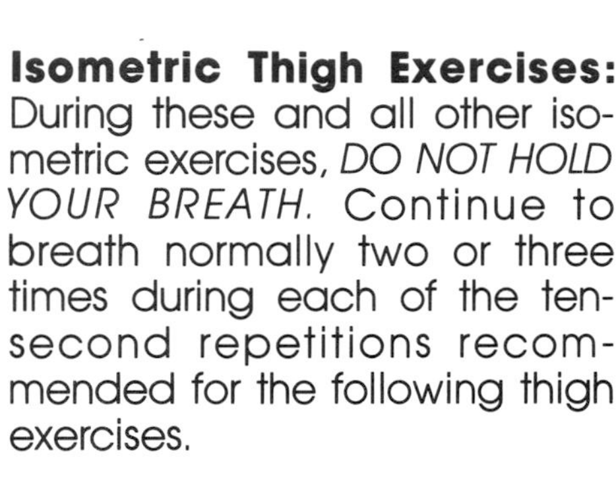

Isometric Thigh Exercises: During these and all other isometric exercises, *DO NOT HOLD YOUR BREATH.* Continue to breath normally two or three times during each of the ten-second repetitions recommended for the following thigh exercises.

Back of Thighs

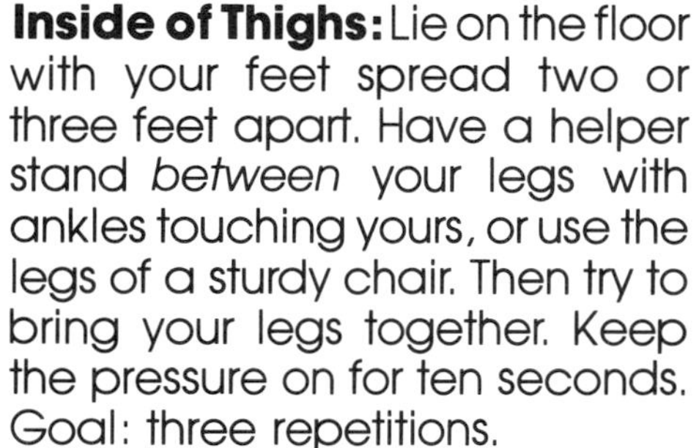

Inside of Thighs: Lie on the floor with your feet spread two or three feet apart. Have a helper stand *between* your legs with ankles touching yours, or use the legs of a sturdy chair. Then try to bring your legs together. Keep the pressure on for ten seconds. Goal: three repetitions.

Back of Thighs: Lie on the floor on your stomach. Bend your right knee about 90 degrees. Have your helper hold your ankle. Then try to move your leg to your back and keep trying for ten seconds. Goal: three repetitions per leg.

Outside of Thighs: Lie on the floor with your feet spread apart about two feet. Position your ankles so they are *inside* your helper's. Then try to spread your legs apart. Keep the pressure on for ten seconds and repeat three times.

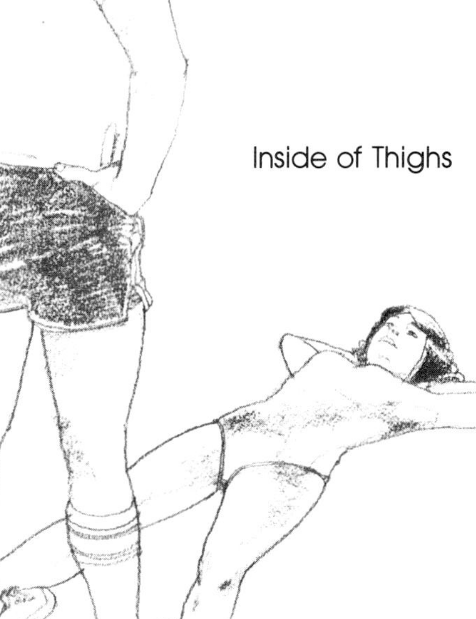

Inside of Thighs

Outside of Thighs

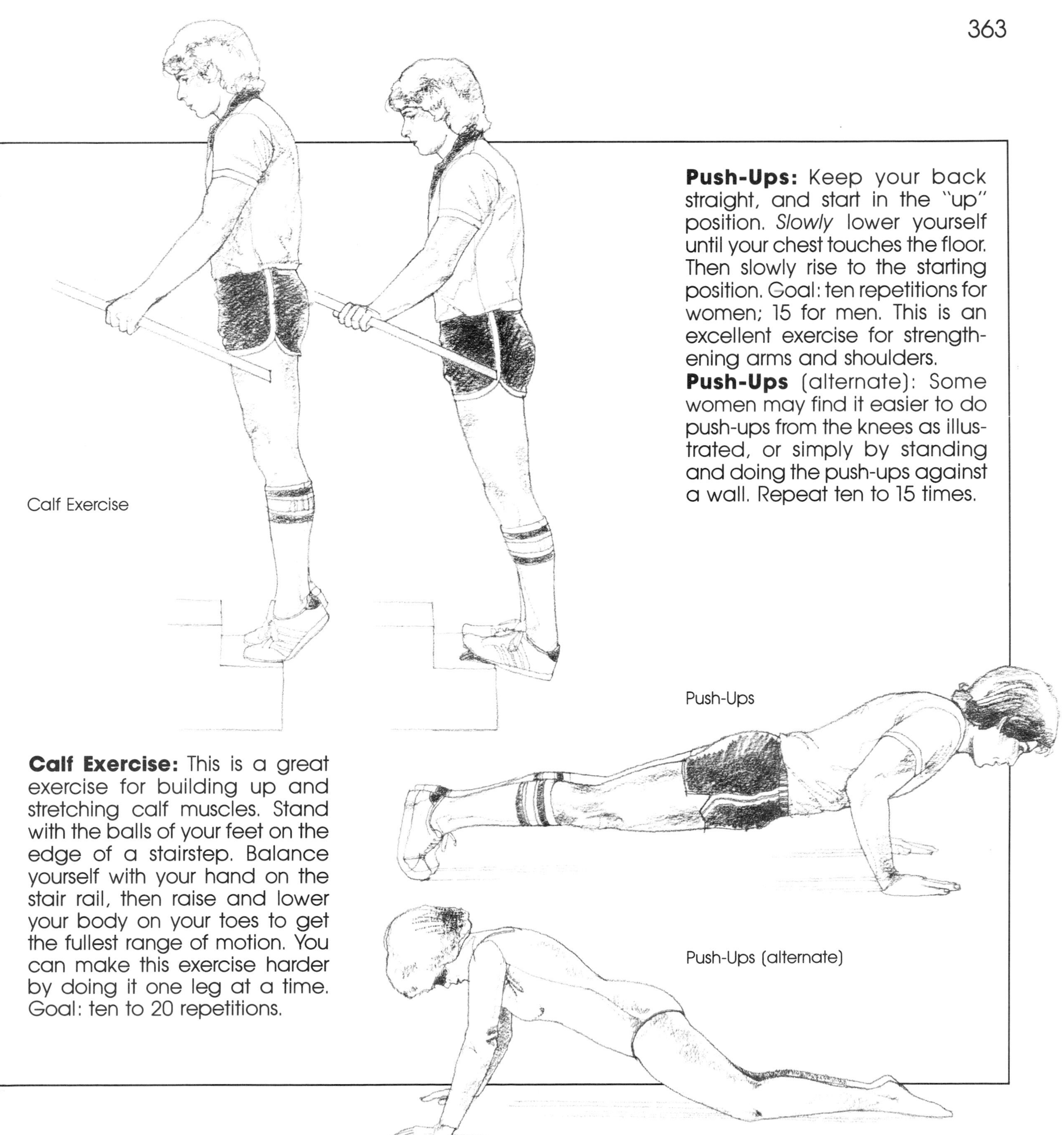

Calf Exercise

Push-Ups: Keep your back straight, and start in the "up" position. *Slowly* lower yourself until your chest touches the floor. Then slowly rise to the starting position. Goal: ten repetitions for women; 15 for men. This is an excellent exercise for strengthening arms and shoulders.

Push-Ups (alternate): Some women may find it easier to do push-ups from the knees as illustrated, or simply by standing and doing the push-ups against a wall. Repeat ten to 15 times.

Push-Ups

Calf Exercise: This is a great exercise for building up and stretching calf muscles. Stand with the balls of your feet on the edge of a stairstep. Balance yourself with your hand on the stair rail, then raise and lower your body on your toes to get the fullest range of motion. You can make this exercise harder by doing it one leg at a time. Goal: ten to 20 repetitions.

Push-Ups (alternate)

Push-Ups (alternate): Another option, especially for men and older boys, is the more-difficult "deep" push-ups done between chairs instead of on the floor. Dip the chest as far as possible between the chairs as shown while your feet rest on a third chair. This is an advanced exercise, and while doing "deep" push-ups, have someone hold the chairs or place them against an immovable object, such as a wall. Repeat ten to 15 times.

Chin-Ups: These exercises are designed to strengthen upper arms. In regular chin-ups, start by grasping the bar with your palms up. Bend your arms until you pull your chin over the bar. Lower yourself till your arms are straight, and repeat. Girls and women should work up to five; boys and men work up to ten. If you find regular chin-ups too difficult at first, stand on a chair and grasp the chinning bar, palms up. Put your chin over the bar with your elbows bent. Slowly lower yourself off the chair till your arms are extended. *A more-difficult variation is to do the chin-ups by grasping the bar with your palms down.* Repeat five to ten times. These variations are designed to strengthen your arms so you will be able to do regular chin-ups.

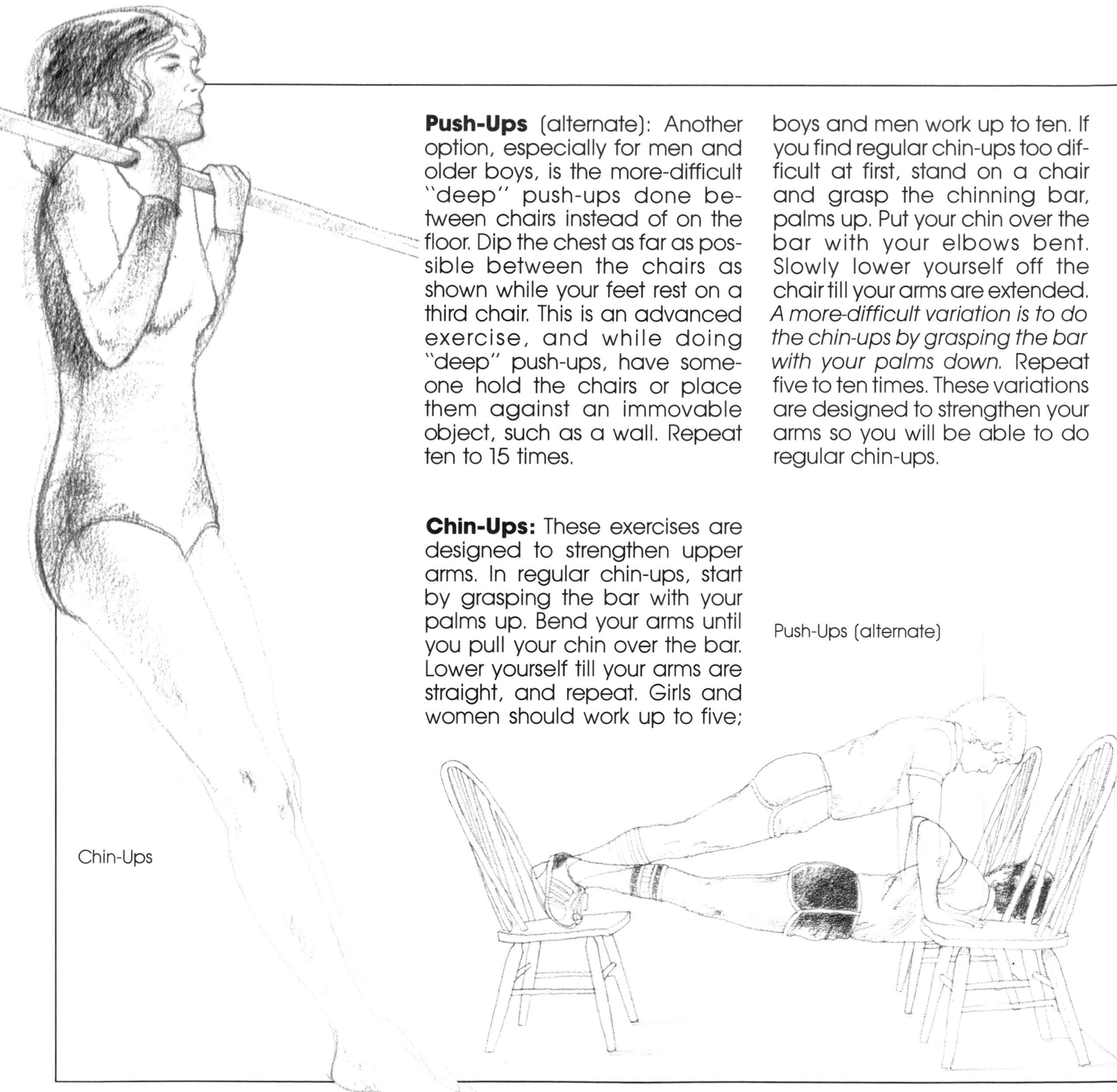

Push-Ups (alternate)

Chin-Ups

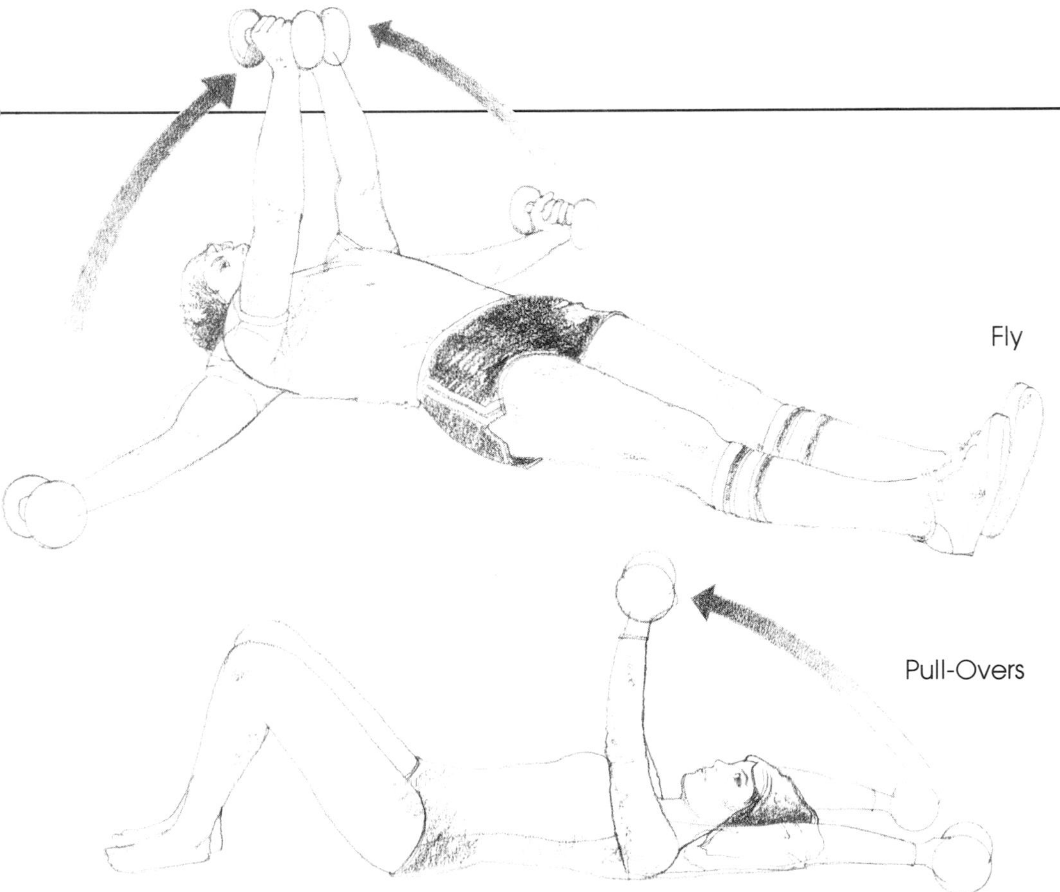

Fly

Pull-Overs

Isometric Chest Exercise: *(Breathe normally throughout this exercise.)* Begin by interlocking the fingers of your hands in front of your chest as shown. Try to pull your hands apart. Hold the straining position for ten seconds and repeat three to five times. Then clasp your hands as shown, and try to push your hands together, again holding the position for ten seconds and repeating three to five times.

Isometric Chest Exercise

Fly: This is good for firming the chest muscles. Lie on your back on a bench or the floor. Hold a weight (a heavy book, a sand-filled container, or a light dumbbell) in each hand. Start with your arms extended above you with elbows slightly bent. *Slowly* lower your arms to the sides and then bring them back up to the starting position. Goal: ten repetitions for men and women.

Pull-Overs: Start this exercise in the same position as in the fly exercise (knees may be bent), except bring your extended arms with weights *slowly* above your head. Bring your arms *slowly* back to the starting position and repeat the exercise ten times.

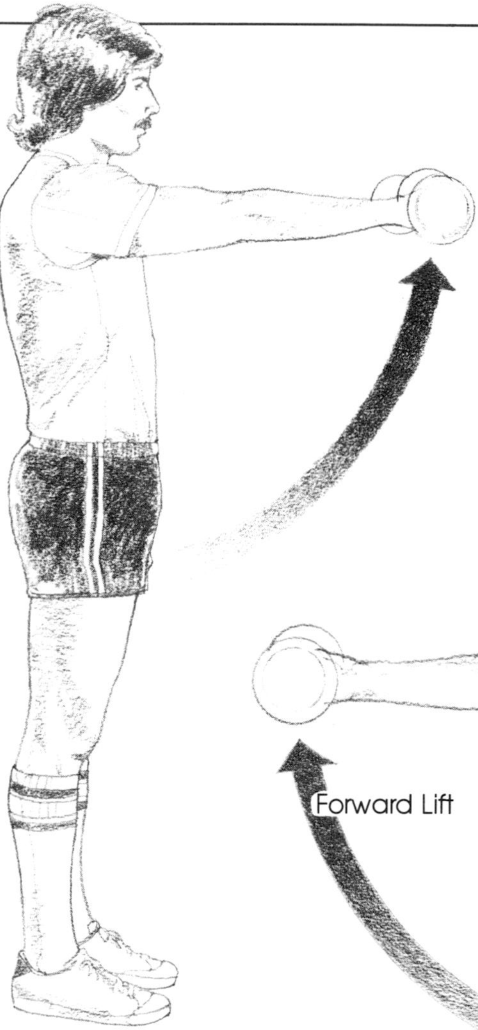

Side Lift: Stand erect with your feet shoulder-width apart and your hands at your sides. Begin by *slowly* raising weights sideways to shoulder level. Keep arms straight. Lower arms and repeat. Goal: ten repetitions.

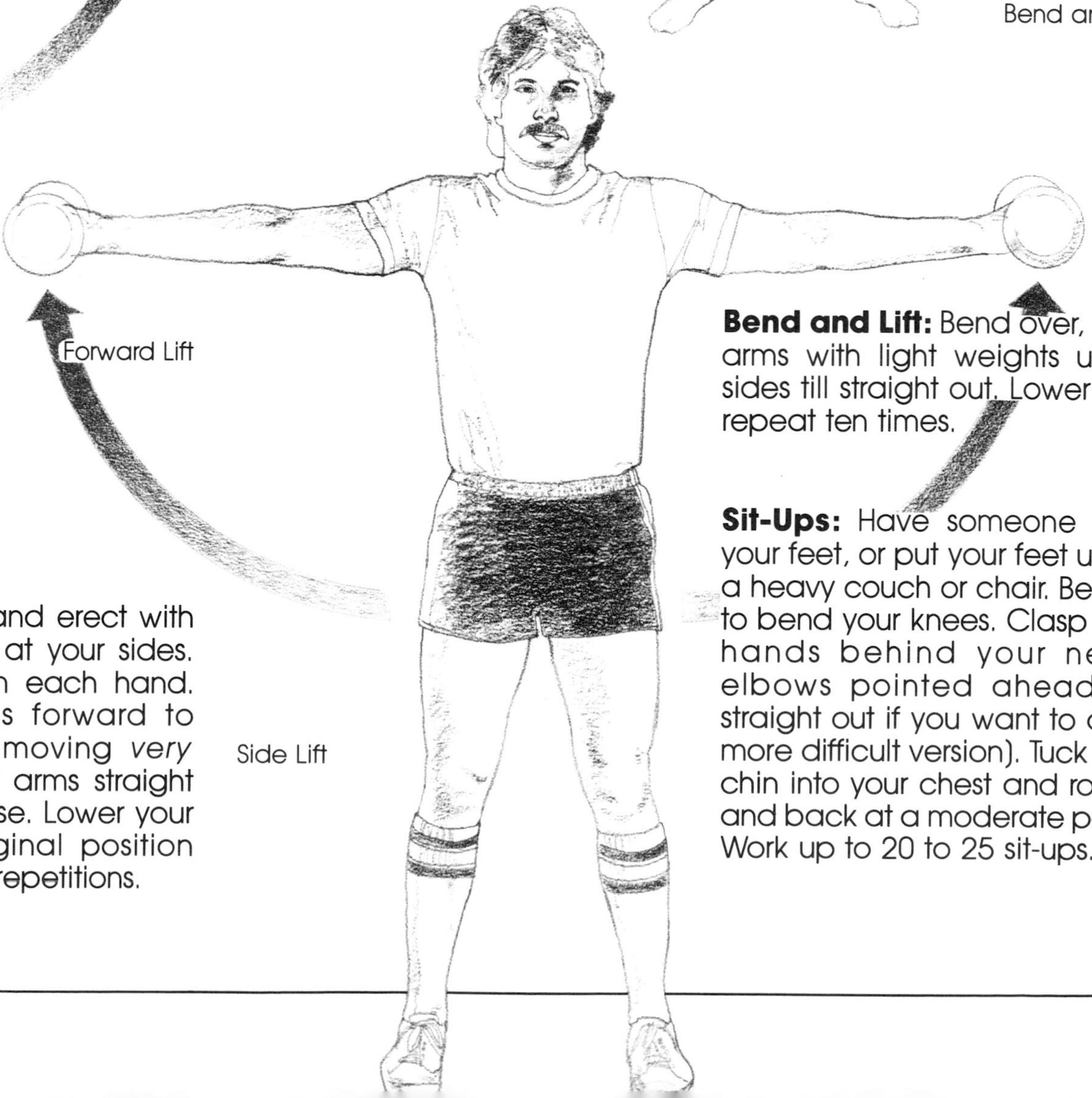

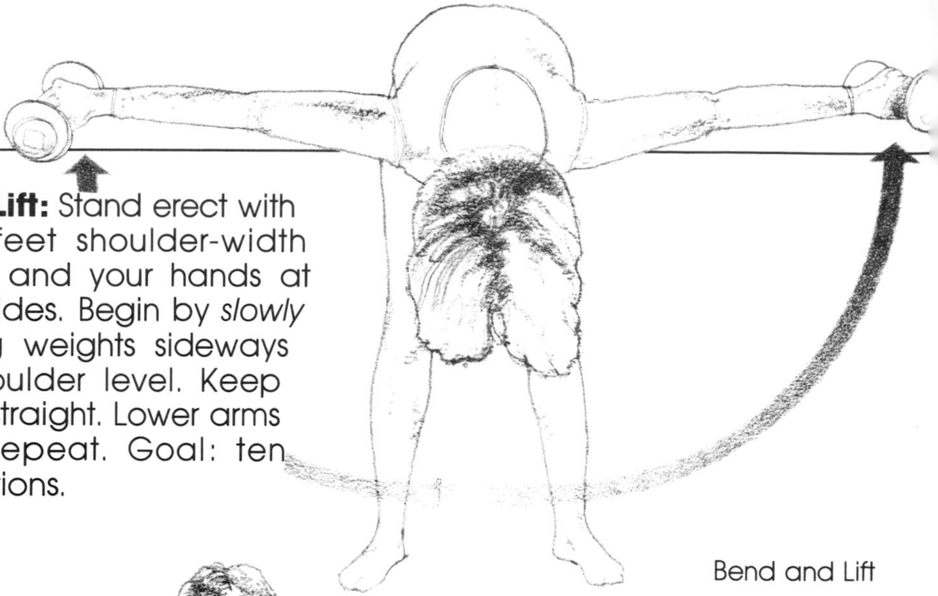

Bend and Lift

Forward Lift

Bend and Lift: Bend over, raise arms with light weights up to sides till straight out. Lower and repeat ten times.

Sit-Ups: Have someone hold your feet, or put your feet under a heavy couch or chair. Be sure to bend your knees. Clasp your hands behind your neck, elbows pointed ahead (or straight out if you want to do a more difficult version). Tuck your chin into your chest and roll up and back at a moderate pace. Work up to 20 to 25 sit-ups.

Forward Lift: Stand erect with your arms down at your sides. Hold a weight in each hand. Raise your arms forward to shoulder level, moving *very slowly.* Keep your arms straight during this exercise. Lower your arms to the original position slowly. Goal: ten repetitions.

Side Lift

Negative Sit-Ups: (See ***Note** on page 369.) Sit with knees bent, and your feet under a chair or couch, or held by your partner. Clasp your hands behind your head, or fold your arms across your chest. Then *slowly* lower your trunk to the floor, taking eight to ten seconds to do it. Sit up again (with help) and repeat the negative sit-up. It's important to lower your trunk very slowly. Work up to ten negative sit-ups.

Head-Knee Curl-Ups: (See ***Note** on page 369.) Lie on the floor with your hands clasped behind your neck and your legs extended. Then slowly curl your head and neck up while, at the same time, raising your legs and bending your knees. The object of this exercise is to try to touch your chin to your knees. Curl up and return to the starting position *very slowly.* Your goal is to work up to a maximum of 20 repetitions. If you want to make this exercise even harder, try keeping your heels off the floor at all times.

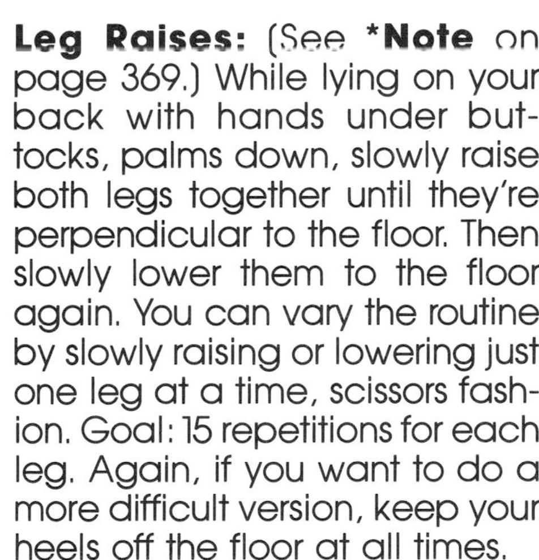

Leg Raises

Leg Raises: (See ***Note** on page 369.) While lying on your back with hands under buttocks, palms down, slowly raise both legs together until they're perpendicular to the floor. Then slowly lower them to the floor again. You can vary the routine by slowly raising or lowering just one leg at a time, scissors fashion. Goal: 15 repetitions for each leg. Again, if you want to do a more difficult version, keep your heels off the floor at all times.

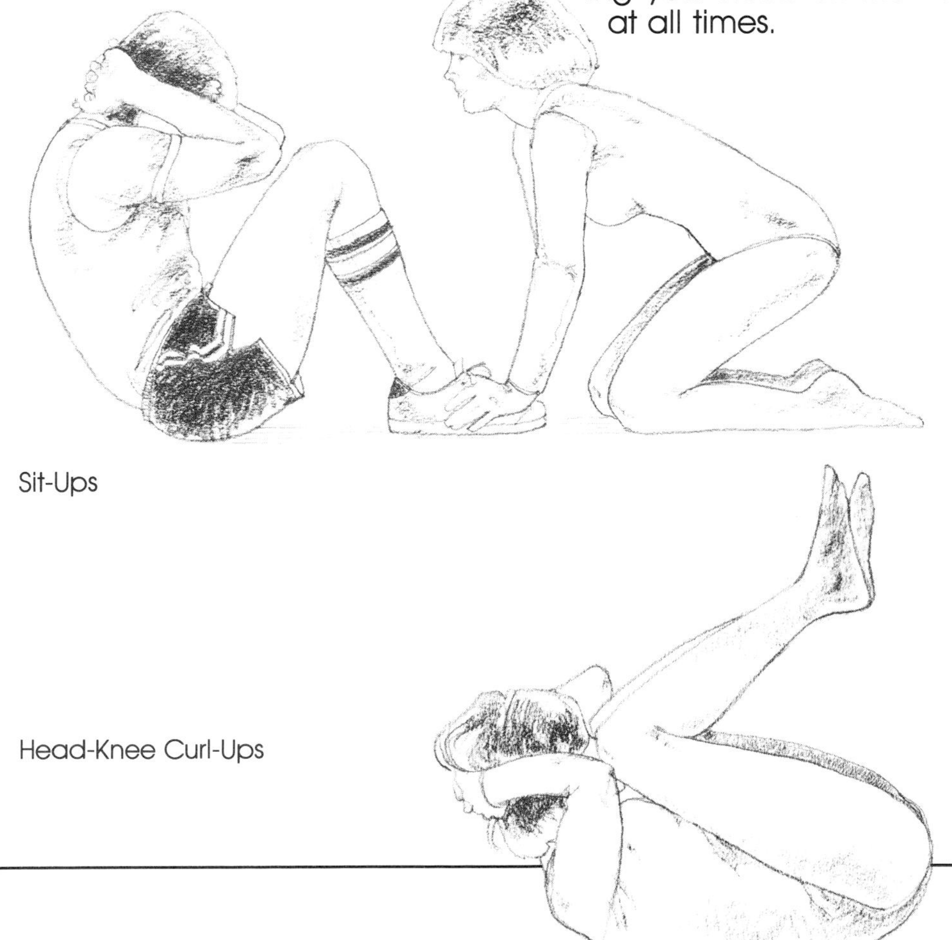

Sit-Ups

Head-Knee Curl-Ups

Sitting Leg Tucks: Sit on the end of a bench or chair as shown. Hold onto the bench with your hands behind you. Bring your thighs up to your chest with your knees bent. Extend knees and legs so your legs are straight; lower them slowly to the floor as shown. Work up to 15 to 20 sitting leg tucks.

Back Lift: (See ***Note** on page 369.) Lie on your stomach with hands clasped behind your neck. Have a partner hold your ankles. Raise your trunk and head as far as possible. Try to work up to raising your chin 18 to 24 inches from the floor. Hold the position five seconds. Goal: three to five times. Start gradually; progress is slow.

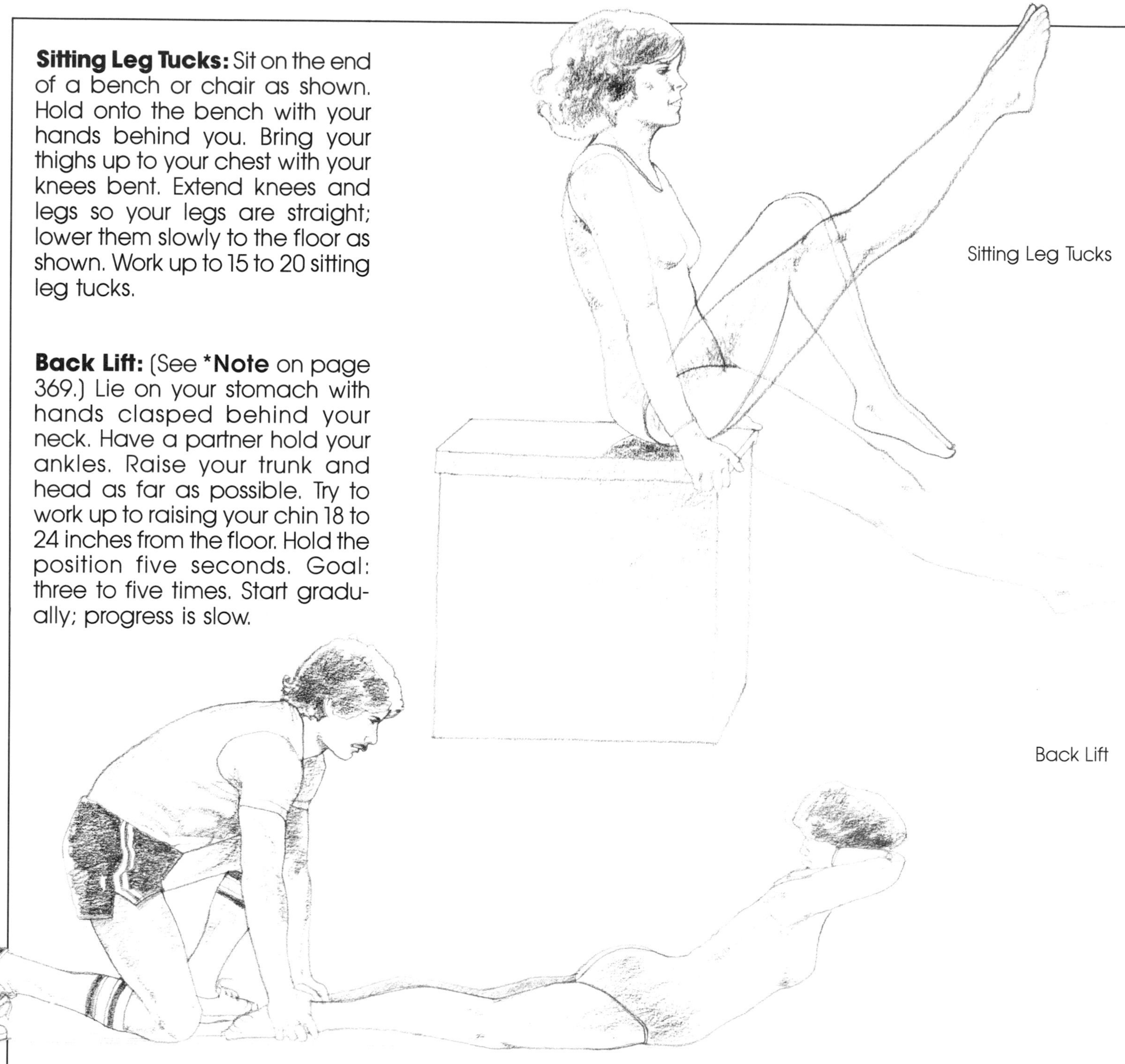

Sitting Leg Tucks

Back Lift

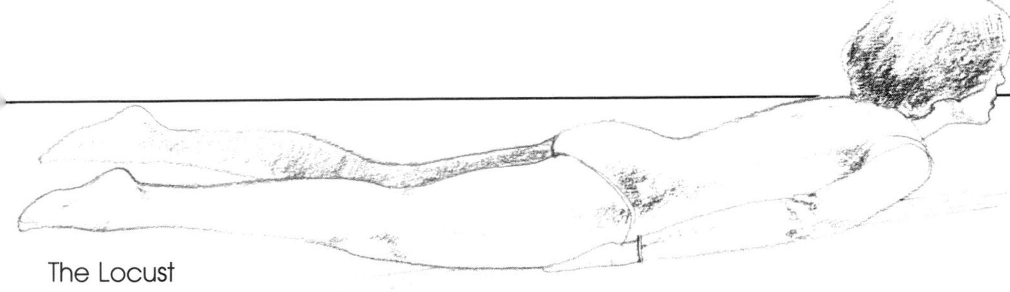

The Locust

The Locust: (See ***Note** below.) Lie on your stomach with palms under your groin and with your chin touching the floor. Push against the floor with your palms; keep legs straight and elevate them as high as possible. Hold the position for five seconds. Repeat five times.

Neck Exercises: *(Breath normally throughout this exercise.)* Those exercises you can do almost anyplace, and they're especially relaxing. Clasp your hands behind your head. Take five or six seconds to slowly pull your head forward while resisting with your neck. Then put your palms against your forehead and, for five or six seconds, push your head back with your hands while resisting with your neck muscles. For the last part of this exercise, put your right hand against the right side of your head. Take ten seconds to push your head to the left while resisting with the neck muscles. Repeat the exercise for left side. Goal: one repetition of each neck exercise.

Neck Exercises

Forearm and Hand Exercise: Squeeze a towel or rubber ball in each hand ten times.

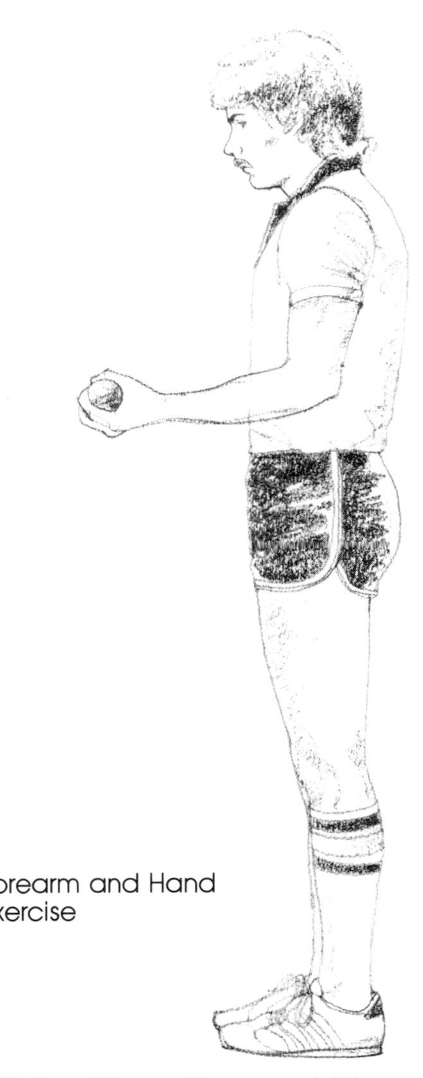

Forearm and Hand Exercise

***Note:** If you have a history of back problems, check with your physician before attempting this exercise.

INDEX

In this index, non-recipe entries are listed in *italic type*. All recipe entries are listed in regular, upright type.

B

C

D

E

F

G

H

I-J

K-L

M

N-O

P

Q-R

S

T-U